THE SECOND WORLD WAR
1939—1945
ARMY

THE DEVELOPMENT OF ARTILLERY TACTICS AND EQUIPMENT

COMPILED BY
BRIGADIER A. L. PEMBERTON, M.C

RESTRICTED

The information given in this document is not to be communicated, either directly or indirectly, to the Press or to any person not authorized to receive it.

The Naval & Military Press Ltd

THE WAR OFFICE
1950

Published by

The Naval & Military Press Ltd
Unit 5 Riverside, Brambleside
Bellbrook Industrial Estate
Uckfield, East Sussex
TN22 1QQ England

Tel: +44 (0)1825 749494

www.naval-military-press.com
www.nmarchive.com

Classified Restricted post-war publication compiled by the authority of the Army Council, the object of which was to preserve the experience gained in weapon development during WW2. This is a valuable volume, which is part of the Official History series. It covers matters not considered in great detail in the main Military series. Very rare in its original and only 1950 printing, with 1000 copies issued.

In reprinting in facsimile from the original, any imperfections are inevitably reproduced and the quality may fall short of modern type and cartographic standards.

"The Art is like to a circle without end; or like to a labyrinth, where a man being well entered in, knoweth not how to get out again, and therefore it must be exercise and industry that must make a perfect gunner."

WILLIAM ELDRED, Mr. Gr. 1646.

FOREWORD

This book is one of a series of volumes, compiled by authority of the Army Council, the object of which is to preserve the experience gained during the Second World War, 1939-1945, in selected fields of military staff work and administration. The author has been given access to official sources of information, and every endeavour has been made to ensure the accuracy of the work as a historical record. Any views expressed and conclusions drawn are those of the author, and do not necessarily reflect those of the Army Council, which, so far as they relate to current training, are to be found in the official manuals, training memoranda, etc., issued from time to time by the War Office.

For the operational background, the reader is referred to the Official History of the War.

THE WAR OFFICE,
January, 1951.

CONTENTS

	Page
ABBREVIATIONS	viii
PREFACE	x

PART I—PRE-WAR DEVELOPMENTS

Chapter		Page
I	The Legacy of the First World War	1
II	The Re-organization of the Artillery	9

PART II—CLEARING THE ATMOSPHERE

		Page
III	France and Belgium 1939–40	27
IV	The Defeat of the Italian threat to Egypt and the Sudan	43
	Section I—Introduction	43
	Section II—The Conquest of Cyrenaica	46
	Section III—The Conquest of Eritrea	54
	Section IV—A.A. and Coast Defence	60

PART III—THE FIGHT AGAINST THE DIVE-BOMBER

		Page
V	The German Drive into the Mediterranean	66
VI	The British Recovery in Egypt	78
	Section I—The Siege of Tobruk	78
	Section II—The Defence of the Egyptian Frontier	87
	Section III—A.A. and Coast Defence	91

PART IV—THE FIGHT AGAINST THE TANK

		Page
VII	The Re-conquest of Cyrenaica	99
VIII	The Retreat to El Alamein	118
IX	El Alamein to Medenine	137
	Section I—The Battle of El Alamein	137
	Section II—The Pursuit to Tunisia	149
	Section III—A.A. and Coast Defence	152
	Section IV—Conclusion	155

PART V—THE FIGHT AGAINST THE MORTAR

		Page
X	Tunisia	157
XI	Sicily to the Winter Line	179
XII	Through the Atlantic Wall	205
XIII	The Pursuit to the Siegfried and Gothic Lines	234
XIV	The End of the War in Europe	256

PART VI—THE WAR IN THE FAR EAST

		Page
XV	The Japanese Offensive	283
XVI	The Defeat of Japan	304
XVII	General Conclusions	327
INDEX		331
LIST OF BATTLE ACTIONS AND ENGAGEMENTS MENTIONED IN THE TEXT		349

MAPS
In separate Map Volume

1. Action at Nibeiwa Camp and Tummar West, 9th December, 1940
2. A.A. Lay-out at Tobruk, 1941
3. Malta H.A.A. Barrage Density, 1942
4. El Alamein C.B. Chart, 23rd/24th October, 1942...
5. Fire Plan for Attack by 9th Australian Division, El Alamein, 28th October, 1942.
6. Artillery D.F. Plan for the Battle of Medenine, 6th March, 1943
7. Outline Plan for 51st Division Attack at Wadi Akrit, 6th April, 1943.
8. Artillery Fire Plan for Attack by 78th Division, 7th April, 1943...
9. Artillery Fire Plan for Attack by 56th Division, at the Garigliano, 17th January, 1944.
10. Dispositions of 56th Division Artillery, 16th January, 1944
11. 13th Corps Artillery Fire Plan for Attack on Gustav Line, 11th May, 1944.
12. A.A. Defence of Mulberry at Arromanches, June, 1944
13. Artillery Fire Plan for 8th and 30th Corps Attacks near Caumont (Operation "Bluecoat"), 30th July, 1944.
14. Artillery Fire Plan for Attack by 1st Corps on Le Havre, 10th September, 1944.
15. A.A. (Anti-Diver) Defence of Antwerp, November, 1944
16. Artillery Fire Plan for 30th Corps Attack in the Reichswald (Operation "Veritable"), 8th February, 1945.
17. Artillery Dispositions and Initial C.B. Plan in Operation "Veritable", 8th February, 1945.
18. Artillery Dispositions and Counter-flak Plan for the Crossing of the Rhine (Operation "Varsity"), 24th March, 1945.
19. Artillery Fire Plan for Assault Crossing of the Rhine by 15th (S) Division (Operation "Torchlight"), 24th March, 1945.
20. Artillery Fire Plan for 5th Corps Attack on the Senio Defences (Operation "Buckland"), 9th April, 1945.
21. Dispositions of 7th Indian Division Artillery during the battle of the Administrative Box, Arakan, February, 1944.
22. Artillery Fire Plan for 2nd Division Attack at Kohima, 4th May, 1944.

TABLES

		Page
A	Comparison of British and German Artillery in 1939	12–14
B	Development of Artillery Radar	24–26
C	List of Artillery Equipments lost in France and Belgium, June, 1940	42
D	Summary of A.A. Actions at Tobruk, April–November, 1941	97–98
E	Times Allowed for the Various Stages of Deployment and Preparation of Fire Plans, June, 1941.	100
F	Comparison of British and German A.Tk. Guns, 1942–43	127
G	Comparison of British and German Heavy and Super-Heavy Artillery, 1943.	179
H	Comparison of A.Tk. Weapons in the Normandy fighting	223
I	Statement of Artillery Weapons Used and Ammunition Expended in Support of Operation "Veritable".	262
J	Number of Guns under Command 12th Corps and Expenditure of Artillery Ammunition at the Crossing of the Rhine.	272–273
K	Re-organization of the Divisional Artillery, India Command, 1943	303

DIAGRAMS

1	The Crooked Barrage	30
2	The Attack by German Tanks on 31st Field Regiment, 13th December, 1941.	108
3	German Tank Tactics, Libya, 1941–42	111
4	Specimen Lay-out of Infantry Brigade Group Defended Area	122
5	Wireless Communications of 6th A.G.R.A. for the Attack on the Gustav Line, 12th May, 1944.	At end of Volume

PLATES

Nos.

1	The Birch gun	
2	The 18/25-pr.	
3	The 9·2 howitzer on the road	
4	The 2-pr. A.Tk. gun	Between pages 54 and 55
5	The 3-in. 20-cwt. A.A. gun in action	
6	The 6-pr. twin Coast Artillery gun	
7	The 8-in. howitzer	
8	A sandstorm in the desert	

Nos.

9	The 25-pr.	
10	The mountains at Keren	
11	View of Italian positions at Keren from 4th and 5th Indian Division gun areas.	Between pages 118 and 119
12	The 2-pr. A.Tk. portee	
13	The 3·7-in. H.A.A. gun	
14	The German 8·8-cm. gun	
15	The 6-pr. A.Tk. gun	
16	The 17-pr. A.Tk. gun	
17	The 4·7-in. medium gun	
18	The 6-in. C.A. gun on Arrol Withers platform	
19	The " Priest "	
20	The 5·5-in. gun	
21	The American S.P. 3-in. M10.	Between pages 182 and 183
22	25-prs. firing a barrage by night	
23	The 7·2-in. howitzer	
24	The original air O.P.	
25	Artillery concentrations near Heidous	
26	The " Sexton "	
27	The 17-pr. A.Tk. gun on the Valentine tank chassis	
28	The S.P. Bofors	
29	The L.C.R.	Between pages 214 and 215
30	The 75-mm. pack howitzer (airborne)	
31	The 32-pr. A.Tk. gun	
32	The 240-mm. gun	
33	The triple 20-mm. L.A.A. Mounting	
34 & 35	The field artillery rocket	
36	The 3·7-in. H.A.A. gun in action in the field artillery role.	
37	The British 9·2-in. railway mounting	Between pages 278 and 279
38	The Reichswald	
39	The " Baby " 25-pr.	
40	The 25-pr. on Jury Axle	
41	Japanese bunkers	
42	View of Ngakyedauk Pass from Hill 1070	
43	Kohima. Objectives of Key 2 and 4, 4th May, 1944	
43A	Carriage 3·7-in. How., Mk. 2P, Towed by Jeep	
44	Kohima. Panorama showing objectives for Operation Key, 4th May, 1944.	
45	Mist in the mountains	Between pages 310 and 311
46	Ferrying guns and mules	
47	25-prs. firing from beached " Z " craft	
48	25-pr. being manhandled through mud on river bank near Rangoon.	
49	The 4·7-in. recoilless gun	

ABBREVIATIONS

A.A.	Anti-aircraft.
A.A.D.C.	Anti-aircraft defence commander.
A.A.O.R.	Anti-aircraft operations room.
A.A.S.L.	Anti-aircraft searchlight.
A.C.M.O.	Assistant counter mortar officer.
A.C.V.	Armoured Command Vehicle.
A.D.G.B.	Air defence of Great Britain.
A.F.V.	Armoured fighting vehicle.
A.F.Z.	Aircraft fighting zone.
A.G.R.A.	Army Group, Royal Artillery.
A.I.	Air interception (radar).
A.L.F.S.E.A.	Allied Land Forces, South East Asia.
A.M.T.B.	Anti-motor torpedo boat.
A.P.	Armour piercing.
A.P.C.B.C.	Armour piercing capped, ballistic cap.
Arty./R.	Artillery reconnaissance.
A.T.M.	Army Training Memorandum.
B.A.A.	Brigadier, Anti-aircraft.
B.C.H.Q.	Bombardment Control Headquarters.
B.E.F.	British Expeditionary Force.
B.M.R.A.	Brigade Major, Royal Artillery.
B.R.A.	Brigadier, Royal Artillery.
C.A.	Coast Artillery.
C.A.G.R.A.	Commander, Army Group, Royal Artillery.
C.B.	Counter battery.
C.B.O.	Counter battery officer.
C.C.M.A.	Commander, Corps Medium Artillery.
C.C.R.A.	Commander, Corps Royal Artillery.
C.D.	Coast defence.
C.H.	Chain (radar).
C.M.	Counter mortar.
C.M.O.	Counter mortar officer.
C.P.O.	Command Post Officer.
C.R.A.	Commander, Royal Artillery.
D.F.	Defensive fire.
D.P.	Dual purpose.
D.R.A.	Director of Royal Artillery.
F.A.	Field Artillery.
F.D.L.	Forward defended locality.
F.O.B.	Forward observer bombardment.
F.O.O.	Forward observation officer.
F.O.U.	Forward observer unit.
F.S.	Flash spotting.
G.A.F.	German Air Force.
G.C.I.	Ground controlled interception.
G.D.A.	Gun defended area.
G.H.Q.	General Headquarters.
G.L.	Gun laying (radar).
G.P.O.	Gun position officer.
G. (Ops)	General Staff, operations branch.
G.O.R.	Gun operations room.

H.A.A.	Heavy anti-aircraft.
H.E.	High explosive.
How.	Howitzer.
H.Q.R.A.	Headquarters, Royal Artillery.
I.A.Z.	Inner artillery zone.
I.F.F.	Indicator friend or foe.
L.A.A.	Light anti-aircraft.
L.C.P. (L.)	Landing craft personnel (large).
L.C.S. (M).	Landing craft support (medium).
L.C.S. (R).	Landing craft support fitted with rocket projectors.
L.C.T.	Landing craft tank.
L.C.T. (R.)	Landing craft tank fitted with rocket projectors.
L.M.G.	Light machine gun.
L. of C.	Lines of communication.
L.V.T.	Landing vehicle tracked.
L.W.	Light warning (radar).
M.G.A.A.	Major-General, Anti-aircraft.
M.G.R.A.	Major-General, Royal Artillery.
M.M.G.	Medium machine gun.
M.N.B.D.O.	Mobile naval base defence organization.
m.p.h.	miles per hour.
m.p.i.	mean point of impact.
M.T.	Mechanical transport.
M.V.	Muzzle velocity.
O.P.	Observation Post.
P.A.D.	Passive air defence.
Q.F.	quick firing.
R.A.	Royal Artillery.
R.D.F.	Radio direction finding.
R.H.A.	Royal Horse Artillery.
R.M.	Royal Marines.
r.p.g.	rounds per gun.
r.p.g.p.d.	rounds per gun per diem.
R./T.	Radio telephony.
S.E.A.C.	South East Asia Command.
S.H.A.E.F.	Supreme Headquarters, Allied Expeditionary Force.
S.L.	Searchlight.
S.L.C.	Searchlight control (radar).
S.P.	Self-propelled.
Tac./R.	Tactical reconnaissance.
U.S.	United States.
V.H.F.	Very high frequency.
V.P.	Vulnerable point.
V.T.	Variable time.
W./T.	Wireless telegraphy.

PREFACE

This book is a historical study, by a single author, of the evolution of artillery tactics and equipment during the Second World War. It is based on contemporary reports and war diaries, and therefore reflects contemporary opinion; sometimes official, sometimes unofficial, but emanating from "the man on the spot". It is not to be regarded as indicative of modern official doctrine—with which indeed it may sometimes conflict—but rather as a background to the study of such doctrine as given in current text-books.

Being the work of a single author, it must also reflect, in places, his personal opinions. To compensate for this, it has been furnished with copious references, so that the reader may know—if he cannot always consult—the sources from which the account of an action, or the development of a doctrine, have been taken. Most of the references are indeed to war diaries and reports, which are accessible only to those who can visit the official archives.

Intended primarily for reference purposes, the book has been provided with a detailed index and, in addition, a list of actions referred to—not always by name—in the text. In this way, it is hoped the reader will be enabled to trace without difficulty the evolution of any particular artillery technique, or the significant artillery feature of any particular battle, with which he happens momentarily to be concerned.

PART I

PRE-WAR DEVELOPMENTS

NOTE:—The nomenclature of the artillery unit was changed in 1938 from brigade to regiment. For the sake of simplicity, the term regiment has been used throughout this book.

CHAPTER I

THE LEGACY OF THE FIRST WORLD WAR

The Evolutionary Cycle

It is well known—but often forgotten—that the weapon with which the gunner fights is the shell. Gunnery, reduced to its simplest terms, is the art of delivering shell at the right place, at the right time, in the right quantity, and of the right quality to achieve the desired object. The problem of artillery tactics is to resolve the conflict that is inherent, in the first two of these two processes, between speed and accuracy, and in the last two between mobility of manoeuvre and range on the one hand and weight of shell on the other.

This conflict is never completely resolved. At one time speed and mobility will be in the ascendant, at another accuracy and shell-power; and between these two extremes the development of artillery tactics moves in a continuous cycle. At any point on this cycle, the particular method then in vogue tends to become an obsession with those who practise it, and thus to acquire a false aspect of originality, and universality, through the suppression of what had gone before. For the same reason, and because of the effort required to change from the manufacture of one type of equipment to that of another, successful solutions are apt to perpetuate themselves without regard to changing conditions, and thus eventually to lead to failure: whence the witty observation that "nothing misleads like success".

The designs of artillery weapons used by both sides in the Second World War differed little in their general principles from those of their 1914-18 predecessors. It will therefore be convenient to begin a study of tactical developments during the Second World War by tracing the main lines of evolution that lead down to it from the First.

The Influence of Trench Warfare

During the greater part of the First World War, the defence had proved itself superior to the attack, and this had been due in the main to three things: the spade, the wire obstacle and the machine-gun. At first hopes were pinned on the gun as a means of restoring mobility to the battlefield, by opening lanes through the wire and then overwhelming the defenders as the infantry advanced to the assault. It seemed to many that "the effect of a bombardment by hundreds of guns for several days would crush all resistance; the enemy infantry and machine-gunners would either be slain or buried in their trenches and shelters, or cowed into surrender, so that it would be necessary only to march forward and take possession."[1]

Experience proved, however, that this idea was wrong. The wire was not always cut, and the material effect on the remainder of the defences was disappointingly small and often quite disproportionate to the amount of ammunition expended. The moral effect, though great, was fleeting. Good troops would recover quickly from the shock of a bombardment, and an excessive amount of debris or shell holes would interfere with the mobility of the attacker, at the same time offering cover to the machine-guns and other weapons of the defence.

It appeared, therefore, that there was an optimum weight and duration for an artillery bombardment, beyond which the expenditure of ammunition was not justified by the results obtained. The point had not been scientifically investigated before the war ended, but there was some reason to believe that the optimum figures had been reached in the fighting round Valenciennes at the beginning of November, 1918, when 87,774 rounds of all natures were fired on a single brigade front in the space of 48 hours.

Covering Fire

It followed that the object of the artillery in the attack must be to neutralize the enemy defences for just so long as to "assist the other arms to maintain their mobility and offensive power."[2] To achieve this object, three types of fire were developed: concentrations, barrages, and smoke screens.

The choice between the first two would be determined by the accuracy with which the enemy dispositions could be located. If air and ground reconnaissance had produced a detailed knowledge of where the main concentrations of enemy troops were, the best and most economical method of covering fire would obviously be concentrations of shells in those areas, The fewer they were, and the smaller in size, the greater would be the density of fire that could be brought upon them, and hence the greater the degree of neutralization achieved.

Where accurate information of the enemy dispositions was not available —and this was thought likely to be the rule in moving warfare—recourse would have to be had to the barrage. Provided that its shape and direction were kept simple, it could be quickly applied, but it was costly in ammunition and could only cover a limited front (560 yards for a field regiment). In 1938 it was laid down that the ammunition required for a barrage to support an attack in position warfare would "often amount to as much as 500 rounds for each field gun and a proportionate number for the heavier natures."[3]

One of the most difficult questions to decide was how to control the duration of a concentration or the rate of movement of a creeping barrage. The ideal was obviously to use direct observation, so that the fire of the artillery could be made to conform exactly to the movements of the attacking troops. With the means of intercommunication then available, however, this was found to be an unattainable ideal, and the solution generally adopted was a compromise between the flexibility of control by observation and the certainty of control by a timed programme, by which the attacking troops were made to conform to the movement of the covering fire. The time limits of each concentration, or the length of the pause on each line of a moving barrage, were fixed, but a certain number of troops or batteries—usually one-third of the total—were considered as superimposed. Such units were free to abandon their allotted task at any moment in order to engage opportunity targets observed by the O.P. In default of such targets, they would be used to add density or depth to a barrage, or density to a concentration.

In 1918, the normal rate of advance of a creeping barrage was 100 yards in four minutes. On occasion, however—such as the attack on the St. Quentin Canal in September, 1918—this speed might be doubled, and in post-war years, as the load on the infantryman was reduced, the normal rate became fixed at 100 yards in three minutes.

In view of the fleeting moral effect of an artillery bombardment, the effectiveness of covering fire, and particularly of a barrage, depended largely on the closeness with which it was followed up by the assaulting troops. " In the French Army, where the artillery is, or was, the dominant arm . . . . the infantry were told that unless 10 per cent. or 15 per cent. of their casualties were caused by the fire of their own guns, they were unlikely to be successful."[4] British doctrine never went to this length, though in practice, during the First World War, attacking infantry had on at least one occasion been ordered to keep within 25 yards of the barrage. Then, with the post-war emphasis on mobile warfare, attention had been diverted to other things and, before 1939, no specific distance had been mentioned in the training manuals.

If time, or the supply of ammunition, was short, the only possible form of covering fire might be a smoke screen. The smoke shell of the 25-pr., introduced in 1938, was regarded as a weapon of great potentialities, and it was then considered that the correct use of smoke in all conditions was " to give depth to the covering fire of the attack, thus economizing in guns and ammunition, and to screen the flanks."[5] It might also be used to support a rapidly mounted attack—say, by an armoured formation or by an advanced guard—or before an attack to draw fire and discover the enemy's counter-preparation areas.

The main weakness of this method was its dependence on weather conditions. If the wind was gusty or very strong, the use of smoke might be impossible, and in certain other circumstances it might be uneconomical. It was therefore always necessary to have alternative H.E. tasks prepared to meet last minute changes in the meteorological conditions.

Defensive Fire

In the defence, a distinction was drawn between " counter-preparation ", fired in anticipation of an attack, and " defensive fire " brought down during the actual assault. For the former, predicted concentrations were considered suitable, the selected targets being the enemy's probable forming-up places and forward communications. For the latter, observed fire was to be used whenever possible, but standing barrages on selected portions of the front, or concentrations on the most probable lines of approach, were to be worked out beforehand in conjunction with sector commanders, and light signals arranged by means of which these S.O.S. tasks could be put into operation immediately they were required.

Counter-Battery Fire

With the growth in importance of the artillery during the First World War, counter-battery work had acquired a new significance, and a technique had been developed that depended for full efficiency upon centralized control at the corps level. The counter-battery staff, which consisted of a C.B.O. and two assistants, received its information from four main sources: air reconnaissance, shelling reports from troops in the forward areas, and locations of hostile batteries obtained by the flash spotting and sound ranging batteries of the survey regiment. Good communications were therefore of great importance, and in the absence of such communications—as, for example, in the early stages of an encounter battle—control would have to be decentralized to divisions.

The allotment of guns for counter-battery work was made by the C.C.R.A., and guns so allotted could not be diverted to other tasks without his authority. The rôle was normally filled by medium artillery, but for destructive shoots heavy howitzers were required, and against guns not dug in, field artillery, with its high rate of fire, could be very effective. Where quick action was necessary, and the location of hostile batteries was not accurately known, smoke might be used against their O.Ps.

The executive control of counter-battery fire was usually delegated to the commander, corps medium artillery (C.C.M.A.), who, under the C.C.R.A., commanded all heavy and medium artillery in the corps, and whose headquarters was the centre to which all information about the hostile artillery was sent.

Predicted Shooting and Artillery Survey

The heavy concentrations required for covering, defensive and counter-battery fire led to the widespread use of predicted instead of observed shooting; and predicted shooting meant survey.

The oldest and simplest form of artillery survey is registration by shooting, in which the gun itself is used as a rangefinder. Its disadvantages are twofold. Firstly, its results are immediately applicable only to the gun—or at most the battery—that did the ranging. Secondly, it eliminates, or reduces, the possibility of surprise. Hence the development of instrumental methods, beginning with the battery or troop director and rangefinder, and ending with the theodolite of the surveyor.

Owing to the conditions under which artillery survey was initiated, the relationship between these various instrumental methods was not at first fully appreciated. During the stalemate on the Western Front from 1915-18, large-scale maps were plentiful and topographical detail was usually ample for the purpose of resecting a position.

With the return of peace, and the absence of any indication of where the next war might be, the large-scale map could no longer be relied on. In 1925, attention was drawn to the importance of " silent registration "—with the aid of a rangefinder, a director and an artillery board—as a means of locating possible target areas where no large-scale map was available. At the same time a campaign was started for the popularization of survey methods and the extermination of the belief that survey itself was a " black art ". In 1929 the regimental surveyor became a recognized part of the unit establishment, and a simple drill was worked out for the application of artillery survey to really mobile operations. The first step in this process was to be a combination of registration by shooting, registration by instruments, and such rough survey as was possible at the O.Ps. of batteries already in action. Starting from this foundation, a complete survey system would gradually be built up with the help of regimental survey parties, the R.A. survey company, and the field survey companies, R.E. To speed up the development of the specialist superstructure, arrangements were made in 1937 for small observation parties from the R.A. survey company to accompany the leading artillery regiments in an advance.

As usual, the regimental officer, in the process of becoming survey-minded, was sometimes inclined to become survey-obsessed. The use of the 1-inch map for the location of targets or the measurement of switches was neglected, and in general there was a tendency towards stickiness and delay in mounting an attack while waiting for survey operations to be completed.

Nevertheless, great progress had been made. Once deployment had been completed, the massed fire of a whole divisional artillery could be brought to bear on a selected area within 30 minutes of the receipt of the orders ; and with the introduction of the 1/25,000 map in 1936—consequent upon the crystallization of the world political situation—quick concentrations of fire became possible even in the early stages of an encounter battle. The accuracy of a concentration fired off the map was not expected to be as good as that obtained by the usual survey methods, but it was deemed sufficient to meet the requirements of moving warfare.

Making the Guns Shoot Together

It was, of course, no use putting the guns of a regiment, or of a division, in harmony with each other by survey methods, unless the shell could be relied on to fall in the expected place. To make sure of this, it was necessary to have an accurate knowledge of the muzzle velocity of every gun, of the ballistic properties of the ammunition being used, and of the effect on each gun's performance of changes in the meteorological conditions.

Calibration for M.V. is a process that should be continuous, and carefully recorded, throughout the whole life of a gun ; because no one group of rounds can be relied on to give an accurate answer, and because the M.V. found with one charge will not necessarily indicate the correct M.V. for all other charges. This was clearly appreciated and often emphasized in training memoranda during the period 1927-39 ; but it was a difficult point to drive home in peace-time, with limited supplies of ammunition, no appreciable wear in the guns, and no casualty list to show the penalty for an inaccurate bombardment. In 1938 it was observed that inattention to calibration was still a " noticeable feature among officers ".[6]

The disturbing effects of badly stored or sorted ammunition were also fully realized but not easily obviated. For " proximity " shoots—that is, the engagement of targets close to one's own troops—it was a strict rule that the nature and lot number of the ammunition used should remain constant. In general, too, it was recognized as an ideal that each unit should be homogeneously equipped with regard to propellants. In practice, however, this was often impossible owing to the variety of ammunition that had to be accepted from the makers, and the storage limitations in Ordnance depots.

"Meteor" was another of the unseen factors that, if neglected, could have a disastrous effect on shooting, but that was difficult to demonstrate convincingly in peace time. From 1928 onwards the issue of a meteor telegram was an obligatory part of all artillery exercises, but mistakes in the calculation of the correction of the moment were frequent, and a satisfactory method had not been found for estimating local variations in meteorological conditions. Meteor telegrams were issued by the meteorological branch, R.A.F., at G.H.Q. and covered wide geographical areas and considerable periods of time.

For these reasons, predicted shooting was acknowledged to have considerable limitations, and stress was laid on the importance of good observation as a means of adjusting any errors found in the opening rounds of a bombardment.

Harassing Fire

Harassing fire was another form of artillery activity for which a special technique had been developed during the First World War. Its main object was to interfere with the enemy's plans by disrupting his communications, and to lower his morale by disturbing the rest and threatening the safety of those in rearward areas. It was therefore the function, primarily, of medium and heavy artillery.

Shooting with Air Observation

The exploitation of the aeroplane as a means of observing artillery fire was a natural consequence of the conquest of the air. The technical difficulties, however, were considerable, and the procedure evolved during the First World War, when conditions were relatively static and both aircraft and wireless instruments were primitive, was complicated and slow. Improvement was gradual but continuous, and by 1938 the number of drills had been reduced in effect to two.

Even so the technique was not easy, and constant practice was required by both airman and gunner if successful results were to be obtained. For example, the clock code system for reporting the fall of shot, though easy to learn and use, was liable to be upset if for any reason the air observer had his "clock" incorrectly set. Again, the ground strips used for indicating to the air the progress of events at the battery had to be familiar to the airman and accurately placed by the battery personnel.

In mobile warfare, when working with an unallotted battery whose identity and location were unknown, the air observer would not know when the battery was ready to fire, and a fixed time interval (four minutes) had therefore to be adhered to between the notification of the target and the firing of the first ranging rounds. If the guns did not fire at the right time, the airman would not be in the right place to observe and the rounds would probably be missed. Success therefore depended on a continuous wireless watch by all ground units concerned and a timely response by the appropriate battery to the air observer's call.

All this demanded a high degree of specialization on the part of the arty/R pilot. As the threat of war with Germany increased, and the size of the German Air Force became manifest, the R.A.F. naturally became preoccupied with other things, and its ability to supply the requisite number of specialists for this task appeared to be doubtful. Moreover, opinion in the R.A.F. inclined to the belief that close observation of fire from the air in enemy back areas would be impracticable in future wars. Without complete local air ascendancy, which was felt to be an unlikely contingency, observer aircraft would soon be driven out of the sky by modern fighters.

Meanwhile, with the spread of aviation, there had been a natural desire on the part of the gunner to get into the air himself, not merely as a passenger —that had been done before—but as his own pilot. The difficulty was to find a suitable aircraft. After an unsuccessful start in 1936, trials were in progress on the eve of the war to ascertain the possibility of controlling artillery fire by the use of a flying O.P.

A.A. and Coast Defence

As the offensive power of aircraft increased, a new form of artillery came into being. At first, aircraft speeds were relatively low and the A.A. gun could be laid direct on the target, with deflections estimated by the G.P.O. and applied on the mounting as in coast and field artillery. There was even the story of a gun, defending London against one of the earlier German air attacks, that pursued the enemy at full speed down one of the main city thoroughfares.

By 1930 the situation had completely changed. To keep pace with aircraft performances, the A.A. gunner was having to discard his old-fashioned sighting arrangements and use modern methods comprising mechanical predictors, which worked out the deflections automatically and then passed them electrically (Case III) to the guns, thus enabling them to be laid by follow-the-pointer methods.

Meanwhile the development of night flying had led to the introduction of the A.A. searchlight (A.A.S.L.), manned, like the defence electric light (D.E.L.) of the coast defences, by R.E. personnel. Thus A.A. gunnery had grown progressively less like field, and more like coast, gunnery.

As a result of the almost complete command of the seas by the Allied Navies, coast artillery was little used in the First World War. Yet it could not be dispensed with, and it had to adjust itself to modern conditions: firstly, by the introduction of more modern heavy and medium equipments, capable of firing to greater ranges than had hitherto been considered necessary, and of a light twin equipment to deal with high-speed coastal motor boats; secondly, by the introduction of a new system of rangefinding called the Fortress System; and thirdly by improving the fire control instruments and data transmission system necessary for the engagement of targets at both long and short ranges.

Conclusion

The First World War had added greatly to the complexity of artillery equipments and gunnery methods. A new type of artillery—" A.A."—had been created. Six distinct kinds of shell—shrapnel, H.E., gas (chemical), smoke, star and incendiary—were in use by the field artillery. Heavy and super-heavy artillery, though not new in principle, had acquired greatly increased scope by additions to their range and shell-power.

If the early promise of the tank (*see* p. 16) was to be fulfilled, and mobility was to be restored to the battlefield, some simplification, both of equipments and of methods, seemed likely to be required.

List of References

[1] " Military Operations in France and Belgium ", 1916, Vol. i, p. 34.
[2] Arty. Training, Vol. III, 1928, p. 14.
[3] Arty. Training, Vol. II, Pamphlet No. 6, 1938, Sec. 15.
[4] Journal of the R.A., Vol. LXXX, 1943, p. 274.
[5] A.T.M. No. 20, April 1938.
[6] Memo. on the Training of the R.A., 1938.

CHAPTER II

THE REORGANIZATION OF THE ARTILLERY

PLATES RELEVANT TO THIS CHAPTER

Nos.
1. The Birch gun.
2. The 18/25-pr.
3. The 9.2 how. on the road.
4. The 2-pr. A.Tk. gun.
5. The 3-in. 20 cwt. A.A. gun in action.
6. The 6-pr. twin Coast Artillery gun.

The Close Support Gun

In spite of the recognized need for simplification, there was one direction in which circumstances at once compelled the acceptance of a fresh complication: close support of the leading infantry in the attack. The gunner might—and often did—argue that the shell was what did the damage, and that the closeness of the support given did not necessarily depend on the closeness of the gun itself. Provided that the shell fell on the right spot, what did it matter where it was fired from?

The proviso was an important one, and, with inter-communication still dependent mainly upon cable, it was not easy for the gunner to make his fire conform to the movements of the troops he was supporting. In some of the big attacks at the end of 1918, the artillery, as often as not, would "cock on" a couple of hundred yards to the supposed range to prevent mishaps.([1])

The only way out of the difficulty appeared to be short "lines", and these in turn demanded a small, inconspicuous weapon with a high trajectory. In mobile warfare especially, the infantry commander felt that he needed some kind of a gun under his immediate control for brushing aside troublesome opposition during the advance. In 1920, therefore, it was decided to introduce one light regiment, armed with 3.7-in. hows., into each divisional artillery.

The Mechanization of the Artillery

This gave a certain degree of flexibility to the fire of the divisional artillery in the early stages of the encounter battle. The next step was to increase its mobility of manoeuvre. Mechanization of the artillery began in 1927 with one field regiment and one light battery attached to the Experimental Armoured Force.

At the same time the British Army led the way in the development of self-propelled (S.P.) field artillery by the production of a single battery of "Birch guns" (S.P. 18-prs.). Though basically sound, as proved by later war experiences, this equipment had suffered from defective planning. It had been rather vaguely designed as a S.P. 18-pr. instead of as a S.P. close support weapon, with clearly defined tasks and characteristics. The 18-pr. itself was never an ideal close support weapon, owing to its single charge, and in the Birch gun it was given a limited elevation.

The idea therefore failed to mature and, possibly, a prejudice was formed in the minds of users against S.P. artillery. When the Armoured Force was broken up in 1930, the Birch guns were discarded. They were regarded as an unnecessary complication, and it was thought better to concentrate on the development of the normal towed equipment. Some difficulty was being experienced in the production of a suitable tractor, and it was not until 1937 that the first two divisional artilleries were completely mechanized.

Gun groups could now move at 15 m.p.h. and cover 100 miles a day—including the occupation of a position—if the roads were reasonably clear.

The Development of Wireless

Meanwhile the development of wireless was making possible a new flexibility of control in keeping with this new mobility of manoeuvre. In 1928, R/T sets were first issued for trial to two field regiments; but it was not until 1938 that wireless equipments and drill could be relied on for the control of artillery fire. Then, for a time, their popularity was such that the use of cable was frequently neglected.

The Armoured O.P.

It remained to improve the liaison between the guns and the troops they were supporting. In 1929 it was laid down that the F.O.O. should normally be the battery commander, and although this ruling was subsequently relaxed, it was continually emphasized that he should be an officer of experience and that he should normally control the fire of the guns.

For obvious reasons the F.O.O. could not be tied to an infantry headquarters, and, if he was to move about with any freedom in the forward area, he must have some form of protection for his vehicle. In April, 1939, it was decided that scout carriers, suitably modified, should be provided for use as armoured O.Ps. in field and medium regiments.

The Reorganization of the Field Regiment

As a result of the improvements in survey (*see* pp. 4, 5) it became possible on occasions to use the regiment as a fire unit. First introduced in 1929, regimental control was actually being tried—not very successfully—against moving targets by 1931. In 1937 the regiment was finally recognized as the unit, both administratively and tactically, in the application of fire.([2])

This 24-gun fire unit, however, though good enough for a set-piece battle, was still too slow in operation for effective use in moving warfare. The battery, therefore, remained the normal fire unit, and attempts were made to speed up the procedure for deployment and for bringing the guns of two or more batteries into harmony with each other.

The two main weaknesses of the existing system were felt to be the absorption of regimental, battery and troop commanders in administrative detail, and the clumsiness and unreliability of the procedure for producing a regimental concentration. It was impossible to get more than six guns (one battery) on to one target until the whole of the regimental survey had been completed, and the means provided for checking calculations and correcting inaccuracies—particularly in predicted fire—were inadequate.

To remedy these defects, experiments were first carried out with the linking of batteries by graphical methods, so that zero lines, etc., could be in harmony from the start, and two batteries could be ranged and shot almost as if they were one. Then, in 1938, the field regiment was reorganized. Instead of four 6-gun batteries each of three sections, it was in future to consist of two 12-gun batteries each of three troops.

To relieve the regimental commander of some of his administrative burdens, and to assist him in the deployment of the regiment in war, a second-in-command was introduced into the establishment. At the same time the administrative work in batteries was greatly reduced by the addition of a quartermaster to the regimental staff. What was left was centralized at battery headquarters, so that the troop commander was relieved of practically all his administrative responsibilities.

To reduce the risk of inaccuracies at predicted fire, all calculations were centralized in the hands of a technical staff at battery headquarters, which was also made responsible for linking the three troops together. The drill for this was carried out in four (later reduced to three) stages, at the end of which the battery could be used as a single fire unit. It was in fact a partial substitute for the work of the old regimental survey party, which was now removed from the establishment. By its means, it was hoped, the production of a 12-gun concentration would be hastened at the expense, if need be, of a delay in the concentration of the whole regiment.

The tactical advantages claimed[3] for the three troop organization were that it facilitated control of movement on roads and across country; that, by enabling the guns of a unit to be placed in action in groups of four, it eased the problem of concealment from the air and increased the efficiency of the anti-tank defence of the gun position area; and that it allowed independent action by a troop to deal with a minor emergency. The establishment of wireless sets was, however, sufficient for only two of the three troops to set up their own O.Ps. The commander of the third troop could only act as a reserve O.P. for the battery.

The Simplification of the Divisional Artillery

The development of the 3-in. mortar as a battalion close support weapon, combined with the improvement of wireless, had rendered the light regiments (*see* p. 9) superfluous. In 1935, therefore, it was decided that these units should be reorganized as army field regiments. Only in India did the 3.7-in. how. remain in the divisional establishment, in the traditional form of a mountain artillery regiment designed primarily for use on the north-west frontier. This regiment was organized on a pack basis and took the place of one of the three field regiments in the normal home establishment of a divisional artillery.

By this time developments on the Continent of Europe had made it necessary to increase the range and hitting power of the divisional artillery, and the design of new equipments offered an opportunity for further simplifications in organization and tactics through the unification of equipment.

The first thing to tackle was the shell. During the First World War, the variety of projectiles in use had become embarrassingly large (*see* pp. 7, 8), and here was a chance of eliminating at least one superfluity by the abolition of shrapnel. The shrapnel shell, introduced in an era of deep infantry columns, in which its long beaten zone was capable of producing great lethal effect, had progressively lost its value as infantry formations were extended. Like Charles II, however, " it was an unconscionable time dying," and it was not until 1935 that it was finally eliminated from the field artillery. H.E. then became the normal field gun projectile, with smoke and carrier shell as its auxiliaries.

All three of these shells function most effectively when the angle of descent is steep and the remaining velocity low; in other words, when fired from an equipment of the howitzer type; and the standardization of this method of fire enabled a single weapon to take the place of the old 18-pr. and 4.5-in. how. It was to be a gun-howitzer, for which the G.S. specification laid down a weight in action of 30-cwt., a cross-country mobility comparable with that of the 30-cwt. six-wheeler, a projectile weighing between 20 and 25 pounds, and a range of at least 12,000—later increased to 15,000—yards.

For several reasons, economic and military, it was decided that the design of the new equipment must allow the conversion of existing 18-prs., of which there was a large stock and of which the later marks had heavy carriages that were capable of taking a more powerful gun. As a result of this decision, and of the limitation imposed on the weight of the equipment in action, a maximum range of 13,400 yards had eventually to be accepted. It was found that a range of 15,000 yards was impossible with a 30-cwt. carriage, and that a shell designed to travel this distance would not be interchangeable with that of the converted 18/25-pr. The maximum range accepted for the latter, which could not fire supercharge, was 11,800 yards.

The Army was now on the way to getting a field gun that was as good as, if not better than, its German equivalent (*see* Table A). The recognition of German air superiority had caused priority to be given to the manufacture of A.A. guns for the air defence of Great Britain (A.D.G.B.), and, with the limited industrial capacity then available, production of 25-prs. was naturally slow. By the outbreak of war only 78 guns, and no carriage, had been delivered; but approximately 1,000 18-pr. Mks. 4 and 5 carriages were converted to take the 25-pr. Mk I by August 19th, 1939, and these went a long way towards equipping the B.E.F. with suitable weapons.

TABLE A
Comparison of British and German Artillery in 1939
I. FIELD ARTILLERY

	German 10·5 cm. gun/how.	British 25-pr. gun/how.	Remarks
Weight in action (tons)	1·98	1·75	(i) The figure for the 25-pr. refer to the new (Mk. II) equipment, which was not available for the 1939/40 operations in France and Belgium. The Mk. I (converted 18-pr.) weighed 1·56 tons in action and had a maximum range of 11,800 yds. In 1941 the German 10·5 cm. was stepped up to give a maximum range of 13,450 yds. (ii) The German 8·8 cm., sometimes compared with the 25-pr., was designed as an A.A. gun and its greater M.V. should therefore be compared with that of our 3·7 in A.A.
Weight of shell (lb.)	32·65	25	
Calibre (ins.)	4·13	3·45	
M.V. (top charge–f.s.)	1,552	1,750	
Maximum range (yds.)	11,675	13,400	
Degrees, elevation	−6° to +40°	−5° to +40°	
,, traverse	56°	4° L to 4° R on top traverse. 360° on platform	

II. Anti-Tank Artillery

	German 3·7 cm.	British 2-pr.	Remarks
Penetration (mms.) at 500 yds.	36	53	Against homogenous armour at 30°
,, ,, ,, 1,000 ,,	27	40	

III. Medium Artillery

	Gun		Howitzer	
	German 10·5 cm. K. 18	British 4·5-in.	German 15 cm. SFH. 18	British 5·5-in. gun/how
Weight in action (tons)	5·39	5·7	6	5·7
Weight of shell (lb.)	33·4	55	95·7	100
Maximum range (yds.)	20,860	20,500	14,570	16,000
Degrees, elevation	0° to +45°	−5° to +45°	−1·30° to +45°	−5° to +45°
,, traverse	64°	60°	64°	60°

Note: The German K.18 and SFH.18 had, like our own pieces, a common carriage.

IV. Heavy Artillery

	Gun		Howitzer	
	German Nil	British 6-in. Mk. XIX	German 21 cm. Mrg. 18	British 8-in.
Weight in action (tons)		11·4 with limber 10·2 without limber	18·5	10·1 with limber 8·95 without limber
Weight of shell (lb.)		100	249	200
Maximum range (yds.)		18,750	18,263	12,400

V. H.A.A.

	German 8·8 cm. Flak 18 & 36	British 3·7 in H.A.A.	Remarks
Weight in action (tons)	5·5	7·5 to 8	
Weight of H.E. shell (lb.)	20	28	
Calibre (ins.)	3·46	3·7	
M.V. (f.s.)	2690	2600	
Maximum ceiling (ft.)	34,773	41,000	
Rate of fire (r.p.m.)	15/20	8/10*	* Later increased to 20 by use of automatic ramming gear.

VI. L.A.A.

	German 3·7 cm. Flak 18 & 36	British Bofors 40 mm.
Weight in action (tons)	1·53 (36)/1·72 (18)	2·0 to 2·5
Weight of H.E. shell (lb.)	1·4	2
Calibre (ins.)	1·45	1·58
M.V. (f.s.)	2690/2610	2700
Maximum ceiling (ft.)	13,775	23,600
Rate of fire (r.p.m.)	80/140	120

Note: The principal German L.A.A. weapon was the 2 cm., which was not strictly comparable with any British type.

VII. LIGHT COAST ARTILLERY

	German	British
Calibre	37 mm.	2·444 in.
Weight of shell	1·64 pounds	6 pounds
M.V.	3,280 ft./sec.	2,300 ft./sec.
Rate of fire	80 r.p.m.	70 r.p.m. (twin mounting)
Weight of gun and mounting	2½ tons	10 tons
Maximum range	7,200 yards	5,500 yards

VIII. MEDIUM COAST ARTILLERY

	German	British
Calibre	149 mm.	6-in.
Weight of shell	100 pounds	100 pounds
M.V.	2,640 ft./sec.	2,900 ft./sec.
Rate of fire	7 r.p.m.*	7·5 r.p.m.
Weight of gun and mounting	35 tons*	37 tons
Maximum range	21,800 yards	24,500 yards

* These figures are approximate.

IX. HEAVY COAST ARTILLERY

	German	British
Calibre	238 mm.	9·2 in.
Weight of shell	327 pounds	380 pounds
M.V.	2,657 ft./sec.	2,825 ft./sec. (supercharge)
Rate of fire	3 r.p.m.*	3 r.p.m.
Weight of gun and mounting	130 tons*	130 tons
Maximum range	29,200 yards	31,300 yards (with supercharge)

* These figures are approximate.

The Modernization of Medium Artillery

In the programme of modernization, medium artillery had to take precedence below both A.A. and field guns, and progress before the war was therefore very slow. The first step was to increase the mobility of existing equipments—60-pr. and 6-in. how.—by the substitution of pneumatic for steel tyres. As a second step, attempts were made to obtain increased range: in the 60-pr. by relining it to 4.5 inches, in the 6-in. how. by designing a new piece to fit on the existing carriage.

The 60-pr. conversion proved successful, but the 6-in. how. project was a failure. In its place a 5-in. piece was proposed, to satisfy a G.S. demand for long range, but in January, 1939, it was agreed that the specification should include a shell of 90-100 lb., a range of 16,000 yards, and a weight of equipment not exceeding five and a half tons. Out of this specification there was evolved, in the spring of 1939, the 5.5-in. gun/how., which was finally approved for production in August of that year. Meanwhile, the Director of Artillery had been urging that the existing stock of 76 converted 60-pr./4.5-in. guns was inadequate, and, largely on his own initiative, had proceeded with the design of a new 4.5-in. equipment that was to fit the same carriage as the new 5.5-in.

These two new weapons, the 4.5-in. gun and the 5.5-in. gun/how., with approximately the same shell-power as their predecessors, gave a substantial increase in range. The first could throw a 55-lb. shell up to 20,500 yards, the second a 100-lb. shell up to 16,000 yards, as against the 16,000 yards range of the 60-pr. and the 9,800 yards range of the 6-in. how. with the 100 lb., and 11,400 yards with the 86-lb. shell.

Thus, at last, medium artillery had been brought into line, on paper, with continental developments (*see* Table A), but it was to be a long time before the weapons themselves materialized. It was in fact realized in December, 1938, that, as a result of the priority given to A.D.G.B., the Army would continue to be equipped for the next two years with medium artillery that was outranged by modern German artillery.

"Pneumatization" was largely completed before the war, and finished during the summer of 1940. In September, 1939, however, production of the new equipments had not even started, and when it did start, a further set-back was incurred through the failure of the first carriage on proof; a failure that was at least partly attributable to the late decision to mount a 5.5-in. instead of a 5-in. gun/how. The production of ammunition had also been adversely affected, and by the outbreak of war no delivery of either type, 4.5 in. or 5.5 in., had been made.

Heavy and Super-Heavy Artillery

For its heavy and super-heavy artillery the Army in 1939 had to rely on veterans of the First World War, such as the 8-in., 9.2-in., 12-in. and 18-in. hows., and the 6-in. and 9.2-in. guns. These were essentially siege pieces, designed to reduce systematic and strong enemy positions. They were of great weight, slow in and out of action, and entirely unsuited to a war of movement. The 9.2-in. how., for example, weighed 21 tons, moved in three loads at a road speed of 3 m.p.h., and took from five to twelve hours to get into action. The 9.2-in. gun and the 18-in. how. were railway mounted, the 12-in. how. both towed and railway mounted.

Designs for a new 8.8-in. how. and 6-in. gun had been discussed in 1925-26, but nothing came of them; and later, when modernization began in earnest, heavy artillery was naturally put at the bottom of the list. With the growth of air support, long-range guns were not so necessary as they had been in 1914-18. They were in fact regarded as something of a luxury that would have to wait until the re-equipment of divisional and corps artilleries had been completed.

In the summer of 1937, when the subject was reviewed, it seemed unlikely that the R.A.F. would ever have enough aircraft to undertake effective ground operations, and the question of a new heavy gun and howitzer was perforce re-opened. The difficulty, as in medium artillery, was to strike a balance between range and shell-power. On April 25th, 1938, when the matter was finally discussed by the Chief of the Imperial General Staff's Specification Committee, it was considered that the normal role of heavy artillery would continue to be the shelling of distant communications and the disruption of strong defences. For the first of these tasks the primary requirement was range; for the second, shell-power. Hence, it was decided that two types of weapon would be required: a gun, firing a 100-lb. shell to a maximum range of 26,500 yards; and a howitzer, with a 300-lb. shell and a maximum range of 16,000 yards.

After some discussion it was decided to proceed with designs for a 7.85-in. how. and a 6.85-in. gun, but before either of them could materialize there was another change of policy. On January 2nd, 1939, the 7.85-in. how. was dropped in favour of a new and more mobile 9.2-in. how., and by October, 1939, the 6.85-in. gun had also been abandoned.

When war broke out, therefore, there was no modern equipment in sight. The best that could be done was to improve the mobility of those already in existence. The 1st—and only—Heavy Regiment, which had previously been equipped with the old 9.2-in. how., was re-armed in April, 1939, with twelve 8-in. hows. (three batteries) and four 6-in. guns (one battery) on pneumatic-tyred carriages.

Anti-Tank Defence

It was the tank that had restored mobility to the battlefield—after the gun had failed to do so (*see* p. 2)—by neutralizing both the machine-gun and the wire obstacle. At a conference of army schools held at Camberley in January, 1938, it was agreed that " neither infantry nor guns are suitable for cutting wire, save in very exceptional circumstances."

What the gun could do, however, was to stop or turn aside the tank, and it was not long before a special type of equipment (2-pr.) was introduced for this purpose. Originally, it was intended to be a purely infantry weapon, and, for mobility and ease of handling, it was mounted on a low-wheeled carriage suitable for traction by M.T. The 25-prs. of the divisional artillery were to be responsible primarily for their own self-defence against a tank attack, though it was accepted that on occasions individual guns might have to be sited for the anti-tank defence of forward areas. For this purpose they were eventually provided with a special armour-piercing (A.P.) shot, though not until many valuable months had been lost trying to meet a G.S. requirement for A.P. plugs in H.E. shell.

The 2-pr. was a good gun and compared very favourably with its German equivalent, the 3.7 cm. (*see* Table A). When, therefore, in 1938, a start was made with the formation of anti-tank regiments, R.A., each consisting of four batteries with 12 guns to a battery, the same weapon was adopted.

By this time it had become evident that a heavier anti-tank gun would soon be required to compete with tanks carrying up to 70 mm. of armour, and to meet this requirement a 6-pr. equipment was under development. A pilot gun was ordered in April, 1938, but the design was not clear until April, 1940. Carriage design was started towards the end of 1939 but was not cleared until early 1941.

Before the introduction of the anti-tank regiment, R.A., the responsibility for the organization of anti-tank defence had been clearly defined. In the area occupied by the forward infantry it lay with infantry brigade commanders. Behind this area artillery commanders would be responsible for organizing a second line of defence; and behind this again the general staff would arrange for centres of resistance, and for the protection of roads, bridges and other defiles.([4])

With the introduction of the anti-tank regiment, R.A., this doctrine was gradually modified, though by the time the war broke out the new division of responsibility had not been finally enunciated. Some valuable experience had, however, been gained on manoeuvres. In the siting of F.D.Ls., for example, allowance had to be made for the anti-tank guns, and this sometimes meant a change from forward slope to rear slope positions. In the siting of the guns themselves, it was found, anything in the nature of a " thin red line " along the front was to be avoided, and " areas covering the most likely lines of approach should be allotted to troops with the guns disposed in depth."([5])

From the earliest days, instructions for the handling of anti-tank guns had aimed at controlling the natural tendency to fire too soon and too fast. It was perhaps the same tendency that had induced Wellington to order his riflemen to withhold their fire until they could see the whites of the enemy's eyes. But there was another argument against opening fire at long ranges with anti-tank guns. The gun was stationary and the tank could move. Thus, by prematurely disclosing its position, the gun would expose itself to the risk of being out-manoeuvred and shot up from the rear.

In 1926, therefore, it was laid down that the most suitable rate of fire for the 18-pr. was 8 to 12 r.p.g.m., and that the most effective range for engagement was between 1,000 and 400 yards. For the siting of anti-tank guns, defiladed positions on reverse slopes were recommended, and a field of fire of 500 yards was accepted as adequate. At the same time, the engagement of tanks with indirect fire, while they were assembling behind their own lines in preparation for an attack, was regarded as feasible, and field batteries were trained in this form of fire.

Co-operation with Armoured Forces

Although it was clear from the start how the gun might hinder the tank, it was not so easy to decide how it might help the latter to preserve its momentum in the attack. In 1930 the chance of developing a S.P. field gun was allowed to slip (see p. 9); and in 1931, when the formation of mobile divisions was first adumbrated, the gun was not considered as a means of close support. Mechanized field and medium artillery was to be included in the division, but was to be used chiefly for the attack on a prepared position.([6])

By 1937, when the first mobile division was actually formed, this policy had undergone a change. The R.H.A., whose normal role had always been co-operation with mobile troops, was now equipped with the 3.7-in. how., and it was two such regiments (mechanized) that provided the artillery for the mobile division. Included in their tasks was " the support by fire of the attack of the tank brigade ".([7])

For this work the 3.7-in. how. proved itself unsuitable. Its anti-tank performance, in particular, was inadequate ; and when, as a result of exercises held in England in 1938, the mobile division was reorganized as an armoured division of one light armoured brigade, one heavy armoured brigade and a support group, its artillery was completely rearmed. It now consisted of one regiment of 25-prs. and one L.A.A. and anti-tank regiment, comprising two batteries of Bofors and two of 2-pr. anti-tank guns. These two regiments, with two motorized infantry battalions, formed the bulk of the support group, whose main roles were now considered to be the safeguarding of flanks and communications, the securing of defiles in rear of the armoured brigades, and the provision of a screen behind which the latter might rest.

A.A. Defence

In 1933 the A.A. defence of the field army was provided by a single air defence brigade, which was designed chiefly for the day and night defence of a base port, or ports. Its main armament was the 3-in. 20-cwt. A.A. gun, another veteran of the First World War, whose performance had been greatly improved by the development of a travelling platform and a modern system of fire control that gave it an effective ceiling of 18,000 feet. For defence against low-flying attacks there was one anti-aircraft light machine gun section to each battery. Illumination for night firing was provided by a searchlight battalion, R.E., with an establishment of 96 lights.

By 1936 the increased performance of aircraft had necessitated consideration of a new and bigger gun, with a heavier shell and a higher ceiling (see Table A). In July of that year the War Office agreed to take a number of naval 4.5 in. A.A. guns for the defence of ports, about which the Admiralty had expressed concern. For future production, however, a newly designed 3.7-in. gun was accepted as the standard, and in October, 1936, it was ruled that all equipments should be on a fully mobile basis. Later on it was found impossible to produce mobile carriages fast enough to meet the demands of war and a static mounting was accepted for A.D.G.B. and ports abroad. For the field force it was decided to retain some of the large existing stock of the 3-in. 20-cwt. equipment, which was nearly a ton lighter than the 3.7-in. and was likely to prove adequate for the defence of forward areas.

Meanwhile airmen had been developing two methods of bombing that evaded the zone in which the predictor-laid A.A. gun was effective : by flying so low that the angular rates of change were beyond the capacity of the predictor mechanism, or by diving at the objective and so upsetting one of the basic A.A. assumptions, that the target would maintain a constant height. Both methods, incidentally, enabled the airman to dispense with his own rather complicated sights and thus made his problem easier.

Such attacks represented a serious menace to the small V.P. and something had to be done to stop them. Hitherto the emphasis had been on volume of fire in the engagement of low-flying aircraft, and the General Staff had been unwilling to accept a weapon of the gun type. The prevailing idea was to produce a stream of tracer bullets that could be directed on a simple hose-pipe system and might be expected to have a moral as well as material effect upon the attacker. Now aircraft were being equipped with armour proof against the small arms bullet, and it was agreed that destructive effect should be given more consideration. In June, 1936, the War Office lifted their ban on research on calibres greater than 0.5-in., and plans were made to adapt the Vickers 2-pr. naval gun for army purposes. The eight-barrelled mounting, as then fitted in H.M.'s ships, was not suitable for use ashore, but a twin mounting was designed that gave a combined rate of fire of 120 rounds per minute. This was essentially a static weapon, and there remained the problem of producing a mobile gun of similar performance. In view of the urgency of the requirement, it was decided in 1937 to adopt the Bofors 40-mm. gun, which was already in production in Sweden. It had a high rate of fire and an excellent field carriage, and when fitted with a No. 3 predictor and a power operated remote control system, its effect was superior to that of the 2-pr. twin. Production of the latter was therefore limited to 60 equipments.

The operation of the predictor depended on the use of a generator, which had to be carried in a separate vehicle, and some doubts were expressed regarding its suitability for mobile warfare. Its performance at practice camp was, however, so impressive—one hit in every three or four rounds instead of one in 33, which was the best that could be expected with the forward area sight or any other form of "eye shooting"—and war was so obviously imminent that it was decided to order enough to cover the requirements of the field army.

To avoid damage to ground installations from falling projectiles, the shell were fitted with a self-destroying element that functioned after a time of seven seconds. For this and other reasons, the effective range of the gun was limited to 2,500 yards, which was equivalent to a ceiling of about 4,000 feet.

By 1939, further improvements had become necessary in the system for dealing with the high level bomber. The main weaknesses were the uncertainty of a timely pick-up, owing to the increasing height and speed at which level bombing attacks were to be expected, and the difficulty of measuring height correctly. Moreover, even if picked up in time, the modern aircraft would not remain for long a suitable target. It was only during the final run-up to the point of bomb release, which was calculated to last between 30 and 45 seconds, that the high level bomber was forced to behave uniformly. At any other time during his approach or withdrawal, he could, and would, take evasive action; if not continuously, at least whenever he saw the flashes of A.A. guns or realized that he was being accurately fired at.

The policy was, therefore, to concentrate guns for the defence of vital and vulnerable areas, the number of which would be kept as low as possible by the use of dispersion, concealment and other P.A.D. measures. It was laid down in 1939 that, for the most important areas, a 16-gun density should be the aim; and that, for areas of less importance, a 4-gun density should provide sufficient deterrent effect.([8])

The minimum defence of a single V.P. against low-flying or dive-bombing attack was generally accepted as a troop of four Bofors, and since, for administrative reasons, it was undesirable to split the troop, it was laid down that all such weapons should be allotted in terms of troops rather than of individual guns.

Since an attack might come from any direction, lay-outs were generally circular in shape, with the guns evenly spaced in rings around the area to be defended; and as the height of attack increased, the outer ring was pushed further and further out and lay-outs in consequence became very scattered. Hence difficulties were experienced over local protection, inter-communication and administration.

Searchlight lay-outs in particular covered a vast area and were very expensive in men and material. Apart from the inadequacy of sound location, which was then the only means of initial pick-up at night, the effectiveness of the searchlight itself seemed likely to be greatly reduced by the nascent practice of "doping" the under surface of a night bomber so that it would not reflect the light of a searchlight beam. It was indeed the opinion of the experts that nothing less than a whole searchlight battalion (96 lights) would suffice for the effective defence of a single base port or similar area.

For this reason it was thought by some that the role of the A.A.S.L. as an aid to the A.A. gun against high-flying targets was finished. In ·A.D.G.B. the searchlights were used mainly in the aircraft fighting zone (A.F.Z.), in which enemy bombers were to be intercepted by fighter aircraft before they came within reach of the defended area. When employed in this way, beams that failed to illuminate a target might still act as valuable pointers, and perhaps even disclose to the night fighter targets that could not be seen by a ground observer.

Then came radar, which promised to solve the problem not only of early warning of the approach of aircraft, but also of laying the guns on an unseen target. By the time war broke out both these projects were well advanced, but no radar set was ready for issue to B.E.F. units for their move across to France; and when it did appear, towards the end of 1939, the first radar set was not effective for unseen fire (*see* Table B).

Against very low-flying aircraft, radar was ineffective even as a warning device, and intercepting fighters were further handicapped by the impossibility of getting into the best position for attack. Fortunately, at night, the dazzle effect of a searchlight could still be very embarrassing. As an alternative means of defence, the R.A.F. were developing the balloon barrage, but this could not be flown in the vicinity of an airfield. It might therefore, it was thought, "sometimes be advisable to allot 6 or 12 lights for the defence of a small vulnerable area against low-flying attack, relying mainly on moral and dazzle effect."([9])

The A.A. Barrage

In field artillery, the barrage had been introduced to neutralize an enemy whose precise position could not be determined (*see* p. 2). The A.A. barrage was not strictly comparable, since its role was to deter, not to neutralize. It was in fact more akin to the defensive fire of the field artillery (*see* p. 3). Yet it owed its origin to the same factor: inability to fix the exact position at which the shell should burst; either because the target could not be seen, owing to cloud or darkness, or because its future position could not be accurately predicted on account of its evasive action (*see* p. 19).

It was in 1918 that A.A. barrages were first used, for the defence of London. The idea was revived in 1927, and again in 1938, but an up-to-date drill for field army units had not been worked out in any detail.

Co-operation between Guns and Fighters

The experience of years in coast artillery had taught the importance of good early warning and identification systems to avoid misunderstandings between the fixed (artillery) and mobile (naval) defences. Since neither could be entirely relied on, certain restrictions had to be imposed on the liberty of action both of guns and ships.

In A.A. defence the need for such restrictions was even greater. In an A.F.Z. absolute priority had to be given to the fighters, and gun fire was prohibited. At the heart of a defensive system, on the other hand, there was usually a zone—such as the inner artillery zone (I.A.Z.) over the centre of London—where the position was reversed and guns were free to fire at any aircraft not identified as friendly. In between these two extremes were places where some form of compromise was necessary. Over some gun defended areas (G.D.As.) flying might be banned to all but fighter aircraft; over others, definite heights and routes might be laid down for the passage of friendly bombers, etc. As a further safety precaution, recognition signals were introduced, as in coast defence, to enable an aircraft to establish its identity when approaching such areas, when off course and uncertain of its position, or, in the last resort, when actually being engaged by the ground defences.

A.A. Defence in the Forward Areas

There were now two distinct types of A.A. gun, and the distinction was henceforth to be recognized in the nomenclature and organization of A.A. units. The 3-in. and 3.7-in. guns were classified as heavy (H.A.A.), the 2-pr. and A.A.L.M.G. as light (L.A.A.), artillery; and, in conformity with this new development, the L.A.A. element was withdrawn from the H.A.A. regiment and separate L.A.A. regiments were raised. At the same time the air defence brigades, now increased to two, were renamed A.A. brigades.

The scale of L.A.A. defence in the field was still small—one regiment out of three in each A.A. brigade—but it was beginning to be recognized that special L.A.A. units would have to be provided for the forward areas, if the latter were to get their fair share of the A.A. "umbrella".

Though defence of V.P.s was regarded as the primary role of A.A. guns, there were other tasks that had to be considered, such as the engagement of reconnaissance aircraft, the protection of movements, or the defence of the forward infantry and field gun areas. No special allotment was made for this purpose, but it was agreed that there should be "a varying number of A.A. guns in the forward area to deal with reconnaissance aircraft and high bombing", and that these would "also be of value against low-flying attacks."[10]

It was recognized, however, that the engagement of a reconnaissance aircraft might do more harm than good by disclosing the whereabouts of our own forces without preventing the information from getting back to the enemy commander. The policy was, therefore, not to engage a single reconnaissance aircraft unless it was so low that it might be presumed to have detected the presence of our forces, and a "kill" could reasonably be expected if A.A. fire was opened.

In view of the dissimilarities between A.A. and field artillery tactics, the control of A.A. defence measures was accepted as a direct responsibility of the general staff. Since A.A. defence was an area problem, it was considered "impracticable in general to include anti-aircraft units in particular formations of a field force." A.A. brigades and units, if allotted to corps or divisions, would normally receive their orders direct from the general staff, and the A.A. commander would "act as adviser on anti-aircraft matters in the same way as the C.R.A. on field artillery problems."[11]

Coast Defence

Before the outbreak of war, certain steps, already mentioned, had been taken with the object of bringing the Coast Defences into a more up-to-date state.

These included the introduction of three modern types of equipment (*see* Table A), a new range-finding system, a new data transmission system and improved fire control instruments. In addition, experimental and development work was proceeding on radar for coast artillery (*see* Table B).

Owing however to the great cost of installing new coast artillery equipment and to its low priority compared to other branches of the artillery, little progress with the modernization or the reorganization of the coast defences was actually made earlier than 1939.

Conclusion

In spite of the inevitable complications resulting from the development of anti-tank and A.A. artillery, considerable progress had been made with the simplification of equipment and drills. The mechanization of artillery and the improvement of wireless had laid the foundations for a new standard of mobility, both of manoeuvre and of fire. The armoured O.P. and the air O.P. were on the point of being realized, and the S.P. gun, though temporarily in abeyance, had proved itself to be a practical proposition. In A.A. defence, the discovery of radar promised to reduce, if not to eliminate, the gap that had developed between the powers of the attack and the defence.

The disquieting factor had been the length of time required to get policy decisions and therefore to start on the development and production of the new equipments. It had taken five years or more of discussion to clear the design of the 25-pr. and the 3.7-in. A.A. gun, and the problem of heavy and super-heavy artillery was never really satisfactorily settled.

There were, probably, four main causes of these delays: the age-old controversy between range and shell-power, about which gunners themselves are frequently unable to agree; the development of air bombing, which distracted attention from heavy and super-heavy artillery until it was found that the R.A.F. was unlikely to be able to undertake effective ground operations (*see* p. 16); financial restrictions; and the oft repeated assurance that there would be "no war for ten years", which must sometimes have acted as an inducement to postpone difficult decisions.

List of References

[1] Military Operations in France and Belgium, 1918, Vol. v, p. 47.
[2] Memo. on the Training of the R.A., 1937.
[3] Arty. Training, Vol. II, Pamphlet No. 2A, 1940, p. 1.
[4] Arty. Training, Vol. III, 1928, pp. 82, 83.
[5] Journal of the R.A., Vol. LXVI, No. 1, April 1939, p. 105.
[6] "Modern Formations", 1931, p. 26.
[7] F.S.R., Vol. II, 1935, p. 4.
[8] Manual of A.A. Defence, Vol. II, Pamphlet No. 1, 1940, pp. 31, 34.
[9] *Ibid*, p. 45.
[10] A.T.M., No. 20, April 1938.
[11] Manual of A.A. Defence, Vol. II, Pamphlet No. 2, 1940, p. 15.

TABLE B
DEVELOPMENT OF ARTILLERY RADAR

Set	Role	Date on which		In Supply from	Performance on medium bomber	Remarks
		Experimental work started	Development of Equipment started			
(1)	(2)	(3)	(4)	(5)	(6)	(7)
A.A. No. 1—						
Mk. I	Local warning and aid to visual control. Modified to embryo unseen fire control.	Nov., 1936	Oct., 1938	Aug., 1939 to April, 1941	Pick-up range 30,000 yds. Fire control 14,000 yds.	Commonly known as G.L. I. Modification for unseen fire control started August, 1940. Replaced by G.L. II.
Mk. II	Local warning and unseen fire control.	Spring, 1939	Aug., 1939	June, 1940 to Aug., 1943	Pick-up range 50,000 yds. Fire control 14,000 yards.	Commonly known as G.L. II. Continued in use throughout war for various purposes including "putting on" A.A. No. 3.
A.A. No. 3—						
Mk. II	Unseen fire control	Nov., 1940	Spring, 1941	Dec., 1942 to April, 1945	Pick-up and fire control at 27,000 yds.	Commonly known as G.L. III. A Canadian set (Mk. I) was issued in Nov., 1942.
Mk. III	ditto	—	—	Sept., 1943 to Mar., 1945	As for G.L. II	Commonly known as Baby Maggie. An emergency set designed to cover delay in production of G.L. III.
Mk. IV	ditto	Jan., 1942	End of 1944	Early 1946 *et seq.*	Pick-up and automatic follow from 36,000 yds. to 1,000 yards. Could continue following to and through the zenith.	Prototype for Mk. VII. A few sets only ordered for emergency use.
Mk. VII	ditto	—	—	—	—	Fully designed auto fire control, developed in Canada. No delivery by end of war.

A.A. No. 4— Mks. II & III	Local warning and "putting on" G.L. III.	Autumn, 1941	Spring, 1942	1943/1944	Pick-up range 25 miles for targets at 3,000 ft. 45 miles for targets at 15,000 ft.	Commonly known as L.W. The Mk. I set was part of the Canadian type G.L. III set. It was not satisfactory.
Mk. V	Local warning, tactical control and "putting on".	—	Mar., 1944	May, 1944, to end of war.	Pick-up range 50,000 yds. at height up to 25,000 ft.	Commonly known as Gorganzola. A special provision for 21st Army Gp. "Normandy" operations.
Mk. VI	Local warning and tactical control.	—	—	End of 1945 et seq.	—	No delivery by end of war.
A.A. No. 2— Mks. I and II	Direction and control of A.A.S.L.s.	April, 1940	Sept., 1940	Sept., 1940 to Feb., 1941	—	Emergency types for use during development of Mk. III.
Mks. III to VII	ditto	—	Nov., 1940	April, 1941 to Dec., 1943	Pick-up range 15–18,000 yds.	Standard service type commonly known as S.L.C.
Mk. VIII	ditto	Autumn, 1942	Early 1944	Sept., 1944 to Feb., 1945	Automatic following to 18,000 yds., and probably more.	Emergency type, and prototype of Mk. IX.
Mk. IX	ditto	—	—	Jan., 1946 et seq.	ditto	No delivery by end of war.
C.D. No. 1— Mks. I to III	Anti-invasion, tracking surface craft, convoy protection.	Late 1938	Aug., 1939	Dec., 1940 to Sept., 1941	—	Permanent structures, commonly known as C.D./C.H.L.
Mk. IV	Long range cover, and tracking of surface craft.	April, 1941	May, 1941	July, 1941 to Aug., 1942	Pick-up range dependent on height of site. Extended to horizon and a little way beyond.	A mobile set adapted from Naval type 271. Twelve emergency sets only available up to March, 1942.
Mk. V	ditto	—	Mar., 1942	Sept., 1942 to Feb., 1944	ditto	Transportable: operated in container or transferred to permanent structure (as Mk. VI).
Mk. VI	Long range cover, and tracking of surface craft, and low aircraft.	—	—	Sept., 1942 to July, 1943	ditto	Emplacement or tower.

TABLE B. DEVELOPMENT OF ARTILLERY RADAR—continued.

Set (1)	Role (2)	Date on which		In Supply from (5)	Performance on medium bomber (6)	Remarks (7)
		Experimental work started (3)	Development of Equipment started (4)			
C.A. No. 1—Mk. I	Coast artillery battery fire control.	Late 1938	Late 1938	—	Pick-up at 40,000 yds. Accurate fire control at 36,000 yds., if horizon permitted.	Cancelled and modified as Mk. II.
Mks. II & III	ditto	Autumn, 1941	Late 1941	Aug., 1942 to June, 1945	ditto	—
Mk. IV	Coast artillery battery fire control and fall of shot observation.	Early 1942	Winter, 1942/3	Mar., 1944 to May, 1944	As above, plus fall of shot observation.	Commonly known as "Charlie". Six sets only produced (by R.R.D.E.). Production proper did not start before end of war.
C.A. No. 2—Mk. I	Coast artillery fire commander's set.	—	July, 1941	July, 1941 to Feb, 1944	As for C.D. No. 1 Mks. IV–VI, with expanded range presentation added.	This set showed a picture, in range only 1,000 yds each side target.

PART II

CLEARING THE ATMOSPHERE

CHAPTER III

FRANCE AND BELGIUM, 1939-40

Plate Relevant to this Chapter
No. 7. The 8-in. howitzer.

Equipment Difficulties

On 3rd September, 1939, the artillery rearmament programme was still very far from completion. A number of converted 18/25-prs. had been issued, but no new 25-pr. equipment, and anti-tank ammunition for field guns was completely lacking (*see* pp. 16, 17). There was a shortage of 2-pr. anti-tank guns; the bulk of the medium artillery was equipped with the 6-in. how. and had in consequence a quite inadequate range; and the production of an up-to-date heavy artillery weapon had not started.

The situation was aggravated by French insistence on a degree of military support far in excess of what had been agreed to. By November, 1939, the supply of converted 18/25 prs. had run out and divisions had begun to arrive armed with 18-prs. and 4.5-in. hows. The attempt to equip new formations had also led to a general shortage of transport, which could only be overcome by the requisitioning of large numbers of civilian vehicles.

Instead, therefore, of the simplification that had been hoped for, there was a complexity of equipment that greatly increased the difficulties both of administration and training. Many of the T.A. regiments were still unfit for active service, and divisions armed only with the 18-pr. or 4.5-in. how. were likely to find themselves at a serious disadvantage in action owing to their lack of range. It was, moreover, impossible to ensure that ammunition railheads were suitably stocked unless the armament of all divisional artilleries was approximately the same.

For these reasons it was decided, in January, 1940, to reorganize the whole of the field artillery so that every division should, as far as possible, have two 18/25-pr. regiments and one mixed 18-pr. and 4.5-in. how. regiment.

The difficulties experienced in A.A. units were no less severe. The priority given to A.A. weapons in the production programme had been directed primarily to meet the needs of A.D.G.B. (*see* p. 12), and the troubles encountered in the production of the mobile 3.7-in. mounting had naturally fallen more heavily upon field force units. The number of 3-in. 20-cwt. equipments available had also been greatly reduced by issues to other countries, such as Egypt. But it was in L.A.A. units that the deficiencies were most serious. The recency of the decision to adopt the Bofors gun and to increase the L.A.A. defences in the forward areas (*see* p. 21) had particularly affected the corps L.A.A. units, which had no A.F.G. 1098 and only about six guns each, equipped with Polish course and speed sights that were unfamiliar to the detachments.

In the A.A. brigades, transport was not only mixed in quality but inadequate in quantity. Most of these formations were on a "base and forward" establishment, which allowed only a limited degree of mobility to the H.A.A. guns, and even on this reduced scale there was, in March, 1940, still a deficiency of 15 tractors out of a total establishment of 106. Efforts to overcome this difficulty, and to make the A.A. lay-outs fit the needs of the moment, resulted sometimes in complicated transfers between A.A. units, helped out by loans from corps resources.

Inadequacy of War Establishments

Nor was it only equipment that was lacking. During the inter-war period of financial stringency, reductions had been made in the war establishments of many units. The comparable strength of a field brigade in the First World War was 27 per cent. greater than that of a field regiment in 1940. In R.H.A. regiments the figure was 31 per cent., and in medium regiments 63 per cent.

As a result the numbers available were found inadequate to cope with digging and the humping of ammunition, the maintenance of reliefs, and the provision of signallers and crews for L.M.Gs. and anti-tank rifles. On 7th May, 1940, an increase of establishments was asked for by the C.-in-C., and on 17th May, it was approved in principle by the War Office.

The Period of Waiting

That these weaknesses were not more seriously and immediately felt was owing to unexpected delays in the development of the German offensive in the West. During this period of waiting the situation in which the B.E.F. found itself, and the nature of the fighting in which it seemed likely to become engaged, were very different from what had been envisaged in peace training. "The type of war we must now consider" said a training memorandum of December, 1939,([1]) " is not the highly mobile type, but a more ponderous war of masses."

During the occupation of the Lille sector by 1 and 2 Corps, artillery dispositions bore a marked resemblance to those of the First World War. Alternative, roving and dummy gun positions were revived, and orders were issued that battle positions were only to be used after the main attack had started. For harassing fire and opportunity shoots in the early stages of the battle, special positions were to be constructed.

The same principle was applied to the preparation of O.Ps. Forward O.Ps., alternative O.Ps. and rear O.Ps.—for use in case the front line was overrun—were all to be prepared in advance and kept properly concealed and operable.

Once the lay-out had been completed, as the war showed no sign of coming nearer, training was started along the lines of the anticipated war of masses. Special attention was paid to the preparation of barrages and counter-battery programmes, and to the current drill for the check of all predicted fire.

The normal rate of advance of a barrage was still 100 yards in three minutes for an infantry attack (*see* p. 3), but had been increased to 100 yards in one minute for a tank attack; and to meet this increase in speed, an alteration had had to be made in the size of each "lift".

The determining factor in calculating the size of a lift was the rate at which the required density of fire could be built up. With the 25-pr., it was not possible to put down an adequate number of shell on any one line in less than two minutes. Hence, for a rate of advance of 100 yards in one minute, the minimum size of a lift would be 200 yards.

The density and depth of a barrage would of course depend on the number of guns and the amount of ammunition that could be dumped in the time available. A trial at the School of Artillery, Larkhill, in May, 1940, showed that 500 r.p.g. was the maximum that a troop could dump and make ready to fire in one night under average conditions.[2]

The time required to produce the data for a barrage was estimated as :—

- (a) For a single regiment, three hours after the receipt of orders at regimental headquarters, assuming that the guns were already in action.
- (b) For a divisional artillery, 10 to 12 hours after receipt of orders by the C.R.A.
- (c) For a corps artillery, 24 hours after receipt of orders by the C.C.R.A.

These times did not take into consideration the time required for the dumping of ammunition, or for the moving of guns, if this was necessary.[3]

During the inter-war period, it will be remembered, no specific ruling had been given regarding the distance at which infantry should follow behind a moving barrage. Now it was stated that they could move up to within 150 yards of a 25-pr. barrage fired over their heads, or up to within 200 yards of a barrage fired in enfilade.[4]

The Crooked Barrage

Simplicity had always been an important feature of barrage plans, and for this reason it had been laid down before the war that " fire should be put down as far as possible in straight lines at right angles to the line of advance."[5] In the type of warfare now envisaged, however, absolute simplicity was difficult to achieve. " In large scale attacks on a wide front, especially if launched from an entrenched position, a straight starting line, and hence a straight opening line, will seldom if ever be obtainable."[6] Infantry dispositions had to conform to natural features, which seldom run in continuous straight lines, and a crooked starting line might, it was felt, have to be accepted as a lesser evil than the withdrawal of the forward infantry in certain sectors, or the staging of a preliminary attack in order to smooth out irregularities.

It was therefore decided to introduce a standard drill for the crooked barrage, and for this purpose two alternative methods were laid down : the wheel and the echelon. In the wheel, the attacking troops were automatically brought square on to their objective by the barrage, and all units were timed to reach the objective simultaneously ; but those on the outside, who set the pace, had to move faster than those on the inside. In the echelon, the lines of the barrage remained parallel throughout and all units were therefore able to advance at the same speed, but they did not all reach the objective simultaneously. (*See* Diagram 1.)

DIAGRAMMATIC ILLUSTRATION OF THE CROOKED BARRAGE

(i) The Wheel Method.

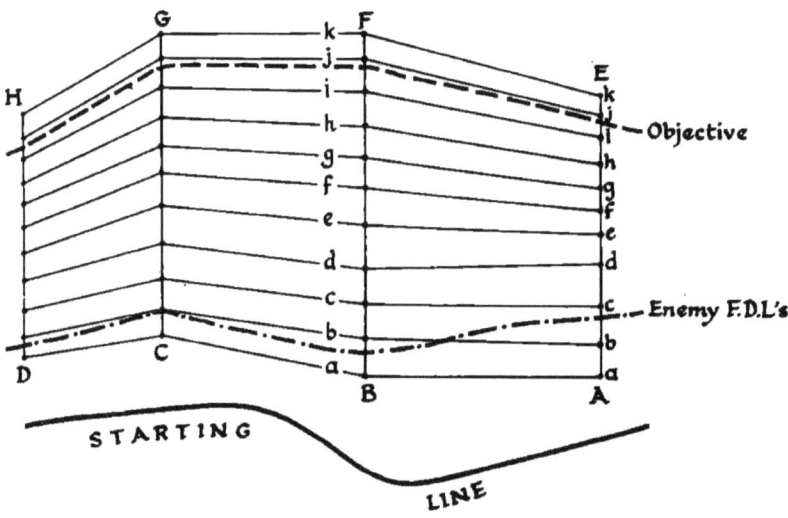

(ii) The Echelon Method.

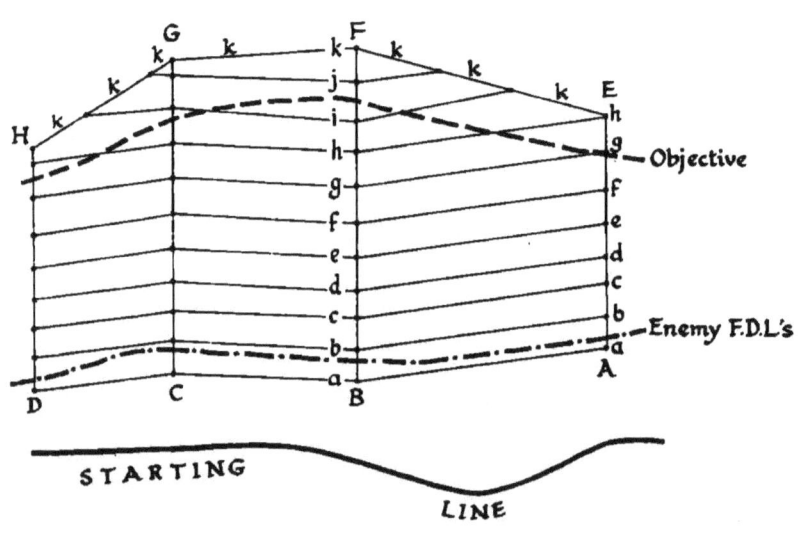

The Base Ejection Smoke Shell

The introduction of the base ejection hexaclonthane smoke shell was another development of this period. Experience showed that this projectile had two great advantages over its predecessor, the white phosphorous smoke shell: the smoke was less inclined to pillar, and it continued to be emitted from the container for some time after landing, instead of being discharged in a single puff. Its main disadvantage was that, at low angles of descent, the containers tended to bounce and thus to cause inaccuracy or gaps in the screen. In mountainous country, too, the difficulties inherent in the vagaries of wind currents were added to by the tendency for the containers to roll down hill.

In general, however, the shell was a success and its introduction increased the uses to which artillery smoke screens could be put. The use of a moving smoke screen as a substitute for a creeping barrage was not much advocated, owing to the risk of interference with the movements of one's own troops; but selected areas could be blinded in succession as the infantry or tanks advanced, and in mobile warfare this might lead to a valuable saving of time and ammunition.

Heavy and Super-Heavy Artillery

In the first contingent, the one available heavy regiment had been recently rearmed with 6-in. guns and 8-in. hows. modified to make them really mobile (see p. 16). The supply of these equipments soon ran out, however, and later heavy regiments had to be equipped with the cumbersome 9.2-in. how. To them were added a small quantity of super-heavy artillery in the shape of 9.2-in. guns and 12-in. hows., the former on railway mountings. The remainder of the existing stock of super-heavy equipments was used for the defence of Great Britain.

Soon after the outbreak of war, the Admiralty offered heavy guns from obsolete battleships for mounting on land carriages. The offer was, however, declined on the grounds that "these monster equipments had a very limited practical or even moral effect on land operations", and that, for long range harassing fire, "the possibility of the bomber was being considered".

Shooting with Air Observation

In April, 1939, attempts were being made to increase the number of previously unlocated targets that could be dealt with in the course of a single sortie. During the winter of 1939-40, trials were continued, using regimental concentrations on fresh locations given in G.N.F. (guns now firing) calls, and this method was found to give satisfactory results.

Some progress was also made with the development of the air O.P. An experimental flight of the R.A.F. was formed at Mailly and two batteries were attached for trials; but the latter had not been completed when, on 10th May, the artillery units had to be withdrawn for the advance into Belgium, and the whole scheme came temporarily to a standstill. Whatever the promise of success in the future, it was evident that no flying O.P. could hope to live in the air until some measure of local air superiority had been achieved; and for the time being the R.A.F. had to concentrate upon winning the battle of Britain.

Anti-Tank Defence

"When the 1st Corps arrived in the sector assigned to the B.E.F. in the first week in October, an almost continuous tank obstacle already existed in the form of a ditch covered by concrete blockhouses built to mount anti-tank guns and machine-guns."(⁸) Behind this obstacle a defensive system was organized on principles that had been taking shape as experience was gained in the handling of the 2-pr. In attack or defence, initial orders as to the location and deployment of anti-tank batteries or troops would be issued by the infantry commander under whose orders they had been placed, and their role would be complementary to that of the recently introduced brigade anti-tank company of nine 25-mm. guns. Subsequent action by the anti-tank regimental commander, acting in accordance with the divisional commander's instructions, would ensure co-ordination between the different brigade lay-outs, between forward 25-prs. and the rear 2-prs. of infantry brigade sectors, and between anti-tank weapons in general and the siting of minefields or the development of natural obstacles.

The principles to be observed in the siting of anti-tank weapons remained the same as before: guns to be sited singly, on reverse rather than on forward slopes, defiladed from the front, and either within an infantry locality or protected by the fire of neighbouring localities. A field of fire of more than 800 yards was not considered essential, and in general fire was to be held until the range had closed to two or three hundred yards.

During the preparation of the frontier defences, the excessive length of divisional frontages (about 10,000 yards) caused the disposition of anti-tank guns to average about one gun to every 180 yards, as compared with the 34 yards favoured by German opinion at that time. The general policy was to form, in depth, a succession of barriers of interlocked arcs of fire, with minefields laid to cover the more obvious lines of tank approach and to shepherd the attackers into areas covered by anti-tank weapons; but, with the numbers available, the concentrations of anti-tank fire in such areas was inevitably small. In fact, so stretched were the resources, it was difficult to avoid some of the evils of the "thin red line".

Last, and most important of all, it was generally agreed that the guns must be sited primarily for the destruction of tanks, and not merely for the defence of localities. It was a happy reminder, amid so much that was purely defensive, that the gun is predominantly an offensive weapon.

The Temporary Break-up of the Support Group

On the outbreak of war our armoured forces were only in embryo with regard to organization and training. The 1st Armoured Division in the United Kingdom was still far from complete in equipment, and the 2nd, which did not form until January, 1940, had only a token issue of light tanks for training. After 3rd September, 1939, priority for all equipment coming from production was given to units composing the first contingent and successive increments of the B.E.F. There was therefore little available for the expansion and training of the forces at home. Moreover, the anticipation of a war of masses on the Western Front caused attention to be focussed on "I" tanks rather than on armoured formations associated with highly mobile warfare. Further consideration was indeed given to the role of an armoured division, as a result of which it was again reorganized into two homogeneous brigades each of three armoured regiments and a support group. But the first of these divisions was not destined to move to France until the middle of May 1940, and in the meantime its 25-pr. regiment had been sent on in advance to make up some of the deficiencies in field artillery, and its motorized battalions went to Norway. Hence the support group never had a chance of continuing its training, or functioning in battle, in its proper role.

The Revival of Wire Cutting as a Task for the Artillery

The development of the anti-tank ditch and minefield had considerably reduced the efficacy of the tank as a means of breaching wire defences, and had thus led to a reversal of the decision arrived at in 1938 (*see* p. 16). The disadvantages of the gun as a wire cutter had in no way diminished, but no better substitute had yet presented itself, and it was therefore once again invested with this difficult role. Calculations, based on experience in the First World War, showed that, with 25-pr. H.E., one direct hit would be required for every five square yards of wire to be destroyed.

The Growth of A.A. Defence

The original A.A. component of the B.E.F. was of modest dimensions, and its activities and problems could be controlled without much difficulty by G(Ops), at G.H.Q. (*see* p. 22). Two A.A. brigades and four L.A.A. regiments—totalling 72 H.A.A. guns, 84 L.A.A. guns, 192 L.M.Gs. and 96 searchlights—would not stretch far when it came to putting up the A.A. umbrella. With French assistance, however, it was just possible to provide cover in accordance with pre-war doctrine, though in few if any places did the scale of H.A.A. defence come up to the standard of a 16-gun density (*see* p. 20).

One L.A.A. regiment was placed under command of each of the two corps, one was allotted for the defence of R.A.F. component aerodromes, and the fourth—which was not included in the first contingent—was distributed among important L. of C. installations. Of the two A.A. brigades, one was made responsible for the defence of the base ports, the other of the move forward to the concentration area and, subsequently, of maintenance railheads and G.H.Q., to which was allotted one H.A.A. and one L.A.A. battery.

The lack of radar was disappointing and was one reason for the omission to use Le Havre as a main base port for the initial stages of the concentration. It was rectified towards the end of 1939, when the first radar sets began to arrive. Though unfitted for the engagement of unseen aircraft, they could generally be relied on to give early warning of an attack from seawards and thus assist the guns to obtain a timely pick-up.

Because of the doubts that prevailed regarding their efficiency in a gun zone (*see* p. 20), the searchlights were used at first in support of Fighter Wing, R.A.F., to illuminate an A.F.Z. covering the exposed northern flank of the B.E.F.

By the end of 1939 it had become apparent that the size and complexity of the A.A. problem was too much for the small and non-technical staff available in G(Ops.) at G.H.Q. The arrival, actual or impending, of two new A.A. brigades had almost doubled the A.A. resources, but their relative immobility was a source of embarrassment (*see* p. 28) and their quantity never really caught up with requirements.

In December, therefore, a M.G.A.A. was appointed to act as adviser to the C.-in-C. in A.A. matters, and to command all A.A. formations and units except the corps L.A.A. regiments and those units allotted to the Advanced Air Striking Force for the defence of its aerodromes. With its heightfinders and predictors, its searchlights and sound locators, and now with its radar, A.A. was a very technical arm, which had grown up so quickly that it was largely unfamiliar to senior artillery officers of the field army. Perhaps for this reason, control by the M.G.R.A. was not considered feasible.

About this time a change took place in the policy for the employment of searchlights. Owing to the insistence of the French on freedom of fire for their A.A. guns against unseen targets—and partly to the lack of British fighters—the A.F.Z. had become of little value, and on 3rd March, 1940, it was decided to discontinue it. Thereafter the bulk of the searchlights was deployed in gun zones, with the remainder assisting L.A.A. guns in the defence of aerodromes against low-flying attack by night or in dealing with enemy mine-laying aircraft at certain ports, for which purposes experience in A.D.G.B. had shown them to be very valuable.

Early in 1940, the A.A. defences of Boulogne and Le Havre were reinforced by balloon barrages, each of 24 balloons. These units were under the R.A.F. Component for command and administration, except at Boulogne after 16th March, when the Admiral du Nord placed all the A.A. defences of the port under the command of the local (British) A.A. regiment. This was a solitary instance of unified command that was not usual in the British Service except in dire emergency, and it was not repeated in this campaign.

In April, 1940, trials were begun, under the supervision of the R.A.F., to investigate the possibility of using the dazzle effect of searchlights for the defence of a small V.P. (*see* p. 20). They had not been completed when the battle opened, but the results had been very promising and searchlights were used in this way during operations with excellent results.

In the same month the A.A. intelligence system was greatly improved by the opening of an A.A. operations room (A.A.O.R.) at Arras. Here information of the movements of all aircraft—friendly, hostile and unidentified—was received from the R.A.F. " filter room " and passed to G.O.Rs. in all the defended areas. This helped to simplify the difficult problem of identification at gun positions, and to ease the strain on A.A. detachments by doing away with the necessity for keeping guns constantly in a state of immediate readiness for action.

To minimize the risk of friendly aircraft being engaged in error, detailed instructions had been issued in October, 1939, which forbade A.A. units from firing on aircraft that followed certain prescribed routes or made certain prescribed signals unless they were definitely identified as hostile. Units other than A.A. were not to open fire on any aircraft until it had committed a hostile act or had been definitely identified as hostile.

Lastly, an attempt was made to produce a better organization for the A.A. brigade. The original organization which was designed for the defence of a base port (*see* p. 18), had proved unsuitable for the requirements of the present campaign. The use of a high percentage of the A.A. resources on mobile and scattered tasks in the forward areas, and the initial divorce of the searchlights from the guns (*see* p. 33), had necessitated the breaking up of A.A. brigades; and this had led to difficulties in the distribution of the ancillary services, which were aggravated by the despatch of so high a proportion of units on the base defence, *i.e.*, semi-static, establishment. For the future a new organization was devised, in which each A.A. unit had associated with it its own quota from the Royal Corps of Signals, Royal Army Service Corps and Royal Army Ordnance Corps.

In pre-war days, when G.O.Rs. and A.A.O.Rs. were in their infancy, wireless had been omitted from the establishment of a H.A.A. regiment. This omission proved a serious handicap, since distances between G.O.Rs. and gun positions were sometimes great and cable could not be relied on. It was therefore made good in the new establishment.

The German Break-Through

When at last the war came it was not the war of masses that had been expected, but the war of movement that had been the subject of so much of our pre-war training. There was, however, one important difference. Instead of attacking, the B.E.F. had to fight a very difficult type of defensive campaign against an enemy who had had every opportunity of bringing his own methods of warfare to perfection.

Contrary to the opinions formed at the time, the Germans do not appear to have had a preponderance of armour in the theatre as a whole. It was through the concentrated use of tanks, and the intimate co-operation of all arms within the armoured division, that they achieved their main effects. Motor cyclists, armoured cars, motorized infantry, anti-tank guns, lightly armoured and heavily armoured tanks, and field artillery appeared in rapid succession, closely supported by bomber aircraft acting in an artillery capacity. Even in impromptu attacks, calls for air assistance were mostly answered within 25 minutes, and the resultant bombardments were reasonably accurate and had the advantage of placing the fire to conform with the observed movements of the assaulting troops.

The Inadequacy of Our Anti-Tank Defences

So far as they went, our anti-tank equipments and training may be said to have been vindicated. Given a fair chance, the 2-pr. had proved itself capable of stopping the German tank of those days, and the 18/25-pr. had also some notable successes to its credit. One field regiment armed with this gun " was consistently successful in knocking out German medium and light tanks so long as it withheld its fire until the enemy was within 600 yards and conserved its A.P. shot."(⁹)

The resources available were, however, inadequate. " Our anti-tank armament was more ample than that of the French, but did not extend further back than the division. No guns were available for the defence of corps or rearward areas . . . except by withdrawing weapons from the formations to which they had been allotted in War Establishments."([10])

Nor was it absolutely certain that the 2-pr. had been thoroughly tested. Two-thirds of the enemy tanks encountered had been light tanks, which had been concentrated for use in the main thrust *via* Cambrai and south of Arras ; and if the Germans had not already increased the strength of their tank armour, it was to be expected that they would do so now that they had had a chance of studying the exact capabilities of the equipments they had captured from us.([11])

It was therefore most desirable that the production of the new 6-pr. anti-tank gun (*see* p. 17) should be hastened, and that the number of anti-tank weapons in the corps should be increased. Recommendations for the future included the introduction of a corps anti-tank regiment, the equipment of one battery in each divisional anti-tank regiment with S.P. mountings, and the addition of an anti-tank platoon of three guns to every infantry battalion.([12])

The Failure of the New Field Artillery Organization

The speed at which things moved after the initial German breakthrough put a severe, and sometimes fatal, strain on organizations and equipments designed to meet other conditions. The three-troop field battery, intended primarily for the attack, proved unsuitable for the very difficult type of defensive campaign that the B.E.F. was now engaged in. It was awkward to handle, and the delay in the production of a regimental concentration imposed by the removal of the regimental survey party had not been counter-balanced by the expected increase in mobility of fire of the 12-gun unit (*see* p. 11).

Such at least was the general opinion, and in conformity with this opinion, it was decided to reorganize the field regiment into three batteries, each of two 4-gun troops, and to reintroduce the regimental survey party. At the same time the scale of armoured O.Ps. was increased from two to six for each regiment—*i.e.* one to each troop.

Yet there was one C.R.A. who considered that no other organization would have made the situation appreciably better. In fact, whatever the faults of the system, it could be argued that the extent of its failure was partly owing to the effects of eight months' inactivity and the defensive attitude that had accompanied it. During this period of waiting there had been a tendency to revert to the more deliberate methods of trench warfare and to the production of fire plans that were unnecessarily complicated. In the short campaign that followed it, all these methods went by the board. The system for the higher control of artillery was not seriously tested. Concentrations of fire by more than one regiment were rare, since frontages were generally large and counter-attacks were on a relatively small scale. Moreover, units themselves gradually became dispersed as the result of continued retirement along crowded roads. In the later stages of the withdrawal, commanders of isolated troops and single guns placed themselves under whoever they found in command and fought on, sometimes in an infantry capacity and on at least one occasion for the rescue of their own guns.

Some Weaknesses of the Counter-Battery System

Counter-battery work, like everything else, was quickly decentralized. On the line of the DYLE, where flash spotting and sound ranging batteries were in action and arty/R sorties were available, several hostile batteries, including A.A., were engaged. Even at this stage, however, the amount of arty/R that could be provided was disappointingly small, and before long it ceased to function altogether. Army co-operation aircraft, even if available, could not operate with any confidence in a sky that was almost completely dominated by the enemy (*see* p. 7).

Flash spotting and sound ranging units were also soon reduced to impotence. Like H.A.A. regiments (*see* p. 35), these units had somehow been overlooked when wireless was being introduced into the artillery, and they were therefore still dependent on a vast network of cable, which took a long time to lay and to reel in. They suffered, in consequence, from a lack of flexibility and found it impossible either to keep pace with the movements or to cover the fronts of the widely extended formations they were supporting.

The remedy was clear: to introduce wireless for certain technical communications within sound ranging and flash spotting batteries. In heavy artillery, however, there were weaknesses that could not be so easily cured. Experience with the 9.2-in. how. had confirmed—if confirmation were necessary—that it could never attain the mobility or handiness necessary in modern warfare, and the projected development of a more mobile weapon of this nature (*see* p. 16) was therefore abandoned. At the same time the General Staff objected to the short range of the 8-in. how. and demanded a maximum of 15,500 yards. The result was a lined-down 8-in.—or 7.2-in.—how. with a 200-lb. shell, for which approval was given on 21st November, 1940.

Wireless Disappointments

During the prolonged defensive period, drastic restrictions had been imposed on the use of wireless, and this, combined with the shortage of charging plants, led in some units to a lack of practice in wireless methods, which was now to have serious repercussions.([13]) The promise, inherent in the development of wireless, of greater flexibility of control was partly neutralized. On more than one occasion a breakdown of communications—due to cut cables, the unreliable working of wireless, and the inadequate range of the No. 1 set—prevented the supporting artillery from responding effectively to calls for help from the infantry. In such circumstances all that could be done was to resort to the nearest pre-selected defensive fire task, and this did not always succeed in putting the shells where they were needed. Furthermore, the preparation of these defensive fire tasks themselves was sometimes delayed through the attempt to co-ordinate them at too high a level in the first instance, instead of letting them be arranged and registered on a provisional basis between battalion and battery commanders.

The Threat of the Mortar

The failure of arty/R, and of sound ranging and flash spotting, had forced counter-battery officers increasingly to rely on information received from normal battery O.Ps.; and this had, incidentally, proved of some assistance in dealing with the enemy infantry guns and mortars, which were lavishly and skilfully used, and which made a considerable impression on troops unaccustomed to their methods. In future, it was clear, more attention would have to be paid to this problem. As an immediate response, it was recommended by the Bartholomew Committee that the infantry's own resources for the provision of rapid fire support should be increased by raising the number of 3-in. mortars in the battalion from two to six; but it was generally felt that this alone would not suffice, and that special counter-mortar measures would have to be included in the counter-battery organization.

The Dive Bomber

If the concentrated use of tanks had been the decisive factor in the German breakthrough, the dive bomber had played a scarcely less impressive part in the subsequent exploitation of victory.

The dive bombing attack, which usually followed a period of preliminary high level bombing, and which was characterized by a skilful use of sun and cloud, achieved its success more by its suddenness and unexpectedness than by the material damage that it caused. The latter indeed was often remarkably slight. It was the moral effect that counted, and this was enhanced at first by the attachment of noise-producing devices to the bombs —and sometimes to the aircraft itself—which caused them to utter a screaming note while in flight. Later this became almost a source of comfort to experienced troops, who learned to know by the sound whether, and when, it was necessary to take cover. But to inexperienced troops, and to the civilians who swarmed upon the roads over which the B.E.F. had to carry out its withdrawal, the noise was apt to be unnerving.

Basically, the idea was not new. The threat of the dive bomber had been recognized some time before the war began (*see* p. 19), and it was believed, not unreasonably, that this threat could be successfully countered by one or two Bofors guns sited in the immediate vinicity of the V.P. to be protected. In theory, the directly approaching diver presented the simplest of gunnery problems, and, provided that the layer had cool nerves and could hold his fire until the target was within hitting range, the chances of its timely destruction were high.

In practice, however, there were several reasons why this theory was often unfulfilled. The attacker, by diving out of the sun, might make himself invisible to the defender; and once the bombs had started to land, the gunner might be blinded by smoke and dust. Moreover, in this campaign particularly, L.A.A. guns could not be everywhere, and the crossing diver produced angular rates of change that were beyond the capacity of the Bofors equipment.

Later, as the Germans developed their technique for using the dive bomber as a counter-battery weapon, and as the supply of Bofors guns increased, the defence of field artillery positions became one of the major commitments of British L.A.A. units. In the meantime, something had to be done to improve the performance of the H.A.A. gun, not only in its own defence, but as a deterrent against the approach of enemy bombers towards the area it was covering.

Experience showed that H.A.A. fire could break up large formations of bombers and thus facilitate the work of defending fighters, or, if no fighters were available, prevent the accurate bombing of objectives. On such occasions, a barrage directed at the position occupied by the leading aircraft of a formation at a selected moment was found to have a decided moral effect upon the remainder.

It was indeed evident that the deterrent effect of A.A. fire was not necessarily to be measured, as some had believed, in terms of actual hits or of the number of aircraft destroyed. Under peace conditions at practice camp, the moral effect of A.A. fire was hard to gauge or to illustrate, and there was perhaps a natural tendency to concentrate exclusively upon accuracy, and to dispose the H.A.A. guns in positions worked out with mathematical precision relative to a theoretical line of bomb release. Now, though accuracy was still very desirable, it was proven that an A.A. unit could afford a good measure of material security to a V.P. without scoring a single hit upon the enemy aircraft.

For example, during the final evacuation of Dunkirk, a H.A.A. troop was retained in action at the base of the mole as a reinforcement to the four Bofors guns in action on the mole itself. A shrapnel and H.E. barrage was laid on along the line of the mole at a height of 3,000 feet, and was fired whenever a " circus " of dive bombers appeared and started to circle the objective preparatory to " peeling off " for the bombing dive. The results were completely successful. In the first attack the aircraft " peeling off " were forced to take evasive action, and on each repetition of the performance they were induced to go higher in order to pull out above the barrage. Their bombs all fell wide of the target.

Thus, in addition to dealing successfully with medium bombers, at heights mostly between 12,000 and 8,000 feet, this H.A.A. troop formed the backbone of the defence against the much advertised dive bomber; and all this had been achieved without any noticeable material effect upon the enemy. " I personally ", said the C.O., " did not see any aircraft shot down by the guns under my command at Dunkirk."

The circumstances were of course peculiar, and it is possible that the enemy was not prepared to risk losses in the air and did not therefore pursue his attacks as relentlessly as he might otherwise have done. Nevertheless the results showed that the moral factor did not operate entirely to the advantage of the attacker, and they offered a hope that the measure of the dive bomber had already been taken.

The " Hedge-Hopper "

The very low level attack—which, fortunately, was not much used by the enemy at this time—was not so easy to deal with. In the first place, not only were the early radar sets unable to follow a target (*see* p. 20), but they could not even detect an aircraft approaching at a very low height. Hence early warning of this type of attack could not be relied on, and the Bofors, if it did not happen to be pointed in the right direction, could not be swung round fast enough to engage the enemy before he had dropped his bombs. Again, the " hedge-hopper ", like the dive bomber, was a difficult type of target to simulate under practice camp conditions, so that the gunnery problem had not been thoroughly studied.

There was, it is true, a compensating factor that could have been exploited with more experience. Because of his low height, the pilot of a "hedge-hopper" was forced to make his approach along some well-defined feature, such as a railway or river line, in order to be sure of finding his objective. There was therefore a good chance of siting L.A.A. guns so that every "hedge-hopper" could be taken on by at least one gun as a head-on target. Nevertheless the feeling remained that the Bofors did not quite fill the bill, and that there was a need for a lighter and handier weapon for dealing with these snap targets.

It was also clear that the danger from dive bombing and low-flying aircraft in the forward areas had been underestimated and that in future divisions would have to include a L.A.A. regiment. In addition, the provision of a dual purpose A-A. and anti-tank weapon was considered, for issue to "protective" companies and platoons of corps, divisions and brigades, and to A.A. platoons of infantry battalions. This project was, however, abandoned, owing to the difficulty of obtaining a suitable weapon. The only 20-mm. guns then in production—the Hispano Suiza and the Oerlikon—were all required for the R.A.F. and the Royal Navy; and the Bofors (40-mm.), even if available in sufficient quantity, was regarded as an artillery piece unsuitable for use by the infantry.

The Night Bomber

The danger of the "hedge-hopper" lay in the inefficiency of radar warning systems at very low altitudes. The night bomber, which usually flew at a considerable height, could be detected as easily as the day bomber, but could not be accurately followed by the early radar sets. It could not therefore be intercepted by fighters or engaged by A.A. guns unless it could be illuminated and rendered visible by searchlights.

Fortunately, the achievements of A.A.S.Ls. in gun zones had been encouraging. In the Lille area, as a result of constant practice from about 8th May onwards, searchlight work reached a very high standard. Several illuminated aircraft were shot down by gun fire and by fighters, in spite of the smallness of the illuminated zone, and also by the L.M.Gs. of the searchlight detachments themselves.

Results had, in fact, shown that, contrary to the expectations of pre-war experts (*see* p. 20), a lay-out of even one searchlight battery was of value; and as the application of radar to the searchlight made headway, its effectiveness could be expected to increase considerably. On the other hand, the four-battery searchlight regiment of 96 lights, and a strength of some 1,480 personnel, had proved itself too unwieldy for mobile operations. It was therefore decided that in future it should be reduced from four to three batteries.

Conclusion

With the evacuation of Dunkirk and the collapse of France, the British Field Army in Europe was faced with a new situation. Bereft of its equipment, it was confined to a purely defensive role in the United Kingdom, while the R.A.F., supported by the guns of A.A. Command, lessened the striking power of the Luftwaffe.

Meanwhile the artillery of the B.E.F. was preparing for the day when it would again go overseas. Its losses in material had been particularly heavy. The artillery equipments left behind in France after Dunkirk (*see* Table C) represented nearly 60 per cent. of our " world " stock at that time, including nearly all the available modern, or modernized, equipments. It was therefore many months before existing units could be fully equipped again, and still longer before any newly raised unit could hope to take the field.

Yet the balance was not all on the debit side. Along with the good things that had been lost, some useless lumber had been swept away. A new heavy equipment had at last been decided on, fire plans had been simplified, and shortcomings in radio and radar were being attended to. In the cold wind of adversity the atmosphere had cleared, and the main tasks of the artillery in the fighting that was to come could be distinctly seen. There were three main opponents to be overcome: the dive bomber, the tank and the mortar; and in subsequent chapters an attempt will be made to show by what means, and with what success, these opponents were severally tackled.

List of References

[1] R.A.T.M. War No. 1, December 1939.
[2] A.T.M. No. 32, May 1940.
[3] Arty. Training, Vol. II, 1934, Supplement No. 2, 1940, p. 11.
[4] A.T.M. No. 32, May 1940.
[5] Arty. Training, Vol. III, 1928, p. 44.
[6] Arty. Training, Vol. II, 1934, Supplement No. 2, 1940, p. 6.
[7] R.A.T.M. War No. 1, December 1939.
[8] 1st Despatch, C-in-C, B.E.F., 25th April 1940, para. 12.
[9] A.T.M. No. 41, October 1941.
[10] 2nd Despatch, C-in-C, B.E.F., 25th July 1940, para. 60.
[11] " Our Armoured Forces ", by Lt.-Gen. Sir G. Martel, p. 72.
[12] Report of the Bartholomew Committee.
[13] R.A.T.M. War No. 2, July 1940.

TABLE C

TABLE SHOWING THE ARTILLERY EQUIPMENTS LOST IN FRANCE AND BELGIUM, JUNE, 1940

	Field Artillery			Anti-Tank Artillery			Medium Artillery				Heavy Artillery				Super-Heavy Artillery		
	25/18 prs.	18- prs.	4·5" how.	Total	2- prs.	25 mm.	Total	6" how.	4·5/60 prs.	60- prs.	Total	6" gun	8" how.	9·2" how.	Total	9·2" gun	12" how.	Total
With 40 Field Regts. (incl. R.H.A. Regts.)	632	216	96	944	—	—	—	—	—	—	—	—	—	—	—	—	—	—
With 10 Anti-Tank Regts.	—	—	—	—	432	48	480	—	—	—	—	—	—	—	—	—	—	—
With 14 Medium Regts.	—	—	—	—	—	—	—	176	32	16	224	—	—	—	—	—	—	—
With 3 Heavy Regts.	—	—	—	—	—	—	—	—	—	—	—	12	12	24	48	—	—	—
With 3 Super-Heavy Btys.	—	—	—	—	—	—	—	—	—	—	—	—	—	—	—	2	4	6
Reserves	72	—	—	72	77	50	127	45	—	3	48	1	1	3	5	—	—	—
GRAND TOTAL	704	216	96	1,016	509	98	607	221	32	19	272	13	13	27	53	2	4	6

CHAPTER IV

DEFEAT OF THE ITALIAN THREAT TO EGYPT AND THE SUDAN

PLATES RELEVANT TO THIS CHAPTER

Nos.
8. A sandstorm in the desert.
9. The 25-pr.
10. The mountains at Keren.
11. View of Italian positions at Keren from 4 and 5 Indian Division gun areas.

SECTION I.—INTRODUCTION

The Shadow of Dunkirk

Before pursuing the train of thought outlined at the end of the last chapter, it will be convenient to turn aside for a moment and consider the two campaigns fought against the Italians for the defence of Egypt and the Sudan.

The great Duke of Wellington used to ascribe his victories over the French marshals to the fact that they planned their campaigns as if they were making a fine set of harness, while his plans were made of rope, so that if anything went wrong he could tie a knot and carry on. In the campaigns that form the subject of this chapter, it would perhaps be fair to say that General Wavell's plans had to be made of elastic.

With the collapse of France and the entry into the war of Italy on 10th June, 1940, the scene and nature of the British Army's main activities had undergone a complete change. Instead of a continuous front with its Maginot Line, and its miles of natural and artificial anti-tank obstacles, there were the vast open deserts of Western Egypt and the Sudan. Beyond them were large enemy forces in Libya and Italian East Africa, which outnumbered the British garrison in the proportion of about ten to one.

After a review of all the factors, it was decided to put on a bold front and to harass the enemy, and delay his preparations, by the use of small mobile columns endowed with as much fire power as could be made available. Like everything else at that time, however, artillery equipments were very scarce. From 3rd September, 1939, to 10th May, 1940, the pick of everything had been sent to France and there was little left over for the Middle East. Now all of this had been lost and the home country itself stood in danger of invasion, so that the prospect of an early improvement in the situation was not great.

When the war with Italy began, there was no artillery at all in the Sudan, and in Egypt there were only two R.H.A. regiments—one of which was equipped with anti-tank guns, the other with 18/25-prs.—three field regiments and one medium regiment. Of the two formations available for operations, the 7th Armoured and the 4th Indian Division, only the first had its full establishment of artillery. The 4th Indian Divisional Artillery had no anti-tank regiment and no third line transport. The medium regiment was equipped with 8×60-prs. and 8×6-in. hows. which were still fitted with steel instead of pneumatic tyres, and it had neither second nor third line transport so could not operate more than 25 miles from railhead.

It was not until November, 1940, that the "pneumatization" of this regiment was completed, and that the first 25-prs. for the field regiments began to arrive. Until then equipments were very mixed. There were 18/25-prs., 18-prs. Mks. IV and V, and 4.5-in. hows., many of which belonged to the Indian Government and were due for return to India as soon as they had been replaced by 25-prs.

The organization of units was equally mixed. Some regiments had two batteries each of two four-gun troops, some two batteries each of three four-gun troops, and some two batteries each of two six-gun troops. Uniformity of organization was in fact deliberately sacrificed in order to make the best possible use of the equipments that were available.

In October, 1940, authority was given by the War Office for field regiments to convert from the two-battery to the three-battery establishment (*see* p. 36) as far as was possible within their own resources. In practice, however, this proved to be an empty favour. N.C.Os. and specialists for the third battery were hard to find, and eventually, many months later, the reorganization had to be completed by the despatch of trained personnel from the United Kingdom.

There was no R.A. survey unit in the Middle East, and no equipment for the Australian and New Zealand artillery survey units that were forming there. Nor was there likely to be any for a long time. This was a serious handicap, since recent experiences in France and Belgium had shown that the allotment of arty/R sorties was often impracticable or on a much smaller scale than formation and artillery commanders had been led to expect (*see* p. 37). It was therefore important to develop to the utmost alternative methods for the engagement of targets concealed from ground observation, such as predicted shooting and sound ranging.

The amount of A.A. artillery available in May, 1940, when hostilities became imminent, was pathetically small: 8 × 3-in., 32 × 3.7-in. and 12 Bofors; and the efficiency of even this small force was seriously reduced by the shortage of predictors, heightfinders and telescopes identification, and by the complete lack of radar. Fortunately, however, some reliance could be placed on Egyptian A.A. and coast defence units.

Lastly, there was a general shortage of ammunition. Thus the three main characteristics of artillery—mobility of manœuvre, mobility of fire and density of fire—were all adversely affected. Altogether it was a difficult situation, which could only be surmounted by careful planning, frequent improvization and some unorthodoxy.

Some Peculiarities of Desert Warfare

Climatic and topographical conditions in the desert were peculiar. Amid its almost featureless expanses, defensive positions were not easy to find and, when found, could seldom be regarded as secure about the flanks. Hence the linear position, already weakened even in European warfare by the penetrative powers of armoured and airborne units, was often impossible to hold, especially with the small forces that were available and that could be kept supplied. In its stead there grew up a system of all-round defence, in which a force of all arms disposed itself around a nucleus of guns.

It was characteristic of the "inhospitable" desert that its fairest promises were often belied by hidden or unpredictable obstacles. Thus freedom of manœuvre, though unrestricted by artificial developments, waterways and mountains, and unhampered by teeming populations, was sometimes unexpectedly and drastically reduced by dust storms, sand drifts or rocks—and, in the coastal areas, by mud after a sudden heavy shower. Worst of all perhaps, to the inexperienced, was the difficulty of finding the way. Sun, stars and compass were the only reliable means of keeping direction, and some form of navigation was essential for even the shortest journeys. On a dark night it was hardly possible to move at all without headlights, except on roads or on marked and lighted tracks. It was usually found necessary to appoint a navigator in addition to the battery leader.

Once an objective had been reached, or contact with the enemy had been made, deployment was generally easy. But again the absence of natural obstacles was counter-balanced to some extent by the wide dispersion, and consequent difficulty of control, imposed by the lack of concealment from the air. A solution was found in the use of flag signals, and in the simplification of movement and deployment drills by a reduction in the number of tactical groups. For example, the "G" party of battery headquarters, gun groups and ammunition groups sometimes travelled together in one main body, the O.P.s moving with the reconnaissance element of the unit which was being supported.

The chief factors affecting gunnery were the difficulty of observation and the introduction of inaccuracies through violent changes in meteor. Observation of fire became impossible in a dust storm, which might sometimes continue for 48 hours, and it was extremely difficult in the mid-day mirage and in the morning and evening mists that so often arose in the desert. At other times visibility was remarkably good, but full advantage could not be taken of this fact owing to the lack of high ground from which to observe. The most obvious way out of the difficulty, air observation, though facilitated by the ease of finding landing grounds, was seldom practicable owing to the difficulty of locating targets from the air in such a featureless country, and to the shortage of aircraft. Hence recourse was often necessary to the simple and old-fashioned expedient of an observation pole or ladder.

Even when he had found an O.P. from which he could see, the gunner was still handicapped by the lack of distinct features. This made zones of observation difficult to define, and opening ranges and lines for observed shooting difficult to estimate ; and if, for the sake of surprise, it was desired to omit registration and use predicted shooting, there was the risk of complete failure owing to the vagaries of meteor.

Anti-tank defence was equally affected. In France and Belgium, where tanks could not often be seen beyond a range of 800 yards, the ideal position for an anti-tank gun had been found to be "on the reverse slope of a hill with a field of fire of 5-600 yards to the crest".([1]) In the desert, tanks would begin to see each other at 2,000 yards, and although there was sometimes a "saucer" in which some degree of concealment could be found for a defended locality, the tendency was, naturally, for opening ranges to increase. Secondly, owing to the lack of anti-tank obstacles, guns had to be deployed within supporting distance of each other and lay-outs tended inevitably to revert to the "thin red line". Thirdly, even if a convenient saucer could be found, something had to be done to prevent the enemy armour from approaching its rim, or from occupying hull-down positions on some other commanding crest; and this led sometimes to the siting of anti-tank guns in concealed positions on a forward, instead of a reverse, slope.

Intercommunication was surprisingly difficult. There were few permanent cables, and atmospheric conditions were often so bad, especially at night, that the use of wireless had to be confined to low frequencies and short distances. Even the value of despatch riders was restricted by the need for skilled navigation, the distances to be covered, and the difficulty of negotiating the rough desert country on a motor-cycle. They were, therefore, usually replaced by liaison officers. .

Yet with all its strangeness and superficial hostility, the desert could be —as Arab wisdom put it—" a fortress to him who knows it", if " a grave to him who does not ". It was perhaps because the British soldier treated it like a good democrat, and tolerated what he could not change without violence, that it was kinder to him than to his totalitarian opponents who, if they were Italians, tried to over-civilize it, or if they were Germans, tried to drill it into obedience.

SECTION II.—THE CONQUEST OF CYRENAICA

Developments in the Armoured Division

The scheme for the defence of the western frontier had been drawn up at a time when a French offensive from Tunisia could be anticipated as a means of relieving Italian pressure on Egypt. It was therefore founded on aggressive action by the Mobile Division—as it was then called— operating from a fortified base at Mersa Matruh.

The original composition of this division was one cavalry brigade, one tank group and a pivot group, which consisted of one R.H.A. regiment and one battalion of motorized infantry, and which, as its name implied, was not intended for intimate participation in the armoured battle. By the time war broke out with Italy, however, this policy had undergone a change. The Mobile Division had become the 7th Armoured Division, and the Pivot Group had become the Support Group composed of two R.H.A. regiments (one armed with anti-tank guns, the other with 18/25-prs.) and two motorized infantry battalions. The anti-tank guns, issued at the end of 1939, were 37-mm. Bofors, which could be carried in and if necessary fired from a 15-cwt. truck, and which were considered to be particularly suitable for highly mobile operations in the desert. The number of these guns available, and the amount of ammunition, was strictly limited, and their hitting power was inferior to that of the 2-pr.; but, as 2-prs. were not available, they were accepted as a useful stop-gap.

Notwithstanding the collapse of France, it was decided to place a small force on the frontier and to use it aggressively, as soon as possible after the outbreak of war, against the Italian frontier posts. This force consisted of one light tank regiment, one armoured car regiment (the divisional cavalry regiment) and the whole of the support group. The strength and composition of the columns sent out followed no fixed pattern. Groupings were made to suit the needs of specific operations, and frequently a troop of guns would accompany a cavalry squadron or a motorized infantry company on patrol.

It was not until September, when the Italians began to advance in strength across the frontier, that the artillery of the support group had an opportunity of functioning as a whole. Then, for five days, from 13th to 17th September, it was offered a series of targets such as gunners usually only dream of. The enemy moved in columns of several hundred vehicles, with tanks, anti-tank guns and artillery in front and on the flanks, and lorried infantry in the centre. When engaged, they deployed their artillery and tanks, and sometimes their infantry, and advanced slowly in rigid lines.

The withdrawal of the small British force in face of these superior numbers " was effected with admirable skill, and there is no doubt whatever that very serious losses were inflicted on the enemy, both by the artillery, which was boldly and effectively handled, and whenever opportunity offered, by machine-gun and small arms fire ".([2]) In particular, a dangerous turning movement by about 50 medium Italian tanks had been brought to an immediate halt by fire from two R.H.A. batteries at a range of 2,000 to 2,500 yards.

Having established themselves at Sidi Barrani, the Italians again relapsed into inactivity, and our own forces, which were still too weak to assume a general offensive, reverted to the harrassing tactics of the preceding period. Once again it became a war of small mixed columns, which usually included a troop of 18/25-prs. and another of anti-tank guns.

It will be seen that the role of the support group in these operations had not been entirely in accordance with pre-war ideas (*see* p. 18). This was owing partly to the difficulty, already mentioned, of holding ground in the desert, and partly to the habitual use of small mixed columns, which, if not obligatory, was at least justified by the successes that had been achieved. It was, moreover, supported by a tradition that dated back to Alexander the Great, if not further.

The resultant dispersion of the divisional artillery, and the constant changes in its distribution to meet the exigencies of the moment, gave rise to numerous tactical and administrative problems that called for the presence of an artillery adviser at divisional headquarters. The commander of the support group was not—as he was in the United Kingdom—an artillery officer, and a temporary solution of the difficulty was therefore found in the appointment of two regimental officers from the divisional R.H.A. units to act respectively as C.R.A. and B.M.R.A.

The Battle of Sidi Barrani, 9th—11th December, 1940

By the beginning of December, the Western Desert Force was ready for its first set-piece offensive. Some of the worst transport deficiencies had been made good, a number of field artillery units had been re-equipped with the new 25-pr., and among the armour available was a battalion of " I " (Matilda) tanks, which could be regarded as impervious to everything except an anti-tank mine or a direct hit by an air bomb. The enemy, too, by his faulty dispositions and by the general inertia of his troops, seemed to invite attack. The fortified camps that he had prepared in the vicinity of Sidi Barrani were not within supporting distance of each other, and the size of their garrisons was such as to offer a reasonable chance of their being overwhelmed in detail by the forces available for the attack. Furthermore, their defences were incomplete on their northern and north-western faces, where the supply columns entered, and absence of anti-tank mines in this area offered a favourable opening for the initial breakthrough.

The technique for the attack was to be based on the " I " tank as the main assaulting arm, with infantry for mopping up, and fire support directed towards the general demoralization and deception of the enemy, and towards the protection of the tanks at their point of entry into each camp. For this purpose, accuracy was considered of less importance than speed and intensity in the application of fire.

On 25th—26th November, a " dress rehearsal " was held in the desert well clear of the intended scene of operations. Facsimiles of the three enemy camps were prepared and the artillery went through each stage of the fire plan using live ammunition, though in ignorance of the real significance of what they were doing. To all but a select few it was no more than a training exercise to study the methods of attack to be employed against " an entrenched camp in the desert ".

The assault was planned to take place in two stages, with a fresh infantry brigade operating in each. All available artillery was formed into a divisional artillery group, which was made administratively self-supporting with the help of a Royal Indian Army Service Corps officer and the use of the senior regimental quartermaster as Brigade Transport Officer. H.Q.R.A. was to accompany each of the attacking brigades in turn, and as it had no signal section of its own, it was provided by Divisional Signals with one W/T set, which communicated with all S3 trucks of regiments on a single frequency.

The strength of the divisional artillery group was 56 field guns (25-prs. and 18/25-prs.), 8×6-in. hows. (now fitted with rubber tyres), 8×60-prs., 24 anti-tank guns (Bofors) and 16 L.A.A. guns (Bofors). Covering fire for the first attack, on Nibeiwa Camp (see Map 1), was to take the form of H.E. concentrations, beginning on selected points on the perimeter and later searching 500 yards inwards. One field battery was detailed to move with the " I " tanks and cover their breakthrough using a mixture of smoke and H.E.

The timed programme was to begin at zero hour, when the tanks went in, and was to continue for 20 minutes, by which time the leading battalion was expected to cross the perimeter. The ammunition allotment was 50 r.p.g., which was to be dumped in gun areas before first light. Subsequent support was to be by observation on enemy outside the perimeter.

In order to preserve the element of surprise, the attack was to start at dawn and the time available for artillery preparations was therefore very short. Although a survey troop R.A. had by now arrived, and had been used for the calibration of all guns, its employment in the initial stages of the attack was out of the question. Reliance had therefore to be placed on a brief preliminary registration, for which only 15 minutes were allowed.

The problem was complicated by the difficulty of identifying one's own shell bursts, and by the mixture of cloud and haze that had accompanied the

Map 1

ACTION AT NIBEIWA CAMP AND TUMMAR WEST, 9 DEC 40

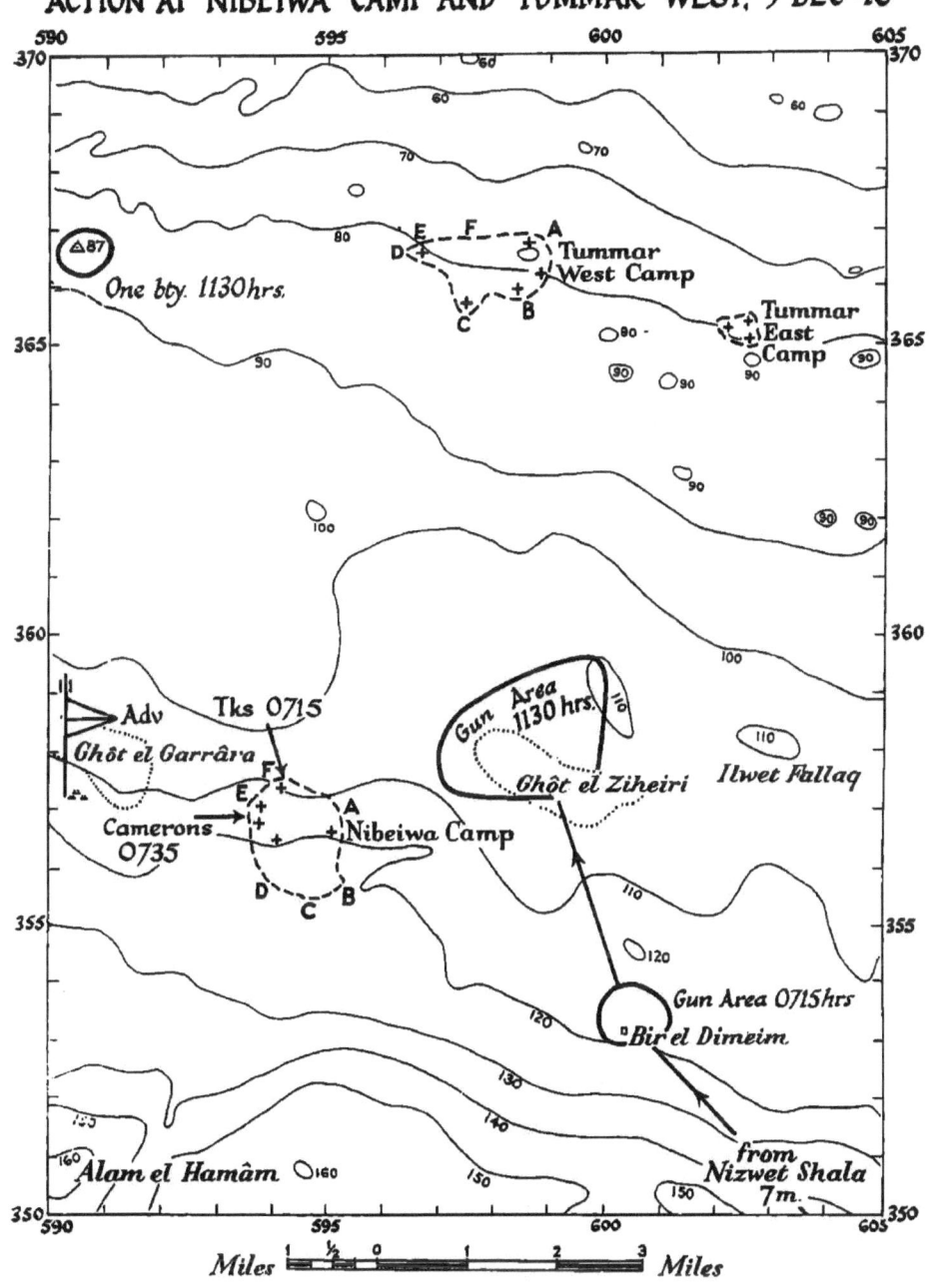

Legend:—Enemy battery positions shown thus:— +
Initial artillery tasks—

NIBEIWA— A–C one med regt
B–C one fd regt
C–D one fd bty
D–E one fd regt
F one fd bty
(on close sp of tks)

TUMMAR WEST—A–B one med regt
B–C one fd regt
C–D one fd regt
E one fd bty
F one fd bty
(in close sp of tks).

dawn. Nevertheless, registration was completed in time and the resultant concentration of fire was described by captured Italian officers as "*molto formidabile*". Twenty minutes later the tanks were through the perimeter, and in little more than an hour the whole camp had virtually fallen.

In the afternoon the same tactics were repeated against the Tummar camps with similar results. On this occasion more time was allowed for registration, but otherwise there was little change in the artillery plan. A dust storm added to the confusion caused by the concentrations of artillery fire, and all resistance was speedily overcome.

It was a decisive victory, and its suddenness and completeness may have been partly responsible for the subsequent rapid collapse of Italian morale. It is therefore worth emphasizing the methods by which this initial victory had been achieved: secrecy and care in preparation, simplicity in planning, and speed in execution. So thoroughly had the plan been worked out, during and after the "dress rehearsal", that on the first day the only orders to be given to the guns were the time of zero hour and the orders for batteries to move for the attack on Tummar West. So carefully had the time-table been worked out that the infantry were on their objective before the enemy had had time to recover from his initial surprise and from the effects of the artillery bombardment.

Capture of Bardia and Tobruk, 19th January, 1941.

It had been a victory also for British equipments, especially the Matilda tank and the new 25-pr., which here made a brilliant debut. It was not to be expected that so neat and exemplary a battle would repeat itself. As the campaign proceeded, the dwindling supply of "I" tanks, the greater strength of the fortifications at Bardia and Tobruk, and the increased activity and efficiency of the enemy artillery turned the course of operations into more familiar channels.

"The diminished resources of infantry tanks necessitated the bold employment of infantry both in assault and exploitation", and consequently "a high expenditure of ammunition for their protection "([3]) This meant a heavy dumping programme and, as the ammunition (some 300 r.p.g.) had to be brought up by road from Mersa Matruh, a delay of 16 days in the launching of the attack on Bardia. Thus the use of surprise was confined to the precise time—and perhaps place—of the main assault.

To conceal the former, advantage was taken of the presence of the R.A. survey troop to eliminate registration. For this it was necessary not only to fix targets, which was relatively easy owing to the inelasticity of the Italian defence system, but also to make sure of a reliable meteor correction. The existing system for the provision of meteor telegrams (*see* p. 6) did not extend far enough downwards to meet the needs of desert warfare, so R.A. survey was made to fill the gap. A suitable range was found and measured, and meteor deduced by comparing the length as calculated by survey methods with that obtained from the shooting of calibrated guns.

To conceal the place of assault, the attacking troops and their supporting artillery were not moved into position for the attack until immediately before zero hour. In the meantime the usual diversionary threats were directed against other sectors, while previously selected battery positions were fixed as unostentatiously as possible. Under cover of a patrol of light tanks, small survey parties moved out in advance of the F.D.Ls. and fixed bearing pickets in ground that was not under observation of the enemy.

By this time the 4th Indian Division was on its way to the Sudan, where General Wavell had planned to liquidate the threat from Italian East Africa before the current campaigning season ended in the following May. Its place was taken by the 6th Australian Division, whose artillery was temporarily reinforced by the 25-pr. regiment from the support group. A second medium regiment had also arrived with $16) \times 4.5$-in./60-pr. guns, and this and other reinforcements brought the total number of guns available to the respectable figure of 122.

Here, then, was enough artillery and ammunition for a barrage on the accustomed lines. It was to be a standing barrage on the 1,500 yard length of perimeter chosen for the attack, and it was to begin as the infantry crossed their starting line about 1,500 yards further back. At $Z+36$, fire was to lift to concentrations covering the bridgehead and forming a box to cover the further penetration by tanks. Then, as the infantry pushed through behind the tanks, they were to be supported by counter-battery fire from the medium artillery and by observed covering fire from the R.H.A. and field batteries.

The results were generally successful, though some discomfiture was caused by the unexpected activity and effectiveness of the enemy artillery. For the capture of Tobruk, therefore, a more prolonged and elaborate fire plan was put into effect, with more emphasis laid on counter-battery work. On 16th January a four-day harassing programme was begun by the artillery of the support group against the western perimeter, and by the medium guns firing from the east against Tobruk town. To this were added night bombardments by the R.A.F. on centres of communication in the rearward area ; and, on the night of 20th-21st January, a bombardment of the western sector of the defences by the Royal Navy, assisted by beacons lit by the support group.

Then, at 0540 hours on 21st January, the attack was launched against a point on the southern face of the perimeter where the anti-tank ditch was shallow and the minefield could be easily removed. It was carried out in three phases: a break-in by one infantry battalion to open a gap for the " I " tanks (now reduced to 16) ; an advance by the " I " tanks to the first objective, which involved the reduction of eight miles of defended posts and the silencing of some 12 battery positions ; and a further advance to a second objective by a fresh infantry battalion, without tank support, at the unusually fast rate of 100 yards in one minute. Covering fire for all three phases took the form of a creeping barrage, with the usual subsidiary concentrations, and a heavy counter-battery programme. Indeed, as the " I " tanks entered the gap, every gun—less those on flank protection—was employed on the neutralization of hostile batteries.

The results were most satisfactory. The enemy batteries were generally ineffective, and within two hours of crossing their starting line the infantry—who had followed behind the barrage at the regulation interval of 150 yards (see p. 29)—had gained the whole of the second objective. The strength of the supporting artillery for this battle was 146 guns and 20 howitzers, and the ammunition fired by the 25-prs. averaged 223 r.p.g.([4])

Odd Jobs for the Guns

In most campaigns some miscellaneous tasks are found for the artillery, and the gunner, whose motto is " Ubique ", is usually ready enough to attempt them. This campaign was no exception. The first of such demands was for the destruction of enemy land mines at Sidi Barrani. In the event, none of these objects was destroyed by artillery, and the conclusion arrived at was that anti-tank and anti-personnel mines were unlikely to be subject to sympathetic detonation, and that " the clearing of a passage through a minefield by shell fire is not a practicable proposition ".([5])

Wire cutting by the artillery, which had been revived (in theory) in France during the winter of 1939-40 (*see* p. 33), was impossible here in the Western Desert if only because of the shortage of guns and ammunition. In fact official opinion considered it " again established that artillery covering fire is not a satisfactory answer for cutting wire ".([6]) A more efficient means was found in the " bangalore torpedo ", a 12-foot length of 3-in. water pipe, packed with high explosive, which was launched into position under the enemy wire and there exploded. Originally a sapper task, it was before long undertaken by the infantry.

Attempts were made to deal with anti-tank obstacles by artillery fire, but these proved unsuccessful. Here again experience showed that bombardment by guns, or by aircraft, could not be relied on to clear a passage either for tanks or for infantry. Such obstacles could, in fact, be " effectively dealt with only by special assault parties."([5])

It is worth noting, in passing, that German artillery doctrine at this time taught that concentrated artillery fire could make gaps in anti-tank obstacles, and that although guns could only destroy well-placed anti-tank minefields at a prohibitive cost in ammunition, the 105 how.—and better still the 210 mortar—could do the job much more economically. In practice, however, neither of these theories was convincingly demonstrated against British forces in the field.

It was obviously not going to be long before the anti-tank gunner was asked to turn his hand to something else besides the destruction of tanks. One of the earliest, though not the first, of such demands was made during the fighting at Bardia, when, in the absence of enemy tank activity, a gun of the 3rd R.H.A. (anti-tank) Regiment engaged a troublesome pill-box, using H.E.-filled A.A. shell, and put it out of action with ten rounds.

The Pursuit to the Tripolitanian Frontier

During the battles of Sidi Barrani, Bardia and Tobruk, the 7th Armoured Division had been operating against the enemy L. of C., preventing the arrival of reinforcements and the withdrawal of troops already in the forward area, and generally helping to mislead the enemy commanders as to the intended point of attack. The tactics employed were a continuation, on a larger scale, of those used in the original harassing operations between June and November, 1940.

By 3rd February it had become evident that the Italians were in full retreat from Cyrenaica and it was decided to use the whole of the 7th Armoured Division—the effective strength of which was by now reduced to 40 or 50 cruiser and about 80 light tanks—in an attempt to cut their line of retreat between Benghasi and Agedabia. As time was short, a mixed column of motorized infantry with strong artillery support was sent forward to join the 11th Hussars (the divisional cavalry regiment), and by 0730 hours on 5th February the leading troops of this combined force had reached their objective near Beda Fomm without opposition, after a desert march of 150 miles in 30 hours.

During the next two days, enemy columns made repeated attempts to fight their way through this small British force, but were broken up one after the other by the fire of tanks, 25-prs., Bofors (anti-tank) and Breda (L.A.A.) guns. During the night 6th-7th February our anti-tank guns were down to 8 r.p.g. when, despite the difficulties resulting from the wear of vehicles and the lack of spare portees, a second battery reached the scene of action in time to meet the last and most determined Italian attempt at a breakthrough just before dawn.

The attack was made by a M.T. column $11\frac{1}{2}$ miles long and headed by 30 M13 medium tanks. Two Bofors guns engaged the tanks at a range of 150 yards, knocking out the leader and damaging seven others before they themselves were overwhelmed.

Their action had turned the enemy tanks off the road and destroyed the momentum of their attack at a critical moment when, in the half light, it was impossible for them to see how little there was in front of them. The fighting continued for some time, but the Italians never again came within sight of success. By 0900 hours their whole force was surrounded by the formations of the 7th Armoured Division and all resistance had ended.

Conclusion

Thus ended a campaign which was compared at the time with the story of the Spanish Armada. It had shown what could be done by a small, mobile and highly trained army against a far larger but less elastic force operating in an element to which it did not take kindly, and driven largely by the relentless will of a proud and distant dictator.

In preserving the elasticity and striking power of that small army, the artillery had played no small part. The outstanding feature of its activities had been the success of the new 25-pr. The 2-pr. had also done well; notably in the hands of the infantry at Bardia and of the R.H.A. at Derna, where, on 26th January, three tanks and one armoured car had been put out of action at a range of 2,000 yards.

In the Armoured Division the value of close artillery support had been clearly demonstrated. " The fear that the presence of artillery units would cramp the style of the A.F.Vs. is groundless ", was announced officially. " The two are complementary."([7]) In the United Kingdom, after Dunkirk, the number of 25-prs. in the support group had been raised from 16 to 24, and the mixed A.A. and anti-tank regiment had been replaced by two homogeneous regiments, one A.A. and one anti-tank. On 29th January, 1941, a similar reorganization was ordered by the C.-in-C., Middle East, and one additional R.H.A. regiment, armed with 25-prs., was allotted as corps troops in support of the two armoured divisions then under his command—the 7th and the 2nd.

There had also been some failures. The armoured O.P., though entirely justified in principle, was lacking both in quality and quantity. The scale of one per battery was found, as in France and Belgium, to be quite inadequate ; and the vehicle then in use, the Bren carrier, did not afford sufficient protection to compensate for its slowness. In fact the general opinion among F.O.Os. was that, if they could not have a light tank, they would rather use an ordinary open truck and chance it.

At Bardia and Tobruk aerial photos and good maps of the enemy's positions were available, but these were of little use owing to the impossibility of locating one's position accurately in such featureless country. Survey was undoubtedly a great help to the gunner, but there were times when close support from the air would have been of inestimable value ; and, unfortunately, there was as yet no sign of " that dove-tailing of inter-service tactical activity to which the Germans and Italians have accustomed us ".[8]

Wireless establishments, especially in the infantry, were insufficient to compete with the extended frontages and depths of desert warfare, and this inevitably handicapped the gunner in his attempts to provide intimate and continuous fire support.

SECTION III.—THE CONQUEST OF ERITREA

Preliminary Operations

Meanwhile steps had been taken to dispel the threat to the Sudan from the Italian forces in East Africa. Like Egypt, it was not an easy country to attack by land. A belt of desert some two to three hundred miles wide covered the most likely objectives ; and here the Italians had also to face the possibility of a large scale rebellion in Abyssinia, if they moved too many of their regular forces out of the country.

In these circumstances it was again decided to adopt an offensive-defensive policy and to rely on the mobility and experience of our own small forces to bluff the enemy into an over-estimation of their strength. In August, 1940, a field regiment of 18-prs. and 4.5-in hows., less one battery, and one section of Bofors anti-tank guns were sent from Egypt to enhance the effect of these harassing operations. On 10th September, and again on 18th September, one field battery, with a suitable escort, moved out from Butana Bridge and shelled the Italian defences at the frontier town of Kassala, which we had had to evacuate.

The 5th Indian Division had now arrived in the Sudan and, to cover its concentration, a special force was formed consisting of the local Sudan Defence Force unit of motor machine-guns, the divisional cavalry regiment, one troop of Bofors anti-tank guns, and one troop of 18-prs. This force, known as " Gazelle ", was to play an important part in the subsequent offensive.

By the beginning of November, 1940, there were two brigades of the 5th Indian Division available for active operations, and it was possible to strike in earnest at the second of the two permanent encroachments made by the Italians on Sudanese territory. This was at Gallabat, which lay on the Abyssinian frontier. The attack was carried out on 6th November, by one infantry brigade supported by one field regiment with 4 × 18-prs. and

Plate 1—The Birch Gun.

Plate 2—The **18/25 pdr.**

Plate 3—The 9·2 in. how. on the road.

Plate 4—**The 2 pr. a.tk. gun.**

Plate 5—The 3-in. 20-cwt. A.A. Gun in action.

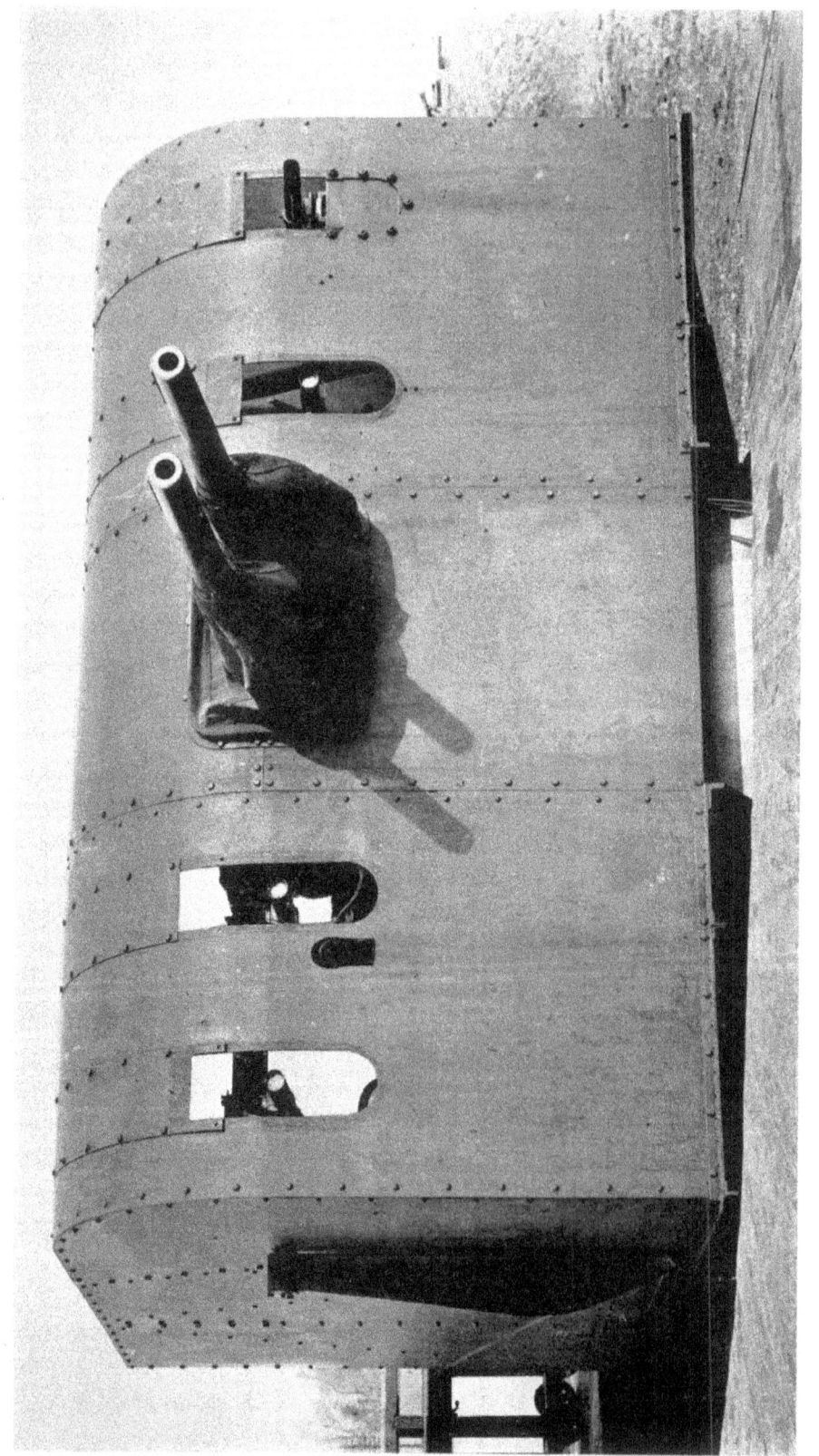

Plate 6—The 6-pr. twin Coast artillery gun.

Plate 7—The 8-in. how.

Plate 8—A Sandstorm in the Desert.

10 × 4.5 in. hows. The Italians, it was believed, were unaware that we had any guns in this area, and it was therefore desired to keep their presence secret as long as possible. Without survey, and without a reliable map, registration could not be dispensed with, but an attempt was made to achieve surprise by synchronizing it with a preliminary air bombardment.

Though the attack itself was a success, it was found impossible to hold the ground that had been won, owing to' the enemy's superiority in the air and to our own lack of A.A. guns. With the aid of the artillery, however, it was possible to deny this ground to the enemy. The infantry therefore withdrew to a less exposed position within artillery range of the disputed positions, and a destructive shoot was immediately carried out by the field guns. On the night 9-10th November, the enemy tried to re-enter Gallabat but were driven back by our defensive fire, and thereafter they maintained a respectful distance.

For the next two months a series of raids was undertaken by our troops in this area. By changing the units, and the nature of the artillery, it was hoped to create the impression of an impending offensive. At the same time mobile columns were formed here and on other possible approaches, each with its own small quota of guns, and each with the same role: to harass the enemy whenever and wherever possible and to keep him guessing where the main offensive was likely to develop.

The Advance to Keren

As a result of the victory at Sidi Barrani on 11th December, 1940, the safety of Egypt from that quarter had been assured and it was possible to transfer the 4th Indian Division and one squadron of "I" tanks to the Sudan. With this addition to our forces, it was intended to begin a general offensive with an attack on the Italian positions at Kassala and Tessenei, which stood across the main routes leading into Eritrea.

In spite of his superiority in the air, the vulnerability of the railway—which ran for a considerable distance close and parallel to the Eritrean and Abyssinian frontiers—and our complete lack of A.A. guns, the enemy did little to interfere with our movements. On receipt of information that Kassala was likely to be evacuated, the date of the attack was put forward from 8th February to 18th January without waiting for 4th Indian Division and the tanks to complete their concentration; and when it was found that the enemy had slipped away, Gazelle Force, with its artillery component reinforced by one troop of 3.7-in. hows. of the Sudan Regiment, was sent off at once in pursuit of him. It was followed—across country at times—by one battalion of 4th Indian Division with one field regiment, plus one troop, in support.

Thanks to the arrival of some Hurricanes, the enemy had now lost his supremacy in the air. His air force, though occasionally seen, never interfered with our daylight operations, whereas the movements of his own ground troops had all to be confined to the hours of darkness. The Italian commanders were also disagreeably surprised by the cross-country mobility of our mechanized columns and guns. Tracks and defiles that they had thought to be impassable, and had therefore left only weakly defended, were successfully negotiated and the demoralized enemy either surrendered or fled into the mountains.

As a result the advance was very rapid and the action of the artillery was largely of an opportunist nature. Enemy armour showed little initiative and its only attempt at aggressive action—by five Italian Mk. II tanks—was quickly disposed of by the machine-guns and Bofors anti-tank guns of Gazelle Force.

On another occasion a field battery experienced a brief flash-back to the romantic age of warfare when it was unexpectedly charged from one flank by a body of about 50 enemy horsemen. Beginning at a range of 400 yards, this charge was only finally broken when within 30 yards of the guns.

Amid the general success, there were two sources of dissatisfaction: the difficulty of giving close artillery support in the scrubby and featureless country that was now being met with, and the inadequate range of the 18-prs. and 4.5-in. hows. with which some of the field regiments were still armed. Among the mountains of Eritrea suitable gun positions were sometimes very scarce, and on at least one occasion full use could not be made of the available artillery owing to the impossibility of finding enough sites within effective range of the enemy positions. Had all units been armed with 25-prs. more rearward positions could have been used with effect.

Thus eight months after the evacuation of Dunkirk, its effects were still being felt. It was not until April 1941 or later that the last of the old equipments had been replaced in far-off Eritrea.

The First Attack on Keren

Nothing, however, could stop the impetus of 4th Indian Division's advance until it came with a bump against the immensely strong defensive position with which nature had barred the approaches to Keren. Precipitous mountains, with razor-backed tops, made artillery support a matter of extreme difficulty (*see* Plate 10). The enemy infantry, comfortably dug in on the rear faces of these ridges, were practically immune against shell fire, since any projectile that skimmed the crest would go sailing away for hundreds of yards into the valley beyond. Even at extreme Charge II ranges the trajectory of the 25-pr. was unable to compete with this problem. O.Ps. might be as much as 3,000 feet above the guns they were observing for, and a change of five minutes in line was sometimes sufficient to alter the fall of a round by as much as 500 yards.

The Italians had cleverly exploited these difficulties by equipping their troops with large numbers of light anti-personnel bombs, which could be used at a range of about 12 yards without endangering the thrower. The moment our artillery concentrations lifted beyond the crest, the enemy would leap up and hurl their bombs with great effect against our troops before they had had time to close.

They had also taken advantage of the almost perfect facilities for observation that they enjoyed. Everywhere our positions, infantry and artillery, were completely overlooked, and heavy casualties among our gun detachments were only avoided by good digging, camouflage, and the frequent use of alternative positions.

Owing to the nature of the terrain, it was impossible to use armoured O.Ps. and casualties among O.P. parties were heavy. Some critics were of the opinion that F.O.Os. would have done better to keep back with forward battalion headquarters until the situation had stabilized, but the C.R.A. 4th Indian Division thought differently. Since all our F.D.Ls. were on narrow ridges he considered that it was imperative that O.Ps. should be in the front line.

Finally, the Italians had secured themselves against the action of the dreaded " I " tanks by blocking the road in the steep-sided Dongolaas Gorge that led up to Keren through the centre of their position.

In spite of all these difficulties, a gallant attempt was made by 4th Indian Division to rush the position, or to find a way round, and snatch a victory before the enemy had had time to collect himself and to consolidate his defences. But it was of no avail. A *coup de main* in the dark without artillery support, and two determined daylight attacks supported by heavy artillery concentrations, failed after coming within an ace of success. Between five and six thousand shells had been fired, but they had not enabled the infantry to cross the last few yards to their objectives. There was nothing left but to withdraw to the ground that had been won on the lower slopes near the entrance to the gorge and await the arrival of 5th Indian Division.

Artillery Preparations for the Attack by 4th and 5th Indian Divisions

By 20th February the artillery resources had been increased by the arrival of a survey and a sound ranging troop. The latter was not equipped with wireless (*see* p. 37), nor was it accompanied by a flash spotting troop ; but in the relatively static conditions of this battle the lack of wireless was not a serious handicap, and some flash spotting facilities were provided by improvising a section of four posts and a plotting centre from the sound ranging and survey troops. They proved a valuable, and very necessary, supplement to the work of the sound rangers, since the high hills made sound ranging difficult at all times, and meteorological conditions made it practically impossible between 0900 and 1700 hours.

Another difficulty was the extreme variation in meteor conditions. Meteor corrections were very great during the middle of the day—on one occasion amounting to over 1,200 yards—and they tended to be inaccurate. A partial solution was found by shooting at a datum point at various times throughout the day, over a period of a week, and deducing a percentage error from the combined results.

With the arrival of a medium battery on 21st February, there were 16 × 6-in. hows. available for counter-battery work, which was centralized under the C.R.A. 4th Indian Division, with an improvized staff. *Pro-formas* for hostile shelling reports were issued to all artillery and infantry units, though it was some time before their use was fully mastered, and practised, by troops accustomed to the simple techniques of highly mobile warfare.

Another element of counter-battery work that had suffered some deterioration was shooting with air observation. In the United Kingdom where better facilities existed, further progress had been made with the acceleration of the procedure. Previous improvements had aimed at increasing the rate at which fresh targets could be engaged by using map spottings combined with regimental concentrations (*see* p. 31). Now a method was devised by which ranging could be carried out more quickly. Instead of waiting for an observation on the first salvo before firing a second, the shoot was initiated by three primary salvos followed by four opening rounds (two of them smoke) with a 600 yard spread. Thus observation was made easier for the airman and the time taken to find the correct range was considerably shortened[9].

To carry out this procedure successfully, however, required constant practice on the part of both airman and gunner. In Eritrea this had not been possible owing to the shortage of Lysander aircraft, and the problem had been further complicated by the difficulty of recognizing the country from the map, which sometimes led to the photographing of wrong areas. Nevertheless, after a few days' practice, some very successful shoots were conducted.

By this time enemy A.A. fire was plentiful and one field regiment was permanently allotted to the task of keeping down their fire. Another, and peculiar, feature of counter-battery work in these operations was the neutralization of enemy pack guns, which, coming into action on top of steep ridges, were easy to see but often extremely difficult to engage. It was a problem that entailed the use of a very deliberate procedure with single guns.

On our side, one L.A.A. battery had arrived early in February and was disposed between the L. of C., advanced landing grounds, gun areas and the forward infantry. It was an extensive task for one battery and it resulted sometimes in troops being broken up into two gun sections. Yet, small and scattered as this A.A. contingent was, it exerted an appreciable effect upon the subsequent conduct of the battle. During the initial fighting at Keren the enemy air force had again become aggressive, and the presence of even two L.A.A. guns in the forward area afforded a definite encouragement to our own troops, and their shooting had a noticeably deterrent effect upon the activities of enemy aircraft.

While 5th Indian Division, with its artillery, was training behind the line for mountain warfare, and working out its plans with the aid of models of its selected objectives, positions were being prepared and a heavy dumping programme carried out by R.A. units and the ammunition company of 4th Indian Division. Including holdings in unit echelons, 600 r.p.g. were immediately available for the 25-prs., and the supply of other natures of ammunition, though on a smaller scale, was still considerable.

For technical (crest clearance) reasons, gun positions had to be concentrated on the floor of the Hagas Valley, where, as stated above, they were entirely overlooked by enemy O.Ps. to the north and east (*see* Plate 11). Communications between O.Ps. and guns were therefore long—four to seven miles, of which about three miles lay along the hillside—and altogether some 250 miles of cable were on the ground. Wireless from O.Ps. to troops was available as a stand-by, and this worked well by day, but was unreliable at night owing to atmospherics.

The Capture of Keren

In selecting the objectives for the main attack on 15th March, the provision of adequate covering fire during the final stages of the assault was the determining factor. Fort Dologorodoc, which stood near the centre of the enemy position on the east side of the Dongolaas Gorge, had previously been avoided because it was completely overlooked by the heights on either side. It was now included in the plan of operations because of its relatively gentle rearward slopes, which offered facilities for close support by the artillery.

To assist in this matter, the infantry were provided with screens, as used during the 1914-18 war and on the N.W. frontier of India, to indicate their positions to the gunners; but now, as then, these devices were not popular with the infantry, who found them an encumbrance to movement and a source of gratuitous information to the enemy. They were not therefore much used and were generally disposed of at the first convenient opportunity.

As before, covering fire was to take the form of concentrations followed by observed shooting once a particular crest had been captured. With the two divisions operating on opposite sides of the Dongolaas Gorge, the problem was to produce the greatest possible density of fire at the critical time and place. In the absence of a C.C.R.A., arrangements for mutual assistance between the two divisional artilleries were co-ordinated by the C.R.A. 4th Indian Division, who had been in the area since the beginning and was familiar with the whole of the terrain. In the initial attack by 4th Indian Division on the commanding heights west of the gorge, its artillery was to be reinforced by 36 guns of 5th Indian Division Artillery. In the subsequent attack by 5th Indian Division on Fort Dologorodoc, 56 guns of 4th Indian Division Artillery were to switch over to its support.

In spite of all the care that had been taken, and the dash with which the assault was carried out, the success gained was only partial. Fort Dologorodoc was taken and held, but the attempt to gain the hills beyond it was frustrated, and on the opposite side of the gorge the heights of Sanchil and Brigs Peak remained as unattainable as ever. An appeal from 4th Indian Division for an air bombardment of their rearward slopes could not be met owing to the obscurity of the situation in that area and the difficulty of identifying our own troops from the air.

After repeated failures, therefore, it was decided to withdraw 4th Indian Division to its original positions, while consolidating the hold of 5th Indian Division on Fort Dologorodoc, and then try a thrust up the centre of the gorge under cover of a small—and, technically, rather difficult—barrage fired by the one available mountain battery. The attack went in early on 25th March and after two days' stiff fighting the enemy resistance began to crumble. Eight fiercely sustained efforts to recapture Dologorodoc had cost him heavy casualties—to which our defensive fire had greatly contributed—and had finally broken his will to continue the fight. On the morning of 27th March our infantry, advancing now behind a normal artillery barrage, broke through the defences beyond Dologorodoc, and by 0800 hours two troops of tanks were in Keren.

"The battle of Keren was won. It had been won by the tenacity and determination of commanders and troops, by whole-hearted co-operation of all ranks. . . . and by the continuous support given to infantry by the

Royal Artillery, who, between 15th and 27th March, fired over 110,000 shells borne by 1,000 lorries from railhead over 150 miles away."([10]) There was still some stiff fighting to be done, but in it no new artillery lessons would be brought out. With the fall of Keren the fate of Italian East Africa had been sealed and 4th Indian Division was free to return to Egypt, where its presence was now badly needed.

Conclusion

Once again the elasticity and endurance of a small professional army had been fully demonstrated. In spite of its old equipments, the artillery had in general done what was required of it ; and on occasion a positive virtue had been made of necessity, as when, by ringing the changes between the 18-pr. and the 4.5-in. how., the enemy was encouraged to believe in an impending offensive where none was intended (*see* p. 55).

The increasing size of artillery bombardments was reflected in the dumping programmes: 50 r.p.g. at Sidi Barrani, 300 at Bardia, and 500 at Keren; which, to those who are interested in such calculations, may give a check on the relative values of the moral and material factors in war. At Sidi Barrani the surprise achieved was almost complete ; at Bardia much less ; at Keren almost nil. After making a generous allowance for all the other factors, it is still an impressive example of what surprise means in terms of economy of ammunition.

The main weakness had lain in the lack of an efficient system for the provision of close support in difficult country. More mountain artillery might have helped, but it was generally agreed that aircraft would do the job better, once a means had been found for indicating the positions of our own troops to the bomber.

Looking back, there was ground for much satisfaction. If Dunkirk had cleared away the mists, these last two campaigns had let in the sunshine. But the " elastic " was growing thin, and with the development of the German thrust in the Mediterranean it would be stretched to the breaking-point.

SECTION IV.—A.A. AND COAST DEFENCE

Cutting the Suit

By the middle of May, 1940, the threat of air attack against Egypt had become serious, and on 18th May a B.A.A. arrived from England to act as adviser on all A.A. and C.D. questions and to take command of all A.A. and C.D. units in the Middle East—except those of the Egyptian Army and the South African Forces—that were not under command of subordinate formations.

The amount of the British A.A. resources at that time was very small (*see* p. 44), and it was therefore inevitable that conflicts should arise between the various claimants for A.A. protection. The Royal Navy argued that the security of Egypt depended on the maintenance of the Fleet in the Mediterranean, which in turn was largely dependent on an efficient A.A. defence at Alexandria. They therefore wanted to increase the defences at this place at the expense of Cairo or the Western Desert. The Army maintained that the removal of guns from the Western Desert might have a serious effect on operations there, where the L. of C. was very vulnerable to air attack. Others felt that Egyptian opinion should not be outraged by the removal of guns from Cairo, and the R.A.F. were naturally concerned about the protection of their airfields.

It was not long before other claimants began to enter the field. By the middle of July demands were coming in from the Sudan for A.A. defences at Port Sudan and Khartoum, and Somaliforce was pleading for H.A.A. guns at Berbera, where continual air attack was "having a demoralizing effect on the people including the garrison".

Indeed, as fast as A.A. reinforcements arrived, new demands for A.A. protection were put forward. On 4th November, 1940, one H.A.A. and one L.A.A. battery had to be sent to Crete. The following day the O.C. Troops Cyprus asked for A.A. defences for the tightly packed towns of Nicosia and Famagusta. On 13th November the Senior Naval Officer Suez Canal pressed for increased A.A. defence of his area, and on 15th November, the Signal Officer-in-Chief Middle East asked for A.A. defences for the wireless transmitting station at Abu Zabal and the receiving station at Maadi, which provided communication to all parts of the Empire and possessed no stand-by equipment. On 21st November, the B.A.A. was informed that the defence of the Palestine Potash Company was vital to the war effort.

It was, in fact, evident that some co-ordination was necessary, and that the peace time system of controlling sub-allocations of A.A. guns from Whitehall was too cumbersome. On 25th September, a standing Inter-Service Air Defence Committee had been formed at G.H.Q., M.E., and on 6th December it was decided by the Chiefs of Staff that the sub-allocation of guns in the Middle East should be made by G.H.Q. with the advice of this Committee.

In November, 1940, an interesting innovation was made by placing passive air defence under the B.A.A., who organized it as a separate section of the A.A. and C.D. branch under the control of a G1. This was a logical application of the principle that "the state of preparation of the P.A.D. scheme will be the foundation upon which the air defence plan is built".[11] It was not, however, the normal method of dealing with P.A.D. in the British Army, and it was not repeated in other theatres.

Development of the A.A. Barrage

The main problem in the rear areas was the defence of the all-important harbour of Alexandria. Like all artificial harbours of its type, it had to rely for the protection of its anchorages on guns sited beside or behind the vulnerable area. Early pick-up was therefore vital, and, for the defence to be really effective, it was necessary that every H.A.A. gun position should be provided with its own radar set feeding data direct to the guns. Unfortunately such a set was still not available, and so, as the ammunition situation improved, a procedure was worked out for what was known as a "geographical barrage".

Rudimentary barrages of this nature had been used in France and Belgium (*see* p. 39), and the idea had been developed in A.A. Command and applied with some success during the Battle of Britain. The principle employed was to put down a line of shell bursts through which the attacking aircraft must fly if they were to bomb the vulnerable area effectively. The location of this barrage would, of course, depend on the height at which the enemy was flying and the direction from which he was making his approach. Since his liberty of manoeuvre was usually quite unrestricted, it was necessary to prepare gunnery data for a series of lines, at suitable vertical intervals, surrounding the whole of the vulnerable area; and to select, at the appropriate moment, the particular line or lines that seemed likely to give the best results. With the aid of information received from the R.A.F., it was hoped to pick up the enemy sufficiently early, and to plot his position, course and speed with sufficient accuracy, to enable a correct selection to be made.

The number of aircraft shot down by this method was naturally small, but so long as the ammunition supply held, the deterrent effect was considerable.

Defence of the Suez Canal

Another important and difficult problem was the A.A. defence of the Suez Canal. The chief threat here was from mine-laying aircraft, and it was estimated that, to give full protection against this form of attack, it would be necessary to establish about 100 observation posts along the canal, each equipped with a L.A.A. gun, and to augment them with balloons and searchlights over certain sections.

The number of personnel required for such a system was found to be prohibitive, and the solution finally adopted was to locate single searchlights at intervals of 2,200 yards along the canal bank, with one row of flanking lights on each side of the canal at a distance of 2,500 to 6,000 yards (determined largely by administrative factors) and at intervals of 5,500 yards. Fighter aircraft, stationed in the vicinity, formed the mainstay of the defence, and the exposure of searchlights was strictly controlled so as to avoid their accidental illumination.

A.A. Defence in the Western Desert

Until the end of October, 1940, the only A.A. artillery in the Western Desert was a troop of H.A.A. guns at Mersa Matruh. For L.A.A. defence the field army had to rely entirely on anti-aircraft light machine guns. On 31st October, the 7th Armoured Division was joined by a combined L.A.A. and anti-tank regiment in accordance with the existing organization in the United Kingdom (*see* p. 18). In December, the first L.A.A. regiment proper arrived, and for the battle of Sidi Barrani each of the three infantry brigade groups had one troop of this regiment under command, with (attached) a R.A.F. observer post of four other ranks and a wireless set whose object it was to give warning of air activity. Thereafter, as fresh units arrived, they were allotted to formations on a similar scale, and sub-allotted by them to the various small columns that were formed, and reformed, from time to time in accordance with the tactical situation.

In January, 1941, a H.A.A. regiment and an A.A. brigade headquarters arrived in the Western Desert, and the latter took control of all A.A. units in the coastal area, itself receiving orders direct from the " G " staff at Corps Headquarters and keeping the C.C.R.A. informed of A.A. dispositions. In the inland area, a lieut-colonel A.A. was attached to the staff of the C.R.A. 7th Armoured Division, with purely advisory duties. The command of H.A.A. units allotted to the Division was exercised by the C.R.A.; that of L.A.A. units was delegated to brigades.

In the rearward areas priority was given to supply ports, and then to R.A.F. landing grounds. Owing to the number of the latter (eight), the strength of the defences at each was very slight. There was practically no H.A.A., and the L.A.A. allotment never exceeded two Bofors or Bredas to each landing ground, manned by A.A. personnel at four of the landing grounds and R.A.F. personnel at the other four. Transport was provided on a pool basis, and on the advance of a squadron to a new landing ground, L.A.A. guns and personnel were ferried up to the new positions.

In the forward areas the priority of tasks for A.A. guns allotted to a division was:—

(a) The field artillery area, which included the forward troops, field gun positions and wagon lines.
(b) Divisional M.T. areas.
(c) Reserves and advanced landing grounds.
(d) Forward dumps.

It was found that the first of these tasks required one H.A.A. battery, and the remaining tasks another two; so that, for reasonable protection, an allotment of one H.A.A. regiment to each division was necessary. L.A.A. tasks were generally the same as for H.A.A., except that L.A.A.—unlike H.A.A.—guns were included in every small column. This led to the splitting up of L.A.A. batteries into sub-units of three, two or even one gun under a N.C.O. It made supervision by the troop commander difficult, but tactically, as in Eritrea (see p. 58), it justified itself by results, and it helped to keep the number of vehicles in each column down to a minimum.

Later, an attempt was made to ease this situation by a change in the organization of the L.A.A. battery. The 4-gun troop, on which the war establishment was based, was not only an imitation of field artillery custom, but had a tactical justification. The minimum number of L.A.A. guns required for the defence of a single point was considered to be four, of which three were to be disposed in the form of a triangle around the V.P. and one at the centre to take on the dive bomber (see p. 38). Recent experience in A.D.G.B. and elsewhere had shown, however, that the gun at the centre was usually blinded by dust and smoke from bombs falling on and around the objective. It was therefore eliminated from the normal lay-out, and as a result a 3-gun troop could be regarded as tactically effective. This meant that a L.A.A. battery of 12 guns could now defend four separate points instead of three, and the idea was quickly exploited by reorganizing the battery into four troops instead of three.

On the whole enemy air activity was not great, and there were times when A.A. units were not required for their normal role. On such occasions the A.A., like the anti-tank, gun was quickly turned to other purposes. The long range of the H.A.A. gun, and the shortage of medium artillery at this time, resulted in its being used against distant enemy O.Ps. and for long range harassing fire; its success in this role produced a certain local enthusiasm, and a request for A.A. guns to be supplied with items of field artillery equipment such as directors. This was at first resisted by the authorities, but the local enthusiasm persisted and their issue became more general.

As the advance progressed, a temporary warning system was organized along the coast. A G.O.R. at R.A.F. Sector Operations Room was connected by land lines to the A.A.D.Cs. and Naval Officers in charge at all ports, and to all guns and selected A.A.S.Ls. In inland areas, reliance had to be placed on spotters located as far out from the guns as possible.

The Coast Defence Problem

Owing to the supremacy of the Royal Navy in the Mediterranean at this time, coast artillery was not called upon to play an active part in operations. There were, however, certain important tasks—such as the examination service for the control of merchant shipping and the interception of contraband—that had to be kept going, and since mastery of the seas could never be absolute, some defence was essential at the more important ports as an insurance against a fleeting bombardment of shore installations or a surprise torpedo attack by light surface or underwater craft against ships in harbour.

The equipment and personnel for most of these tasks at ports that had been a peace-time responsibility of the British Government—*e.g.*, Suez, Port Said, Haifa—had been worked out in some detail and were gradually collected and installed as the war proceeded. The equipment was old but was generally regarded as adequate, except in the case of the A.M.T.B. defences. For the latter role a twin 6-pr. equipment had been designed and produced in small quantities before the war began (*see* p. 7), but none had yet reached the Middle East. As a stop-gap, use was made of a variety of equipments, from the .5-in. machine-gun to the 12-pr. Q.F., most of which dated back to before the First World War.

As operations developed, and new ports came under British control, defences had to be hastily improvised and coast artillery equipments became still more varied; and as the supply of trained coast artillery personnel ran out, men from field army units and other sources were brought in to make good the deficiency. By February, 1941, the burden of coast defence was being borne by Egyptian Army units at Alexandria and Port Sudan, a King's African Rifles battery at Mombasa, a Cypriot battery at Famagusta, British coast defence units at Port Fuad, Port Tewfik, Haifa and Aden, with a mixture of Army, R.N. and R.M. personnel at Suda Bay in Crete. At Tobruk and Benghasi a mixture of British and captured Italian equipments was being temporarily manned by the men of a yeomanry regiment, who had been specially trained for the purpose.

As yet no organization had been designed to meet the coast artillery commitments entailed by the capture of new harbours. There was, under the control of the Admiralty, a mobile naval base defence organization (M.N.B.D.O.) that had been brought up to date during the Abyssinian crisis of 1935-36, but it was still short of equipment and in any case was intended only—as its name suggested—for the temporary defence of a new fleet anchorage pending the installation of permanent defences by the Army. For the latter it was still necessary to go through the peace-time procedure of treating each new commitment on its merits. This, of course, meant considerable delays while reconnaissances were being carried out and demands for suitable equipments were being referred to the War Office. In most cases these equipments were mounted on a central pivot bolted to a concrete foundation, and their installation was therefore a matter of time and of technical skill.

List of References

(¹) Arty. Training, Vol. II, Pamphlet No. 2A, 1940, Sec. 3, 7, vi.
(²) Despatch by C-in-C, M.E., August 1939 to November 1940, para. 34.
(³) Despatch by C-in-C, M.E., December 1940 to February 1941, para. 30.
(⁴) Middle East Training Pamphlet No. 10, Pt. II, pp. 20-24.
(⁵) A.T.M. No. 39, April 1941.
(⁶) Middle East Training Pamphlet No. 10, Pt. III, p. 64.
(⁷) *Ibid*, p. 63.
(⁸) *Ibid*, p. 40.
(⁹) R.A.T.M. War No. 3, January 1941.
(¹⁰) Report by Lt.-Gen. Sir Wm. Platt, December 1940 to August 1941.
(¹¹) Manual of A.A. Defence, Vol. II, Pamphlet No. 1, 1940, p. 16.

PART III

THE FIGHT AGAINST THE DIVE BOMBER

CHAPTER V

THE GERMAN DRIVE INTO THE MEDITERRANEAN

PLATE RELEVANT TO THIS CHAPTER
No. 12. The 2-pr. A.Tk. portee.

The Effect of German Air Superiority

In dealing with the Italian threat to Egypt and the Sudan we had possessed certain definite advantages. The Matilda tank had dominated the battlefield, the 2-pr. and 25-pr. between them had easily held the Italian armour, and our troops in general were highly trained and displayed a greater aptitude for work in the desert than the enemy. In the air the Italians had done little to exploit their numerical superiority.

As a result victories had been won that were perhaps comparable, both in speed and completeness, to those that the Germans had been winning in Europe. Now we were at grips with the Germans again and were to feel once more the effects of German air power, which, in the public imagination at any rate, was epitomized in the dive bomber. There could indeed be no doubt that the dive bomber, as used by the Germans, had proved a definite success. Both in Poland and in N.W. Europe co-operation between attacking air and tank squadrons had been complete, and the dive bomber had been freely used as close support artillery and as long range harassing artillery for the disruption and demoralization of the enemy's administrative services. It was not the weight of the bombardment so much as the speed and intensity with which the attacks were delivered that had won the victory: a characteristic that is also to be found in the British plans for the battle of Sidi Barrani (see p. 50).

It has been estimated that 500 fighters would have saved Sedan in May, 1940, "because the German dive-bombers could have been mastered by so considerable a force."[1] Even a moderate number of A.A. guns, if properly equipped and realistically trained to meet the psychological conditions of air warfare, might—as subsequent events were to show—have greatly reduced the extent of the disaster. Neither fighters nor guns were available, however, in sufficient quantity, and now, in the Middle East, history was about to repeat itself.

The Shadow of Dunkirk Grows Darker

Before the blow fell, the strength of the British position had been seriously weakened. The despatch of an expeditionary force to Greece had caused a heavy drain on the forces in Cyrenaica, as a result of which the desert experience that had been accumulated during the victorious campaign of the preceding months had been largely dissipated. The 6th Australian Division was on its way to Greece, the 7th Armoured Division had had to be withdrawn to rest and re-equip, and the 4th Indian Division was still in Eritrea. In their places were new formations that were unaccustomed to the desert and in varying states of unreadiness for war.

There were still only three medium regiments in the whole of the Middle East, of which one was now in Eritrea and the other two under orders for Greece. Two-thirds of their armament was made up of the old, short-ranged 6-in. how., and the remaining third of converted 4.5-in./60-prs. The new 4.5-in. gun had only just started to come off production, and issues were being held up through a shortage of essential stores.

Anti-tank units were also very short of their proper equipment. The delivery of 2-pr. barrels had not been sufficient to allow the release of any equipments for the Middle East since 12th January, and a number of batteries had to make do with 37-mm. Bofors and captured enemy equipments. At the end of 1940, the conversion of one factory from 2 to 6-prs. was considered, but it was estimated that only 100 of the larger guns would be obtained instead of 600 of the smaller. The proposal was therefore abandoned and it was decided that 6-pr. production must come from new capacity.

Meanwhile in Germany, as had been expected, advantage was being taken of the information gained by examination of captured British equipments. In the pre-war design of their tanks the Germans had wisely made allowance for a probable further increase in the size of the armament and the thickness of the frontal armour. Now these increases were being put into effect in order to gain a superiority over the British tanks armed with the 2-pr. At the same time, thanks to the adequacy of their existing stock of 37-mm. anti-tank guns, it was possible for them to proceed at once with the mass production of a more powerful weapon.

As yet none of the new equipments had made its appearance on the battlefield, but the day of their arrival was not far off. When it came, the Matilda tank would cease to dominate the infantry battle, the British cruiser tanks would find themselves outgunned in the armoured battle, and anti-tank units would sometimes have to resort to desperate measures to get within effective striking distance of the enemy.

The Loss of Cyrenaica—April, 1941

The main danger at the moment, however, lay in the air, where, as early as 12th February, the Germans had begun an offensive from Libya. There was no effective defence, since practically all available fighter aircraft and A.A. guns were required for the campaign in Greece. By the third week in February the use of Benghasi as a port had become impossible and all supplies except petrol, landed at the small subsidiary port of Derna, had to be brought from Tobruk over 200 miles away.

By the end of March, the enemy superiority in the air had been definitely established. There were in the forward area about 200 German and a similar number of Italian aircraft, but on the British side the available resources allowed only a daily average of three Hurricanes for tac/R, five Blenheims for strategical reconnaissance and day bombing, six Wellingtons for night bombing, and a few Lysanders for use in safe areas. One fighter squadron covered the forward areas and protected Benghasi, another protected Tobruk.

The A.A. defences were equally meagre. At Tobruk there were no more than 16 H.A.A. and 12 L.A.A. guns, and in the forward area only 16 L.A.A. guns. These were unable to prevent serious damage being done by the German air force to A.F.Vs. and transport. Indeed from early March the enemy air superiority in the forward zone was so marked that moves had mainly to be carried out by night.

On 31st March, Rommel launched his attack in some strength and quickly overpowered the weak British armour that lay in front of him. Harassed by vigorous dive bombing and machine-gun attacks, and with its petrol supply columns decimated by enemy air action, the 2nd Armoured Division had, by 7th April, practically ceased to exist. The way to the frontier was open, and it was left to the forces in Tobruk to hold the enemy there and to give time for the assembly of reinforcements for the defence of Egypt. Meanwhile the 2nd Support Group, which had successfully withdrawn from its frontier covering position at Mersa Brega, and had been reinforced by elements of the 7th Support Group, was still further withdrawn to the Egyptian frontier with orders to delay the enemy there. For this purpose it was organized in three mixed columns, each containing a battalion or less of motorized infantry, one or more troops of 25-prs., and one troop each of anti-tank and L.A.A. guns.

Thus, within the space of a fortnight, our forces—except those in Tobruk—were back where they had started the previous autumn; but not in the same strength. For some months at least our defences would be much weaker in nearly all the things that mattered: A.F.Vs., artillery, anti-tank guns and A.A. weapons.

German Air Superiority Again Makes Itself Felt in Greece—April, 1941

When, in November, 1940, it was decided to send an air striking force to Greece, the amount of A.A. artillery available to accompany it was minute; and when the ground forces followed in March, 1941, the A.A. resources were still deplorably small: two H.A.A. and four L.A.A. batteries, of which only two of the L.A.A. batteries were fully mobile. Of this small force, half was locked up on airfields, leaving only one H.A.A. and two L.A.A. batteries for the defence of the 1st Armoured Brigade, the 6th Australian and the New Zealand Division—which, when the battle opened, were distributed over a front of about 35 miles—and a L. of C. that was 300 miles long and extremely vulnerable to air attack. There was therefore no H.A.A. artillery with divisions, and, until the withdrawal of the 1st Armoured Brigade into reserve, no L.A.A.

In the air the enemy superiority was even greater than in Cyrenaica. The total serviceable strength of British aircraft was 80, and part of this had to be allotted to the support of the Greek forces fighting in Albania. On the other side the Germans were reported to be able to mass 800 aircraft on the eastern front, and the Italians had 160 based in Albania and a further 150 based in Italy but operating over Albania. For co-operation with the Army we had one Army Co-operation squadron, but it rarely had more than one Hurricane serviceable at a time, and it was impossible to use its other aircraft in the face of opposition.

In these circumstances it was necessary to rely very largely on passive air defence measures, including dispersion, and to accept certain administrative inconveniences resulting therefrom. In the forward areas in particular, where the supply route was a single-track railway from the advanced base at Larissa, there was a tendency to keep " a little of everything everywhere." The confusion was increased by a heavy earthquake, which robbed the base of local facilities on which it might otherwise have counted, and by the lack of trained personnel for the care and supply of ammunition.

Enemy air action began almost at once and followed a definite routine, which aimed first at the destruction of ports and quays and the interception of sea communications; then at the gaining of air superiority; then at the destruction of M.T. parks, petrol, supply and ordnance store depots; and finally at the machine-gunning and bombing of roads and communications. On the night of 6/7th April, as the German forces were approaching the main allied position on the Aliakhmon line, a heavy raid was directed against the Piraeus, where the A.A. defences consisted of only 24 H.A.A. guns (20 Greek and 4 British) and about 15 L.A.A. guns (8 Greek and 7 British), with some Greek searchlights. The damage done to the docks was such that the port had to be closed for two days and the shipping programme slowed down.

During the first two vital days of the withdrawal from the Aliakhmon line, enemy air action was fortunately prevented by mist and low clouds, but from Larissa southwards columns on the road suffered air attack without respite. The R.A.F. could do little to help, since they had themselves suffered a heavy disaster. On 15th April, 14 of their Hurricanes, and all 16 of their Blenheims, had been caught undispersed on the ground on the Larissa airfields and had been totally destroyed. The Greek observer system, which at first had functioned well, had broken down completely during the withdrawal, and the fighters and A.A. guns could therefore no longer rely on early warning. The only G.L. (radar) set had proved a failure, apparently owing to the height and iron ore content of the mountains.

By 20th April, it had become clear that the whole of the Greek mainland would have to be evacuated, and to cover this operation, 4 H.A.A. guns were sent to Corinth Bridge, and 4 H.A.A. and 12 L.A.A. guns to Argos, where the few remaining Hurricanes had been concentrated. It appears, however, that owing to a misunderstanding the aircraft landed at an airfield other than that which had been notified to the A.A. commander. They were, therefore, left temporarily undefended, and on the evening of 23rd April they were surprised by a sudden air attack, and, being again undispersed, were easily destroyed on the ground.

Thus the plans for the evacuation had to be hurriedly altered to allow for the absence of fighter protection. Less use had to be made of the Attica beaches, and more of the Peloponnesus, which gave a shorter sea voyage to Crete and Egypt.

The final disaster occurred at Corinth on 26th April. Under the new plan, the bridge at this place, which offered the only practicable route into the Peloponnesus, became of vital importance. For its defence an A.A. lay-out of 8×3-in., 4×3.7-in and 16 Bofors had been installed, of which the latter covered the area down to Argos as well as the immediate vicinity of the canal. After a heavy "strafing" of these defences on the 25th, the main enemy attack was delivered shortly before 0700 hrs. on the 26th. While 20 to 30 Ju87s. dive bombed the canal, 80 to 100 Me110. fighters covered the whole area with machine-gun and cannon fire.

The attack lasted about half-an-hour, at the end of which time the A.A. defences had been completely silenced. Then came the paratroops. About 800 of them were dropped in the next half hour, and they quickly overcame the canal defences. The H.A.A. unit could do little against them, as a battery at that time had only 5 L.M.Gs. and 30 rifles on its establishment.

Because of the failure of the German air force to interfere with the evacuation by the night bombing of the beaches, the losses in personnel were less than might have been expected, but the losses in equipment were crippling. Practically no artillery, transport or heavy equipment was brought out, and altogether at least 8,000 vehicles had been destroyed or captured.

The Loss of Crete—May, 1941

On 1st November, 1940, when the 14th Infantry Brigade (two battalions only) was sent to Crete, there seemed to be no immediate threat to the island, and " the only requirement was to secure Suda Bay as a refuelling base for the Navy."(^{2}) It was however realized that, if the mainland were overrun, the use of the island by British forces would be limited by the scale of air attack that might be brought to bear on it from Greek airfields.

Air defence was therefore vital, and the A.A. requirements were accepted as 56 H.A.A. guns, 48 L.A.A. guns and 72 A.A.S.Ls., with more added if the airfields and other facilities were developed. In fact, at the time of the evacuation of Greece, there were only 16 H.A.A. guns (3.7-in.), 36 Bofors (of which 12 were static), and 24 A.A.S.Ls. To these were added, on the eve of the battle, 16 × 3-in. guns of the M.N.B.D.O., which had arrived from the United Kingdom to take over the defences of Suda Bay.

The situation was aggravated by the dispersion of the sites to be defended. All the useful harbours in Crete—Suda Bay, Heraklion and Retimo—lay on the exposed north coast and were connected by a single main road that followed the coast and was still under construction. Of airfields there were only two: at Maleme (near Suda Bay) and Heraklion (about 80 miles east of Suda Bay), with a third possible site near Retimo about mid-way between the two.

The defences fell naturally, therefore, into three groups: Heraklion, Retimo, and the Suda Bay-Maleme area, each of which, owing partly to lack of transport, had to fight as a separate force. The majority of the H.A.A. guns and all the searchlights were concentrated for the defence of Suda Bay, and were controlled by a G.O.R. at Canea, which was linked to a Greek observer system (by civil lines only) and to a R.A.F. radar set at Maleme. Of the L.A.A. guns, 22 were allotted to the defence of the airfields, 10 at Heraklion and 12 at Maleme; with a section of 3-in. guns at each place to prevent the enemy bombers from taking it easy just out of range of the Bofors. The remaining 14 Bofors were included in the defences of Suda Bay.

For the rest, reliance was again placed mainly on P.A.D. measures. In anticipation of airborne attack, instructions were issued to the effect that all troops, whether in reserve or forward positions, must be well dug in and concealed. During air attack both weapons and men were to be under cover, and troops in concealed areas were not to open small-arms fire unless they had been located and were being attacked, or unless the aircraft was about to land.

For ground defence, artillery support was on a very feeble scale. Units arriving from Greece came without their equipment, and the only weapons available were some 40 Italian and French 75-mm. and 90-mm. guns, many of which were without essential stores, plus a last-minute addition of one troop of 3.7-in. hows. (portee).

From 14th May, the enemy began to turn his attention to A.A. gun positions, but the material effects of his attacks were not great. By 20th May the total A.A. casualties from air raids were only 6 killed and 11 wounded. No Bofors had been irreparably damaged and the heavy guns were all serviceable, though some predictors and heightfinders had been damaged by near misses and by machine-gun fire.

Meanwhile, in the air, the situation had been deteriorating. By 19th May, the strength of the R.A.F. in Crete had been reduced to three Hurricanes and three Gladiators in operational condition at Heraklion, and one Hurricane at Maleme. Such a force was too small to give effective cover, and the A.A. guns, trying to engage the enemy by normal instrumental methods, had met with little success against the evasive tactics of the dive bombers. The shipping losses had in consequence been serious, particularly at Suda Bay, where there were now 13 damaged ships in the harbour. It was therefore decided to evacuate all aircraft from the island, to base the A.A. defence at Suda Bay on a real " A.A. umbrella "—in the form of a barrage—over the pier, and to allow only two ships in the harbour at a time, both actively discharging at the jetty.

The effect of these measures was very satisfactory. Thereafter not a single dive was carried out as well as usual, not one bomb hit either ship or jetty, and several aircraft turned right away and discharged their loads well wide.

At Heraklion airfield, which was situated in a large open plain and was defended by some 3,500 troops, the L.A.A. guns were withdrawn from the normal perimeter lay-out and dispersed in specially selected positions with orders to hold fire until the expected parachute attack began. At Maleme they remained in their original positions: partly, it appears, because the environs were hilly and much obstructed by olive groves, so that they offered few good gun positions; partly because of the weakness of the local infantry garrison (one under-strength battalion) and the resultant difficulty of finding positions that were covered against ground attack; and partly because of the cover they gave to the adjacent beach and foreshore.

At about 0700 hrs. on 20th May, the main German assault began with an air bombardment, which was heaviest at Maleme and in the Suda Bay-Canea area, where the A.A. locations were fairly accurately known. At Maleme, in particular, the Bofors positions around the edge of the airfield were very obvious, and they were therefore quickly enveloped by clouds of dust and smoke. Moreover, since they had been sited to give the normal 360 degrees arc of fire at every gun position their detachments were exposed to attack by machine-gun or cannon fire from behind while engaging another target in their primary arc. This had a bad effect on morale, already lowered by long periods of duty, constant attacks, and still more constant warnings. Thus the enemy was able to break through the A.A. defences, and, having once landed, he could not be denied the use of the airfield by the action of the ground artillery. The latter consisted mainly of a battery of 75-mm. guns, which were without adequate transport, communications or sights, and which, when cut off from their F.O.O., became practically useless.

There remained the possibility of ejecting the enemy from the airfield by an infantry attack. During the night 21st/22nd May, the New Zealanders succeeded in recapturing almost the whole of the ground lost, but intense daylight bombing the next day forced them to withdraw, and the enemy continued to pour in his troop-carrying aircraft regardless of the fire of our 75-mms. It was estimated that as many as 600 of these troop carriers were landed in one day.

At Heraklion the attack had been successfully held, and during the nights 21st/22nd and 22nd/23rd May attempts at a sea-borne invasion had also been frustrated by the Royal Navy. But the loss of Malame airfield had been decisive. By 26th May the enemy had some 30-35,000 troops on the island, and early the next day General Freyberg decided that evacuation was inevitable.

The Dive Bomber at its Zenith

The dive bomber was now at the height of its fame and power. It had not, in reality, been responsible for all these German successes, but it had played a prominent part in the most spectacular of them. Its moral effect, enhanced by the popular, and almost pathological, emphasis laid in peace on the anticipated horrors of air warfare, could not be adequately countered by preparatory training, which could not provide the realistic conditions necessary; nor had it figured prominently in the previous war experience of most of the A.A. units. During the battle of Britain every available A.A. unit, whether of the field force or otherwise, was placed at the disposal of A.A. Command and served its turn in one of the many gun defended areas. In some of these areas there was plenty of action to be had, but the conditions under which it was waged were peculiar. Thanks to Fighter Command, and to radar, the German bombers seldom loitered or came down low over their objectives, and direct attacks on the A.A. guns were rare.

In these long periods of one-way shooting the need for protection was easily forgotten, especially when emplacements were frequently built by a contractor or taken over complete from a preceding unit. In less critical situations, and with more seasoned troops, the failure to dig might not have had such untoward results; for the casualties inflicted by the dive bomber were still remarkably small. But things were going badly here in Crete; the A.A. defences were inadequate; and the scale of attack was very heavy. Transport was short, movement difficult, stores hard to come by; and gun detachments were suffering from undertraining and strain and were sometimes short-handed. If, therefore, morale was to be fostered, protection was of the first importance. To achieve it, some thought, a sacrifice might even be made of the all-round field of fire.

Alternative L.A.A. Lay-Outs

At the same time sight was not lost of the fact that the gunner's best means of self-defence was his gun. The problem was so to organize a defensive system that the guns within it would be self-supporting; a subject on which the existing manual of A.A. defence gave little guidance. In its composition, consideration had not been given to a situation in which no fighter cover existed and a direct assault on the A.A. defences was to be expected.

To remedy this omission, a training instruction was issued to the effect that, when little or no fighter cover was available, L.A.A. guns and V.P.s should be sited in groups. Within these groups the guns should be disposed in pairs or more so as to provide mutual support against a concentrated air attack. When adequate fighter cover was available, and only "tip and run" raids were likely, guns could again be spaced singly so as to cover the normal airfield lay-out.[3]

For repelling an attack by airborne troops it was evident that all gunners should be armed with rifles or tommy-guns. A proposal to this effect had in fact been made as a result of the campaign in France and Belgium, but the lack of equipments had so far prevented it from being implemented.

The Need for a Reliable Early Warning System

Twice, in Greece and again in Crete, the early warning system had broken down, and it was evident that in operations of this nature—and indeed in all fully mobile operations—L.A.A. units should be capable of providing their own early warnings, either by the use of visual look-outs or of special radar instruments. For this purpose the G.L. set was of little use. Designed primarily for use with H.A.A. guns, it could deal only with individual aircraft, or formations of aircraft, and could provide no information of the general tactical situation in the air. It was also inaccurate at low angles of sight and could not therefore be relied on for early warning of a low-flying attack.

For tactical purposes the R.A.F. had developed a set known as the G.C.I., which could be used for the control of fighter interceptions at night. The main feature of this set was a plan position indicator (P.P.I.), which showed on a luminous screen a trace of all aircraft within 50 miles of the instrument. By fitting a special device, known as I.F.F., to friendly aircraft, it was possible to determine (though not always reliably) which of these machines were hostile; and having selected the aircraft to be engaged, the controller could obtain from another part of the apparatus its approximate height, and could thus complete the information required to effect an interception.

A set of this nature, adapted for use at specially low heights, was obviously what was needed for the tactical control of L.A.A. guns, and investigations were soon in progress. It was not however until the middle of 1943 that the new set—the A.A. No. 4—came into production (*see* Table B). In the meantime reliance, it seemed, would have to be placed on greater dispersion of grounded aircraft, and other P.A.D. measures, at airfields.

At the same time it was more than ever doubtful whether the Bofors alone could deal with the very low and fast attack; an attack that had become much more deadly with the development of the cannon-firing fighter. In open country, and in a clear atmosphere, it might just be possible to get the guns pointing in the right direction before the attack came in; but in close country, and under a cloudy sky, as events in Greece had shown, the enemy could sometimes do his work of destruction and disappear before the defences had had time to engage him.

The Need for Flexibility in the Defence

The loss of Crete was probably only a matter of time and of the losses that the Germans were prepared to accept in order to capture it. Whether the cost could have been made prohibitive remained a subject of controversy. It was considered by some that the presence of a regiment, or even a battery, of 25-prs. at Maleme might have made it impossible for the Germans to land on the airfield; and that our lack of artillery support in general was one of the chief reasons why pockets of paratroops were able to hold out with their lavish supply of tommy-guns, heavy machine-guns and mortars.

It was also arguable that the failure to change the L.A.A. dispositions at Maleme after the R.A.F. had withdrawn, made things unnecessarily easy for the attackers. Instead of the normal airfield defence, it was now the denial of landing grounds to the G.A.F. and the destruction of troop-carrying aircraft that were of prime importance; and these objects might have been more easily achieved by a redisposition of the guns. For example, they might have been sited in troop (4-gun) groups on the hillsides, with the maximum of cover and with orders to hold the fire of at least the majority of the guns until the arrival of the troop carriers.

The need for flexibility in the defence, and for a constant review of the A.A. situation, was clearly laid down in the manuals.[4] On the other hand, there seemed at the time to be good reasons for leaving the guns where they were (*see* p. 71); and to these reasons must be added the fact that, as the attack actually developed, the identification and engagement of troop carriers would not have been easy. Ju.88s. were used for fighting as well as carrying, and in any case the Germans had such reserves that as soon as guns opened fire they would have been attacked and forced to concentrate on their own self-defence. From this point of view, comparison with the later A.A. defence of Tobruk (*see* p. 83) is hardly justifiable.

Some Field Artillery Problems

In Greece alone had field artillery been available in any quantity, and here the wide frontages that had to be held usually limited artillery support to co-operation in the defence of a pass, and precluded the use of anything bigger than a regimental concentration in any one area. The situation was further complicated by the mountainous nature of the terrain and the lack of good roads. Movement and supply by M.T. was difficult, and suitable gun positions, even for 25-prs., were scarce owing to crest clearance problems. The medium guns (4.5-in./60-prs.) were even more restricted in their choice of positions, and the long range of these guns, so valuable in a retreat, had often to be sacrificed by bringing them into action far behind the front line. The 6-in. hows., on the other hand, although they could clear the crests, could not reach far enough.

This, added to the lack of air observation, made counter-battery work very difficult. The Germans moreover possessed the great advantage of being able to use masses of dive bombers as a substitute for artillery support. In the circumstances it was fortunate that so much of the terrain, being mountainous, made accurate dive bombing very difficult.

Sound ranging and wireless, like radar, suffered from the disturbing effects of the mountains. Communication by R/T. was particularly difficult, and this necessitated the frequent use of cable. Owing to the difficulty of finding forward gun positions, enormous lengths of wire had to be laid and could not be salvaged in the withdrawal. Thus stocks of cable were rapidly exhausted, and by the time of the evacuation many units seemed to be on the verge of impotence through the lack of a means of communication.

These problems were very similar to those that had been encountered in the mountainous regions of Eritrea and Abyssinia; and now, as then, the need was felt for a proportion of mountain artillery. On 7th February, 1941, the B.R.A., Middle East, had proposed the formation of a mountain regiment with Cypriot drivers, and the 2nd Mountain Regiment—without mules or drivers—was in due course sent out from the United Kingdom. It did not arrive, however, until 15th May, by which time Greece had been evacuated; and when its British personnel were introduced to the mules, some lack of harmony was noticeable. The mules, which had been recruited from South Africa, Cyprus and India, were reported to be "wild and to have an intense dislike of white men."

Development of the Portee Anti-Tank Gun

The idea of carrying the anti-tank gun in a truck, as an alternative to towing, seems to have originated with the French 25-mm. equipment, which had been issued to the infantry brigade anti-tank companies in 1939 (see p. 32) and which was so flimsy that it could not be towed over long distances. The portee principle was again applied to the 37-mm. Bofors ordered for the Sudan shortly before the outbreak of hostilities with Germany and subsequently issue to the anti-tank regiment of 7th Armoured Division; and it was then that the idea of firing from the truck was first introduced (see p. 46).

By January, 1940, it had been generally accepted that a portee anti-tank mounting was required, and a meeting was held at the War Office to draw up the G.S. specification of the vehicle for the 2-pr. It was agreed at this meeting that the gun should be capable of moving either portee or towed, but that firing from the vehicle was not necessary.

In the Middle East, however, the idea of firing from the vehicle was still popular, and arrangements were therefore made locally for the conversion of a Ford 30-cwt. chassis to enable it to take the shock of discharge and to allow of all-round—or nearly all-round—traverse for the gun.

Against the Italians this method of using anti-tank guns had proved highly successful, and it was now being repeated against the Germans. In campaigns such as these, when the Army was constantly in retirement, it offered the advantage of a quick "get-away." It also proved useful sometimes to have a mobile reserve capable of firing from its portee. And, though primarily intended for use in the desert, it was quite effectively employed in Greece, where conditions were on the whole very favourable to anti-tank defence. For example, in the mountain defiles, where long stretches of road could be enfiladed, tanks could be stopped by 25-prs. at a range of 9,000 yards; or, during periods of in-fighting, ideal opportunities were offered for surprise action by 2-prs.

Perhaps the most successful action of this type occurred at the Proasteion Ridge on 13th April, during the withdrawal from the original Aliakhmon position. The fighting started with a morning attack by enemy infantry, which was broken up by 25-prs. firing direct over open sights. This was followed by the first massed attack from the air, during which the whole position was heavily dive bombed and machine-gunned; and at 1900 hrs. the assault culminated in a thrust by about 30 light and medium tanks, with infantry support, against the village of Mavropage, which was at the time the headquarters of the 1st Armoured Brigade. A troop of anti-tank guns defending the entrance to the village, drove the enemy into a nullah and in the dusk knocked out eight tanks for the loss of one gun, one truck and one man wounded. The 25-prs. again came into action over open sights and, with the aid of our own tanks, the position was held. Altogether the enemy had been so severely handled that neither the S.S. Hitler nor the armoured formation that was with them made a move for the next 36 hours.

Throughout this fighting firing from the portee position had been freely practised. " It is quite possible," said one anti-tank regimental commander, " for a quick troop leader or section serjeant with an eye for country, by skilful use of ground, to avoid casualties and do considerable damage by engaging tanks over open sights for a few minutes, rapidly withdrawing under cover, changing his position and repeating the dose.([5])

A tactical success like that at the Proasteion Ridge gave weighty support to this argument, and for the time being at any rate the portee continued to be favourably regarded.

Conclusion

In all three of these campaigns air superiority had been the deciding factor. Having command of the air, the enemy could use his dive bombers and fighters as he pleased; and in exploiting this advantage, he continued to display the most intimate co-operation between air and ground forces. Calls for assistance from supporting aircraft were made by radio, ground strips and signal cartridges, and " were acted upon quickly and efficiently. The action taken made it impossible for our troops to launch an offensive, and even defensive positions were quickly made untenable, if observed to be holding up the enemy advance."([6])

On the other hand, our troops were not only devoid of air support, but also of adequate A.A. defences. The number of A.A. guns available was generally far too few, and what guns there were were often ineffective owing to the lack of radar. There is no doubt that, as a means of air defence, radar was one of the outstanding successes of the war. It had enabled Fighter Command to repel the daylight attacks on Great Britain and was now on the point of endowing the night fighter also with the means of victory. But in A.A. defence its full potentialities were not to be developed until the war was nearly over. From the time when the War Office was informed of the possibility of its application to A.A. problems, over a year was absorbed in preliminary investigations before actual experimental and development work could be started. Then, when—late in 1936—its application to A.A. gunnery was actively pursued, technical difficulties were encountered that added greatly to the delay in production. The C.H. radar station, as used for daylight interceptions by the R.A.F., represented radar at its simplest: detection over a wide zone and long range, with no greater accuracy than was required to put a squadron or flight of fighters at approximately the same height and within visibility range of the enemy. For the engagement of unseen aircraft by A.A. guns a much greater degree of accuracy and continuity of following was required. In fact, to provide a complete solution of this problem, the A.A. radar set had to be part of a continuous transmission system that ended only at the gun itself. But in 1937, when the problem first presented itself, a large number of mechanical predictors were already in existence, or on order, for the ordinary visual fire control system. Hence the development of a suitable predictor was not immediately proceeded with, and it was not until 1944-45 that it finally came into being.

List of References

[1] "The Second World War", by Maj.-Gen. J. F. C. Fuller, p. 81.
[2] Despatch by C-in-C, B.L.F. in M.E., 7th February to 15th July 1941, p. 21.
[3] A.T.M. No. 42 of January 1942.
[4] Manual of Anti-Aircraft Defence, Vol. II, Pamphlet No. 1, 1940, Sec. 11, para. 2 (v) and Sec. 17, para. 4 (iii).
[5] War Diary, 102nd (N.H.) A.Tk. Regt. R.H.A., May 1941.
[6] Report of Inter-Service Committee, Pt. I, p. 48.

CHAPTER VI

THE BRITISH RECOVERY IN EGYPT

Plate Relevant to this Chapter
No. 13. The 3.7-in. H.A.A. gun.

SECTION I.—THE SIEGE OF TOBRUK

Rommel's Attempt at a Coup-de-Main

On 10th April, when Rommel began to probe the Tobruk defences, the situation was critical. The original, and only defensible, perimeter was nearly 30 miles long and in a state of dilapidation in many places. To hold it there was only the 9th Australian Division, reinforced to a strength of four infantry brigades, with three R.H.A. regiments (25-prs.) and an army field regiment (18-prs. and 4.5-in hows.) in support. The total number of field guns available was 72, or one to every 800 yards of frontage. Since, however, the perimeter was semi-circular and the guns centrally placed, it was possible to concentrate the fire of at least 40 guns on any threatened area without change of position.

The immediate problem on this occasion was anti-tank defence. The infantry posts in the perimeter were often as much as half-a-mile apart and there were not nearly enough guns to give one to each post. Infantry companies had only anti-tank rifles, though some had appropriated captured Italian 75-mm. and 90-mm. guns—mostly without sights and instruments—and had emplaced them in the forward areas in anti-tank positions. The divisional anti-tank regiment, which had lost one battery in the withdrawal, was variously armed with 2-prs., 20-mm. Breda A.A. and anti-tank machine-guns and 20-mm. Solothern anti-tank rifles. In addition there were two batteries of the 3rd R.H.A. Regiment; one armed with 2-prs., the other with 37-mm. Bofors.

With such limited resources, it was impossible to prevent the enemy tanks from breaking through the perimeter almost wherever they chose. The plan of defence was therefore aimed at limiting their subsequent activities by the siting of anti-tank guns and minefields in depth and by the retention of one R.H.A. battery, armed with 37-mm. Bofors, in mobile reserve. The field guns were well dug in and so sited as to be mutually supporting and to provide a solid core to the anti-tank defences. Behind them again were the A.A. guns round the harbour, of which the Bofors (40-mm.) and Breda (20-mm.) were equipped with a proportion of A.P. ammunition and were prepared to act as a last line of defence in the event of a tank breakthrough.

For the delivery of his *coup de main* Rommel had assembled some 200 or more tanks, of which about half were German and included some of the new Mark III and IV models. The former carried 30-mm. of armour, reinforced by strengthening plates in front and rear, and were equipped with a 5-cm. gun firing a 4½-lb. shell that could penetrate the British cruiser tank at a range of about 1,400 yards. The Mk. IV, or close support, tank was less heavily armoured and carried a low velocity 7.5-cm. gun for use primarily against infantry and other unarmoured troops. There were also some 8.8-cm. A.A. guns, which, though manned by the Luftwaffe and primarily intended for A.A. defence, had a good telescopic sight and could, if well placed, be used effectively against tanks. They were very mobile and hence well suited for work with an armoured division.

After the usual preliminaries—probing for the weak spots, air attacks on the defending artillery, and feint attacks on other parts of the perimeter—Rommel launched his first real assault on the centre, or southern, sector during the night 13th/14th April. Infantry broke through the wire and established a bridgehead, through which, about half-an-hour before dawn, passed 38 tanks of the leading German battalion. After advancing about three-quarters of a mile, they halted in a depression and waited for daybreak.

During this pause the 37-mm. Bofors of the reserve battery were ordered up to engage them as soon as it was light enough to see. So when they resumed their advance, they were harassed by Bofors and engaged by 25-prs. over open sights as they came in view of the field artillery positions. Once again advantage was taken of the ability to fire from the portee position. To compensate for their inadequate hitting power, the Bofors were driven at top speed to within about half-a-mile of the enemy, where they would swing round, fire a few shots, and then race off again. At first these "mosquito" tactics took the enemy by surprise, but subsequent attacks were progressively less effective and more expensive.

Nevertheless, as a result of good timing and co-operation by all arms, the defence as a whole was most successful. After a fierce duel with the 25-prs., the enemy tanks were halted some 500 yards or more from the battery position, and when the survivors swung eastwards in an attempt to work round the flank, they came under fire from two guns of a neighbouring anti-tank regiment. After suffering further casualties, they broke off the attack and withdrew to a safer distance, only to be struck on the flank by a small force of British tanks that had been held in hand against such an opportunity.

Back on the perimeter, the Australian infantry, unperturbed by the passage of the enemy armour, had held their ground and dealt effectively with the infantry and other supporting arms, in some instances by calling for defensive fire from the artillery on top of their own positions. Thus isolated from their own infantry and guns, and attacked on all sides by British tanks and guns, the leading enemy battalion lost heart and by 0730 hrs. was hurrying back through the wire.

The Organization of Tobruk Fortress

The attempt at a *coup de main* had failed and it was not until the end of April that Rommel was ready for a second, stronger and more thoroughly organized, attempt to take the fortress. Meanwhile steps had been taken to give greater depth and solidity to the defences. About two miles behind the perimeter, or Red Line as it was now called, a new Blue Line was constructed, consisting of a continuous minefield covered by barbed wire and by anti-tank and machine-gun fire from a series of platoon posts at intervals of about 500 yards. By degrees minefields were added between these two main lines, until in the end there were mines almost everywhere. The field gun area was situated behind the Blue Line, and the anti-tank guns were distributed between the Red and the Blue Lines. All 25-prs. were given an anti-tank role, and alternative positions were surveyed, dug and made completely ready for occupation.

The strength of the artillery had been increased by the arrival of 25-prs. to replace the 18-prs. and 4.5-in. hows. in the army field regiment (*see* p. 78), and of a troop of 60-prs. Many Italian guns of various calibres, and in varying degrees of serviceability, were also manned—not always by artillery personnel—and proved a useful, if sometimes unpredictable, addition to the fire power of the fortress. Altogether there were nearly 100 field and 113 anti-tank guns, with 14 disabled tanks dug in at suitable places for anti-tank defence.

The weakest point of the artillery defences was counter-battery. Apart from the troop of 60-prs., there was no medium artillery. Facilities for air co-operation were also scanty. In the early days there were some Lysanders available, but they could not keep in the air without an escort of three Hurricanes, which had to be taken from their main role of defending the harbour. After the departure of the Lysanders some success was obtained with Hurricanes using two-way R/T. and shooting with an allotted battery. But even this ceased when the last five Hurricanes were themselves withdrawn on 26th April. With a total fighter strength of 13 for the whole of the Western Desert, it was imperative that the R.A.F. should husband their resources.

There was now no means of obtaining arty/R or air photographs, nor was there at this time any sound ranging or flash spotting unit in the fortress. The accurate fixation of hostile batteries was therefore impossible, and counter-battery work had to be confined to neutralization shoots based on hostile shelling reports and information received from patrols outside the wire. Destructive shoots would in any case have been difficult owing to the unreliability of meteor telegrams. These were produced at Maaten Bagush, away behind the Egyptian frontier, and approximate adjustments had to be made for conditions at Tobruk. Hence all forms of predicted shooting were certain to be inaccurate.

The Second, and Main, Axis Attack on Tobruk

In pursuance of the preparations that had been going on ever since the previous fighting died down on 17th April, the new attack was launched against the western sector, where there was a commanding feature generally known as Medauur. Profiting by their experience on 14th April, the enemy set out to establish a wide bridgehead before attempting to make a deep armoured thrust. On the evening of 30th April, after a preliminary bombardment by Stukas, followed by artillery concentrations, enemy infantry and sappers advanced through the dust clouds and the gathering darkness and cleared gaps in the minefields and wire on either side of Medauur. Owing to the rupture of all communications, it was impossible to keep touch with the company on the hill, and hence to put down defensive fire. It was not until the morning mist cleared about 0800 hrs. that the situation could be verified. Enemy tanks seen moving about on Medauur were engaged by the field regiment in support of this sector, but they continued to advance until they came to grief on a recently installed minefield. The main attack then turned southwards, pursued as before by artillery concentrations, and was again halted, this time by a counter-attack by 14 British cruisers.

There was now a lull in the operations while the German tanks returned to Medauur for more fuel and ammunition. When the attack was resumed in the afternoon, after another attempt by Stukas to soften up the field gun and perimeter areas, attention was redirected to the extension southwards of the bridgehead. Some progress was made, but all attempts by the enemy tanks to lead a major drive down the line of posts were defeated by artillery fire. Finally, all progress came to an end when, late in the afternoon, a small mixed force of British tanks counter-attacked from the south-east.

An attempt by the Australian infantry to regain Medauur failed. Owing to the enemy command of the air, the battalion detailed for the attack was seen and shelled as it debussed and was therefore unable to adhere to the prearranged time programme. Observation from ground O.Ps. was difficult, and the battalion, left behind by the artillery concentrations, was met and held by the fire of the enemy tanks and infantry.

The situation was therefore still critical; but, fortunately, there was a heavy duststorm next day, which prevented the enemy from making a serious attack and gave the garrison time to bring up fresh infantry and more guns, and to form a new switch-line to contain the enemy salient. In the words of an eye-witness, this was "a gunners' day even more than May 1st; their heavy fire disorganized any plans the Germans had of renewing the attack when the storm abated. All through the 2nd, very little stood between the Germans in the Salient and the guns that harassed them so persistently."[1] But the line held and by 3rd May the initiative had definitely passed to the defenders. That evening another counter-attack was made by the reserve brigade supported by three regiments of field guns and a section of medium artillery. Again it ended in failure, owing partly to delays in starting and the failure of the infantry to keep up with the timed concentrations.

The Germans therefore remained in possession of Medauur, and continued to do so throughout the remainder of the siege. But their losses had been heavy and, in view of the impending invasion of Russia, a repetition of such losses could not be accepted. Rommel was ordered on to the defensive by the German Supreme Command in the Mediterranean.

"Once again the German armour had been defeated, and this time the effectiveness of minefields plus artillery fire in stopping tanks had been clearly demonstrated. Thirty-nine of the German tanks had been destroyed or disabled by mines or shells, only seven by the British tanks. This was the first time that any major attack had been broken by these tactics."[2]

How many of these disabling shells had come from the 25-prs., and how many from the anti-tank guns, cannot be stated with certainty. Nor had the stopping power of a 25-pr. concentration been precisely determined. Sometimes it had checked a tank advance, sometimes it had not, but its general effect had undoubtedly been demoralizing. "Officers who served in the Great War" wrote a lieutenant of the 5th German Tank Regiment in his diary "are all saying: 'Yes, it was like that in 16-18.' What we experienced in Poland and on the Western Front was only a promenade in comparison."

It was almost certainly an exaggeration, but it probably reflected faithfully the feelings of both sides at the time. A much needed victory had been won by British arms against the might of the Wehrmacht, and its magnitude must have seemed all the bigger at a time when German preoccupations elsewhere were not known. It was just the kind of situation in which the effects of success may be most misleading (*see* p. 1), and it needed a cool judgment to avoid a misplaced confidence in the power of indirect artillery fire to stop tanks.

Organization of the A.A. Defences

Having failed for the second time to capture Tobruk, the enemy now tried to wear down the resistance of the garrison by air attacks aimed at the closing of the harbour. During this period, although a measure of air superiority had been won by the R.A.F. over Libya as a whole, no fighter aircraft could be allotted specifically to the defence of the fortress. The whole burden of air defence had therefore to be borne by the A.A. units.

The A.A. resources consisted initially of 16 mobile 3.7-in. guns, 6 mobile Bofors, 12 static Bofors (with predictors), 42 Bredas (of which about 30 per cent. had transport and could be used portee), and 8 A.A.S.L.s manned by the Royal Wiltshire Yeomanry. There were also 2 Italian searchlights, and later an addition of 8 static 3.7-in. and 4 static 102-mm. Italian guns (without instruments) was made to the H.A.A. defences. By this time, however, two of the mobile 3.7-in. were disabled as the result of prematures, so that there were never more than 22×3.7-in. guns in action.

The above were organized in two commands: one for the defence of the harbour, the other for the defence of the field gun areas and formation headquarters around the perimeter; the whole under the command of the 4th A.A. Brigade, which came directly under Fortress Headquarters (*see* Map 2). For early warning the G.O.R. had a call on the local R.A.F. radar set, and the H.A.A. units between them could muster two G.L. Mk. I. Though modified for the engagement of unseen targets (*see* Table B), these instruments could not be sited at the gun positions by day owing to the danger of destruction by dive bombers. In any case, there was only one H.A.A. predictor fitted to receive G.L. data. They were therefore placed in specially selected positions and used for the control of predicted barrages. At night four mobile 3.7-in. guns, controlled by the solitary suitable predictor, were moved into action alongside one of them.

The perimeter defences were provided by three Bofors and 32 Bredas, or just over half the total number of L.A.A. guns available, which were disposed on an area basis. There was no permanent protection for the troops in the front line, but arrangements were made for some of the mobile 3.7-in. guns to move into the field gun area when necessary.

The Defeat of the Dive Bomber

Thus the general strength and up-to-dateness of the A.A. defences were about the same as they had been at Athens and Suda Bay. It was a disappointingly small display of power for the twentieth month of the war, but in the circumstances it was to prove just adequate. Between 13th April and 5th May considerable numbers of enemy aircraft were destroyed, and neither the field guns nor the A.A. guns themselves were ever silenced. If the harbour was seldom usable by day, it was at least kept more or less continually in action by night. Indeed the efficacy of the A.A. defences was evidenced by the determined efforts made by the enemy to annihilate them. Under cover of diversionary attacks by medium bombers and fighters, the Ju.87s. would go for the A.A. positions, as many as 50 sometimes being employed against the H.A.A. guns.

At first, as at Crete, there were a few unpleasant surprises. Some of the units were inexperienced in this type of warfare, gun emplacements were not always solidly constructed, and troop commanders or spotters sometimes failed to detect or to appreciate the significance of the dive bombers' preliminary tactics. Thus left unattended to, with nothing to disturb their aim, the latter were able to place their bombs with a fair amount of accuracy; and raw detachments, shocked into taking cover behind ill-built emplacement walls, suffered casualties from near misses and a subsequent loss of morale.

Fortunately, however, the enemy attacks were not pressed as intensely as in Crete, and before long a satisfactory answer to the problem of the dive bombing attack had been found. It was based on the reassuring effect of sound material protection combined with the moral stimulus of aggressive action. Guns were well dug in and a definite drill, known as the "Porcupine", was evolved, by means of which the guns could start hitting back from the very beginning.

There was a critical moment in this type of attack, when the first dive bomber was at a height of about 4,000 feet. It was found that a ferocious burst of fire at this moment would usually cause a premature release of the bombs, with a consequent loss of accuracy, and would often turn the following aircraft away altogether. Hence, on receipt of warning of the approach of dive bombers, the four guns of a troop would point outwards at an elevation of about 60 degrees, each covering an arc of 90 degrees so that between them an all round defence was provided. At the critical moment the guns would start firing with a very short fuze, so as to make sure that the shell burst in front of the enemy, and they would go on firing until the attack was over. Meanwhile any Bofors, Bredas, rifles and even revolvers in the position were brought into action by spare officers, batmen, cooks, etc.; and no one with a weapon was allowed to "go to ground".

The same aggressive principle was applied in the organization and handling of the L.A.A. defences. The German technique of using returning bombers—or later, after the Hurricanes had gone, fighters—to shoot up the L.A.A. guns from behind, was met by the disposal of light automatics among the Bofors to deal with all such attacks.

At the same time passive air defence measures were not neglected. In particular, the use of dummy positions was brought to a fine art. To make the deception complete, these dummy positions were equipped with dummy guns, dummy men, trucks and ammunition dumps, and finally with dust producers, which were made to synchronize with the firing of the real guns in the same locality.

The main object of the A.A. defences, however, was to defend the fortress, and their self-defence was never allowed to become more than a means to this end. To protect the harbour against dive bombing attacks, the plan adopted was similar to that used during the later stages of the operations at Suda Bay (*see* p. 71). All but four of the H.A.A. guns were detailed to take part in a "harbour barrage", which was prepared at varying heights and was controlled by an officer at an O.P. in direct communication with the G.O.R. The remaining four 3.7-in. guns acted as "swingers" for the engagement of opportunity and unexpected targets. While the harbour barrage was in operation, it had priority over all other tasks, and not more than one gun in each H.A.A. troop was allowed to be used for self-defence.

L.A.A. guns detailed for the engagement of dive bombers would all face away from the vulnerable area when awaiting attack. As the enemy approached, the guns nearest to him opened up so as to give the maximum volume of fire at long range, while those on the far side of the area swung round and engaged the bombers with accurate predictor methods as they flattened out after their dive.

The combined effect of all these measures was highly successful. By the end of May the A.A. guns had definitely won their battle with the dive bomber, and the enemy now concentrated his attention on high level bombing. Owing to the proximity of the guns to the vulnerable area, and to the presence of seasonal cloud and haze, engagement by ordinary instrumental methods was rarely possible. A daylight G.L. controlled barrage was therefore introduced and divided into four sectors, to each of which was allotted one 4-gun H.A.A. position. It was thin, but it sufficed. By the end of July daylight attacks had become very rare and irresolute, so that small ships were again able to use the harbour by day.

There were still the night bomber and the minelayer to be disposed of. Against the former a G.L. controlled barrage was used, as for the day bomber. The minelayer, however, by approaching at a much lower height, often escaped detection by the G.L. sets. It was therefore dealt with by a barrage controlled by information received from the H.A.A. gun positions and from three listening posts established within 1,000 yards of the harbour. Eight searchlights were used to illuminate the barrage, which was thickened up by short bursts from the L.A.A. guns, firing to sight if possible. "This produced as terrifying a spectacle as could be raised with the equipment available", and, "when the barrage was fired in time, planes took care to avoid it".[3]

"At the end of six months Rommel had little to show for all his expenditure of aircraft, bombs and personnel. In more than 750 raids enemy bombers sank only seven ships and a few auxiliary lighters in the harbour, and five of these ships were sunk in the first six weeks before the A.A. defences reached their full strength."[4]

It was conclusive evidence that A.A. guns, resolutely and intelligently handled, could not only keep themselves in action but could also keep most of the enemy bombs off their objectives; and this with little assistance from up-to-date methods of fire control. The radar equipment available was scanty and primitive, and the L.A.A. (No. 3) predictor, on which such high hopes had been set, had not been altogether a success. In the opinion of the Commander 4th A.A. Brigade, it was an admirable instrument in the hands of a well trained detachment, but took a considerable time to establish a reputation for efficiency if issued to partly trained troops, who might lose confidence in it and revert to the forward area sight.

Despite these shortcomings, considerable casualties had been inflicted on the enemy air force (*see* Table D); and, what was more important, the moral factor in the duel between ground and air had been brought into better perspective. If it was not true that, as one experienced G.P.O. expressed it, given adequate warning and a well trained detachment, the moral factor was bound to operate against the dive bomber, it was true that with A.A., as with other troops, attack was the best form of defence. "Those who manned every weapon they could use when attacked from the air, instead of going to ground, survived to fight another day—not only with skins intact but with tails up."([5])

The Revival of the Rocket

During the latter half of the siege some use had been made of rockets in the A.A. role. As a weapon of war the rocket was not new. It was first used against the British Army in another famous siege, at Seringapatam in 1799. At that time it had little but a moral effect, since it contained no charge except the propellant. Adopted and developed by the British, it was introduced into both land and sea services, but was later abandoned owing to its inability to keep pace with the increasing accuracy of the gun.

It had, however, two great advantages over the gun: no recoil and no wear of the "piece". Hence the equipment could be kept light and was cheap to produce and easy to handle. It was the first of these qualities that led to its revival in the early days of the war as a quick means of filling the gap in our A.A. defences. In the engagement of unseen targets, the accuracy of the gun was of little value without a corresponding degree of accuracy in the radar set that controlled it; and in September, 1940, when the first G.L. sets were received in A.D.G.B., their performance was very erratic. In fact the situation was so unsatisfactory that officers discarded R.D.F. and resorted to working out their own data from range tables and from heights broadcast from G.O.R., and sometimes in desperation they fired wildly into the searchlight intersections. In such circumstances a multiple-barrelled rocket projector, which could make up in volume what it lacked in accuracy of fire, promised to be of some utility.

As an immediate measure, however, far greater importance was attached to the use of the rocket—now known, for reasons of secrecy, as the U.P. (unrotated projectile)—as a stop-gap to cover the vast deficiencies in Bofors production. The battle of Britain was in full swing and dive bombing attacks on targets in the United Kingdom seemed imminent. To meet this threat, an extremely simple single-barrelled projector was produced on a large scale; but, perhaps fortunately, it was never put to the test as a L.A.A. weapon. In the face of a still active Fighter Command, the enemy dive bombers seldom ventured upon the scene, and the A.A. rocket was left to develop along more rational lines.

There were two separate lines of development, both of which were eventually represented in the A.A. defence of Tobruk. The first was a multiple-barrelled projector that discharged rocket projectiles which released a number of small parachutes each trailing a length of piano wire with a small bomb on the end. The effect was to create a miniature, and temporary, balloon barrage, which, if correctly timed and placed, was quite effective. The second fired a H.E. shell, which differed from the ordinary

H.E. shell only in its greater explosive content, rendered possible by the lower peak acceleration of the rocket, which permitted a considerable reduction in strength and weight of the projectile casing. The intention was to make a 4-barrelled and a 9-barrelled type for mobile use in the field, and a 24-barrelled type for use in A.D.G.B.; but pending the completion of these multiple-barrelled designs, some of the existing single-barrelled projectors were formed into H.A.A. batteries and used for predicted shooting with the aid of a G.L. set.

As a means of bringing the burst nearer to the target, consideration was given to a photo-electric (P.E.) fuze, which was activated by a change in the intensity of the light falling upon it. The idea was that, as the shell came within the shadow cast by the aircraft, the fuze would operate and the shell would be detonated. In practice, however, there were too many other shadows that might have the same effect; such as clouds, smoke from the barrage, etc. In addition, firing towards the sun would give rise to prematures, and of course the fuze would not function at night. The project was therefore finally abandoned.

A further disadvantage of the rocket lay in the unreliability of its propellant. This was apt to be unstable above a certain temperature, and after a voyage round the Cape and exposure to the summer climate of Tobruk, it sometimes behaved rather oddly.

As a substitute for the A.A. gun, therefore, the rocket had not made a successful debut.

Field Artillery Developments after 4th May

As the siege progressed, some slight additions were made to the artillery in Tobruk, and on 3rd June the counter-battery organization was strengthened by the arrival of a flash spotting and a sound ranging troop, and on 9th June a counter-battery officer was appointed from the 1st Australian Corps Headquarters. But the most pressing need—for more medium artillery—could not be satisfied, since G.H.Q. had none to spare.

The enemy, on the other hand, had by this time collected a number of 15-cm. and 8.8-cm. (A.A.) guns, together with some French 240-mm., and after the failure of his attempt to close the harbour by air action, began to try the effect of artillery bombardments. The 60-pr. troop and one troop of 25-prs., assisted by one of the 149-mm. coast defence guns, were given the primary task of engaging these guns whenever active; and on two occasions a special night bombardment was arranged, in which all three Services co-operated. In this way a temporary relief was sometimes obtained from the enemy's bombardments, but his guns were too well dug in and the garrison's counter-battery resources—including meteor arrangements (*see* p. 80)—were too slight to achieve really destructive effects.

Before long the threat of the mortar, already experienced in France and Belgium (*see* pp. 37, 38), had begun to make itself felt again. At first neither infantry nor artillery were in a position to deal satisfactorily with this problem. At night, when the German mortars did most of their shooting, the use of artillery was not deemed advisable owing to the impossibility of concealing the gun flashes. Later, a few guns were moved into special emplacements each night and engaged the flashes of enemy mortars with some success. Captured Italian mortars, with a longer range than the British, were also used with effect. But these were no more than palliatives, and the major problems of the mortar remained unsolved. That they were not more actively investigated at this time was probably owing to the fact that the desert offered few opportunities for the use of mortars on a large scale, so that their full potentialities were not readily appreciated.

SECTION II.—THE DEFENCE OF THE EGYPTIAN FRONTIER

The Shortage of Equipment and Manpower

While Tobruk held out preparations went forward, with many ups and downs, for the counter-stroke that was to relieve it. This was a period of kaleidoscopic changes in the military situation. There was trouble with the Vichy French in Syria; there was a rising in Iraq; there was the German invasion of Russia; all of which affected in one way or another the security of our position in the Middle East and made inroads on the already slender resources for the resumption of the offensive in the Western Desert.

The artillery situation was serious. In June 1941 there were in the Middle East only four field regiments available as corps and army artillery, and these had all been used up in the defence of Tobruk and the Egyptian strongholds of Mersa Matruh and Maaten Bagush, and in the reorganization of the 7th Armoured Division. There was no anti-tank regiment for the Cavalry Division (in Palestine) or for the defence of the long and vulnerable lines of communication in the Western Desert and Trans-Jordan—now rendered necessary by the trouble in Syria and Iraq—and existing regiments were short of 116×2-prs. The three available medium regiments were all armed, or being rearmed, with 6-in. hows., which were of small value in the Western Desert. Some American 155-mm. hows. had been offered, but their performance promised to be little better.

Shortage of equipment was nothing new. The situation caused by our unpreparedness in 1939, and by the losses at Dunkirk, had merely been aggravated by further heavy losses in Cyrenaica, Greece and Crete. But now there was a deficiency of manpower too. In June the newly arrived 2nd Mountain Regiment had to be reduced to a training cadre, and in September, when attempts were made to come into line with the new home establishments by raising the number of batteries in the field regiment from two to three, and the number of guns in an anti-tank regiment (other than the armoured divisional regiments) from 48 to 64, it was manpower that was' the limiting factor. The average shortage of artillery personnel in the Middle East was in the neighbourhood of 7,000.

Fortunately, however, owing to the open nature of the terrain, the 6-gun troop provided a temporary solution of the gunnery problem without the need for an additional battery headquarters and staff. It was as easy to handle in the desert as a 4-gun troop, and by reducing the number of troops in the battery from three to two, it simplified the procedure for obtaining a battery concentration and thus speeded up the preparation of fire plans.

The Development of the "Jock" Column

After the withdrawal of the Support Group to the Egyptian frontier in the middle of April, the system of defence reverted to that of the preceding autumn, which was based on the bold use of small mobile columns. Known eventually as "Jock" columns after their most skilful exponent, Lieut.-Colonel J. C. Campbell, D.S.O., M.C. (later Major-General J. C. Campbell, V.C., D.S.O., M.C.) of 4th R.H.A., their main tasks were to strike at the enemy's supply lines and to harass his flanks and rear. In their earliest form they consisted of a squadron or less of tanks or armoured cars, a troop (six guns) of 25-prs., a troop of anti-tank guns, and a company of motorized infantry. Later on one or two Bofors were sometimes included in an A.A. role.

Their methods of operation varied, but were usually based on a fire unit of four 25-prs., which was brought into action in a previously selected position of observation. The remaining two 25-prs. and two of the anti-tank guns were kept on wheels to meet a threat from either flank, while the other two anti-tank guns were used as escort to the 25-pr. O.P.

The essence of their tactics was boldness and speed of manœuvre. Provided they were quickly engaged, enemy columns could be broken up and driven off. If, however, the enemy did not advance directly towards the guns, but moved round them with boldness and in open formation, a troop of 25-prs. could not hope to stop him. Everything depended, therefore, on the achievement of an initial surprise and the receipt of continuous information from our own patrols to ensure a timely and orderly withdrawal.

Artillery Concentrations *versus* Tanks

By mid-June, the 4th Indian Division had returned from Eritrea and a fresh attempt was made to relieve Tobruk. The general plan was for the 4th Indian Division to advance and seize the defiles at Halfaya, and then Fort Capuzzo, with the help of the 4th Armoured Brigade, which was now composed of Matilda tanks. The rest of the 7th Armoured Division was to protect the operation on the left flank and exploit any success towards Tobruk.

Capuzzo was captured by the infantry and "I" tanks without much difficulty, but it soon became apparent that the strength of the enemy armour in this area was much greater than had been expected. The Matildas, used as cruisers, were a failure and many "were knocked out by 88s before they knew what had hit them."[6] The 7th Armoured Brigade on the left, after an initial success, found itself outnumbered and outgunned; and when the enemy counter-attacked it was forced to give way. Turned aside, but not stopped, by artillery concentrations, the enemy tanks continued to work round the open left flank and soon began to threaten the security of all our troops in the Capuzzo—Halfaya area. On 17th June, therefore, the 4th Indian Division was ordered to withdraw to its original positions.

Once again it had been shown that artillery concentrations of the strength then practicable in the Western Desert, though they might delay or divert an armoured attack, could not stop a really determined enemy. Such fire did not knock out tanks, even when they were stationary, and it was very expensive in ammunition. The conclusion arrived at after this battle was, therefore, that the use of concentrations should be confined to the engagement of tanks advancing through defiles (*see* p. 75), or of enemy supporting tanks whose leaders were being engaged by our anti-tank defences.

The Problem of the 2-Pr.

Contemporary developments in anti-tank doctrine in the United Kingdom had emphasized the need for tactical mobility equal to that of infantry. To achieve this mobility, three requisites were prescribed: reconnaissance and battle procedure must be speeded up, and the gun must be capable of moving rapidly across country and of being carried rapidly across obstacles.(7)

In accordance with these requirements, the home pattern portee had been designed to admit of the gun being brought into action on its own wheels off the truck in not more than two minutes. In practice, however, it was found to take longer, and after the withdrawal from Capuzzo the C.R.A. 4th Indian Division pressed for the issue to his divisional anti-tank regiment of the Middle East pattern truck from which the guns could be fired.

With this extra mobility, the 2-pr. could give a good account of itself in harassing operations against the enemy's flanks and rear, and in covering a withdrawal or the movement of a convoy. In the main battle, however, when mobility could not always be exploited and something more than deterrent effect was required, its performance no longer inspired universal confidence. Sometimes it did well, as at Capuzzo on 16th June, when three troops, with an approximate expenditure of 250 rounds, claimed to have destroyed or damaged 16 enemy tanks. On the other hand, accounts were being received from some units of shot that had bounced off the enemy armour, and of gun detachments that had been shot up by the 7.5-cm. guns of the Mk. IV tanks at ranges beyond the effective reach of the 2-pr.

It was evident that the time had arrived for the introduction of the new 6-pr., if indeed it was not—as some thought—long overdue. In its absence the burden of anti-tank defence would have increasingly to be borne by the 25-pr.

The Need for S.P. Artillery

Two points stood out as the result of these operations: the German habit of avoiding the armoured battle and enticing our tanks on to his own anti-tank guns; and, in the attack, the use of the Mk. IV tank, with its 7.5-cm. gun, to destroy or neutralize the opposing anti-tank guns. The answer to both these stratagems appeared to lie in the development of S.P. artillery. The German panzer divisions themselves included 15-cm. assault guns, which consisted of the standard 15-cm. infantry howitzer mounted on a light tank chassis, and it was now agreed that a similar weapon was required in the British Service for the support both of armoured and infantry formations.

Since the need was urgent and some obsolete Valentine tanks were available, an order was placed with the Ministry of Supply in October, 1941, for the mounting of 100×25-prs. in an armoured box on the Valentine chassis. This improvized equipment, known as the "Bishop", had several disadvantages: the maximum elevation that could be given to the gun was 15 degrees, which was equivalent to a range of only 6,400 yards (with Charge 3); the internal traverse was limited to 8 degrees, and to put on bigger switches it was necessary to move the chassis; the vehicle was high and conspicuous, and had insufficient mobility for the effective support of cruiser tanks. It was therefore unsuitable for use with armoured formations and could only be regarded as a convenient stop-gap pending the development of something better.

Even more pressing, perhaps, was the need for a S.P. anti-tank gun. As early as August, 1940, such a gun had been asked for by the Director of Army Fighting Vehicles for incorporation in the armoured division, and there was some support about this time for the idea—later developed by the Americans—that it should be used in an aggressive manner as a tank-destroyer. In September, 1941, however, when the G.S. policy was finally enunciated, the role envisaged was purely defensive in character. The reasons given for the development of the S.P. anti-tank gun were:—

(a) To enable long marches to be carried out without detriment to the equipment.

(b) To get better performance over rough country than could be obtained with a towed gun.

(c) To provide a "hit and run" weapon.

(d) To facilitate the movement across country of reserve guns to threatened areas.

The first equipment to be produced was a S.P. 2-pr. on a Loyd carrier, which was lightly armoured and had a 225 degree traverse. It was the intention to issue these equipments to 25 per cent. of the anti-tank artillery in armoured divisions and 100 per cent. of the anti-tank platoons in reconnaissance battalions; but various modifications were found necessary and production on a large scale was never begun. Finally, in December, 1942, it was abandoned as a result of the introduction of more powerful anti-tank weapons.

Attempts to Improve the Armoured O.P.

At Sidi Barrani, the carrier O.P. had proved unpopular and the proposal had been made that it should be replaced by a light tank (*see* p. 54). At Capuzzo the field regiment supporting the "I" tanks was provided with some of these tanks for the use of its F.O.Os.

The experiment was not a success. The Matilda was too slow and it was found difficult to control the driver. In addition the F.O.O. had to carry out the duties of one of the crew and could not therefore concentrate his attention on his own job. Since the carrier was insufficiently armoured, and the light tank obsolescent and liable to break down, it appeared that for the support of armoured units, both "I" tanks and cruisers, the best available vehicle, at any rate in the desert, was the armoured car. The ideal solution, however, was to produce a new vehicle specially designed for the purpose; and investigation of this project was immediately begun.

The difficulty was to produce a design that would suit all tastes and all conditions. There are few subjects on which it is easy to get a unanimous opinion from "users", and the armoured O.P. was certainly not one of them. It might indeed be said that the problem was never completely solved while the war lasted.

The Reorganization of the R.A. Survey Regiment

The reorganization of the survey regiment, approved in August, 1940, as a result of the experience gained in France and Belgium, had allowed for a headquarters and three batteries: one for survey, one for flash spotting, and one for sound ranging. Each battery was composed of two troops, which in mobile operations could be allotted one to each of two divisions.

Survey troops were responsible for the fixation of bearing pickets and control points, and the calculation of the co-ordinates of targets and other points selected from air photographs. They could also produce "known ranges" for A.A. and other units wishing to test their height and range-finders or to calibrate their guns. Flash spotting troops were divided into observation sections, which used a long base for the location of hostile batteries, and ranging sections, which used a short base for the control of air burst ranging. Sound ranging troops were used for the location and engagement of hostile batteries, preferably while the latter were still firing.

This organization was based on homogeneity of equipment and training within the battery, and it worked very well under European conditions where survey was normally a corps function and batteries spent most of their time under the control of the regimental commander. In the Middle East, however, it had proved less suitable. Here the fighting had nearly always been on single divisional fronts. It was therefore desirable that the battery should be capable of performing all three functions and thus of working as an independent unit. With this object in view, the establishment of the survey regiment was changed—at first locally, then universally—from three batteries of two troops each to two batteries of three troops each: one survey, one flash spotting and one sound ranging.

SECTION III.—A.A. AND COAST DEFENCE

The Western Desert

While in Tobruk the attacks of the German and Italian air forces had been held and finally defeated, the situation on the Egyptian frontier was less satisfactory. Here the operations of our mobile columns were still liable to serious interference from enemy air action, which sometimes forced the troops to leave their guns and vehicles and seek shelter.

After meeting the requirements of Tobruk, which naturally had first priority, there was very little to cover the formations in the Western Desert. The H.A.A. resources were limited to three batteries, one of which was armed with semi-mobile 3-in. guns, and these were all used up in the defence of the Matruh stronghold and of airfields. Of L.A.A. regiments there were two, plus one Australian battery and some machine-gun batteries of a South African A.A. regiment.

Once again, therefore, units were widely dispersed in order to give some A.A. defence to all claimants, including the small mobile columns, of which there were at one time as many as five in operation. Thus the L.A.A. regiment allotted to the 7th Armoured Division found itself working on a frontage of 30 miles and a depth of 60 miles, and had great difficulty in maintaining its communications.

In the early days in France, conditions had been so static that L.A.A. units had been robbed of their wireless sets to enable H.A.A. units to keep touch with their G.O.Rs. Now conditions were so mobile that even the restored No. 11 sets were inadequate. Their range was too short for communication between regimental headquarters and batteries, and the despatch riders on a motor-cycle, intended for keeping touch between battery headquarters and troops, could not operate in the desert (*see* p. 46). Hence a more powerful set (the No. 9) had to be provided for linking regiments to batteries, and the No. 11 set was relegated for use between batteries and troops.

Unsuitability of the No. 3 (L.A.A.) Predictor for Use in Mobile Operations

At Tobruk the No. 3 predictor had proved of doubtful value in the hands of inexperienced troops (*see* p. 84). In the Western Desert it was found that —as had been foreseen by the Bartholomew Committee—it was unsuitable for fully mobile operations.

The extent of its unsuitability was the subject of some controversy. Its devotees insisted that its presence need not delay the opening of fire with the forward area sight, and that, once in action, it greatly improved the accuracy of the shooting. It was, moreover, much more robust than some critics seemed to imagine; and a good many of its failures might be attributed to lack of preliminary training in field operations.

The fact remained, however, that its use entailed the provision of an extra vehicle and made the L.A.A. gun more difficult to conceal in action. It was, therefore, finally decided that it should not accompany the gun in highly mobile operations, but should be brought up whenever a position was likely to be occupied for more than 48 hours.

The Growth of the A.A. Barrage

As a result, perhaps, of the resistance of Tobruk, and of the persistent R.A.F. bombing of Benghasi, enemy air attacks on Egyptian bases were relatively few and unsustained. Throughout the eight months that Tobruk was besieged, only 22 attacks were made on Alexandria and 21 on the Suez Canal ports.

In dealing with these attacks the A.A. defences had still to rely mainly on the barrage. Although some G.L.II radar sets had arrived, there were certain technical difficulties that often prevented them from being used for the continuous engagement of unseen targets. For example, the G.L.II would not work reliably unless the ground around it was dead level up to a distance of about 50 yards. Such positions were of course not easy to find, and to overcome this difficulty a wire structure, known as a "mat", was introduced, which, if laid over the ground about the G.L. cabin and accurately levelled, would produce an artificial reflecting surface of the required quality. Alternatively, a "water mat" might be created in certain areas by flooding the surrounds and thus producing a level water surface.

In general, however, the accuracy obtained was disappointing and, for lack of anything better, there was a gradual elaboration of the simple geographical barrage described in Chapter IV (*see* p. 61). At Alexandria the basic barrage line was approximately a circle of 4,200 yards radius, centred on the entrance to the inner harbour and divided into sectors of 1,200 yards. At first this was very successful in preventing the mining or bombing of the harbour and Great Pass; but here as elsewhere, once the enemy had grown accustomed to it, he developed the habit of diving underneath it. To counter this, the guns were ordered to fire their second and third rounds at reduced elevations.

As an additional measure, extensions—known as " whiskers "—were made to the circumferential barrage lines to cover objectives of particular importance within the defended area. Then, in August, 1941, it was found necessary to make a further addition to deal with the persistent attacker who was not deterred by the initial burst of fire. This took the form of a " swinging following barrage ", in which the guns, after firing the prescribed number of rounds on the selected outer barrage line, swung to an inner line on which it was calculated that the attack could be forestalled.

Co-operation with Fighter Aircraft

The best that could be said of these barrages was that they tended to frighten away, or at least to disturb the aim of, any but the most determined attacker. In an overseas theatre of war like the Middle East, where vulnerable areas were comparatively small and the defence of the civil population was not a major problem, the effect of the guns was generally adequate.

In the United Kingdom, with its large industrial population, the situation was very different. There, the inability of the guns to keep off the night bombers had led to the hastened development of a new radar technique for night fighter interceptions.

Since the range of an instrument that could be carried in an aircraft was small, it was necessary to use a ground set, known as a G.C.I.(see p. 73), for the initial location of the enemy and for the control of the fighter until it had been brought to a point at which its own (A.I.) set would be effective. G.C.I. stations were set up to cover the approaches to the main vulnerable areas, and a " tally-ho " procedure was evolved by means of which a selected night fighter patrol could be ordered off the " cab rank " and sent in pursuit of a particular raider.

So promising were the results obtained, that to avoid interference with the operations of the A.I. fighters, it was decreed that on certain nights, known as " fighter nights ", the A.A. guns would either remain silent or else limit their fire to a certain height below which the A.I. instrument was not likely to be reliable. From the psychological point of view, this sometimes had unfortunate results. The civil population, hearing the bombs come down, would misinterpret the silence of the guns, and a certain amount of avoidable ill-feeling and loss of morale would result. It was also arguable that, although the silence of the guns might enable the night fighters to add slightly to the size of their " bag," it would at the same time give a free run to those of the enemy bombers who did get through and thus make their bombing more effective. For this reason the Navy insisted on maintaining the barrage at main fleet bases like Alexandria, though they eventually agreed to limit its height to 7,000 feet and to fix geographical boundaries outside which the fighters had absolute freedom of manoeuvre.

Meanwhile radar had been applied to the control of the A.A.S.L. and a new technique had been evolved for searchlight controlled fighter interceptions. The industrial heart of Britain was surrounded by two searchlight belts: an outer, or " indicator ", belt in which lights were widely spaced and were intended to indicate the approximate height, position and course of approaching aircraft; and an inner, or " killer ", belt in which lights were spaced at 6,000 yards and were intended to provide continuous illumination of targets until they had been intercepted and destroyed by the night fighters. The latter, in anticipation of an attack, would station themselves singly in " fighter boxes " lying at right angles across the killer and indicator belts, and would " orbit " round beacons, which were sited one at the centre of each box, and which consisted of a vertical beam with a coloured searchlight beside it to enable the fighter pilot concerned to recognize his own beacon.

The number of searchlights required, though less than that formerly deployed in A.D.G.B., was still large, and the method was not therefore generally applicable to overseas theatres. In the Middle East, for example, searchlights were used in conjunction with fighters only for the defence of the Suez Canal, and here the number of lights available was too small to be really effective. Moreover, even if more searchlights could have been provided, there would have been considerable administrative difficulties in maintaining a second line of flanking lights, particularly to the east of the canal, where the ground was " soft desert " without roads or tracks.

It was not until the Beaufighters, equipped with the new A.I. sets, began to arrive at the end of August that the situation became really satisfactory.

Coast Artillery in Action at Malta, 25th-26th July, 1941

In July, 1941, an attack on Malta by Italian " E " boats and midget submarines gave to the coast artillery a chance of proving the efficacy of the new 6-pr. 10-cwt. twin equipment, with its high rate of fire, efficient weight of projectile, auto-sight, ease and speed of applying corrections, and deadly accuracy at short range. Owing to slowness in production, no directors were in action in this battle. All equipments were fought by auto-sights.([8])

The Italian intention was to attack with torpedo a British convoy that was believed to be in Grand Harbour, and at the same time to make a small subsidiary attack on the submarine anchorage in the Marsamuscetto. The attacking force consisted of two main components: nine " explosive motor boats ", each carrying one man and one torpedo; and two " human torpedoes ", each with a complement of two men and a detachable explosive bow.

For the approach voyage these tiny craft were carried in two parent ships; the first, and larger—which carried the explosive motor boats and their flotilla leader—towing the second, with two large " escort and rescue " M.T.Bs. in close company. The convoy left Augusta (about 90 miles N.E. of Malta) at 1815 hrs. on 25th July, and at about 2300 hrs., when 14 miles N.E. of Valletta, the explosive motor boats were disembarked and the human torpedo carrier was slipped. The larger carrier then withdrew towards Cape Passero, while the remainder of the attacking force, with one of the rescue M.T.Bs. towing the human torpedo carrier, moved at 5 knots to a point 7,000 yards N.E. of St. Elmo. Here the two rescue M.T.Bs. took up a rescue position, while the carrier, followed by the explosive motor boats at minimum speed in line ahead, proceeded to a point about 900 yards N.E. of St. Elmo, and there, under cover of a 15-minute air attack on Valletta, launched its two human torpedoes to the attack.

It will be seen that the essence of the enemy tactics was:—
- (*a*) The maximum use of carriers for the remote approach.
- (*b*) A slow and silent close approach.
- (*c*) Air attack to conceal the close approach and to prevent defence searchlights exposing.
- (*d*) A very short and rapid dash to the objectives.
- (*e*) The use of very small and economical attacking craft, and the simultaneous attack in numbers.

For the radar detection of such attacks the defence had to rely on the C.O.L. sets of the R.A.F., as no Army sets were yet available for Malta. With their aid, the comparatively large M.T.B. carrier was picked up at a range of 45 miles, but the small attacking craft themselves could only be reliably detected at very close range, and no assistance was in fact obtained from this source.

For visual purposes there were two pairs of observation lights, one on each flank of the harbour entrances; an illuminated area composed of one movable dispersed (30 degree) fighting light per 6-pr. equipment, each with a definite zone of responsibility; and, behind this again, two 16-degree beams serving two "silent" equipments, one at each entrance, with a zone of responsibility confined rigidly to the immediate neighbourhood of its own entrance.

The existing doctrine, laid down in the Manual of Coast Defence, was that, when enemy surface craft were known to be near, sufficient searchlights should be exposed to ensure that no craft could approach without detection. On the other hand, since that manual was written, there had been over a year of air bombing by a numerically superior "Luftwaffe", which had perhaps led to over-emphasis of the virtues of concealment and to a natural reluctance to disclose the position of the defences or to do anything that might assist the enemy to make a successful landfall.

Hence, though the sounds of motor engines had been heard to seawards intermittently since 2200 hrs., only two exposures of the defence lights were made between then and 0330 hrs., both without results; and during the enemy air attack, which began at 0413 hrs., no light at all was exposed. It was not indeed until 0444 hrs. that the alarm was given by one of the gun lookouts, who saw a small craft about 300 yards away. Almost immediately, as the illuminated area lights exposed, the bridge span at the shore end of the St. Elmo breakwater was blown up by the first human torpedo.

It was the only success achieved by the attackers. Within two minutes the main attack by five of the explosive motor boats, in line ahead at 100 yards intervals, had been engaged—at an opening range of about 800 yards —and routed. Three of the boats were sunk and the other two disabled at an average cost of 28 rounds of 6-pr. for each target destroyed. The remainder of the attackers were engaged, with less precision, by both Bofors and 6-prs. at ranges of about 3,000 yards; and by 0600 hrs. the cannon-firing Hurricanes of the defence had appeared to attack the retreating survivors and to turn the enemy defeat into a complete disaster.

Altogether it was a most encouraging demonstration of what could still be done by alert and well-trained look-outs and gun detachments, and by a well-arranged distribution of fire scheme.

Conclusion

With the diversion of German air effort towards the Russian front, the situation in the Middle East and in N.W. Europe had ceased to be critical. There were still some fierce battles to be fought by the A.A. guns; notably that over Malta, which will be discussed in a subsequent chapter; but in general it could be said that the air attack had been mastered.

In achieving this result, both fighter and A.A. gun had played a part—individual rather than collective. During the daylight battle of Britain co-operation had been at its simplest and best. While the fighters intercepted and defeated the enemy bombers, the A.A. guns helped to beat off attacks against their airfields. Against the night bomber, co-operation was more difficult. Radar was still in its infancy, and both R.A.F. and Army were perhaps too intent on their own problems to pay much attention to combined action. Thus, at the start, reliance was placed largely on the gun, in the belief that G.L. was more advanced than A.I. and S.L.C. (*see* Table B), and that it would enable the gun to master the unseen target. When it failed to do so, confidence was transferred to the A.I. set in the aircraft and the guns were sometimes silenced altogether while the fighters roamed at large over the gun defended areas. At the same time radar-controlled searchlights were brought into action in the aircraft fighting zone and visual—or "bull's-eye"—interceptions were used to supplement the scanty resources of A.I. fighters.

Later, as resources increased and technique improved, co-operation became much closer. Meanwhile, in overseas theatres especially, the A.A. defences had a heavy burden to bear; a burden that was rendered all the heavier by the omission to develop radar with a suitable predictor for A.A. purposes when the opportunity first presented itself (*see* p. 76). That it was borne successfully was due in large measure to a greater realism in training, which had fostered the spirit of aggression and the calculated acceptance of dangers that were often more imaginary than real. The threat of the dive bomber had been met and held, and before long it would be eliminated altogether by the growing superiority of the R.A.F. When that happened, the Germans would find themselves the dupes of their own early successes. Misled by the ease with which their dive bombers had shocked a divided Europe into submission, they would neglect to prepare—until it was too late—against the day when its magic would cease to work.

List of References

[1] "Tobruk", by Chester Wilmot, p. 146.
[2] *Ibid*, p. 147.
[3] Report on Operations of 4 A.A. Bde., 7th April to 9th October 1941.
[4] "Tobruk", by Chester Wilmot, p. 275.
[5] A.T.M. No. 43 of May 1942.
[6] "History of the 4th Armd. Bde.", by Brig. R. M. P. Carver, p. 9.
[7] A.T.M. No. 41 of October 1941.
[8] "The Battle of Valletta, 25th-26th July 1941", by the Coast Artillery School.

TABLE D
SUMMARY OF A.A. ACTIONS AT TOBRUK, APRIL—NOVEMBER, 1941

	10-30 April	May	June	July	August	September	October	November	Remarks
(a) No. of a/c engaged during month by types:—									
Ju 87	386	277	123	79	217	46	113	84	
Ju 88	120	168	79	127	82	64	25	23	
ME 109	83	143	55	48	34	15	27	27	
ME 110	37	28	31	43	16	2	12	1	
Dorniers	11	—	—	—	—	—	—	—	
Heinkel III	4	6	1	—	1	1	—	—	
Henschel	4	12	4	10	9	5	7	3	
CR 42	—	13	13	—	—	—	—	—	
G 50	—	1	18	7	29	13	20	4	
S 79	—	10	6	2	3	8	—	2	
ER 20	—	—	—	—	—	12	—	2	
Unidentified	32	74	132	126	205	240	309	124	
TOTALS	677	734	462	442	596	406	514*	274†	*Includes 1 Ju 52 †Includes 4 Ju 52

	10-30 April	May	June	July	August	September	October	November	Remarks
(b) Casualties to A.A. personnel due to enemy action:									
Killed	8	2	5	1	2	19	4	—	
Wounded ...	53	19	10	9	5	29	5	3	
(c) Casualties to enemy aircraft,									
by H.A.A.: destroyed ...	6	2	2	3	2	—	—	—	
probably destroyed ...	4	4	2	3	2	1	3	1	
damaged ...	7	6	8	10	7	3	1	1	
by L.A.A.: destroyed ...	31	17	10	4	11	1	2	4	
probably destroyed ...	12	22	10	2	10	3	4	1	
damaged ...	36	39	11	18	30	8	10	—	
(d) Ammunition expenditure,									
by H.A.A.: total number of 3·7 rds. fired	8,230	7,385	7,291	6,699	8,295	7,454			
average number of rds. per a/c destroyed ...	823	1,231	1,823	1,116	2,074	7,454			
by L.A.A.: total number of 40-mm. rds. fired	7,168	8,962	3,504	4,234	8,071	3,406			
total number of 20-mm. rds. fired	18,713	23,628	9,019	5,755	11,480	5,727			
average number of rds. per a/c destroyed ...	602	836	626	1,655	931	2,283			

PART IV

THE FIGHT AGAINST THE TANK

CHAPTER VII

THE RECONQUEST OF CYRENAICA

Plate Relevant to this Chapter
No. 14. The German 8.8-cm. gun.

The Speeding Up of Fire Plans

After the failure at Capuzzo in June 1941 there could no longer be any doubt that the Matilda tank had ceased to dominate the infantry battle. In the subsequent months, therefore, much attention was given to the problem of how to provide quicker artillery support for " I " tanks in the moving battle. A " pocket gun " moving alongside the G.P.O., and a mobile aiming point in the form of a suitably decorated cable truck, were the customary bases of all such fire plans, and with their aid it was found possible to get off the first round within about five minutes of coming into action.

Meanwhile, in the United Kingdom, there had been a general speeding up of procedures for the application of artillery fire in the armoured division: quick barrages and smoke screens, and quicker methods for the engagement of targets by air observation. The essence of the quick barrage was the preparation in every unit of a standard barrage lay-out that could be applied to all but the most unusual fire support tasks, and that required no more than the co-ordinates of a selected point or points in the area to be neutralized before the calculation of gun programmes could begin. Its effect was to halve the time required for the production of these programmes after the receipt of orders at battery command posts (*see* Table E). The quick smoke screen procedure, introduced for use with the 25-pr., reduced the time taken to produce an effective screen to ten minutes, including the registration of a point or points of origin when little was known about the zone and the wind could not be ascertained without shooting.

This increase in simplicity and speed was of necessity achieved at the cost of some sacrifice in accuracy. The shape of the standard barrage could not be expected to fit exactly the lie of the ground or the dispositions of the troops to be covered. It was therefore considered that the distance of the infantry or tank start line from the opening line of the barrage might have to be as much as 500 yards.([1])

Air observation, which had already been subjected to a series of modifications (*see* pp. 31, 58), was now still further speeded up as the result of the development of two-way wireless communication. This allowed a closer liaison between ground and air than had existed before, and the increasing strength of the R.A.F. had enabled more attention to be given to the specialist training of army co-operation squadrons. The rather clumsy clock code procedure was abolished and pilots were taught to conduct simple shoots direct from the air. In future they were to give corrections, not observations, and to adjust the fire of the guns in the normal way by bracketing for range and line.

At the same time "ladder ranging" was introduced to speed up the engagement of important targets in zones not adequately registered by shooting or by silent methods. This procedure, which had long been in use in the Royal Navy and latterly in coast artillery, was particularly valuable at long ranges when the time of flight of the shell was considerable. Instead of waiting for the first round to fall before the next pair of elevations was ordered, the third and subsequent rungs of the ladder were fired while the first two were still in the air. Thus time was saved at the cost of a possible slight increase in ammunition expenditure. Though feasible for a terrestrial observer only over level surfaces where observation of all rounds could be guaranteed, the system was generally applicable to shooting with air observation.([2]) In practice, however, the system never came into general use.

In counter-battery work the speed factor caused attention to be focussed on neutralization by concentrations, or by air bombardment, as opposed to destructive shoots. Normally, a 2:1 numerical superiority was regarded as the minimum required for effective neutralization.

In the defence also a simplification of procedure was achieved by the abolition of counter-preparation (*see* p. 3). Under modern conditions it was found that the distinction between counter-preparation and defensive fire was often artificial and was apt to cause confusion.([3])

TABLE E

TIMES ALLOWED FOR THE VARIOUS STAGES OF DEPLOYMENT AND PREPARATION OF FIRE PLANS

(FROM R.A.T.M. WAR No. 4 OF JUNE, 1941)
(Since cancelled)

Unit	Operation	Time Allowed (mins.)
Troop	(1) To advance 1 mile from R.V. and fire first round, with short wireless communication to O.P.	15
	(2) To come into action on line of march and be ready to fire on R/T orders from B.C.	8
Battery	(1) To advance 1 mile from R.V. with short wireless communications to two O.Ps. ready to fire.	25
	(2) Link shoot, from guns in action to troops ready for link shooting.	8
	(3) Silent registration of eight points and preparation of panoramas.	20–40
Regiment	(1) To advance 1 mile from R.V. with short wireless communications to O.Ps. and orientation by R.S.O. of all battery directors.	45
	(2) Regimental barrage (10 lifts) from receipt of traces at battery command posts to the production of gun programmes.	80
	(3) Regimental quick barrage, from receipt of co-ords. and detail of barrage to the production of gun programmes.	30–40
Divisional Artillery	(1) Meteor worked out at two ranges and on two lines, and the results plotted as a graph.	25
	(2) Alteration of target records on change of grid involving bearing and fixation (with five targets).	25

Note.—The above table was subsequently cancelled because it did not prove to be a reliable guide.

Increased Importance of Observed Fire

As a result of this emphasis on speed there had been simultaneous developments in the use of wireless and of the armoured O.P. "Observed fire," it was now stated " and fire as a result of observation, have become of much greater importance."(⁴) By the use of wireless on their own artillery "net", O.Ps. could keep in continuous touch with the guns and with one another, so that fire could be brought down, stopped, lifted and corrected with far more assurance than heretofore. Henceforth a battery commander could control the movement of his O.Ps. and decide which of them, at any moment, was to be the "control O.P." and direct the fire of the guns.

In addition to the set on the artillery net, every armoured O.P. was in future to be equipped with a No. 18 set on the infantry net, for communication with battalion or company headquarters. Thus all O.Ps. would know what was going on in the battalion they were supporting, fire plans could be quickly arranged, and small fire plans could be " largely controlled by observation in accordance with actual progress rather than on a rigid time basis."(⁴) Even so, however, it was considered desirable, if time permitted, to arrange a brief timed programme ; and for large scale planned attacks, such a programme was essential.(⁵)

Improving the Accuracy of Artillery Shooting

One of the greatest causes of inaccuracy, both in the Western Desert and in Eritrea, had been the unreliability of meteor telegrams. By firing at a datum point and comparing the "hitting range" with the surveyed range, it was possible to deduce the correction of the moment ; but in unmapped or featureless country like the desert, a suitable datum point could not always be found, and some other means had to be discovered for obtaining this correction. One obvious method—already practised by the Germans—was to make the shell burst in the air instead of on the ground, so that the position of the burst could be easily and accurately fixed by cross observation from selected O.Ps. manned by the ranging sections of flash spotting troops.

In February, 1941, this method of air burst ranging was officially recognized as a means of overcoming errors in meteor telegrams caused by "rapid changes of temperature or wind, and by delays in transmission."(⁶) It could also be employed for the calibration of guns from their battle positions, and for the engagement, by day or by night, of targets that were out of sight from ground O.Ps. but that could be accurately located from air photographs or maps, or by sound ranging sections. Furthermore it offered a chance, to be exploited later, of producing quick concentrations in difficult country ; and it could be conducted from O.Ps. that were behind a crest and could therefore be surveyed and occupied without interference from the enemy.

To produce an air burst, however, it was necessary to have a special time fuze (No. 210), which had not been contemplated when the new artillery equipments were introduced in 1938, and in November, 1941, the supply of these fuzes was only just beginning.

The importance of calibration within the unit had been greatly increased by the circumstances of mass production and the haste with which the new equipments had had to be issued. It was obviously impossible for every gun to be calibrated by absolute methods before it reached the troops, and it was therefore laid down that their relative M.Vs. should be obtained by comparative calibration in units before they went into action for the first time.

Thus steps had been taken to compensate for variations in the behaviour of the guns and of the weather. It remained to ensure that no error was allowed to creep in through faults in the ammunition. Neglect of this factor could upset the accuracy of an artillery concentration, and thus cause unnecessary loss of life to the infantry, just as surely as the failure to calibrate or to apply a meteor correction; and experience showed that such neglect was not uncommon. " Insufficient attention " said a training memorandum of this period " is being paid to the care and preservation of ammunition."[1]

Wire Cutting and Mine Exploding

This was a period of active experimentation in which everything that a gun might reasonably be expected to do was given a trial. Soon wire cutting and mine exploding reappeared among the list of artillery activities. For example, on 6th November the Polish Artillery at Tobruk was ordered to cut two or more lanes in the enemy wire as a preliminary to an artillery demonstration designed to prevent the enemy from reinforcing his forces on the frontier. The demonstration as a whole was a success, but among the lessons learned, or relearned, was that " wire cannot be completely cut by artillery fire, even with a very large expenditure of ammunition."[7] It was also expensive in time and inimical to secrecy; in short, a method that should " only be adopted as a last resort."[8]

It was the same with mine exploding. A trial carried out by the New Zealand Division on 23rd October with a field gun and howitzer barrage showed " conclusively that this method of clearing minefields was impracticable."[9] A similar conclusion had been arrived at by the C.R.A. 4th Indian Division after the battle of Sidi Barrani (see p. 52).

Direct Air Support

" In November, 1941, a British army for the first time took the field against the Germans with a superiority in numbers, for the first time we possessed an imposing array of tanks, for the first time the Army enjoyed full air support."[10]

Mere numbers, it is true, were as yet no reliable index of fighting value. The tanks were completely, and the fighter aircraft partly, outclassed by those of the enemy. The artillery, too, was still very weak in anti-tank equipment. Units were armed mainly with the 2-pr., which was completely outranged by the German 5-cm.; the balance of their establishment being made up by the temporary issue of 18-prs. or 75-mms.

Field artillery units, though now homogeneously equipped, were still in the process of converting to the three-battery establishment and could not complete this process owing to the lack of trained specialists and N.C.Os. To get over this difficulty, the War Office had been asked to include in future drafts a proportion of such personnel to act as a nucleus for the formation of the third battery in each of the unconverted regiments.

Counter-battery facilities were poor, owing to the short range of the 6-in. and 155-mm. hows., with which seven of the ten available medium batteries were still armed, and to the lack of survey equipment. The only sound ranging troop then in contact with the Germans was without the radio link that had been found so necessary in France and Belgium (see p. 37).

To compensate for this lack of weight and range in its artillery, the Eighth Army could rely on substantial support from bomber and fighter aircraft, though the methods of applying such support were still in their infancy. During the operations in East Africa in May and June, 1941, a small "close support group" of one flight each of army co-operation, fighter and bomber aircraft had helped to maintain the impetus of the advance, but at the end of the campaign it was reported that we had "still not discovered any satisfactory rapid method of marking our leading troops." Indeed it was clear that the term "close support" was misleading. Targets could not be safely engaged within 500 yards of our own troops, and only then if they were easily recognized from the air, since, in the face of enemy opposition, it was impossible for pilots to cruise round and find them.

Hence the nomenclature was changed from "close support" to "direct air support", and in a Middle East directive issued on 30th September, 1941, it was pointed out that air bombardment was generally less accurate than artillery fire and that, compared with the latter, it could not be sustained for any length of time and did not increase in accuracy as it proceeded. Nor could it yet be applied by indirect methods when visibility was impaired by mist or cloud.

Preparations for the Offensive

In preparation for the coming operations, the offensive spirit had been sedulously fostered. Jock columns, so often used with success in Eritrea and in the Western Desert, continued and even extended their activities during October by sending out ambushing and sniping parties, of a section or troop of 25-prs. escorted by armoured cars or motorized infantry, to harass the enemy defences along the line of the frontier. In the coastal area assistance was given both by the bombers of the Fleet Air Arm and by the guns of H.M.'s ships, when available. On 13th November, a naval liaison officer and F.O.O.—the latter an officer of the Royal Artillery specially detailed for this purpose—joined 13 Corps Headquarters.

For the first time, too, a fair proportion of A.A. units was available for use in the forward areas. Indeed the Commander, 4th Indian Division, in a special order of the day on 17th November, was able to say: "We are now at full strength in our supporting arms. We have in the Division no less than 102 anti-tank guns with 64 South African anti-tank guns behind them, 56 × 25-prs., and 36 × 40-mms.: a total of 258 guns in the Divisional area, quite apart from any "I" tanks allotted, with which we can kill the German "panzers" should they come our way."

Dispersion of the Artillery

Yet it soon became evident that this business of destroying tanks was to be conducted in the face of great difficulties. The armoured offensive, which had begun with the object of bringing the enemy to battle by seizing ground that was vital to him, ended with a series of isolated actions by each of the three armoured brigades in turn. Thus the available guns were split up among a number of different columns and the artillery as a whole was not able to do itself justice.

On 21st November the Support Group, operating with the 7th Armoured Brigade at Sidi Rezegh, secured a foothold with one battalion on the escarpment overlooking the airfield from the north, and made a show of gaining contact with the Tobruk garrison, which had broken out towards El Duda. It was the first infantry attack to be made by a motor battalion in the Middle East, and it was supported by a 4-minute concentration by 42 × 25-prs., following a preliminary smoking of the enemy O.Ps.

By this time, however, Rommel had correctly appreciated the situation and was rapidly concentrating his panzer divisions in the Sidi Rezegh area. The Support Group and the 7th Armoured Brigade were isolated, and for the next two days they had to bear the brunt of an attack by the bulk of the enemy armour. The Support Group, though much stronger in field guns than in January, 1941—it now had 56 × 25-prs. instead of 24—was not designed for a prolonged defence. Moreover its position on the airfield was entirely overlooked by the enemy in the escarpments on either flank. It was therefore under continuous heavy shell fire from enemy Mk. IV tanks and medium artillery.

After fighting for two whole days against heavy odds, these two formations withdrew from Sidi Rezegh on the morning of 23rd November. The field guns of the Support Group had put up a "terrific" fire against the enemy tanks, but 56 × 25-prs. were not enough to stop a really determined armoured attack. The anti-tank guns, which were too few in number to allow many to be grounded, kept up a running fight from their portees and inflicted a number of casualties upon the enemy, but they themselves suffered heavily in the process.

On 23rd November, the 5th South African Brigade, which was moving up from the south to relieve the Support Group, was overrun and practically annihilated, and on 25th November, the 1st South African Brigade was attacked at Taib-el-Esem. This Brigade was in a prepared position and had evolved its own "moving box" tactics for dealing with enemy armour. Field and anti-tank guns were distributed within the box in troop positions that were mutually supporting and that could give all-round protection to the perimeter. While on the move, armoured cars reconnoitred up to 5-6 miles on all sides, and one was allotted to each field artillery troop as a mobile O.P. Whenever the Brigade halted, slit trenches were dug immediately, and the desert was "turned into a fortress in a very short time."[11] A hard-hitting fire unit was formed in each battalion, consisting of one troop of anti-tank guns, one platoon of heavy machine-guns, and one section of mortars, with one troop of field guns ready to accompany the unit, if necessary, and throw an oncoming attack into confusion. The anti-tank defences were further supported by L.A.A. guns moving at the apices of equilateral triangles about the centre of the box.

By these methods two heavy armoured attacks were successfully repulsed and at no point did the enemy succeed in penetrating the perimeter. A third attack was broken up, with the aid of the 4th Armoured Brigade and its two R.H.A. batteries, before it had started. Then, as their ammunition was exhausted, the South Africans withdrew under cover of darkness.

The remnants of 30 Corps now collected and reorganized in the Gabr Saleh area.

The 25-Pr. to the Rescue

Back on the frontier, the 4th Indian Division had taken up the offensive on 22nd November with an attack on the enemy positions at Sidi Omar. The operation resembled in many ways the attack on Nibeiwa and the

Tummars which the same Division had carried out successfully the year before (see pp. 48, 49). There were two separate localities, Omar Nuovo and Libyan Omar, which were to be attacked in succession by an infantry battalion preceded by "I" tanks and covered by artillery concentrations on selected portions of the objective. But there was no surprise, and the Italian battalion garrisoning the area had been stiffened by a company of picked German infantry supported by a number of field guns and two or three 88-mm. A.A. guns dug in and prepared for an anti-tank role. The tanks were late in crossing the start line and ran on to an unsuspected minefield; the counter-battery organization failed to locate or to neutralize the 8.8-cm. guns, which inflicted further heavy casualties on the "I" tanks; and in the later stages of the attack, after the first objective had been taken, the infantry were unable to keep up to the timed programme, which, owing to the lie of the land, had had to be substituted for observed shooting. As a result progress was slow and costly, and it was not until several days later that the last of the enemy pockets in Libyan Omar had been liquidated.

Meanwhile Rommel was initiating a powerful counter-stroke with his 15th and 21st Panzer Divisions right through to the frontier. The brunt of the attack fell upon the 4th Indian Division, whose artillery had been carefully instructed regarding the measures to be taken in just such an eventuality. On 21st November, the C.R.A. had issued an order emphasizing again that "the primary object of these operations is to destroy enemy A.F.Vs." and that it was therefore "our object to lure enemy tanks within decisive range and then destroy them . . . NOT to engage them at extreme range and deflect them away from our defences."

Now, four days later, these tactics were to be severely tested. At 0910 hrs. on 25th November the 1st Field Regiment was in action at Bir El Hurush about three miles S.E. of Sidi Omar, when some 30 enemy Mk. III and Mk. IV tanks appeared from the south and were engaged in strict accordance with the C.R.A's. instructions. The attack was made in open order so that all the tanks could fire simultaneously, and from a flank so that at least one of the 25-pr. troops could not use more than half its guns. The enemy fire began at a range of 2,000 yards and was indiscriminate at first, but gradually became more accurate, the tanks stopping as usual to fire their guns but not their machine-guns.

The 1st Field Regiment bore this fire in silence until the range had closed to 800 yards or less. Then they opened up at the leading enemy tanks and for the next ten minutes an intense artillery duel took place, as the result of which the attack was brought to a standstill at a range of about 500 yards. Withdrawing to a hull-down position about 500 yards further back, the enemy continued the duel for another ten minutes and finally made one more attempt at a head-on charge. This time they were immediately engaged with a great volume of fire and after advancing about 300 yards they had had enough. They now withdrew rapidly to the south and east pursued by the fire of the whole Regiment and of another field battery in the vicinity.

Altogether the engagement had lasted about 45 minutes, during which time seven enemy tanks had been knocked out, all at ranges of less than 700 yards, at a cost of 5 × 25-prs. and two Bofors (of the supporting L.A.A. unit) put out of action by direct hits, 18 men killed, 44 wounded and four missing.

During the remainder of this day enemy tanks continued to appear in varying numbers and were engaged by the medium guns and howitzers as well as by the 25-prs. But never again did they make a serious attempt to rush the battery positions. By this action the guns had saved a great quantity of transport and other units in and behind the gun area.

On at least two occasions during this enemy counter-thrust the 2-pr. portee was able to show what it could do when conditions were favourable. On 24th November a few tanks and a battery of anti-tank guns carried out a running fight to enable a mass of " B " echelon transport and other equipment of 30 Corps to escape by Maddelena. Making good use of ground and of their mobility, firing sometimes off their own wheels and sometimes off the portees, the anti-tank gunners were able to keep up with the tanks and achieved their object without the loss of a single gun, though some vehicles were knocked out and casualties to personnel were heavy.

On 26th November two troops, protecting 13 Corps Headquarters on the march towards Tobruk, were sent to head off a mixed enemy column that was following the same route on its return from the abortive thrust towards the frontier. It was early morning and the enemy tanks made good targets against the rising sun, so that the two troops, opening fire at a range of 200-300 yards, were able to inflict several casualties upon them. For half an hour a running fight was kept up, during which the guns withdrew gradually westwards and forced the enemy to move southwards. The latter were kept in sight the whole day, but did not again attempt to come to close quarters.

Opportunities of this kind were rare, however, and in the main battle the 2-pr. was completely outclassed, as witness the action fought by the New Zealand Division at El Duda. On 27th November this Division had recaptured Sidi Rezegh, taken Belhamed on the ridge to the north of it, and joined hands with the Tobruk garrison at El Duda. By now Rommel had recalled his armour from the frontier and the German tanks, cruising about very slowly outside the effective range of the 2-prs., shelled the position with their 7.5-cm. guns and gradually goaded the anti-tank gunners into opening fire. Then, when satisfied that all the anti-tank guns had been located, they knocked them out quickly with their 7.5-cms. and their supporting artillery. If, on such occasions, our " I " tanks moved out to counter-attack, the enemy tanks would give ground, again keeping outside the effective range of the 2-pr., and would try to draw the " I " tanks on to their own anti-tank guns or on to previously prepared minefields.([12])

After a gallant resistance the New Zealand Division was forced to withdraw during the night 1st/2nd December and moved back to the rear areas to refit; but the offensive was now resumed by the 4th Indian Division and the 22nd Guards Brigade, with the remaining tanks of the 7th Armoured Division collected in the 4th Armoured Brigade. On 5th December the enemy armour was attacked near El Gubi, where it stood astride the proposed axis of advance of the British forces. The attack was a failure, the greater part of the enemy forces remaining inaccessible behind a powerful screen of artillery and anti-tank guns; but as fresh British units came up the enemy was outflanked and forced to withdraw north-westwards.

Though Tobruk was relieved, the enemy was not routed, and on the Gazala position his armour made several violent counter-attacks, in the course of which the 4th Indian Divisional Artillery was again severely tested. While preparing to attack the southern flank of this position, the infantry of the 7th Indian Infantry Brigade were caught in an awkward position and the supporting artillery regiment was forced to come to their assistance by opening fire at a range of about 4,000 yards. As a result it became involved in a duel, in the open, with about 40 enemy tanks and their supporting artillery. In the course of this duel the enemy were able to approach within 5-cm. and small arms range of the nearest battery, which was consequently silenced; but the other battery of the regiment took up the fight, assisted by anti-tank and L.A.A. guns, and after being engaged over open sights at a range of about 700 yards, the enemy halted, changed direction and withdrew. Altogether some 12 to 14 tanks—about half of them Mk IVs—had been disabled, though many of them were subsequently recovered by the enemy during the night.

A little later another determined attack, on a similar scale, was made against a battalion of the 5th Indian Infantry Brigade, which was being supported by the 31st Field Regiment. After beating off several tank attacks during the afternoon of 12th December, with the loss of one of its troops, the Regiment was engaged the following afternoon by a force of about 40 enemy tanks supported by infantry and guns. The attack, which was preceded by heavy artillery concentrations, came in from the south in two groups, one directed towards each flank of the regimental area (*see* Diagram 2). Several 25-prs. were knocked out by direct hits from 7.5-cm. guns, and as the range shortened, machine-gun fire from the tanks, combined with air bursts and mortar fire, knocked out most of the detachments. Before long " D " Troop had been overrun, and then " E " Troop, taken in flank from the south and charged in front by the second group of tanks from the west, suffered the same fate. " B " Troop, continuing the fight alone, lost all but one of its guns.

Some " I " tanks, which had been brought up to strengthen the defences the previous evening, and some 2-prs., which had been taken off their portees and dug in in prepared positions, did their best to hold off the enemy but could make little impression on his tanks as the ranges were too great. Thus the 31st Field Regiment was practically annihilated, but by its self-sacrifice it had saved the rest of the column. The enemy withdrew, and on the following evening began to evacuate the whole of the Gazala position.

From now on things moved rapidly and quick fire plans became the order of the day. During this period a new method was evolved that reduced still further the time required to produce artillery support in a moving battle. A troop of guns, while on the march, would keep its O.P. informed by R/T of the bearing on which it was moving; and the O.P. would keep as far as possible to the same bearing. By mutual arrangement between the O.P. officer and the G.P.O., the approximate distance between O.P. and guns would be known, so that, when a target was spotted, an opening range and bearing could be quickly estimated. By this method a round could be discharged within two minutes of receiving the order to come into action (*cf.* Table E).

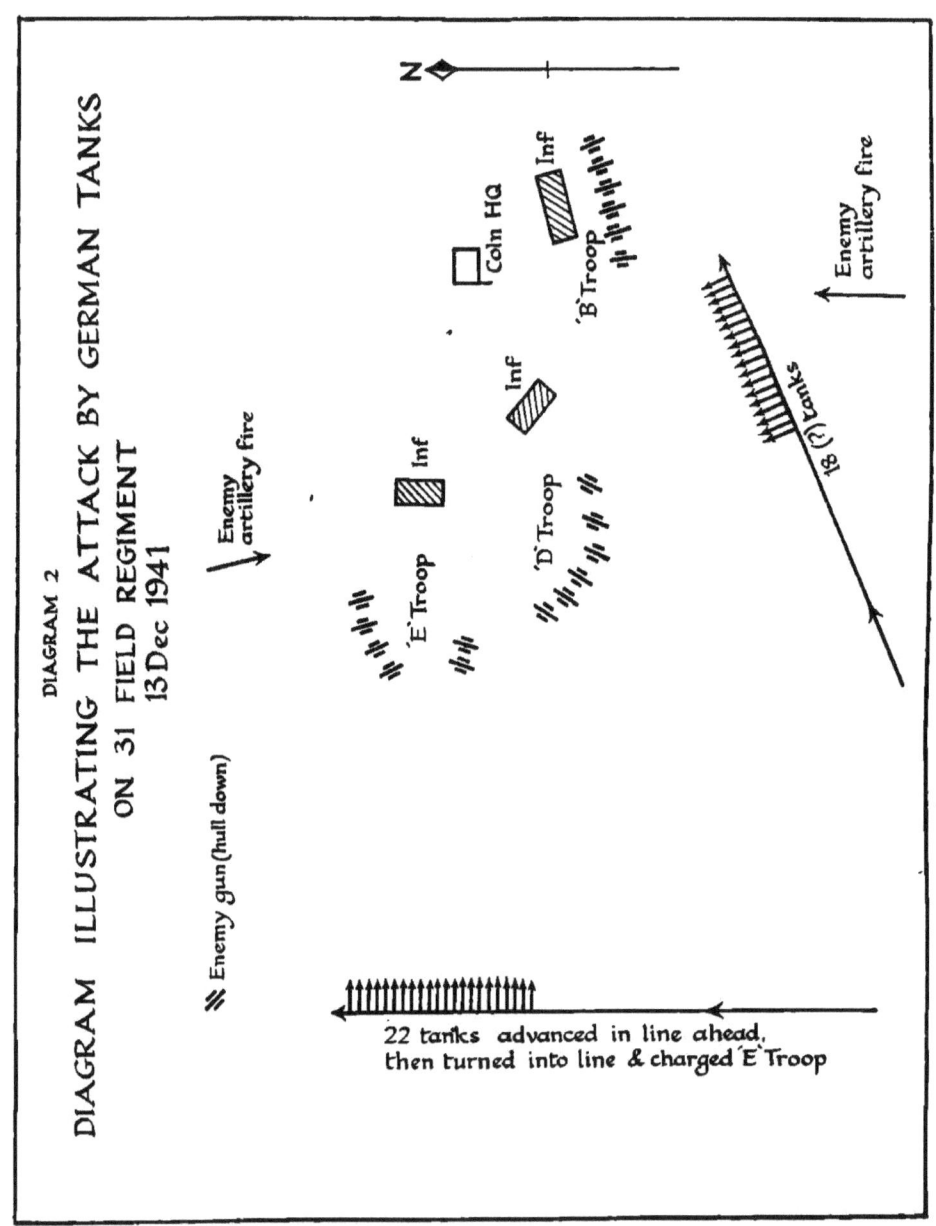

It remained only to clean up the enemy pockets on the Egyptian frontier. The biggest task here was the reduction of Bardia, which was entrusted to the 2nd South African Division and the 1st Army Tank Brigade, supported by 104 × 25-prs. and 40 medium guns and howitzers. The latter were formed into a medium artillery group, which included 24 of the 25-prs. and was provided with its own survey facilities and counter-battery staff, and was supported by the 451st A.C. Squadron, R.A.A.F. Counter-battery information was fuller than ever before in this theatre, including air photographs (right up to date), sound ranging and flash spotting locations, air spottings, hostile shelling reports, and sound and flash bearings from ground O.Ps. and infantry. When the attack was launched in the early hours of 31st December, every known hostile battery received at least three bombardments with a concentration of not less than 2:1, and up to 14:1 for the most troublesome.

The second noteworthy feature of this operation was the use of " I " tanks by night. In view of their vulnerability, it was the only sure way of operating against the unlocated anti-tank gun, and as there were no minefields within the perimeter, conditions were exceptionally favourable. As an additional precaution, smoke was put down by the artillery to screen the flanks of the attack.

The immediate results were satisfactory and by mid-day the main objectives had been captured; but an enemy counter-attack forced the infantry to withdraw and it was not until 2nd January, 1942, that the garrison finally surrendered after a considerable pounding from the air as well as from the ground forces. On 31st December, 81 light bomber sorties were combined with a naval bombardment, and on 1st January, 1942, a further 45 sorties hastened the collapse of enemy resistance.

German Tank Tactics

Since the enemy had been driven from Cyrenaica with the loss of two-thirds of his army, we could fairly claim a victory; but it had to be admitted that in the handling of armoured forces, and especially of their artillery component, we still had something to learn from the Germans. The opinions of those who had served with armoured formations in France and Belgium had been divided on this subject, and as late as March, 1942, it could be said that many had failed to recognize " till quite recently the vital importance of the closest co-operation between tanks, artillery and infantry in the employment of armoured forces."[13]

German tactics, on the other hand, as exemplified during the recent fighting, were admirably calculated to exploit the superiority of their tanks, both in armour and armament, and their ample supply of supporting weapons. They were based on the most intimate co-operation between the tanks and the supporting arms, and on the assumption that the primary role of the tank was to kill infantry. The purely armoured battle was as far as possible avoided, and on meeting our tanks in strength the Germans would withdraw and endeavour to lure our armour on to their own anti-tank weapons.

For this purpose a battle drill had been evolved which centred on a " moving box " similar to that employed by the 1st South African Brigade (*see* p. 104). In the defence this box contained all the supporting arms: field, 5-cm. anti-tank, 8.8-cm. A.A. and 15-cm. close support guns, of which the latter were sometimes carried on S.P. mountings. In the advance the tanks would move ahead of the box in two echelons, each accompanied by some of the field guns. If the enemy were met while on the move, the box would halt and take up a position for all-round defence, while the tanks deployed on a wide front and withdrew gradually to positions on either side of the box, where they would await attack. If the latter was pressed home, the wing that had been attacked would withdraw once more, past the flank of the box, to a position from which it could engage its pursuers frontally with its 7.5-cm. guns, while the 5-cm. and 8.8-cm. guns of the box engaged them in enfilade. Finally, the disengaged tanks would swing round from the other flank and engage the attackers from the rear (*see* Diagram 3).

In the attack—which usually took two or three hours to mount—the Mk. IV tanks would take up a position about 2,500 yards from the objective, and hull-down if possible, from which they could pin the defences with their machine-guns and engage any visible anti-tank guns with their 7.5-cms. Under cover of their fire 5-cm. anti-tank guns, heavy machine-guns and 15-cm. close support guns would deploy and engage the anti-tank guns of the defence. Behind this covering force the tanks would form up for the attack, followed by the box, disposed as shown in Diagram 3, with the infantry all riding in their trucks. On arrival at the objective, some of the tanks would drive straight through, the remainder staying behind and assisting the infantry to mop up. Finally, when success had been achieved, the covering force would move forward into the captured locality to stiffen the defence, and the tanks would be withdrawn and serviced near what had now become the rear face of the locality.[14]

The essence of this drill was simplicity and speed. Within the box the various units were disposed in a stereotyped pattern, with anti-tank and A.A. guns covering the flanks so that, if caught on the move, the box could be organized for all-round defence with very little loss of time. It was not thought out on the spur of the moment, but was gradually evolved after some costly "Balaclava" charges had been made against our guns without much previous reconnaissance. Nor, of course, was the idea a new one. It had been used most effectively by an earlier master of mobile warfare, Tamerlane, in his campaign across the Russian steppes.

The Gun as the Primary Tank Destroyer

"Renown" wrote someone "awaits the commander who first, in this war, restores the artillery to its prime importance upon the battlefield from which it has been ousted by heavily armoured tanks."[15] By January, 1942, it might be said, this restoration had almost been accomplished; and now, in the lull between the enemy's expulsion from Cyrenaica and his anticipated counter-offensive, steps were taken to increase the effectiveness of our anti-tank defences by applying some of the lessons learned in the recent fighting.

There was one quality in which our tanks were superior to the enemy's, and that was speed. In the 1st Armoured Division, which had relieved the 7th Armoured Division on the frontier, advantage was taken of this fact to produce a new battle drill based on the gun as the primary tank destroyer. In the desert, where movement was practically unrestricted, it was difficult to force one's opponent to give battle against his will; so a leaf was taken out of the German book and attention was directed to "luring the enemy on to the guns while the tanks move to a flank and counter-attack."[16]

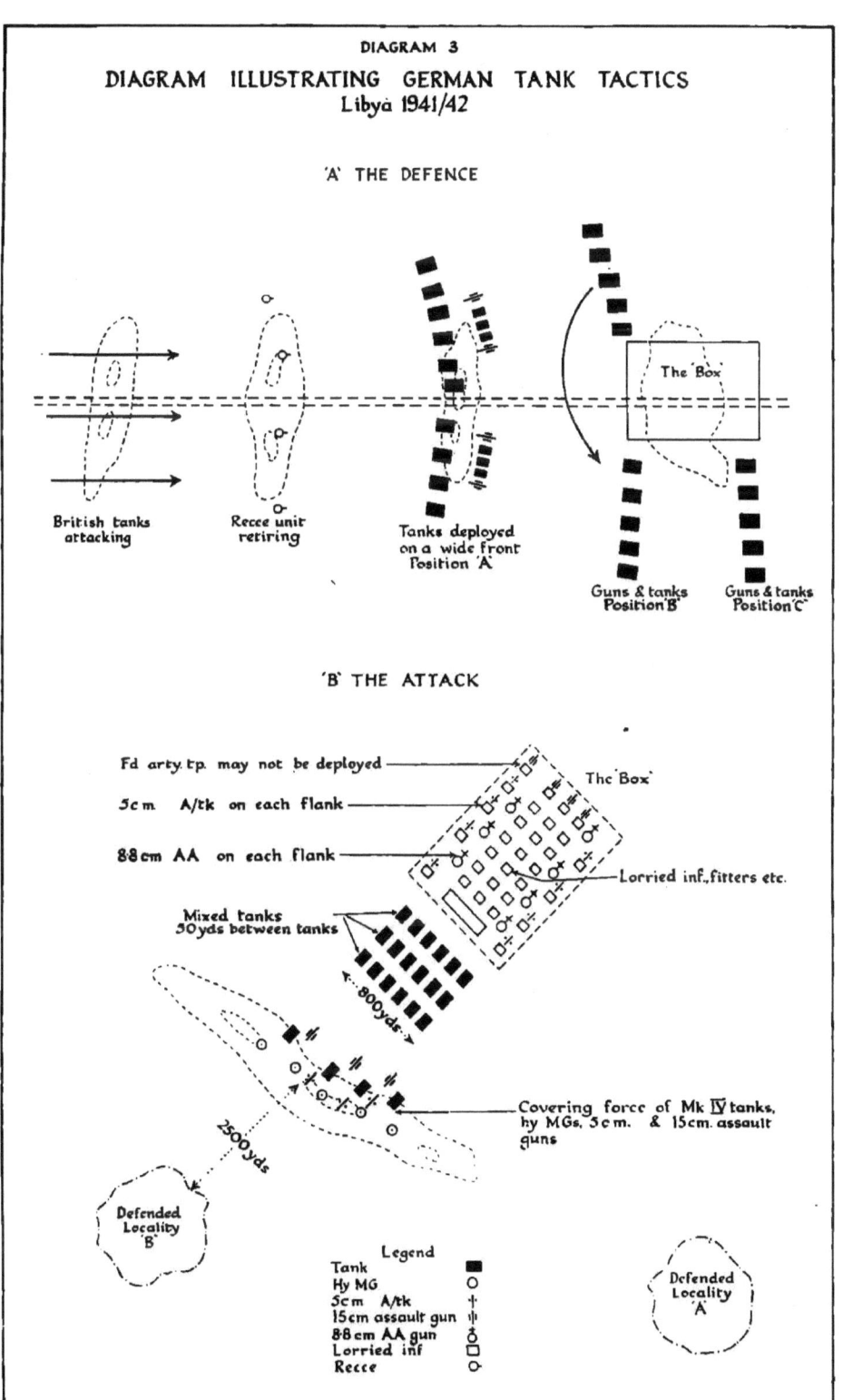

In the advance a portion of the 25-prs. were to be allotted a primary anti-tank role, and the armoured brigade was to move in arrowhead formation, each regiment having its own share of close support and primary anti-tank artillery. In the defence some 25-prs. would be allotted a primary anti-tank role whenever they could be spared, and the lay-out of all anti-tank weapons would be co-ordinated by the C.R.A. or senior R.A. commander.

The same principle had been adopted in the 4th Indian Division, where it was explicitly laid down that " in mobile operations, anti-tank defence must be based on our field artillery"([17]) Guns were invariably to be dug in, and other arms were to be disposed so as to include the defence of field gun positions. Tanks, when used in a defensive role, were to be located in rear of field gun positions, and any attempt by such supporting arms to engage enemy tanks at extreme range was forbidden.

To counter the enemy artillery preparation, field or medium artillery only was to be used, with the object, not of breaking up the attack before it got under way, but of neutralizing the fire of 5-cm. and 7.5-cm. guns in accordance with normal counter-battery methods. The intention was in fact to let the assaulting tanks come in to ranges at which their destruction could be assured. For this purpose, if conditions permitted, smoke was to be used to deny observation to the enemy and to force him to close prematurely.

In dealing with the assaulting tanks, maximum ranges for opening fire were laid down as 1,200 yards for field artillery and 800 yards for anti-tank artillery and tanks. The latter figure was however soon greatly reduced for the 2-pr (*see* p. 128). L.A.A. guns were only to engage the enemy tanks in an emergency and then not beyond a range of 400 yards. The infantry were to play no part in this tank action, their role being to deal with any enemy infantry who might be moving in co-operation with the tanks.

New Anti-Tank Dispositions

To give effect to these principles, and to counter the enemy habit of attacking gun positions from the flanks, a standard lay-out was adopted which allowed for a 360 degree arc of fire at every gun position and mutual support between troops. Troop positions were disposed in the form of a diamond with sides of about 800 yards, and any available anti-tank guns were sited on their flanks. Within the troop, guns were sited in a semi-circle at intervals of 60 to 70 yards.

As the enemy tanks approached, one of the troops not directly threatened would put down a smoke screen—if the wind was favourable—300 to 1,000 yards in front of the troop that was being attacked, thus preventing the enemy support tanks from shelling the guns from hull-down positions and allowing the remainder to be engaged at a range favourable to the 25-pr. If the wind was unfavourable, the supporting tanks would be taken on by indirect fire directed from a flank O.P.

A second troop would deal with lorried infantry both when in their trucks and after they had debussed. All other guns would withhold their fire until the assaulting tanks were within 1,200 yards; and in engaging these tanks, the opening rounds would be placed beyond rather than in front of the target, to avoid obscuration of the latter by dust. Many a good shoot, it was found, had been spoiled by the failure to observe this precaution.

In accepting a field of fire of 1,200 yards Middle East formations were departing from the original figure of 500 yards (see p. 17), which was still adhered to as the standard for other theatres.[18] The difference was the result of the peculiar topographical conditions in the desert, and it increased the need, already perceptible, for better sighting arrangements for the 25-pr. The efficacy of this gun when laid direct was reduced in a misty atmosphere —so common at dawn or dusk—owing to its dependence on the dial sight, which had a high power of magnification. To get over this difficulty, a modified open sight was introduced in January, 1942, for engaging tanks when atmospheric conditions prevented the use of the dial sight.[18]

The Misuse of the 2-Pr Portee

Though inevitable in the circumstances, this use of the 25-pr. was far from desirable. It diverted too many of the field guns from their proper role and thereby took most of the punch out of the regimental concentration.

The root cause of all the trouble was the inadequacy of the 2-pr. as an anti-tank weapon in face of modern German armour. Effective only up to 600 yards, if as far as that, it was forced to open fire at 800 yards or more in order to minimize the effects of enemy machine-gun fire. Then a Bren gun was mounted on the portee and used to induce the enemy tanks to close down. But it was no more than a palliative. The fact remained that the German tanks had the range of the 2-pr. and in open country like the desert could choose their own time to make an end of it.

Under-powered as it was, it might still have done its job if it had been available in sufficient quantities. Three regiments, each of 48 or 64 guns, to a division were required, according to the estimate of one C.R.A. at that time, to make up for the lack of natural anti-tank obstacles and the impracticability of creating artificial ones in fast-moving desert warfare.

But no such numbers were, or were ever likely to be, available; and the thinner the resources, the greater the urge to make existing equipments as mobile as possible. So the portee continued in favour, and in spite of numerous official reminders that it was not a cruiser tank, it was often so used. As a result the casualties in anti-tank units had been very heavy, and they had not been justified by the amount of damage inflicted on the enemy. Hitherto our tank losses from enemy anti-tank guns had been "out of all proportion to their losses from our anti-tank guns", and the reason for this inequality had not lain solely in the superiority of German weapons and armour. It was at least partly because the enemy grounded his anti-tank guns, dug them in, and then lured our tanks on to them.[19]

It was questionable whether the existing policy for the siting of anti-tank guns was not in need of modification. Official doctrine laid down that they should be sited singly, in mutually supporting positions—which in the desert meant about 800 yards apart—and " so disposed in depth as to take increasing toll as the hostile A.F.Vs. advance and thus bring their forward movement to a standstill."[20] But in these operations the German tanks had usually attacked in mass and it had not been possible to oppose them with an adequate volume of fire with guns so dispersed. It was therefore considered that a better method would be to site them in groups of four to six covering an area about 300 yards square.[21]

A.A. in the Ground Role

Owing to the early mastery of the air by the R.A.F., A.A. guns were not always fully occupied in their normal role, and as in December, 1940 (*see* p. 63), there was a natural eagerness to find employment for them against ground targets. Despite their inadequate laying arrangements for this purpose, some useful work was done. During the fighting round Tobruk, for example, 3.7-in. H.A.A. guns had effectively harassed enemy traffic along the by-pass and had engaged several hostile batteries. In recognition of this fact, a low angle range table was prepared and finally issued in May, 1942.

L.A.A. guns had also done good service as emergency anti-tank weapons. Though destructive effect could not be relied on above 400 yards, it was found that by firing alternate rounds of A.P. shot and H.E. shell, considerable moral effect could be obtained from the H.E. tracer, which might sometimes justify the opening of fire at a range of 700 yards.

Organization and Command of A.A. in the Field

For the first time in operations in the Middle East, a formation headquarters—Eighth Army—was provided with a B.A.A. and staff on parallel lines to the B.R.A. It was in keeping with the system that had been initiated in France in 1939 (*see* p. 34) and repeated at Cairo in May, 1940 (*see* p. 60), and it was reported at the time as having been an "unqualified success." Within the division, the L.A.A. regiment was placed under command of the C.R.A., and this was also admitted—sometimes with a faint hint of surprise on the part of A.A. unit commanders—to have worked well.

The 3-gun troop organization, though satisfactory under the conditions then obtaining, was not considered likely to produce a positive deterrent effect against a more numerous and powerful enemy. For this and other reasons it was decided that in future a L.A.A. troop should consist of 6 guns, and the divisional L.A.A. regiment of three batteries each of 18 guns.

At first the fighter landing grounds absorbed a large proportion of the available army A.A. artillery; and as each successive advance of these landing grounds might be over 100 miles, or a two-day journey for A.A. units, some 50 per cent. of the guns were out of action (on the move) for 48 hours at a time. Later, considerable A.A. resources had to be allotted to the ports of Tobruk, Derna and Benghasi to enable them to be developed; and by the time Benghasi had been captured, the army A.A. was so stretched that a L.A.A. battery had to be taken from the 4th Indian Division to assist in the defence of this place.

The presence of L.A.A. units with divisions had been of great value, though they suffered sometimes from abuse owing to their comparative novelty and a widespread ignorance of their capabilities. L.A.A. commanders were not always informed of the course and bearing of a move, or of the policy to be adopted if attacked, and were sometimes ordered to place their guns in bad tactical positions. Extravagant demands would also be made on the A.A. gunner by those whom he was supporting. Thus fire would be asked for against aircraft at 5,000 feet, and complaints would be raised that the L.A.A. gunners were "not trying" if, for the sake of accuracy, they engaged a target with single shot instead of blazing away at "auto". This was embarrassing to the gunner, who was already deeply concerned to prevent waste of ammunition by the premature engagement of targets. Owing to the absence of H.A.A. guns in divisional areas, the natural tendency to fire at aircraft that were out of range was greatly accentuated, and in the opinion of one C.O. " the waste of ammunition on aircraft flying outside the 3,500 yards self-destroying range of the 40-mm. by L.A.A. as a whole is prodigious, sometimes almost criminal."[22]

Demand for a 20-mm. L.A.A. Gun

During December, when enemy air activity had begun to increase again—though still confined largely to forward areas—it was found that casualties from low-flying attacks with cannon guns and machine-guns were proportionately greater than those from dive bombing or level bombing attacks. Such attacks were also more difficult to deal with. Appearing suddenly over a crest at heights of 30 to 100 feet, or diving out of the sun, the enemy fighters would come in at great speeds and take continuous and violent avoiding action, which made them extremely difficult to hit, especially as there was no early warning system.

Owing to the mobility of the operations, and the need to keep down the number of vehicles to an absolute minimum, predictors had been left behind in most cases; and in any event they were of doubtful value against this type of target. Existing forward area sights, on the other hand, were designed to deal with targets at a range of 1,000 to 1,500 yards, and with speeds not exceeding 250 m.p.h., whereas fighters were now attaining speeds of 400 m.p.h. and, owing to the absence of H.A.A. guns in divisional areas, Bofors were required to engage targets up to 3,000 yards. A new and enlarged forward area sight was designed to deal with this situation, but there were some who felt that the only satisfactory answer to the low-flying attack was the introduction of a 20-mm. gun to supplement the Bofors, and a demand for such a weapon was put forward by 30 Corps.[23]

Protection of L.A.A. Guns

One of the most vexed questions with which the L.A.A. gunner had to deal was the degree of protection and concealment that was possible, and desirable, for his guns in the field. Field artillery commanders who had known what it was to be attacked from the air without the means of retaliation were at first sometimes perplexed by the A.A. gunner's predilection for hill-tops, which in the desert were not only conspicuous but often also unfit for digging. Then the disillusionment experienced by the A.A. units in Greece and Crete had tended for the moment to swing opinion to the opposite extreme. Next came Tobruk and the defeat of the dive bombers; and now, with fighter cover once more over their heads and the enemy in retreat before them, the A.A. gunners acquired a renewed confidence in the protective power of their own weapons. Deception was not neglected. On the contrary, a new and mobile form of dummy position was devised that could be carried about in large quantities and erected in about five minutes. Protection was also insisted on whenever circumstances permitted. But, in one unit at any rate, a gun pit was no longer regarded as indispensable. When movement was frequent, they said, it was better not to dig a pit and make the Bofors conspicuous. If it was dug as a matter of course, the men would often be tired out when the nature of their job required speed, alertness and quick reactions. Psychologically a pit was comforting, but when the detachments were used to pits, the reaction of having to fight in the open, which was normal during movement, was all the more disquieting. " The answer, therefore, appears to be, build breastworks where tank attacks are likely, and only dig pits when it is certain that the troop will settle for more than 48 hours in any one position."[22]

Conclusion

" This was probably one of the fastest-moving and most exciting battles that had ever been fought "[24], and the attention given to the acceleration of fire plans had no doubt been well repaid. But there were still some glaring weaknesses in the equipment and handling of the artillery.

In the armoured battle, heavy casualties had sometimes been suffered from encounters with enemy anti-tank screens, which were met unexpectedly and which could not be neutralized owing to the absence or misuse of the supporting guns. Trouble also arose from the use of infantry and anti-tank guns apart from the armour, so that they were not present when required to take over and hold ground won by tanks, which could not therefore be withdrawn for maintenance and resting of the crews.[25]

Owing to the nature of the operations, attacks on prepared positions had been few. Where they had occurred, artillery support had been hampered by the difficulty of locating the enemy strongholds, which, like our own, had no parapet and merged imperceptibly with the surrounding desert. Hence area shoots alone were possible in support of the attack, and success was more than usually dependent upon the closeness with which the infantry and tanks could follow up the artillery concentrations.

After the failure at Sidi Omar (see p. 105) much thought was given to this problem in the 4th Indian Division and an improved technique was worked out for the support of " I " tanks in the future. Its outstanding features were more close support for the tanks, more attention to counter-battery work during the initial stages of the breakthrough, and a combination of timed programme and observed covering fire for the subsequent follow-through by the infantry.

The arrangements made for the co-operation of H.M.'s ships in the coastal sector had not been a great success. During the period of these operations the Royal Navy had been busily engaged at sea and it had not therefore been possible to allot suitable ships to co-operate with the Army. Moreover, owing to the menace of air attack, bombardments could only be carried out at night. The naval F.O.O. was therefore never used as such, and it appeared unlikely that he could ever have functioned successfully from corps headquarters. A bombardment, it was found, took 24 hours to arrange, and the F.O.O. had to remain at corps headquarters until times and frequencies had been fixed. This meant that he could not reach the forward areas in time to observe, and it was clear that if the F.O.O. party was to work properly, the Naval Liaison Officer should in future be with divisional, not corps, headquarters.

Air support had undoubtedly been very helpful in a general way and had sometimes produced material as well as moral effects. But it still took three hours from the initiation of a request for support to the arrival of the bombers, owing—among other causes—to the distance of the bomber landing grounds from the target area and to delays in communication resulting from the unsuitability of the existing wireless equipment for work on the move. And " only one thing could make the bomb-line system work, namely the demonstration of such accuracy by the R.A.F. light bombers that the local commanders could have absolute trust in them. This happy state of affairs had not yet been reached."[26]

The outstanding feature of this period, however, had been the failure of the 2-pr. gun. Driven to unorthodoxy by lack of range and hitting power, our anti-tank gunners had suffered heavy casualties without achieving commensurate results. The temptation to misuse the portee carriage had perhaps been checked, but pending the arrival of the 6-pr., the 25-pr. had had to be called in to bolster up the anti-tank defences. Thus one unorthodoxy had been replaced by another, and artillery tactics as a whole continued to suffer. Seldom indeed had so much hung on a G.S. decision as on that taken in 1940 when the production of the 2-pr. had been given priority over that of the 6-pr. (see p. 67).

List of References

[1] R.A.T.M. War No. 4 of June 1941.
[2] R.A.T.M. War No. 5 of January 1942.
[3] A.T.M. No. 40 of July 1941.
[4] A.T.M. No. 41 of October 1941.
[5] Arty. Training, Vol. II, Pamphlet No. 3, 1941, Sec. 6 (3).
[6] A.T.M. No. 38 of February 1941.
[7] War Diary, C.R.A. 70 Div., November 1941.
[8] Arty. Training, Vol. II, Pamphlet No. 3, 1941, Sec. 7 (4).
[9] War Diary, C.C.R.A., 13 Corps, October 1941.
[10] Despatch by C-in-C, M.E.F., November 1941 to August 1942, p. 2.
[11] Lessons from Cyrenaica, No. 12, by 1st South African Bde.
[12] Lessons from Cyrenaica, No. 9, by Eighth Army.
[13] Telegram from V.I.C.G.S. to W.O. from Cairo, 22nd March 1942.
[14] Journal of the R.A., Vol. LXIX, No. 4, pp. 310-312.
[15] A.T.M. No. 42 of January 1942.
[16] H.Q.R.A. 1 Armd. Div. Training Instruction No. 1 of 20th January 1942.
[17] 4 Ind. Div. Instructions on " Fire Control, A.Tk. Defence ", 23rd December 1941.
[18] R.A.T.M. War No. 5 of January 1942.
[19] R.A. 50 Div. Trg. Instr. No. 4 of 22nd March 1942.
[20] Arty. Training, Vol. II, Pamphlet No. 3, 1941, Sec. 13.
[21] Report by B.R.A., Eighth Army.
[22] War Diary, 57 L.A.A. Regiment, December 1941.
[23] Report by 30 Corps on Operations, December 1941.
[24] " Our Armoured Forces ", by Lt.-Gen. Sir Gifford Le Q. Martel, p. 129.
[25] *Ibid*, p. 160.
[26] " The Desert Air Force ", by Roderic Owen, p. 90.

CHAPTER VIII

THE RETREAT TO EL ALAMEIN

PLATES RELEVANT TO THIS CHAPTER

Nos.
15. The 6-pr. A.Tk. gun.
16. The 17-pr. A.Tk. gun.
17. The 4.5-in. medium gun.
18. The 6-in. C.A. gun on Arrol Withers platform.

Reorganization of the Armoured and Infantry Divisions

The disappointing results of our armoured offensive in November and December, 1941, had led to much argument. It was agreed that failure had generally been a result of inferior tactics as well as of inferior equipment, and official opinion inclined to the view that " our existing divisional and brigade organization did not allow of that very close co-operation on the battlefield between the armoured corps, artillery and infantry which was essential to success."([1]) Hence a remedy was sought in the reorganization of British formations in the Middle East.

The main idea was to give every brigade—armoured, motorized and infantry—its own permanent allotment of artillery and engineers. In the armoured division this meant the abolition of the support group and the reorganization of the division into one armoured and one motorized infantry brigade group. At the same time the appointment of a C.R.A. was finally authorized, in April, 1942.

In the infantry division, curiously enough, the effect of this new organization on the position of the C.R.A. was just the reverse. Although in the armoured division his existence was at last officially recognized, in the infantry division he was suddenly threatened with extinction. Since he was now left without any unit under his immediate command, there was a tendency in certain quarters to restrict him to the technical training of field regiments and the allocation of artillery personnel. Simultaneously there was a move to abolish the appointment of C.C.R.A. on the grounds that, under modern conditions, army field regiments were invariably placed under command of divisions and there was therefore nothing for the C.C.R.A. to command. His advisory functions could, it was suggested, be adequately performed by the Brigadier, General Staff, who would be capable of supplying the corps commander with such information as he required on R.A. matters.([2])

Both these proposals were successfully resisted. With regard to the C.R.A., it was pointed out that although in the desert he might rarely have to take command of the divisional artillery as a whole, there was no knowing when centralization of control might again become necessary, and it was therefore important that every C.R.A. should be able to practise himself in the exercise of his normal functions.

The same argument applied to the C.C.R.A., and in addition both commanders were soon to become responsible for A.A. defence within their own formations. In May, 1942, the divorce of A.A. from field artillery was terminated and it was laid down that, in any field force, the M.G.R.A.,

Plate 9—The 25-pr.

Plate 10—**The Mountains at Keren.**

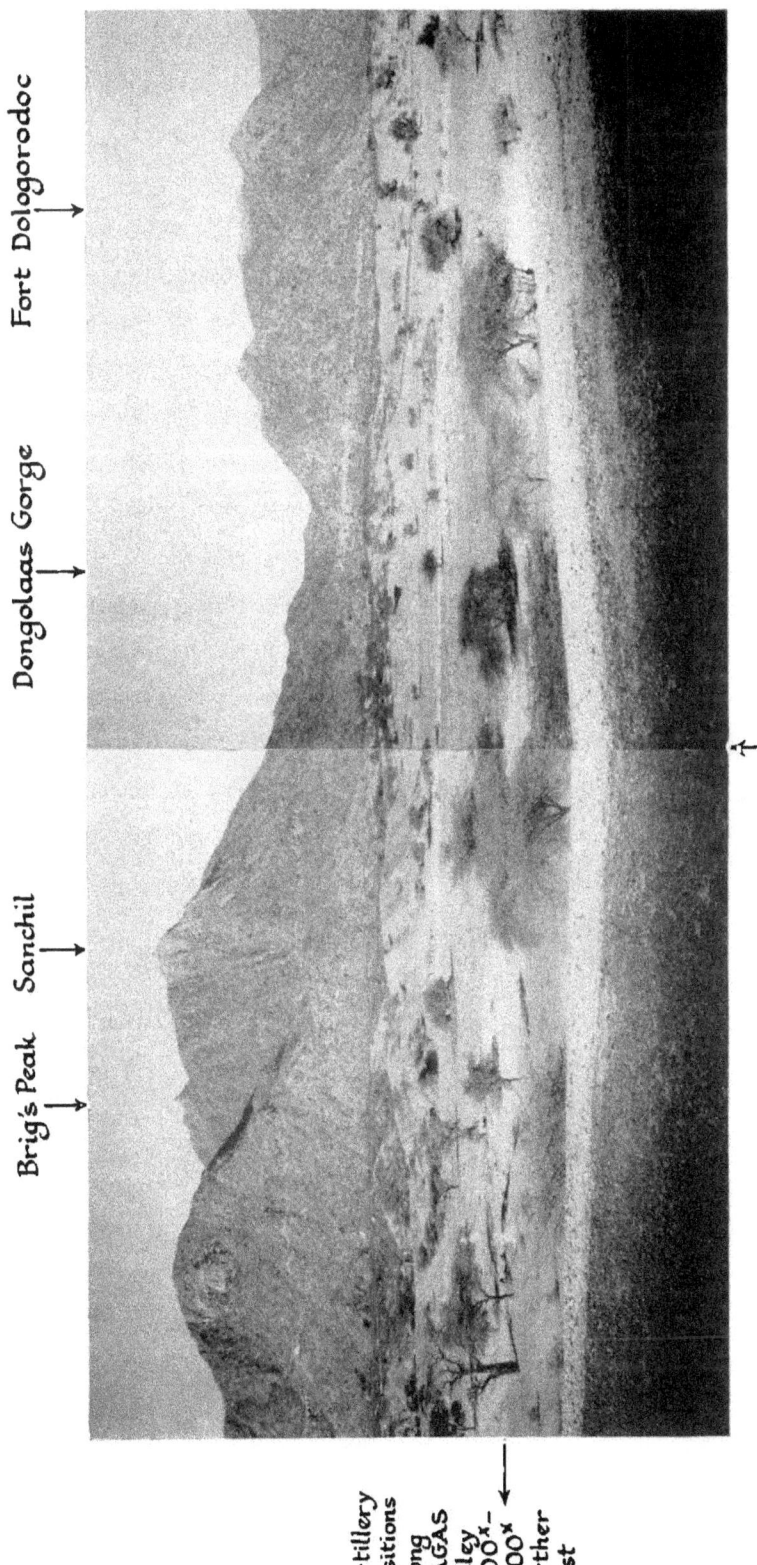

Plate 11—View of Italian positions at Keren from 4 and 5 Indian Division gun areas.

Plate 12—**The 2-pr. A Tk Portee.**

Plate 13—The 3·7-in. HAA gun.

Plate 14—The German 8·8-cm. gun.

Plate 15—**The 6-pr. A Tk gun.**

Plate 16—The 17-pr. A Tk gun.

B.R.A., C.C.R.A. and C.R.A. were to be responsible for advising their respective commanders on the employment of A.A. units and for the co-ordination of all artillery resources in the formation.(³)

At the same time—and partly, at least, because of the shortage of manpower—it was decided that anti-tank regiments should be broken up and their guns distributed among R.H.A. and field regiments. A start was made with the artillery of the armoured divisions, and as the 6-pr. had now begun to arrive in the forward areas, the reorganization of the 25-pr regiments was made to coincide with the re-equipment of anti-tank batteries. It was not, however, until much later that the process could be completed, and then the 2-pr. had to be retained in several batteries owing to the shortage of 6-prs. There were other units besides the artillery—notably the motorized infantry battalions of the armoured divisions—who had strong claims upon the new weapons, whose rate of appearance was inevitably delayed by the hazards of a long sea journey and the difficulties of reassembly and testing after disembarkation.

Jock Columns Again Active

With the entry of Japan into the war in December, 1941, all hope of carrying the offensive into Tripolitania had vanished and a situation had arisen similar to that of the year before. The object now was to keep a watch on the enemy's movements, to prevent his reconnoitring our own positions, and to harass him generally. For this purpose the Jock column was again brought into use. The 1st Support Group, which had taken over from the 7th Support Group, had been quickly initiated into the methods of its predecessor, and between it and the 201st Guards Brigade some eight small columns, each based on a 25-pr. battery, were formed to cover the 25 odd miles of front. In addition there was with the Guards Brigade a battery of medium artillery, which was brought forward for the engagement of hostile batteries and strong points.

For about ten days these small offensive columns kept up a show of force along the frontier, moving out at first light from their night leaguers and occupying gun positions and O.Ps. from which to harass any movements seen in the enemy's lines. Then, on the night 20th-21st January, 1942, Rommel began his anticipated counter-offensive. With a force of about 35,000 men and 100 tanks he broke through our defensive screen and moved at great speed down the main road, undeterred by the fire of our guns, which at Agedabia poured some 3,000 × 25-pr. shells into his advancing columns without being able to check them.

Having reached the line Tmimi—Mechili, however, the enemy was in no condition to pursue his offensive, and for the next four months he remained with outposts on this line and his main forces some distance in rear of it. Once again, therefore, conditions became favourable for the employment of Jock columns, and the need for offensive action happened at this time to be particularly acute. The situation at Malta was becoming desperate. Supplies were running out and it was evident that the enemy were preparing for an assault. Having lost the airfields in the Benghasi and Derna areas, the R.A.F. were no longer able to defend the island in strength, and the only hope was to replenish its ammunition and supplies by sea before the Axis attack was launched.

For this purpose a large convoy was despatched in March, and to cover its final approach to the island, the Eighth Army was ordered to undertake a limited offensive against the enemy's forward landing grounds at Tmimi and Martuba. Resources did not permit an attempt to capture and hold the airfields, so resort was made to the 25-pr. to deny their use to the enemy. Martuba, for example, was to be dealt with by a field battery, with suitable escort.

If it did nothing else, this raid attracted to itself a considerable number of enemy aircraft and thus diverted their attention from the convoy. But the weakness in A.A.—and anti-tank—defence, which was an unavoidable feature of the Jock columns, became very evident in operations of this nature and gave rise to much criticism. It was clear, the critics thought, from the experience of the past two years that these columns could not press home an attack against anything but very weak resistance, nor could they deny ground to the enemy for more than a very limited time. Moreover, their continuous employment led to dispersion of resources and imposed a heavy strain on commanders, troops and vehicles, especially in the artillery.([4])

Their supporters, however, still claimed that they were the only possible means of waging an active war in the desert; and to the counter claim that they were vulnerable and liable to quick annihilation they would reply by quoting General Campbell's dictum: "You can always go south in the desert." There were even some gunner officers who preferred to dispense with an infantry escort altogether and thus avoid the necessity of having to provide anti-tank defence for a larger area; for at this time, it should be remembered, the infantry had no weapon of their own that was effective against enemy tanks.

On one point at least all were agreed. So far as enemy tanks were concerned, the role of the Jock column was defensive, not offensive. "A column" it was said "does NOT go out to destroy tanks but to destroy 'soft-skinned' troops."([5]) Yet it must be ready to defend itself against tanks, and it might on occasion be used as a bait to entice the enemy armour back on to prepared defences.

The Development of the Defensive Box

On 2nd February, the decision had been taken to stand on the Gazala line and to hold Tobruk as a forward base for the subsequent renewal of the offensive. For that purpose the Eighth Army now began to dispose itself in a series of localities, sited and prepared for all-round defence, which, in continuation of an idea that had already become prevalent during the preceding period, were popularly known as "boxes". The basic principles of the system were that boxes should be within supporting distance of each other and of the armoured formations that were held in reserve to deal with the enemy tanks.

Within the box the core of the defence was provided by the field artillery, the anti-tank guns, both R.A. and infantry, as a rule being distributed around the perimeter. The difficulty was to provide the requisite amount of artillery. "I was satisfied" said the C.-in-C. "that the Eighth Army had enough infantry to deal with any situation likely to arise. . . . But I wished that it could have more field artillery, as there was no reserve of guns at the disposal of the two corps commanders or of General Ritchie himself."([6]) In fact there was, in the whole of the Middle East, on 31st May, a reserve of only 24 × 25-prs., which represented no more than 2 per cent. of the equipments that would be in this theatre by August, 1942.

The worst shortage, however, was as usual in anti-tank guns. On 27th April, the M.G.R.A. reported a total deficiency of 1,039 of these equipments, of which 120 were due to the Eighth Army. To make matters worse, many units, both R.A. and infantry, were in the process of changing from the 2-pr. to the 6-pr., and many of them had not yet had time to become really familiar with the new weapons.

It was therefore more important than ever that full use should be made of what guns there were; and here a difficulty arose—largely, it seems, through the excessive length of front to be held in relation to the number of troops available. (50 Division, for example, held a front of about 30 miles.) In order to obtain the necessary depth, defended localities were sometimes prepared on a battalion basis, with boxes measuring about 3,000 yards around the perimeter and situated some 4-5,000 yards apart; that is, within field artillery supporting range of each other.

At no time convenient from an artillery point of view, this dispersion of units was doubly inconvenient now, when field guns were required to assume a primary anti-tank role in order to compensate for the shortage of 6-prs. Later on, after much experience had been gained in the use of this kind of defended area, a specimen lay-out was produced for an infantry brigade group (*see* Diagram 4). The ideal situation for such a lay-out was inside a depression, or "saucer", so placed that it could not be overlooked from hull-down positions within 7.5-cm. range, or from points suitable for use as artillery O.Ps. The 25-prs. would then be sited in mutually supporting positions inside the saucer, with the anti-tank guns around the rim. But such positions were, naturally, not easy to find.

The Battle for Tobruk, 27th May—10th June, 1942

The efficacy of these boxes was soon to be put to the test. While the Eighth Army had been preparing for a resumption of the offensive early in June, Rommel was being heavily reinforced from Italy, and on 27th May he himself launched a powerful attack.

His plan was to move the bulk of his armour round the southern end of our minefields at Bir Hacheim, whence it was to move north on El Adem, destroy our armour, and then turn west against the rear of the Gazala position. Meanwhile the Italians were to capture Bir Hacheim and to carry out a frontal attack on the Gazala position in conjunction with the armoured attack from the east.

The start of this attack came as a surprise. The 3rd Indian Motor Brigade and an Indian field regiment, which had recently been brought up from Egypt, were still in the process of digging themselves in in a box S.E. of Bir Hacheim. Two of the 25-pr. batteries had been given a primary anti-tank role, and there were in addition 32 anti-tank guns, of which eight had been kept in mobile reserve. The position was naturally a strong one, but mines had not yet been laid and the guns, which had only arrived in the box at 1700 hrs. the previous evening, had not had time to register before dark.

DIAGRAM 4

Diagrammatic lay-out for an Infantry Brigade Group Defended Area, comprising three mutually supporting battalion areas in open country.

Note:- One Army Tank Squadron and one MG Company are included in the lay-out

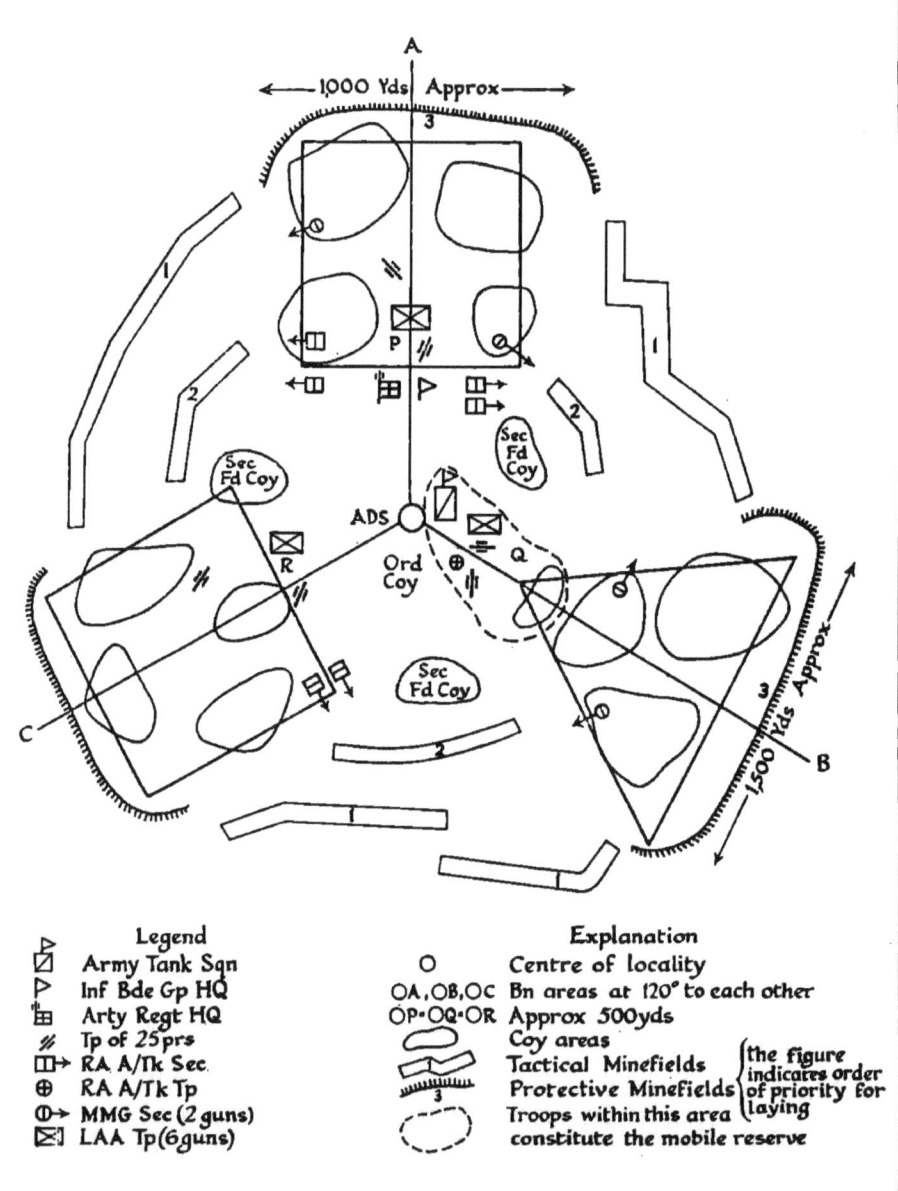

Legend		Explanation	
▷	Army Tank Sqn	O	Centre of locality
⊠	Inf Bde Gp HQ	OA, OB, OC	Bn areas at 120° to each other
▷	Arty Regt HQ	OP·OQ·OR	Approx 500 yds
⫽	Tp of 25 prs	⬭	Coy areas
⊡→	RA A/Tk Sec	⌇⌇⌇	Tactical Minefields
⊕	RA A/Tk Tp	⌇⌇⌇3	Protective Minefields (the figure indicates order of priority for laying)
⊙→	MMG Sec (2 guns)	⬭	Troops within this area constitute the mobile reserve
⊠	LAA Tp (6 guns)		

When, at dawn on 27th May, the Brigade Commander found himself confronted by practically the whole of the Afrika Corps, he had to make a rapid appreciation, and having decided to stand his ground, he resolved that he, not the enemy, should begin the battle. The field regiment was ordered to open fire with all its guns and it proceeded at once to engage the enemy M.T. and artillery. The enemy, inconvenienced but not checked, overran the box and swept on, though not before the field regiment had taken a heavy toll of their tanks. In particular, one troop, holding its fire until the range had closed to about 600 yards, claimed to have knocked out 21 enemy tanks before it was overrun.

The next box to go, that of the 150th Infantry Brigade at Ualeb, had been occupied much longer; but it was in a very isolated position between the southern end of the main Gazala line and the Free French position at Bir Hacheim, and the soil was limestone rock, which could not be dug without the aid of a power excavator. Its garrison was therefore forced to fight at a disadvantage and was eventually overrun.

In the hope of retaining the initiative and blocking the retreat of the enemy armour, an attempt was made to recover the lost ground and repair the gaps in the minefield. Owing to the relative weakness of our armoured forces, it was decided that the only chance of success now lay in an infantry attack on the enemy salient supported by as many guns as could be made available.([7]) One R.H.A. and three field regiments were concentrated for this purpose, and under cover of a heavy artillery bombardment the 10th Indian Infantry Brigade, advancing in the moonlight during the early hours of 5th June, seized the first objective with little or no opposition.

But it had been a "blow in the air". The enemy had withdrawn his forward troops either before or during the preliminary bombardment, and the 22nd Armoured Brigade, following through in the daylight, was engaged first by artillery and then by increasing numbers of tanks and anti-tank guns. Little progress could be made and as the day wore on the armour was withdrawn and the 10th Indian Infantry Brigade, with its three supporting field regiments and the 22nd Armoured Brigade Support Group, with one R.H.A. regiment, were left to hold the ground that had been won.

This ground contained no "saucer", but was a long, gradual slope, and the guns were therefore very exposed. They were also very congested, and were overlooked from a ridge that ran around the western, or enemy's, side of the defended area. The soil was not suitable for digging, and there were no mines or wire to protect the four separate boxes into which the defences were divided. These positions had been hastily occupied, without a thorough preliminary reconnaissance, and there was no co-ordination of the anti-tank defences.

When, therefore, the enemy resumed his attack at first light on 6th June, the situation soon became desperate. The British armour was unable to intervene in the battle in time to save the position, and the whole force, including four field regiments of 64 guns and more than 100 anti-tank and L.A.A. guns, was lost.

Thus an all-too-rare attempt to use the concentrated fire power of the artillery had ended in disaster. But we still had air superiority and at Knightsbridge and elsewhere there were boxes that were well organized and within supporting distance of the remains of our armour. The Knightsbridge Box, established after a three day reconnaissance of an area covering some 50 square miles, stood on high ground that had a shallow depression in the middle and that could only be overlooked from a distance. The saucer was pear-shaped, about half-a-mile long and a quarter of a mile wide, and within it positions had been dug for the garrison, which consisted of one R.H.A. regiment, an anti-tank battery, two L.A.A. troops, and one battalion plus one company of infantry. The soil was sandy and every vehicle was dug down nearly to roof level in its own narrow pit, so that the field of fire across the box was clear and the position invisible, or nearly so, from all but the air. A thin surround of dannert wire, and still thinner minefields consisting of old mines dug up from Tobruk, covered the perimeter, within which were sited machine-gun positions and platoon and artillery O.Ps. Anti-tank guns (6-prs.) were emplaced 200 yards behind the perimeter, with a core of four 25-pr. troop positions and six L.A.A. (Bofors) guns in the shallow saucer. Later, two 3.7-in. H.A.A. guns were added to the defences and did useful work in a ground role.

For days, while the armoured battle raged around it, this box defied the attempts of the enemy to overrun or overawe it. Attacked by tanks, and bombarded both from the ground and from the air, its garrison was never silenced and was withdrawn only when a general retirement had been decided on.

On 18th June, the enemy captured Gambut and with it the only airfield from which fighter aircraft could operate for the close defence of Tobruk. On 20th June the attack on Tobruk itself began.

The troops available for its defence were more numerous than the year before; one more motor and three more infantry battalions, the same number of field guns, nearly three times as many medium guns—29 instead of 10—and half again as many anti-tank guns—41 × 2-prs. and 25 × 6-prs. instead of 19 × 2-prs. and 25 × 37-mms. But as the holding of the fortress had not been part of the original plan, half the garrison, including most of the artillery, had been used for the fighting up in front and, when hurried back into their defensive positions, arrived piecemeal and tired and were in no way ready to meet an immediate and determined attack.

Information regarding these operations has yet to be sifted, and a comparison of the artillery dispositions and tactics with those of the year before, interesting though it would be, is at present scarcely possible. Whatever the cause, the collapse was rapid and the enemy armour, breaking through the perimeter, destroyed the field guns in their defensive positions one after another.

Reorganization of the Division into Battle Groups

The immediate reaction to these disasters was a revulsion of feeling against the box and dissatisfaction with the existing organization of the infantry division. Too much time, it was thought, had been spent " digging holes in the desert " to the prejudice of training, and there was too much " soft stuff " in the infantry division that served only as an encumbrance in a desert battle.([6])

In any case some reorganization was necessary, as formations had become disorganized and, owing to the heavy losses in guns, there was a great shortage of field and medium artillery, of which the latter was now reduced to 8 × 4.5-in. guns and 16 × 155-mm. hows. The first requirement was to build up as quickly as possible a hard hitting, highly trained battle force for mobile operations, which could act as " our mainstay both in offence and defence."([9]) For this purpose the remaining armour was to be regrouped temporarily into one armoured division of two armoured brigades, each of two mixed regiments, and one division of two motor brigades and one light regiment of Stuart tanks. Artillery was to be provided, when available, on the basis of eight or ten field batteries to each division plus the normal anti-tank element.

Infantry divisions were to be reorganized forthwith into battle groups, each to consist of one battery of 25-prs. and one infantry battalion, less two companies, with ancillary troops. Two or three of these groups would be commanded by a brigadier with a skeleton brigade headquarters, and three brigade groups by a skeleton divisional headquarters. The idea was that each division should establish three or four " defended O.P. areas ", which should be held by infantry and anti-tank guns and be not more than 10,000 yards apart, and that within this framework the rest of the division should operate as battle groups.([10])

The Retreat to El Alamein.

The problem now was to find a secure position on which, with our reduced forces, we could finally check the enemy's advance. What was needed was a " Torres Vedras," and nowhere other than at El Alamein, already reconnoitred on General Wavell's instructions in June, 1941, could this requirement be satisfied. Here the tired Eighth Army could rest, with its right flank on the sea and its left flank on the impassable Qattara depression, while it made good its losses and prepared to turn the tables upon an almost equally exhausted enemy.

For some time the situation remained critical and on 1st July occurred what might be described as the last battle of the boxes. The 18th Indian Infantry Brigade Group was occupying a box in the Deir El Shein depression near the west end of the Ruweisat Ridge. A composite field regiment, with a total of 23 × 25-prs.—had moved into the box at about 0700 hrs. the same day, in anticipation of the despatch of a mobile column, or—to use the newly approved nomenclature—a battle group. There was therefore a large amount of transport in the area, which could not be adequately dispersed in the space available, and the rocky nature of the ground made digging very difficult. The total number of anti-tank guns available, including those of the infantry, was 33 and they were distributed in the usual manner between the three battalion sectors of the perimeter.

Shortly after the guns had moved into position, the enemy began to shell the box from the north, and as the fire became more intense, tanks appeared from the same direction and, under cover of a dust storm, broke through the defences on that side. A counter-attack, supported by seven Valentines, drove them back temporarily to the perimeter, but it was impossible to save the box without outside assistance, which was not forthcoming. By late evening the whole position had been overrun. " Only one infantry battalion survived the attack, but the stand made by the brigade certainly gained valuable time for the organization of the El Alamein line generally."([11])

The matter was clinched on the two following days, when field artillery fire effectively blocked the gap left by the loss of Deir El Shein. Thereafter the initiative passed to the Eighth Army, and between 10th and 27th July four separate attacks were made, in each of which some ground was gained. On no occasion, however, could the initial success be followed up owing to the lack of fresh and well-trained troops with which to maintain the momentum of the attack. On the other hand, the artillery—except medium—available was now numerous, and with its aid the ground taken was securely held. Several strong enemy counter-attacks were broken up, sometimes by 25-pr. concentrations and sometimes by anti-tank guns operating in front of the armoured brigades.([12])

Thus by the end of July, the situation had become more or less stabilized, and a full month was to elapse before Rommel made his next and last desperate attempt to force a break-through.

The Race Between Gun and Armour

Throughout this fighting the Germans had continued to enjoy a marked superiority in tank and anti-tank equipments. Only some 240 of our 630 tanks had a gun heavier than the 2-pr. or 37-mm., whereas of the enemy tanks nearly all had 5-cm. or 7.5 cm. guns. The 6-pr. anti-tank gun was also only available in limited numbers, and most of these did not arrive until the very eve of Rommel's offensive, so that they had to be used in battle without preliminary practice or trials.

Owing to the delay in the production of the 6-pr., emergency measures had been taken to increase the performance of the 2-pr. By the introduction of a lighter and specially strengthened shot, and by the fitting of a ballistic device in the form of an unrifled muzzle attachment, it was found possible to achieve a very large increase in hitting power. But this modification, known as the " Littlejohn converson ", did not take effect in time to be of use to the R.A.

Meanwhile the Germans had been increasing the strength of their protective armour. Indeed, as early as April, 1941—that is, about eight months before the 6-pr. had begun to come off production, and a year before it had reached the Eighth Army—the British authorities had decided that, to keep pace with the probable development of tank armour, a further large increase would have to be made in the hitting power of the new anti-tank gun.

As with the 2-pr., attempts were first made to improve the penetration of the existing projectile. There were three ways in which that could be done: by increasing the M.V., by the use of a ballistic cap to increase the performance of the projectile, and by improving the material of which the A.P. shot was made. Eventually, however, it was agreed that the correct solution was to increase the calibre of the gun. By mid-April, 1941, the design of a new 17-pr. 3-in. tank and anti-tank gun had been initiated. It was to have a muzzle velocity of 3,000 feet per second and a penetrative capacity of 125 mms. at 600 yards, and for anti-tank purposes it was to be mounted on a split trail carriage with a 60 degree traverse, the whole weighing about $2\frac{1}{2}$ tons. A wooden mock-up of this equipment was ready by August, 1941, and in view of the urgency of getting production started, an immediate order was placed for 500 equipments without waiting for a pilot model to be made and tried out. It was hoped that the first 200 of these equipments would be ready by the end of 1942, and as they could not be accommodated in any existing tank turret, it was decided to issue them to corps anti-tank regiments, R.A.

With the introduction of the 17-pr. and the provision of high velocity shot for all British anti-tank guns, the advantages so long enjoyed by the Germans were about to be taken from them (*see* Table F). But the immediate military situation was serious and something had to be done to tide over the interval that must elapse before the production of the 17-pr. got into its swing. With this object in view, 100 old 3-in. 20-cwt. A.A. guns were collected, provided with a special 12½ lb. shot, and mounted half in Churchill tanks and half on 17-pr. carriages, the production of which was in advance of that of the guns. The Churchill mounting was handicapped by its small internal traverse—only 7 degrees—and the guns so mounted were allotted for home defence only. Of the remaining 50 on 17-pr. carriages, 25 were allotted to the Middle East and 25 to Home Forces.

Some Further Modifications of Anti-Tank Tactics

TABLE F

Comparative Table of British and German Anti-Tank Guns, 1942/43

Gun	Plate	Range (Yards)	Penetration (mm) 30° angle of attack
5-cm. German	Homogeneous ...	500	65
		1,000	53
8·8-cm. German ...	do. ...	500	112
		1,000	103
		2,000	86
6 pr. British	do. ...	500	75
		1,000	63
17 pr. British ...	do. ...	500	123
		1,000	113
		2,000	93
25 pr. British	do. ...	500	62
		1,000	54

The tactical effect of the increasing thickness of frontal tank armour was to induce the anti-tank gunner to engage his target from a flank rather than head-on. Thus the basic principles of anti-tank defence had been increased from two to three: defilade, enfilade and depth.

During the previous period there had been a tendency to use anti-tank guns for protecting the flanks of the field guns. This was now discouraged and a return was made to the old principle that the field and anti-tank gun lay-outs should be complementary, the former adding depth to the anti-tank dispositions as a whole. For the local protection of a field artillery troop, use was made of medium machine-guns. Sited one on each flank of the troop, these guns would help to keep the enemy tanks closed down and would engage enemy infantry that might be riding on them or following up the attack in lorries.

The 25-pr. was, however, still the backbone of the defence and the diamond (or square) formation of troops within the regiment remained the rule. Experience had shown the danger of the isolated box, and for the future it was laid down that brigade defended areas were to be within anti-tank supporting distance of each other; that is, not more than 2,000 yards from outer perimeter to outer perimeter.

In the last resort artillery personnel must, it was obvious, be prepared to deal with enemy tanks and other units that had succeeded in penetrating the gun position area. It followed that the issue of personal weapons to field artillery units could no longer be delayed (*see* p. 73). In June, 1942, it was agreed by the War Office that in all such units every man should have either a pistol, a machine carbine or a rifle; and within each unit special tank-hunting parties were to be trained.

In the siting and handling of anti-tank guns the two main problems remained the same: to reconcile the conflicting claims of all-round defence and concentration of fire at the vital points, and to decide when to take advantage of the maximum range of the gun and when to withhold fire in order to make certain of a kill. With regard to opening ranges, the figures now laid down were 500 yards for the 2-pr. and 800 yards for the 6-pr.[13] But these were a guide only and each individual gun detachment would usually have its own instructions based on local conditions and on the principle that "the closer the tank the safer the gun." Once battle had been joined and there was reason to believe that other tanks would not enter the area, all guns were free to engage any tanks within maximum range—*i.e.* 600 yards for the 2-pr. and 1,600 yards for the 6-pr.[14]

For the support of a tank attack, German doctrine, advocated but not much practised by us in 1941, was now adhered to. According to this doctrine the primary role of the anti-tank gun was to cover the flanks of the attack, and, once the objective had been taken, to assist the infantry in the consolidation of the position.

When supporting infantry, the chief problem was the follow-up in the night attack. It was found inadvisable for anti-tank units to advance into a position until it had been secured by the infantry and guides had been sent back to lead the guns in to company areas, where they would be put on the ground and resited as early as possible the next morning. Even this, however, was difficult if the force was in close contact with the enemy, especially with the 6-pr., which could not be manhandled over large distances and which was very conspicuous either when towed or carried portee.

For all the above tasks firing from the portee was now strongly discouraged. In defensive positions guns were to be dug in and concealed, and portees to be taken clear of the position. In the attack guns were to be grounded and towed at least from the forming-up area. For protecting O.Ps., column headquarters and "B" echelons, or as a mobile reserve in a defensive position, for engaging the flank of an enemy attack or shepherding it into the main gun zones, the use of the portee was still allowed; but even for these tasks it was generally agreed that the gun could do better if fired from the ground.

Medium Artillery in the Desert

Except for the reduction of the enemy strongholds at Bardia, Sollum and Halfaya, there had been few occasions on which medium artillery could be used to full effect during the initial offensive by the Eighth Army at the end of 1941. This was partly because of the short range of the 6-in. and 155-mm. hows. with which several of the batteries were still equipped.

By May 1942 the situation had been improved by the arrival of more 4.5-in. guns, and the first consignment of the new 5.5-in. was on its way. Almost immediately, however, these advantages were offset by a serious loss of 4.5-in. guns from prematures. Suspected lots of shell had all to be returned to the base for examination, and as a result the medium batteries were restricted to essential counter-battery tasks until the problem had been investigated and an adequate supply of reliable ammunition had been assured.

It was during this period that the practice became established of using B.B.C. time signals for the synchronization of counter-battery and other concentrations. It had already been used with success in combined operations along the coastal sector, and it was now given a more general application.

The superiority of the sudden and concentrated burst of fire over the desultory bombardment had long been recognized, and if the number of guns involved was large and the times of flight of the shell were very different, it was found desirable that the time laid down in orders should indicate the moment, not at which the guns were to open fire, but at which the shells were to arrive at the target. Thus originated the T.O.T. (time on target) procedure, which subsequently became very popular.

The problem was how to synchronize timings under moving warfare conditions in the desert, where telephone lines were impracticable and wireless emissions had often to be banned in the interests of secrecy. The solution was to listen in to the B.B.C. time signals and to regulate the fire in accordance with them.

The Development of Air Support

Throughout these operations, the R.A.F. had maintained their superiority in the air and much valuable experience had been gained in the handling of Army Air Support Control. Ground level attack had proved to be the most accurate method of giving close support, and the speed with which calls could be answered had been greatly hastened. During the fighting round Knightsbridge, for example, the quickest time achieved was 35 minutes from the initiation of the request to the arrival of the aircraft.

The once dreaded Stuka, on the other hand, when confronted by British fighters, had proved to be "a crow masquerading in eagle's feathers." On many occasions these aircraft were induced to jettison their bombs before reaching their targets, whereas the British fighter-bombers, needing less escort and able to fend for themselves once their bombs had been dropped, demanded less and did more. ([15]) And after the fighter-bomber came the tank-busting Hurricane, which was first used during this fighting.

Thus the threat of the dive bomber, which was first parried by the A.A. guns in May and June 1941, was finally eliminated by the fighters a year later. The main problem that remained to be solved was the indication of targets to the air. During static periods, artificial landmarks could be created in the form of letters of the alphabet laid out on the ground and used as reference points, from which targets could be indicated by means of a bearing and distance. For moving warfare, coloured smoke appeared to be the ideal means of indicating target areas from the ground, and steps were accordingly taken to produce suitable smoke candles and projectiles for use in guns and mortars. Although this meant that targets must be within range of the artillery, which could normally be expected to engage them more accurately than could bomber aircraft, the moral effect of the 250-lb. air bomb was considerable and was especially valuable in this theatre, where medium artillery was scarce and heavy artillery non-existent.

The Growth of A.A.

By the autumn of 1942 British fortunes in the Middle East had reached their nadir and in spite of our growing strength in the air, the demands for A.A. defence were very heavy. Indeed a high proportion of these demands was directly associated with the growth of the R.A.F. and the resultant large number of airfields to be defended. In March, 1942, there were deployed in the Middle East, excluding Malta, 300 H.A.A. and 600 L.A.A. guns, of which approximately 12 per cent. of the heavy and 50 per cent. of the light guns were absorbed in the defence of airfields. By 1st August, 1942, the total had reached 490 H.A.A. guns, 840 L.A.A. guns and 170 searchlights, and still the demands were far from satisfied.

The Defence of Airfields

In spite of the high proportion of A.A. guns allotted to the defence of forward airfields, the casualties among grounded aircraft were heavy enough to cause concern to the home authorities. Situated as they were within range of enemy fighters, they were liable to surprise attacks by low-flying aircraft armed with cannon guns, and as experience in Greece had shown, the results of such an attack could be devastating. Dispersion of aircraft pens and the improvement of the early warning system might help to keep down losses, but radar coverage was not easy to achieve in the desert, when conditions were very mobile. Not only was the accuracy of the delicate R.A.F. radar sets upset, but the to-and-fro movements of the front line made the erection and maintenance of a screen very difficult. During the lull in the fighting at the beginning of 1942, Tobruk was provided with better equipment and mobile sets were installed at Gambut and Gazala. "At the same time an organization bearing some resemblance to the Royal Observer Corps submitted visual reports from the El Adem area."[16]

Early warnings obtained in this way were passed to A.A.O.Rs. and broadcast thence to the guns either by firing a specified number of rounds from a selected gun position or by the use of the local sirens. In general, however, it had come to be accepted that the destruction of aircraft on the ground was "a normal feature of air warfare which must be faced by both sides at all times."[17] The losses might indeed have been greater had it not been for certain peculiarities of the desert, which happened to be favourable to the defence. By day, for example, the flatness and bareness of the terrain robbed the would-be hedge-hopper of much of his surprise effects, and at night, even in bright moonlight, the pilot had great difficulty in locating his objective, so that by the simple expedient of withholding fire the defence could often obtain complete immunity.

The Menace of the Low-Flying Attack

It was not only airfields that had suffered from low-flying attacks with cannon and machine-guns. Such attacks had played a large part in the disruption of our communications and the general discomforture of our forces during the withdrawals from Cyrenaica, Greece and Crete in 1941, when the number of A.A. guns available had been entirely inadequate ; and although the situation had now greatly improved, there were still occasions when, in pursuit of an important object, enemy aircraft would persist with a low-flying attack in the face of A.A. fire. It then became necessary to increase considerably the strength of the A.A. defences, especially in the desert, where the engagement of multiple targets was very difficult in an atmosphere rendered thick by the dust of many bomb bursts. For the same reason attention was again drawn to the need for a sight that would enable the laying of the L.A.A. gun to be controlled by one man, and for a gun that was handier than the Bofors.

The Defence of the Railway

From 7th March, 1942, onwards the cannon-firing Me110 was also used against the single railway that fed the Eighth Army area. These attacks were directed chiefly against the locomotives, which, if hit in the boiler, were easily brought to a standstill. Here in the rearward areas, however, a number of counter-measures were possible. Fighter protection, with a properly organized early warning system, was provided ; static A.A. defences were installed at all the major stopping places and L.A.A. guns (Bredas and L.M.Gs.) were mounted on all the trains. Armour plating was fitted to the locomotive boiler and cab, and, later, balloons were attached to the trains and covered by quadruple .30 Brownings mounted in front and rear of them. As a final precaution, the railway was operated by night only, except during moonlit periods, when it was found better to work by daylight.

The problem was on the whole similar to that presented by the defence of the Suez Canal, and the experience gained there had naturally been of value. It was not long before an efficient system of defence was in operation and the attempt by the enemy to disrupt this vital supply line had been frustrated.

The A.A. Defence of Malta

The highlight of this period from the A.A. point of view was the defence of Malta. During November and December, 1941, an entire "Luftflotte" was transferred to Sicily and air attacks on Malta became very heavy. From the end of March to the beginning of May, 1942, the weight of these attacks was such that the fighter defences were greatly reduced in efficiency and the burden of air defence, as at Tobruk in the previous year, was borne largely by the A.A. artillery.

Numerically, the scale of A.A. defence that had been provided was most imposing: 112 H.A.A. guns, 144 L.A.A. guns and 79 searchlights. This gave a H.A.A. gun density over the main target area of 80, or five times the figure laid down in the training manuals for V.Ps. of the greatest importance (*see* p. 20 and Map 3). On the other hand, the radar equipment available (G.L.II) did not allow of the continuous engagement of unseen targets, which had therefore to be dealt with by the rather primitive methods of predicted and geographical barrages (*see* pp. 61, 82).

Fortunately, visibility in these parts is generally good and the net result was satisfactory. During April, 1942, the A.A. guns destroyed 102 enemy aircraft for certain, and for the whole period September, 1941, to June, 1942, their score was 175 as compared with 477 shot down by the fighters.[18]

In keeping with the unusually large share of responsibility that fell to the guns, the latitude allowed to them was rather greater than was customary elsewhere at that time. Briefly, there were three phases, of which the first allowed absolute liberty of action to the guns, and the second and third restricted H.A.A. to heights above 6,000 feet and L.A.A. altogether in certain areas when friendly aircraft were taking off or landing. When night fighters were operating within 10 miles of the coast, a fourth phase might be added to any one of the other three, restricting H.A.A. to a height of 10,000 (later changed to 14,000 feet). If an A.I. (radar) equipped fighter was in visual or instrumental contact with an enemy aircraft approaching the island, guns would not engage; but if the fighter was not in contact, it would be directed away from the G.D.A. in time for the guns to be able to engage.

As elsewhere, the general policy for night operations was laid down by the R.A.F. controller, but the night A.A.D.C. was entitled to use his own initiative if, in his opinion, this policy " would fail to secure the safety of vulnerable areas, and more particularly, of H.M. ships in harbour."[19]

Attempts to Improve the Accuracy of A.A. Fire

The A.A. barrage, however effective it might be, was expensive in ammunition, and by the autumn of 1942 the stocks of Bofors ammunitions in the Middle East had become dangerously low. Moreover there was a danger that, in H.A.A. units at any rate, the growing preponderance given to barrage fire might " lead to weakness when engaging targets by normal methods."[20]

Although, therefore, it was still accepted that the number of aircraft shot down was not a true gauge of the degree of A.A. protection provided, it was nevertheless emphasized that " the aim should be to achieve the maximum destructive effect consistent with the preventive roll."[21] The key to the problem lay in the production of better sights for the Bofors and a more accurate form of radar for the H.A.A. gun. After much experimentation, both in units and at the School of Artillery, the first of these objects was at last achieved by the production of the Stiffkey Stick. Though theoretically no more accurate than the forward area sight, or any other form of " eye-shooting ", it was simpler to operate and had the great advantage of enabling one man to control the laying of the gun both for line and elevation. Under trial in September 1941 it was found to give results not much inferior to those obtained with the No. 3 predictor, and if the trial itself was too short to be scientifically conclusive, there were practice camp records to show that the superiority of the predictor over the forward area sight had decreased as the war progressed. The cause of this deterioration was uncertain, but it might reasonably be attributed to the gradual decline in the standard of personnel that is a common feature of all wars.

In H.A.A. defence some improvement in accuracy had been obtained in A.D.G.B. during 1941 by the introduction of a semi-automatic plotter, which had the effect of enabling each separate gun position to undertake a series of predicted shoots on information supplied by its own G.L. set instead of confining itself to participation in a brigade or regimental barrage. But this plotter had not yet reached the Middle East and in any case was not suitable for use in mobile units.

Apart from prediction errors, meteor facilities in Cyrenaica were far from adequate. The same difficulty had been encountered in France and Belgium in 1940, and as a result a meteor expert had been added to the establishment of the H.A.A. regiment. But that was on paper only. In reality the supply of experts was so limited that it became necessary to pool Army and R.A.F. resources in certain instances and use the pooled personnel on an area basis.

But perhaps the greatest need of the H.A.A. gunner was for flashless propellant. As the ceiling of the bomber aircraft had increased, the A.A. gun had been more and more seriously handicapped by its own flash, which not only revealed its position to the enemy but also enabled the latter to take avoiding action before the shell could reach him. For many years attempts had been made to overcome this disadvantage by the elimination of the flash, but all had failed. Now at last the problem had been at least partially solved, and by the middle of August, 1942, the new flashless—or, perhaps more correctly, less-flash—propellant was beginning to arrive in small quantities in the Middle East.

New A.A. Weapons

It was, however, evident by this time that the necessary increase in effectiveness of A.A. fire could not be achieved merely by increasing the accuracy of the existing weapons. As aircraft performance had improved, the amount of sky to be covered had outgrown the capabilities of a single type of H.A.A. and L.A.A. gun. Experience in A.D.G.B. had also shown that a single hit from a Bofors would not necessarily destroy an enemy aircraft, and for this reason a more powerful weapon had been demanded. The outcome was a new "intermediate" A.A. gun in the form of a twin 6-pr.

At the same time demands had come from the Middle East for a longer burning tracer for the Bofors to make use of the deterrent effect of the L.A.A. fire at greater ranges (*see* p. 84). As an interim measure it was decided to link four Bofors, thus equipped, to a Vickers (H.A.A.) predictor, and so to produce a fire unit capable of engaging enemy aircraft effectively up to a height of 10,000 feet, especially at night when the moral effect of the tracer was known to be considerable.

There was another gap to be filled in at very low levels, as witness the demand by 30 Corps (*see* p. 115), soon to be substantiated by experience in A.D.G.B. It was therefore decided to make an issue of 20-mm. guns for reinforcing the L.A.A. defences at main airfields, ports, railheads and field maintenance centres. These guns were not to be part of unit establishments, except in coast batteries, but were to be held in the nearest convenient ordnance depot and issued temporarily for the use of units allotted to the defence of the above areas.

There was, however, a grave technical defect in the ammunition supplied with these weapons. Developed, as it had been, for use with the Royal Navy and the Royal Air Force, it contained no self-destroying element and was therefore a source of great inconvenience and some danger to ground units in the vicinity. The siting of the 20-mm. gun was in consequence limited to areas in which its field of fire was over the sea or over unoccupied land.

A.A. Searchlights in the Ground Role

By July, 1942, attempts were being made to find a ground role for the A.A. searchlight. The similarity between desert and naval warfare had often been remarked upon, and as the atmosphere was extremely clear, except during sand storms, there appeared to be good prospects for the employment of a mobile projector carried on its own generator as a self-contained unit.

It was not a new idea. Searchlights had been used with success on the Asiago Plateau in the 1914-18 war, their role being to put a "light box" round a small sector of the enemy front line during the course of a raid by our own forces, and so to expose any attempt by the enemy to reinforce the threatened area. More recently, a proposal had been put forward for the use of a small pack-transported projector in perimeter camps on the N.W. Frontier of India as a means of defeating the nocturnal sniper.

The suggestions now made for the use of the A.A.S.L. in the desert were more ambitious and embraced almost every kind of night operation. In the attack they were to undertake a preliminary search for enemy tanks, transport and mine-laying parties, or to assist the attacking troops to maintain direction by illuminating a salient feature in the enemy's lines. In the defence they could again reveal the location and movements of enemy tanks, transport and infantry, and could assist in preventing the recovery by the enemy of any tanks that had become immobilized within range of the searchlight beams. In support of a raid they could repeat the tactics of the Asiago Plateau, and in all three types of operation they could enable the artillery to make use of observed fire. Finally, they could be used in conjunction with the air to illuminate, or to indicate the direction of, the target to be bombarded.

Such at least was the theory. The uses accepted as practicable by 13 Corps in September 1942, however, were confined to the covering of minefields in static positions and assistance to the R.A.F. in night bombing.

Development of the Mobile Coast Battery

The need for a mobile coast battery had been felt almost from the first in Cyrenaica and had been amply confirmed by the course of the recent operations, during which the situation changed so rapidly that ports were subject to sudden variations in importance or in ownership. It was moreover desirable to have a unit that could be moved by road in an emergency. At Benghasi, for example, in December 1941, the 4th Indian Divisional Artillery had had to take over the responsibility for coast defence and to retain it for many days owing to the delay in the arrival of proper coast artillery equipments. Although the latter reached the port by sea on 8th January, 1942, their disembarkation was held up by a variety of causes—mines in the harbour, lack of a suitable crane, shortage of tugs, rough seas, and the priority given to R.A.F. petrol—with the result that they were still in their lighters when the enemy began his offensive.

In March 1942, therefore, a conference was held by the M.G.A.A. in Cairo and it was agreed that a suitable unit would be a combination of 6-in. guns on Arrol Withers platforms, such as were used by the M.N.B.D.O., and Bofors for use in the A.M.T.B. role, the latter to be equipped with a No. 3 predictor modified to function at an angle of 5 degrees depression.

Conclusion

The hopes entertained at the beginning of this period had not been fulfilled. " The superiority of 8 to 5 in artillery with which the Eighth Army accepted battle on 27th May " had " failed to produce the results expected."[22] Granted that, tank for tank, the Germans were better armed, it was generally felt that our superiority in numbers, and particularly in artillery, should have discounted this with proper handling.

What had gone wrong? Committees and individuals debated this question at great length, and the reasons for failure were finally stated to be as follows:—

(a) The dispersion of the artillery among small bodies not under command of the highest artillery commander who could exercise collective control.

(b) The failure to make a fire plan based on adequate reconnaissance.

(c) The confusion in the minds of many officers resulting from the dual role of the 25-pr. as field and anti-tank gun.

(d) The improper use of anti-tank artillery. In spite of all that had been written and said on this subject there were still " far too many instances " of anti-tank guns being knocked out through being " fired portee when the situation did not justify it."[23]

(e) The difficulty experienced by the infantry, under desert conditions, in protecting the guns from close range small arms fire.

At least two of these factors could probably be traced to the operation of a psychological factor already alluded to (see p. 1). The success of the Jock column in earlier campaigns had apparently led to a false appreciation of its value and to a consequent dissipation of artillery resources. The brigade group (see pp. 118, 125), intended as an antidote to this tendency, was itself in fact a dissipation of artillery power. Thus, in spite of the appointment of a C.R.A. in the armoured division, nothing had been learnt about the control of the divisional artillery, since regiments were always grouped with their respective brigades.[24]

It was the same in the infantry division, where the divisional artillery was scattered among brigade and battalion boxes, which were sometimes too far apart to be self-supporting. With the arrival of the 6 pr., the technique of anti-tank defence began to improve, but by this time the Germans had again increased the protection of their Mk III tanks by the use, among other devices, of hollow frontal armour. Thus the advantages gained by the introduction of this new gun were not as great as had been hoped for, and there were some who thought it would have been preferable—if it had been possible —to eliminate the 6-pr. altogether and go straight to the 17-pr.

In the midst of so much disappointment, comfort might be taken from the growing success of direct air support and of the final defeat that had been imposed upon the enemy dive bomber. The slowness of the Germans in providing a substitute, and in countering the activities of our new fighter-bombers, showed at least that the hypnotic effect of easy successes was not peculiar to the British mentality.

List of References

[1] Despatch by C-in-C, M.E.F., November 1941 to August 1942, p. 100.
[2] War Diary, M.G.R.A., M.E.F., May and June 1942.
[3] A.T.M. No. 43 of May 1942.
[4] C.R.M.E./35221/M.T. 1 of 11th April 1942.
[5] War Diary, H.Q.R.A. 50 Div., March 1942.
[6] Despatch by C-in-C, M.E.F., November 1941 to August 1942, p. 76.
[7] *Ibid*, p. 82.
[8] Minutes of Army Commander's Conference at Matruh, 22nd June 1942.
[9] M.8A/4210/GSD of 24th June 1942.
[10] " The Battle of Egypt ", by G.I., M.T., Eighth Army.
[11] Despatch by C-in-C, M.E.F., November 1941 to August 1942, p. 92.
[12] War Diaries, 5 Ind. Div. R.A. and 1 R.H.A. Regt., July 1942.
[13] A.T.M. No. 44 of October 1942.
[14] 4 Ind. Div. R.A. Training Instruction No. 3 of 30th September 1942.
[15] " Desert Air Force ", by Roderic Owen, p. 88.
[16] *Ibid*, pp. 92, 126.
[17] Cable from V.C.I.G.S. at Cairo to War Office, March 1942.
[18] War Office Digest No. 5 of 30th August 1942.
[19] A.A. Defence Instructions by C.R.A. Malta, 10th May 1942.
[20] A.A. Notes 1942, No. 1.
[21] Minutes of M.G.A.A.'s Conference at G.H.Q., 17th-18th August 1942.
[22] Eighth Army Training Instruction No. 1 of 1942.
[23] Report of C. of I. on Operations in W. Desert, 27th May-2nd July 1942.
[24] War Diary, M.G.R.A., M.E.F., December 1942.

CHAPTER IX

EL ALAMEIN TO MEDENINE

PLATES RELEVANT TO THIS CHAPTER

Nos.
- 19. The " Priest ".
- 20. The 5.5-in. gun/how.
- 21. The American S.P. 3-in. M10.
- 22. 25-prs. firing a barrage by night.

SECTION I.—THE BATTLE OF EL ALAMEIN

Restoration of the Divisional Organization

It was not only in the air that the Germans were beginning to experience the penalty that is attached to prolonged success. It seemed that a series of spectacular victories won by " blitzkrieg " methods had led to a neglect of purely infantry tactics. Their infantry had " lost their old skill in handling their personal weapons " and had tended to degenerate into mere " tank followers ".[1]

Now, in Egypt, this weakness was to contribute more than anything else, perhaps, to their eventual downfall. In the Eighth Army, after a brief period of misgiving, confidence in the offensive power of the infantry had been restored. Given adequate artillery support, it was affirmed, infantry could still attack successfully in enclosed or hilly country. In the desert it was more difficult, but even here it was not impossible, provided that the attack was made under cover of darkness or of smoke and that there were no uncut wire obstacles or anti-personnel minefields covered by the fire of enemy small arms that could not be neutralized.[2]

The first step was to rehabilitate the divisional organization, and with it the executive powers of the C.R.A. In future the armoured divisional artillery was to consist of three regiments of 25-prs., of which one was to be S.P.; one 64-gun anti-tank regiment; and one 54-gun L.A.A. regiment. The infantry divisional artillery was to be the same, except that at first none of the field regiments would be S.P.

Thus the field and anti-tank regiments were again separated and the old organization of the divisional artillery was revived. At the same time the use of the battle group was banned. It had proved in practice " an indifferent compromise between the offensive tactics of the Jock column and the defensive tactics of the box ".[3]

This did not mean that the mobile force of all arms and the all-round defended area were taboo. Both were orthodox tactical expedients of long standing, and both were particularly applicable to desert warfare. But the methods of applying them were in future to conform more closely to the principle of concentration. In the infantry brigade group defended area, for example, at least half—later increased to three-quarters—of the available 25-prs. were to be sited in indirect fire positions for use primarily in the normal field artillery role.

The Battle of Alam El Halfa
30th August-6th September, 1942

For the moment the emphasis was on the defensive. In August, 1942, the enemy could still count on the superiority of his armour, and after the July attacks by the Eighth Army had failed to drive him from his position in front of El Alamein, it became a practical certainty that he would take the offensive once more in a final attempt to complete his drive on Suez.

His difficulty was going to be to find room in which his armour could manoeuvre. If, as seemed likely, he was to repeat his customary movement round the southern flank, it would be necessary for him to include the commanding Alam El Halfa ridge as one of his first objectives; and General Montgomery, taking advantage of this fact, had planned to receive the attack on ground "not only selected and prepared by the defenders, but dominated by their artillery and at the mercy of their air forces. It was hoped also that the technical superiority of the German tanks would be largely offset when they found themselves forced to attack well dug in British armour ".[4]

In accordance with this plan there were in the area some 16 medium, 240 field and 200 anti-tank guns, besides the guns of nearly 400 tanks and over 100 anti-tank guns manned by the infantry. It was the biggest concentration of fire power that had been achieved in the desert since the war began, and at every important stage of the ensuing battle it was able to exert a decisive influence upon the course of the operations.

By 5th September the battle was virtually over and the drive on Egypt had been finally held. It had been done, in Roman fashion, largely by sitting still and letting the enemy batter himself in vain against a carefully selected and strongly fortified position. Above all it had been done by the concentrated use of fire power. In General Montgomery's own words, the concentrated fire of artillery had proved itself to be still " a battle-winning factor of the first importance ", and for this reason " command must be centralized under the C.R.A. so that he can use the divisional artillery as a 72-gun battery when necessary ".[5]

Attempts to Revive the Close Support Gun

The crisis had passed and thoughts could now be turned to the offensive. There were two main problems to be dealt with: the anti-tank screen and the minefield. On 17th July, 1942, it had been estimated that for every one of our tanks knocked out by German tanks, three had been knocked out by anti-tank guns; and in the anti-tank mine another protective weapon had appeared that was as great a menace to modern armour as the buried spikes of Darius had been to the cavalry of Alexander.

At El Alamein, fortunately, the enemy minefield was relatively thinly sown with anti-personnel mines and only lightly covered by wire. There was therefore reason to hope that it could be forced by an infantry assault of the old-fashioned type supported by a really heavy concentration of artillery fire. Once penetration had been achieved, however, and our armoured formations had passed through the gap, the whole situation would be changed. Thereafter knowledge of the enemy's dispositions would become increasingly scanty and his anti-tank guns in particular would remain silent and concealed until our tanks were at close quarters. If, therefore, they were to be successfully neutralized, there would have to be the closest liaison between the artillery tank O.Ps. and the units they were supporting, and an assurance that some guns of the divisional artillery would always be in action.

The problem was in fact not unlike that presented by the machine-gun in and after the 1914-18 war which had led in 1920 to the introduction of a special close support weapon into the artillery of the infantry division. Subsequently rendered superfluous by the development of the mortar and of wireless, the pack (or light) regiment had been abolished after a few years (*see* p. 11); but during the present war the superiority of the German mortars and the disappointing results of wireless inter-communication between guns and forward infantry had brought the subject of the close support gun to the fore again, and with it the controversy of whether or not such a weapon should be part of the divisional artillery. There were, in September 1942, three types of weapon in being or under discussion for this role: the S.P. field gun on a tracked chassis, the light S.P. infantry gun, and the portee field gun.

The advocates of the infantry gun chose as their weapon the S.P. 95-mm, and the proposal was that four of these guns should be included in every infantry battalion and armoured regiment. But this gun never came to anything and need not therefore be further discussed.

The demand for a portee field gun had originated in July 1942, in the Middle East and had not been connected primarily with the close support role. It was intended for the normal support of desert columns, whose mobility had hitherto been handicapped by the inadequate performance of the existing field artillery tractor. Owing to the nature of the terrain, and the distances to be covered, it was to be equipped with wheels; but the idea, once germinated, offered other possibilities, and a tracked portee equipment was now under consideration as a close support weapon in theatres other than the Middle East.

In the end, however, both projects were abandoned on account of supply difficulties. All available chassis of a suitable type were already earmarked for heavy, medium and A.A. artillery, and plans had been drawn up for the production of a new universal type of tractor that promised to give the desired increase in power and performance. It was therefore agreed by all concerned to forgo the provision of a portee field gun.

Thus, for the moment at any rate, the S.P. field gun was the only artillery weapon available for close support, either of armour or of infantry. Whether it should be regarded as a " close support " or as a normal field artillery weapon, was open to question. To the gunner the distinction between the two was more apparent than real (*see* p. 9), and he was therefore inclined to shy at the term " close support ", which was " connected in the minds of most with the use of small units such as troops, or even sections, well forward with the leading elements of the units being supported ". This was " the antithesis of the correct use of artillery, the cardinal principle of which is concentration of fire ".[*]

Moreover both armoured and infantry units were now equipped to deal unaided with immediate opposition. In the former there were the Grant, and later the Sherman, tanks, whose 75-mm guns could fire up to a range of 8,000 yards, and whose inclusion in armoured regiments gave to the latter for the first time the means both of dealing with enemy anti-tank guns and of fighting on equal terms with the enemy armour. Indeed it was not long before armoured units were to develop their own methods of indirect fire.

In the infantry division the 2-in. and 3-in. mortars, if properly sited and handled, could engage all located enemy positions within their range, no matter how enclosed the country; and as for hitting power, the 3-in. mortar could put down 200 lb. of projectiles in one minute at rapid fire, as compared with 125 lb. by the 25-pr. at intense rates. Thus for short periods the six 3-in. mortars of a battalion could bring down a greater weight of fire than an 8-gun field battery, and yet they were "flexible, easily controlled, and easily concealed ".([7])

The "Priest"

Although, therefore, the S.P. regiment was to some extent a specialized form of artillery, primarily suited for the close support of armour, it was generally agreed that it was capable, with certain limitations, of carrying out the normal tasks of horse or field artillery, and that it should form part of the divisional artillery. In this capacity it had several advantages. It could move out of—but not into—action and change position quicker than towed artillery, and its greater cross-country mobility gave it a better choice of positions in difficult and roadless country. Its armour, too, made it less likely to be pinned to a position under fire, while its armour and heavy machine-gun combined made it less dependent on an infantry escort.

The problem was to find the right weapon. The hastily improvized Bishop had several serious disadvantages (*see* p. 89) and in the absence of any suitable British substitute, it had recently been supplemented by the American S.P. 105-mm M7, familiarly known as the "Priest", which was mounted on a Grant chassis and fired a 35-lb. shell to a range of 10,500 yards. With its greater shell power, range and internal traverse (about 40 degrees instead of 8 degrees), the Priest was definitely an improvement on the Bishop, and in addition its greater speed enabled adequate support to be given to cruiser tanks. It suffered, however, from certain technical disadvantages. The life of the piece proved to be much shorter than had been expected, and the recuperator was also subject to rapid wear and was very vulnerable owing to the thinness of its casing. Its introduction led moreover to undesirable complications in the ammunition supply. It was therefore ultimately to be replaced by a new design of S.P. 25-pr.

Extension of the Artillery Wireless Net

The contention that all field artillery is close support artillery could be sustained only if there was the closest liaison between the guns and the formations or units they were supporting. During the fighting in November and December 1941, artillery tank and armoured O.Ps. had been put into direct touch with armoured and infantry units by the addition of a No. 19 or No. 18 set to the No. 11 set supplied for intercommunication within the battery and regiment, and by October 1942, a definite drill had been laid down for the indication and engagement of targets selected by the infantry.

At the same time, steps were taken to improve the facilities for the co-ordination and concentration of artillery fire within the corps. In

August 1942, large scale exercises were held in the 13th Corps to practise and perfect the working of the C.C.R.A.'s net, so that information could be quickly passed from F.O.Os. to corps headquarters and the C.C.R.A., in touch with the situation on the whole front, could direct the fire of the corps artillery in accordance with the needs of the moment. For this purpose he was provided with a roving set, with which he could maintain touch with units while on the move and so avoid becoming tied to his own headquarters.

Thus even the 72-gun fire unit did not mark the limit of artillery hitting power, given good wireless drill and maintenance.

Preparations for the Offensive

With the arrival of 300 Shermans in September, the Eighth Army at last found itself in possession of a tank that was "equal in armour, armament and performance to the best tank in the Afrika Corps".[8] In quantity, too, its tank resources were nearly double those of the enemy. But before this advantage could be exploited, it was necessary to make a gap in the defences which the enemy had been busily strengthening since the failure of his last offensive. The operation would therefore have to begin, "like a battle of the 1914-18 war, with the assault of an entrenched position in depth and it would not be until that battle had been fought and won that we should be able to proceed to the more swift-moving clash of armoured forces which had distinguished the decisive campaigns of this war ".[9]

In this initial attack much would depend on the amount of artillery support that could be made available. During September and October two medium regiments and six additional field regiments had arrived from the United Kingdom, bringing the total number of guns of these two categories in the Eighth Army up to nearly one thousand; and one of the main features of the plan was so to dispose this artillery as to bring the greatest possible concentration of fire, under centralized control, against the principal point of attack.[10]

For the initial stages of the operation, the preparation of fire plans was greatly assisted by the quantity and quality of air photographs that were available. Under semi-static conditions, such as now obtained at El Alamein, vertical photographs, frequently repeated, could give an accurate picture of the enemy dispositions as complete as his camouflage arrangements would allow. In fact so accurate and detailed was the knowledge of these dispositions that covering fire could mostly be given in the form of concentrations on all prepared defended localities, arrangements being made for the fire to lift from locality to locality at an average rate of 100 yards in three minutes.

Counter-battery work assumed a more than usual importance owing to the enemy preponderance in medium and heavy artillery. It was believed that, on the main front of attack, he could dispose of 200 field, 40 medium and 14 heavy guns (*see* Map 4); and calculation showed that it would not be possible to neutralize all these guns during the progress of the attack. It was therefore decided to put all available artillery on to counter-battery work for 15 minutes before zero hour, with concentrations on the main front of attack of up to 20:1 and never less than 10:1. It meant risking the loss of surprise, and for this reason it was viewed with some misgiving by infantry commanders, but it was generally agreed afterwards to have been justified.([11])

Once again owing to the excellence and amplitude of the air photographs provided by the R.A.F., and the check maintained on hostile artillery activity by flash spotting and sound ranging sections, the dispositions of the enemy guns had been fixed with considerable accuracy. It only remained to ensure, as far as could be, that these dispositions were not altered on the eve of the offensive. Hence for over two weeks before "D" day, counter-battery activities were confined to silent registration, with an occasional destructive shoot against a particularly troublesome hostile battery, and neutralization shoots against what were obviously roving guns.

Since the infantry attacks were all designed to take place by moonlight, and much use was to be made of regimental, divisional and even greater concentrations, it was evident that special importance would attach to the initial accuracy of the fire. In the interests of secrecy, registration was restricted to one gun to each regiment, and this only on essential points; but as ample time was available for preparation, all guns were calibrated, accurate and frequent meteor telegrams were issued, and all units were put in harmony with each other by being brought on to a permanent grid. Finally, ammunition for the opening bombardment was carefully prepared and dumped at gun positions, so that when the advance began, artillery units would be able to move forward with their echelons full. Throughout the coming battle no restriction was to be imposed on ammunition expenditure for any of the major attacks, and in 12 days' fighting the 824 × 25-prs. in action were to fire between them over a million rounds, with an average of 102 r.p.g. a day. The medium rates were even higher: 133 r.p.g. for the 4.5-in., and 157 for the 5.5-in.

The Battle of El Alamein, 23rd October-5th November, 1942

The immediate effect of our preliminary counter-battery bombardment was impressive. By 2200 hours, when the infantry were due to begin their advance, all hostile guns had been silenced, and they were kept in this condition until daylight by air attacks, first by Wellingtons and Albacores and then by night fighters, which shot up the flashes of any guns that opened fire. As a result the enemy's forward defences were captured without serious opposition. On the main position, however, a much sterner resistance was encountered. By this time the enemy artillery was beginning to reassert itself and from now on our infantry casualties were due more to gun and mortar fire than to bullets.([12])

During the subsequent "dog-fight" in the north, C.B. intelligence was never quite up to date and results were therefore not as good as might have been hoped for; but when Rommel, rejoining his army from Europe on the 26th, hurriedly concentrated his armour and tried his old game of a massed tank attack out of the afternoon sun, his armoured formations were broken up by continuous air bombardment and heavy shell fire before they could get to grips.

It was now the turn of the Eighth Army to resume the offensive, and on the night 28-29th October, an operation was carried out by the 9th Australian Division to exploit a salient that had been created to the south of the road and railway during the previous fighting, to isolate the enemy troops on the coast, and to draw attention away from the preparations for the main breakthrough to the west. Artillery support, provided by thirteen R.H.A. and field and three medium regiments, was—as usual up to this point —by concentrations timed to lift ahead of the infantry. What was unusual was that the lines of fire of the guns were mostly at right angles to the direction of attack, and that at one time the guns were firing directly in the face of the advancing infantry (*see* Map 5). The operation was only partly successful but was completed by the 26th Australian Infantry Brigade on the night 30th-31st October with little change in the artillery plan.

For the final breakthrough on the night 1st-2nd November, a preliminary counter-battery bombardment by the whole of the artillery was prepared on the same lines as those used with such success in the initial attack on 23rd October. Thereafter, as the knowledge of the enemy's dispositions was necessarily incomplete, 192 guns were to put down a creeping barrage over the 4,000 yards of front, while a further 168 were to shell known and likely enemy positions in the path of the advance and on either side of it. Finally, all available guns were to be concentrated in support of the 9th Armoured Brigade's attack on the Rahman track, which ran from north to south behind the enemy front and formed his main lateral line of communication.

Once again the enemy put up an unexpectedly stiff resistance after being subjected to so gruelling a bombardment, and at dawn on 2nd November the 9th Armoured Brigade found itself on the muzzles of the familiar and powerful anti-tank screen on the Rahman track, instead of beyond it as had been planned. There then ensued the largest armoured clash of the battle, which began with a gallant attack by the 9th Armoured Brigade and ended in the final discomfiture of the Afrika Corps. The German tanks, forced to pit themselves in two groups against our massed armour and artillery, sustained losses that were crippling.

The anti-tank screen, however, still held, and this had to be cleared before the victory could be exploited. A fresh infantry brigade was brought up from the 4th Indian Division, and at 0230 hours on 4th November it attacked behind a hastily arranged but extremely effective creeping barrage. The attack was completely successful and within a few hours the Eighth Army had started for the third and last time the pursuit to Agheila.

Covering Fire and the Principle of Concentration

The results of this battle showed that infantry, unsupported by armour, could still gain its objective without undue casualties if covered by really heavy concentrations of artillery fire.[11] The weight of fire produced can be seen from the following three examples. On the night 30th-31st October, the attack by the 26th Australian Infantry Brigade northwards across the railway and main road was supported by some 360 field and medium guns. The attack by the 151st and 152nd Infantry Brigades on the night 1st-2nd November was covered by about 320 guns, and that of the 5th Indian Infantry Brigade on the night 3rd-4th November by 270 guns.

The handling of the 72-gun fire unit was now being reduced to a fine art. Standard concentrations were evolved in which the fire of batteries and regiments was either superimposed on a single map reference and subsequently moved about as necessary, or distributed over an area that was defined by a single map reference and the bearing of the front of the concentration. The latter method, known as a " Stonk ", afterwards became very popular.

A similar drill was adopted for the creation of large smoke screens, which were put down on the enemy's F.D.Ls. either to induce him—not always successfully—to disclose his defensive fire plans, or to play on his nerves. For example, on one occasion the 4th Indian Divisional Artillery, at first light, laid a screen 1,500 yards long and 800 yards deep.

The creeping barrages used in the later stages of the battle were, thanks partly to the flatness of the terrain, kept extremely simple and were usually accompanied by concentrations by the medium, and some field, regiments on known and suspected strong points in the barrage lane. In one night attack, where there was no clearly defined start line and the enemy was some distance away, the opening line of the barrage was put down on a marker line some 1,500 yards in front of the enemy and was maintained at a very slow rate of fire for 55 minutes in order to let them get up to it. This technique proved very successful and was repeated, with equal success, on a second occasion.

Yet there were times when the covering fire, in spite of its intensity, failed to produce the results that had been expected. As in the 1914-18 war—which this battle closely resembled—so now, the killing effect of artillery fire was disappointing to those without experience. Indeed several formations reported that " the number of enemy dead and wounded found by the leading troops was surprisingly light, and that enemy automatic weapons quickly opened up when the barrage or concentrations had passed."([13])

This is an old lesson that training exercises can never really teach and that has to be relearned by every new formation as it goes into battle. The essence of it is that the infantry must keep close enough to the barrage to ensure that the enemy may be engaged before he has had time to recover from the demoralizing effects of the artillery fire. Attempts to specify a distance have sometimes been made (*see* pp. 3, 29), but distances are difficult to estimate on the battlefield with enemy shells adding to the confusion, and a more general guide—laid down during the First World War and by at least one formation after El Alamein—was that, if covering fire was to be effective against a first class enemy, some risk of casualties from our own guns must be accepted.([14]).

Having once got the infantry at the right distance from the barrage, there remained the problem of how to keep them there. This problem was twofold: first to adjust the pace of the barrage to that at which the infantryman could be expected to move; second to arrest or recall the barrage whenever the advance of the infantry was held up.

The standard rate of advance for a creeping barrage was still 100 yards in three minutes (*see* p. 28), and although the terrain here was easy, the enemy defences were strong and were held in places by some of the best German infantry. There was therefore no suggestion of increasing this rate.

In the matter of recalling a barrage, the Eighth Army was better off than its predecessors of the First World War. In 1916-18, once the barrage had started, there was no means of stopping or recalling it if the infantry were held up. Now, thanks to the closer liaison between gunner and infantryman resulting from the use of wireless, it could sometimes be done. But only sometimes. It was not yet considered feasible in anything larger than a brigade attack;([13]) and even then communications might fail and the guns have to remain silent owing to ignorance of where the infantry were, as happened on at least one occasion at El Alamein.([15]).

Even by day it was not always easy in the desert to determine the position of the leading infantry. Indeed formations would sometimes differ by over 1,000 yards in their estimates of these positions, and the best method of deciding between them was to make use of artillery survey, either by shooting on to an adjoining feature and deducing its co-ordinates, or by getting the troops concerned to put up a predetermined signal and having it resected by a flash spotting section. It was, however, some time before the other arms could be convinced of the reliability of such methods.

Once an objective had been reached, covering fire became defensive fire, and here an addition was made to the existing procedure in order to allow full scope to the principle of concentration. Besides the ordinary D.F. and S.O.S. tasks arranged between infantry brigades and their supporting artillery regiments, special divisional tasks were prepared before each attack and adjusted as soon as the infantry dispositions were known. These tasks were named and passed to flank and supporting divisional artilleries, so that calls for fire—which could be made by battalions, brigades, F.O.O.s and artillery liaison officers—would be answered immediately by the supporting regiment and subsequently by a really heavy concentration.

The Success of our Counter-Battery Measures

In order to make the best use of the limited resources in medium artillery, all three regiments were placed under command of 30 Corps carrying out the main attack in the north; and at varying stages of the attack up to four field regiments were added to this medium artillery group, which was provided with buried cable communications and was commanded by a C.O. taken from one of the regiments to perform the duties of the now defunct C.C.M.A.

As many of the enemy batteries were beyond the range of the 25-prs., the majority of the bombards had to be carried out by the mediums, which were in consequence kept very busy. During the initial attack medium batteries were firing more or less continuously for 20 hours and their ammunition expenditure exceeded 300 r.p.g. Indeed so great was the wear of the guns, and so rapid their loss of M.V., that it was found necessary, in a battle of this magnitude, to have them calibrated every third day.

Taken as a whole, our counter-battery measures proved most successful and may be said to have played a considerable part in the ultimate victory. The chief factor contributing to this success had been the air photograph. By " D " day a complete photographic plot of the whole front had been prepared, and thereafter new batteries could be easily located by comparing day-to-day photos with this original plot. Meanwhile printing facilities had been increased and the process of interpretation and distribution had been greatly speeded up. Before the battle, the time interval between the taking of a photograph and its receipt at the counter-battery office was about 36 hours. After the battle had started, special copies of prints were in the hands of the counter-battery staff four to five hours after the aircraft had landed.

The weak point in the system was the absence of air observation. Our mastery of the air was not yet so complete that arty/R aircraft could operate over enemy territory without a strong fighter escort; especially the aircraft then allotted to army co-operation squadrons for this purpose. Hence, once the initial programmes had been fired in each attack, counter-battery shooting depended largely on information from flash spotting troops, artillery O.Ps. and hostile shelling reports. By careful organization and quick dissemination of this information, some good work was done, but the fact remained that the neutralization shoot with predicted fire was an extravagant and not always reliable method of dealing with hostile batteries whose position could not be fixed with absolute accuracy.

Improvements in the Meteor Organization

With the growth of the divisional concentration, the supply of accurate and regular meteor information had become of increased importance. In the summer months the correction to be applied to the 25-pr. at long ranges might be as much as 700 yards. It was therefore a factor that could not be ignored, and it was met by the provision in each corps of a mobile meteorological unit, in which was included a wireless section, so that forecast upper air temperatures and winds might be received from a R.A.F. forecasting unit. Forecast winds were particularly useful during the winter months, when the prevalence of clouds often precluded the use of balloon observations at the higher altitudes.

During the El Alamein battle, meteor was issued every two hours, but in mobile operations the frequency of issue was greatly reduced owing to the difficulty of transporting the hydrogen cylinders for the balloons.

The Anti-Tank Gun Comes into its Own Again

At Tobruk and at Fort Capuzzo in April and May 1941, it had been proved that an artillery concentration could sometimes delay or divert a tank attack, and now at El Alamein the same experience was repeated. The concentrations fired were usually regimental, but on one occasion the fire of two divisional artilleries and three medium regiments was put down on a map square in which some 60 tanks of the 21st Panzer Division were temporarily halted. The casualties inflicted on the enemy by these bombardments were generally slight, but the moral effect, as some of our own armoured brigades could testify, was undeniable. It not only induced the enemy tanks to withdraw or change direction, but it also made them close down and prevented them from refuelling and replenishing ammunition in the forward area, as they had previously been accustomed to do.([11])

At Stalingrad, where another great allied victory had recently been gained, such concentrations had in fact played an important part in the Russian scheme of defence. Stretched thinly as it was along the western bank of the Volga, the city offered little depth to the defence and was therefore peculiarly susceptible to attack by the familiar "blitzkrieg" method: a swift penetration by tanks, supported by aircraft and artillery and followed by the encirclement and annihilation of each isolated sector. To counter this, the Russians massed a numerous artillery on the far side of the river and prepared successive zones of fire by heavy, medium and field guns, in which powerful concentrations could be brought down on the enemy as he advanced to the attack. They did not expect that such fire would stop the enemy altogether, but they did expect that it would disorganize and delay him, and perhaps even cause him some losses, thus rendering him an easier target for the anti-tank guns concealed within the defences.([16])

From this point there was no getting away, that the final antidote to the tank attack must be the anti-tank gun. For a year or more the 25-pr. had filled the breach in our anti-tank defences and had more than once staved off disaster; but, except at short ranges, it was not a really good killer of tanks. The provision of anti-tank shot (see p. 17) had in fact been intended only for self-defence, and it is perhaps a tribute to the designers, and to the skill at improvisation acquired by British gunners during the lean years between 1939 and 1942, that confusion had arisen regarding the relative importance of the field and anti-tank roles (see p. 135), and that the B.R.A. Eighth Army now found it necessary to issue a warning that, as an anti-tank weapon, the 25-pr. was " far inferior to the 6-pr.".([11])

In the armoured division, anti-tank resources had been greatly strengthened by the arrival of the Sherman tank and the new S.P. 6-pr. equipment known as the " Deacon ". The former was armed with a gun that, as a tank destroyer, was surpassed only by the 8.8 cm gun of the enemy. The latter was a thick-shielded 6-pr. with a central pivot mounting, carried on a 4-wheeled chassis. It was issued on the scale of one battery to each regiment as originally proposed in 1940 (see p. 36), and was found useful as a mobile anti-tank reserve, especially when operating in conjunction with the carrier company of the M.M.G. battalion. It was not, however, an unqualified success, owing to its size and the difficulty of digging it in and concealing it. Arrangements were therefore made for it to be replaced in armoured divisions by the American S.P. 3-in. M10.

The Problem of the Enemy Anti-Tank Screen

During the infantry attacks the enemy anti-tank guns had presented no great difficulty. Some had been hit by the barrages and concentrations and all had been quickly overrun by the infantry. In fact General von Thoma, commanding the Afrika Corps, subsequently attributed his defeat more than anything else to the destruction of over 50 per cent. of his anti-tank guns by our artillery fire.

In the armoured battle, however, the problem of the anti-tank screen had not yet been completely solved. The enemy, as usual, was quick to build up new screens to stem a break-through, and these sometimes inflicted heavy casualties upon our armour before they had been finally mastered. Although training instructions issued on 17th August had insisted that priority must be given to the neutralization of anti-tank weapons, and had emphasized the value of smoke for this purpose, there was still a tendency in some formations to neglect its use and to advance to the attack without making a pre-arranged fire plan.([11]) In such circumstances the time lag between a tank squadron being held up and the F.O.O. being able to bring down effective fire might vary from five minutes to five hours, depending on whether the guns were in action or not, the number of the enemy anti-tank guns, the nature of the ground, and the degree of visibility. Yet in at least one armoured brigade—the 23rd—the soundness of the official doctrine had been amply demonstrated, and as a result the proportion of smoke shell carried by its artillery regiment had been increased to 33⅓ per cent.

The conclusions to be drawn appeared to be as follows. Against carefully prepared and dug positions in depth, it would always be necessary to mount a full scale infantry attack heavily supported by artillery. Small anti-tank localities, with a preponderance of small calibre anti-tank weapons, might be dealt with direct by armoured units, supported by concentrations from at least one artillery regiment. Lastly, the hastily constituted anti-tank screen, not dug in, could first be neutralized by M.M.G. fire and then knocked out, gun by gun, by the Sherman tanks and by the S.P. units of the supporting artillery. For the present, however, it had to be accepted that the anti-tank gun was still the most serious menace to the tank, and that the enemy still had the advantage of superior equipment, including ammunition and sights.([13])

The Need for Flashless Propellant and Time Fuzes

The increasing frequency of night operations had brought into prominence the need for flashless propellant. There were three different reasons for eliminating the flash of a gun, each affecting a different type of artillery. In H.A.A. defence, the flash warned the airman he was being fired at and enabled him to take avoiding action before the shell could reach him. In L.A.A. and anti-tank defence it gave away the position of the gun, and by night had a blinding effect upon the layer. In field artillery work of all natures it exposed the gun to observation by enemy flash spotters.

Unfortunately, it had not been found possible to eliminate flash without increasing the amount of smoke created, and thus seriously handicapping the layer when engaging a target by direct fire. For the engagement of tanks by day, therefore, the introduction of flashless propellant seemed likely to do more harm than good, and in December, 1941, its provision for the anti-tank gun, which had hitherto been given top priority, was removed from the list altogether.

In August, 1942, opinion underwent another change. An incidental advantage of the flashless propellant was that it caused less wear to the gun and thus increased the life of the barrel; an important consideration in the case of a high velocity weapon like the anti-tank gun. To it experience was shortly to add yet another advantage: a reduction in muzzle blast and a consequent reduction in the amount of dust thrown up on firing. In October, 1942, therefore, the 6-pr. and 17-pr. anti-tank guns were reinserted in the priority list for flashless propellant immediately above the 25-pr., which meantime had dropped from third to eighth place to make way for certain coast and A.A. guns.

Another outstanding feature of the El Alamein battle had been the extent of the enemy's entrenchments, and this had led to a demand for time fuzes for use with air burst H.E. against troops in slit trenches and under light cover, and against partly dug in anti-tank guns. Indeed opinion in the Eighth Army was now emphatically in favour of air burst H.E. as a lethal weapon, and a request was made for 15 per cent. of all field and medium artillery ammunition to be time fuzed.([17])

Section II.—THE PURSUIT TO TUNISIA

The Advance to Tripoli

With the final collapse of the enemy resistance on 5th November, the nature of the fighting underwent a complete change. It was open warfare again of the most mobile type, in which the chief obstacles to progress were rain, which saved the enemy from complete encirclement at Matruh; mines, which the enemy used at Agheila and elsewhere in prodigious quantities and with consummate skill; demolitions; and a lengthening of the L. of C. Bardia 11th November, Tobruk 13th November, Tmimi 14th November, Martuba 15th November, Derna 16th November, Benghasi 20th November. One place after the other was entered by our leading troops practically without opposition, while the R.A.F. pounded away at the enemy columns from landing grounds that were often in advance of our own main bodies and protected only by armoured cars.

A brief stand by the enemy at Agheila in mid-December offered an opportunity for the latest sound ranging equipment to prove its worth. A "base" was deployed in 5½ hours, and in 11 days this base obtained about 60 per cent. of the hostile battery information given in the C.B.O.'s list. Later, however, as the advance became more rapid again, the value of the new radio link was largely neutralized by electrical faults caused by movement over rough country.[18]

At one time it appeared to be touch and go as to whether the Eighth Army would get to Tripoli before its supply system broke down. Ten days was the time limit allowed, according to administrative calculations, for the advance from Buerat to Tripoli, and by 17th January the advance was becoming "sticky". General Montgomery therefore decided "to accelerate the pace of operations, and to give battle by night as well as by day, in order to break through the Homs—Tarhuna position and secure my objective".[19]

Orders were given for attacks to be carried out by moonlight, including the occupation of positions and registration by the artillery. The resulting fire plan was not a good one, but the infantry were able to attack under it and to gain ground "many hours earlier than they would have done otherwise". Experience showed that it was possible to observe the fall of 25-pr. shell under a full moon up to 500 yards.[20]

Quick Fire Plans

This was a period of sudden action and fleeting targets, in which speed rather than accuracy or weight of fire was the main consideration. For three months, war in the desert reassumed the characteristics that had distinguished it before the stalemate set in at El Alamein: navigation by compass, night leaguers, Jock columns (now known as pursuit columns), "pistol" or "pocket" guns (*see* p. 99), etc.

In its earlier stages, the pistol gun procedure had been used chiefly for snap actions by individual troops. Now it was being applied to the battery and even to the regiment. In the first case, the O.P. would nominate the "control troop" and both troops would drop into action where they were, the linked troop making a rough correction to allow for its estimated displacement.[21] In the second, one gun per battery would be included in reconnaissance groups, and on coming into action the regimental survey officer would fix the position of one of these pistol guns and would fire from it two groups of air bursts about 40 degrees apart and at a mean range (say 6,000 yards). The C.P.O.s or G.P.O.s of other troops would lay their directors on these air bursts and from the measurements thus obtained deduce their own positions relative to the pistol gun. In this way the gun was used as a quick means of putting all batteries on to the same temporary regimental grid.[22]

During the pursuit, considerable risks were taken in keeping pistol guns and reconnaissance groups well forward. At Buerat, for example, they were about 35 miles ahead of the main body of the artillery and actually came into action behind a thin armoured car screen.[23]

The next step was to adapt the " stonk ", or standard divisional concentration, to the conditions of moving warfare. While the "control regiment" was registering the target, a survey beacon would be erected in a prominent position in its area and its co-ordinates, and later those of the target as found by registration, would be passed by R/T to the B.M.R.A. for broadcasting to all units. In this way the whole divisional artillery could be brought immediately on to the same grid and in desert country it was expected that all guns would be ready to fire one hour after their trails were on the ground, but in broken country, where regimental bearing pickets were not intervisible, this time would be increased.[24]

The Arrival of the 17-Pr. and Decline of the Portee Anti-Tank Gun

By the end of January, 1943, the first 17-prs. were ready for issue at the R.A. Base Depot. Carefully camouflaged to resemble the 4.5-in. medium gun, they were secretly despatched to join the Eighth Army in the forward area.

The anti-tank gunner now had a good margin of superiority over the German tanks and unorthodox equipment like the portee could at last be dispensed with. Except in the motor battalion and S.P. battery of the armoured division, all anti-tank guns were in future to be towed. In the former alone was the 6-pr. portee now to be seen. Elsewhere the 3-ton portee, designed for the carriage of the 6-pr., was replaced by a 15-cwt. armoured truck. This vehicle was not ideal for the purpose, since it could not carry the whole of the detachment or of the 1st line ammunition, but it was the best that could be provided.[17]

It was fortunate that these more powerful equipments arrived when they did, for circumstances were now dictating a reduction in quantity of the anti-tank guns with field formations. The size of the anti-tank regiment, which had so recently been increased to 64 guns as the result of battle experience, was about to be reduced owing to the shortage of manpower. In November, 1942, information had been received from the War Office that anti-tank regiments could not be maintained on an establishment of more than 48 guns.

The Battle of Medenine, 6th March, 1943

The Eighth Army, hurrying forward to relieve the pressure on the 2nd U.S. Corps in Tunisia, had become rather over-extended, and at Medenine, on 6th March, 1943, Rommel launched against it the 21st, 10th and part of the 15th Panzer Divisions fresh from their success in the Gafsa sector.

Six days earlier General Montgomery, foreseeing the possibility of such a move, had instructed 30 Corps to prepare a defensive position on high ground N.W. of Metameur (*see* Map 6). For a few days the situation seemed critical, but by 4th March the 2nd New Zealand Division had joined the 7th Armoured and 51st (H) Divisions and there were some 400 tanks and over 500 anti-tank guns in position round Medenine. By 6th March, the whole position had been thoroughly organized.

Centralization of artillery command had been made possible by the laying of cable to all batteries, and the rapid dissemination of information was ensured by the use of the alternative wireless link. The flexibility essential to a defensive battle had also been preserved. Although the whole of the corps artillery was controlled by the C.C.R.A., fire orders were normally delegated to Cs.R.A. and below according to the state of the communications at the time and the amount of information available. Defensive fire plans had been carefully prepared and an ample supply of ammunition had been dumped at battle positions.

The anti-tank defences had been co-ordinated by anti-tank regimental commanders working in conjunction with their neighbours on either flank, so that practically no line of approach was left uncovered. Depth was also given to the defences, which were backed up by three armoured brigades held in readiness in rear of the corps position. Thus no artillery other than anti-tank had to be deployed in an anti-tank role and the full weight of the field and medium artillery could be used for orthodox purposes.([25])

Many of the anti-tank guns were sited purely to kill tanks and not to protect the infantry. Thus one battery was in action in front of the F.D.L.s and had to be protected by infantry patrols at night and by machine-gun fire in daylight. All guns of this battery were so sited that they could not see enemy tanks until they were at very close range. They had a very good day's shooting.

Divisional L.A.A. artillery was used mostly to protect gun areas, and the 12th A.A. Brigade defended the advanced landing grounds. Since the latter were only a few miles from the enemy lines, alternative anti-tank positions were prepared for all guns and were occupied during the battle. In fact the concentration of A.A. units in this area formed a part of the defensive scheme for the south-western flank of the Eighth Army, which at this time was rather ill-defined and exposed to attack.

Thus the defence as a whole was well balanced and the results achieved were quick and decisive. The initial enemy air assaults were repulsed without difficulty and with very little loss to the defenders; and when, at dawn on 6th March, the enemy debouched from the Matmata Mountains, he was met by troops who were fresh and thoroughly primed for battle. The field and medium artillery hit him at long range and broke up some of his attacks before they had even started; the anti-tank guns dealt at short range with the remainder. Sometimes the enemy tanks would not face the fire of the 6-prs. and would gradually become penned up in some sheltering wadi, only to be struck again by defensive fire and impromptu concentrations from the field and medium guns.

It was all over in a day. After four major attacks, the first in the early morning mist, the enemy drew off in the evening with the loss of 52 tanks, which represented probably one-third of his total tank strength on the southern front and perhaps nearer half of those engaged in the battle. Our casualties were light and we lost no tanks. In fact only one armoured squadron had had to intervene in the fighting. It was a gunner's battle, in which the anti-tank guns of the infantry had co-operated most effectively with those of the R.A., and both had fitted in neatly with the rest of the artillery fire plan.

"This action proved conclusively that if infantry are well dug in with their anti-tank guns properly concealed, and if they are well supported by artillery fire, they have nothing to fear from a tank attack even though they are not protected by wire or mines ".([3])

SECTION III.—A.A. AND COAST DEFENCE

A.A. Defence

Owing to the superiority that had been established by the R.A.F., enemy air activity was relatively slight except in the forward areas in the early stages of the battle and again from 16th to 25th November, when both R.A.F. and Army had temporarily outrun their maintenance services. Dive bombing attacks gave way by degrees to low-flying attacks by fighters and medium level bombing from 7,000-9,000 feet by formations of Ju87's with fighter escorts, and in general enemy aircraft showed a marked disinclination to come within range of the Bofors guns. Attacks on the railway changed at the beginning of the battle from daylight fighter sweeps and reconnaissances to night attacks by single aircraft, and the damage done was negligible. Action against the ports and landing grounds was on a very small scale.

The distribution of the existing resources varied considerably as the operations proceeded. On 13th August, 1942, the strength of the A.A. defences in Egypt, excluding Egyptian Army units, was 220 H.A.A. guns, 447 L.A.A. guns and 107 searchlights, which were allotted as follows:—

	H.A.A.	L.A.A.	S.Ls.
Eighth Army	—	228	—
Landing grounds in Eighth Army area	32	96	12
Railway Protection in Eighth Army area	8	12	—
Alexandria—Aboukir	26	29	4
Cairo and Delta	48	72	3
Canal Zone	106	110	88

By 23rd October, the number of divisions in the Eighth Army had risen from 6 to 11 and the L.A.A. guns with divisional regiments to 408. Then, as the pursuit got under way, this figure fell again to 220, and the landing ground defences increased, having reached by 30th November, a total of 56 H.A.A. and 168 L.A.A. guns.

After the capture of Tripoli, when Eastern Mediterranean Command took over all static A.A. defences, the appointment of B.A.A. at Headquarters Eighth Army was abolished and the A.A. staff was added to that of the B.R.A. In order to maintain continuity of liaison with the R.A.F., the 12th A.A. Brigade became permanently responsible for the defence of landing grounds, for which purpose a considerable force of infantry and armoured units had sometimes to be placed under its command.

The Use of the Decoy

As an additional precaution during the El Alamein battle, a dummy landing ground lay-out was prepared near Amiriya, on lines similar to those that had been so successful in A.D.G.B. It consisted of two main portions: a dummy flare path covered by a Bofors battery normally disposed, with a master gun in telephonic communication with the nearest H.A.A. position; and, eight miles away to the south, a dummy H.A.A. lay-out, complete with flash simulators. In the former, decoy bonfires were prepared and manned by R.A.F. personnel, working under the control officer of the local R.A.F. group. In the latter were included two genuine 4-gun H.A.A. positions, which were controlled from the G.O.R. and which fired at an increased rate so as to produce a shell density comparable to that of the total number of positions represented.

Experience soon showed that this dual control system was unsatisfactory, and it was therefore agreed that the whole lay-out should be operated by the L.A.A. battery commander on the spot, working on general information and instructions from the A.A.D.C. Fire was opened by the two H.A.A. gun positions on orders or information from the G.O.R., and this was the signal for the flash simulators and Bofors to be brought into action, followed—after the first attack had been made—by the ignition of the decoy bonfires.

Early Warning

At the beginning of this period the resources of the R.A.F. filter room at Dekhaila were available for A.A. units defending both landing grounds and railway. Later, as the Army advanced, the speed with which R.A.F. radar stations were established, and the closeness of the co-operation between R.A.F. and A.A. units—due partly perhaps to the retention of the same A.A. brigade on landing ground defence duties—enabled a satisfactory degree of cover to be maintained over rearward areas even during periods of great mobility. Divisional units had as usual to rely on their own air sentries.

The main difficulty was still the detection of the low-flying attack. In A.D.G.B., during the summer of 1942, the consistent evasion of the R.D.F. screen by the enemy "hedge-hoppers", in their tip-and-run raids against coastal targets, had led to new developments. On 26th September, 1942, it was decided to link R.A.F. C.H.L. stations along the coast, which were more effective against low-flying aircraft than R.D.F., direct to L.A.A. troop headquarters. Visual O.Ps. were also tried, and demands were placed for No. 208 R/T sets to ensure the immediate passage to all guns of information obtained in this way. In March, 1943, six light warning sets (*see* Table B) were deployed along the coast, and in April, 1943, a system of colour plotting was introduced to give the distance of the enemy from the coast, plus a 2-figure map square plot sent to the G.O.R. to help to get the guns pointing in the right direction.

As a result, between 7th May and 6th June, 1943, A.A. Command destroyed 25 enemy aircraft as against 17 destroyed by the R.A.F., and the Germans promptly called a halt to their attacks. In the Middle East, however, nothing of this sort had yet materialized, and the best that could be done was to experiment in the back areas with a modified G.L. Mk I, which was never seriously tested owing to the absence of enemy air action.

Improvements in A.A. Fire Control

By 22nd November, the 12th A.A. Brigade, defending the landing grounds, had become very extended. It reached, in fact, from Mareopolis to Msus, a distance of approximately 700 miles. Hence wireless became of increasing importance, and it was now applied for the first time to the control of H.A.A. gun-fire from G.O.Rs. for the early defence of landing grounds. Since R/T was impossible at night owing to atmospheric conditions, a system was evolved for the passage of plots and orders by W/T to gun stations.

In base areas improvements were effected in the fire control system with the aid of new equipment and new methods that had arrived from the United Kingdom. Most of the H.A.A. gun positions were now equipped with G.L. Mk. II, and the rather clumsy and uneconomical predicted barrage was gradually being replaced by the A.D.G.B. method of independent site control with the aid of the semi-automatic plotter. At the same time advantage was taken of the new searchlight radar equipment (S.L.C.) to produce beam intersections which, if G.L. failed, could be laid on direct by the H.A.A. guns. In future the G.O.R.-controlled barrage was to be retained only as a last resort against the ordinary raider, or as a means of engaging a massed attack, which was likely to upset the accuracy of individual G.L. sets.

In the Canal Zone beam intersections were also used as a substitute for the L.A.A. barrage. Here searchlights were disposed so as to produce cones of light directed, like the guns, at the intersection of two master beams, each equipped with the S.L.C.

During the period 1st-8th September, ten searchlights, with three S.L.Cs., were put at the disposal of the R.A.F. for use in conjunction with night fighters. It was a method that had been used with some success in A.D.G.B. as a supplement to A.I. interception in its early stages (*see* p. 96), and it seemed to offer prospects of even better results in the clearer atmosphere of Egypt.

In the event, however, the number of targets that presented themselves was too few to test either of these systems effectively; though a searchlight battery was included in the defences both at Tobruk and Benghazi, and in one raid on Tobruk the enemy was successfully illuminated and induced to jettison his bombs wide of the target.

A.A. in the Ground Rôle

Because of the general preponderance of our field artillery, few opportunities arose for the use of A.A. guns in the ground rôle. At El Alamein the idea had occurred of using the 3.7-in. H.A.A. gun to destroy derelict tanks left behind on the battlefield and thus to prevent their subsequent recovery; but before a suitable tractor could be found to take the gun up to its selected position in the forward area, the breakthrough had been accomplished and the need for such action no longer existed.

One very useful rôle was found for the L.A.A. gun by taking advantage of its tracer ammunition. Single guns, placed about 300 yards behind the starting line, were used to indicate the line of advance during the night attacks and thus greatly helped the infantry to maintain direction; and once this technique had become known to the enemy, it served as an added means of deception when staging a feint attack.

Coast Defence

By the time the offensive started one coast battery had been organized on a semi-mobile basis. Equipped with 6-in. and 12-pr. guns, it was brought into action on the narrow isthmus west of Dekhaila airfield ready to engage any enemy tanks that might cross the skyline. After the pursuit had started, its guns were moved forward on tank transporters and emplaced for the defence, successively, of Mersa Matruh, Benghazi and Tripoli. Behind it other coast defence units were installed by taking existing equipments—6-in., 4-in, 12-pr. and 6-pr.—and personnel from Egypt and Syria; and at the minor ports of Bardia and Derna—of which the former was only used while Tobruk was being reconditioned—A.M.T.B. defences were provided by the Bofors guns of a L.A.A. unit.

SECTION IV

Conclusion

During these six months the restoration of the gun to its earlier position of importance upon the battlefield had been finally assured. With the 6-pr. now available in adequate numbers, and the 17-pr. beginning to make its appearance, the tank had been mastered and the 25-pr. was able to revert to its proper rôle. It was not, of course, the final victory. That would have to be won by the Sherman and its successors, just as the final victory over the dive bomber had been won by the fighters of the R.A.F. But it was the foundation on which a successful offensive could be based.

For three years the Army had been struggling against difficulties imposed by lack of preparedness and the collapse of allies, and confusion had been increased by an almost continuous sequence of reorganizations. To mention only the most important of those that had concerned the artillery, there were the reorganizations of the field regiment in 1938, 1940 and 1942; the armoured and infantry divisional artilleries in 1940 and 1942; the A.A. brigade and searchlight regiment in 1940; and the L.A.A. and anti-tank regiments in 1940, 1941 and 1942. Now most of these troubles were over. Equipment was becoming plentiful, reorganization was in abeyance, and orthodoxy was restored to power.

Meanwhile the enemy, having lost the advantage of superior equipment and having been deprived of the initiative, was being induced to repeat some of the faults we had made in certain earlier operations. At Alam el Halfa and Medenine had had paid heavily for his over hasty attack with armour against a carefully prepared position, and he continued to make use of battle groups after their usefulness appeared to have ended.[13]

There were, however, two ways in which he was still able to baffle us: by his use of the minefield and of the anti-tank screen. At El Alamein we had been able to force a bridgehead with infantry and artillery, but this was partly because of the relatively small number of anti-personnel mines used by the enemy and the thinness of his wire obstacles. It was evident that in future, if armoured formations were to act as more than weapons of pursuit, and were to get forward in face of even hastily organized and weak anti-tank gun opposition, they must use smoke and rapid concentrations of artillery fire to neutralize the enemy detachments, while the tanks moved forward to positions from which their final assault upon the guns could be covered with their own machine-guns.[26]

The day might also come—in fact was soon to come—when greater attention would have to be paid to the control of counter-battery fire. At El Alamein the counter-battery organization had worked well, but the efficacy of our counter-battery fire was still severely limited by the lack of an air O.P. and by the continued inability of arty/R aircraft, despite our air superiority, to function without a strong fighter escort.

During the pursuit to Tripoli, it was found possible to produce a divisional concentration within about one hour of the guns coming into action, and a quick barrage within two hours as compared with the 10-12 hours considered necessary in 1939 (*see* p. 29). The two main factors contributing to these successes had been the " air burst grid " (*see* p. 150) and the improvement of wireless equipment and drill. By putting bursts in the air and warning other units (by wireless) when and where to look in, it was possible to put a whole regiment, and even a whole divisional artillery, into sympathy from the beginning, thus avoiding the inconvenience and delay of conversion from battery to regimental, and later to divisional, grid.

The traditions and fighting spirit of the Jock columns lived on, and there was one battery at least that could claim never to have been on a grid until it had reached Buerat. In general, however, the principle of concentration had been firmly re-established. The lore of the desert had proved, on closer acquaintance, to be not incompatible with normal artillery doctrine.

Now the desert had been left behind and the Eighth Army stood on the threshold of Tunisia, which by comparison was almost Europe. Here, and later in Sicily and Italy, there would be few opportunities for the large scale use of armour, but many for the exploitation of the mortar.

List of References

[1] Note by General Freyberg quoted in Official (Preliminary) Narrative of War.
[2] " Tactical Handling of Inf. Divs. in the Middle East ", C.R.M.E./37467/M.T.1 of 17th August 1942.
[3] " The Battle of Egypt ", by G.I., M.T., Eighth Army.
[4] Official (Preliminary) Narrative of the War, Sec.   , p. 41.
[5] Notes on Last German Attack on El Alamein, by Comd. Eighth Army, 7th September 1942.
[6] Report by 1 R.H.A. on the " Priest ", as edited by M.G.R.A., M.E.F., 23rd December 1942.
[7] A.T.M. No. 44 of October 1942.
[8] " The African Campaign from El Alamein to Tunis ", Despatch by F. M. Alexander, Vol. I, p. 17.
[9] *Ibid*, p. 25.
[10] *Ibid*, p. 26.
[11] R.A. Notes on El Alamein, by B.R.A. Eighth Army.
[12] Report by Corps Lessons Committee on the Fighting from 23rd October to 5th November 1942.
[13] M.E.T.M. No. 8, Lessons from Operations, October-November 1942.
[14] Report by 1st South African Division on Fighting from 30th September to 10th November 1942.
[15] Summary of Arty. Operations in 9 Aust. Div., 23rd October-4th November 1942.
[16] " From Tunisia to Normandy ", by Maj.-Gen. H. Rowan-Robinson, p. 28.
[17] War Diary, M.G.R.A., M.E.F., January 1943.
[18] R.A. Notes No. 6, App. " D ".
[19] " El Alamein to the R. Sangro ", by Field Marshal Montgomery, p. 36.
[20] " Notes on Lessons Learned During Advance from El Alamein to Tunis ", by C.R.A. 51 (H) Div.
[21] 4 Ind. Div. R.A. Training Instruction No. 3 of 30th September 1942.
[22] War Diary, 7 Armd. Div. R.A., December 1942.
[23] Arty. Lessons, Eighth Army, El Alamein to Sousse.
[24] 4 Indian Div. R.A. Instruction of 25th November 1942.
[25] " The R.A. Story of Medenine ", by B.R.A., Eighth Army.
[26] " Lessons from Recent Operations ", from War Diary, M.G.R.A., M.E.F., 29th December 1942.

PART V

THE FIGHT AGAINST THE MORTAR

CHAPTER X

TUNISIA

Plates Relevant to this Chapter

Nos.
23. The 7.2-in. how.
24. The original Air O.P.
25. Artillery concentrations near Heidons.

The Reappearance of Heavy Artillery

When the First Army set out for North Africa in the autumn of 1942, it was the first British army since the B.E.F. of 1939-40 to take with it a proportion of heavy artillery ; and, judged by the standards of the First World War, the proportion was still small. The growing strain on our industrial resources had early set a limit to the amount of artillery that could be produced and priority had naturally been given to A.A. and mobile field artillery equipments (*see* p. 12). Planning, also, had been complicated by the conflicting claims of range and shell power, and by uncertainty regarding the amount and accuracy of the fire support to be expected from the R.A.F. Until air superiority had been won, air observation for long range artillery was out of the question, and without it the guns would lose much of their value. By the time it had been won, it seemed possible that the air bombing of small targets might have so improved in accuracy as to render long range artillery superfluous.

It is not surprising, therefore, that the development of heavy artillery made halting progress. On 21st November, 1940, the 7.2-in. how. had been accepted as the sole heavy artillery weapon partly because of the need for quick production (*see* p. 37). The carriage, originally intended to be built to a new design, was to be developed from the existing common carriage of the 6-in. gun and 8-in. how., of which large quantities were available in the U.S.A. out of stock surviving from the First World War. Owing to technical difficulties, production started slowly and in the end the converted carriage was not entirely successful.

In December, 1942, owing to the greatly reduced scale of heavy regiments accepted by the General Staff for the period ending 31st December, 1943, it became possible to consider an improved carriage. The policy was that the 7.2-in. how. should continue to be the only heavy artillery weapon, with the 6-in. gun and 9.2-in. how. in reserve in case of need.([1]) By this time, however, demands were beginning to come in from the Middle East for long range artillery to compete with the German 17-cm. and 15-cm. guns, and to meet these demands arrangements were eventually made for the provision of 155-mm. and 8-in. guns from the U.S.A. At the same time the 7.2-in. how. was adapted to the 155-mm. carriage, which, by virtue of its greater strength, allowed an extension of the " piece " and a consequent improvement in its performance. None of these improvements took effect, however, until after the Tunisian campaign had ended.

The Introduction of the A.G.R.A.

The introduction of heavy, and the increase in quantity of medium, artillery raised the question of how these, and other, non-divisional artillery units were to be commanded. At Bardia in January, 1942, and more recently at El Alamein, a medium artillery group had been formed and a commander and staff had had to be improvised (*see* pp. 109, 145). Now it was felt necessary to create a permanent organization for this purpose.

The question was, should it be on a corps or army basis? The C.C.M.A. had gone, and in the autumn of 1942 it was agreed that the majority of non-divisional artillery units should be regarded as army troops, to be allotted to lower formations as required. To make the system flexible, a number of group headquarters were formed and allotted to armies on the scale of one to each corps, the composition and sub-allotment of each group being determined by operational requirements. On 26th November, 1942, the army group R.A. (A.G.R.A.) and its commander (C.A.G.R.A.) were officially sanctioned, and the latter became responsible to the C.C.R.A. for all counter-battery arrangements within his area.

The Development of Air Observation

In the flat, open desert, with no long range artillery, air observation had been desirable but perhaps not essential. In broken country like Tunisia, with some heavy and a considerable amount of medium artillery, and with an increasing emphasis on counter-battery fire, it was to become practically indispensable.

Fortunately, with the growth of the R.A.F. and the achievement of air superiority in the European and Mediterranean theatres, it was also possible. Despite a good deal of opposition, based on mistrust of its ability to function in war, the air O.P. had at last materialized. Air O.P. squadrons, organized in three flights each of four aircraft, were normally allotted at the rate of one to each corps. Within the corps, flights could be sub-allotted one to each of two divisions, with the third flight under command of the C.C.R.A. or of the affiliated C.A.G.R.A. Within the division or A.G.R.A., sections of single aircraft were temporaily allotted to regiments in accordance with the situation; the organization being such that a section could remain under command of a regiment or battery, and detached from its flight, for a considerable period.

Since the flying personnel were all R.A., the air O.P. was in effect " neither more nor less than an artillery O.P. capable of moving quickly in three dimensions ", and the pilot was intended to be " as much a part of the regiment as any battery or troop commander ".[2] As such, he could be entrusted with the control of a regimental or divisional concentration, which he would exercise through the medium of his parent regiment.[3] In practice, however, changes were frequent and regiments had constantly to work with different pilots.

The aircraft was very " manœuverable " and so could be kept in close proximity to regimental or battery headquarters; but in the air it was expected to be very vulnerable, owing to its slow speed and lack of armament and armour. If so, it would depend for its security on cover provided by our own air force or A.A. artillery, and on its ability to make a quick descent and " squat " in the face of an attack by enemy fighters. For this reason its activities were subject at first to three restrictions: it was to keep 1,000 yards or more behind our forward troops; it was not to fly above 600 feet; and it was not to keep in the air for more than 20 minutes at a time.[4] Almost from the start, however, these restrictions were lightly regarded by pilots, who soon learned to rely on warnings of approaching enemy aircraft obtained from special air sentries at battery and troop command posts and passed by R/T direct to the air O.P.

Nevertheless the air O.P. was only a supplement to, and not a substitute for, the arty/R aircraft of the army co-operation squadrons, whose functions, especially counter-battery work, remained very much the same as before. Arty/R requirements were submitted by the C.C.R.A. to the general staff at corps headquarters, times were agreed during which sorties would be required, tasks were allotted to pilots in order of priority, and the responsibility for answering air calls was allocated to selected artillery units. For the engagement of distant targets "mission" sorties would have to be arranged, and they would often have to be provided with special fighter cover.

Terrain and Climate

Northern Tunisia, apart from the coastal plain in the east, is a country of high mountains with narrow plains between the ranges which offer a very limited scope for armoured action. The mountains, through which the First Army had to fight its way to the Tunisian plain, were wild and rugged, strewn with boulders and, in the northern sector, often covered with a dense scrub that limited visibility to a few feet. Tracks were few and bad, and paths had sometimes to be cut through the scrub with the aid of axes and knives.

In the south-east, where the mountains met the coastal plain, the country was flatter, with big upstanding rocky hills and ridges rising out of it and offering ideal defilade for the enemy 8.8 cm. dual purpose guns. Except in the northern sector, around Tebessa and Le Kef, woods suitable for cover were very scarce. The olive groves, though tempting at first, suffered from two serious disadvantages: in wet weather the ground beneath them became so muddy as practically to immobilize any unit sheltering there, and the height of the foliage was such as to blind both guns and tanks.[5]

Throughout the greater part of the campaign the weather was extremely bad. The rains began early in December, less than a month after the initial landings in North Africa, and continued until early April, reaching a maximum in March. During this period rain, mist and mud played a constant part in military operations and often forbad movement altogether to formations that were not adequately equipped with pack transport.

Enemy Tactics

In short, conditions could hardly have been more favourable to the enemy, who, in his conduct of the defensive battle, made full use of reverse slopes, thus sometimes catching our leading infantry unawares and making it difficult for us to provide them with adequate artillery support. His machine-guns were cleverly sited in positions immune from our artillery fire, and he was amply equipped with mortars, which as usual he used most effectively, especially against features that had just fallen into our hands and were still in process of consolidation.

In the hills, wire and mines were not much used. The former was apt to give away a position that might otherwise have escaped detection. The latter could not be transported in sufficient quantities on the number of pack mules that were available. In the later stages of the fighting, however, among the foothills on the coastal plain, the enemy again made use of elaborately organized minefields, which were sometimes skillfully concealed amid the corn crops.

The Need for Mountain Artillery

It was not the first time we had encountered such conditions. In Greece and in Italian East Africa the need for mountain artillery had been felt, and from November, 1941, onwards, attention had been directed towards the creation, in the United Kingdom, of a small number of mountain divisions capable of operating in countries as far apart as northern Norway and North Africa. The artillery of each division ought, it was thought, to contain one mountain regiment, but owing to a shortage of 3.7-in. hows. and pack animals, this could not be provided.

By November, 1942, the policy had undergone a change. The idea of a special mountain divisional establishment was abandoned, and the divisions selected for training in this role, now reduced to two, were to adhere as closely as possible to the normal organization, so that they could, if necessary, be used in a normal role. The new tactical conception was that operations off a M.T. axis would usually be confined to outflanking movements on a man-pack basis against light opposition, and on an animal-pack or sledge basis as resistance stiffened. These turning movements would normally be undertaken within range of the divisional artillery on the road and, thanks to the development of wireless, could be adequately supported from there. For this reason a relatively small proportion of mountain artillery could be accepted, and this would be allotted primarily for close support of the infantry.

This conception coincided more or less with that which had been formed in the India Command apropos of operations in the jungle. On 11th January, 1942, G.H.Q. India had issued instructions for a " mixed transport division ", with a normal artillery component of one mountain, two field, one anti-tank and one L.A.A. regiment, and an allotment of animal transport companies sufficient to enable two brigades to operate on a " fighting pack scale " just off the road, or one brigade group to operate away from the road for a limited period on a " hard scale ".([6])

For the fighting in North Africa, the First Army was provided with two light batteries armed with 3.7-in. hows., which though mechanized and not pack-transported, were reported to have " paid a splendid dividend in the mountains, where they proved themselves to be the best close support weapon obtainable."([7]). The Eighth Army had no such provision, and although the lack was sometimes felt, it was remarkable how readily this desert born army adapted itself to mountain conditions, both here and later in Sicily and Italy.([8])

In fact it is probably fair to say that, in Tunisia, light artillery was a luxury rather than a necessity. What was essential was a really mobile O.P. party and a good W/T set. The field artillery at that time was equipped with 21 and 18 sets, of which the former were difficult and heavy to carry and the latter had too short a range to communicate between O.Ps. and guns. It was therefore necessary to equip O.P. parties with pack transport for the carriage of the heavier and more powerful sets, and when this was done no difficulty was experienced.

The Race for Tunis, 8th November-27th December, 1942

"The First Army was the first British force to be sent abroad with a good supply of A.A. artillery, both heavy and light."(⁹) Yet still, at the start of the campaign, the A.A. umbrella was very thin in the forward areas. The general policy had been to concentrate on the protection of beaches, ports and airfields.

There was also a complete lack of suitable airfields in the forward areas, and the result was to give the enemy a temporary command of the air, of which he was quick to take advantage. During the bitter fighting from 26th November to 3rd December that preceded our withdrawal from the Djedeida area, he put in low level and dive bombing attacks which, though not very intense judged by later standards, had considerable moral effect owing to the inexperience of the troops, the absence of our own aircraft, and the shortage of A.A. guns. The usual combination of infantry, armour and Stukas proved too much for our light forces operating at the end of a very long L. of C., and in spite of some good work by the 6-prs., and some of the 25-prs. in an anti-tank role, the 11th Infantry Brigade Group was overwhelmed and the bulk of its artillery captured. Torrential rain, starting on 23rd December, put an end to the offensive operations of 5 Corps and left them on the wrong side of the Medjerda valley with the important Longstop feature in enemy hands.

The Build-Up of the First Army, 28th December, 1942-27th March, 1943

The race for Tunis and Bizerta had been lost and there followed a period of build-up, during which both sides tried to hold on to or seize ground that offered advantages for the future. "We were mainly on the defensive, suffered from an acute shortage of infantry, and were often hard perssed in the mountainous country. . . . Our greatest asset was our preponderance in artillery, and the front seemed at times largely held by artillery fire alone."(¹⁰)

To make full use of this artillery fire, survey was essential, since maps were non-existent or unreliable. Only two R.A. survey troops were landed in the early convoys, but the speed and accuracy of their work was such that Cs.R.A. and Cs.C.R.A., or their representatives, were soon able to shoot large numbers of guns with almost the same facility that a battery officer could shoot a single troop. To prevent waste of ammunition, and to derive full value from the increased flexibility of the fire control system, a procedure had been introduced whereby special O.Ps. manned by senior officers (majors or lieut.-colonels) were superimposed upon the normal O.P. layout, and were empowered to initiate and control a quick observed divisional concentration. If the range was known, ranging might be dispensed with. If the location of the target was doubtful, the O.P. would use the first troop to report ready for ranging and give "all" corrections, using yards for line as well as range.(³)

Employed for the first time by the 6th Armoured Divisional Artillery at Bou Arada early in January, 1943, this system was most effective in breaking up repeated German attacks by massed artillery fire. As the war proceeded, however, it became more and more the practice to fire large unobserved concentrations—as indeed had been done at El Alamein mainly owing to the difficulty of getting good observation.

After a gallant performance by the air O.P. squadron near Medjez in the face of local enemy air superiority, air observation was not much used during this period. The air O.P., by rendering valuable service at a critical period when the race for Tunis was seen to have failed, had defeated its critics and established its claim to survival; but the view now obtained from our ground O.Ps., especially those overlooking the Medjerda valley, was so good that the need for an air O.P. was not acute. It was therefore decided to husband our scanty resources.

Arty/R, on the other hand, which would have been very useful at the longer ranges, was interfered with by several factors. At first there was our inferiority in the air. Then, when the air situation had improved, the activities of arty/R sorties were hampered by equipment difficulties. Until the obsolescent Hurricanes could be replaced by Mustangs, such sorties had to be provided with strong fighter cover, which could seldom be spared from other more important tasks.

By this time the enemy artillery was beginning to indulge in desultory shelling of our infantry positions, and owing to the difficulty of locating hostile batteries in the hills, special retaliatory shoots, known as " strafe " targets, were directed against the enemy infantry whenever our own infantry was being shelled and proper C.B. methods were impracticable.([11])

The German Tiger Tank Makes its Debut

On the southern portion of the front, where the French 19th Corps was fighting at a great disadvantage owing to its lack of modern equipment, the enemy scored a success in the middle of January by a surprise thrust with armour, including some of the new German Mk. VI (Tiger) tanks, in the Bou Arada area. Thanks to the timely arrival of British reinforcements, the attack was held and five enemy tanks, including two Tigers were destroyed in the Robaa valley.

The War Office had had early news of the Tiger, as a result of which 100 × 17-prs., specially mounted on 25-pr. carriages, had been sent out to North Africa to deal with it. At Robaa, however, the 6-pr. had done all that was necessary. By withholding their fire, the anti-tank gunners had caught the enemy armour at a disadvantage and had pierced the Tiger's 80-mm. flank armour at ranges between 500 and 900 yards.

A month later, at Sidi Nsir in the northern sector, German tanks, after a brief initial success, were again held by artillery fire, this time chiefly from field and medium guns. On 26th February an isolated detachment of one infantry battalion and one field battery, which had been placed out as a delaying force to cover the northern approaches to Beja, was overwhelmed, after a gallant fight, by a strong force of enemy armour and lorried infantry. The following day, when the enemy followed up his success with an attack on the main Beja position, he was met by the concentrated fire of field, light and medium guns controlled by the field artillery regimental commander from the infantry brigade commander's A.C.V. Caught on a narrow mountain road, from which there was no egress, the enemy tanks offered excellent targets, and of the 11 that were estimated to have been knocked out, only one had arrived within reach of the 6-prs. There is no doubt that on this day the majority of the victims could be claimed by the 25-prs. and 5.5-in. guns.([12]).

These two successes, won without the intervention of the 17-pr., and followed within a few days by the decisive victory of Medenine (*see* pp. 150 *et seq.*), had marked the turning-point in the long struggle between the gun and the tank. As further proof, if such were needed, examination of one of the derelict Tigers revealed that the 17-pr. possessed an ample margin of power for dealing with this new opponent. In fact, during the subsequent attacks by the 1st Division in the Medjerda area in April and May, 1943, 17-prs. successfully dealt with Tiger tanks that stood back at about 1,500 yards range and shot up our infantry positions.

The Mareth Line and the Wadi Akrit, March—April, 1943

The Eighth Army was now free to develop its assault against the southern end of the enemy's Tunisian stronghold. The main attack on the Mareth Line began at 2230 hours on 20th March and followed the same general lines as at El Alamein. After a preliminary counter-battery bombardment by three medium and three field regiments, the 50th Division advanced to the assault in the moonlight, supported by concentrations and barrages from 48 medium and 256 field guns. We had nothing heavier than 5.5-in. guns, and not very many of them, to neutralize underground concrete fortifications comparable to those of the Maginot line, and we had therefore to rely on a series of "blitzes" on successive forts as they were assaulted by the infantry. The Wadi Zigzaou, which ran in front of the enemy's positions in this sector, was very deep and steep-sided and the bottom was everywhere muddy. It was in fact impassable except to infantry on their feet, and vehicles could only be got across on a causeway made of fascines, which was kept in operation for three days by the sappers under close range machine-gun fire from two forts.

A few 2-prs. but no 6-prs. were able to make the crossing, and it was therefore impossible to hold on to our gains when the 15th Panzer and part of the 90th Light Division counter-attacked on the afternoon of the 22nd. During the night of the 23rd our troops were withdrawn across the wadi under cover of a "box" barrage put down by the 50th and 51st Divisional Artilleries.([13])

The main weight of the attack was now transferred from the enemy's front to his rear by means of a powerful "left hook" to the west of the Matmata Mountains. The object was to force the El Hamma gap between the Gebels Tebaba and Melab, and to cut off the retreat of the enemy from the Mareth position. Instead of waiting for darkness, as had always been done hitherto, the attack was launched out of a setting sun on the late afternoon of 26th March. It was preceded and accompanied by heavy air attacks carried out by 16 Kittybomber squadrons, with 5 Spitfire squadrons as "top cover", the whole controlled, for the first time, from an aircraft flying over the battlefield and from ground O.Ps. containing R.A.F. officers with high frequency wireless sets. The 8th Armoured Brigade in the lead was covered by heavy artillery fire, including the usual concentrations and a creeping barrage, which not only directed the tanks on to their objective but also enabled the supporting aircraft to follow the course of the battle.

This was a thin barrage put down on a front of about 2,000 yards and at a density of only one gun per 100 yards. Behind it the tanks were able to advance through the dust and smoke without losing direction. It also, of course, helped to subdue opposition in front of them, though it could hardly be called a barrage in the true sense of the word.

The New Zealand Division, following behind the 8th Armoured Brigade, quickly overcame the enemy defences and the 1st Armoured Brigade passed through in the moonlight to close the gap behind the enemy. At first light on the 27th, however, it was held up by anti-tank guns on the outskirts of El Hamma and in the subsequent fighting the 15th and 21st Panzer and the 164th Light Divisions put up a fierce resistance, under cover of which the bulk of the enemy forces on the Mareth Line were able to make good their withdrawal.

At the Wadi Akrit, therefore, the Eighth Army again found itself faced by the enemy in a strong position, and this time there was no question of a "left hook". On the east the sea, and on the west the salt marshes known as the Chott El Fedjadj, formed a solid resting place for either flank, and in the gap of 12 to 15 miles that separated them ran a continuous anti-tank obstacle, which consisted partly of the wadi itself and partly of an extension to it in the form of an anti-tank ditch. On its northern side the wadi was dominated by two mountains: in the west the Gebel Fatnassa, separated from the salt marsh by a defile through which ran the road from Gabes to Gafsa; in the east the Gebel Er Roumana, which extends almost to the sea.

"Taken all round it was a very strong position, much stronger by nature than the Mareth Line ".([11]) To capture it, therefore, a full-dress attack by three divisions was deemed to be necessary. As time was pressing, and it would be ten days before the next moonlight period, it was decided to change the technique on this occasion and put in the attack in complete darkness.([8]) The time selected was 0400 hours on 6th April, and covering fire was to be provided by 450 guns.

On the right the 51st Divisional Artillery had a difficult problem and their fire plan was very complicated, comprising a number of concentrations and five barrages, of which one ended with a wheel (*see* Map 7). It was a step towards the crooked barrage (*see* p. 29), which, though taught in 1940, had seldom if ever been used. For the last two and a half years the majority of our fighting had been done in the desert, where the ground was generally flat and barrages could be kept simple and straight. But in Tunisia the conditions were more nearly those of Europe, and from now on the crooked barrage, though avoided whenever possible on account of its complexity, was to figure at intervals in the artillery plan.

The decision to lay a barrage over the Gebel Er Roumana was made against the evidence of air photographs, which showed the hill to be undefended. It was, however, incredible that so dominating a feature could have been neglected by the enemy, and a barrage was therefore ordered. It was well this was done, for the hill was in fact strongly held by the enemy; and it was only because his positions were cut out of the rock and well camouflaged that they had failed to appear on the air photos.

MAP 7

Outline Fire Plan for 51 Div Attack at Wadi Akarit 6 April 1943

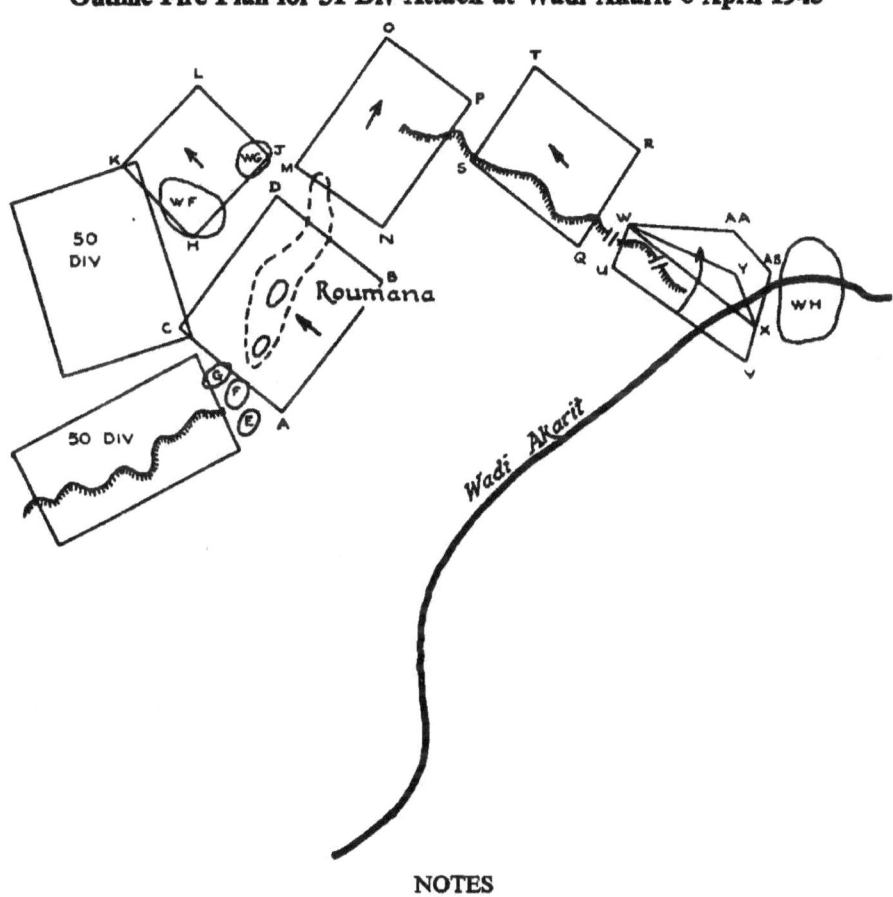

NOTES

152 BDE

Phase I (0415 to 0528)

Barrage A B C D (3 Regts) concentrations E, F and G (1 Regt). Barrage to stand on opening line for 23 mins., then to advance at 100 yds. in 4 mins. for 44 mins. and increase to 100 yards in 2 mins. for last 6 mins.

Phase II (0525 to 0645)

Barrage M N O P (2 Regts), concentrations WF, WG and WH (3 Regts). One Bty to print out start line of barrage for 20 mins., after which full barrage to advance at 100 yds. in 4 mins. for 1 hr.

Phase III (0830 to 0918)

Barrage H J K L (2 Regts). To stand on opening line for 28 mins. then a burst of smoke and Bofors overhead, after which barrage to advance at 100 yds. in 2 mins. for 20 mins.

154 BDE

Phase I (0445 to 0620)

Barrage U V W X-W Y X-W AA. AB, 2 Regts (less 1 Bty) to fire standing barrage on WX and 1 Regt on WY for 15 mins., while 1 Bty prints out opening line UV. Barrage then to advance, in 50 yd. lifts, to WX and swing to WY, to cover "gapping," all 3 Regts participating. Rate of advance 100 yds. in 6 mins.

Barrage to stand on WYX for 5 mins. and then lift to W.AA.AB and stand again for 15 mins., to cover attack by 7 A and SH.

Barrage QRST (2 Regts.) to be fired 95 mins. after receipt of code word "James." To begin with burst of smoke and Bofors overhead and advance at 100 yds. in 2 mins. for 38 mins.

In spite of its complexity, this fire plan was a success. In the centre, on the other hand, the 50th Division were held up on the anti-tank ditch. A request for the repetition of part of the barrage, and the postponement of the second phase of the battle, to enable the infantry to get on to their first objective, had to be refused on account of the interference it would have caused with the programmes of the other two divisional artilleries and of the corps artillery; and in the event the infantry of the 50th Division actually caught up nearly a thousand yards on the barrage during the second phase.

On the left the 4th Indian Division fought their own artillery battle and were not co-ordinated with the remainder of the corps artillery for topographical reasons. The attack was kept silent for as long as possible. Taking full advantage of the surprise thus gained, the darkness, and the broken nature of the country, the infantry brigades pushed ahead, guided, where the going was worst, by a troop of Bofors, which from 0430 hours until daylight fired bursts of tracer at five minutes' intervals. The remainder of the artillery followed up the advance and by 0830 hours was in action in forward positions ready to fire a 30 minutes programme of timed concentrations for the taking of the second objective.

Thereafter control was in the hands of F.O.Os. and liaison officers at battalion and brigade headquarters, who could call for battery, regimental or divisional targets as required. Between 0245 hours on 6th April, and 0200 hours on 7th April, 21 concentrations, varying in strength from one field regiment to four field and one medium regiment, were fired on the orders of the C.R.A.: three to guide the infantry and get them on their objectives; six against enemy mortars, machine-guns and anti-tank guns; five C.B. bombards; five D.F. tasks; one stonk on 1,000 infantry and 30 M.T. vehicles; and one area smoked by one section to guide the Kittybombers on to their target.

The Attack by 78th Division in the Mountains, 7th-23rd April, 1943

The First Army was now getting ready for a major offensive, and as a preliminary measure a series of attacks was carried out by the 78th Division in the mountains, beginning at the Oued Zarga plain and climbing thence up a number of tangled spurs to end at the village of Heidous. It was chiefly an infantry battle, but it included some artillery features of interest. The initial attack was made in the early darkness, at 0400 hours on 7th April, on a three brigade front (*see* Map 8). The artillery available included 130 × 25-prs., 32 × 5.5-in. and 12 × 7.2-in. hows., the bulk of which was divided into three groups: right, centre and left. Apart from a silent attack by 2nd Hampshire Regiment on the extreme left, support was given in the form of concentrations fired by all groups on targets selected by brigade commanders. At zero hour the infantry were to be just short of their first objectives and closing up to within 150 yards of the concentrations, the end of which was to be indicated by the firing of one round air burst by all guns that could do so.

In order to achieve the maximum amount of fire support for the infantry, the 78th Divisional Artillery was absolved from all counter-battery commitments for this operation. Any necessary counter-battery bombardments were to be carried out by the flanking divisions, which could use for this purpose those of their guns that had been placed in support of the attack.

In the later stages of the fighting, occasional use was made of a creeping barrage, at a rate of advance of 100 yards in five minutes, or of a smoke screen to blind enemy O.Ps. on high ground overlooking the advance. In the main, however, owing to the mountainous nature of the country, artillery support continued to be by observed concentrations, most of which were impromptu and were called for and controlled by O.Ps. specially equipped with pack transport.([11]).

The Final Breakthrough

Everything was now ready for the final breakthrough into the Tunisian plain. On 22nd April, after repelling a spoiling attack by the enemy, the infantry of 9 Corps advanced and succeeded in making a gap for the armour to pass through. But " we were not quick enough, and a strong enemy anti-tank screen in broken country north-east and north of Sedkret el Kourzia and near Djebel Kournine prevented eventually all further advance."([10]) The attack by 9 Corps was therefore broken off and a readjustment of forces was made for the final blow.

It was to begin in the dark at 0330 hours on 6th May, and was to be carried out by two divisions—the 4th British and 4th Indian—on a front of only 3,000 yards, supported by 444 guns out of a total of 652 in the area at the time. For the capture of the first two objectives support was to be by timed programme, that for the first objective including a creeping barrage by five field regiments at a rate of 100 yards in three minutes. Thereafter concentrations were to be fired at call, and to facilitate calling for repetitions of these concentrations, all were given names.

The barrage was to dwell for 30 minutes on the opening line to enable the infantry to complete an approach march of about half a mile to their start line. The density of the barrage was only about one 25-pr. to 22 yards, but the quantity of shell falling in the narrow area of the attack was very great : 216 guns on the 4th Indian, and 188 on the 4th, Division front.([15])

At $Z-10$ hostile batteries were to be attacked in turn with heavy concentrations, starting with the most troublesome, and thereafter concentrations at a 10 : 1 density were to be put down on known hostile batteries during selected phases of the attack. Ammunition was dumped on a scale of 550 r.p.g. for field, 350 for medium, and 200 for heavy guns. During the next 24 hours the 25-prs. fired on an average 368 r.p.g., or four more than were fired in the El Alamein battle.([15])

The fire plan started on time and the infantry attack went smoothly. At dawn the scorpions and Churchill tanks came up and the covering fire was deepened by an air bombardment of unprecedented intensity, which included over 2,000 sorties of all types—bombers, fighters and tank-busters. Under this tremendous hammering the enemy morale began to crumble and by 1100 hours the final objectives, up to a depth of 5,000 yards, had all been taken.

The 6th and 7th Armoured Divisions passed straight through to complete the victory, and anti-tank artillery, including 32 × 17-prs., was detailed to line the sides of the break-in.([16]) Close behind the armour went a divisional artillery and an A.G.R.A., under the command of the C.C.R.A. 9 Corps, ready to support either division in case of need, or, should their advance be held up, to take up positions for the support of an attack by the infantry who were following in rear of the artillery group. It soon became evident, however, that organized defences were not likely to present a serious problem and that infantry were more urgently required that artillery. Not until 12th May, when the 6th Armoured Division made its final attack southward from Bou Ficha, was concentrated artillery fire again to be required. Remnants of the enemy, hemmed in between this division and the Eighth Army positions at Enfidaville, were still showing fight. But a simultaneous artillery bombardment from both sides, arranged by wireless, combined with an air bombardment by the Western Desert Air Force, produced an early display of white flags and this marked the end of all organized resistance.

The Predominance of Our Artillery

Thus ended a task that had been begun under very different circumstances in the winter of 1940-41. Then a small and ill-equipped but highly trained army and air force, with little supporting artillery, had by cunning and audacity outmanoeuvred and outfought an Italian army and air force many times its size. Its very success, however, had led—as always—to over-confidence in some of the methods it had employed, and at the same time had stung the Germans into a reaction with which these methods were less well suited to deal. There followed a period of hard fighting for the defence of Egypt, in which the dive bomber and the tank were successively held while the Eighth Army adapted itself to the German system of battle groups.

Now, with greatly increased forces and an ample supply of field artillery, the battle group had been discarded and a return had been made to the principles that had guided our earlier citizen armies of the First World War. Significantly, the first resounding success had been won in a battle that had resembled very closely those of the previous era of positional warfare; a battle of simple plans and limited objectives, backed by a heavy preponderance of artillery fire concentrated at the main point of attack.

In Tunisia, the First Army had been experiencing its baptism of fire and learning, as most democratic armies do, by its own mistakes. Its opponents had begun the campaign with three great advantages: a long military training that extended almost as far back as the cradle; a wide battle experience in other theatres; and a terrain that put a premium on delaying tactics and professional skill in the handling of small formations and units. There had therefore inevitably been some critical moments, in which it might fairly be said that the situation was saved by the predominance of our artillery. In fact, during the defensive battles of February and March, artillery fire was almost the sole reserve, and it was freely and effectively used to hold the front against both tank and infantry attacks. (⁹)

During the subsequent offensive, when our air forces had won the mastery of the sky, it was surprising how many guns could be massed together for the support of an attack in this type of country without being detected by the enemy, and how boldly they could be handled after zero hour without incurring serious casualties. For the final battle we had 650 guns arrayed against 250 of the enemy's, and the technique for controlling the fire of all these guns had been steadily improving. Flexibility of control had been increased by the use of senior observers (*see* p. 161) acting as C.R.As.' or C.C.R.As.' representatives, and of liaison officers from reinforcing artillery regiments at the headquarters of assaulting formations, each equipped with wireless on the A.G.R.A. or divisional artillery frequency and endowed with the right to call for the fire of the whole of his group or divisional artillery. The problem was now rather to control the number of F.O.Os. so that excessive expenditure of ammunition could be avoided and commanders could rest assured that what O.P. parties there were were all accurately informed of the immediate situation in their vicinity.

The main weakness of the system was in fact still the difficulty of making the supporting fire conform to the movements of the assaulting troops when the latter could not conform to a prearranged time programme. To exploit the flexibility inherent in modern wireless equipments, new tactical terms had been introduced by the infantry to indicate to the gunner the degree of flexibility required in the artillery fire plan. Thus " varied by observation " meant that the fire plan might be changed on the initiative of the artillery observer, and " modified on call " meant that subordinate infantry commanders might vary the fire plan by direct orders to artillery O.Ps. If neither of these terms was used, the fire plan was assumed to be rigid.([17])

Communications in fact were now the limiting factor in quick artillery concentrations([18]), and improvements were required both in existing wireless sets and in wireless technique within units. The original system, by which a field regiment was allotted seven wireless frequences, had led to the overcrowding of the ether and it was not until improved wireless discipline had rendered possible the acceptance of a single frequency that the control of artillery concentrations could be further speeded up.

The Mortar and the Machine-Gun

Flash spotting and sound ranging had both given disappointing results, partly because of technical troubles associated with the mountains, and partly because the enemy gunners, making use of their superior range, usually kept well back and in positions defiladed behind high ground. Flash spotting was also adversely affected by the occasional use of flashless propellant by the enemy. For counter-battery work, therefore, reliance had to be placed chiefly on vertical air photographs.

Fortunately the opposition put up by the enemy artillery was slight, owing partly to the neglect of the artillery arm following upon the early successes of the dive bomber, and partly to administrative difficulties caused by the continuous sinking of supply ships by the Royal Navy. A far more serious problem was presented by the mortar and the machine-gun. The silent flight of the mortar bomb, and its power of searching into gullies, added greatly to its demoralizing effect. In fact it was believed to be responsible for 43 per cent. of our neurotic cases, which was equivalent to the combined effects of shelling and air bombardment.([19]) In the final stages of the campaign the enemy made use of a six-barrelled, rocket-firing mortar—the " nebelwerfer "—which fired its rockets at half-second intervals from ranges of up to 6,000 yards and produced a beaten zone of about 200 yards by 400 yards.

The machine-gun was equally difficult to locate and it was largely due to its fire, and that of the hidden sniper, that the rate of advance of the barrage had had to be reduced to 100 yards in four or even five minutes. The physical exertion of movement in this country had also an effect, and towards the end of the campaign the infantry expressed a preference for concentrations and barrages to lift 200 yards at a time, instead of 100 yards as heretofore, so that they could have a longer pause at the end of each bound.[11].

Although the proper answer to the enemy mortar was still considered to be artillery fire, there was general agreement that the handling of our own mortars was capable of much improvement. Modifications were made to the 3-in. mortar to increase its range, and a 4.2-in. mortar—first used in action by the 66th Mortar Company R.E. at El Alamein—was introduced to add weight and range to the punch of the infantry supporting weapons. As a result the control of mortar fire was approximating more and more to that of artillery, and in some divisions 4.2-in. mortar platoons were being trained by the C.R.A.

The Use of Air Bursts for Moral and Lethal Effect

At El Alamein air burst H.E. had been in considerable demand for use against hostile batteries and troops in trenches or under light cover (*see* p. 148). Now many were convinced of the value of air bursts for moral effect. A psychiatrist's report from the New Zealand Division proved that a large percentage of the men disliked the unheralded air burst, such as that of the high velocity 8.8 cm., more than anything else except perhaps the mortar.[20]

Unfortunately time fuzes were not easy to make and production had lapsed when shrapnel was abolished in 1935 (*see* p. 11). The gunnery problem presented by the use of a time fuze was considered too difficult to be mastered by citizen armies, and for the sake of simplicity H.E. shell were provided with impact fuzes only. When, therefore, in March, 1940, time fuzes were demanded by the 1st Canadian Division for use with the 25-pr., some difficulty was experienced in getting production going. After trials at Larkhill in August, 1940, had shown that " any divisional artillery should be able to carry out air burst ranging accurately ",[21] it was decided—in October, 1940—to manufacture both a mechanical and a chemical (powder ring) type of fuze; but the usual difficulties and delays were encountered and it was not until the latter half of 1943 that the supply became really satisfactory. There were indeed still some who argued that H.E. with delay action bounce was better than time burst H.E., and it was not until October, 1943, that an official pronouncement was made in favour of the latter for use against troops in slit trenches.[22]

In the meantime the 3.7-in. H.A.A. gun was there to fill the breach. It was the high velocity and the time fuze of the H.A.A. shell, more than anything else perhaps, that was responsible for the growing popularity of this weapon in the ground rôle.

Co-ordination of Artillery and Air Support

In the desert, co-ordination between artillery and aircraft had been comparatively easy. The creeping barrage acted as an excellent moving bomb line, and as the observed engagement of opportunity targets beyond it was impossible owing to smoke and dust and to the absence of arty/R and the air O.P., it was most desirable that the fighter-bombers should give support in the area immediately in front of it. This was what was done so successfully at El Hamma (*see* pp. 163-4), and it presented no particular difficulty in the desert, where targets were as a rule easily identified.

In Tunisia conditions were very different. "It rapidly became obvious that in this new landscape the targets which the Desert Air Force had come to expect would never be found. In the woods and orchards and broken ground of Tunisia, pilots would have to be induced to carry out a task quite new to them—the bombing of targets which they could not see."[23] It was not easy, and without the use of smoke shell it would have been almost impossible. A design in four colours—red, blue, green and yellow—had been cleared in November, 1942, but the first issues could not be expected to reach the Middle East before the end of this campaign.

During the operations by 10 Corps at Enfidaville on 25th and 26th April, raids were made by light bombers against enemy gun areas with some success. Information was supplied each night by the C.B.O., and as the raid went over, a line of artillery smoke (white) was put down on the southern edge of the area. "No one particularly liked these targets—least of all the air crews. But they seemed to pay a reasonable dividend; fire lessened for a time, the guns shifted, and photos proved that a number of direct hits and many near misses on gun pits had been scored."[23]

On other occasions the guns were able to direct the new tank-buster aircraft on to their objectives; and on 12th May, for the final air attack on the 90th Light Division, hemmed in in the coastal sector between the First and Eighth Armies, the northern and southern limits of the area to be bombed, which at one point was within 1,500 yards of our own troops, were marked by lines of 25-pr. smoke each 2,000 yards long.

The Night Attack

The restrictions imposed on planning by the use only of moonlight periods for the night attack had already become intolerable (*see* p. 164). Hence thoughts had begun to turn, as in the past, to the creation of artificial moonlight. The star shell was the traditional method of obtaining nocturnal illumination, and in the First Army a recommendation was made for the reintroduction of such a shell for the 25-pr. There was, however, no suitable star shell in existence, and it would be many months before one could be produced in quantity.

Searchlights had been used by the Italians at Amba Alagi in 1941, and more recently a proposal had been put forward for their use in the Eighth Army (*see* p. 134). It was also reported that the Russians had developed a technique for the use of "blinding headlights" on their tanks, and it was evident that night attacks by tanks, at least in moonlight, would become more frequent. To meet such attacks, 2-in. mortars and bombs illuminating were issued to anti-tank units on the scale of one to each section.

The Problem of the Minefield

Apart from the mortar, the clearing of minefields was now perhaps the greatest problem that faced the gunner. The enemy, in preparing his defensive lay-outs, would site his foremost posts in narrow slits very close to the minefield. If not neutralized by artillery fire, these posts would prevent the use of detectors by the assault parties. If, on the other hand, they were engaged by the guns, the shell fragments, scattered over the minefield, would also make the use of detectors impossible. Moreover anti-tank mines would be sensitized in such a way that they all became anti-personnel mines.

For the same reasons, attempts to clear a way through a minefield by artillery concentrations were no more successful than they had been in 1941 (*see* p. 102). Hence the development of the "Scorpion", an armoured vehicle that threshed its way through the minefield and was not therefore hampered in its work by the effects of an artillery bombardment.

The Air O.P.

The air O.P. had been a definite success, and far less vulnerable than had been anticipated. The fact was that the enemy Stukas and their fighter escorts were usually too intent on picking up their objectives and getting away again to look around for stray air O.Ps. The latter had therefore been able to perform many useful functions and had proved particularly valuable for the conduct of registration shoots and of neutralization shoots against enemy A.A. guns that threatened to be troublesome to our supporting aircraft, and for watching the front for a counter-attack. On one occasion an air O.P. had shot the whole of the 6th Armoured Divisional Artillery; on another, a 7.2-in. how. battery had been shot by moonlight; and during the moonlight attacks on 21st and 22nd April reconnaissances had been carried out over the enemy lines to discover which of the known hostile batteries were active.([18])

The main difficulties were the lack of adequate oblique photographs and the broken nature of the country. The former was not satisfactorily overcome until the air O.P. was equipped to take such photographs itself. The latter made the location of small targets, such as infantry, mortar and machine-gun posts, very uncertain.

Artillery Support of Tanks

With the arrival of the Sherman tank, a new technique for an attack by armoured units had been developed. Instead of going in behind a heavy barrage or concentration, which took insufficient count of the hidden anti-tank gun and minefield, the Shermans used their 75-mm. guns, as the Germans had used theirs, for mutual support, while the artillery registered likely anti-tank gun positions and stood ready to engage when required.

In general the Priest had fulfilled the hopes that had been aroused by its earlier performance in the desert. Owing to its nondescript appearance, and to the flashless propellant with which it was equipped, it could operate, amid the dust and smoke of battle, in places where the 25-pr. would probably have got into trouble. It could therefore keep close up behind the armour, where it was sometimes used by single guns. Indeed it was recognized that the S.P. regiment belonged " really more to the armoured brigade than to the C.R.A." This was " an evil which must be accepted ", and which, " granted good co-operation between C.R.A. and armoured brigadier ", need cause no trouble.([15])

In the infantry division the role of the tank had undergone a complete change since the winter of 1940-41, when the Matilda was at the height of its fame. As a result of the greatly increased use of minefields by the enemy, it was now seldom possible for tanks in an assault echelon to precede the infantry at tank speed. Even when the assault echelon with tanks leading was used successfully, the infantry were apt to be held up by machine-gun and mortar fire before reaching their objective, thus losing the value of the artillery covering fire. Against a prepared position, therefore, neutralization was primarily the task of the artillery, and the tanks of the assault echelon would often follow in close support of the infantry, where they suffered fewer casualties from mines and could see what they were doing.([24])

Anti-Tank Ammunition

Attempts to improve the penetrative power of anti-tank ammunition had been continuous. The first step was to fit a special cap to the nose of the shot and thus prevent shattering at oblique angles of impact. Shot thus fitted was known as armour piercing capped. A further development was the fitting of a streamline ballistic cap over the armour piercing capped shot. This second cap improved the ballistics of the shot and resulted in higher down-range velocities and increased penetration of armour. The shot fitted with both caps was known as A.P.C.B.C., and production began for the 2-pr. in February 1943, for the 6-pr. in April 1943, and for the 17-pr. in August 1943.

By April 1943, as the result of trials with the 6-pr. in the U.S.A., opinion again veered regarding the value of flashless propellant for anti-tank guns. The smoke given off by this propellant was once more adjudged too serious a hindrance to the observation of the trace and strike, particularly in tank equipments, and on 31st May anti-tank guns were removed for the second time from the priority list.

A.A. Lay-Outs in the First Army

By the first week in December, 1942, the number of A.A. guns, including American, at the disposal of the First Army was 88 heavy and 174 light, in addition to those with divisional L.A.A. regiments. The majority of these weapons were distributed between ports and communication centres on the L of C, with 8 L.A.A. and 4 to 16 H.A.A. at each place. As new convoys arrived, there was often a complete reshuffling of A.A. resources and it was found quite impossible to keep regiments, or even troops, permanently under the same commander. Though tactically open to criticism, this dispersion of A.A. resources was practically inevitable for reasons of morale. It had in fact been a common feature of previous campaigns, when the enemy had command of the air and troops had not yet become accustomed to air attack.

The most striking change in policy since 1940 was the reliance on dispersion and concealment alone to protect dumps, and the consequent release of guns for the A.A. defence of forward areas. Formation headquarters were at first protected, but they were not attacked, and it was soon decided that they too might rely on passive air defence measures. Located, as they often were, in isolated farmhouses, they would simply have invited attack by surrounding themselves with a tell-tale L.A.A. lay-out.

In the later stages of the campaign, as the R.A.F. began to dominate the sky and the enemy's air effort was more and more restricted to the immediate vicinity of the front, the handling of the A.A. artillery became more aggressive. The ancient controversy about the relative importance of deterrent and lethal effect in the application of A.A. fire was temporarily stilled. For the present, at any rate, it could be definitely stated that " the object of A.A. artillery is to kill Germans."([9]) By February, 1943, one-third of the H.A.A. and half the L.A.A. guns were in the forward area, and A.A. units were instructed to adopt the most offensive policy possible ; pushing guns up into unexpected places, laying ambushes, etc.

A.A. Organization In and Behind the Eighth Army

In January, 1943, it was decided to apply the air defence system as it existed in the United Kingdom to the whole of the Eastern Mediterranean—including Tripolitania, Cyrenaica, Egypt and the Levant. In pursuance of this policy the M.G.A.A., Mediterranean Expeditionary Force, was, on 13th March, 1943, appointed Commander A.A. Group, Eastern Mediterranean, and made responsible as such to the R.A.F. officer acting as air defence commander.([25]) Thereafter the Inter-Service Air Defence Committee established in September, 1940 (see p. 61) passed out of existence and was replaced by the Joint Operations Staff, which periodically laid down priorities for the Air Defence Commander, Eastern Mediterranean, to enable him to prepare plans for the distribution of the available air and A.A. resources. These plans were then submitted to the Cs.-in-C., through the Joint Operations Staff, for their approval.

An exception was made at first in the case of Tripoli, which, at the request of the Commander Eighth Army, was allowed to remain temporarily under his control. This port was vital to the operations of the Eighth Army and it was agreed that the number of guns then allotted to it—64 H.A.A. and 60 L.A.A.—represented the minimum scale of defence that could be accepted.

Within the Eighth Army, the 12th A.A. Brigade had continued to be responsible for the defence of airfields and advanced ports, and had gradually perfected its system for the prompt provision of defences at new landing grounds during the pursuit. A regimental group of one heavy and two light batteries was earmarked for each new landing ground, and the Brigade Intelligence Officer, with wireless, moved forward with the leading troops to report on the state of the going. As soon as all necessary information was available, the regimental group was sent forward, usually at night, and reached its destination before the main routes had become crowded. For example, during the New Zealanders' left hook round the Mareth Line, a regimental group made its way to El Hamma along the Hallouf road 36 hours before that road was officially opened to traffic.

At times the resources of this Brigade were very strained. Before the attack on the Mareth Line there were five fighter wings requiring protection, all within 20 miles of the enemy front line ; and at one specially important landing ground the scale of defence had to be raised to three heavy and three light batteries.

The Unseen Target

The greatest A.A. problem was still the production of effective fire at night. In the First Army, G.L. equipment was not included in the earlier convoys, and after it had arrived the hills in some places made it of little use for anything except early warnings. Thus barrages had to be used, and at first they were very thin owing to the small number of guns available.

Yet they sufficed. At Bone, for example, which was heavily and persistently attacked during December, 1942, 16 H.A.A. and 24 L.A.A. guns gave a useful backing to the night fighters and materially helped to bring these attacks under control. Since sites suitable for continuous following by G.L. II could not be found, plots were transmitted *via* the 66th A.A. Brigade Command Post to the guns, including those of H.M. ships, and concentrations were fired at predicted points about 30 seconds ahead of the last position indicated by the target plots. If G.L. lost the target, concentrations were fired at the centre of a 1,000 metre square and at a height chosen in accordance with the best information available.([26])

If the gunnery was primitive, the system of tactical control had been improved by the introduction of a mobile G.O.R., which was equipped with its own light warning set, plotting gear sufficient to serve 12 H.A.A. positions, and wireless and line telephony for broadcasting. This organization was of particular value in an assault landing, when it would act as an early warning centre by filtering and broadcasting information received from the R.A.F., the R.D.F. ship, its own L.W. set, and sometimes the L.A.A. sets of L.A.A. regiments.([27])

A.A. Smoke Screens

In June, 1940, when the threat of heavy air attack on the United Kingdom was felt to be imminent, the Chiefs of Staff had invited the Ministry of Home Security to accept responsibility for area smoke screening of vulnerable targets at night. Screening was in full swing early in 1941 and by the end of that year some 9,000 Pioneer Corps personnel were engaged on this task alone. In 1942, when the enemy made his great attempt to neutralize Malta by intensive bombing, smoke again rendered good service and was used, for the first time, by day as well as by night.

The first steps to screen ports in North Africa were taken by the Royal Navy, but the responsibility was soon handed over to the Army. Operationally, A.A. smoke units were under the control of local A.A.D.Cs., who would be advised by the naval commander whether and when smoke was to be made.([28])

At first there was some distrust of the new weapon on the part of A.A. commanders, who felt that the activities of their guns were likely to be seriously restricted. · Experience showed, however, that it was possible to site L.A.A. guns so that their arcs of fire were not interfered with, and H.A.A. guns with G.L. control were not of course affected.

The Sun Barrage

The attack out of the sun had long been a favourite ruse of the enemy dive bomber, and to counter it the 12th A.A. Brigade had instituted what was known as a "sun barrage". Friendly aircraft were instructed never to approach their own landing-grounds from this direction, and any aircraft that did so was automatically classified as hostile. As soon, therefore, as aircraft were plotted or heard approaching from out of the sun, a barrage was put up on their anticipated line of dive. L.A.A. guns fired 40 rounds at "auto", sweeping five degrees each side of the sun, and H.A.A. shell were set to burst at a range of 4,200 yards from the centre of the vulnerable area. After two attacks by Me109's on the newly opened Tamet landing ground in January, 1943, in each of which one aircraft was shot down by these methods, the enemy gave it up. The sun barrage had evidently proved the solution to this problem.([20])

Use of the L.A.A. Gun for the Warning of Road Convoys

During the period 27th February-12th March, 1943, men, equipment and supplies had to be rushed from Tripoli to the Medenine area along a single road. Convoys were required to travel by night and day, and, as there was no moon, headlights were used as far as Ben Gardane except when enemy aircraft were in the vicinity. To inform convoys of the presence or approach of enemy aircraft, the guns of a L.A.A. battery were distributed along the route at intervals of about nine miles and were fired in accordance with air raid warnings received from the G.O.R. at Tripoli. Acting upon this signal, all convoys would then stop, douse headlights, and wait until the "all clear" had been given by two bursts of six rounds "auto" at one minute intervals.

The Success of the Radar Controlled Searchlight

For the first time in the Middle East S.L.Cs. had been in action continuously over a period of some weeks against diving and low-flying targets. At Tripoli, experience showed that for the defence of a small vulnerable area a lay-out of 24 A.A.S.Ls., including 8 S.L.Cs., would ensure the illumination of a high proportion of targets for long enough to enable the guns to engage them effectively.

Thus the radar-controlled searchlight had proved a most valuable supplement to the radar-controlled H.A.A. gun at low angles of elevation where G.L. was unreliable. As a result the primary rôle of the A.A.S.L. was now in co-operation with L.A.A. guns.([29]) At the same time results obtained with S.L.C. were so good that, at the request of the R.A.F., and with the help of U.S. reinforcements, two illuminated aircraft fighting zones were formed in the First Army area, to act as a second line of defence to the more distant operations of radar-controlled night fighters.

The outcome of these successes was the creation, in May 1943, of six composite L.A.A./S.L. batteries, each equipped with 12 Bofors and 9 searchlights, for the defence of airfields and other targets.([28])

Coast Artillery

Included in the order of battle of the First Army were six coast batteries; three armed with 6-in. guns, and three with Bofors and searchlights; the latter with a primary A.M.T.B. and a secondary A.A. rôle. In the early stages of the campaign these guns were placed—as coast artillery had always been, and continued to be, in the Eighth Army—under the control of the local A.A. commander. Later, however, the command of all the port defences in the First Army was centralized under G.H.Q. and was exercised through fire commanders appointed in each port.([28])

In the Eighth Army, where the rate of advance was still necessitating the opening of new ports at short notice, H.A.A. and L.A.A. guns were given a secondary anti-ship rôle in order to hasten the installation or increase the strength of the coast defences. At Sfax, for example, where the first A.A. batteries arrived within 1½ hours of its capture, the A.A. defences—40 heavy and 38 light guns—were mostly given coast protection as a secondary rôle and were supplemented in due course by 8 × 75 mms. and 8 × 6-pr. anti-tank guns with the Free French, and by 4 × 18-prs., 2 × 6-in. guns and 2 coast artillery searchlights of a coast battery, all under command of the 12th A.A. Brigade.

Conclusion

This period, like its predecessor, had been one of great tactical progress. Equipments and ideas that had been hatching in some cases since 1938 had at last come to life. The 7.2-in. how. was in action on the ground, the air O.P. in the sky. Ideas set in motion by the early successes of the enemy had, after some initial doubts and delays, been brought to fruition. The use of air bursts, the co-ordination of air and artillery support, and the improvement of anti-tank ammunition had put us on a level with the enemy in these most important aspects of artillery fire.

We had however done more than merely imitate the enemy. In the massed use of artillery we had developed a technique with which he was at first unconcerned and later unable to rival; unconcerned, because of his over-confidence in the dive bomber, and unable to rival because of the effect on his industries of our air attacks and sea blockade. From El Alamein onwards we had adopted a policy of expending shells rather than lives; a policy suggested, if not dictated, by the growing strain on our manpower resources.

In the use of the night attack also we had led the way. Restricted at first to periods of moonlight, it promised to become independent of such restrictions through the development of artificial illumination by star shell or searchlight.

In the air, the long struggle for supremacy was about to be finally decided in favour of the Allies. As a result the emphasis would shift permanently from defence to attack, and A.A. defence would lose a great deal of its importance before a complete solution of its main problems—the unseen target and the "hedge-hopper"—had been found. Yet there would often be periods, especially in campaigns that started with an assault landing, when local air superiority would be lost. Coinciding with all the worst difficulties on a purely army level—shortage of troops, ammunition and supplies; hard defensive fighting; no mail and no tents—this period would put a heavy strain on morale, which even the most experienced troops would endure better if sustained by the sight and sound of their own A.A. guns in action. It might indeed be said that "no weapon—the fighter not excluded—has such wide publicity value as the A.A. shell. The burst is seen by thousands, all of whom praise and criticize it with an interest as truly personal as the interest taken in the efforts of the company cook."[30] It was therefore important that criticism should be informed and not ignorant; all the more so because of the characteristic differences in appearance of A.A. and field artillery fire. The latter often looked better than it really was, the former worse.

The main weakness in artillery tactics at this moment was the inability to maintain intimate contact with assaulting troops and hence to overcome the opposition of the enemy close support weapons, especially the mortar. It might be—as it had been in the case of the dive bomber and the tank—that the final answer to the mortar would have to be sought in the improvement of our own mortar equipments and technique. Yet much could also be done by improving the means of intercommunication and the cross country mobility of O.P. parties and guns. Lack of power and portability were the two most common defects of wireless equipments; lack of power and of armour the most serious weaknesses of artillery transport. Until these defects had been remedied, really close and continuous support—whether by concentrations or barrages, or by anti-tank guns during the consolidation of a captured position—could not be guaranteed.

For the immediate future, therefore, the chief hopes of the artilleryman, both field and A.A., lay in the ether. Radar and radio were the means by which his next great successes were to be achieved.

List of References

[1] W.O. File 51/Guns/2612.
[2] Arty. Training, Vol. II, Pamphlet No. 4, 1942, App. IV.
[3] R.A.T.M. War No. 6 of September 1942.
[4] Arty. Training, Vol. II, Pamphlet No. 3, 1941, Sec. 11.
[5] " Lessons of the Tunisian Campaign ", by British M.T. Directorate (N.A.).
[6] W.O. File 20/Misc/2039.
[7] " Lessons "—Supplementary Report by C.R.A. 78 Div.
[8] " El Alamein to the River Sangro ", by Field Marshal Montgomery.
[9] War Diary, B.R.A., 1st Army, December 1942-May 1943.
[10] " Operations in N.W. Africa "—Despatch by General Anderson.
[11] War Diary, R.A. 78 Div., February-May 1943.
[12] War Diary, R.A. 46 Div., March 1943.
[13] War Diary, R.A. 50 Div., March 1943.
[14] " The African Campaign from El Alamein to Tunis "—Despatch by Field Marshal Alexander, Vol. II.
[15] R.A. Notes No. 6.
[16] First Army Notes on Medjerda Battle.
[17] R.A.T.M. No. 7 of March 1943.
[18] " R.A. Experiences and Lessons, 6th April-12th May 1943 ", by 9 Corps.
[19] Report of W.O. Observer in N. Africa, May 1943.
[20] Arty. Lessons, Eighth Army, El Alamein to Sousse, issued by M.G.R.A., M.E.F., on 9th August 1943.
[21] Report by C.R.A., 1 Canadian Div., 29th August 1940.
[22] R.A.T.M. No. 9 of October 1943.
[23] 79994/1/M.T., R.A.F., of 19th September 1943.
[24] " Lessons from N. Africa ", G.H.Q., M.E.F., B.M./M.T.1/75 of 22nd May 1943.
[25] G.H.Q., M.E.F., 3808/M.O.1 of 13th March 1943.
[26] War Diary, 66 A.A. Bde., December 1942.
[27] R.A. Notes No. 2.
[28] R.A. Notes No. 5.
[29] Report No. 8 on Experiences in Employment of A.A. Units in the Middle East, 28th June 1943.
[30] Paper by B.R.A., First Army, quoted in R.A. Notes No. 8.

CHAPTER XI

SICILY TO THE WINTER LINE

PLATES RELEVANT TO THIS CHAPTER

Nos.
26. The "Sexton".
27. The 17-pr. A.Tk. gun on the Valentine tank chassis.
28. The S.P. Bofors.
29. The L.C.R.

Increasing Emphasis on Medium and Heavy Artillery

During the past eight months, the predominance of our artillery over that of the enemy, begun at El Alamein, had been steadily maintained. There still remained, however, one serious weakness. The artillery as a whole lacked balance. Overwhelmingly strong in field guns, it was deficient in medium and heavy. The development of direct air support had not yet rendered long-range artillery superfluous, and it was therefore imperative to introduce new weapons.

By August 1943 American 155-mm. guns, which threw a 95-lb. shell to a range of 26,000 yards, were becoming available (*see* p. 157), and in future heavy regiments were to consist of two batteries of these guns and two of 7.2-in. hows. The short range of the 5.5-in. medium gun was also about to be remedied by the introduction of a lighter (80-lb.) shell. But for the attack on Festung Europa still heavier shell and longer ranges would be required, and to meet this requirement a pool of 12-in. and 9.2 in. hows., and U.S. 8-in. guns and 240-mm. hows., was to be provided in each main theatre (*see* Table G). Maintained, when not in use, by a small detachment of specialists, these weapons would be issued as occasion demanded for the temporary re-equipment of selected field or medium regiments.[1]

TABLE G

Comparison of British and German Heavy and Super-Heavy Artillery, 1943

Equipment	Wt. in Action (tons)	Wt. of Shell (lb.)	Max Range (yds.)
Guns			
British 155–mm. (US)	15·8	95	26,000
8–in. (US)	31	240	35,000
German 17–cm.	17·2	149·6	30,375
		138·16	32,375
15–cm.	12	94·6	27,000
		95·7	27,000
Hows			
British 7·2–in.	10·25	202	16,900
12–in.	72·8 Rly.		
	44·2 Rd.	750	14,350
240–mm. (US)	28·9	360	25,000
German 21–cm. Mk. 18	16·4	249	18,260

The 9·2-in. gun on a railway mounting went "hand in glove" with the 12-in. how.
Figures for 9·2-in. gun on rly mtg. ... 86·3 tons, 380 lb., 25,000 yds.

It was the best that could be done with the manpower resources that were available. By August 1943 the ceiling of the R.A. in the army expansion programme had been reached. Henceforth increased artillery requirements would have to be met by transfers of units between theatres or by changing the equipment of certain regiments. Since the need for more medium artillery was urgent, it was decided that one of the two army field regiments provided for each corps should be converted to medium ; but the permanent inclusion of a medium regiment in the armoured divisional artillery, though generally accepted as desirable, could not be offset by equivalent reductions elsewhere and had therefore to be forgone.

For fighting up the spine of Italy it seemed likely that some mountain artillery would be of value, although experience in Tunisia had shown that, provided O.Ps. were put on a pack basis, existing equipments could usually do all that was required. To make more certain of this, incremental charges were produced for the 25-pr., which, if added to charges I and II, would give much the same crest clearance and angle of descent as the 3.7-in. how. at the shorter ranges. Thus equipped, the ordinary field regiment would be capable of engaging targets up to $7\frac{1}{2}$ miles from a road. If supporting fire was likely to be required beyond that range, recourse would have to be made to pack artillery ; and this meant the introduction of a pack-portee 3.7-in. or 75-mm. (American) how. as an alternative to the 25-pr.

So began a system based on what became known as the " golf bag principle ". Given easy access to a number of special weapons, a single unit was enabled to suit its action to the needs of the moment—or, to continue the metaphor, " to play each shot with the appropriate club ". Before long this principle would be extended to cover the assault landing, in which the field regiments of the assaulting divisions would be temporarily re-equipped with " Priests ".

The Development of S.P. Artillery

The S.P. gun was now definitely established and the period of improvisation was over. By August, 1943, the Bishop and the Deacon were officially recognized as obsolescent, and by the end of the year the new S.P. 25-pr., the Sexton, had begun to make its appearance. In view, however, of the popularity of the Priests—which was largely due to their being equipped with time fuzes—it was decided not to replace them until their life had expired. Among units at home, preparing for the invasion of France, the Priest would be used for the assault landing and the Sexton for normal purposes, such as the support of an armoured division.[2] In theatres abroad, the Priest was to continue in use for all purposes, and some of these weapons were actually retained in service in Burma up to and after the end of the war.

The Sexton was a Canadian designed and manufactured equipment consisting of a 25-pr. gun on a Ram 2 tank chassis. The full range achieved with the field carriage (13,400 yds.) could be attained, and this was a decided advantage over the Priest. In mobility the two equipments were about equal, but the interior lay-out of the Sexton was superior to that of the Priest and more ammunition could be carried. In addition, the complications entailed by the U.S. type of sight were obviated and it was no longer necessary to rely upon the U.S.A. for ammunition.

For anti-tank work, immediate requirements were to be met by the U.S. 3-in. M.10, which consisted of the 3-in. A.A. gun (M.7) mounted on a medium tank chassis of the M.4 (Sherman) type. The gun was mounted in a roofless turret with a 360 degree traverse. The chassis had considerably thinner armour than the standard tank. A total order for 1,500 of these equipments was placed, and the first issues were made to units in the Middle East in June, 1943.

Meanwhile work was proceeding on a G.S. specification for a S.P. 17-pr. with all-round traverse, which was originally sent to the Ministry of Supply in September, 1942. In the summer of 1943, various alternative mountings were considered and it was finally decided to use the A.30 chassis, similar to that of the Challenger tank, which it was hoped might be ready for issue by the latter half of 1944. In the event, however, the earliest production models did not become available until December, 1945. Some 17-prs. were mounted on the Valentine tank chassis and issues began in October, 1944, in time to render good service both in France and Italy. About the same time arrangements were made for the 17-pr., which had a better performance than the U.S. 3-in. gun, to be substituted for the latter on the M.10 chassis.

In February, 1943, the S.P. Bofors had made its debut and corps and divisional L.A.A. regiments in the United Kingdom were being issued with 18 S.P. equipments out of their total establishment of 54. The advantages of this equipment were that it could fire on the move and that it was more " manœuvrable " in a defile than the towed equipment. It was, on the other hand, more conspicuous and was at a disadvantage in the forward areas owing to the time required to dig it in. It was therefore normally used for the defence of columns, the protection of forward troops in a mobile battle, the exploitation of " roving " positions, and harassing shoots against ground targets where it was necessary to move in and out of action quickly.[3]

The appearance of so much S.P. artillery had made it desirable to distinguish between the role of the tank and the S.P. gun. In contrast to the American policy, the idea of seeking out and destroying enemy armour was discouraged. A suitable role for the S.P. anti-tank gun, it was thought, was the engagement of tanks that stood off and neutralized our forward localities ; or, when employed with armoured formations, to help in the defence of pivots or localities held by the infantry.[4]

The S.P. field gun was not designed for firing on the move, was not armed with machine-guns, and was not intended for the destruction of enemy tanks. It was to be used as an anti-tank weapon only in an emergency.[5]

In accordance with this policy, armoured divisional and corps troops anti-tank regiments were to consist of two batteries of 17-prs. S.P. (or 3-in. M.10's in lieu) and two batteries of 6-prs. wheeled. In the infantry and mixed divisional regiments there were to be no S.P. guns and each battery was to consist of two troops of 6-prs. and one troop of 17-prs. wheeled ; except in the India Command, where all anti-tank units were to remain for the time being on a 6-pr. basis.

The Problem of the Assault Landing

The opposition to the landings in North Africa had been brief and it had therefore been possible to use existing port facilities almost from the start.

It was evident that in the forthcoming operations against Sicily a greater strain would be placed on the organization for the launching and support of an assault landing.

The system for the control of naval gunfire had made considerable progress since the autumn of 1941, when its use in the coastal sector during the relief of Tobruk had not been altogether successful (*see* p. 116). The chief improvement had been the inclusion of a R.A. bombardment liaison officer in each of the bombarding ships, whose duty it was to advise the captain on the military aspects of the plan and to keep him in touch with the progress of the battle. He also assisted the ship's gunnery officer in the solution of technical problems and at direct fire was responsible that the ship engaged the correct target. A senior bombardment liaison officer was allotted to the staff of an assaulting force, with the task of assisting the senior artillery commander and staff gunnery officer in framing the bombardment plan, and of allotting F.O.Os. and bombardment liaison officers. In action his place was in the headquarters ship with the naval force commander, whom he kept advised of the military situation and assisted in the redistribution of ships and F.O.Os.

Each F.O.O. could communicate on a separate spotting frequency with the bombarding ship allotted to him, and on the bombardment calling wave with the headquarters ship, through which he could call for fire if no bombarding ship had been allotted to him. As a rough guide, a 6-in. or 8-in. cruiser was considered to be the equivalent of one medium regiment, with a range of 19-29,000 yards; a destroyer of one or two field batteries, with a range of 16-20,000 yards.

The tasks normally allotted were the neutralization of hostile batteries or defended areas, attacks on large bodies of troops or transport, and major destructive shoots. Counter-attacks, if important, could also be engaged. For example, at Narvik in 1940 and in Libya in 1941, German attacks had been halted and turned by ships' fire.(⁶)

The crucial moment in an assault landing was of course the final approach to the shore, the last " nasty ten minutes " when the ships' guns had to lift from the beach and the assault craft had to rely on whatever covering fire they could provide for themselves. To fill in this gap, two new types of supporting weapon had been devised: the landing craft rocket and the landing craft gun. The former, armed with a battery of rocket projectors, would accompany the leading flights of the assault and sweep the beaches as a prelude to the final touch-down. Though not very accurate, it produced a large beaten zone and its moral effect was very great. The L.C.G. was a converted L.C.T. armed with a couple of 4.7-in. naval guns. It was used on the flanks of the assault to deal with the more troublesome of the beach defences. It suffered, however, from two severe limitations: the craft had to be moored before the guns could fire, and any but the smallest degree of traverse had to be applied by moving the craft itself.

Increased Facilities for the Use of Smoke and Map Shooting

Hitherto artillery smoke shell had not been extensively used: in the desert, because H.E. shell and even normal troop movements produced more than enough obscurity in the form of dust clouds; in Tunisia, because of the tendency for the smoke canisters to roll down the mountain sides; and in

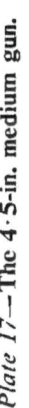

Plate 17—The 4·5-in. medium gun.

Plate 18—The 6-in. Coast artillery gun on Arrol Withers platform.

Plate 19—The " Priest ".

Plate 20 — The 5·5-in. gun.

Plate 21 — The American S.P. 3-in. M10.

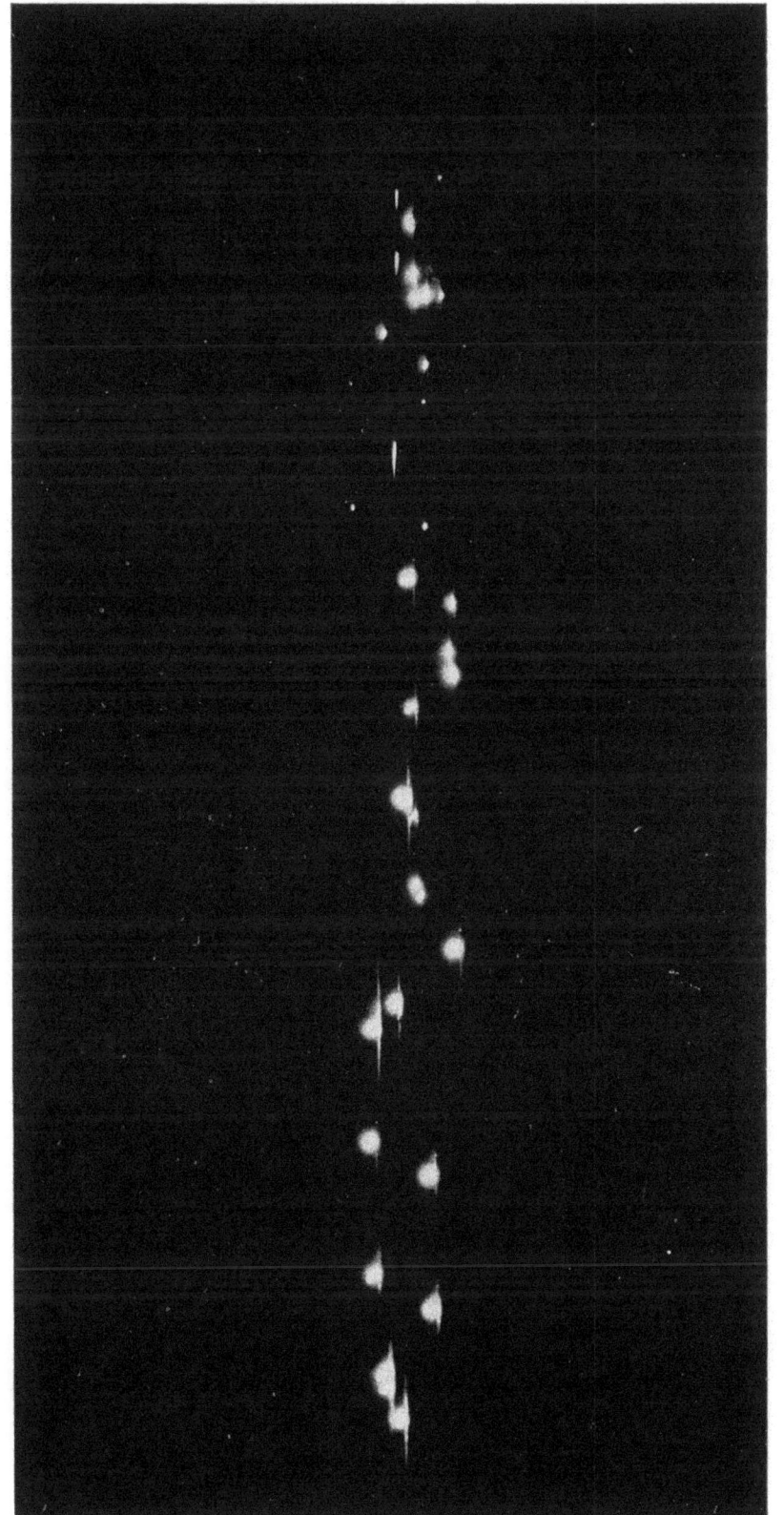

Plate 22—25-prs. firing a barrage by night.

Plate 23—The 7·2-in. how.

Plate 24—**The original air O.P.**

Plate 25—Artillery concentrations near Heidons.

both because of meterogical conditions, which sometimes made the behaviour of smoke unpredictable. With the transfer of operations to the European theatre, the opportunities for using smoke would be greater.

Another advantage lay in the quantity and quality of the maps to be expected. The country over which the First and Eighth Armies had been fighting was not well mapped, and topographical difficulties, such as the lack of detail in the desert and the irregularity and inaccessibility of some of the mountain features, made the provision of good maps almost impossible in the time available. As a guide, the accuracy of a 1/25,000 map might vary from 25 metres, for the best, to 100 metres for the worst; and it was only when the best maps were available, and the country was rich in map detail, that G.P.Os. would be able to fix their guns off the map with sufficient accuracy for predicted concentrations.

From El Alamein onwards the use of the vertical air photograph for artillery purposes had been steadily developing. Now that the facilities for air photography had improved, its application to military problems was being carefuly organized. There were three types of photograph that were available to the gunner; the vertical pin point (V.P.P.), covering a small area or point of particular importance; the vertical line overlap (V.L.O.); and the stereo pair (S.P.), which gave " relief " to the picture and was of particular value to the C.B.O. for the detection and examination of enemy gun positions.

Where maps were non-existent, V.L.Os. were accompanied by gridded traces, known as " skeleton block plots ", which, if superimposed on two successive photos, would enable the co-ordinates of a point that was identifiable on both photos to be found by geometrical methods.([7]).

The Attack on Pantelleria—11th June, 1943

As a preliminary to the invasion of Sicily it was decided to capture the tiny island of Pantelleria, which had been strongly defended by the Italians and which constituted a possible threat to the communications of the allied invasion force between Sicily and North Africa. The force allocated to the assault was one division, with an artillery component of only one field battery and one anti-tank troop. It was the kind of operation that lent itself peculiarly to air and sea support, and full advantage was taken of this fact by the R.A.F. and the Royal Navy. From D-10 onwards the island was subjected to air atttacks of increasing intensity, working up to a climax of 2,000 bombers on " D " day. A test bombardment by the Royal Navy on D-3 met with a feeble response from the shore batteries, and when the assault went in at 11.55 hours on 11th June, little opposition was encountered.

It was the first defended place to be reduced to surrender in this war as a result of air and naval bombardment alone; yet in spite of the intensity and duration of the air attack—which between 6th June and the surrender dropped 4,656 tons of bombs—the material damage done to the enemy artillery was not great. Of 109 guns inspected, only 16 were found to be definitely damaged, though nearly all command posts, fire control apparatus and communications had been rendered inoperative.

The Invasion of Sicily, 10th July, 1943

Everything was now ready for the assault on Sicily. Landing places had been selected so as to get the maximum value out of the air forces based on Malta and an early opportunity of capturing new airfields ashore and thus ensuring continuous fighter cover; a formidable array of ships' guns was prepared to cover the establishment of the beachheads, and the first moves inland, through the medium of the bombardment liaison unit; and airborne and other troops had been detailed for the destruction or neutralization of the enemy coastal batteries.

The initial assault was to be made in the dark and so timed that the supporting weapons—infantry carriers and 6-prs, R.A. 6-prs. and 17-prs, Priests and Shermans—would beach at or shortly before first light. F.O.Os. from the bombardment liaison unit were to accompany the leading battalions, and pre-arranged targets for ships' guns included a number of suspected enemy batteries. Yellow smoke or flares were provided for indicating the positions of our own troops to the air, and as a further precaution a bomb-line, representing the predicted line of forward troops, was laid down every two hours for use in case all other means of communication failed.

On the whole the results were satisfactory. The moral effect on the enemy of the landing craft rocket came fully up to expectations and the S.P. guns proved of great value in the early stages of the landing, since they were able to come into action in the water before the beach had been captured and cleared. Eight screw guns (3.7-in.), which were all that could be obtained, were also unloaded and brought into action at the water's edge.

The Italian garrisons manning the beach defences put up little resistance. By first light all the landings had been successfully accomplished, and during the first day the Eighth Army made no contact with any of the Italian mobile divisions or with German troops.

The Defence of the Beachheads

There were two main sources of danger to the beachheads: tanks and aircraft; and as events turned out, it was only the latter that materialized on the Eighth Army front. To meet it, the first esential was an early warning system; and since naval, military and air force units were involved, this system had to be intelligible to all three Services. A standard grid—the Mediterranean Area Fighter Operations Grid (M.A.F.O.G.)—was therefore introduced for the broadcasting of all radar warnings, and a standard air warning code was published and used for the passage of the usual operational details.

The very low-flying attack still presented difficulties, and the problem of warning, and controlling the fire of, L.A.A. guns was not yet satisfactorily solved. In March, 1943, the light warning radar set (*see* Table B) began to make its appearance, and this undoubtedly eased the situation by providing each L.A.A. unit with a local warning system of its own; but it was not the complete answer, nor had the latter been found before the war was over.

It was therefore unfortunate that no suitable 20-mm. L.A.A. gun was yet available for dealing with snap targets. The Oerlikon, which had no self-destroying element in its ammunition, proved a menace in the hands of any but properly trained A.A. troops and was in consequence withdrawn from all non-A.A. units in Sicily, never again to come into general use. Its successor, the Polsten, suffered at first from the same disability.

Chemical Warfare (Smoke) companies were included in the beach defence organizations to afford cover to landing craft on the beaches and to help screen ships at sea in an off-shore wind. Owing, however, to the limited supply of smoke-producing material, the ordering of a smoke screen was restricted to dawn, dusk and the periods during which a night raid was in progress. At Syracuse, between 14th and 31st July, smoke screens were operated during 18 raids, varying in strength from 6 to 40 aircraft, and during this period only one ship was sunk in the harbour.

In general, the A.A. defences of the beachheads were not severely tested. What enemy air activity there was was largely directed against shipping lying off the shore waiting to unload.

Decline of the Enemy Air and Armoured Forces

During the first eight days of the campaign many determined low level attacks were made against our field artillery areas and infantry positions, as well as vital roads and bridges; but by 18th July such attacks had practically ceased.[8] By this time our own mounting offensive in the air was beginning to make itself felt, and "not only were we virtually unhindered by enemy aircraft, but we were able to keep up a relentless pounding of the hostile troops and L of C."[9]

German armoured units too had lost a great deal of their former effectiveness. The process of deterioration, which had first become noticeable in Tunisia, had continued and the general opinion was that the efficiency of the armoured formations now being encountered was only about 60 per cent. of that of the old Afrika Corps.[10]

Unfortunately, except in the Catania Plain, this was a country more suitable for infantry than for armour. Hence tank actions were on a very small scale and the bulk of our anti-tank, as of our A.A., artillery was held back in order to reduce congestion of traffic in the forward areas.[11]

Close Support Difficulties

The difficulty of finding good gun positions, especially during the final phase of the operations, was even greater than in Tunisia. In the fighting round the foot of Etna, for example, stone walls, terraces, lava and the existence of but a single road made it almost impossible to deploy the whole of a divisional artillery against each successive objective, or to find room for the medium artillery decentralized to divisions from A.Gs.R.A.[12] Here S.P. guns again proved particularly valuable, since they were able to get into good positions on the hillside terraces by pushing down the walls in front of them.[13]

In such country decentralization of the artillery was often necessary. The normal amount of support allotted to a division was four field and one medium regiment, but there appears to have been no standardized system of calling for fire (by radio) at that time. Partly perhaps for this reason, there was a tendency to allot a few tanks—usually about a troop—for the moral support of the leading infantry. Anti-tank guns, now seldom fully engaged upon their normal role, were likewise made to serve on occasions as close support weapons, either to silence enemy machine-guns or to destroy strong points in the form of fortified farm-houses or concrete pill-boxes. The same sort of thing had happened previously in the first Cyrenaican campaign against the Italians, and for similar reasons (*see* p. 52). It was to be repeated later in Italy and Normandy.

For the set-piece attack, the timed programme remained the most favoured method of giving close support. The key to success lay in the ability of well trained infantry to " lean on the barrage ", and the current dictum now was that " unless the assaulting troops are sufficiently close behind the barrage to close with the enemy within two minutes of the barrage lifting, the barrage is wasted."([13])

Counter-mortar and Counter-battery Difficulties

The enemy was not strong in artillery, but what guns he had were boldly handled to cover his withdrawal, and as usual his mortars and nebelwerfers were both numerous and skilfully concealed. In these large tracts of broken country they often remained unlocated in spite of our use of arty/R, air O.Ps. and hostile shelling reports (shelreps). Increasing interest was therefore taken in the development of our own mortar technique, especially in conjunction with the new 4.2-in. mortar. This weapon had proved more accurate than had been expected and was acquiring some popularity.

Counter-battery fire was also hampered by the difficulty of locating hostile gun positions. The enemy resorted at this time to a high measure of single gun harassing, mostly with S.P. equipments, which were frequently moved. Suitable ground for full length flash spotting and sound ranging bases was seldom obtainable, and air O.Ps. were sometimes handicapped by the lack of landing grounds in the vicinity of gun areas. The use of air photographs was also restricted at first by the difficulty of communication with the airfield at Malta from which the photographic reconnaissance unit was operating.

In these circumstances progress was necessarily slow, and under cover of his rearguard actions the enemy was busily evacuating the pick of his army across the narrow straits of Messina. Attempts to deny him the use of these straits by air attack were frustrated by powerful A.A. gun defences which he had erected to cover his movements. Thus the victory won was not annihilating. With as little delay as possible, the pursuit had to be resumed and the two allied armies had to set out upon their long stern chase up the peninsula of Italy.

The Crossing of the Straits of Messina

The first step was to cross the straits of Messina and secure a foothold in Calabria. These straits were only a few thousand yards wide and as soon as the Sicilian shore was in our hands, the Eighth Army had set to work to establish an artillery supremacy across them. The problem was complicated by the fact that the deployment of the artillery for the support of the crossing had to be carried out on a single road, parts of which were in view of the enemy on the opposite shore. Moreover, the time factor necessitated the movement of guns by day as well as by night. It was therefore essential to work out, and to implement, the counter-battery plan as a prelude to the deployment of the field artillery in support of the crossing.

By 3rd September, when the operation was due to begin, the hostile artillery had been completely dominated. Of the 114 enemy guns that had been located from time to time, not more than 50 appeared to be still in position at the time of the crossing. Against them we had been able to mass 288 × 25-prs., 48 × 4.5-in., 32 × 5.5-in., 12 × 155-mm. guns, 36 × 155-mm. hows, and 8 × 3.7-in. H.A.A. guns, in addition to some 17-prs. which were used for "concrete busting" between San Giovanni and Cannitello on the afternoon of D-1.

In the final programme during the night of 2nd/3rd September some 29,000 rounds were fired—of which 25,000 were 25-pr.—representing a total weight of ammunition of just under 400 tons.([14]). Not more than five enemy gun positions replied to our bombards, and the amount of shell fire directed against the assaulting troops of 13 Corps was very small. "The Italian coastal troops and their supporting artillery surrendered after firing a few shots and the only German fire reported was spasmodic long range shelling from guns sited inland. These were quickly silenced by air attack."([15])

The Landing at Salerno

Concurrently with the operations in the heel of Italy, the American Fifth Army, with 10 Corps under command, was landing at Salerno in the Bay of Naples. For the first time in an operation of this sort, serious opposition was encountered. A German division happened to be located in the vicinity and had organized itself in readiness to meet an attack. The actual coast defences themselves were lightly held, and small mobile columns—consisting, as in Libya and elsewhere, of an infantry company, machine-guns and mortars, 8.8 cm. guns, and generally two or three tanks—lay back ready to counter-attack wherever a serious penetration had been effected, and thus to gain time for the deployment of larger forces and the occupation of strong defensive positions further inland.

As in Sicily, the Allied plan was to land in the dark under cover of a naval bombardment, which was timed to begin 15 minutes before "H" hour. For the first five minutes the beaches were to be bombarded by destroyers. Thereafter support was to be continued by the various types of landing craft armed with guns, rockets and mortars. From "H" hour until first light, supporting fire was to be confined to the flanks of the beaches. Subsequently, cruisers and destroyers, with allotted F.O.Os., would be "at call".([16])

In preparation for this operation an addition had been made to the bombardment control organization. Bombardment liaison officers (Intelligence) and bombardment calling wave parties were permanently located at corps and divisional headquarters, with duties which included the sending of sitreps to ships, the arrangement of any attachments that might be required, and the answering of questions from army or ships. They were also to keep touch with F.O.Os. whenever possible.([17])

Air support was at first confined to fighter patrols from bases in Sicily, supplemented by Seafires of the Support Carrier Group. It was hoped that Montecorvino airfield would be captured on "D" day (9th September), but this hope was not fulfilled and it was not until D + 3 that tactical bombing support became possible through the establishment of two landing strips near the beach, from which Spitfires could operate and give fighter cover to the bombers. Arty/R could not be carried out until some days later, when the tac/R squadron was established on the mainland.

The beaches at Salerno were steep, so that landings could be made dry-shod; but beyond them lay uneven sand dunes covered with scrubby grass, which merged into reclaimed land extending to a depth of some four miles and patterned with small fields divided by dykes and narrow unmetalled roads bounded by steep ditches. In this difficult country the Priests again rendered excellent service. By H + 80 the first field battery was in action ashore, and in the confused fighting that followed these guns were occasionally used with success for the stalking of troublesome enemy tanks. They were also of great assistance in clearing out coast defence guns from the flanks and rear, working in very close touch with the leading infantry.[18]

It was from 12th to 14th September that the situation was at its worst. Only a narrow bridgehead had been established and this was everywhere overlooked by the hills, which rose steeply from the coastal plain. The enemy, relying on his demolitions to delay the advance of the Eighth Army, was rapidly reinforcing his defences at Salerno, whereas we could expect no reinforcements until about 16th September. His tanks were infiltrating our positions in small numbers and, once inside, were very difficult to deal with owing to the lack of anti-tank gun positions with anything like an adequate field of fire.[19]

In these circumstances much depended on the continuous support of the Royal Navy. Fortunately, the absence of enemy long range coastal batteries, and the comparative immunity of the Fleet from air attack, made such support possible. With the aid of the air O.P., a large number of shoots were carried out by cruisers, destroyers and monitors, in the course of which enemy gun positions, tanks, M.T. and infantry were successfully engaged. Targets registered by daylight were sometimes engaged " blind " at night from positions marked by buoys and located again in the dark by the use of radar.[20] Communication was by relay through a F.O.O. ground station, which had to be temporarily equipped with a No. 19 set in order to get the necessary range. Later, F.O.Os. received No. 22 sets for this purpose.

When the situation became really serious, battleships were rushed to the scene in spite of the danger from the new radio-controlled bombs with which the enemy had been scoring some successes. The support that they gave, supplemented as it was by as much of the strategical Air Force as could be brought to bear, was considerable. At the same time the defensive fire put down by the artillery ashore was responsible for breaking up several threatening attacks, including the first big attack by tanks on 15th September, which was stopped by divisional concentrations. Finally, on 16th September, when the newly arrived 26th Panzer Division launched a series of disjointed attacks along the whole front, the gunners were given opportunities reminiscent of Graziani's advance into Egypt (*see* p. 47). As one brigade commander put it, " the enemy moved about the front in vehicles or on foot in the open without any covering fire and we just shot them to hell with our artillery."[19]

Thereafter the situation began to improve. The supply of ammunition was now assured and more extensive harassing fire tasks could be carried out on the enemy L. of C. From 9th to 30th September the 46th and 56th Divisional Artilleries engaged some 1,815 targets, of which 159 were divisional, 637 regimental and 803 battery targets, and 216 were harrassing fire tasks.[21] Naval guns continued to be of great value for the engagement of targets beyond the range of field and medium equipments.

By contrast, the German artillery support during this operation was poor. Although the beaches and landing craft generally were within range even of 75-mms, and excellent observation was afforded by its commanding positions in the hills, the effect of the enemy artillery was remarkably small.([10])

A.A. Defence at Salerno

Considerable air opposition had been expected, and a large force of A.A. guns was therefore landed on " D " day. Each of the three beach groups was supported by 8 H.A.A. and 18 L.A.A. guns, and a H.A.A. regiment and part of a divisional L.A.A. regiment, intended for the defence of Montecorvino airfield, were superimposed on the beach group lay-outs as a result of the failure to capture the airfield. By D+3 the balance of divisional L.A.A. artillery had been landed, giving a total of 48 H.A.A. and 162 L.A.A. guns within the bridgehead.

When the first follow-up landed on D+6, the battle was still in full swing within 4-5,000 yards of the beaches and there was a definite congestion of A.A. units. That night, therefore, when the right flank of 10 Corps was penetrated by the enemy, one H.A.A. and one L.A.A. regiment were formed into an infantry battalion and for four days this force, known as "Gunnerforce", was kept in being as a mobile reserve to operate in a counter-attack role.

With the arrival of the Corps L.A.A. regiment in the fourth follow-up, the A.A. resources of 10 Corps were completed. They were divided into three groups; the Naples Port Defence Group of 4 H.A.A. and 4 L.A.A. batteries; the Airfield Group of 1 H.A.A. and 1 L.A.A. regiment; and the Subsidiary Port Group—for Castellamare and Torre Annunziata—of 2 H.A.A. and 2 L.A.A. batteries. From this stage onwards A.A. dispositions were based on normal port and airfield defence lay-outs.([21])

A regimental commander, landed in the assault with the elements of an A.A.O.R., was able from the start to co-ordinate the defences of all three beaches. Fire plans allowed for five types of barrage:—

(1) Directional, in which all guns fired in a single named direction at a predetermined quadrant elevation (Q.E.).

(2) Porcupine (see p. 83), in which all guns fired outwards at a given Q.E. and range.

(3) Umbrella, in which lines of fire intersected approximately over the centre of the vulnerable area.

(4) Sun, which was fired in the direction of the sun to harass unseen targets diving out of the sun (see p. 175).

(5) Anti-torpedo, which was fired across the anchorage at 3,000 feet, but not below.([22])

In the early stages of the operation, balloons ashore were operated by the R.A.F. and controlled by the Sector Air Defence Commander independently of the A.A. Commander. This was not satisfactory and arrangements were subsequently made through Fifth Army for the control of balloons in the Naples area to be vested in the Commander 12th A.A. Brigade, thus reverting to a unity of command that had once before been achieved at Boulogne on the orders of the Admiral du Nord (see p. 34).

Two Pioneer smoke companies were included in this Brigade, and although enemy air activity was not enough to necessitate the use of much A.A. smoke, some success was obtained with a 3-ton truck used as a mobile screen to cover fires started at night; and on 19th and 22nd September, when enemy shelling of the beaches became heavy, a linear smoke screen was laid out to hide them from known enemy O.Ps. in the mountains.[23]

Enemy Delaying Tactics

At first the enemy's tactics were much the same as in Sicily: delaying actions in which the main weapon was the machine-gun, supported by mortars and S.P. guns, and in which our own artillery was frequently prevented from keeping up with the infantry by the skilful use of demolitions. In the low-lying coastal country, with its abundant cover in the form of orchards, crops, walls and ditches, the chief role was played by the S.P. gun, with up to half a dozen machine-guns dug in round it. If our advance was led by tanks, these guns, usually very well concealed, held their fire until the range had closed to 80-100 yards and, after knocking out one or two tanks in the leading troop, made a rapid get-away before they could be outflanked.[10]

Here the Priest was again in its element, and the need for more S.P. anti-tank guns was frequently felt. What was needed was a weapon that could move across country by a covered route to a position from which enemy tanks could be engaged by surprise. For lack of it, anti-tank protection had become perhaps the most important role for tanks in support of infantry.[24]

By early October the Allied advance along the whole front was being solidly contested, while further back, along the lines of the Rivers Sangro and Garigliano, a winter line was being prepared by the enemy on both sides of the Apennines, backed on its western half by the strong Cassino position. At the same time Allied resources in manpower and material, especially landing craft, were beginning to be drained by preparations for the campaign in N.W. Europe. Thus the armies in Italy were committed to a long " slogging match " with little possibility of amphibious operations against the enemy's flanks, and, as always happens on such occasions, the artillery moved up in the batting list.

The Problem of the River Crossing

During the next eight months the Fifth and Eighth Armies were to gain repeated experience in the conduct of an opposed river crossing. First there was the Volturno, which separates the flat coastal plain about Naples from the rocky, terraced mountains that rise sheer behind it. Since the enemy held all the good vantage points, it was decided to rely on secrecy and surprise for the main crossing and to use the artillery in the initial stages for the purposes of deception. While the 56th Division made a subsidiary and noisy attack at Capua, and the 7th Armoured Division established a small bridgehead in a loop of the river to the westward, the 46th Division on the extreme left, starting about half an hour after the other two, crossed in silence at a place where the natural difficulties in the way of such an operation made the achievement of surprise all the more likely. Its artillery firing concentrations on the right flank, helped to heighten the illusion that the main assault was being made at Capua.([25])

The difficulty on such occasions was to get the 6-pr. anti-tank guns, whether infantry or R.A., across the river for the immediate defence of the captured bridgehead. S.P. field guns were in some instances able to fill the gap by sniping enemy tanks from across the river, and in the subsequent fighting the air O.P. was used to great advantage as a means of overcoming the limitations placed on ground O.Ps. by the close and wooded nature of the country. Nothing, however, could entirely take the place of the front-line anti-tank gun, without which an early foothold had sometimes to be abandoned by the leading infantry.

It was the same when, a fortnight later, the Eighth Army came up against the Trigno, except that to the ordinary difficulties of an opposed river crossing were now added the immobilizing effects of rain and mud. A battalion bridgehead, seized by the 78th Division during the night 22nd/23rd October, could not be immediately exploited, and when a full scale assault was put in ten days later, the anti-tank guns were unable to ford the river and without them the infantry were unable to hold their first objective in the face of a daylight tank counter-attack. The enemy was thus able to break off the fight and retire in good order across the Sangro.

The winter line, on which he now stood, was strongest near the sea, where it had been under construction since early October. The main defence works were established along an escarpment, about 150 feet high, that rose abruptly from the plain about 2,000 yards to the north of the river. Close to the south bank there was another line of steep hills, which gave good observation and which was held by the enemy as an outpost to the main position.

Yet it was precisely here that the Eighth Army had to launch its attack. On the left and in the centre, where the defences were weaker, an assault was impossible owing to snow and mist and to the lack of communications. The plan was, therefore, to break into the enemy defences on the Sangro Ridge on a narrow front, beginning with an infantry penetration and following it up with an armoured breakthrough.

This plan was spoilt by bad weather, and as it became evident that the use of tanks in large numbers could not be relied on, a new plan was prepared which comprised a series of very limited operations each supported by the whole weight of 5 Corps Artillery. The assault, which was timed to begin at 2130 hours on 28th November from a bridgehead previously established by the 78th Division, was preceded by two deceptive bombardments on the front of the neighbouring Corps, fired on 24th and 25th November, and by the usual preliminary C.B. bombardment to restrict the enemy shelling of the bridges and the maintenance routes. The initial attack was carried out by a brigade of the 8th Indian Division under cover of a barrage by four field regiments and concentrations by another four field and two medium regiments.

The advance was to be at the rate of 100 yards in five minutes and was to be carried out in two phases, each involving one battalion, with Mozzagrogna and Santa Maria as their respective objectives. In fact, however, the latter part of the operation failed owing to the cratering of the roads by the enemy, which delayed the infantry and prevented the supporting arms, especially tanks, from getting forward. It was not until the morning of 29th November that Santa Maria was finally taken by a combined infantry and tank attack put in from a new direction. The ascent at the point selected was particularly steep and the enemy, relying on the ground to stop tanks, had not sited any 8.8 cm. guns in this area. The attack, therefore, moving forward under cover of a barrage by two field regiments and concentrations by four field and two medium regiments, was completely successful. The next day operations were resumed and Fossacesia was taken after an intense bombardment by six field and three medium regiments and three H.A.A. troops. By last light on 30th November the 4th Armoured and 38th Infantry Brigades were firmly consolidated on the ridge from the sea to Santa Maria.

The Eighth Army had smashed its way through this very strong line in three days, during which the artillery had fired over 600 r.p.g. 25-pr., 350 r.p.g. 4.5-in., and 327 r.p.g. 5.5-in.

The Failure to Break Through the Winter Line

The forcing of the Sangro, it was hoped, would be followed by a rapid advance to Pescara, whence the whole of the German winter line could be rolled up by a drive on Rome. Ortona was the first objective, and to get there another difficult river line, that of the Moro, had to be crossed. On 10th December the 1st Canadian Division succeeded in establishing a bridgehead, but when the armour tried to pass through, it was held up by heavy fire of all kinds as it approached a steep gully that lay across the line of advance and formed an almost complete anti-tank obstacle crossed by only one road. Under cover of its precipitous sides the enemy had constructed weapon pits that were almost immune from damage by shell fire. Mortars of 3-in. and 4.2-in. calibre were in fact the only weapons that the Canadians could use with significant effect against these positions, and they were not enough to force the passage. It was not until several days later that the position was turned from the west, and not until seven days later still that—with the aid of 25-prs. firing in the upper register (*see* p. 241)—the last of the defenders were ejected and Ortona was reached.

The Germans were still fighting hard and at Ortona there was some extremely tough street fighting, in which little use could be made of the large quantities of artillery available. Hence tanks and anti-tank guns were employed in direct fire tasks while the field artillery harassed the coastal road in rear of the town and the heavy artillery was turned on to the destruction of strong points.([26])

Meanwhile the New Zealand Division had been experiencing some equally hard fighting in their attempt to take the key town of Orsogna. A battalion of the 6th New Zealand Brigade worked its way into the town on the night 3rd-4th December, but was driven out again at first light by an enemy counter-attack with 10 tanks, against which the defensive fire of the artillery proved ineffective. A second attack on 7th December, carried out in daylight and covered by an artillery barrage and an air bombardment in front, and by artillery smoke screens on the flanks, was no more successful. The supporting tanks were held up by demolitions and the anti-tank guns by the rain-sodden ground. A third and fourth attack, the latter staged by 13 Corps and supported by the whole of the Corps Artillery, were necessary before the main objectives could be taken, and even then conditions remained confused and difficult.([27])

In January, some further progress was made by the 1st Canadian Division after stiff fighting, during which a particularly troublesome centre of resistance was engaged as a corps target by nine field, five medium and one heavy regiment, receiving altogether 14,640 rounds within the space of 20 minutes. There was, however, no breakthrough. On this front it was clear that stalemate had occurred and that little further progress could be expected until the winter was over.

The Attack on Monte Camino

On the west of the Apennines the Fifth Army had in early December made a preliminary and successful attack on Monte Camino, an outpost of the Cassino feature, which formed the central bastion of the winter line. It was a deliberate operation designed to show how a large, semi-isolated mountain mass should be captured, and the role of the artillery was correspondingly massive. Preparations for the battle included the dumping of 800 r.p.g. for the field guns, and when the 167th Infantry Brigade went into the attack at 1730 hours on 2nd December, it was supported by the whole artillery of two corps, the 10th British and the 2nd U.S. During the next 75 minutes 1,329 tons of ammunition fell on four areas each about 500 yards square([28]), and this undoubtedly hastened the capture of a very difficult feature. By 6th December, 10 Corps had captured the summit of Monte Camino, which it had almost secured on the 3rd but failed to hold against counter-attacks, and on 9th December the capture of Rocca d'Evando brought it level with the Garigliano along the whole of its front.

The Crossing of the Garigliano

For the turning of the Garigliano line it had been decided to carry out a landing at Anzio, and as a preliminary to this operation a strong assault was made on the river line itself by 10 Corps. The enemy in the hills to the north enjoyed excellent close observation of the river line, especially from two commanding positions at Castelforte and Minturno. It was therefore important initially to secure a bridgehead at each of these places to cover the rafting across of supporting weapons and vehicles. Both operations were to be carried out in the dark; that on the left, at Minturno, in silence by the 5th Division; that on the right, at Castelforte, where the enemy overlooked the scene of action at close range, by the 56th Division supported by all the available artillery.

The action fought by the 56th Division contained several interesting features from the artillery point of view and is therefore worth recording in some detail. The attack was made by two brigades, one on each side of Castelforte. The possibility of using the whole of the artillery for the support of each operation in turn was considered, but was ruled out by the time required—approximately eight hours—for the leading infantry to reach the river, force a crossing and capture their objectives on the far side. Separate allocations were therefore made to the two brigades, the majority of the medium and all the heavy artillery going to the 167th Infantry Brigade on the left, whose task was to secure the key feature of Damiano (*see* Map 9).

Great care was taken during the preparatory period to build up an accurate picture of the enemy dispositions. Infantry brigade intelligence officers, in conjunction with representatives from the supporting field regiments, would make daily analyses of air photo information supplied by 56 Division and reports of infantry patrols and of infantry and gunner O.Ps. Results were checked by the intelligence officer R.A. at divisional headquarters, augmented by information received through counter-battery channels, and modified as necessary to accord with subsequent observations.

The task of moving in the artillery, and of building up the large dumps of ammunition required for the attack, had to be carried out at night, since the gun positions, though partly concealed by olive groves, were mostly on forward slopes under observation from the hills beyond the river (see Map 10). In selecting them, the controlling factor was the supply of ammunition, which necessitated the use only of positions in the immediate vicinity of the few existing roads and metalled tracks.

The secret introduction of reinforcing artillery called for a large amount of predicted fire, and as the available maps were too inaccurate to be relied on, a number of control points were selected in the enemy area and their co-ordinates deduced from air photographs by a special co-ordinate section, provided by the C.C.R.A. and attached to the C.B.O.

Before reconnaissances could be made of the river bank, the enemy had to be ejected from his positions in the Maiano bend, and as these positions were completely devoid of cover and were overlooked at close range by enemy O.Ps. on the hills behind them, it was desirable that the period of occupation by our own infantry should be as short as possible. Hence the time allowed for the final " tying-up " of the fire plan was reduced to the absolute minimum.

The greatest threat to the success of the operation was felt to be the combination of mortar and machine-gun fire against the crossing-places. It was therefore decided to use the heavy and medium artillery for counter-mortar tasks during the first half-hour, and thereafter to switch them on to half-an-hour's intensive counter-battery fire.

The advance of the 167th Infantry Brigade up to the river bank was to be made in silence, with the artillery standing by ready to fire a pre-arranged neutralization programme in case of emergency. During the crossing and initial establishment of bridgeheads, a series of very heavy concentrations was to be put down on selected enemy localities; the field artillery dealing with machine-gun positions close at hand, with three regiments concentrated on each in turn, and the medium and heavy artillery with the more distant positions that were adjudged likely to contain mortars.

While the infantry were assembling on the far bank, the main line of resistance was to be given a very heavy pounding by medium and heavy artillery, and the advance to the final objective was to be covered by a heavy barrage with the usual concentrations on the flanks. This barrage consisted of five rows: the first 25-prs; then two more rows of 25-prs. at 200 and 300 yards plus; then 5.5-in at 500 yards plus; and finally concentrations by 7.2-in lifting in turn from one selected locality to another. It was timed to advance very slowly (100 yards in 15 minutes), owing to the extremely difficult nature of the country, and white phosphorus shells were used to mark the flanks to assist in maintaining direction.

The whole operation was to be covered by a heavy interdiction programme carried out by naval and air bombardment, as a result of which it was hoped practically to isolate the battle area during the first days of the assault.

At first things went well. Complete surprise was obtained, the fixation of forward enemy defences was accurate, and although the infantry were unable to keep up with the barrage on the terraced slopes of Damiano, it had done its work so thoroughly that little interference by fire was encountered.([29]). The attack had started at 2100 hours on 17th January, 1944, and by the evening of 18th January the leading infantry were on their final objectives.

The trouble, as usual, was to consolidate and reorganize the captured positions. Owing to the almost complete absence of arty/R, counter-battery work was difficult and anti-tank units suffered considerable casualties in trying to get across the river under heavy artillery fire. The interdiction plan too had failed owing to bad weather, so that the enemy was able to recover the initiative. Between 19th and 22nd January he staged a series of counter-attacks against Damiano, where our initial advance had failed to secure adequate observation for our artillery O.Ps.

In these circumstances it was decided " to use the guns without regard to expenditure of ammunition or exhaustion of personnel "([29]) until the left flank could be reinforced and reorganized. The main artillery policy was to break up counter-attacks by means of what used to be known as " counter-preparation " (see p. 3); that is, the engagement of likely concentration and forming-up areas. Owing to the lack of ground observation, and the inability of air O.Ps. to detect an incipient counter-attack in such broken country, much of the fire had to be " blind ". On 22nd January the 56th Divisional Artillery answered 20 calls for D.F. and engaged 75 " U " targets (divisional concentrations) between 0945 and 2115 hours.

Thus the front was held and the enemy was forced to abandon his counter-attacks and rush reserves to Anzio, where a landing had been effected in the early hours of 22nd January.

The Landing at Anzio

This operation had achieved almost complete surprise, so that oppposition was negligible and the port of Anzio was taken practically undamaged. Between 23rd and 29th January, however, four heavy air attacks were made on the port and beaches, in the course of which several warships and transports were sunk or damaged. The A.A. defences were then increased by the addition of extra A.A. guns, a balloon barrage and a smoke screen over the port ; and fighter aircraft were operated from a reconstructed landing strip in the beachhead.([30])

Meanwhile the enemy had been rapidly concentrating his forces in his attempt to eliminate the bridgehead. By 30th January no less than eight German divisions, with 180 tanks and a formidable artillery, had assembled and were deploying south of Rome. There followed a succession of violent counter-attacks, in the defeat of which the artillery naturally played an important part. Indeed the last main German assault was virtually " nipped in the bud " by artillery counter-preparation. Forewarned of an impending offensive, the guns spent the whole night "working over" concentration areas, routes forward and assembly areas, with the result that the attacking troops never really got under way.

This was true counter-preparation, as practised in the First World War. It was not fired in response to a call from the leading infantry, but was initiated by the local infantry and artillery commanders as the result of information received from "I" sources. It is probable that battalions in the line knew little of what was going on beyond the fact that they liked the sound of the shells going over in satisfactory quantities.([31])

Air support was also provided on a large scale, and on 17th February allied aircraft dropped 952 tons of bombs; the heaviest weight ever recorded in the history of direct air support in the Mediterranean.([32])

The situation now developed into a stalemate and the troops at Anzio were to remain cooped up in their bridgehead for many weeks to come. During this period the A.A. units—of which all the H.A.A. were American and one-third of the L.A.A. British—maintained a defence that "deserves to rank with that of Malta and Tobruk."([17]) G.L.III (*see* Table "B") and its American equivalent were now in action, and the resultant increase in efficacy of A.A. shooting was perhaps reflected in the "score book." From 22nd January to 6th May, 1944, 203 enemy aircraft were shot down and 112 more probably destroyed.

In addition to the A.A. smoke screen at night, a "haze" was also made to act as a daytime screen between the harbour and all German O.Ps. This, combined with the fact that the enemy found himself mostly looking into the sun, helped to counterbalance his possession of the high ground, so that in spite of his unusual strength in artillery, his shooting was not very effective.

Some Ammunition Problems

It had by now become evident that the Allies could no longer rely on being able to make full use of their superiority in armour and air power. Tanks and aircraft were too frequently immobilized by rain and mud. Even if the weather was fine over the battlefield, landing grounds might be unserviceable as the result of local floods or storms, or cross winds might prevent the air forces from operating.([27])

Hence an unexpectedly heavy burden was placed upon the artillery and ammunition expenditure mounted rapidly. At the same time new types of projectile and propellant had added to the complexities of gunnery and to the burdens of the administrative staff. Time fuzes and flashless propellant, though still not plentiful enough to meet all demands, were now well-established items in the ammunition supply, and the latter had been of special value at the Garigliano, where so many of our gun positions were exposed to enemy observation.

Another impending development of the night battle was the night marker shell, which was designed for indicating targets to the air. Lastly, there was the propaganda shell, which had brought the gunner into line with the prevailing trends of psychological warfare. It was perhaps a logical development of artillery fire, the effect of which had always been predominantly moral, but its ballistic properties were different from those of the H.E. shell and its use therefore necessitated the provision of special gunnery data.

Complexity of design also meant increased risks of confusion in the handling and storing of ammunition to which had to be added the neglect that inevitably crept in when troops were tired and time was short. The practice of dumping ammunition at gun positions, essential though it was, was expensive both in material and in labour.

It was moreover impossible to comply fully with the regulations for the segregation of natures and lots of propellant in depots, echelons and units. At gun sites, in particular, the delivery of large lots could not be ensured owing to the number of trans-shipments that were necessary. Later on, in fact, after the Normandy landings had started, ammunition arrived in Italy from all over the Empire and lots were inextricably mixed up. It was found quite impossible to sort them out, and eventually the attempt to do so was abandoned.

Even if the ammunition was all the same, guns were apt to develop considerable differences in wear during periods of prolonged activity. Calibration, therefore, had become a very live issue, and it was decided to provide one calibration troop to each theatre or army group; but, owing to lack of equipment, it was impossible immediately to conform to this scale. As a temporary solution it was agreed that a pool of standard guns should be provided and calibrated in each theatre. From this pool single guns would be issued as required to units, who would then be responsible for carrying out a comparative calibration of the remainder of their guns.([33])

But calibration and care of ammunition would be of no avail unless reliance could be placed on a steady and accurate supply of meteorological information. To be reliable, meteor telegrams had to be right up to date, and with no meteorological unit below corps headquarters (see p. 146), this was not always possible. Hence in July, 1943, an agreement was reached between the War Office and the Air Ministry, in accordance with which meteorological units were to be reorganized so as to provide, among other things, a section with each divisional artillery and A.G.R.A. capable of conducting balloon ascents and receiving broadcast upper air temperatures.([34])

Efforts to Extend the Use of Air Observation

After every precaution had been taken to ensure the accuracy of the opening rounds, there was still no absolute guarantee that the fire would be effective or that ammunition would not be wasted. Some experienced gunners were, it is true, in favour of predicted shooting as opposed to ranging by observation; but there were occasions on which the verification of results from the air was very desirable, if not essential.

The instrument that was readiest to hand for this purpose was the air O.P., which was now being successfully used for the conduct of counter-battery shoots; the spotting and engagement of flak areas during the operations of our close support bombers; the checking, and if necessary correcting, of smoke screens; the reconnaissance of gun areas; and the testing of unit camouflage and concealment schemes.([35]) By December, 1943, a definite procedure had been laid down for the control of large observed concentrations by the air O.P. acting as a " commander's representative ".([36])

Nevertheless the air O.P. had its limitations. It was difficult to get it into the air in time to spot an active hostile battery, owing to the habit adopted by the enemy of firing only a few rounds at a time. In the mountains, too, its range of vision was often severely restricted.

Hence there was an increasing demand for arty/R missions. As the result of experience in Tunisia, the procedure for arty/R shoots had been still further simplified. The new procedure, known as the "agreed point method", was based on the assumption that all targets must be prearranged in greater or lesser degree, and it did not therefore allow for the impromptu shoot or LL call. The agreed point was the target, if its location was accurately known; if not, a prominent feature within the area to be searched; or the centre of the area, if no such feature existed. The initial salvo was fired on the agreed point and the pilot corrected the fire of the ranging troop on to the target.([37])

This method was used with success and was regarded as really practical, especially if vertical photographs were available for the indication of targets to pilots.([21])

The Fighter-Bomber in the Counter-Battery Rôle

Despite these efforts, the effect of our counter-battery bombards had on the whole been disappointing. Reports by air O.Ps. had revealed inaccuracies in predicted C.B. fire, and they had been confirmed by examination of vacated enemy gun positions during the advance up the Italian peninsula.

On the other hand, counter-battery resources had been considerably strengthened by developments in the use of the fighter-bomber. In Tunisia, the employment of light bombers in this role had been rather hesitantly practised (see p. 171). Now, with the aid of gridded air photographs, fighter-bombers were getting definite results. Heavy gun positions, pin-pointed by the flash spotters, could be attacked "with a fairly reasonable chance of obtaining hits, whereas before the use of photographs, unless there was an outstanding natural landmark nearby, the chances of hits were very small."([38])

By combining the use of the gridded air photograph with that of a mobile army/air ground O.P., close support aircraft could be briefed in the air and so directed on to opportunity targets. The method employed, which involved the use of a "cab rank" in the air and a "rover" control station on the ground, was developed after the crossing of the Trigno and was a natural evolution of the control system used at El Hamma (see p. 163). The aircraft detailed for the "cab rank" would fly to some easily distinguishable landmark and there orbit overhead for 20 minutes, or until given further instructions from the ground.

The ground O.P. was in direct contact with the headquarters of the attacking brigade and with the aircraft by radio, and copies of the appropriate gridded air photographs were carried by both ground controller and pilot. When, therefore, calls for assistance came in from the headquarters of the attacking brigade, targets could be indicated at once to the supporting aircraft. The system was particularly effective against enemy guns liable to change sites overnight.([39])

Increasing air support naturally gave rise to further developments in counter-flak as an aid to the operations of the supporting aircraft. The idea of including enemy A.A. artillery in the counter-battery programme was not new. It had been used, for example, at Keren and at the Dyle (see pp. 58, 37). But now that close air support had become a regular feature of military operations, counter-flak shoots—known popularly as "Apple Pies" and timed to take effect as a preliminary to the bombing dive—had developed into a definite procedure; a procedure rendered easier by the fact that A.A. batteries were the simplest to spot from the air—although the use of flashless propellant was making even this task more difficult—and that their periods of activity were determined by the operations of our own attacking aircraft.

"Concrete Busting" Becomes a Normal Artillery Rôle

During the fierce fighting at the Tobacco Factory near Battipaglia, in the Salerno battle, the 25-pr. had proved incapable of dealing with the many concrete emplacements that the enemy had constructed there. In the street fighting at Ortona, and in the frequently encountered strong point based on some mountain village, the same difficulty was experienced. Indeed the mountain village, dominating ground that was vital to the attacker, required a special technique for its reduction. Within the strong point itself, the houses were so solidly constructed that even a direct hit from a field gun caused little damage; and, covering it from flanks and rear, were cunningly sited machine-guns and mortars that were also practically immune to shell fire. Hence there was little scope for the use of normal artillery support in the attack. By day smoke was uncertain, and by night an artillery programme only served to warn the enemy that an attack was in progress, or impending, without being able to do him much damage.

In the tank or anti-tank gun, with its solid shot, there was to hand a means of destroying the houses before the attack began.([40]) The 17-pr. had already been used successfully against Italian pill-boxes in the Messina crossing (*see* p. 187), and from now on the use of the anti-tank gun as a "concrete buster" became increasing prevalent. At the same time steps were taken to produce a weapon that could do the same job at long range. In November, 1943, a design was approved for a "common pointed" shell for the 12-in. how., weighing about 750 lb. and specially intended for the attack of concrete.([41])

The Gapping of Minefields and Wire Obstacles

With the introduction of new types of gun and shell, artillerymen again turned their attention towards the problem of the minefield and the wire obstacle. Trials were carried out at the School of Artillery with 5.5-in. guns and 7.2-in. hows. against minefields. The former, at a range of 5,350 yards, were able to clear a gap 100 yards long and 20 yards wide with an expenditure of 3,000 rounds spread over a period of five hours. The latter, at 8,000 yards, were not a success. The pattern was not sufficiently close, and the tendency was to displace mines without detonating them. These results agreed fairly closely with current German doctrine.

A gap about double the above size could be cleared from the air at a cost of 960 × 50-kg. bombs, but neither shelling nor bombing could guarantee that all mines were neutralized. This still had to be done by engineer parties. Moreover, in battle, ranging was likely to be difficult owing to the lack of definition in the edges of minefields.

Some success had been obtained, more economically, with the very sensitive fuzes of the 20-mm. and 40-mm. L.A.A. shell. Tests showed that, at a distance of 40 yards, tellermines could be detonated by the 20-mm. H.E. incendiary shell even when the cover of the mine was four inches below ground level.

Other trials, carried out with the 40-mm. gun, showed this to be a promising form of wire cutter. For example, at 800 yards one gun could cut a gap 10 to 12 feet wide in deep wire; and 6-pr. anti-tank guns, firing H.E. with modified 244 fuze, did as well, if not better.

The Preservation of Elasticity in the Artillery Fire Plan

The net result of all these developments was a considerable increase in the weight of metal that could be delivered in support of an attack. The difficulty was to prevent increasing weight from causing clumsiness. Attempts to introduce originality into the barrage had seldom met with success. For example, a very natural desire for secrecy and speed in the attack had sometimes prompted the selection of start lines in front of our own F.D.Ls.—where they could not be marked with tape—and the omission of pauses whether on the opening line or afterwards. The results, however, were generally accepted as confirming the opinion that start lines should be in our own territory, and that the barrage should dwell on the opening line and subsequently at variable intervals worked out to suit the ground and the degree of resistance expected.

Originality was therefore very difficult to attain. Indeed so important was it to maintain simplicity that the only "fancy touches" regarded as admissible were the "two-way" and the "dummy" barrage, both of which were expensive in ammunition. In the former, the fire would start on the enemy reserve positions and creep back to the opening line, where, after a pause, it would reverse its direction and cover the infantry advance in the normal manner. In the latter, a false barrage would be put down some time before zero hour in the hope that, when the real attack started, the enemy would not man his positions.([42])

Success depended therefore, as ever, on the closeness with which the infantry followed up the barrage, and this was sometimes adversely affected by confusion between enemy defensive fire and our own barrage. Thus, on one occasion, a large artillery programme was stopped during an attack because of a report of "short shooting", which subsequently proved to have been enemy shelling.([43])

But if the barrage was difficult to apply successfully, concentrations were even more so. Concentrations "at call" might be, and often were, worked out beforehand in immense detail so that every conceivable form of opposition was allowed for. It was, however, often impossible to implement them owing to lack of information regarding the whereabouts of our own troops, which was partly as a result of the unreliability of R/T in the mountains and in the volcanic conditions that prevailed in many parts of Italy.

To overcome this difficulty, various systems were devised such as "terror concentrations" and the process known as "lifting out". The object of the terror concentration was to "drench" a series of targets in turn, with repeat "doses" administered at irregular intervals, so that the enemy would be paralysed and would be induced to stay underground for much longer than the usual few minutes after a barrage or simple concentration lifts. Up to 400 guns might be used on a single target, and allowing three "doses" for each, about six targets could be dealt with by one such group in two hours.

"Lifting out" was chiefly applicable to the support of an attack in which the infantry could approach close to their objective under cover and make a surprise assault. The procedure was for all guns, mortars and machine-guns to concentrate on the objective for five to ten minutes at a rapid rate, thus producing an intense and stupifying burst of fire, and thereafter to lift, some forwards and some sideways, to cover mortar and flanking fire positions as the assault went in.([44])

Command and Control of A.A. Defences

After some trial and a little error in North Africa, operational control of A.A. brigades was invariably exercised through gunner channels except where an air defence commander had been appointed (see p. 174). Knowledge of A.A. artillery, its capabilities and methods, was spreading, and the retention of two separate gunner commanders was no longer considered either necessary or desirable([45]); an opinion contrary to that held by the American authorities, who argued that the roles of the A.A. and field artillery were entirely distinct and were unlikely to be expertly appreciated by one and the same commander.

Sector air defence commanders, when appointed, controlled the issue of air raid warnings and the operations of fighter aircraft and balloons direct; and the fire of A.A. guns and the exposure of A.A.S.Ls. through the A.A.D.C. At ports and in beach defences, the decision whether or not to use smoke was made each evening by the naval officer in charge and communicated to the sector air defence commander, who had the right of veto if the creation of smoke was likely to hinder the operations or jeopardize the safety of our own aircraft.

The degree of control exercised over the guns depended on the nature of the area being defended. Following the home pattern, those areas that could most suitably be defended by A.A. guns were classified as "inner artillery zones" (I.A.Z) and all friendly aircraft were normally prohibited from flying over them, so that almost complete freedom of action could be allowed to A.A. units. Even here, however, it was possible for the R.A.F. controller to stop the guns from firing, in case of need, by issuing the order "Hold Fire".

In other gun defended areas (G.D.A.) three conditions had to be fulfilled before unseen aircraft could be fired at: a warning must have been issued, the aircraft must not be showing I.F.F., and the guns must be in direct communication with a G.O.R. so that fire could be stopped immediately, if required. At airfields special instructions were compiled in agreement with the local air force commander.([46])

Early in November, 1943, it was decided to establish a powerful A.A. defence for the United Nations Conference, which was due to assemble at the Mena House Hotel, outside Cairo, on 21st November. Begun as an exercise on 9th November, this operation involved the movement and installation of 48 H.A.A. guns, 72 L.A.A. guns and 18 A.A.S.Ls. A smoke company was also deployed, and a squadron of balloons held in readiness under the orders of the A.A.D.C. A decoy lay-out was arranged in the area of the Sakhara Pyramids about ten miles to the south, and altogether some 450 miles of cable were laid.

Developments in Radar

In July, 1943, G.L. III had at last begun to make its appearance, and in Italy its performance had been very satisfactory. From the technical point of view, its main advantage over G.L.II was its independence of the reflected ray from the ground, and hence of the " mat ", artificial or natural (*see* p. 92). It was therefore much easier to site, and it also showed a high degree of immunity from ground clutter even in mountainous districts.

Its main disadvantage was its narrow field of " view ". Although most useful for the engagement of a target, it was less capable than G.L.II of finding the target in the first instance. Its operator had in fact to be told where to look, and for this purpose it had to be accompanied by a " putter-on " in the form of a L.W. set similar to that used for the early warning at A.A.O.Rs. and in L.A.A. units.

The radar control of searchlights and of air interceptions had also continued to make progress, which resulted in a closer collaboration between night fighters and guns. Hitherto there had been a rigid system by which, on " fighter nights ", the guns were forbidden to fire at all or were restricted to a certain height laid down in advance (*see* p. 93). In October, 1943, as the result of experience in the Tyne and Tees defences, a much more elastic system was introduced. The height of the gun/fighter boundary, instead of being laid down beforehand, was agreed on at the beginning of an engagement and was made to approximate to that of the highest raid in progress at the time. Thus full use was made of the guns, and the fighters, flying above the boundary, with the aid of their A.I. gear could look down into the G.D.A., follow the enemy aircraft, and drop down and intercept them after they had emerged from the area.[47]

The application of radar to coast artillery problems was a natural development which had been put into effect in the United Kingdom early in 1941. Its extension overseas proceeded more slowly, but by March, 1944, early warning cover against surface vessels had been provided in all defended ports in the Middle East, and one fire control set was in process of installation at Haifa. A second set, just arrived, was provisionally allotted to Aden.[48]

By this time " counter-radar " was getting into its stride, and both sides were using specially treated paper strips, known as " window ", which were thrown out in large quantities by some or all of the attacking aircraft and which caused confusing responses in the radar receiving sets and made it difficult to track the real enemy. Electrical disturbances in the atmosphere might also give rise to false signals, and even if aircraft were picked up and correctly identified, communications between the sector operations room and G.O.R. might be temporarily out of order.

At Bari, on the night of 2nd/3rd December, 1943, all three of these adverse factors were in operation, and as a result a skilfully timed attack by about 30 enemy aircraft was able to penetrate the defences, which included fighter aircraft and an A.A. component of 52 H.A.A. guns, 78 L.A.A. guns (34 of which were 20-mms.) and 32 A.A.S.Ls. Three enemy aircraft were shot down, but the attack as a whole was successful. Seventeen ships with 30,000 tons of cargo were sunk—mainly through the explosion of two ammunition ships— and although the port was not permanently damaged, five working days were lost.[30]

Conclusion

The outstanding feature of this period had been the successful accomplishment of an assault landing in the face of serious opposition. The fighting at Salerno had shown the practicability of an operation that since Gallipoli had seemed to offer little hope of success. Increased flexibility of control bestowed by radio and radar, armoured mobility in the shape of the tank and the S.P. gun, and the moral effect of the rocket had each played its part in the victory, and by providing the means of tactical exploitation, had restored in full the strategical value of sea-power.

Once ashore, however, strategical mobility was reduced to a minimum by the nature of the terrain and by the increasing absorption of shipping resources in the preparations for Operation "Overlord". The fighting, therefore, had inevitably developed into a simple slogging match, in which massive fire plans were at a premium and deception had often to take the form of "Chinese attacks", or dummy fire plans, in which large quantities of ammunition were expended. The promised opportunities for the increased use of smoke (*see* p. 183) had to some extent been realized, especially for the screening of bridging operations following the assault of a river line. Maps, on the other hand, had sometimes been disappointing, and the value of predicted fire had been further diminished by errors in meteor and other ballistic factors.

In air defence, the full fruits of radar were at last beginning to be harvested, although the engagement of unseen high level targets by H.A.A. guns was handicapped by the lack of an electronic predictor and by the recent introduction of "window", and there was no means at all of laying a gun on an aircraft diving out of the sun or carrying out a low-flying attack by night. The immediate benefits lay rather in the growing intimacy of co-operation between ground and air components.

Similarly, in the application of radio to direct air support in the attack, great progress had been made; progress that had been foreshadowed at El Hamma in March, 1943, but that had to wait for its fulfilment until unchallenged air supremacy had been obtained. It was one of the many tactical expedients which, perceived only as an unattainable ideal in the hour of greatest need, took substance and added strength to an army already in the ascendant.

In the armoured battle also we continued to be on top. Tiger and Panther tanks were now often committed to a purely defensive and stationary role as hastily improvized pill-boxes, and even in this role they could usually be put out of action by the 17-pr.

Against the third of its chief opponents, the mortar, the gun had been less successful. The development of a new technique and of a special counter-mortar organization was to be one of the major advances of the succeeding period. Meanwhile an eleventh-hour attempt was being made by the enemy to strengthen his neglected artillery arm, with the result that counter-battery work threatened to become as important, and as difficult, as it had been in 1916-18.

List of References

(¹) R.A. Notes No. 7.
(²) R.A. Notes No. 8.
(³) War Diary, R.A. 56 Div., June 1944.
(⁴) A.T.M. No. 46 of October 1943.
(⁵) A.T.M. No. 45 of May 1943.
(⁶) Combined Operations H.Q. Monthly Information Summary, No. 4, Pt. II, August 1943.
(⁷) R.A.T.M. No. 9 of October 1943.
(⁸) War Diary, 18 L.A.A. Regt., July 1943.
(⁹) "The Conquest of Sicily", Despatch by Field Marshal Alexander.
(¹⁰) Notes on Operations, Italy, 17th November 1943.
(¹¹) Notes on Operations, Sicily, 16th November 1943.
(¹²) War Diary, R.A. 78 Div., August 1943.
(¹³) Notes on Operations, Sicily, 23rd August 1943.
(¹⁴) War Diary, 30 Corps C.B. Staff.
(¹⁵) "El Alamein to the Sangro", by Field Marshal Montgomery.
(¹⁶) R.A. 46 Div. Operational Instruction No. 3 of 29th August 1943.
(¹⁷) R.A. Notes No. 17.
(¹⁸) Notes on Operations, Italy, 15th December 1943.
(¹⁹) Report by 201 Gds. Bde., 9th-18th September 1943.
(²⁰) Notes on Naval Bombardment by F.O. Levant and E.M., 30th June 1943.
(²¹) Misc. R.A. Notes on Ops. and Eqpt., 9th-30th September 1943 by R.A. 10 Corps.
(²²) 12 A.A. Bde. Standing Instructions for Beach A.A. Defence, 20th August 1943.
(²³) "Use of Smoke in Operation Avalanche", 16th November 1943.
(²⁴) Notes on Operations, Italy, 3rd December 1943.
(²⁵) "Operations of British, Indian and Dominion Forces in Italy", Pt. I, Sec. C.
(²⁶) Notes on Operations, Italy, 31st March 1944.
(²⁷) "Operations of British, Indian and Dominion Forces in Italy", Pt. I, Sec. B.
(²⁸) Notes on Operations, No. 23, 28th January 1944.
(²⁹) Report on Forcing of Garigliano by C.R.A. 56 Div.
(³⁰) "Operations of British, Indian and Dominion Forces in Italy", Pt. I, Sec. A.
(³¹) Note by C.R.A. 56 Div.
(³²) "The Desert Air Force", by Roderic Owen, p. 212.
(³³) R.A. Notes No. 11.
(³⁴) W.O. File 79/Mob/5966.
(³⁵) Reply from A.F.H.Q. to War Office and School of Artillery Questionnaire.
(³⁶) G.H.Q., M.E.F., 1064/1/R.A. of 27th December 1943.
(³⁷) R.A. 10 Corps Standing Orders for Arty/R Shoots, 2nd October 1943.
(³⁸) D.O. Air Co-op Circular No. 12, G.H.Q., M.E.F., 18th January 1944.
(³⁹) "The Desert Air Force", by Roderic Owen, p. 201.
(⁴⁰) Report on Mountain Warfare, G.H.Q., M.E.F., 14th January 1944.
(⁴¹) R.A. Notes No. 10.
(⁴²) Mins. of Cs.R.A. Conference, Eighth Army H.Q., 22nd January 1944.
(⁴³) 10 Corps Training Instruction No. 1 of 4th November 1943.
(⁴⁴) Notes on Fire Plans, by C.R.A. 56 Div.
(⁴⁵) R.A. Notes No. 13.
(⁴⁶) 12 A.A. Bde. Standing Operational Instructions, February 1944.
(⁴⁷) R.A. Notes No. 9.
(⁴⁸) Report No. 10 on Employment of A.A. and C.D. Units in M.E., March 1944.

CHAPTER XII

THROUGH THE ATLANTIC WALL

Plates Relevant to this Chapter

Nos.
30. The 75-mm. pack how. (airborne).
31. The 32-pr. A.Tk. gun.
32. The 240-mm. gun.
33. The triple 20-mm. L.A.A. Mounting.

The Development of Airborne Artillery

After four and a half years of war and some two years or more of undisputed allied air supremacy in the West, production was in full swing and the flow of material from the factories had increased from a mere trickle into a mighty torrent. There would still be shortages of important stores at certain times and in certain places, owing to temporary breakdowns in the distributive system, but on the whole artillery resources were now adequate, both in quantity and quality, for the task that lay ahead of them.

Included in the preparations for the new drive into N.W. Europe was the employment, for the first time, of a complete British airborne division in its normal role. It was in July, 1938, that Germany had begun to form her first airborne division, for anticipated operations in the Sudetenland, with an artillery component of one troop of four Skoda guns. By the end of 1940 this component had been raised to an artillery battalion of three troops, one A.A. battalion of four troops, and an anti-tank battalion of four companies; and a "Flieger" corps had been formed, consisting of one "Flieger" and one infantry division. After the attack on Crete, German airborne troops were not much used in their proper role—owing, apparently, to Hitler's lack of faith in them—until, early in 1943, information of allied progress in this direction brought about another change of policy.

The formation of the first British airborne formation had been initiated immediately after Dunkirk, and on 11th November, 1940, a War Office plan for an airborne "aerodrome capture group" included two sections each of 4 × 3.7-in. hows. and two L.A.A. troops each of 4 Bofors or Hispanos. For another year, policy remained in a state or flux. Then, towards the end of 1941, the 1st Airborne Division began to form. Its artillery was at first embodied in the air-landing and parachute brigade groups, but on the 15th December, 1941, it was removed from them and formed into divisional troops. It then consisted only of one independent light battery, armed with 8 × 3.7-in. hows. By September, 1942, two anti-tank batteries had been added, and a H.Q.R.A. was formed in October, 1942. Originally proposed in July, 1942, when the divisional artillery consisted only of three batteries—one light, one anti-tank and one L.A.A.—this headquarters was a comparatively small affair, intended to command and supervise the training of these three independent batteries. It was commanded by a lieut.-colonel and organized on a non-operational basis, since it was considered "most unlikely that the artillery in this formation will ever be used in such a way as to necessitate centralized control."[1] It was not until October, 1944, that the rank of the commander was upgraded to that of brigadier.

Meanwhile it had been decided to replace the 3.7-in. how. by the American 75-mm. pack how., which was more easily available and was considered to be slightly more suitable. Anti-tank batteries, which had originally been armed with 2-prs., were to be re-equipped with 6-prs. as soon as the axles of the latter had been modified to fit into the Horsa glider. For A.A. defence, use was still made of 20-mm. Hispanos and 40-mm. Bofors, the latter requiring some dismantling for carriage in the Horsa and therefore taking longer to come into action after landing.

In January, 1943, the 1st Airborne Divisional Artillery still consisted only of one light battery, armed with two guns, and two anti-tank and one L.A.A. battery nearly at full strength. On 13th February, 1943, the light battery expanded to form the 1st Air-landing Light Regiment, but the anti-tank regimental headquarters was not formed until some time later.

The evolution of artillery policy, like the growth of the units themselves, proceeded gradually. Battle experience began at the Primasole Bridge in Sicily in July, 1943, when 12 guns of the 1st Air-landing Anti-Tank Battery accompanied the 1st Parachute Brigade, together with two parachute naval bombardment units and a F.O.O. from the 1st Air-landing Regiment for liaison with 13 Corps Artillery. The possibilities of air support as a substitute for artillery support in airborne operations were not at this time fully appreciated, and opportunities for fresh experience were slow in coming. When, on 9th September, 1943, the Division at last went into action as a formation, it was to seize Taranto by a sea-borne operation that met with no opposition. After pursuing the retreating enemy as far as Foggia, the bulk of the Division returned to the United Kingdom in November, leaving behind the 1st Air-landing Light Regiment to serve as part of 13 Corps Artillery until the following February. During the subsequent advance northwards, this unit, with its 75-mm. pack hows. drawn by jeeps and its special training in dealing with demolitions and mines, was most useful as a means of close support when demolitions held up the less mobile 25-prs. Indeed on one occasion the guns were broken down into pack and carried into action on the top of Churchill tanks; as once before, in the First World War, the guns of an Indian mountain battery had been carried—by mule loads—in Ford vans during the final pursuit of the Turks in Mesopotomia.

Incomplete as they were, these operations had helped to crystallize policy. A Chiefs of Staff memorandum of 30th September, 1943, based on experience in Sicily, suggested that " airborne forces should be used in conjunction with a main attack by land, sea or air, and supply a means of turning the enemy's ever-open flank by using the door over the top."

Meanwhile, in May, 1943, the 6th Airborne Division had begun to form, and it was in accordance with this principle that it was to be used in the Normandy landings. It was to be flown in on the night of " D "-1/" D " and was to seize and hold vital river and canal crossings on the left flank of the beachhead.

Since its own artillery was limited to an air landing light regiment of 24 × 75-mms., one air-landing anti-tank regiment and one L.A.A. battery, it was obvious that additional fire support would be required if it was to hold for any length of time the positions it was to win by the speed and unexpectedness of its initial assault. At first this would have to come entirely from the Royal Navy, but after 1000 hours on "D" day it was expected that further help could be given by the 3rd Divisional and 1st Corps Artilleries.(²)

The problem was how to control this supporting fire. At first a tentative arrangement was made by taking officers from divisional and A.G.R.A. regiments, training them in parachute jumping, and then using them as a pool on which to draw for special occasions. It was from similar origins that had been evolved the bombardment troops—now expanded into a bombardment unit of three troops—for the control of ships' guns during an opposed landing from the sea. So, by June 1944, there had been created a Forward Observer Unit R.A. (Airborne), which, though slightly less elaborate than the bombardment unit, contained the same two essential elements: one for observation, the other for liaison. It was organized as a headquarters and three sections, each providing six forward observers airborne; four to act as observers, and two as liaison officers to man a rear link. The intention was that each section should work with a brigade, with one forward observer airborne to each battalion and one spare. The liaison officers would act as artillery representatives at brigade headquarters, and be responsible for the retransmission of fire orders direct to the guns of the ground forces.(³)

Covering Fire

For geographical reasons, the amount of air support that could be given to an operation across the Channel was very much greater than anything yet attempted, either in the form of interdiction or of direct support. A technique had still to be worked out, however, to make the latter effective. Although, in North Africa and Italy, much experience had been gained in co-operation with the Tactical Air Force, the subject was still in its infancy so far as large-scale bombardments by the Strategical Air Force were concerned. For the indication of targets, the use of smoke by the artillery had proved of value, but there was always the risk that the enemy might confuse the issue by putting down smoke on our own localities. The provision of coloured smoke in four varieties (see p. 171), though primarily intended to ensure an effective contrast with any type of background, would also go part of the way towards meeting this risk by making possible the use of a colour code that could be changed from one operation to the next. Equally, if not more, important was accurate timing by the R.A.F., so that the enemy would not get more than two minutes' warning of an impending air attack.

For the assault landing itself, naval covering fire could also be on an unprecedently large scale; and, better still, improvements had been made in the system for maintaining fire support of the leading troops as they approached the beaches. The artillery of the assault divisions had been specially equipped with S.P. guns, which were carried by troops in L.C.Ts., from which they were to give covering fire to the first flight of the assault. Each regiment had a F.O.O. embarked in a L.C.P.(L) or L.C.S.(M), who went ahead to observe the fire and who was in wireless communication with a fire control officer (F.C.O.) embarked in the control L.C.T. of the regimental group. To assist in the preparation of gunnery data, each group of L.C.T. had attached to it a navigational leader equipped with radar for giving a navigational fix.(⁴)

On completion of the run-in, regiments were to stand by off shore while the beaches were cleared, and to fill in the time interval between their last rounds afloat and their first rounds ashore, which was expected to be at least 90 minutes, a Royal Marine Armoured Support Group was formed and equipped with 95-mm. hows. mounted in Centaur tanks.

Once ashore in force, concentrations and other forms of covering fire would follow procedures that had now been fairly well standardized. Concentrations could be of any width, but could not exceed 200 yards in depth if troops were to cross the ground after them and to reach their objectives before the effects had worn off. If a greater depth had to be covered, two or more concentrations would be ordered at suitable timings.([5]) Barrages were kept as simple as possible, with a depth of 400 yards and an overlap of 400 yards on each flank of the attack. As always, a barrage was accompanied by concentrations within and on the flanks of its line of advance, and sometimes concentrations were combined with a light directional barrage such as had been used at El Hamma (*see* p. 164).

When time did not permit the detailed preparation of a barrage, a moving stonk, which had a standard frontage of 525 yards, could be used by giving the origin and axis in the normal way and arranging for it to move up its axis by lifts at the appropriate intervals and speed. In some formations, amplifications were made to the stonk in order to produce a quick area shoot for special occasions. For example, at the Garigliano, R.A. 56 Division used what they called a "pattern target" to comprise the fire of four field, two medium and one heavy regiment. It was normally laid out in the form of pairs of adjacent stonks by the field and medium regiments, with intervals of 200 and 300 yards between the pairs, and a fourth line 500 yards beyond the third pair (mediums), which was taken on as a 1,200-yard stonk by the heavy regiment.([6]) Thus:—

	G		hy regt
F	Axis ↑	E	2 med regts
D		C	2 fd regts
B		A	2 fd regts

D.F. tasks were treated as area tasks requiring nothing less than a regiment, and were applied as a rule on a frontage equal to that of a stonk. In an emergency, therefore, fire could be put down quickly in the form of a standard stonk. Each task was given a number, and a group of tasks was sometimes given a code name so that all could be fired together. Blocks of numbers were allotted to divisions, infantry brigades and battalions, so that mortar tasks included in the brigade fire plan could be given numbers.([5])

Counter-Mortar

The major artillery problem at this time was the neutralization of hostile mortars. In the United Kingdom the approach to the subject had been conditioned by the desirability of avoiding any addition to war establishments. An attempt had therefore been made to combine the counter-mortar with the counter-battery organization. In Italy this had proved unsatisfactory, since the enemy guns and mortars were sited in entirely different areas.([7])

It was necessary to decentralize the organization of counter-mortar measures down to divisions and brigades. The solution proposed was to appoint a C.M.O. to each division and an A.C.M.O. to each brigade, taken—in the first instance anyhow—from the body of the divisional artillery and put through a preparatory course of training in the corps counter-battery office.

For the location of hostile mortars, every possible means was given a trial: mortar reports (moreps) on the lines of "shelreps" (see p. 186), artillery and mortar O.Ps., air O.Ps., flash spotting and sound ranging sections ; and since the normal sound ranging instruments proved insufficiently sensitive, even when pushed well forward, a new instrument, known as the "four pen recorder", was designed and issued on the scale of four to each survey regiment for counter-mortar work.

Attempts had also been made to use radar for this purpose, but so far nothing had come of them. Trials carried out with the G.L.III in 1943 had been so unsuccessful that the idea had been temporarily abandoned, pending the development of a more suitable set. Revived at the end of the year in connection with the artillery preparations for the invasion of North-West Europe, it was again held in abeyance as savouring too much of the defensive at a time when, by order of the higher command, attention was to be devoted exclusively to consideration of the offensive.

Increasing use was made of our own 4.2-in. mortars, and the allotment of tasks between them and the guns was usually made, on the infantry brigade level, by the C.O. of the supporting field regiment. If, however, the divisional commander wished to use all his 16 mortars in the initial fire plan, the C.R.A. would himself co-ordinate by dealing direct with the mortar company commander or the C.M.O.([8]) The 3.7 H.A.A. gun, with its time fuzes, was considered particularly efficacious, and forward H.A.A. troops were linked to the counter-mortar organization and placed at the call of the C.M.O.

Artificial Moonlight

The increasing use made of night attacks, and the undesirability of confining such operations to moonlit periods, had brought into prominence the need for some form of artificial moonlight. In the United Kingdom successful trials had been held with 25-pr. and 3.7-in. how. star shell, and the production of both types was in hand. It had also been decided to develop a star shell for the 3.7-in. H.A.A. gun, which could then be used to provide illumination when not required to make any other kind of contribution to the fire plan.

The chief source of artificial moonlight was, however, to be the searchlight. Trials had been carried out both in the United Kingdom and in Italy, and certain principles had been established. Battle experience had shown that the optimum period for a night attack was that of "half moon", and the object of illumination in the attack was generally therefore to produce the effect of half moon over the enemy position and the assaulting troops. In addition, it might be required to produce as bright a light as possible over selected areas for limited periods; for example, to light up the objective for a final assault after an approach in darkness.

In the defence, the object was to illuminate the ground in front of the foremost troops; and at other times light was required to make work possible at night which otherwise could only be done by day, and to economize in time and effort spent on activities which were hampered by darkness. It was, for example, of great assistance to transport operating over bad roads, and it was later much used in this way during the fighting in the Apennines.

As yet, however, the possibilities of the A.A.S.L., when used in such rôles, had not been fully explored. In the days of German air supremacy, the risks involved had seemed prohibitive, and it was only slowly that people came to realize what liberties could be taken now that the "boot was on the other leg."

Co-operation with Tanks

The tendency to increase the proportion of S.P. guns had been steadily persisting. A proposal was put forward about this time that an extra S.P. field regiment should be provided for each independent armoured or tank brigade. 21 Army Group also pressed for the development of a S.P. medium equipment, to be used in support of armoured divisions; thereby reviving a demand that had been raised by the 7th Armoured Division in 1942. The requirement was not however supported by experience in Italy, and as no specification or design for such an equipment existed, it was left to M.Gs.R.A. to initiate a demand in the normal way through their respective theatre commanders.

For co-operation with tanks, a new technique had been devised for the use of air O.Ps. Flights working with armoured formations, and with infantry divisions with armoured brigades in support, would assist tanks in locating themselves, keep the tank commander informed of the "going" and of what was "round the corner", and shoot the field regiments supporting the tanks through the F.O.Os.' net. For this purpose, aircraft were netted on the tank F.O.O. frequency, with a "flick" on the tank commander's frequency.(⁹)

The closeness with which armoured troops could follow artillery covering fire was a matter of some discussion about this time. During an exercise on the Sussex Downs in the winter of 1941-42, some Churchills had got in among the 25-pr. barrage without harm to themselves; and in July, 1943, a formal demonstration on these lines took place at the School of Artillery, Larkhill.

Here, it seemed, was an ideal method of combining the neutralizing effect of artillery fire with the armoured mobility of the tank. The suppression of the enemy anti-tank guns could actually go on simultaneously with the attack by our own armour.

As usual, however, there were disadvantages, as well as advantages, to be considered. While in the barrage, the tanks had to close down, and this was felt by many to outweigh the advantages derived from the prolongation of the covering fire. The method was, therefore, seldom if ever deliberately used in battle.

Anti-Tank Developments

As the race between gun and armour continued, a design was proposed for a 32-pr. anti-tank gun, which was originally to have been mounted on both towed and S.P. carriages. Owing, however, to its great weight, the former type of mounting was soon abandoned, and the production of the latter was delayed by the lack of a suitable chassis. This equipment was therefore still in the experimental stage at the end of the war in Europe, and in the subsequent fighting in the Far East it was unnecessary because of the comparatively thin armour of the Japanese A.F.Vs. There were moreover indications that it would ultimately be better to design improved high velocity shot for the 17-pr. rather than undertake the re-equipment of anti-tank units with a new heavy gun. The "small hole" rather than the "big hole" was in fact to emerge as British anti-tank gun policy in 1945.

In conformity with this policy, the performance of anti-tank ammunition was further improved by the production, in the summer of 1944, of a new device known as the "discarding sabot", or D.S. shot. In this projectile, a tungsten carbide core was enclosed in a light metal casing, or sabot, which separated into segments on the shock of discharge and which was discarded as the projectile left the muzzle of the gun. The armour penetration achieved at normal impact at a range of 1,000 yards was 146 mm. with the 6-pr. and 231 mm. with the 17-pr. On the other hand, where A.P.C.B.C. could penetrate, it did greater damage inside the tank and was less likely to pass straight through a lightly armoured target. In consequence, both kinds of shot had to be retained in the service ; A.P.C.B.C. for use when penetration was certain, and D.S. for special occasions.[10]

Developments in A.A. Defence

Owing to the existence of A.D.G.B., the preparations for the Normandy offensive could be made under cover of air and A.A. defences very much stronger and more up-to-date than anything that had been available in overseas theatres. Since the Germans had ceased their daylight attacks by fighter-bombers in June 1943, and had switched (as in September 1940) to night attacks, much experience had been gained in the conduct of G.C.I. and S.L. controlled interceptions (see pp. 93, 94). As a result, what had been two rival systems were gradually woven into a flexible and co-ordinated whole, the effectiveness of which was still further increased by the introduction of faster night fighters in the form of Mosquitos.

In the autumn of 1943, experiments in the Milford Haven area had shown that night fighters, aided by S.L.C. controlled searchlights at 6,000 yards spacing, could intercept successfully without individual control from sector. Since the minimum of R/T communication with the aircraft was required, a high concentration of fighters was possible and interception was quick. It was in fact a promising form of defence for isolated strong points, beaches and ports subsequent to an assault landing.[11]

As far as guns were concerned, the main advances of 1943 had been technical rather than tactical. Accuracy of fire had been improved by the introduction of mechanical fuzes and flashless propellant (which reduced the possibilities of evasive action), volume of fire by the development of remote control gear and the mechanical fuze setter for the 3.7 in., and "ceiling" by the installation of the first 5.25-in. equipments.

There had also been a fundamental change in the functions of the G.O.R. Before the advent of an efficient G.L. equipment, unseen targets had of necessity been engaged by barrages controlled direct from the G.O.R. But with the introduction of G.L.III and the arrival of the first electronic predictors in October 1943, engagements were once more conducted from individual gun positions, and the G.O.R., now equipped with a modified form of G.C.I. set (*see* p. 73), was restricted to general tactical control and the passage of information upon which the fighting of the battle depended.

At first the fighter-bombers had had to make their night attacks from considerable heights, but with the introduction of radio altimeters and other navigational aids, it soon became possible for ordinary air crews to fly blind at night at heights of 300-500 feet. Thus the low-flying attack, which by day had been practically mastered with the aid of the 20-mm. gun and other devices (*see* p. 153), had again become a menace by adapting itself to night conditions. On 18th May 1944, therefore, it was agreed by the Weapon Development Committee that unseen fire control systems should be developed for both light and intermediate guns, with the latter as first priority.

Preparations for the Resumption of the Offensive

As a prelude to the assault on the Atlantic Wall, it was decided to launch a full-scale offensive in Italy. The plan was to deceive the enemy into expecting a sea-borne attack from the west of Rome and then to strike hard at the focal point of his defences at Cassino.

The difficulties likely to be encountered in this attack were considerable. The enemy positions in the hills were known to have been thoroughly prepared for all-round defence and to contain pill-boxes, armoured emplacements, casemates, sangars and trenches. Their armament included a large number of medium machine-guns and mortars, and it was estimated that, out of a total of about 400 guns and nebelwerfers on this front, some 230 could fire into the Cassino sector and about 150 could take part in the actual battle for Monte Cassino. All were well dug in, and the mortars had been particularly troublesome in previous battles.([12])

In order to achieve an adequate concentration of force west of the Apennines, 5 Corps was left to hold some 30 miles of front between the sea and Palena with only two divisions and an armoured brigade. To deceive the enemy, the Corps Commander kept most of his formations up, using his artillery positions, organized for all-round defence, to add depth to the infantry lay-out. A show of aggression was maintained by confining the use of mines and wire to close approaches that could not be covered by fire, and —so long as the ammunition supply lasted—by subjecting the enemy to a carefully thought out weekly programme of harassing fire.

Unfortunately, about this time there was a serious shortage of ammunition, which necessitated the restriction of ammunition expenditure on the whole front to 15 r.p.g.p.d. for 25-prs. and 10 for medium artillery, in order that the necessary reserves might be built up.([13]) For in the fighting that lay ahead, the concentrated use of field and medium artillery would be the keynote to success. "The location of the enemy's positions" wrote the C-in-C "will be difficult; his troops will be well posted and skilfully concealed. Only by a lavish expenditure of ammunition shall we be able to overrun them without suffering heavy casualties. . . . The troops with which we are now fighting are not as experienced and well-trained as those with which we started. . . . The effect of this is that attacks against stiff resistance must be helped forward by artillery."

In the air, allied supremacy was almost complete. Nearly 4,000 aircraft of operational type were available in Italy and the near-by islands, as against which the Luftwaffe could muster only 700 in the whole Central Mediterranean theatre, and of this number less than half were based on Italy.([12])

The Attack on the Gustav Line

The Liri Valley was chosen as the main point of attack because, though narrow, it was regarded as the most suitable part of the front on which to make use of our great superiority in tanks and artillery. For this very reason it was the obvious approach, and it involved a frontal attack on prepared defences with little possibility of effecting a tactical surprise or even of finding positions for the supporting artillery that were not completely overlooked by the enemy from his observation posts on Monte Cassino.

The total number of guns available was 1,060 for the support of an attack by two corps; the 2nd Polish on the right, with Monte Cassino as its objective; 13 Corps on the left, with orders to cross the River Gari (Rapido) and drive up the Liri Valley. The battle was to begin at 2300 hours—half an hour before moonrise—on 11th May, with a 40-minute counter-battery and counter-mortar bombardment, and artillery support throughout was to be on a lavish scale. In the Polish Corps sector, where transport difficulties were acute, abnormally large quantities of ammunition had to be dumped in the forward area—1,090 r.p.g. for field, and 700 for medium, artillery—much of it in full view of the enemy on Monte Cassino and Monte Cifalco. In 13 Corps, 600 r.p.g. were dumped for field guns, 350 for medium, and 200 for heavy guns.

By strict attention to camouflage, by restricting all moves to the hours of darkness, and by keeping guns in new positions silent until the attack had started, some degree of secrecy was maintained. Indeed, as at the Garigliano, hardly a shell fell on the artillery positions before the attack opened.([12])

In form, the preliminary bombardment differed noticeably from the usual practice. The counter-battery role, including the engagement of nebelwerfers, was performed by medium and heavy artillery only, while the field and H.A.A. guns dealt with hostile mortars and forward localities. Hostile batteries were subjected in turn to group salvos, in which as much as seven tons of ammunition was sometimes delivered simultaneously on to one target. Some H.A.A. guns were also used to supplement the 7.2-in. hows. for the air burst engagement of nebelwerfers.([14])

This new departure was the result of necessity rather than of choice. Owing to the limited number of long range guns that were available, their use had to be confined largely to counter-battery work.([15]) Even so it would not have been possible to compete with certain of the German 17-cm. guns, which outranged all our artillery, without the opportune appearance of some American 8-in. guns.([14])

To cover the infantry across the Rapido, 17 field and 2 medium regiments of 13 Corps Artillery fired a creeping barrage, at a rate of advance of 100 yards in six minutes, while counter-battery bombardments were continued on a reduced scale (*see* Map 11). The infantry of the Polish Corps were not to attack until 1¼ hours later, and during the interval the greater part of the artillery allotted to the Corps was to shell the infantry positions in the path of the attack. Then, when the attack went in, it was to be supported by concentrations from all types of weapon, with additional close support by 16 flame throwers and 72×4.2-in. mortars, the latter manned by the personnel of superfluous anti-tank units.[12]

As the attack developed, arty/R aircraft were to carry out an average of 12 missions daily, thus providing almost complete cover over the whole battle area. It was the first occasion on which complete coverage of this kind had been given, and the results were very satisfactory. Between 12th and 25th May, 134 missions were carried out, of which 127 were successful. Of 109 targets engaged, 32 were G.N.F. (guns now firing) and some were tanks, flushed from cover and pursued with fire while close support bombers were called to the spot through the "rover" control station (*see* p. 198).

Air O.Ps. were also active. For this battle the 13 Corps front was divided into two sectors, each covered by one flight under the control of the C.B.O. at 6 A.G.R.A. headquarters. An Army Air Support Control tentacle was also installed at these headquarters, by means of which the C.A.G.R.A. was able to co-ordinate the activities of air O.Ps. and arty/R sorties, and to pass good targets, such as the tanks referred to in the previous paragraph, to the "rover" controlled aircraft[14]

The preliminary counter-battery bombardment was of some assistance to 13 Corps in its crossing of the Rapido, especially to the 8th Indian Division on the left. The 4th Division, on the right, had a more difficult time; and when the Polish Corps began its attack on Monte Cassino, the effects of the bombardment had worn off altogether. As a result the latter Corps suffered heavy casualties and had to be withdrawn to its start line at 1400 hours on 12th May.

Meanwhile 13 Corps had run into unexpected difficulties. The preliminary bombardment had not been very successful in dealing with mortars, machine-guns and small arms, and from the moment of setting foot across the river the leading troops plunged among a thick and continuous network of pill-boxes, wire, minefields and concrete emplacements. In the course of some very confused fighting the infantry lost the barrage, and by the first light on 12th May, only a shallow bridgehead had been secured.

In these circumstances it became more important than ever to blind the enemy observation posts on the Monastery feature and to neutralize the machine-guns and mortars that lay behind it. From first light 12th May onwards, continuous smoke screens, which could be stopped at call, were put down on its north-western and south-western slopes by the 3rd Carpathian and 4th British Divisional Artilleries; and four separate heavy battery concentrations were fired by 7.2-in., 8-in. and 240-mm. hows. during the attack of 2 Polish Corps and subsequently at hourly intervals during daylight. In addition, smoke generators, operated by a L.A.A. regiment, were used to screen the river crossings, artillery positions and supply routes. Altogether some 800 tons of smoke were used on these two corps fronts between 12th and 18th

Plate 26—The "Sexton".

Plate 27—The 17-pr. A Tk gun on the Valentine tank chassis.

Plate 28—The S.P. Bofors.

Plate 29—**The Landing Craft, Rocket.**

Plate 30—The 75-mm. pack how. (Airborne).

Plate 31—The **32-pr.** A Tk gun.

Plate 32—The 240-mm. howitzer.

Plate 33—**The triple 20-mm. LAA mounting.**

May, and 135,000 smoke shells were fired in five days.([16]) But the complete screening of so commanding and steep-sided a feature was impossible to achieve. As so often before, the smoke canisters were found to roll down the mountain side and thus create unpredictable gaps in the screen.

On 17th May, 2 Polish Corps put in a fresh attack on Monte Cassino without the delays that had cost them so dearly on the previous occasion. After a 20-minute counter-battery and counter-mortar bombardment, followed by concentrations for 40 minutes on the enemy infantry positions, the two assaulting divisions moved off at once at such a speed that the leading infantry escaped most of the enemy defensive fire. The fighting was hard, but the objectives were gained and held.([12])

The Attack on the Hitler Line

The Gustav Line had been broken, but behind it lay the Hitler Line, which, though sketchy in the mountains, was even more elaborate than the Gustav Line in the valley. The Forme D'Aquino was supplemented as an anti-tank obstacle by a discontinuous anti-tank ditch, with minefields covered in front and in rear by thick belts of wire. On the fringe of the line were numerous semi-mobile armoured pill-boxes, and behind them an intricate system of concrete gun emplacements and satellite weapon pits, all linked by tunnels and communication trenches.([12])

Against this position, the 1st Canadian Corps was able to bring the fire of 810 guns of all types, of which 76 medium and heavy were allotted exclusively to counter-battery, and 52 guns and mortars to counter-mortar, roles, leaving 682 guns to provide covering fire for the infantry. By midnight 19th/20th May about 1,000 shells an hour were crashing on to known enemy positions, and this programme continued at varying timings and rates of fire until the opening of the attack at 0600 hours on 23rd May.

The assault was made by three battalions on a 2,000 yard front, covered by a creeping barrage on a 3,000 yard front, which advanced at the rate of 100 yards in five minutes to the first objective, where it was to pause for an hour before going on, at 100 yards in three minutes, to the final objective. The operation was successful and by 1800 hours the Hitler Line had been pierced, but the casualties had been heavy and the Corps Commander, in his subsequent report on the battle, concluded that 2,000 yards was too narrow a frontage for an attack by three battalions, since it allowed the enemy to concentrate his artillery and mortar fire.([12]) On the other hand, it enabled very heavy concentrations to be put down by our own artillery. Thus on one occasion a target was engaged simultaneously by 19 field, 9 medium and 2 heavy regiments. The "time on target" was 33 minutes after the request had been received from the C.R.A. 1st Canadian Division, and the total weight of ammunition fired was 92 tons, made up of 3,509 rounds from 668 guns.([17])

The difficulty lay in keeping the enemy artillery under control. As usual, for some time after the completion of the counter-battery programme, hostile batteries remained inactive. When they did come to life, however, at about 0930 hours, they could not easily be silenced again. Air O.Ps. and arty/R aircraft were hampered by poor visibility until about 1300 hours, and the C.B.O. was therefore forced to resort to the periodical bombardment of selected groups of hostile batteries. There was also trouble with the meteor corrections. During the pause on the first objective, it was reported that meteor had changed by 200 yards since the start of the programme, and under such conditions the accuracy of predicted shooting was not likely to have been very great.([18])

The Pursuit to Lake Trasimene

After the collapse of the Hitler Line, the Germans were forced to undertake a hasty withdrawal. From Rome northwards for over 100 miles, the country was little suited to the delaying tactics that they had employed so successfully hitherto. In consequence the allied tactics changed from the deliberate infantry attacks of El Alamein, Medjez El Bab and Cassino to the armoured thrusts and quick fire plans of the pursuit to Tripoli and Tunis.

From the artillery point of view, the outstanding feature of this new pursuit was the increase, both in quantity and performance, of the medium and heavy artillery. In the early stages of the breakthrough, the mobility of such units was not generally appreciated. As a matter of fact, medium—and on reasonably good roads, heavy—regiments were practically as mobile as field regiments, although the heavy equipment did of course take longer to get in and out of action. It required about four hours preparatory work before it could fire from a new position.([19]) In particular, the tractor was very efficient and compared favourably with the field artillery tractor, which had always been under-powered.

This welcome influx of medium and heavy artillery in the forward areas was not, however, an unmixed blessing. Their presence on the roads sometimes caused traffic blocks at critical times, and the need for control of road movements was one of the major lessons of this part of the campaign.

The main weakness lay at first in the organization of air observation. There was at that time only one wireless frequency for a corps front, and this caused such delays in the answering of demands for sorties that by the time the aircraft had arrived on the scene, the tactical situation had completely changed and the sortie was useless. In the latter stages of the pursuit, when more frequencies were available, the time lag was considerably reduced; but it still took, on an average, one to two hours to get a sortie into the air. Further improvement, it seemed, would have to be effected by providing direct wireless communication between aircraft and guns, and between guns and landing ground.

Again, owing to the distance of the landing ground from the battlefield, pilots sometimes had very little time for observation and many shoots were never completed owing to lack of petrol. Hence the air O.P., with its shorter take-off, was more than ever in request, and arrangements were made for a small pool of bulldozers in each A.G.R.A. to facilitate the rapid construction of landing strips.([20])

In particular, it was used to shoot medium artillery against the enemy S.P. delaying guns. For this purpose, pilots on the main Fifth and Eighth Army fronts were now habitually flying at 4,000 feet and above, often over enemy territory, and operational sorties averaged from 45 to 60 minutes. It must however be remembered that the conditions were abnormal and that similar liberties could not be taken in the Anzio beachhead.([21])

As usual in the pursuit, the intercommunication system was subjected to a searching test, which was felt the more acutely because it followed a prolonged period of semi-static warfare. Among other things, the signals organization of an A.G.R.A. headquarters had not kept pace with the evolution of its functions. Now generally accepted as the hub of all the artillery communications in the corps (*see* Diagram 5), this unit badly needed—and in due course received—a signals company of its own.[22]

Another effect of the deliberate attack had been to impose an excessive degree of caution upon F.O.Os. and upon those responsible for answering requests for fire by air O.Ps., and a certain rigidity in the control of fire plans. For example, there was the "shell line", which resembled in purpose the bomb line that had been introduced about the time of the invasion of Sicily (*see* p. 184). Within this boundary, the artillery of one formation was not allowed to fire on the front of a neighbouring formation without first obtaining the permission of the C.R.A. or C.C.R.A. concerned.

In a rapid pursuit such restrictions were burdensome, and an attempt was made to abolish them.[20] The shell line, though retained, was made less restrictive. Its location coincided with the day's objective, and beyond it all fire was to be unrestricted. Within it, divisional and corps concentrations were not to be called for on the front of flanking formations without reference to the C.R.A.'s representative concerned.[23]

The Normandy Landings

By 14th June, the Germans had succeeded in regrouping their forces in Italy to meet the main Allied thrust north of the Tiber, and on 17th June the weather broke and steady rain fell for the next four days. This, combined with the growing scarcity of good roads, slowed down the advance, and it was clear that from now on increasingly heavy opposition was to be expected.

Meanwhile the invasion of Normandy had begun and the final proof had been given that modern fire power, properly organized, had solved the problem of the assault landing. There were 32 enemy batteries capable of firing on to the assault beaches, of which 50 per cent. were in casemates of reinforced concrete six feet thick. After a preliminary softening by air attacks spread over a period of nearly two months, the most important of these batteries were attacked with 5,300 tons of bombs by British night bombers on the night of "D-1" "D". This was followed by a daylight attack by U.S. heavy bombers, which dropped another 5,900 tons of bombs on hostile batteries and defended localities; and finally by a pre-arranged bombardment by six battleships, two monitors and 22 cruisers.

This ended the preliminary counter-battery programme, and the fire plan was now devoted to the close support of the assaulting troops during the run in and the subsequent advance inland. The enemy defences here consisted of a chain of infantry strong points, which lined the coast at intervals of about 1,000 yards and extended inland to a depth of 200 yards. They were well supplied with supporting weapons in the form of medium machine-guns, mortars and anti-tank guns, and in places they included a French 75-mm. or German light howitzer. Behind this narrow strip, defences in depth were not much developed, since the enemy appreciated that any attacking force would be so weakened by the fire of the coastal defences that it would be easily dealt with by the mobile armoured reserves located in the rear of the beaches.([24])

The fire plan for the neutralization of these defences allowed a "free for all" period during the run in, when 93 destroyers, 147 close support naval craft, the R.M. Armoured Support Group, and the S.P. divisional artilleries would engage pre-arranged or opportunity targets, while medium and fighter bombers engaged areas further inland. During the crossing of the beaches, H.M. ships would continue to bombard opportunity targets as occasion offered, and more intimate support would be given by the R.M. Armoured Support Group.([24])

To deal with the expected counter-attacks by the enemy armoured reserves, it was necessary that strong anti-tank defences should be available as soon as possible, and in view of the difficulty of getting towed guns over the beaches in the early stages, it was decided to equip assault divisional anti-tank regiments with a proportion of S.P. 3-in. M10 guns.

The results of this joint fire plan were on the whole very successful. Although the destruction caused by the massive air and naval bombardment was not as great as had been hoped, the enemy opposition was effectively neutralized for the vital period of the assault, so that the troops were able to get ashore with unexpectedly small casualties and to overcome a strong, if shallow, coast defence system in one day's fighting.

During the run in, ten regiments of S.P. artillery fired 1,800 rounds each in about 30 minutes. Later, on the beaches, they fully lived up to their reputation. In the 3rd Division sector, for example, as the tide came racing in over the flat sand, the guns were soon standing in some feet of surf, and eventually the width of the beach was reduced to 10 yards instead of the 30 yards that had been anticipated. Among the welter of transport edging towards the exits, stranded landing craft, derelict D.D. (duplex drive) tanks and A.Vs.R.E. (Assault Vehicles, Royal Engineers), were over 50 S.P. guns, including 8 Centaurs of the R.M. Armoured Support Group, all firing from the water's edge.([25]) In an operation in which no individual element of the fire plan can be said to have had an important material effect, the S.P. artillery made a valuable contribution to the cumulative moral effect of the successive bombardments by the air and naval forces, and by the rockets and guns of the special close support naval craft.([26])

Another definite success was the F.O.U. (Airborne). Owing to a lack of suitable aircraft for the air lift, the 6th Airborne Division could take with it only one battery of the air-landing regiment, the remainder being brought in by sea on "D" + 7. It was therefore more than ever dependent on outside artillery support, which in this case consisted of the 3rd Divisional Artillery, a medium battery of 4 A.G.R.A., two cruisers and two destroyers. On many occasions, especially during the period of heavy fighting between 8th and 10th June, it was the assistance of this outside artillery that either saved the situation or enabled operations to be carried out; and it was the liaison and observation provided by the F.O.U. (Airborne) that made the whole thing possible. The parachute and gliderborne F.O.O.s were connected by wireless through a common airborne support net direct to field batteries or regiments of the 3rd Divisional Artillery, and the medium regiment of 4 A.G.R.A. In addition, the C.R.A. 6th Airborne Division had a link with the C.C.R.A. 1 Corps.

This system worked excellently while the 6th Airborne Division was sharing the services of the 3rd Divisional Artillery. Subsequently the Division always had two field regiments and one H.A.A. regiment (acting in the ground role) under command, and on occasion a battery or regiment of medium artillery. Incidentally, the provision of ammunition for the 75-mm. pack hows. caused some anxiety in the early stages. Air supply alone could not compete with the ammunition expenditure, which reached a figure of 1,500 rounds (for 8 guns) on "D"+1, 1,300 on "D"+2, and 2,500 on "D"+3; and as the weapon was peculiar to the 6th Airborne Division in the British sector, some difficulty was experienced in finding it on the beaches.([2])

Defence of the Beachheads

One of the most serious threats to our beachheads came from the German long range artillery. The only guns, other than ships' guns, in the British and Canadian sectors able to shoot beyond 20,000 yards were 16 × 4.5-in. and 40 U.S. 155-mm. guns; whereas the German 17-cm. gun had a range of 32,000 yards, and some of their smaller guns could fire up to 25,000 yards. Hence, counter-battery problems assumed a special significance. An air photograph interpretation unit (A.P.I.U.) and a special C.B. organization were set up in England to provide the C.B. offices in Normandy by wireless with the latest information from air photos.

The country in the assault area was such that air observation was essential at all times, and as arty/R aircraft had to operate at first from airfields in England, and pilots would not therefore be properly briefed for the engagement of impromptu targets, the performance of this role had to be left largely to air O.Ps. Landing ground reconnaissance parties of air O.P. squadrons were landed on "D" day, and as soon as the strips were ready, the aircraft were flown across the Channel in batches under the navigational leadership of Fleet Air Arm aircraft.

In the planning of Operation "Overlord", the susceptibility of the beachheads to air attack had weighed very heavily, and the result was perhaps an over-insurance in the matter of A.A. protection.([27]) On "D" day, 23 per cent. of the artillery to be landed was A.A., and by "D"+1 the proportion had risen to 42 per cent., at which level it remained for the next month or more.([28])

The A.A. organization for the initial phase was based on the appreciation that by day the G.A.F. could be taken care of by the fighter aircraft alone, except at heights below 3,000 feet, where the main responsibility for defence would rest with the A.A. guns. By night, the small number of allied night fighters that could be controlled at any one time necessitated heavy concentrations of A.A. artillery round the vital targets.

Administratively, it was clear that the artificial port, or "Mulberry", at Arromanches would be the most vulnerable target until at least one large permanent port had been captured in the British sector. Two A.A. brigades, suitably increased and modified, were allotted to this task and to the defence of some 23,000 yards of beaches. A third brigade, made up to three H.A.A. and three L.A.A. regiments, was detailed to cover the ten airfields of 83 Group, R.A.F.

To meet the threat of very low-flying attacks, triple 20-mm. equipments were provided.[29] They were intended for the defence of small, well-defined V.Ps. and were to be sited as close as possible to the V.P. and not more than 200 yards apart. As the average duration of an engagement would not exceed four to eight seconds, eye-shooting was the only practicable method of fire control.[30]

For the L.A.A. defence of the Mulberry, special arrangements were necessary to get the Bofors and 20-mm. fire suitably distributed over the whole of the vulnerable area. Some of the Bofors were mounted on hollow concrete blocks, known as "phoenixes", or blockships, which had been brought across the Channel and sunk in predetermined positions. Others were mounted on landing barges flak (L.B.F.), anchored in suitable positions within the harbour area. A number of balloons and smoke generators were also afloat on trawlers. Finally, some 20-mm. guns were mounted at the ends of the piers in the Mulberry and manned by personnel of the Port Floating Equipment Company, R.E.

Altogether the strength of the A.A. units deployed on 17th June for the defence of the Mulberry, the adjacent beach maintenance area, and the little harbour of Port en Bessin, was 96 H.A.A., 132 Bofors and 16 × 20-mm. guns, 24 A.A.S.Ls., 76 balloons and 62 Esso smoke generators. Later, the number of balloons was increased to 144 (*see* Map 12).[31]

Two types of L.A.A. barrage were prepared: the umbrella (*see* p. 189) and the radial. In the latter, the guns fired at predetermined points along a named radius emanating from the centre of the V.P. and representing one of the 16 points of the compass; the result being to create a zone of fire roughly along the line of approach of an attacking aircraft. A drill was also worked out, and successfully applied in trials—though never, owing to lack of opportunity, against the enemy—with three L.A.A. batteries each in close formation near a H.A.A. gun position, with orders to fire barrages on data received from the H.A.A. command post, or by following a nominated master gun, either L.A.A. or H.A.A.

Control of unseen fire by L.A.A. guns was exercised by a L.A.A. barrage control officer, situated in a special L.A.A./G.O.R. with its own H.A.A. plotter and radar sets, through battery control posts, which were in direct communication by line and/or wireless with all gun positions. In the early stages of the operation, the use of line was quite impossible owing to the destruction caused by bulldozers, flails and travelling cranes moving about in the harbour area.

Smoke screens were controlled by the A.A.D.C. from the A.A.O.R. through a smoke control post, which was in touch by R/T with section posts on land and trawlers at sea. The R.A.F. had an overriding power of veto on the use of smoke, and the R.N. had to give permission before it could be used, but could not enforce its use against the wishes of the Army (*e.g.* "Q" Movements, Beach).

For the general control of A.A. fire, rules laid down by S.H.A.E.F. before "D" day provided for three types of area: I.A.Zs. as already defined (*see* p. 201); G.D.As., in which precedence was sometimes given to aircraft and sometimes to guns, but which were prohibited to all aircraft other than fighters; and unrestricted areas, where aircraft had absolute freedom to fly and guns might normally fire only on aircraft definitely recognized as hostile. The decision to create a restricted area was to be arrived at by agreement between army groups and the appropriate air force commanders, and 96 hours was to be allowed for the broadcasting of this decision before the restrictions were enforced. All the assault beaches were regarded as I.A.Zs., with a height limitation of 16,000 feet, until the local air force controller was ashore and able to exercise his control in the normal manner.[32]

The efficiency of these arrangements was never seriously tested. Enemy air activity between 6th June and 15th July was virtually negligible, its most troublesome feature being mine-laying off the beaches and harbour entrances beyond the range of shore-based A.A. artillery. To counter this, it was agreed at an Inter-Services Conference held at Courcelles on 5th July that A.A. sloops or Hunt class destroyers should be moored outside the shipping area.

A.A. Searchlights

Plans had been based on the assumption that searchlights would be used for three main roles :—

(1) In conjunction with guns, against aircraft at low or medium heights; over the beaches in the assault phase, and possibly at certain other vulnerable areas later. For this task, four independent mobile batteries, equipped with 90-cm. lights, were considered sufficient.

(2) In conjunction with fighter aircraft, particularly as a means of combating "window". An illuminated belt, or aircraft fighting zone, was to be formed around the assault area by six regiments equipped with 150-cm. lights.

(3) In conjunction with L.A.A. guns for the "canopy" defence of night fighter airfields. Six mobile L.A.A./S.L. batteries, equipped with Bofors guns and 90-cm. lights, were allotted to this role.

In the event, owing to the small scale of enemy air effort, the illuminated belt was not required. The absence of attacks on airfields also released the L.A.A./S.L. batteries for other roles, and experience soon proved them to be most effective for the defence of V.Ps.[33]

The result was a general diminution of importance of the rear, and diversion of attention towards the forward, areas; a tendency that was further accentuated by the revival of interest in the searchlight as a potential source of artificial moonlight. On 15th July, 12 Corps, in their offensive S.W. of Caen, used searchlights in this way for the first time in battle, to support a night attack. The result was satisfactory, and from now on "movement light", as it was called, was increasingly used not only as an aid to fighting, but for airfield construction, bridge building and aiding movement of all sorts. In mid-September, 1944, it was to be used for the first time in Italy, during the fighting on the Gothic Line.

The Effect of the Bocage Country

As the invasion forces moved inland, they entered the "bocage" country, where the "going" was very difficult and facilities for observation often poor. Viewed from above, this country "appears almost continuous forest, but on entering it you discover a labyrinth through small fields and orchards surrounded by high-banked hedges and trees. Apart from a few main roads, these innumerable, narrow, mud (now dust) tracks ran like tunnels through tall thicket hedges, connecting the farms and hamlets. Further south, it all opens up again into pleasant open pasture and corn land, with occasional forests and hills."[34]

In such a terrain, quick fire plans and the immediate organization of D.F. were most important. On 13th-14th June heavy attacks on one of our armoured brigades were broken up very largely by organized artillery support, which included 25-pr. air bursts fired at a range of 400-500 yards against infantry advancing through the bushes.[35] On 1st July, when the Germans made their last and strongest attempt, with five divisions, to break the Second Army salient, they were engaged by massed artillery fire with devastating effect, and all but one of their attacks were dispersed before reaching our forward infantry positions.[36] During this fighting, heavy concentrations were brought down on opportunity targets, and on several occasions the fire of over 300 guns was concentrated on a single area.[37]

In the attack, despite the difficult "going", the rate of advance was faster than had been customary in the mountains of Italy. For example, on 25th June, 8 Corps, acting as part of the southern jaw of the Second Army's main pincer movement on Caen, advanced at the old rate of 100 yards in three minutes against an enemy well concealed in difficult country and covered in front by extensive minefields. Covering fire took the form of a creeping barrage, with pauses, fired by 240 field and 80 medium guns, supplemented by concentrations from five field and one heavy regiment.[38] The attack began well, but, as so often happened, the infantry were held up towards the end of the barrage by machine-guns, 8.8 cm. guns and some Tiger tanks. A second attack on 27th June met the same fate.

With regard to the use of artillery concentrations, there were now two schools of thought: one favouring corps concentrations, the other considering that the divisional concentration could deal with any but the super-target of great rarity.[29] A rather similar problem occurred in the organization of close support bombing from the air. The question here was, to what extent could the diversion of heavy bomber effort from the main strategic role be justified in order to provide covering fire for the Army; and the answer depended to some extent on the closeness with which the assaulting troops could follow up the air bombardment. In the attack on Caen, on 7th July, when this type of close support was tried for the first time and some 2,300 tons of bombs were dropped, it was decided that the bomb line should not be brought nearer than 6,000 yards to the leading troops, and that the defences between the bomber target area and the front line should be dealt with by concentrated artillery fire. During the break-out by 7 U.S. Corps on 25th July, this interval was reduced to 1,200 yards.[39]

Anti-Tank Tactics

Another effect of the "bocage" country was to restrict the use of tanks to small-scale operations and to make them more sensitive to the short-range infantry weapons, such as the P.I.A.T. and the grenade. Nevertheless, as a glance at Table H will show, the A.P. projectile, whether fired from one of our own tanks or from an anti-tank gun, easily held pride of place as the killer of tanks, and it was as important as ever to get anti-tank guns forward quickly to a captured objective; all the more so because of the inadequate killing power of the Churchill tank. The towed 17-pr. was not easy to manœuvre, and it was often 12 to 15 hours before it could be dug in ready for action in its new position. Hence it was decided to perpetuate the S.P. element introduced into anti-tank units for the initial landings (see p. 218). In future, infantry divisional anti-tank batteries were to consist of one troop 17-pr. towed, one troop 17-pr. S.P. (Valentine or M.10), and one troop 6-pr. towed. The idea was that the 6-pr. or the S.P. 17-pr. should be used as the F.D.L. gun, with the towed 17-pr. acting as a " long stop ".[40]

In the fighting in Normandy, where large numbers of air bursts occurred through mortar bombs and shells hitting trees, there was a growing demand for some form of splinter-proof overhead cover to S.P. anti-tank guns. Some experimental " mock-ups " were produced, but that was all.

TABLE H

Comparison of Anti-Tank Weapons in the Normandy Fighting

(from 2 O.R.S. Report No. 17)

Weapon	Percentage of Tanks Destroyed	
	1st Phase (to 7 Aug.)	2nd Phase (8–31 Aug.)
A.P. projectiles	65	63
Hollow charge projectiles	10	2
H.E. projectiles	11	10
Mines	1	0
Rocket-firing aircraft	9	18
Cannon-firing aircraft	4	2
Bombs	0	5

Counter-Battery

Although the enemy had a large number of guns, they fired very little, apparently because of the maldistribution of their dumps and irregular supply.[41] The chief feature of their artillery tactics, as in Italy, was their skilful use of camouflage and of the mobility of their S.P. guns. It was by the exploitation of these factors, and by the studied use of pauses in the British fire to carry out their movements, that their casualties were kept, as a rule, remarkably low.[29]

On the whole, however, our C.B. measures worked well and were much assisted by basic photographic cover provided before the invasion started. Some very heavy concentrations were put down on hostile batteries, amounting on one occasion to 104:1, with an average weight of shell of 20 tons a target. On 30th June, as a prelude to an air attack by 250 bombers on Villers Bocage, a counter-flak programme was fired by 5 A.G.R.A., and similar programmes were sometimes arranged to cover the activities of arty/R aircraft.

The main problem was to get a reliable e.t.a. (expected time of arrival) of the aircraft in time to pass it to the guns. This difficulty was sometimes overcome by the initiation of counter-flak shoots by air O.Ps. when they observed that the enemy flak was worrying our bombers (*see* pp. 172, 197).

The counter-flak programme remained in use till the end of the war and was believed to be very effective. An A.A. gun pit is always difficult to protect against shell fire, and while an air attack was in progress, the enemy A.A. detachments had perforce to man their guns.

The Air O.P.

Even in the "bocage" country the air O.P. proved a great asset. It was often in fact the only means of observation, and it was sometimes used as a check on the heavy mortaring which frequently represented the principal enemy activity by day. A sortie would be kept standing by at instant readiness and on receipt of the first indication of where the mortars were firing from, it would be sent up to search the suspected map square and engage any likely position as a "Mike" target (regimental concentration).[42]

Perhaps for these reasons, the enemy began to take more aggressive counter-action, especially in the eastern sector, where he was very sensitive to our airborne bridgehead east of the Orne, and where his fighters could most easily stalk our air O.Ps. from a variety of directions. On occasion he would attack a single air O.P. with as many as ten fighters, which, flying at 1,000 feet or below, were very difficult to pick up on the radar sets of the early warning system.[43]

Special measures were therefore taken by L.A.A. units to provide for the safety of air O.Ps. A harbour area, some 1,500 yards by 800 yards in extent, was selected within easy flying distance of the area over which an air O.P. was operating, and was defended by a troop of L.A.A. guns, with a ground O.P. manned by an officer and two spotters. Attached to this troop were a L.W. set and one or two 22 sets for communication with the air O.P. squadron advanced landing ground and/or the pilot. On the approach of hostile aircraft, the alarm was given to the air O.P. by verey lights or shell bursts directed behind the aircraft so that they could be seen by the rear observer—the latter a recent innovation of considerable value.[44]

In Italy, night-flying by air O.Ps. had become common on moonlight nights, and casualties from enemy air action had been few. Indeed more casualties had occurred through aircraft being struck by our own shells than from any other cause. The greatest danger occurred, naturally, during the shooting of a fire plan for a major attack, such as that on the Gustav Line. At such times, however, the use of the air O.P. was limited by bad visibility owing to dust and smoke, and by the fact that the bulk of the artillery was firing on pre-arranged targets. Sorties could therefore be restricted until after the fire plan was over. At other times the main danger occurred during heavy impromptu concentrations. This danger was met—but not entirely overcome—by regiments warning pilots when a regimental or higher concentration had been ordered, so that they could take the appropriate avoiding action.[45]

Operation "Goodwood"

On 18th July, as a preliminary to the impending breakout from Normandy, a southward thrust was made by three corps from the bridgehead east of the Orne, with the object, among other things, of threatening Falaise and drawing off the German armour from the area of the intended breakout. 8 Corps, in the centre, was to make the main effort with three armoured divisions, and the whole operation was to be supported by one R.H.A., 16 field, 14 medium, three heavy and two H.A.A. regiments, totalling 776 guns, with additional support from one monitor (2 × 15-in. guns) and two cruisers (19 × 6-in. guns).([46]) The usual preliminary air bombardment was to be carried out by 2,000 medium and heavy bombers, which were to drop some 8,000 tons of bombs on the enemy positions.([47])

The first three miles of the advance ran through a corridor about two miles wide, with the enemy holding both flanks. On the left were enemy battery positions that had been built up since "D" day, with O.Ps. overlooking the corridor.([48]) Hence the counter battery role assumed a particular importance, all the more so as the attack was to be made in daylight.

The artillery fire plan was divided into five phases:—

I. Before "H" - 100 minutes, a counter-flak programme was to be fired to cover the operations of the heavy night bombers.

II. From "H" - 100 to "H", a counter-battery programme was to be fired by 21 naval and 660 army guns, while medium bombers put down a carpet of fragmentation bombs for the last 45 minutes over the area through which the armoured, and the flanking infantry, attacks were later to pass.

III. From "H" to "H" + 80 the bulk of the artillery would be covering the initial assault in direct support of the attacking divisions. The 11th Armoured Division, leading the 8 Corps attack with one brigade up, was to be covered by a creeping barrage fired by 192 field guns on a front of 2,000 yards and advancing at a rate of 150 yards in one minute to a depth of about four miles. Optional pauses were allowed for in the progress of this barrage, in particular at one place where it changed direction.

IV. From "H" + 80 to approximately "H" + 200, to cover the further advance of the attacking divisions, the bulk of the artillery would continue to give direct support, but in the form of concentrations, mostly "on call". A proportion of the guns would revert to counter-battery tasks.

V. After "H" + 200 pre-arranged programmes would cease and some of the supporting artillery would be out of range. Of the remainder, the majority would remain in support of attacking divisions by *ad hoc* methods, and a proportion would continue in the counter-battery role.

In the arrangement of counter-battery tasks, the policy was to neutralize all hostile batteries in range before "H" hour, and to reply with observed fire, directed by an air O.P., to any hostile battery that became active between "H" and "H" + 100. During the later stages of the advance the neutralization of the most dangerous hostile battery areas was to be repeated, and a reserve of artillery was to be kept " on call " for retaliation against hostile batteries that opened fire later on " D " day. Naval guns and fighter bombers were to be used for similar tasks on gun areas not readily accessible to artillery deployed in the two flanking corps areas.[49]

The preliminary counter-flak and counter-battery bombardments were successful, and in the early stages of the operation enemy artillery activity was slight. The initial air bombardment and the artillery programme also succeeded in overcoming the enemy forward defences, and the leading tanks were able to overrun the first enemy gun line and penetrate to a depth of about 4,000 yards. Some 3,000 yards beyond the first gun line, however, was a second, which had remained intact and which could not be penetrated by the 11th Armoured Division. The enemy had known for a long while that the British Second Army contained a large force of tanks and had therefore concentrated his anti-tank artillery on this sector. The A.A. guns emplaced for the defence of Caen also took a hand in the proceedings by firing in an anti-tank role.[48] Hence opposition stiffened during the afternoon, and counter-attacks began to develop. Finally, the operation was brought to an end by heavy rain on the afternoon of 20th July, after a total advance of about 10,000 yards.

Operation " Bluecoat "

Attention was now redirected to the " bocage " country, where, on 25th July, the First U.S. Army began the breakout, assisted, on 30th July, by a powerful thrust from the right wing of the British Second Army. For this operation the armour had been brought round from the left wing, but in view of the terrain, the initial thrust, except on the extreme right, was to be made by the infantry and army tank brigades, with the armoured divisions following through to exploit success.

The operation had to be mounted in a great hurry—less than 48 hours from the time that the preliminary moves were ordered—and if only for this reason, it was necessary to keep the fire plan extremely simple (*see* Map 13). The dumping of ammunition—300 r.p.g. for 25-prs.—was on a relatively small scale for an operation of this kind, and the artillery was rather thinner than usual on the ground.

In the interests of secrecy and surprise, no preliminary air or counter-battery bombardment was to be allowed. 30 Corps, opening the attack at 0600 hours with the 43rd and 50th Divisions, was to take its first objective with air support only and its next three under cover of artillery concentrations, at first timed and later " on call ". 8 Corps, following at 0655 hours with the 11th Armoured and 15th (S) Divisions astride the Caumont—Beny Bocage road, used concentrations alone for the support of the 11th Armoured, and a mixture of concentrations and barrages for the 15th Division.

These barrages had several interesting features. The frontage to be covered was wide—2,300 yards for three field regiments, with two medium regiments superimposed—and in " bocage " country the ground burst of the 25-pr. was not considered of much use against the Germans, who were always well dug in. Hence it was decided to use 75 per cent. of time fuzes (No. 222) in order to get increased moral and material effect.

The rate of advance of each barrage was 100 yards in four minutes, and the larger of the two, in Phase II, was to last for 110 minutes and to include no main pauses. In Phase III, the barrage was to stop 600 yards short of the summit of the hill that was the infantry objective. The infantry and tanks would then pause and prepare for the final assault, which would be preceded by heavy artillery concentrations on the objective.

Once the battle had started, heavy bombers were to attack selected areas ahead of the advance, and throughout the operation considerable use was made of smoke screens to cover the left flank of 30 Corps and to mask the enemy positions on the forward slopes of the high ground St. Martin Des Besaces— Bois Du Homme, which overlooked the whole area.([50]) The operations of the heavy bombers were hampered by low cloud and bad weather, and the 30 Corps attack was soon held up by a stream, the banks of which were steep and heavily mined and the approaches to which were covered by well sited anti-tank guns and machine-guns.

8 Corps was more successful, although the infantry leading the 15th Division attack were delayed by shelling, sniping and mortar fire while *en route* to the start line for Phase II, and the Churchill tanks had to push on alone in order not to lose all the benefit of the artillery barrage. Eventually they crossed the start line from half an hour to an hour after the barrage had opened. On the right they met with little opposition and by mid-day had reached the objective, where they were joined by the infantry two hours later. On the left the opposition was stiffer and it was not until 1530 hours that infantry and tanks were on the objective.

By this time the left flank of 8 Corps had become exposed, owing to the hold-up in 30 Corps, and Phase III was therefore modified. The air attack on the final objective went in, as planned, at 1600 hours, and the Commander 15th Division, appreciating that further opposition was likely to be only from enemy rearguards, decided to push through with one tank battalion, without infantry, supported by artillery concentrations " on call ". The battalion reached the objective at 1900 hours and was joined by the infantry at 2300 hours.

During the next two days, 8 Corps continued to make good progress. Then, however, the opposition began to stiffen and enemy counter-attacks, added to the great difficulty of the country, gradually brought matters to a standstill.

Operation " Totalize "

" The time had come to deliver the major attack towards Falaise, which had so long been the fundamental aim of our policy on the eastern flank."([51]) On 7th August, while the German counter-stroke at Mortain was being parried by 7 U.S. Corps, the First Canadian Army launched an assault with two infantry divisions, each with an armoured brigade in support.

The plan this time was to attack under cover of darkness with the infantry mounted in heavy armoured carriers, which, it was hoped, would enable them to rush the enemy F.D.Ls. and zones of defensive fire. The operation was to begin at 2300 hours with a 30-minute concentration by heavy bombers, in the course of which 3,458 tons of bombs were to be dropped. At " H "+30 the assault was to be launched in eight armoured columns, preceded by gapping teams of assault engineers and flail tanks, and covered by a creeping barrage on a front of 4,000 yards, advancing to a depth of 6,000 yards at a rate of

100 yards in one minute. This barrage was to be fired by nine field and nine medium regiments, and the ammunition allotted was 184,800 rounds of 25-pr., 15,600 × 105-mm., 71,200 × 5.5-in., 4,000 × 7.2-in., 3,000 × 155-mm., and 3,600 × 3.7-in. H.A.A. ; or about two and a half times as much as was fired during the last 12 days of the battle of Keren (see p. 60).

To ensure accurate navigation by night, positions and bearings of thrust lines were fixed by Survey for the leading tanks ; and directional wireless, Bofors tracer and artificial moonlight (provided by one S.L. battery) were also employed to facilitate speed of movement in the dark.[52]

There was to be no intensive counter-battery fire before " H " hour, but between " H " + 100 and " H " + 120 (i.e. at the end of the barrage) and again between " H " + 420 and " H " + 440 (i.e. shortly after daylight), there were to be bombardments by seven field, seven medium, one heavy and one H.A.A. regiment.[53]

The enemy appeared at first to be overcome with confusion, but recovered sufficiently to put down D.F. with artillery and mortars. He was also clever enough to add to the difficulties of a rising ground mist by thickening it up with smoke. Of the navigational aids, the Bofors tracer was reported to be effective, but the searchlights were unable to pierce the dust cloud. As a result some of the columns went astray and did not reach the debussing area until over an hour after the barrage had finished. In general, however, this part of the operation was a success and the first objectives were gained without difficulty.

Mopping up was not so easy, and although some progress was made in the afternoon by the 4th Canadian and Polish Armoured Divisions, after a " softening up " attack by Flying Fortresses, the advance was finally halted before a strong anti-tank screen comprising about 60 dug-in tanks and S.P. guns, supplemented by some 90 × 8·8 cm flak guns sited in an anti-tank role.[52]

Comparison of Air and Artillery Bombardments

After this battle was over, an interesting comparison was made between three parallel battalion attacks on three separate objectives, two of which had—while the third had not—been included in the preliminary bombardment. The first two battalions had difficulty in taking their objectives ; the third, assisted by an artillery barrage, carried out its task more easily.[54]

It was perhaps a sign that the optimum weight of fire support was being exceeded (see p. 2). It was also an inducement to compare, scientifically, the effects of air and artillery bombardments.

" By the time the breakout was achieved, the emergency intervention of the entire bomber force in the land battle had come to be accepted almost as a matter of course."[55] With air support on this scale, it was quite obvious that the bombers could deliver a weight of explosives incomparably greater than anything attainable by existing artillery resources, and that they could also reach targets out of range of the heaviest guns. As with artillery fire, however, it was the moral effect that counted most, and against good troops this was fleeting. By dint of the overwhelming concentration in time of a bombing attack, the neutralization of the enemy defences might be expected to persist for one hour after the last bomb had dropped ; but if the attacking troops failed to follow up the bombardment within this period, the advantage might actually lie with the enemy, whose opportunities for resistance would have been strengthened by the gratuitous presentation of craters and rubble heaps in which to conceal his defensive weapons.(56) For example, at Caen on 7th July, the results of the great air stroke (*see* p. 222) had been very disappointing. The battle that subsequently developed had been as tough as any, and it was felt by those concerned that the effects of the bombing had been to make the capture of the town more difficult by denying " much of it to all but infantry on foot, while leaving plenty of cover for snipers, restricting the number of entrances to be held, and leaving intact a lateral route through the town."(57)

The effect of the ordinary artillery barrage or concentration was of course still more fleeting. Two minutes was the time limit allowed to the infantry to reach their objective after the covering fire had lifted (*see* p. 186). The " terror concentration " (*see* p. 200) might be expected to have a more lasting effect, but as yet no attempt had been made to put it into figures.

Observed *versus* Predicted Fire

The gist of the matter lay in the ability to produce moral effect without creating too much material destruction. From this point of view, air burst H.E. had definite advantages; but the best solution, because it was the most economical, was to shoot accurately.

The subject of accuracy, and of the optimum weight of an artillery bombardment, was at this time receiving much attention from those responsible for artillery policy. There could be little doubt that the system of regimental and divisional concentrations was sometimes being abused. In the words of an experienced officer, recently returned from Italy, " day after day one saw concentrations—regimental at least—being put down on targets which were only troop targets "(58); and this opinion was confirmed by reports from French officers who were living in Normandy at the time of the invasion, and who had therefore had an opportunity of observing the effects of our artillery fire from the " business end ". One of them indeed remarked on the number of casualties caused by observed fire and the slight damage sometimes caused by predicted concentrations(59), which at that time were estimated by one C.A.G.R.A. to represent about 98 per cent. of all artillery fire.

The result was an unnecessary large expenditure of ammunition, which, combined with failures on the part of units to submit ammunition returns, made planning difficult. " It is no exaggeration to say that a promising operation might have to be postponed unnecessarily for lack of information to show whether enough ammunition was available."(60)

Whether results could be more economically achieved by observed fire was still a subject of controversy. The evidence of the French observer, just quoted, implied that they could, and it was in fact the official opinion at this time that " divisional and regimental concentrations without ranging rarely produce satisfactory results, and are only necessary when time is not available for ranging, or when surprise is the dominant need."(61) Yet the opposite school of thought could ask, with some justification, when is surprise not the dominant need in war? It was surprise that had won a total victory at Sidi Barrani at a very small cost in artillery ammunition (*see* p. 60); it was surprise, rather than shell power, that had turned the scale at the Sangro (*see* p. 192); and it was surprise that, in the opinion of the same French observers, had been the most important factor in the application of our artillery fire in Normandy.

It was the old conflict between accuracy and speed (*see* p. 1), and the difficulty of finding a solution was increased by the continued unreliability of meteor and, sometimes, of maps. In spite of improved organization and techniques (*see* p. 197), meteor telegrams could not be relied on, even under normal conditions, to give an accuracy better than 200 yards. In Italy the maps were sometimes quite unreliable, and in France the contour values on the 1 : 25,000 maps sometimes differed from surveyed heights by as much as 30 metres.

Hence the emphasis on observation. But in the "bocage" country, observation was often so poor that ranging on the target was impossible, and even a suitable datum point could not be found in the target area on which fire could be directed to check the correction of the moment. The latter could be found by the use of high air bursts, but subsequently, at fire for effect, errors were likely to creep in owing to the inherent inaccuracy of the powder-filled fuze (*see* p. 170), which was all that was then available.

Because of this inaccuracy, it was not easy to achieve or to maintain the correct height of burst, upon which the superior effectiveness of this type of ammunition depended. The versatile air O.P. was sometimes able to help by flying very low and observing for height of bursts after ranging had been completed.

It was these sorts of difficulties that made some experienced gunners pin their faith to predicted shooting (*see* p. 197). It is interesting to note, however, that the Germans and Russians made relatively little use of predicted fire, relying more on observed shooting. In the opposed river crossing, for example, the Russians found that a timed programme was never satisfactory, and they relied therefore on very careful observation from their artillery O.Ps. and on signals to denote the progress of the assaulting infantry.([62])

Between these conflicting arguments it is not easy to draw a just balance, but perhaps it would be fair to say that, although everyone agreed on the superior merits of observed shooting—provided the observer was efficient and could apply the fire at the right time and place and at the right intensity—there were many occasions on which prediction had to be used because observed shooting was impossible: notably for C.B., barrages, time programmes and D.F. In the British Army, at any rate, no commander was likely to rely entirely on observed shooting in attack or in defence.

Radar as a Counter-Mortar Weapon

By the end of 1943, radar (G.L.III) was being used to improve the accuracy of artillery shooting by the tracking of free balloons, and the deduction of upper wind values, when visibility was too poor for direct observation. But it was as a counter-mortar weapon that it was to render its greatest service to the field artilleryman at this time.

The need was urgent. The normal German infantry division included 57 × 8-cm. and 12 × 12-cm. mortars, with maximum ranges of 2,600 and 6,500 yards respectively, and it was estimated that about 70 per cent. of the British casualties in Normandy were caused by mortar fire. On our side the only special equipment available at the beginning of the operations was the "four pen recorder" (see p. 209), which was still in the early stages of development and could be supplied only to 1 and 30 Corps. Before long thoughts again turned to the possibilities of radar, and experiments were re-started in France with a new expert and immediately began to yield the most encouraging results. Meanwhile in Italy, where, owing to the nature of the country, the enemy mortar was still more of a menace, experiments with radar had also been in progress, and a radar regiment, R.A., was eventually formed.

Later, as the first auto-following radar sets became available (see Table B), the accuracy and speed of location were considerably improved. With the G.L.III, locations involved a certain amount of guesswork, and to avoid gross errors, a number of observations had to be made and the means taken. With the A.A. No. 3 Mk. 5, continuous trajectories could be plotted from the observation of one or two rounds, and a mortar could be located to within 25 yards, even if the initial 2,000 feet of the trajectory was missing. Hence siting of the radar was made easier, and the speed with which a location could be obtained was considerably increased.[63]

Conclusion

Thus at last the mastery of the mortar seemed to be in sight. But not by artillery activities alone. The old idea that the proper answer to the enemy mortar was artillery fire (see p. 170) required some modification. Because of its steeply curved trajectory, the mortar—especially in Italy—was sometimes inaccessible to artillery fire other than air burst H.E., and the use of the latter was restricted by the shortage of time fuzes. It was therefore apparent that a large, if not the major, part of the work would have to be done by our own mortars.

The question was, who should handle them? There was no doubt that, to be effective, their fire would have to be controlled by accurate gunner methods, and from the beginning many 4.2-in. mortar teams had been trained under gunner supervision. Later, as anti-tank units became superfluous, their personnel were sometimes used for this role, and in South-East Asia (see p. 286), mortar regiments were temporarily included as part of the divisional artillery.

Nevertheless, the mortar was predominantly an infantry weapon, and in the organization of the C.M. system the eventual employment of infantry officers as A.C.M.Os. at least had been anticipated (see p. 209), though never actually practised. To those who were reluctant, on the one hand to entrust to non-gunners, and on the other to accept as infantrymen, the responsibility of applying artillery procedures, it could be pointed out that infantry and Royal Armoured Corps officers had already on many occasions successfully directed the fire of their supporting artillery. Indeed in the Norman "bocage" country—and in the jungle—it was often the only method of engaging targets by observation. But it did of course require a well-trained officer to produce results, and "many excellent opportunities were lost by reinforcement and other officers who had not been well trained."([59])

This shortage of trained personnel was not peculiar to the infantry. The war had reached the stage when equipment was plentiful and manpower was severely limited; a characteristic of the closing stages of a war fought by an industrialized democracy. For the past two years, shells had been used in ever increasing quantities to save lives, and it was clear that the policy would have to continue. At the moment the Germans on the Western Front were beaten and disorganized, but when they rallied again behind the Siegfried Line and the Rhine, the problem would have to be faced of how to apply this huge weight of artillery fire, and air bombardment, without making the subsequent progress of our own infantry too difficult.

List of References

[1] C-in-C H.F. No. 72/64/10/G(SD) of 31st July 1942.
[2] History of Airborne Forces.
[3] R.A. Notes No. 17, para. 983.
[4] "Lessons from Overlord," A.L.F.S.E.A. 10050/G(O)1 of 9th January 1945.
[5] R.A.T.M. No. 11 of April 1944.
[6] R.A. 56 Div. No. 263G of 21st January 1944.
[7] R.A. Notes No. 16, para. 876 (c).
[8] Notes on Ops. No. 21 of 3rd June 1944.
[9] 13 Corps Arty. Instruction No. 1 of 26th March 1944.
[10] R.A. Notes No. 22, para. 1277.
[11] Combined Operations Monthly Information Summary, No. 4, Pt. II, August 1943.
[12] "Operations of British, Indian and Dominion Forces in Italy", Pt. II, Sec. B.
[13] A.A.I. 26/2/G(Ops) of 21st March 1944.
[14] 6 A.G.R.A. Report on Liri Valley Battle, May 1944.
[15] Appreciation by C.C.R.A. 13 Corps, 31st March 1944.
[16] Notes on Operations, Italy, No. 30 of 21st August 1944.
[17] Report by C.C.R.A. 1 Canadian Corps, 30th May 1944.
[18] Report by C.C.R.A. 1 Canadian Corps on Ops. of Canadian Arty. in Italy, May-June 1944.
[19] Notes by C.C.R.A. 13 Corps, 26th June 1944.
[20] B.R.A. Eighth Army, Memo. No. 1 of 12th June 1944.
[21] R.A. Notes No. 15, para. 836.
[22] Analysis of Recent Ops. by Canadian Corps in War Diary, R.A. 2 Canadian Corps, June 1944.
[23] R.A. 46 Div. Training Instruction No. 17 of 8th September 1944.
[24] Notes on Ops. 21 Army Gp., 6th June 1944-5th May 1945.
[25] "Assault Division", by Norman Scaife, pp. 77-80.
[26] 2 Op. Research Sec. Report No. 1.
[27] "Normandy to the Baltic", by Field Marshal Montgomery, p. 35.
[28] R.A. Second Army Landing Tables.
[29] Notes on Recent Ops. No. 3 of August 1944.
[30] 80 A.A. Bde., SG30/24 of 9th August 1944.
[31] War Diary 76 A.A. Bde., July 1944.

(³²) S.H.A.E.F. Air Defence Review, October 1944.
(³³) *Ibid*, November 1944.
(³⁴) " Assault Division ", by Norman Scaife, p. 125.
(³⁵) Immediate Report No. 12 of 17th June 1944.
(³⁶) " Normandy to the Baltic ", by Field Marshal Montgomery, pp. 71-2.
(³⁷) R.A. 30 Corps No. RA149 of 3rd July 1944.
(³⁸) R.A. 8 Corps Fire Plan, Operation Epsom.
(³⁹) " Normandy to the Baltic ", by Field Marshal Montgomery, p. 73.
(⁴⁰) War Diary R.A. 21 Army Gp., August 1944.
(⁴¹) " Normandy to the Baltic ", by Field Marshal Montgomery, pp. 66-7.
(⁴²) War Diary R.A. 43 Div., June 1944.
(⁴³) R.A. Notes on Recent Ops., No. 2.
(⁴⁴) Report by O.C. 102 L.A.A. Regt. of 11th July 1944.
(⁴⁵) R.A. Notes No. 21, para. 1200.
(⁴⁶) War Diary, R.A. 1 Corps, July 1944.
(⁴⁷) Notes on Ops. 21 Army Gp., 6th June 1944-5th May 1945, Sec. 2, D.54.
(⁴⁸) Training Instructions 12/285 of 23rd January 1945.
(⁴⁹) R.A. 1 Corps Op. Order No. 6 of 17th July 1944.
(⁵⁰) B.A.O.R. Battlefield Tour, Operation Bluecoat.
(⁵¹) " Normandy to the Baltic ", by Field Marshal Montgomery, p. 92.
(⁵²) *Ibid*, pp. 97-8.
(⁵³) R.A. 2 Canadian Corps Operation Instruction No. 5 of 7th August 1944.
(⁵⁴) 2 Op. Research Sec. Rpt. No. 8.
(⁵⁵) " Crusade in Europe ", by General Eisenhower, p. 297.
(⁵⁶) 2 Op. Research Sec. Rpt. No. 14.
(⁵⁷) *Ibid*, No. 5.
(⁵⁸) R.A. Notes No. 23, para. 1316.
(⁵⁹) A.T.M. No. 51 of November 1944.
(⁶⁰) A.T.M. No. 50 of August 1944.
(⁶¹) A.T.M. No. 49 of July 1944.
(⁶²) R.A. Notes No. 27, para. 1552.
(⁶³) R.A. Notes No. 27, para. 1568.

CHAPTER XIII

THE PURSUIT TO THE SIEGFRIED AND THE GOTHIC LINES

PLATES RELEVANT TO THIS CHAPTER

Nos.
34 and 35. The field artillery rocket.
36. The 3.7-in. H.A.A. gun in action in the field artillery role.

Mountain Artillery in Action in Italy

After the withdrawal of seven divisions from the U.S. Fifth Army for the invasion of southern France, the Eighth Army had become the spearhead of the advance to the Arno. The two corps that led this advance had very different experiences. 13 Corps on the left, once it had broken through the Trasimene position, found itself again in open terrain suitable for the employment of mechanized and armoured forces. 10 Corps, on the other hand, had to force its way into progressively more mountainous country, where the "going" was so difficult that recourse had often to be made to mule transport for the supply of the forward infantry. The Germans, as usual, exploited the advantages of their position by the careful siting of demolitions, tanks and S.P. guns, and by the liberal use of mortars.([1])

In September, 1943, the War Office had decided that one division in North Africa and one in the Middle East should be trained for mountain warfare and should include one mountain artillery regiment of 12 × 3.7-in. hows. and four pack transport companies in addition to normal war establishments. There had also been a proposal to form one or more mountaineer battalions for independent action in the mountains, and to provide them with an artillery element in the form of a special mountain O.P. troop, organized on similar lines to the naval bombardment unit and capable of producing one O.P. party to each mountaineer company. This, however, never materialized.([2])

By early July, two recently converted mountain regiments had joined 10 Corps Artillery, and a third field regiment had been re-equipped with jeep-drawn 75-mm. guns. During the ensuing months these units rendered valuable service, in particular during the attack on the Bibbieni covering position, when both mountain regiments and most of the jeep-drawn 75-mms. were placed under command of the 10th Indian Division for a special role in the mountains.

Quick Fire Plans in the Pursuit

In North-West Europe, where the pursuit was now very quick, the emphasis was, as usual, on simplicity and flexibility in the preparation of fire plans, and on economy of ammunition, if only to save transport. After crossing the Seine, the Second Army covered 250 miles in six days, and in order to compete with the maintenance problem it was necessary to ground 8 Corps, and the majority of the army artillery, in the area of the Seine for some weeks.([3])

While this rapid movement continued, no attempt was made to place guns on a theatre grid. Fixations for divisional grids were obtained from French trigonometrical data supplied by S.H.A.E.F., or direct from map spottings.([4])

To preserve flexibility in the fire plan, increasing use was made of "on call" targets in lieu of timed programmes. Such targets were based on information obtained from air photos, air O.Ps. and other intelligence sources, and were arranged in groups each with its own code name. An individual target, a group or a combination of groups could be called for by the infantry as required, and as the advance progressed groups that were no longer safe to engage would be cancelled.

This system proved very effective in some formations, especially at night([5]), but in others the infantry found it difficult to decide when and where to call for fire. The number of concentrations "on call", including C.B. and C.M. targets, had become embarrassingly large, and the lack of facilities for the combined training of infantry and gunners, together with the heavy infantry casualties, made the system far from infallible.([6]) Moreover, when command was not centralized, there was the risk that one unit, by calling for fire, might discourage another unit that had got on faster. Finally there was the possibility that communications might fail, in which case, if no timed programme had been prepared, the infantry would be without artillery support altogether. Hence it was ultimately agreed that some sort of timed programme was still necessary, and it appeared probable that the best solution of the problem, when the enemy dispositions were not accurately known, would be a combination of barrage and concentrations "on call".([7])

In spite of occasional failures, wireless was helping to ensure continuity of fire support in the fast-moving battle. For example, during a brigade advance, while the supporting artillery regiment was on the move, another regiment could put a set on its "net" and answer calls for fire—on targets indicated by map references—without the delays inherent in the installation of new F.O.Os. and representatives, and in the re-netting of wireless sets on a new frequency.([4])

Barrage *versus* Concentrations

The increased use of concentrations "on call" had affected the relative positions of concentrations and barrage in the general framing of fire plans. There was no doubt that the barrage was expensive in ammunition and that, in the infantry attack especially, its timing was a matter of great difficulty. Experience showed that the rate of advance as planned was seldom achieved in practice. At the Garigliano, even 100 yards in 15 minutes proved too fast up the difficult slopes of Damiano (*see* p. 195); at Cassino the barrage, advancing at 100 yards in six minutes, had begun to leave the infantry behind almost from the start (*see* p. 214); and at Caumont, where the barrage did not begin until Phase II, the tanks had had to push on ahead of the infantry in order to reach and cross the start line before its effects had worn off (*see* p. 227).

There were, however, occasions when the "boot was on the other foot". At Overloon, in October, 1944, after an air and artillery bombardment that only began from 60 to 30 minutes before "H" hour, the infantry complained that the barrage, fired by three divisional artilleries and moving at a rate of 100 yards in five minutes, had held up their advance. German prisoners reported that although their casualties had not been heavy, thanks to the cellars in which they could shelter beneath the ruined houses of the village, "the Tommies were so close on the heels of the barrage that it was too late to start fighting when we emerged."(8)

Also, with tanks and carrier-borne infantry, results had been generally satisfactory. In Operations "Goodwood" and "Totalize" (*see* pp. 225, 227), a rate of advance of 150 yards in one minute by day, and 100 yards by night, had been well maintained; and in the advance by the Guards Armoured Division from the Dutch frontier on 17th September, in conjunction with the airborne attack on Arnhem, the pace was successfully increased to 200 yards in one minute against parachute infantry dug in along the road axis and supported by some S.P. guns.

As a killer, the concentration had the advantage of suddenness and surprise, especially if combined with cunningly regulated periods of silence. By December 1944, T.O.T. concentrations (*see* p. 129) by as many as seven field regiments were being used by some formations in Italy,(9) although for the close support of an attack such large concentrations covered too large an area—about 400 yards by 400 yards—and so kept the infantry away from their objective. In the mountains, where the defences were localized and could rarely be attacked on more than one company front, the support of a battery was usually sufficient, and by careful ranging it was possible to let the infantry get within 200 yards of the objective before the covering fire ceased.(10)

Incidentally, in one such attack, an interesting demonstration occurred of the moral effect of prolonged and accurate shelling of a small defended locality. The target was an enemy position in and around two houses above a 20-foot rocky cliff on a hill top, which had been unsuccessfully attacked after a 30-minute bombardment by a field regiment. As at Keren (*see* p. 56), the infantry had been unable to scale the cliff and were driven off by grenades thrown from the houses above. The next day a new idea was tried out. After careful registration by two 25-prs., the target was engaged continuously by one gun at a time, firing 20 rounds in the hour, from 1000 to 1700 hours, with forward infantry giving observations from a church 300 yards away. At 1900 hours the infantry advanced under a quickly prepared fire plan and met no opposition. According to a statement by one of the only two survivors of the original garrison of perhaps 50, the majority had been unable to stand the shelling and had withdrawn without permission in the middle of the afternoon.

The conditions were of course unusual in that the enemy were not in well-prepared dug-outs or pill boxes, but in a very confined position and under close observation from our forward infantry. Nevertheless, the results achieved were striking and at once invited the question whether they were due more to the prolongation or to the accuracy of the shelling. Claims could be advanced on both sides with sound psychological backing, although those in favour of repetition or prolongation of the stimulus were discounted to some extent by the experience at Cassino and elsewhere, where very prolonged bombardments of much greater weight had failed to demoralize the enemy.(11)

Moreover, on purely psychological grounds, the claims of accuracy appeared to be stronger, since it would effect the vividness of the emotional stimulus, and this was generally accepted as the most potent of all the psychological factors. Investigation of the effects of air bombing had shown that the survivors of a bombardment could be divided into two groups, the "near-misses" and the "remote-misses", of whom the former tended to have their morale lowered by the thought "the next one will get me", whereas the latter might actually be elated by the feeling that "it has happened and I'm safe."([12]) Soldiers, by virtue of their training, will of course be less susceptible to such impressions; but the tendency will still be there, and its existence may afford an argument in favour of the concentration as opposed to the barrage. For the very use of a concentration presupposes some chance of accuracy in the application of the fire, whereas the barrage is generally reserved for occasions on which the enemy dispositions are not accurately known.

Artillery Smoke Screens

One of the quickest and most economical ways of achieving results was the use of smoke screens, as was demonstrated by the First Canadian Army when it resumed its thrust towards Falaise in mid-August. The plan was to by-pass the resistance astride the main road and come down on the town from the N.E., and at 1200 hours on 14th August, as the massed armour moved forward to the assault, both its flanks were covered by smoke screens, and in the barrage that preceded it, smoke was mixed with the H.E.

The results, even allowing for some exhaustion and lowered morale on the part of the enemy, were distinctly encouraging. The casualties suffered by the attacking troops were light and all objectives were quickly taken.([13]) By the end of the day an advance of some five miles had been made and the Canadians were only four miles short of Falaise itself.

Similar results were obtained at the crossing of the Seine and of other rivers, where the enemy defences were not very strong and were quickly rushed with the aid of a judicious mixture of smoke screens and feint bombardments.

Smoke screens were also frequently used in Italy at this time. During the advance to the Gothic Line, 13 Corps, in the course of a hard fight at Arezzo on 15th July, recaptured with the aid of a smoke screen, a key feature that had fallen to an enemy counter-attack. The feature in question, known as "Hill 501", was quickly enveloped in a blanket of smoke and the enemy were ejected by a second attack by the 1st Guards Brigade.

During the September fighting on the right flank of the Eighth Army, 1 Canadian Corps found itself attacking strong enemy positions on the Fortunata Ridge and at Rimini, from which the movements of its own troops were completely overlooked. Once again artillery smoke screens provided a satisfactory solution of the problem, their effectiveness being ensured, as usual, by observation—and if necessary correction—from air O.Ps. During this month the 25-prs. of the 1st Canadian Division fired 25,000 rounds of smoke out of a total of 262,000.([14])

Yet, in the opinion of at least one senior artillery commander, the overall use of smoke in N.W. Europe was less than had been anticipated; and this he attributed to the fact that, in spite of all attempts to simplify the procedure, the production of a quick and accurate smoke screen was still a bit too difficult for the average gunner of this period.

At the other end of the front in Italy, the American Fifth Army halted at the River Garigliano for the winter and depended, for the maintenance of its forward positions, on the use of bridges that were in full view of the enemy. During daylight, therefore, a continuous smoke screen was maintained and behind it movement was able to go on with impunity.

Improved System of Indicating Targets to the Air

One of the many precedents created by the Desert Air Force during the pursuit across North Africa had been the use of beacons as a guide to the night bombers. To this had been added the Pathfinder technique evolved during the air attacks on Germany. Both methods were now employed for the direct air support of 21 Army Group: the former as a navigational check for the heavy bombers, the latter for the medium bombers. An alternative method of marking targets for night bombers was available in the form of the night marker or flare shell (*see* p. 196), which was giving satisfactory results.[15]

By day, the new coloured smoke had also proved quite effective for the indication of targets to close support fighter-bombers, and another new development was the use of ordinary H.A.A. shell bursts for the marking of a bomb line. Originating in experiments by A.A. Command and the Eighth U.S. Army Air Force, this technique was later successfully used in operations.[16] Since the bursts were placed well up in the sky—usually some 3,000 feet below the level at which the bombers were flying—it was particularly valuable in a mountainous country like Italy, where a smoke line on the ground might be very irregular, and in jungle, where the points of origin of the smoke might be invisible to the air on account of the trees.

The Air O.P. in the Pursuit

Throughout this period, the versatility of the air O.P. had continued to grow. It had already been used to shoot medium artillery against the enemy S.P. delaying guns (*see* p. 216), and the efficiency of this system was now increased by the addition to the partnership of a S.P. anti-tank gun. The latter would be tuned in on the air O.P. net, so that it could be sent to intercept the enemy after he had been flushed from cover by the gun fire and thus make sure of the kill.[17]

A rather similar technique was used for the hunting of enemy tanks. In 5 Corps, during November, 1944, two divisional air O.P. aircraft were allotted solely to this task, operating in conjunction with a heavy or medium battery and an armoured regiment or tank battalion, both of which had wireless sets on the divisional air O.P. flight frequency. S.P. anti-tank guns, equipped with R109 receivers, would also listen in to the air O.P. running commentary on the movement of the enemy tanks and be ready to take advantage of any opportunity that presented iteself. Thus a number of enemy tanks were destroyed and the remainder were kept on the move and prevented from acting as strong points.[18]

The facilities for the taking of oblique air photographs, both by day and by night, were continually being developed, and by the end of September, 1944, the radar control of air O.Ps. by night was under active consideration in 21 Army Group. The ideal now aimed at was the round-the-clock supervision of enemy activity in the forward areas.[19] To increase the scope of the air O.P. by making landing easier, the introduction of helicopters was strongly advocated, but the first issue of these aircraft did not take place until after the war in Europe was over.

From Sicily onwards, the need had been felt for air O.Ps. in the early stages of an assault landing. The use of light aircraft carriers for this purpose, though occasionally practised by the Americans in the S.W. Pacific, was not considered feasible for the support of 21 Army Group during the invasion of Normandy. Continued attempts were therefore made to produce an amphibious air O.P. and by December, 1944, a prototype Auster with float chassis was undergoing trials; and other trials were on foot to make the air O.P. completely air portable.[20]

With so many and varied demands being made on the air O.P. organization, economy of flying time became a matter of great importance. From this point of view, the original idea of allotting one air O.P. section to each divisional field regiment (see p. 158) had certain disadvantages. It sometimes resulted in all aircraft being in the air or on the ground simultaneously, and thus caused a waste of flying time or a lack of continuity in observation. A better method was for all sections, and regimental headquarters of artillery regiments, to be placed on a common air O.P. net, with control at H.Q.R.A.[21] Indeed, with the scale of air O.P. resources available in 1944, even the decentralization of flights to divisions was considered by some C.Cs.R.A. to be impracticable, owing to the frequency with which corps changed their composition—there were about 15 divisions in 1 Corps between June and December, 1944—and, sometimes, to the paramount claims of A.Gs.R.A.

Co-operation with Armour

During the final stages of the breakout from Normandy, and especially during the armoured thrusts to the south and S.E. of Caen that preceded the closing of the Falaise gap, the organization and control of the armoured divisional artillery had been well tested. In general, no difficulty was experienced in the exercise of centralized command by the C.R.A., though communication difficulties sometimes necessitated the movement of H.Q.R.A. up to the gun area, thus separating it from the rest of divisional headquarters. When the infantry brigade was leading, H.Q.R.A. moved on one occasion into position beside brigade headquarters (cf. p. 48). When the armoured brigade was leading, it sometimes outran the support of the field guns, which could not be deployed outside the area cleared by the infantry, and it had therefore to depend on medium artillery for its covering fire.[7]

Another echo from the past was the use of the shell to help the leading units to identify their positions on the map. At El Alamein it was the infantry who were assisted in this way (see p. 145). Here in France it was the tanks, which sometimes got lost when travelling across country in the dust clouds raised during dry weather, and which were put "on the map" again by a round or two of smoke fired at a given map reference.[4]

In Italy, when both guns and tanks were supporting an infantry attack, the tank commanders sometimes objected to a creeping barrage from start line to objective, on the grounds that it blinded them and so interfered with the use of their own weapons. They preferred the idea of a standing barrage on the objective. But this did not meet with official approval. " It must be accepted " was the official verdict " that tanks will very seldom be able to use their weapon to the best advantage when accompanying infantry in the attack."(22)

The Handling of an A.G.R.A. in the Pursuit

The mobility of medium and heavy artillery, so convincingly demonstrated during the pursuit to Lake Trasimene (*see* p. 216), was now crowned by the introduction of a pistol gun procedure as developed by the field artillery in North Africa (*see* p. 149). When forced to provide his own temporary grid, the C.A.G.R.A. would nominate a centrally placed regiment as control and the regimental survey officer of this regiment would fix the co-ordinates of the control director and measure the bearing and range to each of the other regimental directors.(23)

At times, such as during the advance of 13 Corps from the Arno to the Gothic Line, the A.G.R.A. units would have to be temporarily decentralized and placed under command of divisions. By the end of September, however, centralized control was resumed in this Corps, and during the attack on the Fiumicino Line by 1 Canadian Corps in October 1944, the strength of the 1st Canadian A.G.R.A. was increased to seven medium, two heavy and one H.A.A. regiment; a record for this—and probably for any— theatre.(24)

The Field Artillery Tractor

In field and anti-tank artillery some difficulty was being experienced with towing vehicles. The field artillery tractor had been a source of almost continuous trouble since mechanization had begun in 1938 (*see* p. 10). In August 1942, the War Office had decided to investigate the possibility of producing a universal type artillery tractor suitable for the 6-pr., 17-pr., 25-pr. and Bofors, but at a meeting on 14th August 1944, the D.R.A. was moved to complain that " after five years of war, the Army still had no satisfactory tractor for field or anti-tank work, and that there was a need to improve the performance of heavy artillery tractors." It was decided at this meeting to develop a new wheeled or partially tracked vehicle for the 6-pr., an armoured tractor for the 17-pr., a wheel and a ¾-tracked vehicle for the 25-pr., and an entirely new heavy artillery tractor.

Counter-Battery

Owing to the use by the enemy, in Italy, of deep and effective shelters for his gun detachments, in which the latter would take refuge as soon as they realized they were being ranged on, the customary counter-battery neutralization shoot was replaced, in June 1944, by a destructive shoot carried out by a single gun and continued until a direct hit or a near miss had been reported by the arty/R or air O.P. pilot.(25)

This method had two disadvantages: owing to the time required to achieve a direct hit or near miss, not more than one shoot could as a rule be carried out by each sortie; and secondly, the guns used on such tasks could not, owing to the shortage of ammunition, be " covered " against the enemy sound rangers by simultaneous shoots from other units.(26) Later, an adaptation of the method was introduced to enable a number of enemy batteries to be engaged within the period of a single sortie. As many aircraft as could be made available, and controlled, were sent into the air together, covered by counter-flak shoots on enemy A.A. batteries within range—and if necessary by fighter aircraft—and allotted each to a particular height and area. Each pilot would do two or three shoots, either consecutively or concurrently. This system, known as a "Festa", was originally designed for the assault on the Gothic Line, and though not actually used there, was later found to be effective in other operations of a similar nature.[27]

The timing of counter-battery fire, when used in a retaliatory role, had always been a difficult problem. There was frequently an interval of 20 minutes or more between the arrival of the enemy shells and the reply of our own guns. Hence it was considered better in some formations to hit back at once at known enemy positions and headquarters— as had been done in Tunisia (see p. 162)—rather than wait until the actual offender had been located.[28]

Counter-Mortar

With the aid of the four pen recorder and of radar, the location of enemy mortars was making considerable strides. Although the location of the smaller mortars, such as the 8.1-cm., still presented difficulties, the larger types of bomb were easy to follow on the radar set, and single trajectories could be picked out even when a large number of weapons were fired simultaneously. As a general guide, it was found in 21 Army Group in November, 1944, that the accuracy of locations was approximately 50 yards for G.L.III, 100 yards for the four pen recorder, and 150-200 yards for listening O.Ps.[29]

Where reliance had to be placed on "moreps" (see p. 209), it was not always possible to determine which of several hostile mortars was firing, and it was therefore necessary to group known mortar positions by areas, for the application of retaliatory bombards. Even when the offending mortar could be accurately located, it was not always easy to engage it effectively. In November, 1943, an attempt had been made to increase the efficacy of the gun as a C.M. weapon by the introduction of what was known as "upper register firing".

If a gun is elevated above 45 degrees, the shell, instead of going farther, will start to drop short. For every target within range of the gun, therefore, there are two possible elevations: one in the upper, the other in the lower, register; and the effect of using the former is to increase the angle of descent and hence the possibility of hitting a mortar tucked away in some steep-sided gully.

Unfortunately, for technical reasons, certain complications were introduced into the process of laying the gun, and the range tables that were immediately available were of approximate accuracy only, while the behaviour of the shell at these high elevations was inclined to be erratic. Moreover, so much digging was involved that the method was not popular, and apparently it was not much used for this reason.

Air burst was an obvious alternative, but here again the inaccuracies of the time fuze made the engagement of close targets inadvisable. For example, the safe distance from our own F.D.Ls. for the engagement of hostile mortars by the 25-pr. was considered to be 600 yards when using air burst or upper register shooting, as compared with 300 yards when using ordinary ground burst. With the 7.2-in. how., which was the most favoured weapon for this role, the corresponding distances were 1,500 and 800 yards.([30])

In France, at this time, enemy 8.1-cm. mortars were customarily sited from 500-800 yards, 12.1-cm. mortars about 1,000 yards, and nebelwerfers up to 4,000 yards behind the F.D.Ls.([29]) It was therefore evident that, for the effective fulfilment of the C.M. role, there would have to be the closest co-ordination between our own guns and mortars, and a careful filtering of all mortar information. If, however, the process of filtering took too long, the enemy mortars would have moved, or their crews would have gone to ground, before fire could be brought down upon them. Hence, in 21 Army Group, C.M. fire was organized in two stages: immediate retaliatory fire, under the control of the A.C.M.O. or C.M.O., against pre-selected enemy "sore spots" in the sector from which the mortars fired; and a deliberate shoot ordered by the C.M.O. as soon as an accurate fixation had been obtained. For this purpose, most divisions had a C.M. group usually consisting of one 7.2-in. battery and one medium troop and/or one H.A.A. battery; though one corps preferred to use a divisional artillery with a call on medium artillery. Infantry guns were considered to be the responsibility of the C.B.O., and nebelwerfers were a border line case with the majority opinion in favour of their being dealt with by the C.M.O. Liaison between C.M.O. and C.B.O. had therefore to be very close, and there were some who thought that the two organizations should be combined. Although this idea was not generally approved, it was the universal custom for the C.M.O. to move with H.Q.R.A.

In a rapid pursuit, C.M. sections were sometimes required to accompany battle groups of the armoured division([29]), and for this purpose the need was felt for a more mobile form of radar set.

In passing, it is worth noting that the German C.M. organization included no C.M.O. or staff of aural observers listening for mortars from unsurveyed O.Ps. They appear to have concentrated all their available men and efforts on the scientific sound ranging of our mortars, and for this purpose had introduced four pen recorders in 1942, some two years before they were introduced in the British Army.([31])

The Attack on the Gothic Line

Although the Gothic Line had been hastily constructed and was not complete by the time our attack was launched, its natural strength made it a formidable obstacle. For the defence of this line the Germans had amassed a considerable amount of artillery. On 1 Canadian Corps front from 25th August to 28th October, 1944, the average strength was 158 field, 56 medium and 14 heavy guns, 36 nebelwerfers and 161 mortars; as opposed to which the Canadian Corps had under command 240 field, 64 medium and 16 heavy guns.([32])

It was estimated in 1 Canadian Corps that 58.7 per cent. of their casualties in this fighting were caused by H.E. shell fire, 11.7 per cent. by small arms, and 7.1 per cent. by mortar fire. It was therefore necessary to allot a higher proportion of guns and ammunition to C.B. tasks, and to make the fullest possible use of air support. The latter was applied in three different ways: the "cab rank" system, with a controller and "cab rank" specially allotted, if possible, to the C.B.O.; and day and night bombing by medium and heavy bombers of known and suspected hostile battery areas.

An interesting action took place for the capture of the Coriano Ridge. Some 50 odd guns took part in this operation and four successive feint bombardments were fired before the infantry, following hard upon a fifth heavy bombardment that closely resembled its predecessors, went in to the assault. The trick succeeded and the effect of the deception helped considerably towards the capture of a difficult objective.

As usual in the mountains, sound ranging locations were fewer than those obtained by flash spotting—3:1 was about the proportion—and in a big battle, like that for the Gothic Line, sound ranging was further hampered by the noise of our own guns firing. The observation of periodical silences by all guns was suggested, but not accepted because of the difficulty of choosing a time when the hostile artillery was likely to be active—but not too active—and when meteorological conditions would be suitable.([32])

On the introduction of artificial moonlight, some fears were felt that the use of searchlights might interfere with flash spotting, but in practice this was found not to be so. In the attack by the 4th Division of 5 Corps near Rimini on the night of 16th/17th September, when the searchlight made its début in this role in Italy, a troop of lights, sited on a reverse slope so as to give indirect illumination of the battlefield, assisted in the capture of a feature from which heavy fire had been directed the previous day. The experiment was deemed a success and searchlights were used several times subsequently on moonless nights, and on nights when there was low cloud, the illumination then being obtained by reflection from the cloud base.([33])

The Capture of Le Havre and Boulogne

In France, while the Second Army had been hurrying northwards from the Seine, the First Canadian Army, with 1 Corps under command, had been reducing some of the strongly defended Channel ports. The first was Le Havre, which constituted one of the strongest fortresses of the Atlantic Wall. It had a garrison of 12,000 and was protected on the east by a flooded valley dominated by high ground, and along the northern perimeter by an anti-tank ditch sited in conjunction with extensive minefields and wire obstacles. Behind the anti-tank ditch was a series of strong points of reinforced concrete, with a large number of machine-guns and 8·8-cms. In the town were two forts, numerous pill-boxes and anti-tank guns sited to cover all the approaches. Of guns capable of use in the ground role there were 108 of 8·8-cm. calibre or over.([34])

Against this 1 Corps could muster two infantry divisions (the 49th and 51st) and some 350 guns, with additional support from the 15-in. guns of two monitors and a heavy scale of air support by Bomber Command. Moreover, there had been several improvements in siege technique since the last attempt at an operation of this kind at Bardia in January 1942 (*see* p. 109). Artificial moonlight had solved the problem of nocturnal movement, the flail tank had provided a valuable means of gapping minefields, and the Kangaroo had added momentum to the infantry assault during its initial passage through the enemy F.D.Ls.

With these and other aids, 1 Corps was able to overcome the defences after 48 hours' fighting. The assault began at 1745 hours on 10th September after the defences had been softened by the heavy guns of the Royal Navy and by a series of air attacks by Bomber Command culminating in a 90-minute bombardment before " H " hour, in which 4,600 tons of bombs were dropped. The operation was planned to take place in four phases: first, a breakthrough by the 49th Division in the N.E. corner of the defences, joined at midnight by the 51st(H) Division on their right; then, in Phase III, the 51st Division would develop its operation to secure certain hostile battery areas and defended areas in the line of advance; and finally, in Phase IV, both Divisions would exploit into the town and crush any remaining resistance within their own boundaries.

To cover the advance of the 49th Divisional flails to the start line, a smoke screen was to be fired by two field regiments, and the subsequent attacks by both Divisions were to be supported by concentrations—at first timed, later on call—and by smoke screens on call (*see* Map 14). An active C.B. policy was in force before " H " hour, and during the operation, in addition to " Apple Pie " shoots against enemy flak units to cover the operations of the bombers, C.B. neutralization programmes, observed and corrected by air O.Ps., were to be fired at the opening of each phase, in particular during the " gapping " of the principal minefields and anti-tank obstacles. Thereafter C.B. fire would be on call, with air observation in daylight. Artificial moonlight was to be provided on call by one searchlight battery, to illuminate the minefield gaps and the routes leading to them.

The maximum number of guns allotted was: for covering fire, six field and three medium regiments, and two 7.2-in. how. batteries; for C.B. fire, two field, three medium and one heavy regiment. The ammunition expenditure allowed was 430 r.p.g. 25-pr., 268 × 5.5-in., 145 × 7.2-in., and 83 × 155-mm., plus a total of 2,200 rounds of 3.7-in. H.A.A., of which 1,200 were to be air bursts for " Apple Pie " shoots.

The first phase, carried out by the 56th Infantry Brigade Group of the 49th Division, was an immediate success. Information obtained before the attack—from air photos, prisoners of war and civilians—was very full, and it had therefore been possible to distribute the supporting artillery fire with considerable accuracy. Subsequent phases were more protracted, owing to the bad state of the " going ", unavoidable congestion on the traffic routes, and delays imposed by minefields and road blocks. By the evening of 11th September, however, both Divisions had reached their final objectives, and the ammunition expenditure had not been heavy. The 49th Divisional Artillery, for example, fired only 260 r.p.g. H.E. and 20 r.p.g. smoke.

Because of our preponderance in artillery, and because of a breakdown in communications, no C.B. fire was attempted by the enemy, whose gunners only came above ground to fire a task and then immediately went below again. Hence harassing fire by us was of little value.[35]

At Boulogne, where the enemy garrison of 9,000 was supported by approximately 90 guns of 75-mm. calibre or over, the battle lasted six days, " chiefly because the hostile batteries and concrete strong points in many cases withstood our artillery and air action and had to be reduced in turn by the ground troops."(36) It was not the weight of support that was lacking. During the preliminary bombardment the R.A.F. dropped over 3,000 tons of bombs, and the initial attack by two brigades of the 3rd Canadian Infantry Division was supported by 344 guns: 120 field, 128 medium, 48 heavy and 48 H.A.A. Some 20,000 rounds were fired during the timed programme, which lasted for 1½ hours, and another 80,000 on C.B. tasks, among which were included some very heavy concentrations of 10 to 15 minutes' duration.(37) Incidentally, the 15-in. and 14-in. coast artillery guns at Dover were able to assist by engaging enemy batteries near Calais, with air O.Ps. observing, and on 17th September, a direct hit was scored on one battery at a range of 42,000 yards.(36) Further attacks on the enemy morale were made by the psychological warfare branch, whose plans included the dropping of leaflets from the air before the attack, and the firing of 40,000 safe conducts into the perimeter during the attack.(37)

The fire plan was probably the most detailed of its kind ever produced. More than 400 points—covering every known or likely strong point, gun position and infantry locality—were included in the list of artillery concentrations; and after the timed programme had finished, a comprehensive selection of concentrations and stonks was placed at the immediate disposal of the infantry.(38) Yet in spite of these precautions, no less than 17 batteries were reported back to the Division as being particularly troublesome, with requests for air or other action; and of the 600 casualties suffered by the Canadians during this operation, the majority were caused by enemy shell fire.

Of 31 air attacks on battery positions subsequently examined, 7 proved to have been on dummies and 11 on empty emplacements. In the remaining 13 attacks, 800 bombs and 200 rockets had put out of action one rangefinder and four guns. C.B. bombardments suffered of course from similar difficulties. Even when the location was accurate, complete neutralization was not always achieved. One 6-gun 8·8-cm. battery fired 2,000 rounds in the ground role in spite of receiving nearly 6,000 shells within a radius of 300 yards.

Nevertheless it was significant that the three battalions which attacked into previously bombed areas captured their objectives in 1½ days or less, whereas two other battalions attacking similar positions without preliminary bombing took five and three days respectively to achieve the same results; and the unit with the best time of all to its credit—under 12 hours—arrived at its objective within three-quarters of an hour of the cessation of bombing.(37)

The Airborne Attack on Arnhem

In the attempt to secure the Arnhem bridges, an air-borne formation was to be used for the first time at a distance from the main ground forces. It was not anticipated that the artillery of 30 Corps, leading the advance of the Second Army, would be in range before the evening of "D"+1; and as events turned out, this did not happen until "D"+4. Meanwhile the 1st Airborne Division had to do what it could with its own small artillery component, supplemented by air bombing and strafing of neighbouring barracks and buildings and of numerous flak positions.

To make matters worse, the number of aircraft available was insufficient to land the Division complete in one lift. Of a total artillery strength of one air-landing regiment and two air-landing anti-tank batteries, only about three-fifths could be accommodated in the first lift, the remainder following in the second lift during the late afternoon of "D"+1. After allowing for forced landings *en route* and other mishaps, the number of guns available for immediate action was 23 × 75 mms., 26 × 6-prs. and 14 × 17-prs.

The light regiment was kept centralized under command of the C.R.A., so as to afford the maximum concentration of fire on any sector. Each O.P. officer had a list of pre-arranged targets to cover all known enemy positions, including 8.8-cm. gun positions, as obtained from air photographs. Owing to the closeness of the country, it was necessary to employ 11 F.O.Os. from a F.O.U. (*see* p. 207) in addition to the regiment's own O.Ps.

For the same reason the anti-tank units became involved in some very confused fighting, and the divisional anti-tank reserve, originally consisting of one 17-pr. troop from each battery and a 6-pr. troop from one battery, proved the mainstay of the defence, varying in strength as odd guns were added to it or despatched on various missions throughout the battle.([39])

It was on 20th September ("D"+3) that the enemy reaction began in real earnest. Intense mortaring and shelling was followed by determined infantry attacks supported by tanks or S.P. guns, all of which were actively engaged by the light regiment. At the bridge, however, things went badly. The 6-prs., caught under direct enemy small arms fire, could not be manned, and the bridge force, shelled by enemy tanks at point blank range, was finally overwhelmed early on the morning of "D"+4.

About 0900 hours on this day wireless contact was made with the artillery of 30 Corps. From then onwards, two R.A. sets were kept permanently on the command net of the 64th Medium Regiment, and owing to the failure of the F.O.U. representatives to establish satisfactory communications, all calls for fire were sent by this means. By the last day (25th September) the enemy was established in a wood within the divisional perimeter and proximity shoots had become common, an unusually large proportion being within 200-300 yards of our own troops. Owing to the closeness of the country, many targets were called for by references to the 1:25,000 map, which on this occasion proved very accurate.

When evacuation was decided on for that night, a ring of fire was prepared about 500 yards from the divisional perimeter. The programme included fairly intensive fire from 2000 to 2300 hours, with spasmodic concentrations between 2300 and 0400 hours. Every available regiment was employed and the results were satisfactory. The enemy made no attempt to follow up the withdrawal and very little interference was experienced from mortars and guns.([39])

Clearing the Scheldt Estuary

During October, the activities of 21 Army Group were largely concerned with the clearance of the Scheldt estuary as a prelude to the reopening of the port of Antwerp. The outstanding feature of the operation, from the artillery point of view, was the attack on the island of Walcheren. "The nature of the terrain, which was closely intersected by dykes and steep banks, did not offer scope for an airborne landing and it was eventually decided that the most effective way to capture the place quickly would be to "sink" it: by breaching the sea dykes which ran round its circumference."([40]) This was expected to render many of the enemy gun positions untenable, and if the breaches were large enough, to enable the assaulting forces to pass through in their amphibious craft and take the defences in reverse.

The breaching of the dykes was successfully carried out by Bomber Command early in October, and on the morning of 1st November two sea-borne attacks were made, one from Breskens to Flushing, the other from Ostend to the Westkapelle area. Both got on to the beaches with comparatively little loss: the former guided through a thick mist by an A.A. No. 3 Mk. II radar netted, through an adjacent 19 set, with the leading "Buffalo" of each column; the latter helped by heavy covering fire from various types of support craft.([41])

Subsequently, however, stiff resistance was encountered and the capture of the island was not completed until 8th November. Casualties were heavy, "since very few of the coastal guns had been silenced beforehand, or even effectively neutralized during the landings."([42]) The town of Flushing was defended by concrete strong points and suicide squads who established themselves in the cranes and gantries of the dock area. In this fighting the 52nd Division, which had been earmarked for a long time for mountain warfare, and more recently for an air portable role, was able to make good use of its mountain guns asembled in the upper rooms of the houses.([43])

On the whole, the effects of the air and artillery bombardments had been disappointing, and an operational research section was ordered to investigate the causes of failure. For a long time past "the accuracy of predicted fire had caused some concern: barrages and concentrations had become enormous, and because of mixed ammunition lots, uncalibrated guns and a number of other defects, it was suspected that they were very inaccurate."([42]) It appeared, however, that the disappointment experienced at Walcheren was the result not so much of inaccuracy of fire as of over-optimism regarding the results likely to be achieved against well-constructed fortifications, and a consequent failure to prepare the fire plan in sufficient detail.

The Rocket as a Field Artillery Weapon

Among the supporting weapons in the Walcheren operation was the "Land Mattress", or multiple rocket projector, which here made its debut in the ground role. First used, in this war, for A.A. purposes (*see* p. 85), the rocket had been quickly adopted by the Royal Navy as a close defence weapon, and it was from this "Sea Mattress" that the field army projector had been evolved. The naval pattern was unsuitable for a ground-to-ground role, because it was very heavy and was designed to fire only at a fixed range of 3,500 yards. During June, 1944, the development of a land service projector was undertaken by the Ministry of Supply. By rotating the rocket, it was found possible so to reduce the weight of the projector that a bank of 40 barrels could be mounted on the General Service 20-cwt. trailer. At the same time the range was increased to 8,000 yards by the use of the 3-in.

aircraft motor rocket in conjunction with the standard 29-lb. naval H.E. shell. The provision of a means of elevation between 30 and 45 degrees gave a variation of range between 6,700 and 8,000 yards, and as this was considered to be insufficient, a further reduction in range was achieved by the provision of circular metal discs, known as "spoilers", which, if fitted over the rocket fuze, would increase the air resistance and so reduce the minimum range to 3,900 yards, and, incidentally, increase the accuracy by improving the stability of the rocket while in flight.

This equipment was still in the development stage when the First Canadian Army asked for a battery of 12 multiple projectors to be used in the attack on Flushing. There was doubt about the advisability of an operational trial at this time, owing to the fear that it might interfere with the filling programme of field and medium artillery ammunition, and to the fact that the fuze (No. 721) had not yet been approved by the Ministry of Supply for use with H.E. shell because of its lack of safety arrangements. Nevertheless, approval was given, and a battery of 30-barrelled projectors was duly delivered[44], manned by L.A.A. personnel, and fired 1,146 rounds in predicted salvos between 0620 and 1220 hours on 1st November. A few days later it did good work in support of the Polish Armoured Division north of Breda[7], and at Venlo, on 3rd December, two enemy defended localities were effectively engaged in support of an attack by the 15th (S) Division.

The accuracy was still much less than that of the gun—the area covered by a battery salvo was approximately 800 yards square—and it took about ten minutes to reload the projector after firing. But all were agreed that, although against battle-hardened men its moral effect might be no greater than that of ordinary artillery fire, against less experienced troops it was pronouncedly so. The First Canadian Army in fact regarded it as a potential counter-mortar weapon of great promise[7], and R.A. 12 Corps, after Venlo, thought the additional fire support provided was "out of all proportion to the size of the unit" and suggested that there was a definite requirement for one rocket battery to each corps.[45]

The Battle of Geilenkirchen

Having cleared the Scheldt and opened the port of Antwerp, 21 Army Group was able to concentrate its attention upon clearing out the enemy pockets west of the Rhine. Among the operations staged for this purpose was an attack by four battalions of the 43rd Division at Geilenkirchen on 18th November, 1944. The supporting artillery consisted of the 43rd Divisional Artillery and the 5th A.G.R.A., and the outstanding feature of the whole operation was the bombardment of Bauchem and the subsequent attack by the 5th Dorsets.

The enemy, about 150 strong, were in open trenches round the village and were subjected to a 4-hour preliminary bombardment in which 184½ tons of ammunition were fired, giving an average density of about 1.8 tons per 100 yards square, or about the same as that at Valenciennes in 1918 (*see* p. 2) and in the Tunis breakthrough. The programme consisted of 10 minutes' artillery (49 tons), followed by 3 hours' mortar fire (49 tons) together with some 20-mm., 40-mm. and 75-mm. tank guns (18 tons), and finally by a little over half an hour of artillery fire (73 tons).

When the attack went in, the enemy offered no resistance. Their line communications had been cut at an early stage, and sub-unit commanders had not moved at all during the bombardment. Their casualties were not known exactly, but were thought to have been about 10 to 15 per cent. In the whole attack our casualties were only seven, of which four were caused by our own shells falling short.

In three other battalion attacks, where successive areas were bombarded for only 20 to 40 minutes with weights ranging from $\frac{1}{4}$ to 1 ton per 100 yards square, the disruptive and moral effect was still considerable. In some places our troops were 30 minutes behind the concentrations, yet no effective resistance was offered. Our own casualties were, however, several times greater than at Bauchem.

In attempting to assess the significance of these results, it had to be borne in mind that the quality of the enemy troops was not high, and that they were fighting in open field defences.([46])

Air Defence Problems in the Pursuit

Shortly after the invasion of Normandy a separate air defence division had been created in S.H.A.E.F. and made responsible for the co-ordination of air defence between naval, army and air forces, and for advice to the Supreme Commander on all matters relating to air defence by ground elements, including P.A.D. and fire defence.([47])

The main problem during the pursuit was to reconcile the conflicting views of army and air forces regarding the need for I.A.Zs. in the forward areas. As soon as the breakout from Normandy had begun, it became evident that the original 96-hour rule for the declaration of an I.A.Z. (*see* p. 221) would have to be modified. The Third U.S. Army, while passing through the Avranches bottleneck, was strongly attacked by the G.A.F. on four successive nights; and since night fighters could not be relied on to intercept these attacks, it was found necessary to instal strong A.A. defences, and to allow the declaration of an I.A.Z. to take effect within 48 hours of its notification to S.H.A.E.F.

The result was to produce a continuous chain of I.A.Zs. from Avranches to Paris, and later from Paris to Antwerp, which seriously interfered with the activities of our bomber aircraft. The latter would have liked complete freedom of manoeuvre in order to evade the enemy night fighters, which were then the most efficient part of the G.A.F. This meant of course the elimination of all I.A.Zs. and reliance on night fighters for the defence of the ground forces.

Army groups, on the other hand, had more faith in strong A.A. defences in the forward areas and wanted I.A.Zs. established at every bridge and bottleneck that was vital to their progress. In the end a compromise was struck and a corridor was kept free for the passage of the bombers.([48])

From the artillery point of view, areas in which there were heavy concentrations of guns were of the greatest importance, since, in spite of all attempts to produce flashless propellant, guns firing by night were still very vulnerable to air attack. Such areas were not likely to be more than four miles square, or to exceed in number one per army at any one time; and in the opinion of the M.G.R.A. 21 Army Group, it was essential that they should be recognized as I.A.Zs., if only for L.A.A. guns.(⁴⁹) It was the same in Italy, where enemy aircraft, acting in a C.B. role, would lurk about over the forward areas waiting for our artillery to open fire, and would then swoop down and drop their bombs on the gun areas.(⁵⁰)

Again, however, the R.A.F. were unable to agree and a compromise had to be found in the acceptance of these areas as G.D.As., provided that the A.A.O.R. concerned was connected to the local R.A.F. controller. This meant that A.A. guns could engage all seen aircraft above 500 feet that were recognized as hostile, and all those below 500 feet that were not recognized as friendly. Unseen aircraft not identified as friendly could be engaged by H.A.A. guns if warning of an impending attack had been received. Otherwise fire would only be opened if a hostile act had been committed. L.A.A. guns were to engage unseen aircraft by pre-arranged barrage only.(⁴⁹)

As the advance progressed, the problem was eased by the notification daily of intended bombing operations for the following night and the issue of " hold fire " instructions by A.A.D.Cs. affected (*see* p. 201). This, combined with better identification of aircraft and the reduction in number of I.A.Zs. owing to the decreasing activity of the G.A.F., made things work much more smoothly ; and finally, in March 1945, the rules for the restriction of flying in the forward areas were further simplified by the laying down of a standard height limitation, which forbade aircraft to fly below 12,000 feet and guns to fire above 10,000 feet.

The complete solution of this problem lay, like that of so many others, in the ether ; that is, in a better system of identification than the existing I.F.F. At first, when the area of operations was confined to the Normandy bridgehead, severe restrictions had had to be imposed on the use of I.F.F. in order to prevent clutter ; and although these restrictions were reduced as more space became available, it was still not practicable to allow large groups of aircraft, such as bombing formations, to use I.F.F., and it was this that made the creation of I.A.Zs. in the forward areas unavoidable.(⁵¹) If a better system of identification could have been produced, not only would restricted areas for flying often have been unnecessary, but a great reduction in liaison staffs, communications and complicated procedures could have been effected.(⁵²)

Scales of Defence—A.A. and C.D.

For active A.A. defence, maximum scales were laid down as follows(^{53}):—

	H.A.A.	L.A.A.	A.A.S.Ls.
Port (handling 7,000 tons or more daily)	48	54	72
Airfield	8	18	—
Rail & River Crossing—Paris	64	96	48
Nantes	16	16	—
Depot Area	16	36	—

The estimated scale of sea-borne attacks was light and could in general be adequately provided against by A.A. units serving in a dual capacity. Thus the custom continued of placing the responsibility for coast defence upon the local A.A. brigade commander, assisted by certain specialist coast artillery personnel. At Boulogne, for example, the 76th A.A. Brigade deployed one

H.A.A. and two L.A.A. troops in a primary coast artillery role, and under its command were a fire commander post, a coast observer detachment, a coast artillery searchlight troop, and half a C.A. radio maintenance detachment.([54])

The local seaward defence commander, appointed by the army group or communications zone commander concerned, was the co-ordinating authority for implementing the agreed Joint Intelligence Staff policy; and the air force commander was responsible for the co-ordination of all radar activities.([55])

In Italy, in September, 1943, arrangements had been made for the early despatch of coast artillery personnel to seize and use whatever enemy equipment they could find in the ports that were occupied. Many coast artillery guns of 90-mm. calibre or less were left by the enemy in good working order, and while they were being prepared for action, interim defences were installed in the form of A.A. guns and S.Ls., and a warning system was provided by naval radar.([56])

In neither theatre were attacks actually made on the seaward defences by anything larger than " E " boats, but in the Scheldt estuary from December, 1944, onwards some useful work was done by both H.A.A. and L.A.A. guns in the engagement of " E " boats and midget submarines. On 12th March, 1945, for example, a total of at least 13 submarines was destroyed, of which the Navy claimed five, A.A. three, and the R.A.F. five.([57]) In these actions, the operations of the naval anti-submarine launches were assisted by H.A.A. radar plotting, which vectored them on to their targets; and both in Italy and in N.W. Europe, A.A. radar and S.Ls., working in unison, helped the navigation of convoys by illuminating and warning vessels that were in danger of running aground or of getting out of the mine-swept channel.([58])

Passive Air Defence

Since the early days of the war, when P.A.D. in the Middle East had been placed under the B.A.A. (*see* p. 61), much valuable experience had been gained in the United Kingdom as the result of enemy air raids. In November, 1942, therefore, when the allied expeditionary force landed in North Africa, a P.A.D. section was included in supreme headquarters and was placed in the charge of an officer lent by the Ministry of Home Security.([59]) Similar arrangements were made for the Normandy landings, and British and U.S. staff officers were assigned for P.A.D. duties at the principal headquarters in army groups and communication zones.([60]) Early warnings were transmitted from A.A.O.Rs. to P.A.D. control centres.([61])

A.A. and Anti-Tank Guns in the Field Artillery Role

After the breakout from Normandy, the overwhelming superiority of the allied air and armoured forces left little for the A.A. and anti-tank gunners to do. Both therefore sought, and found, employment in a variety of other tasks. By December, 1944, the anti-tank gun was being regularly used for the engagement of pin-point targets such as pill-boxes, machine gun posts, snipers in houses and O.Ps., and of soft-skinned vehicles or troops behind light cover; for nuisance value harassing fire; and for the cutting of wire obstacles. Engagement was normally direct and therefore had to be brief, the subsequent withdrawal of the guns being covered, if possible, by a smoke screen fired by mortars or field artillery. Indirect fire might, however, be used against targets obscured by smoke, and for this purpose sight clinometers were issued for 17-prs., but not for 6-prs.([62])

Bofors guns too began to extend their activities beyond the directional and deceptive fire for which they had been consistently used ever since the battle of El Alamein. The extreme sensitivity of the fuze enabled the Bofors shell to produce an air burst effect against enemy under light cover or in woods, where the shell would often detonate on impact with the foliage; and this, combined with its high rate of fire, gave the gun a moral value out of all proportion to its killing power.([63]) At the crossing of the Garigliano, 35 L.A.A. guns had been allotted to the support of the infantry attack([64]), and thereafter such use of the Bofors became increasingly popular. On 30th September, 1944, when the First Canadian Army was holding a line 10,000 yards long on the Antwerp—Turnhout canal with one reconnaissance regiment, a Bofors battery plus one troop was deployed in conjunction with the regiment's 3-in. mortars, and between them they successfully prevented the enemy from crossing the canal and discovering the weakness of the force opposed to them.([7]) Again in October, 1944, the L.A.A. regiment of 1 Corps, with part of the anti-tank regiment and some 600 Belgian troops under command, held a sector of the Corps front about 7,000 yards long, and subsequently advanced about 4,000 yards against the by no means negligible resistance of the German rearguards.

Meanwhile the H.A.A. battery had been slowly winning its way to recognition as a self-contained medium battery when used in the ground role. In Normandy, the first two A.A. brigades to land had, by the end of June, fired over 15,000 rounds against ground targets in support of 1 and 30 Corps. In Italy, between February and July 1944, one H.A.A. regiment had fired only 163 rounds in the A.A. role as opposed to 60,062 in the ground role, of which more than 10,000 were fired against enemy mortars; a fact that elicited from the A.A. brigadier concerned, the reflection that the German 8·8-cm. which had earned in its own army the sobriquet of "maid of all work", could in fact do nothing that the British 3.7-in could not do as well or better. It was therefore, he thought, regrettable that so much scepticism should still prevail regarding the use of the 3.7-in in the field role.([65])

Nevertheless scepticism persisted, and for some time longer the role continued to be regarded as something out of the ordinary, and as requiring the assistance of a parent field or medium regiment in the matter of survey and of the manning and use of O.Ps. It was not until December 1944 that the issue of directors and other technical field artillery stores to all H.A.A. batteries was approved—subject of course to their availability, which could not be guaranteed for some months.([66])

In conformity with this general trend, A.A. brigade headquarters were now being used for other than A.A. purposes. As far back as the autumn of 1942, the 12th A.A. Brigade had been reinforced by infantry and armoured units and charged with the ground as well as air defence of airfields in the Alamein area (*see* p. 152); and at Nijmegen, in October 1944, history repeated itself when the 100th A.A. Brigade, suitably strengthened by the addition of R.E. and infantry detachments, was made responsible for the defence of the bridges against air, ground and riverborne attacks.([67]) During the coastal operations by the First Canadian Army in September and October 1944, the 74th and 107th A.A. Brigades were converted temporarily into A.Gs.R.A. (7); and on 19th September, in Italy, the 2nd A.A. Brigade, consisting of two light and two heavy regiments for use as infantry and field artillery respectively, joined 10 Corps, with the 1st Guards Brigade, to replace the 9th Armoured Brigade.([68])

These achievements naturally gave rise to the question, which was the more useful, the dual purpose gun or the dual purpose gunner? For technical reasons, a really efficient dual purpose weapon was unattainable. The ballistic requirements of the three main types of gun—field, anti-tank and A.A.—were so incompatible that any attempt to strike a compromise would inevitably produce a second-rate weapon. On the other hand, in the man behind the gun there was promise of a much greater degree of adaptability. Not only was the modern soldier better educated than his predecessors, but the service of his weapons, instead of becoming more difficult as they became more complex, had actually been simplified. Hence the combination of alternative guns and dual purpose gunners seemed to assure the more efficient and economical use of both weapon- and man-power.

There was indeed nothing new in the idea that man is naturally more adaptable than his tools. "The best results are not to be expected from one-tool users of any trade or profession, be they mechanics, surgeons, dentists or golfers."([69]) And it was from this idea that had sprung the "golf-bag principle". (*See* p. 180.)

Conclusion

Owing partly to the speed at which operations had moved, neither radar nor sound ranging as a means of locating enemy mortars had progressed very far during this period. The existing A.A. radar set and the four-pen recorder were not suitable for mobile warfare. Hence the counter-mortar problem remained in much the same state as at the beginning of the period.

Meanwhile the counter-battery problem had been brought back into the forefront of the picture. As the frontiers of Festung Europa contracted and the German armament factories—despite the Allied air bombardments—increased their output, the amount of artillery that the enemy was able to concentrate for his last big defensive battles was surprisingly large. At the Gothic Line and at Boulogne the majority of our casualties had been caused by shell fire (*see* pp. 242, 245), and it was evident that in the coming assault upon the Siegfried Line, counter-battery would be of equal, if not greater, importance.

From one point of view, that of counter-flak, it would be more important than ever before. In the past, "Apple Pie" shoots had been confined to the protection of friendly bombers and arty/R aircraft, which, if things became very "hot" for them, could usually take evasive action; but with the growth of the airborne division, the problem took on an entirely new aspect. Hitherto, in Normandy and at Arnhem, the landings had been made in advance of the ground forces and reliance had been placed on surprise, plus what support could be given by bomber and fighter aircraft, to establish the initial bridgehead. Now, as the length of the front diminished, and the probable points of attack became easier to forecast, the amount of opposition likely to be encountered from enemy A.A. guns became increasingly formidable. Possible dropping zones were relatively few in number, and the opportunities for evasive action were, for obvious reasons, strictly limited. Hence the success of an airborne operation might in future depend on an initial thrust by the ground forces so as to bring the selected dropping zones within range of our counter-flak artillery.

But there was a greater obstacle to be met with than the enemy artillery, and that was mud. If the war was to be pressed relentlessly to its conclusion, without the traditional relaxation of effort and resort to winter quarters, movement problems of great difficulty would have to be faced, especially in the lower Rhine valley, where the normal winter floods could be so easily aggravated by the enemy. Since much of this movement would have to be carried out by night, it was fortunate that " movement light ", as provided by the A.A.S.L., had at last established itself as an aid to the night operation (*see* p. 243).

There was another possible source of advantage in the moral effect of the small calibre, high velocity weapons, such as the L.A.A., tank and anti-tank guns. Up to date this had only been used in isolated instances during operations by individual battalions or at most brigades. It remained to be seen what effects it might have if organized on a divisional or corps basis.

Lastly, against a long-prepared position like that of the Siegfried Line, there would be the problem of "concrete busting." Air bombing was generally ineffective in this role, because a near miss, even with a heavy bomb, had little or no effect. Flame throwers were effective against the apertures of concrete pill-boxes, but had a very limited range. Hence there was still a definite need for artillery assistance.

The procedure recommended was descriptively entitled the "pick and shovel method". A 17-pr., firing A.P. shot, was the pick; and the 5.5-in. medium gun, firing H.E., was the shovel that dispersed the rubble. By this method, gaps wide enough to allow the passage of medium tanks could be made in a wall eight feet thick. The 3.7-in. H.A.A. gun, firing a mixture of A.P. shot and H.E., was another good concrete destroyer, and the 155-mm. gun was also effective at ranges up to 1,000 yards.[70]

List of References

[1] Operations of British, Indian and Dominion Forces in Italy, Pt. II, Sec. D, Chaps. II and III.
[2] War Diary, M.G.R.A., M.E.F.
[3] War Diary, R.A. Second Army, September 1944.
[4] C.R.C.A., First Canadian Army, Notes No. 1, October 1944.
[5] War Diary, R.C.A., 1 Canadian Div., October 1944.
[6] R.A. 56 Div. 2741 of 11th December 1944.
[7] C.R.C.A., First Canadian Army, Notes No. 2, February 1945.
[8] "Assault Division," by Norman Scaife, p. 160.
[9] War Diary, R.A. 46 Div., December 1944.
[10] R.A. Notes No. 23, App. "B".
[11] R.A. Notes No. 25, para. 1422.
[12] "The Structure of Morale", by J. T. MacCurdy, p. 12.
[13] War Diary, R.C.A., 4 Canadian Armd. Div., August 1944.
[14] War Diary, R.C.A., 1 Canadian Div., September 1944.
[15] 21 Army Gp/00/458/Ops(A) of 29th August 1944.
[16] R.A. Notes No. 23, App. "C".
[17] R.C.A., 1 Cdn. Corps, Rpt. on Ops., 25th August-28th October 1944.
[18] War Diary, R.A. 5 Corps, November 1944.
[19] 21 Army Gp/17626/4/R.A. of 28th September 1944.
[20] R.A. Notes No. 23, paras. 1341-2.
[21] War Diary, R.C.A. 5 Canadian Armd. Div., September 1944.
[22] Notes on Ops. No. 26 of 17th July 1944.

(^{23}) 10 A.G.R.A. Standing Instructions, August 1944.
(^{24}) Operations of British, Indian and Dominion Forces in Italy, Pt. III, Sec. E, Chap. IV, para. 17.
(^{25}) 2 A.G.R.A. No. GRA/50 of 28th June 1944.
(^{26}) 6 A.G.R.A. No. G/27 of 20th August 1944.
(^{27}) R.A. Notes No. 29, para. 1656.
(^{28}) R.A. 78 Div. RA/322/12 of 1st November 1944.
(^{29}) R.A. 21 Army Gp. Reply to W.O. Questionnaire, November 1944.
(^{30}) R.A. 56 Div. Standing Orders, August 1944.
(^{31}) R.A. Notes No. 27, para. 1575.
(^{32}) R.C.A., 1 Canadian Corps, Rpt. on Ops., 25th August-28th October 1944.
(^{33}) Operations of British, Indian and Dominion Forces in Italy, Pt. III, Sec. E, Chap. III, para. 9.
(^{34}) Notes on Ops. of 21 Army Gp., 6th June 1944 to 5th May 1945, p. 20.
(^{35}) War Diary, R.A. 1 Corps, September 1944.
(^{36}) R.A. Notes No. 21, para. 1206.
(^{37}) 2 O.R.S. Report No. 16.
(^{38}) "Assault on Boulogne, Arty. Picture", by R.C.A., 3 Canadian Div., 20th September 1944.
(^{39}) R.A. Notes No. 23, para. 1312.
(^{40}) "Normandy to the Baltic", by Field Marshal Montgomery, p. 162.
(^{41}) R.A. Notes No. 23, para. 1321.
(^{42}) Operational Research in N.W. Europe, para. 14.
(^{43}) Ops. of 21 Army Gp., 6th June 1944 to 5th May 1945, p. 39.
(^{44}) R.A. Notes No. 28, App. "F".
(^{45}) R.A. 12 Corps, RA/116 of 28th December 1944.
(^{46}) 2 O.R.S. Report No. 22.
(^{47}) R.A. Notes No. 18, para. 1064.
(^{48}) S.H.A.E.F. Air Defence Review, 15th October 1944.
(^{49}) Mins. of Joint Meeting on A.A. Defence, H.Q. 21 Army Gp., 15th August, 1944.
(^{50}) War Diary, R.C.A., 1 Canadian Div., September 1944.
(^{51}) S.H.A.E.F. Air Defence Review, 15th September 1944.
(^{52}) Ibid, 3rd June 1945.
(^{53}) S.H.A.E.F./1033/7/ADD of August 1944.
(^{54}) War Diary, 76 A.A. Bde., September 1944.
(^{55}) S.H.A.E.F. Memo. of 9th September 1944.
(^{56}) R.A. Notes No. 21, App. "A".
(^{57}) R.A. Notes No. 28, para. 1597.
(^{58}) S.H.A.E.F. Air Defence Review, March 1945, and R.A. Notes No. 21, App. "A".
(^{59}) S.H.A.E.F. Air Defence Review, 3rd June 1945.
(^{60}) Ibid, 14th August 1944.
(^{61}) History of P.A.D. in 21 Army Gp.
(^{62}) R.A.T.M. No. 13 of December 1944.
(^{63}) War Diary, C.R.C.A. 2 Canadian Div., October 1944.
(^{64}) R.A. Notes No. 18, App. "A".
(^{65}) Report on Use of 3.7-in. A.A. Gun in Field Role, by 2 A.A. Bde., 14th August 1944.
(^{66}) R.A. Notes No. 23, para. 1350.
(^{67}) War Diary, 100th A.A. Bde., October 1944.
(^{68}) Operations of British, Indian and Dominion Forces in Italy, Pt. III, Sec. B, para. 37.
(^{69}) DG of A/BM/17/44 of 6th June 1944.
(^{70}) A.T.M. No. 49 of July 1944.

CHAPTER XIV

THE END OF THE WAR IN EUROPE

PLATES RELEVANT TO THIS CHAPTER

Nos.
37. The British 9.2-in. railway mounting.
38. The Reichswald.

The Luftwaffe Fights its Last Major Battle in the West

On 1st January, 1945, the Luftwaffe staged its last major offensive in the west. Originally designed to synchronize with the beginning of von Rundstedt's ground offensive in the Ardennes, but postponed owing to bad weather, it was an attempt to neutralize allied air supremacy by an all-out attack on airfields. A force of about 800 F.W.190s, M.E.109s and Ju88s had been collected for this purpose, and the plan was to saturate the defences and to neutralize the warning systems by concentrating the attacks both in time and space. Routes of advance were planned to pass over terrain unfavourable to radar, aircraft were ordered to fly at minimum altitudes, a strict radio silence was enforced, and the operation was to take place early in the morning while the allied aircraft were still grounded.

At about 0900 hours enemy aircraft began to appear over British and American airfields from Eindhoven in the north to Metz in the south, as well as over forward areas. In the British sector these attacks were generally without warning, but in the American sector warning varied from two to six minutes, and in some cases fighters were airborne in time to intercept.

By about 11 o'clock, the battle was over and the Luftwaffe, in spite of some successes against our grounded aircraft, had been decisively beaten. As aircraft claims came in, it became obvious that "the A.A. units had scored their greatest victory."[1] The final confirmed score for allied A.A. gunners on this day was 363 enemy aircraft destroyed and 102 probably destroyed, and thereafter the Luftwaffe was virtually a defeated force.

The Jet Propelled Aircraft

It was a fitting finale to the story of A.A. defence of the field army, and a welcome reminder that the efficacy of the A.A. gun, first manifested in A.D.G.B. and at Tobruk in 1941, had not diminished. Yet behind a justifiable feeling of satisfaction lay some anxiety for the future. In the jet propelled aircraft, with its speed of 500-550 m.p.h., the Germans had an air weapon that was going to cause a great deal of trouble to the A.A. experts. It was calculated that, if a target flew continuously at 600 m.p.h., it would have to be picked up at a range of about 40,000 yards as a direct approacher, and, to obtain a 20-second engagement before it had reached the line of bomb release, the H.A.A. guns would have to be pushed out about 6,000 yards from the edge of the vulnerable area.[2]

In fact, to compete with such targets, it was evident that fully automatic tracking, prediction and gun-laying would be required. The first two could be achieved with equipment then available, the radar A.A. No. 3 Mk.V and the predictor A.A. No. 10; the third, automatic laying, would involve the installation of remote control gear as provided in static—and in the American mobile 90-mm.—equipments. In the meantime, considerable improvement had been effected in the performance of the mobile 3.7-in. H.A.A. gun by the introduction of automatic fuze setting and loading.

With L.A.A. guns, the period of engagement seemed likely to be so reduced that a considerable increase in the depth of the defence zone would be necessary in order to get the requisite number of fire units. This accentuated a tendency, already present in the U.S. Army, for L.A.A. lay-outs, so long associated with pin-point targets, to follow the H.A.A. custom and be based on area defence. The massing of artillery and transport within confined sectors, such as had happened before the breakout at St. Lo and during the preparations for the assault on the Siegfried Line, first brought the matter to a head and led to the evolution of a new system on these lines, with some 12 O.Ps. on a circle of ten miles radius to provide all-round warning.

The advantages claimed for this system were that it avoided the move of L.A.A. units every time the field artillery moved within the defended area, and thus reduced petrol consumption and congestion on the roads, and that it kept more L.A.A. guns in action. It also simplified the signals problem and avoided the disclosure of important localities. On the other hand, it reduced the defences of specific V.Ps., complicated administration, and called for careful staff work to ensure that the field artillery remained within the defended area.(^{3})

Owing to the inadequacy of the H.A.A. gun at low heights, and to the lack of a suitable radar equipment for laying the L.A.A. gun, L.A.A. barrages had become increasingly important. They were based in general on radar information received from a suitably placed H.A.A. position, which was connected by line to the L.A.A. control post. When it was evident to the barrage control officer that a particular aircraft would come within range of his guns, he would predict a square through which it was likely to pass and order this to the guns as the zone of the barrage.

Meanwhile, at the Pisa airfield, in Italy, an interesting experiment had been carried out, which proved the possibility of firing a defensive L.A.A. barrage while night fighters were actually being " scrambled " to deal with enemy aircraft outside the range of the guns. By flying straight out from the end of the runway and not climbing above 300 feet until they were three miles away, two Beaufighters were flown off successfully during the firing of a high defensive barrage. It was also demonstrated that offensive barrages could be fired while fighters were operating above the airfield, by close co-operation between the sector controller and the L.A.A. control post.(^{4}) So far had inter-Service co-operation progressed since the days of " fighter nights ", when A.A. guns had been forced to endure in silence both enemy bombs and local invective (*see* p. 93).

At the same time there were many who now insisted that A.A. units should be independent of the air force with regard to early warning. Liaison between the two Services was still not close enough to ensure the timely receipt of such warnings on all occasions, and by January, 1945, a micro-wave early warning set, with a range of 40 miles on fighter-bombers at 15,000 feet, was available and seemed to offer itself for employment as a mobile A.A.O.R.

The L.A.A. and the Intermediate Gun

Another effect of the high speed jet propelled aircraft was to widen the gap that already existed between the effective zones of the 3.7-in. and the Bofors, and thus to increase the need for the intermediate gun (*see* p. 133). In the field army it was desirable that this new weapon should be equipped with anti-tank and field artillery sighting gears, and it seemed doubtful whether the recently introduced twin 6-pr. would be sufficiently mobile.[5]

There was also a definite need, of long standing, for something handier than the Bofors to deal with the " hedge-hopper ". The early issues of 20-mm. guns had been a failure for two reasons: the lack of a self-destroying element in the shell, and the unsuitability of the field carriage provided. But by March, 1945, the new army pattern of the 20-mm. gun, the Polsten, was available and each L.A.A. troop was in future to contain a proportion of these weapons.

The Flying Bomb

Meanwhile events had been happening which seemed to indicate that in A.A. defence a new evolutionary cycle had begun. As early as December, 1943, A.A. Command had been led to anticipate the appearance of the pilotless aircraft, or flying bomb, and had planned a scheme of defence that was ultimately to involve the deployment of 800 heavy and nearly 2,000 light guns.

The original scheme consisted of three belts; the outer defended by fighters, the next by H.A.A. guns, and the inner or rearmost belt by balloons. The H.A.A. gun belt was composed of four rows of 8-gun stations at 6,000 yards intervals with 3,000 yards between rows. Searchlights were provided as aids both to fighters and H.A.A. guns, and at each gun and searchlight site there was to be a Bofors.

This lay-out did not prove very successful. Although the flying bomb fulfilled precisely the three basic A.A. assumptions of constant height, course and speed, it was far from an easy target for the H.A.A. guns as then equipped and controlled. In fact the method adopted by the enemy in delivering these attacks was very similar to that used by the Luftwaffe on 1st January, 1945 (*see* p. 256). The bombs flew at an awkward height (2,000-3,000 feet) and at a high speed (350-400 m.p.h.) and thus presented angular rates of change that were very difficult to compete with on the hand-controlled mobile mountings that had been used to ensure a rapid deployment. In addition, the enemy had seen to it that the bombs should arrive in clusters, and as far as possible in cloudy weather. Hence visual laying was often impossible and the fullest success depended on the use of an electronic predictor that could follow automatically the movements of the radar instrument.

Since the height of the attacks suited the L.A.A. rather than the H.A.A. gun, the Bofors were later removed from the S.L. positions and redeployed in 4-gun positions in front of the H.A.A. gun belt. Then, on 3rd July 1944, after the attacks had been in progress for three weeks, the mobile 3.7-in. were replaced by power-controlled statics, and about mid-July it was decided to reverse the positions of the gun and fighter zones and to move the entire A.A. belt to the coast so that the guns should get an uninterrupted view.

In the new lay-out, 4-gun L.A.A. positions, equipped for unseen fire, were interspersed between the H.A.A. positions, and orders were also given for the deployment of four twin rocket batteries at 1,000 yards intervals, the whole providing a fire-power of 512 barrels. The fighters, which had previously been allowed to encroach upon the gun zone when in contact with a flying bomb, now kept out of it altogther, except above 8,000 feet, so that the fire of the guns was completely unrestricted up to 6,000 feet.

There was another reason why the guns required an empty stretch of sea in front of them. In the variable time (V.T.) fuze, which had been under development for three years, radar had just made its last, and perhaps most fruitful, contribution to A.A. defence. Operated " electronically " under the influence of the target, this fuze finally solved the problem of fuze setting and produced automatically a burst within effective range of the target. But it was, naturally, liable to random bursts if it passed close to a solid object other than the target, and it contained no self-destroying element. It could not therefore be freely used over friendly and populous country.

Its effectiveness was soon reflected in the score sheets. In the first seven days of the new deployment, the guns shot down 17 per cent. of the targets entering their area, and by the last week in August, when this particular phase of the operation ended, the figure had mounted to 74 per cent. In September, as the result of progress made by 21 Army Group, the enemy shifted his attack from the south to the east coast, and this involved the transfer of the gun belt to a line stretching from Clacton to Great Yarmouth. By the end of November the proportion of bombs destroyed had risen to 80 per cent., at an average ammunition expenditure of 156 rounds a bomb ; a figure, incidentally, remarkably close to that which had been expected against aircraft flying in accordance with the three basic A.A. assumptions, and which had therefore been accepted as the original basis of calculation for H.A.A. gun densities.

In short, the flying bomb had been mastered, and when it was used by the enemy against the recently captured port of Antwerp, the organization of the defences was greatly facilitated by the experience gained in A.D.G.B. Although a few of these bombs had appeared in Normandy, they had caused little inconvenience ; less in fact than might have been caused by descending A.A. shell fragments if they had been engaged by the defences. Hence they were generally left alone. At Antwerp and Brussels, however, they were a real anxiety. Between 12th October 1944 and 30th March 1945, 5,960 of them fell in the Antwerp city area, killing 731 soldiers and 3,515 civilians.(⁶)

The problem was more difficult than that which had been so successfully dealt with by A.A. Command. There was no convenient coast line over which radar and guns could operate unhindered by ground clutter or by the risk of damage to civilian life and property. On the Continent, too, the preoccupation of the tactical air force with other tasks made the provision of fighter defences very difficult. Accordingly, it was decided at the outset that the defence must be exclusively an A.A. task. Certain so-called " Diver areas " for the defence of Antwerp and Brussels were therefore marked out in collaboration with the Air Force and rules were drawn up giving A.A. the utmost possible freedom below 5,000 feet, but allowing for the passage of operational aircraft in distress or other emergency. " Safe " corridors were defined between the various gun areas and at night were marked by S.L. marker beacons.([7])

By the end of November, 192 U.S. and 130 British H.A.A. guns—some of the latter equipped with American SCR 584 radar sets and No. 10 predictors—with 72 British searchlights were deployed on the A.A. Command system (see Map 15), and considerable increases, including some mixed H.A.A. regiments from the United Kingdom, were made later. As in A.D.G.B., performance improved steadily with experience, and during the last seven days of the attacks, ending on 30th March 1945, only 3 per cent. of the bombs got through the defences.([8])

The Long Range Rocket

So ended the V.1. But the enemy still had one more " shot in his locker ": the V.2., or long range rocket. This weapon, first used against Paris and the United Kingdom in September 1944, had again set the A.A. experts thinking. Carrying a 1,000-lb. war head, similar to that of the flying bomb, and launched from sites 170 to 200 miles away, the rockets reached a height of 50 to 55 miles and arrived at a speed of over 1,800 m.p.h. and at an angle of approach of about 45 degrees. They gave no audible warning, therefore, of their coming, and existing radar sets were unable to cope with them. Plans were made for a new radar instrument and the modification of the No. 10 predictor, and, as an immediate counter-measure, air attacks were directed against the launching sites and personnel, and the factories in which the rockets were made. Preparations were also made to bring the A.A. defences into action, though no shooting was actually carried out.

To help in the location of certain suspected sites near Rotterdam, a special organization was set up in 21 Army Group. Sound ranging and flash spotting bases were established near Malines and results were reported, via a mobile air reporting unit (M.A.R.U.) and R.A.F. group filter room, to a special H.Q.R.A. in London.([8]) But it was the advance of the allied armies and the collapse of the Wehrmacht that finally disposed of the V.2. before any serious damage had been done.

Organization of Heavy and Super-Heavy Artillery

During the assault on the Gothic Line, the United States 240-mm. hows. had played a very important role in destroying pillboxes and strong points that were holding up the advance of the infantry.([9]) In 21 Army Group also the heavy shell of both 8-in. gun and 240-mm. how. had filled a definite requirement, though there was still a demand for a weapon with longer range, in preference to great weight of shell, to deal with the German 17-cm.([5])

Now, with the German fronts contracting and the prospect of meeting heavier concentrations of artillery behind well-prepared defences like those of the Siegfried Line, heavy and super-heavy artillery were likely to play an important part in the delivery of what it was hoped might be the "knock-out blow." Hence the number of super-heavy regiments was increased, by conversion of field and H.A.A. regiments, and a super-heavy group headquarters was formed with an improvized establishment similar to that of an A.G.R.A.([10])

The composition of a group was originally intended to be one railway regiment of four 9.2-in. batteries, with a cadre battery of two 18-in. how. sections attached, and a number of road regiments each consisting of one 8-in. gun and two 240-mm. how. batteries.([11]) In October, 1944, it was decided in 21 Army Group that owing to the destruction and disorganization of the railway system in the area of operations, railway regiments could never be effectively employed by them, and that all should therefore be of the road type.([12])

Reorganization of the Airborne Divisional Artillery

In the light of experiences in Normandy and at Arnhem, it was also decided to reorganize and to strengthen the artillery of an airborne division. Although in theory the airborne division was to be committed to battle only for a specific object and then speedily withdrawn, in practice it was apt to " remain in battle until the necessity for re-equipping it for further airborne operations made its withdrawal imperative."([13]) During the advance to the Seine, the 6th Airborne Division consisted of six brigades—airborne, commando and allied—and had under command 140 pieces of artillery, representting one air-landing light regiment, two army field regiments, one H.A.A. regiment (in the ground role), one medium battery, one Centaur tank 90-mm. battery, one Belgian 25-pr. battery, and one Dutch 25-pr. troop.

Experience at Arnhem had emphasized the importance of flying in the division complete in one lift. Of the artillery, the light regiment was required to ensure close defensive fire, for which the ground forces' guns might be at too great a distance. The number of anti-tank guns in the division—two 16-gun batteries, one each for the two parachute brigades, plus 18×6 prs. of the glider brigade—was generally felt to be inadequate. Immediate reinforcement after the landing was required either by parachuted 6-prs. or by a S.P. anti-tank battery from corps or army.([14])

The staff of H.Q.R.A. was therefore increased to make it comparable to a normal H.Q.R.A. in an infantry division; the air-landing light regiment was consolidated from the existing small headquarters and three independent light batteries into a normally constituted unit similar to the infantry divisional field regiment; and a third anti-tank battery was added and a small regimental headquarters was created to co-ordinate anti-tank training and lay-outs. In the European theatre, owing to the now negligible air threat, the L.A.A. element was eliminated in order to provide the personnel for the third anti-tank battery, leaving it open as to whether such an element should be retained for formations operating in the Far East.([15])

The creation of a separate counter-mortar battery for the airborne division was considered but was eventually ruled out. It was decided instead to adapt the forward observer unit (see p. 207) for counter-mortar duties by the addition of a counter-mortar increment, comprising a plotting centre, three listening posts and two sound ranging sections. The latter, which were equipped with one four pen recorder and one radar each, would not be able to land with the initial assault owing to the weight and bulk of the instruments, but it was hoped to provide an air portable radar set that could be flown in very much earlier than the four pen recorder.([16])

The Variable Time Fuze

The conditions of an assault landing, followed two months later by a rapid pursuit across northern France, Belgium and Holland, had had their effect upon the ammunition situation. On 12th November, 1944, one C.R.A. reported that since arriving in this theatre, the ammunition received had been too mixed to sort satisfactorily.[17] This was all the more serious in that, for production reasons, the variety of propellants had increased as the war progressed. As a result some equipment—e.g. the 7.2-in. how.—had no less than ten different types of propellant, each with its own peculiarities.

By January, 1945, a great advance had been made in the effectiveness of air burst H.E. by the adaptation to ground warfare of the variable time (V.T.) fuze (see p. 259). It still suffered, however, from certain disadvantages; its liability to random bursts; its sensitivity to rain, snow and sleet; and its lack of a percussion element, which was apt to make ranging difficult.[12] Its use was therefore subject at first to certain restrictions. It could not, for example, be used for impromptu shoots, and was in general confined to pre-arranged fire plans which could be notified 24 hours in advance.[18]

TABLE I

Statement of Artillery Weapons and Ammunition Expenditure used in Support of Operation "Veritable" (see next page)

	Weapons
Field Guns	576
Medium	320
H.A.A.	72
Heavy	76
Super-heavy	6
TOTAL	1,050

Rockets—one regt. of 12 × 32–barrelled projectors

Bofors	114	
4·2" Mortars	80	
75 m.m. (Shermans)	60	Used in preliminary
17-pdr. Anti-Tank	24	"pepper pots."
M.M.Gs.	188	
TOTAL	466	

Dumping of Ammunition (in 4 AGRA and 3 S/Hy Regt)

25-pdrs.	700 rpg.
5·5"	350 ,,
7·2"	150 ,,
155 mm.	100 ,,
8" Guns	140 ,,
240 mm. How.	80 ,,

Ammunition Expenditure

	Quantity	Weight
(a) Preliminary Bombardment (excluding "Pepper Pots")	91,330 Shells	1,596 Tons
(b) Pepper Pots	145,000 ,, 2,000,000 rds. MMG	520 ,,
(c) Barrage	160,338 Shells	2,793 ,,
(d) Concentrations on 51 (H) Div. Front	54,329 ,,	1,044 ,,
TOTAL		5,953 ,,

The Battle of the Rhineland
Operation "Veritable"

When, on 8th February, 1945, 30 Corps led the 21 Army Group attack on the Siegfried Line and its covering positions in the Reichswald, over 1,000 guns, not counting anti-tank and Bofors (*see* Table I), were to take part in what was, initially, to be primarily an artillery battle. Direct air support, following a comprehensive interdiction programme by the allied air forces, was planned to include the bombing of important places like Goch and fighter bomber attacks on hostile batteries, but it was agreed that the attack would not be postponed more than 24 hours in the event of unfavourable weather, and that air support should therefore be regarded as a bonus rather than play a decisive part in the operation.[19]

As so often before, the concentration of all this artillery immediately before "D" day, and the preservation of secrecy, presented a difficult problem. The gun areas were congested and the roads very bad; and on these roads some 500,000 rounds, weighing 11,000 tons, had to be dumped and camouflaged during the hours of darkness. But equal, if not worse, difficulties had been surmounted at Cassino, the Garigliano and El Alamein, where the enemy had commanding observation and allied air supremacy was not so complete as now. So here, by the exercise of ingenuity and care, the concentration of the guns was punctually effected and secrecy was preserved by making all reinforcing artillery remain camouflaged and silent in special "hides" until last light on "D"-1 day.[20]

In the sequel these precautions were well rewarded. The enemy high command refused to believe in the possibility of an attack from Nijmegen and therefore failed to reinforce the 84th Division, a formation of low category and rather elderly men, which held this part of their front. Their artillery was also weak. Although believed to have a large number of guns available within the area as a whole, they had not apparently disposed more than 114 of them to cover the sector selected for the breakthrough.

In these circumstances it was decided to take full advantage of our great superiority in artillery and to accept the loss of surprise involved in a heavy preliminary bombardment. This was to be followed by a massive corps barrage, with accompanying concentrations, which would blast a way into the German defences for the assaulting formations. Special attention was to be paid to the destruction or neutralization of known concrete defences, for which observed fire was necessary by heavy and super-heavy artillery.

From the gunner point of view, therefore, it was desirable that the operation should begin in daylight, and this happened to fit in well with the rest of the plan. For topographical reasons the attack was confined to the corridor between the Nijmegen—Cleve road and the Reichswald; and for tactical reasons it was necessary to make the initial penetration in great depth, taking as the final objective the Materborn feature, which overlooked the Siegfried defences from the east, at a distance of some 12,000 yards from the start line. In the words of the Corps Commander, "there was no room for manoeuvre and no scope for cleverness. I had to blast my way through three defensive systems, the centre of which was the Siegfried Line."[19] The intention was to penetrate the latter by night, with the aid of artificial moonlight, and in order to give time for a close reconnaissance before the attack went in, it was necessary to deal with the covering position during the previous morning and early afternoon. Hence " H " hour was fixed for 1030 and the preliminary artillery bombardment was to begin at 0500 hours.

The fire plan was designed with three main objects in view: to neutralize all known enemy batteries and mortars; to destroy all known headquarters and communications; and to neutralize localities in the line of advance of our own infantry. Every trick that had been learnt during the last two and a half years was brought into play, and several new ones were added. Close support aircraft were assisted by yellow smoke, as usual, to indicate the positions of forward troops; and by red smoke, fired by the 25-prs., to indicate targets for bombing, with blue and green smoke available if called for. By night, red and green flare shells were to be fired by the 25-prs. to mark targets from five minutes before the expected time of arrival of the aircraft until no longer required[21]; and a new technique for the control of close air support by a mobile radar control post (M.R.C.P.) enabled targets to be engaged in the dark or in cloudy weather without previous warning—such as the arrival of flare shells—and with an accuracy comparable to that achieved by visual methods of level bombing. The chief disadvantage was that the aircraft had to fly straight and level for the last 30 miles or so of the approach, but by maintaining a height of 8,000-10,000 feet they were able to keep out of range of the enemy's light flak, and by flying above the clouds they offered a difficult target to his heavy flak, which in the forward areas was visually controlled.[22]

During the preliminary artillery bombardment, divisional L.A.A. and anti-tank units were associated with the machine-gun battalion in what were known as " pepper pot " groups, which were used intermittently to saturate with fire the enemy defences on the immediate front and flanks of each divisional attack. Except in the 51st Divisional sector, programmes were prepared by the 2nd Canadian Division, which had been in the area for some time and was therefore conversant with the enemy dispositions (*see* Map 16). The principle adopted was for as many different types of weapon as possible to fire on each target, and for fire to be maintained throughout the whole period—except from 0730 to 0740 hours (*see* below)—so that from 0500 hours onwards local reinforcement, ammunition supply and movement would be really difficult. Some difficulty was experienced over siting these groups, since all fire had to be indirect and was not allowed to pass over the heads of our advancing infantry. For the same reason, and because the equipments were not designed for switching, the number of targets to be engaged by each weapon was to be kept to a minimum.

" Concrete busting " was to be carried out intermittently between 0705 and 1230 hours, and a rocket regiment (12 projectors) fired 13 salvos at selected divisional targets at intervals of $\frac{1}{2}$ to $1\frac{1}{2}$ hours between 0500 and 1400 hours. As the effect was more blast than splinter, targets were engaged, as far as safety limits allowed, immediately before the arrival of the infantry in the target area. It was found that, if the same targets were simultaneously engaged by 25-prs. and the latter continued firing after the rockets had lifted, better results were obtained as the enemy were still stunned when our infantry arrived.[19]

The preliminary bombardment for each phase by the remainder of the artillery was to follow the principle of engaging known enemy localities, headquarters and communications with increasing intensity until the morale of the enemy had been shattered. There were to be five bombardments between 0500 hours 8th February and 0100 hours 9th February, in the course of which each target was to receive a minimum of six tons.

Counter-battery fire before "D" day was confined to normal activity by the Canadian artillery already deployed. Thereafter a very active policy was to be pursued, control up to "H" hour being vested in 5 A.G.R.A. and subsequently divided on a geographical basis between 5, 2 Canadian and 9 A.Gs.R.A. with arty/R sorties allotted to each. Included in the preliminary bombardment programme were four counter-battery bombards, in which the 45 known or suspected hostile battery positions were to be subjected to concentrations averaging about 40 : 1 (*see* Map 17). Between 0730 and 0740 hours all fire, including "pepper pots," was to cease and a feint smoke screen was to be laid by eight field regiments across the whole front of 13,500 yards, in the hope that the enemy artillery would be induced to open up and thus expose themselves to location by the sound ranging sections.

Counter-mortar arrangements before "H" hour were prepared by the C.M.O., 2nd Canadian Division, who had 20 O.Ps., 2 radar and 2 M.L. sets in action. Enemy mortars had been active since 15th January, and to deal with them the C.M.O. had a call on ten 7.2-in. how. batteries. After "H" hour divisions were to be responsible for their own C.M. work, each having a call on its direct support medium regiment and on two 7.2-in. how. batteries from an A.G.R.A.[19]

The corps barrage, covering the advance of the three centre divisions, was of great deliberation and intensity, and was to be accompanied by timed concentrations from the heavy guns on suspected enemy localities. Beginning on a reduced scale, with approximately two field regiments in each division firing mixed smoke and H.E., it was to stand on the opening line for 70 minutes while the assaulting formations formed up. Then, as the infantry began their advance, three more field and three or four medium regiments to a division were to be superimposed in four rows to a depth of 500 yards, and the whole barrage (now entirely H.E.) was to move forward in lifts of 300 yards every 12 minutes. Throughout this advance, the two rearmost regiments were to cease firing H.E. one minute before the end of each serial and one gun per troop was to fire one round of yellow smoke as an indication that no more H.E. would be fired on that line and that the infantry could therefore resume their advance.

It was particularly important that there should be no delay at this point because of the size of the lifts, which had been designed to give time to the infantry and armour to make a tactical advance between one lift and the next. In this connection, it was considered that the weight of the bombardment to which the enemy had by this time been subjected would offset the disadvantage of not having the attacking troops permanently close behind the barrage.[19]

The shape of the barrage, though not crooked in the full sense of the term (*see* p. 29), was rendered irregular by the introduction of a slight wheel to meet divisional requirements. Pauses of 30 to 60 minutes were to be made on each of the intermediate objectives, and on the final objective, some 4,000 yards from the opening line, the barrage was to dwell for 30 minutes.

Thus, when the last round was fired at 1600 hours, it would have been in operation for 6½ hours.(²³)

On the right flank, the 51st (H) Division elected for pre-arranged concentrations in lieu of a barrage. Enemy localities in its sector were thought to have been accurately located, and the divisional commander preferred all available fire to be directed on to these selected targets. In addition, the right flank was open and special arrangements were required for its protection. It was therefore agreed that this division should prepare its own fire plan, provided that concentrations on the inner flank conformed to the timings of the barrage. To ensure that there were no gaps, the corps barrage was made to overlap the boundary between 51st (H) and 53rd (W) Divisions by 300 yards.(¹⁹)

Corps (Victor) targets could be answered by all guns within range not engaged on a guaranteed timed programme or D.F. shoot, and during the initial stages of the battle 30 Corps was able, for the first time, to answer a Victor call with as many as 1,000 guns.

In addition to the feint smoke screen between 0730 and 0740 hours (*see* above), genuine protective screens were to be put down by the artillery during the period of forming up and the initial attack, to prevent the enemy from observing these operations from the front edge of the Reichswald; and another, between 1030 and 1600 hours, to cover the left flank of the 2nd Canadian Division. The 51st (H) Division also had a smaller smoke screen, to be fired " on call ", for the protection of its right flank; and throughout the whole operation a continuous smoke screen (not shown on Map 16) was maintained by pioneer smoke companies to meet the threat of observed enemy fire from the right bank of the Rhine. Emission points on the first day, starting just east of Nijmegen, stretched over a distance of 8,000 yards, and they were successively extended until 30,000 yards in all were covered. The total amount of material consumed between 8th and 23rd February was 625 tons of No. 24 generators and 1,000 tons of fog oil.(²⁴)

Altogether nearly 6,000 tons of artillery ammunition were expended by 30 Corps on " D " day, and by midnight all formations had reached the objectives ordered for the day. The counter-battery programme had done its work well. The average number of rounds fired at each enemy battery was 1,117(²⁵), and the enemy artillery, though it put down a volume of fire heavier than any yet met by British troops in this campaign, was never very troublesome.(²⁶) During the ten minutes' silence only one hostile battery was active, and subsequent investigation revealed some 50 guns knocked out or abandoned.(¹⁹)

Between 8th and 23rd February, 58 arty/R sorties were used on 29 missions, and 12 shoots were carried out, of which 6 were effective. Sorties were normally flown at 4,000-6,000 feet and encountered flak of all types up to 8·8-cm., but no fighter opposition. Annotated vertical photographs were used when available, otherwise the 1:25,000 map. No use was made of oblique photographs for this purpose. Hostile batteries in gun pits and pin-pointed on photographs were easily located, and the " agreed point " (*see* p. 198) was almost invariably the target; but guns located by other means were not often found—possibly because they had moved.(²⁷)

The principal difficulties encountered during the first two days' fighting had been mud, mines and flooding. Traffic congestion soon became acute, and the second and third phases of the initial penetration were considerably delayed. The breaching of the Siegfried Line began at 0400 hours instead of 2100 hours, and the final objectives were not reached until dusk instead of daylight on " D " + 1 day, as planned.

Casualties were light on both sides, those inflicted on the enemy by our shell fire amounting probably to not more than 3 per cent. of his total strength. But his troops—particularly those of the 84th Division—appeared to find the moral effects of our artillery fire devastating. Suffering from the nervous strain of the prolonged bombardment, prisoners stated that they had the impression of being opposed by overwhelming forces, which it was useless to resist, especially in their isolated state with no communications and no prospect of reinforcements; because, they said, " during the barrage it was impossible to send runners or to move local reserves."[19]

On the other hand, some of our own infantrymen inclined to the belief that the optimum weight of artillery fire support was being exceeded. " I am more than ever of the opinion ", wrote one battalion commander after the battle was over, " that in mobile operations we are too cumbersome in our fire plans. Often attacks if they had been made silently, would have succeeded more quickly and with less casualties because of the fact that the enemy was not ready for us: yet by firing a long fire plan we told the enemy all about our plans and prepared him for what was coming."

Sometimes, therefore, this critic felt it would pay to start the artillery plan at zero hour " on and behind our final objectives, which nowadays are never very distant . . . . Except in more static conditions, it is very hard to estimate the rate of advance and it was seldom that the infantry kept up with the timed concentrations."[28]

In the thick forest country it certainly was difficult for the infantry to keep close enough to a barrage, owing to the number of premature bursts caused by contact with the trees. On one occasion, during the later stages of the battle, this difficulty was overcome by the use of moving stonks fired in enfilade by a specially positioned field regiment. To avoid premature bursts among the trees, the target height ordered was based on the ground height plus the mean height of the trees. Thus the chance of a short round was restricted to the relatively narrow limits of the 100 per cent. line zone. All data were predicted and the fire plan was entirely successful. The infantry followed close behind the stonks and no round fell among our own troops.[29]

Such were the general impressions of some of those who actually took part in the battle. A more detailed and scientific analysis was subsequently made by an operational research section, and the conclusions arrived at were as follows:—

(a) A density of 650 to 1,300 field and medium shells per kilometre square cut all the line communications in the forward defences.

(b) A density of about 650 field and medium shells an hour per map square, or one or two shells every minute within 200 yards, seems to have been enough to keep officers and everyone else in their shelters.

(c) A density of about 2,600 shells an hour per map square, or about six a minute within 200 yards, seems to have been enough to neutralize the quality of the troops in these defences, which were manned by a second class division.

(d) There was an indication that our own casualties did not fall much with weights of fire over 100 tons per kilometre map square occupied by the enemy.

(e) There was also an indication that the number of shells fired was more important than the weight, and that "pepper pots" represented an economical method of increasing the fire effect.([30])

The Crossing of the Rhine

There remained the Rhine, with a width on the British front of 400-500 yards, increasing sometimes to 1,000 yards or more at high water, and with a current flowing at an average speed of about $3\frac{1}{2}$ knots. The enemy defences here had little depth and were mainly simple earthworks. The strength of his artillery on the 12 Corps front, where the crossing was to be made, was estimated to be only about 50 medium or field guns, though in fact there were probably more. Being sited mostly in very enclosed country, they were very difficult to locate. To this figure must be added a number of guns which the 7th Parachute Division might bring to bear against 12 Corps.([31])

The A.A. defences, by contrast, were formidable. It seemed indeed as if the enemy had anticipated our use of airborne troops in the forthcoming operation—not a difficult guess to make—and to meet it had borrowed heavily from the extensive A.A. lay-out of the Ruhr. The estimate of A.A. guns in the Emmerich—Bocholt—Wesel triangle on 17th March, 1945, was 153 light and 103 heavy. Less than a week later, just before the battle began, these figures had risen to 712 light and 114 heavy.([31])

The technique worked out by 12 Corps was based on an assault landing, and as little time was likely to be available for preparatory training by the formations detailed to undertake the operation, it had to be relatively rigid. It was decided on this occasion to make sure of immediate artillery support for the airborne troops by dropping them within range of our guns on the west bank, and to ensure a rapid junction with the ground forces by timing the air landing to take place after the initial crossing had been effected. The advantages thus gained were considered to outweigh the risks due to the increase in the enemy A.A. defences, and the timing was convenient in that it allowed the crossing of the Rhine to be made by night, and the fly-in of the airborne troops in daylight on the following morning. As was now customary, the difficulties of a night operation were to be mitigated by the extensive use of "movement light".

Owing to the limited ferry resources, guns could not cross the river during the early stages of the battle; and since workshop facilities did not allow of the refitting of more than one S.P. field regiment as an amphibean, and fire support would be required early on deep objectives allotted to the airborne divisions, an extremely forward deployment in the flood plain of the Rhine was adopted (see Map 18). Though the positions at first selected from the map and air photographs were considered at the time to be rather a pious hope, they were in fact all occupied and stocked with 600 r.p.g. of dumped ammunition. Since many of the positions were under enemy observation at 3,000-4,000 yards, a smoke screen was maintained almost continuously over the whole front, and this made flash spotting by our own counter-battery organization virtually impossible.

The assault crossing by 12 Corps was carried out in two stages: Operation " Widgeon " by the 1st Commando Brigade against Wesel, beginning at 2200 hours on " D "-1 day; and Operation " Torchlight " by the 15th (S) Division further north, beginning at 0200 hours on " D " day, 24th March, 1945. Both were to be preceded by a softening bombardment of one or two hours' duration by ten medium regiments, four heavy batteries (7.2-in.) and one super-heavy battery (240-mm.); but the covering fire plans for the two operations were different. The 1st Commando Brigade was to be supported from " H " − 30 to " H " + 30 minutes by a barrage and timed concentrations, fired by the 7th Armoured Divisional Artillery Group and followed by pre-arranged concentrations on call and a 15-minute air bombardment by 200 heavy bombers, which was intended to see them on to their objective. The 15th (S) Division used a very elaborate programme of timed concentrations followed, in the usual manner, by concentrations on call; the whole occupying a total of 706 guns, one rocket battery, and divisional " pepper pots " as in Operation " Veritable " (see p. 264).

Incidentally, it is of interest to note that during Operation " Widgeon ", the mountain regiment of the 52nd (L) Divisional Artillery (see p. 247) again came in useful as a means of providing close support for the 1st Commando Brigade. The only method of calling for fire after the crossing was by 22 sets, carried on stretchers or on " weasels ", and for this reason the organization and equipment of the mountain regiment was better suited to the task than that of the normal armoured divisional artillery regiment.[32]

The form of the 15th Divisional fire plan was influenced by the fact that L.Vs.T. (Buffalos) were to be used by certain of the assault companies, with the object of motoring straight through—as in Operation " Totalize " (see p. 227)—to deep objectives on the far side of the river. Since these L.Vs.T. could not, like pedestrian infantry, wait for the covering fire to lift, it was arranged that all H.E. fire on the front of assault should lift at least 400 yards as the leading craft entered the water at " H " hour. The L.Vs.T. would then take up the task, as they crossed, with their Polstens (20-mm.) and other infantry weapons, while anti-tank guns or tanks on the flanks covered the first half of the crossing by firing A.P. shot at the far bank, wherever this was possible. For the second half of the crossing reliance had to be placed on deception. For 60 minutes before " H " hour, the whole Corps Artillery bombarded alternately, at intervals of a few minutes, the right bank and the rearward localities beyond it, so that when the final lift took place the enemy would be disinclined to leave his shelters and would not reach his firing positions until it was too late.

At night, and with the amount of artillery involved in this operation, covering fire had to be on a timed programme, but timings could be modified in the normal way and the C.O. of the close support regiment had an observer on his net on the near bank to report if, by error, the L.Vs.T. entered the water before " H " hour (see Map 19). As aids to movement, flare shell were used to mark distant objectives and landing places on the far bank, and a searchlight battery provided illumination at and in front of the assembly areas.

The latter was disposed in two banks: one behind the assembly areas and the other forward, to give light for the operations after the crossing.(33)

Counter-battery arrangements were in the hands of the Commander, 9 A.G.R.A. and the artillery allotted for the initial bombardment, from 1800 to 2000 hours on "D"-1 day, was 11 medium, 2 heavy, 1 super-heavy and 1 H.A.A. regiment and 3 U.S. F.A. battalions (155-mm.). During this period some 90 hostile batteries were engaged on the now customary "milk round" system; that is, one at a time by all guns that could bear. From 2000 hours on "D"-1 to 0100 hours on "D" day the bombardment was continued by 1 medium regiment, 4 heavy batteries (155-mm.), 1 super-heavy battery (8-in.), 1 H.A.A. regiment and 3 U.S. F.A. battalions; thereafter, until 0400 hours, by heavy batteries only.(31)

But the high light of the counter-battery plan in this battle was the counter-flak programme fired in support of the air landings (Operation "Varsity"). The time fixed for the drop—known as "P" hour—was 1000 hours on "D" day, and the counter-flak bombardment—following an hour's preliminary bombardment, by all 12 Corps Artillery units that could bear, of enemy localities selected by the airborne divisions from photographic and other intelligence sources—was to begin at 0930 hours. Simultaneously, the R.A.F. were to attack enemy guns that could engage the troop carriers and gliders from positions beyond the range of our artillery.

The artillery problem presented a new kind of difficulty resulting from the order of events laid down in the tactical plan. In this instance, neutralization alone would not suffice, since, in order to avoid the risk of damage to our own aircraft, all guns had to cease fire as the leading units of the airborne formations arrived over the area, and to remain silent until the last aircraft had left the area. This meant practically three hours' silence while over 1,700 aircraft and 1,300 gliders delivered some 14,000 airborne troops in the battle area. Hence some degree of destruction would be required if the counter-flak bombardment was to be really effective. But the destructive effect of the normal counter-battery bombardment was largely confined to communications, and A.A. weapon, which used direct methods of fire, were independent of communications other than the buried cables connecting predictor to gun. The number of rounds that would have to be fired to make sure of a direct hit on a gun or a fire-control instrument was very large and there was not enough artillery to produce the requisite weight of fire in the time available—which in the programme was 30 minutes, but in fact was reduced to 22 minutes by the premature arrival of the aircraft. The most that could be hoped for, therefore, was that the moral effect of the counter-flak bombardment would last for long enough to cover the fly-in of the first flight.

In view of the difficulty of ensuring the timely arrival of the airborne formations, two C.C.R.A.'s representatives were installed: one on the high ground about eight miles west of the Rhine, to give warning of their approach and so enable the bombardment to continue if they were late; the other in an observation tower in the main gun area, to stop the guns firing when the leading aircraft was about to cross this area.

It was intended at first to continue firing on certain targets with all guns whose line of fire was clear of the lanes laid down for the fly-in and the fly-out. Shortly before "D" day, however, "it was made abundantly clear that aircraft could not stick rigidly to these lanes, and that the only safe course was to stop all fire on the frontage covered by the fly-in and the fly-out as long as these continued ", although this meant refusing calls for fire from airborne divisions at times when they were most in need of support.([34])

The arrangements for the reinforcement of the airborne divisional artilleries, and for the provision of additional fire support, were as follows. Taking the 6th Airborne Division as an example, its " organic " artillery consisted of one air-landing light regiment (75-mms.), one air-landing anti-tank regiment (17-prs. and 6-prs.), a forward observer unit (F.O.U.), and the recently added counter-mortar element (see p. 261) comprising a C.M.O. at H.Q.R.A., an A.C.M.O. at each brigade headquarters, and a listening post with each of the two parachute brigades. During the early stages of the operation the 4.2-in. mortar troop of the airborne armoured reconnaissance regiment was in action just in front of the air-landing light regiment and could be called on through any F.O.O. via the R.A. representatives at H.Q. 5th Parachute and 6th Air-landing Brigades.

As soon as the link-up with the ground forces had been effected, this artillery was reinforced by a S.P. anti-tank battery (17-prs.) and a S.P. field regiment. In addition, one medium regiment of the 52nd (L) Divisional Artillery Group was placed in support of each of the centre and right brigade groups, and the remainder of this group was prepared to engage pre-arranged targets on call by the 6th Airborne Division. If additional fire support was required, requests were sent through H.Q.R.A. to 18 U.S. Airborne Corps, which was in charge of the whole airborne operation. Pre-arranged D.F. targets were registered by F.O.Os. of the F.O.U. and the air-landing regiment, and liaison officers from the F.O.U. accompanied the C.R.A. 52nd (L) Division, each of the two medium regiments in close support, and the S.P. field regiment.([35])

A comparison of the effects attributed to these various fire plans is interesting. The air bombardment of Wesel, in support of the 1st Commando Brigade, came down only 1,500 yards ahead of the leading troops and was reported to be very accurate. Its effect was good and by first light the whole brigade, less one battalion, was in the town and had taken 400 prisoners.

In Operation " Torchlight," the right hand brigade reached its final objectives more or less according to plan, but the left hand brigade met with more opposition. Soon after first light it became apparent that the enemy was recovering from the initial bombardment and had reoccupied parts of the bund and houses east of Hubsch. Attempts made before the operation by field and medium guns to destroy certain buildings on the far bank, overlooking the river, had failed, and subsequent attacks to clear up this situation had to be made without artillery support owing to the progress of the airborne operations. M.M.G. support was, however, given and " resistance, which had bordered on the fanatical, began to crumble after the arrival of the airborne troops."([31])

In Operation " Varsity," between 0930 and 0952 hours on 24th March, some 24,000 rounds (440 tons) of ammunition was fired at enemy flak positions; the number of rounds to each target varying from 16 to 1,000, with an average of 242. But the physical damage inflicted was very small, and there were substantial casualties to gliders, crews and loads.

TABLE J

CROSSING OF RHINE (OPERATION "PLUNDER") NUMBERS OF GUNS UNDER COMMAND 12 CORPS

Formation	Mtn 3·7-in.	Fd 25-pdr.	Med 4·5-in.	Med 5·5-in.	Hy 155 mm.	Hy 7·2-in.	S. Hy 8-in.	S. Hy 240 mm.	HAA 3·7-in.	Rocket Bty	Remarks
7 Armd Div.	24	48	—	—	—	—	—	—	—	—	(a) Projectors each of 30 barrels.
15 (S) Div.	—	120	—	16	—	—	—	—	—	12(a)	
52 (L) Div.	—	72	16	16	—	—	—	—	8	—	
53 (W) Div.	—	72	—	64	8	8	—	—	8	—	
3 AGRA	—	—	—	16	44	8	—	—	8	—	
8 AGRA	—	24	—	48	—	—	2	4	—	—	
9 AGRA	—	—	—	—	—	—	—	—	24	—	
100 AA Bde.	—	—	—	—	—	—	—	—	48	—	
TOTALS	24	336	16	160	52	16	2	4	96	12	—

TABLE J (cont.)
AMMUNITION EXPENDITURE, 21st-28th March 1945

Equipment	Allotted	Fired	Percentage
25-pdr.:—			
H.E.	393,120	222,274	56
Smoke	105,840	2,787	2·7
4·5-in.	17,280	7,602	44
5·5-in.	172,800	69,607	40
155 mm. (British)	7,200	4,335	60
7·2-in.	7,920	3,964	50
240 mm.	600	576	96
8-in.	280	176	62
3·7-in. (Ground Role)	43,200	16,573	38
3·7 in. Mtn.	—	5,832	—

It was the same with the air bombardment, which, incidentally, had to end by " P " - 30 to allow the dust to settle before the arrival of the paratroops. An average of over 500 bombs was dropped on each battery, but only one landed in a gun pit and that was empty; and although the moral effect was considerable, it is probable that it had largely worn off by " P " hour or soon after.

Thus the conclusion was that " although the operation succeeded, the anti-flak programme contributed little to its success." The only marked reduction in flak intensity was brought about by the capture of gun positions by the airborne troops themselves.([36]) If to this is added a comparison of the rounds actually fired with those allotted, and dumped, both here and in Operation " Veritable " (see Tables I and J), it might be questioned whether artillery preparations were not now reaching uneconomical proportions.

The Final Offensive in Italy

After a pause during the winter, conditioned largely by a shortage of infantry reinforcements and of artillery ammunition, 15 Army Group launched its final big offensive in the spring with the object of destroying the German armies south of the Po. The plan consisted of a pincer movement by the Eighth and U.S. Fifth Armies, with the former, on the right, beginning the attack some three days or more before the latter.

The Eighth Army had several rivers with high flood banks to cross, and on its right flank was Lake Comacchio, a shallow sheet of water extending for some 15 miles from east to west, and 10 to 15 miles from south to north. On its eastern side the lake was separated from the sea by a spit of land only 1½ miles wide, and the centre of that was flooded, leaving a strip about 800 yards wide on each side. To the west lay the Bastia-Argenta gap, which the Germans had strengthened by flooding large areas on its flanks and by building up a strong defensive system of minefields, entrenchments and defended villages in the narrows north of Bastia. Here, evidently, was the hinge of the whole German defensive system and the biggest problem confronting the Eighth Army.([37])

As a preliminary measure, it was decided to secure the spit of land to the east of Lake Comacchio, and to follow this up by clearing the enemy from the south-western shores of the lake. The first of these operations would, it was hoped, alarm the enemy for the safety of his seaward flank and thus induce him to misplace his reserves before the main blow was delivered against the Senio defences; the second would open a way round the narrows at Bastia and Argenta.

The attack on the spit was carried out on the night of 1st-2nd April by the 2nd Commando Brigade, and to increase the chances of deception, a disproportionate amount of artillery (160 guns) and ammunition expenditure was allotted. For the next preliminary operation, on the south-western shores of the lake on the night of 5th-6th April, the 56th Division had under command six field and three medium regiments, and one heavy battery (7.2-in.), making a total of 196 guns.

It was impossible to find any central area from which 5 Corps Artillery could cover both these operations and the main attack on the Senio defences, which was timed to take place on the evening of 9th April. Moreover, the existing gun positions in this area were laid out on a defensive basis in some depth, and, having been occupied throughout the winter, were well known to the enemy. It was therefore necessary to prepare, in secret, new forward gun areas for 29 regiments for the main battle, in addition to those required for the two preliminary operations.

Movement began on " D " - 10 and was carried out at night under Corps control. Reinforcing artillery was brought directly into silent battle positions. Artillery in the line was moved gradually, leaving " rover " elements to maintain normal activity until " D " day, when they too were brought into their battle positions. The guns detailed to support, in turn, the two preliminary operations in the north, were transferred to their final battle positions on " D " - 1 and " D " - 2.

The attacks by the 2nd Commando Brigade and the 56th Division were completed according to schedule and call for no particular comment beyond the fact that, in the former, radar was used—as at Breskens (*see* p. 247)—to assist in the navigation of the assault craft during their night approach across the lake; and in the latter a new use was found for L.A.A. tracer ammunition as a signal for the beginning of the timed programme. In the past it had been found that the synchronization of watches, by B.B.C. time signals or other means, did not prevent bombardments from opening raggedly, and so it was decided to confirm by a visual signal the moment at which the guns should open fire.

The way was now clear for the main assault on the Senio defences, which were so deep and strong that it was decided to subject them to a preliminary softening by air and artillery bombardment. The dumping programme was in accordance with the heaviest " set-piece " standards: 1,000 r.p.g. for 25-prs., with others in proportion (2/3 for medium and 1/3 for heavy). In addition, up to 450 r.p.g. (for 25-prs.) were accumulated in corps dumps.[38]

The plan was to attack in the evening with two divisions—one north, the other south of Lugo—and to consolidate a bridgehead during the night with the aid of " movement light." Both divisions were to by-pass Lugo, making contact at a corps junction point west of the town. Thereafter the assault was to continue over the R. Santerno, which was laid down as the corps' second objective (*see* Map 20).

The operation began at 1350 hours on 9th April with an attack by 700 heavy bombers assisted by all the latest navigational aids, such as coloured smoke, night marker flares, radar for the indication of targets, and H.A.A. air bursts for the marking of bomb lines. For example, 24 H.A.A. guns of the 12th A.A. Brigade put up a line of air bursts at 15,000 feet—*i.e.* 3,000 feet below the bombers—beginning five minutes before the "expected time of arrival" and continuing for 90 minutes.([38])

This was followed by a 4-hour programme of fighter-bomber attacks combined with an artillery bombardment by over 1,200 guns, and the 3-in. and 4.2-in. mortars of four divisions concentrated for the support of the two assaulting divisions. The object of this programme was twofold: firstly, to stun the enemy by the intensity and accuracy of the attack; secondly, to mislead him as to the time of the infantry assault. In order to meet the first of these requirements, it was calculated that the bombardment would have to continue for at least three hours. To deal with the enemy positions in the vicinity of the river, special arrangements were necessary. These positions were dug into the reverse slopes of 25-feet high flood banks, and they could not therefore be effectively engaged from the front. Advantage was taken, however, of a loop in the river to site some guns for enfilade fire.

To meet the second requirement—deception—recourse was had to the feint bombardment, or dummy barrage (*see* p. 200), already practised with success during the attack on the Gothic line—at the Coriano ridge on 12th September, 1944 (*see* p. 243)—and, on several occasions, by the Russians in the Crimea. The plan was to deliver a series of feint bombardments, each designed to appear as the prelude to an infantry assault, and each followed by an interval of varying length, beginning with a period of harassing fire against known areas of occupation and ending with a ten-minutes' artillery silence, during which some of the fighter-bombers would rake the floodbanks with cannon and machine-guns and others attacked more distant objectives to add depth to the artillery bombardment. In the 8th Indian Division, these feint bombardments were delivered mainly in the form of a standing barrage on the western stop bank of the Senio; in the 2nd New Zealand Division a number of lifts of a dummy creeping barrage were fired, on a system known as "Dragnet," the fire finally returning to the stop banks.([39])

To obviate the risk of casualties to the fighter-bombers from our own shell fire, exact timing was required. A gunner staff officer was therefore attached to the "Rover" controlling station so as to achieve the closest possible co-ordination between successive artillery and aircraft attacks.

At the close of the fifth bombardment period, the artillery paused for two minutes and then put down a standing barrage, with smoke included, beyond the Senio to cover the infantry across the river. At the same time the last squadron of fighter-bombers flew low over the river and kept the enemy's heads down by dummy runs in simulation of their previous attacks.

As the last of the fighter-bombers left, the 8th Indian and the 2nd New Zealand Divisions went forward to the assault (1920 hours); the former covered first by a standing barrage of 28 minutes' duration at about 300 yards beyond the western floodbanks, then by a moving barrage at a rate of 200 yards in 12 minutes to the first objectives, then by timed concentrations—with a short barrage on the right flank—to the second objectives, and finally by concentrations on call to the third objective. The New Zealand Division, which had to attack across endless rows of vines and roads, used Bofors tracer to indicate direction and battalion boundaries, and searchlights to give indirect illumination of the area. Covering fire, as was customary in this Division, was by barrage throughout; standing at first for 10 minutes on a line 400 yards beyond the west floodbank, then for 15 minutes 100 yards further on, and then for 18 minutes on the opening line another 100 yards further on. Thereafter it moved forward at a rate of 100 yards in 5 minutes, on a two-brigade front of 4,500 yards and to a depth of 4,000 yards.

The counter-battery programme began with a 90-minutes' bombardment from 1030 to 1200 hours on " D " day, assisted by air O.Ps. Again between 1600 and 1615 hours—*i.e.*, during the first interval in the preliminary artillery bombardment—the enemy guns were engaged by ten medium regiments; and from 1923 to 2020 hours, to cover the establishment of the first bridgeheads, a C.B. programme was fired by seven medium regiments. Finally, during the assault, C.B., and in the early stages C.M., programmes were continuous.

The enemy made little response to our preliminary bombardment, and the advance of the New Zealanders, who began the battle in possession of the eastern floodbank, was very rapid, although for the first 2,000 yards they were hindered by smoke and dust, which obscured the " movement light " and the Bofors tracer. Progress on the 8th Indian Divisional front was slower. Its right-hand brigade was able to follow close behind the barrage to the first bound and was on the line of the Lugo by 0100 hours on " D " + 1; but the left-hand brigade had difficulty in crossing the Senio, owing to the steepness of the banks, and later met stiff opposition, which prevented it from keeping up with the timed programme.

The use of H.A.A. bursts to indicate the bomb line was not entirely successful. The bombers naturally had some difficulty in timing their arrival exactly, and to deal with this problem, a spotter was installed and ordered to report to A.A.O.R. the appearance of the aircraft over the coast line (cf. p. 270). Even then, however, some bombs still fell on our own troops.([40])

The enemy, though defeated, was not yet routed. The Bastia-Argenta pivot still held, and the 56th Division now resumed its operations to open this bottleneck. " Buffalos "—known in Italy as " Fantails "—which had not been able to operate in the mud of Lake Comacchio, showed more promise in the artificially flooded area South-west of the perimeter dyke, and experiments proved that a 25-pr. mounted in one of these craft could effectively engage visual targets while the craft was in motion, or after it had grounded.

The main feature of interest in this operation, however, from the artillery point of view, was the co-operation between the air O.P. and the " cab rank " control of the fighter-bombers. As early as December, 1944, attempts had been made to increase the elasticity of the " Rover " system by installing the control in a Sherman tank. Owing to technical troubles, the experiment was a failure, but in the spring of 1945 the trials were repeated with more success. The Americans, developing the idea still further, linked " Rover " with a Cub (air O.P.) aircraft working on the same radio frequency as the fighter-bombers and the ground control station, and carrying as its crew a pilot from the 22nd T.A.C. and an artillery officer from one of the Fifth Army divisions. The fighter-bombers thus in effect became flying guns.

" This system, known as ' Horsefly ', produced swift results, but was regarded with disfavour by the R.A.F. as being uneconomical in air support resources."(⁴¹) Nevertheless a step was taken in that direction by equipping each air O.P. flight with its own 22 set working direct from the Rover control station on the ground to the air O.P. aircraft on the flight " stagger " frequency. This enabled air O.P. pilots to call for " cab rank " on any suitable targets, and to brief fighter-bomber pilots almost personally with only one link at the Rover ground station.(³⁸)

The Exploitation of Victory

During the subsequent exploitation of victory by the 78th Division, fire plans consisted almost always of provisional quick barrages issued to units by line. This meant that start lines, finishing lines, intermediate objectives and pauses, " H " hour, etc., could all be left for late decision and issue to regiments within an hour or less of the attack going in. When time permitted, barrage traces were issued in confirmation of verbal orders, mainly for the information of the brigade and battalions being supported.

Smoke was not greatly used, except coloured smoke to indicate air targets. The dumping of up to 200 r.p.g. at about three hours' notice was often necessary, but heavy concentrations of fire were rare and only about 20 " Uncle " targets were fired. This was an occasion when propaganda shell were likely to be most effective, and 100 of them were fired about every other day.

One medium troop was placed on the " H " net of each field regiment so that, in addition to calls for fire being made through A.G.R.A. representatives with C.Os. of field regiments or at H.Q.R.A., the O.Ps. of each field regiment could shoot medium guns direct when opportunity offered.

R.A. survey parties were kept well forward with the leading field regiments and the divisional artillery was invariably on the theatre grid when required.

A continuous air O.P. patrol was maintained each day and besides conducting shoots, these patrols provided useful information on the state of the bridges in the line of advance. Many calls were also made on the fighter-bomber " cab ranks ", which did particularly good work as the enemy guns and transport became penned against the Po.

Conclusion

Germany had been defeated, and the gun, after a period of apparent subjugation by the tank during the dark days of 1940 and 1941, had been restored to a position of great, if not prime, importance on the battlefield (*see* p. 110). In the words of Field Marshal Montgomery, " The Gunners have risen to great heights in this war and I doubt if the artillery has ever been so efficient as it is today."(⁴²)

Thanks to radar, the problem of the mortar was at last on the way to being solved. That the efficacy of our counter-mortar measures had improved may be inferred from the frequency with which enemy shell fire was now being reported as the main source of casualties. In fact radar and the four pen recorder at their best were producing 11 and 8 locations respectively a day, out of a postulated 60 to 80; and it was hoped that with some experience the latter might increase its figure to 15 and the former to very much better. But neither G.L. nor the four pen recorder could move forward and set up in less than about a day, so that for the later stages of an attack and for consolidation, it seemed that hopes would have to be pinned to the air O.P.([43]), although the spotting of enemy mortars from the air had not on the whole been very successful.([44])

It was, however, remarkable what the air O.P. could do, and where it could go, after a little practice. Great developments had taken place since those first tentative trials at Mailly in 1940 (see p. 31), and the air O.P. was now an indispensable element in every artillery organization. A flight of O.P. aircraft had even been towed portee behind the tanks of the Guards Armoured Division in its thrust towards Arnhem.([45])

That the enemy also recognized their value was proved by the growing frequency of his attacks upon them, and to avoid these attacks improvements had been made in the early warning system. At Nijmegen, for example, a wireless set on the air O.P. squadron frequency was placed outside the A.A.O.R., with a remote control set inside, both manned by squadron operators. By this means air O.P. pilots were kept in touch with the local air situation and were able to postpone their take-offs or cut short their sorties if enemy aircraft ("bandits") were in the area and flying below 2,000 feet.([46])

In March, 1945, the establishment of air O.Ps. was increased and their organization was made more flexible. Experience had shown that the flight should be the tactical unit and that each divisional artillery and A.G.R.A. needed a flight for its own use. Hence it was proposed to provide in future one flight of four O.P. aircraft to each infantry division, armoured division and A.G.R.A., and one flight of two O.P. and two photographic aircraft for each army and corps. There was to be a squadron headquarters at each corps, and a wing at each army, headquarters.

Arty/R had also by general consent fully justified itself. In the future requirements might be expected to increase as the ranges of guns increased; and the growing demand for fire to be observed by night seemed likely to necessitate the introduction of a different type of aircraft. The chief problem was still to economize in flying time. For years now the procedure had been cut and simplified, and it was difficult to see what more could be done in this direction. When, therefore, the R.A.F. complained that the shoots took too long, the only remedy left was more practice.([47])

Without air observation, it was certain, counter-battery fire could not be expected to be fully effective. Mounting evidence from the war fronts confirmed what had been learnt in 1918, that " in predicted fire, it is not possible to ensure that the m.p.i. is accurately placed on the target.([48]) Unless, therefore, the fire could be adjusted by observation, the effectiveness of a bombardment could only be guaranteed by searching and sweeping, which involved a considerable expenditure both of time and ammunition.

The point was all the more important because of a suspicion that counter-battery was not being given the attention it deserved. As one infantryman put it—after being wounded in the Reichswald—, " too much time and ammunition is spent in ' stonking ' the enemy before an attack and not enough in counter-battery work when we have reached the objective. Many times we have sat on the objective and had everything thrown at us and our gunners unable to do anything about it, particularly if the objective is being used as an avenue for further advances."([49])

Plate 34—The field arty. rocket.

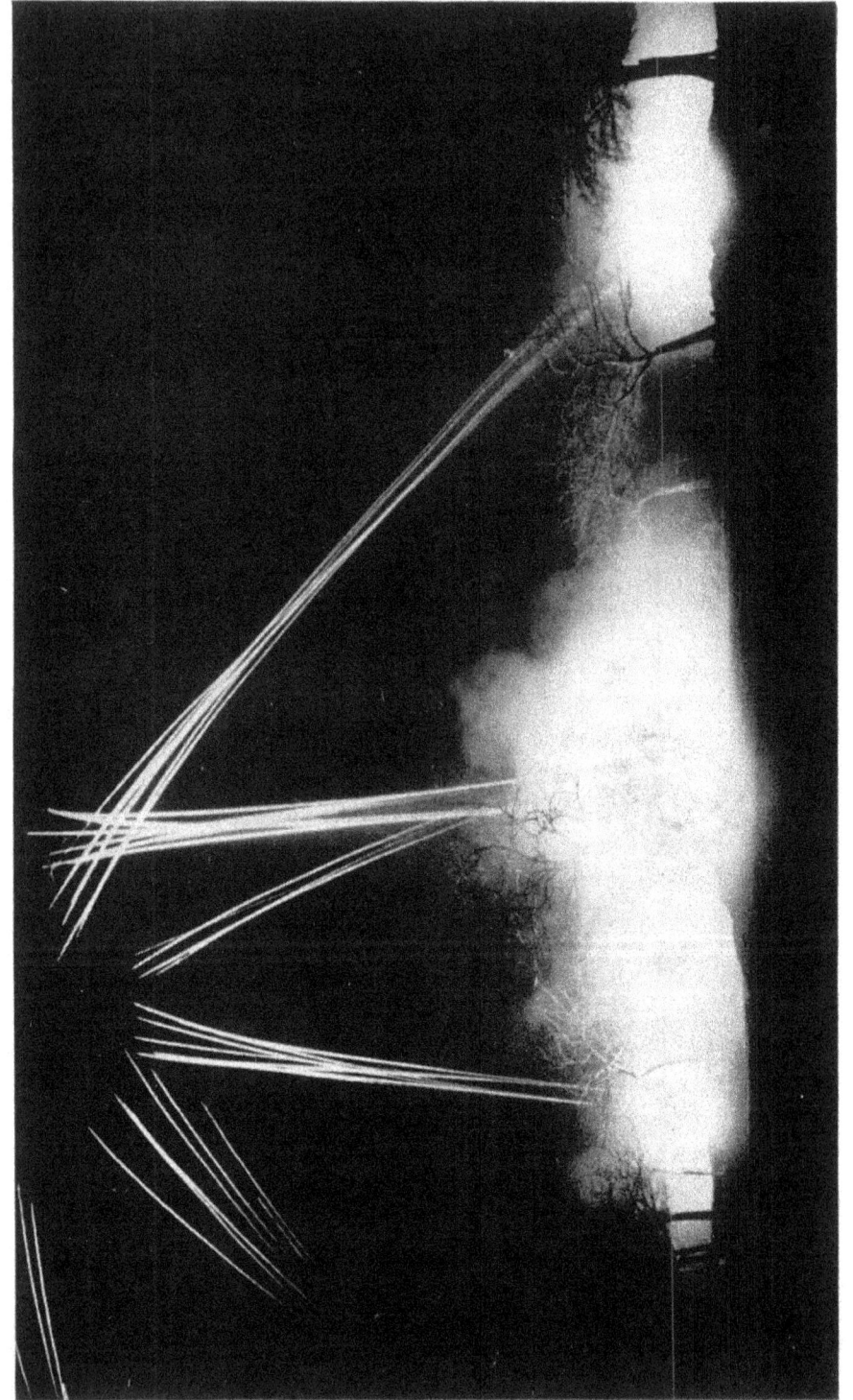

Plate 35—The field arty. rocket.

Plate 36—The 3·7-in. HAA gun in action in the field artillery role.

Plate 37—**The British 9·2-in. railway mounting.**

Plate 38 — **The Reichswald.**

Plate 39—**The Baby 25-pr.**

Plate 40—The 25-pr. on Jury Axle.

Plate 41—**Japanese bunkers.**

This was of course an individual view, which took no account of what was happening to the enemy infantry, or of the difficulty of providing accurate counter-battery fire during the period of consolidation. By this time the enemy guns had moved and many were still unlocated. Flash spotting and sound ranging were virtually impossible amid the noise and confusion of supporting fire, and the subsequent D.F., and new air photos were not yet available. As with counter-mortar measures, therefore, hopes of immediate retaliation hung entirely upon the air O.P. The fact remained that the majority of our casualties were now often caused by enemy shell fire (*see* pp. 242, 245). There were also some reasons for believing that the weight of both air and artillery bombardments of area targets was being overdone. At Bologna in October, 1944, and again at Consondolo (north of Argenta) in April, 1945, 15 Army Group found—like 21 Army Group at Caen (*see* p. 229)—that the air blitz was not always of positive benefit to the ground forces. " The carpet of air destruction could be unrolled, but the German troops failed to suffocate under its folds."[50]

It was the same with the guns. Investigation of the results of artillery fire in the early stages of Operation " Veritable " " gave a strong indication that the immensely heavy bombardments used in the operation were defeating their own ends."[51] It now appeared that the optimum intensity was about 50 to 60 tons per kilometre square per hour, and the optimum duration from three to four hours. It further appeared that what counted most of all was the number of " bangs ", and that this was the reason why the " pepper pot " (*see* p. 264) was so often successful.[52]

In the preparation of fire plans, the choice between barrage and concentrations remained as open as ever. In the hands of practised and skilful exponents, such as the 2nd New Zealand Division, there seemed little that the barrage could not do. It was in fact their normal method of artillery support. Designed to carry the infantry sufficiently far into the enemy position to displace his supporting weapons up to and including his field artillery, its depth was normally 4,000 yards, and the density aimed at was one gun per 25 yards—or, preferably, 20 yards—of attacking front. The time allowed for its preparation, including supplementary concentrations, was about 12 hours after receipt of the divisional commander's orders.

The results achieved speak for themselves. In the series of operations beginning at the Senio (*see* p. 274), four successive barrages carried the Division triumphantly from the Senio to the Sillaro ; and in the opinion of one of its brigade commanders, " provided the troops understood a barrage and kept right up to it, an attack under a barrage seldom failed."[39]

At the Reichswald, centralization of control had been carried to new heights—for this war—by the preparation of a " block barrage " covering the front of several divisions (*see* p. 265). Again the operation had been an undoubted success, but the quality of the enemy troops encountered during this phase of the battle was not very high, and against more formidable opponents results might have been different. Large scale fire plans of this kind were inevitably linked with the assumption that progress along the whole front would be more or less even. In practice, however—as a glance at Maps 11 and 13 will show—the advance of the infantry was often spasmodic and irregular.

There are many factors that determine the result of a battle, and it would be dangerous to make comparisons without a full knowledge of the circumstances, including the state of the ground, of our own troops and of that of the enemy. It is, however, interesting to note that the American Army authorities, impressed by similar experiences of their own, decided to eliminate the " rolling barrage ". They felt that, with modern techniques for the control of massed artillery fire, reliable communications, and adequate air-ground observation, reliance might be better placed on successive concentrations on critical points of resistance.

Reliable communications meant good wireless equipments and drill, and here the two main sources of difficulty were the overcrowding of the ether and the vulnerability of wireless instruments. As the area to be covered had increased, the power and complexity of the set had likewise increased, and with them the chances of interference between neighbouring instruments and the difficulty of concealment and transportation in the forward areas. Hence we find, in June 1945, instructions being issued that an air O.P. should not be on the same net as a large number of ground O.Ps. whose primary means of communication was wireless; and a procedure being introduced for a re-transmission drill from a F.O.O. with a 38 set to a tank O.P. and thence *via* the tank main set (No. 19) to the battery commander, G.P.Os., troop leaders, etc.([53])

Thus the gunner was able to keep touch with the movements of both friend and foe. Indeed, with the development of radar, the location of enemy guns and the tracking of enemy vehicles—except under conditions of heavy rain or snow—became possible. Towards the end of 1942 development was begun on a set to control the fire of coast weapons by comparing the echoes obtained from the splash of the projectiles in the water and from the target itself, and during the summer of 1943 considerable success was achieved by this method against enemy convoys in the Straits of Dover. Early in 1944 it was realized that the same effects might be obtained from the " splash " of ground bursts, provided the radar aerial and the point of burst were inter-visible, and to a lesser extent from the splinters of air bursts. In October 1944, two special radar units were formed, each equipped with a modified C.A. set, and sent, one to 21 and the other to 15 Army Group. Both had some success, and in one American formation, during a 16-day period of enemy inactivity in March 1945, 52 per cent. of the missions fired by the corps artillery were radar located.([54])

It was also possible, by the use of artificial moonlight, to facilitate the movements of our own troops while denying the same facilities—if not indeed causing positive embarrassment—to the enemy. Initially, the normal A.A.S.L. battery was used for this purpose in a secondary role, but later special " moonlight batteries " were formed on local W.Es. in Italy and N.W. Europe. Attempts to standardize the organization were begun on 24th April 1945, and it was generally agreed that these batteries should continue to be manned by the R.A., equipped with special projectors (probably 90-cm.) without radar, and provided on a scale of one battery of 24 lights (subsequently reduced to 16) for each corps.([55])

Fighting lights, used in focus at the lowest possible elevation, would in clear weather give illumination up to 8,000 yards and create shadows that could be used by our own troops for concealment. Movement lights were normally used to give reflected light with the minimum of glare and shadows; working lights to give intense illumination, usually of a small area.([56])

Lastly, the moral, if not the lethal, effect of artillery fire had been considerably enhanced by the development of the V.T. fuze for air bursts (*see* p. 262). Although trials at the School of Artillery showed the lethal effect against an enemy in slit trenches to be no greater than that obtained with the 222 time fuze, if correctly set, the possibility of errors in setting the latter made it less reliable in battle; and as to the superior moral effect of the V.T. fuzed shell, there could be little doubt. Reports by prisoners of war, both in N.W. Europe and in Italy, were most convincing. V.T. fuzed shell, they said, were the most demoralizing and destructive weapon they had ever encountered.([57])

In the sphere of A.A. defence, the introduction of the jet fighter and the flying bomb had set difficult problems to the gunner, but both had so far been satisfactorily solved by methods not differing markedly from those of the past. The flying bomb, behaving as it did in an exemplary if over hasty manner from the H.A.A. point of view, was definitely defeated by the A.A. guns—once the V.T. fuze and the necessary automatic following gear had been provided—with the minimum of assistance from fighter aircraft. Against piloted aircraft, the L.A.A. barrage proved itself still capable of holding off an attack against a vital pin-point target. At Remagen, for example, a total of 442 enemy aircraft were active over the area between 7th and 21st March, 1945, yet no damage was done to this or to any other of the bridges which the Americans had built. Altogether 142 aircraft were destroyed, and 59 probably destroyed, by A.A. fire, and all A.A. artillery commanders agreed that the umbrella barrage put up by the automatic weapons—of which there were 216 × 40-mm. and over 300 × .50 machine-guns —had prevented the enemy from pressing home their attacks on the vital areas.([58])

Against the V.2, or long range rocket, however, existing methods of defence offered little prospect of success and it was perhaps fortunate that the advance of the land forces brought the war to a close before this new weapon had been fully exploited by the enemy.

Now Germany was defeated and a rather different type of warfare was required to bring about a victory over Japan.

List of References

[1] S.H.A.E.F. Air Defence Review, 3rd June 1945.
[2] 100 A.A. Bde., 101/5/G of 2nd November 1944.
[3] S.H.A.E.F. Air Defence Instruction No. 4 of 15th November 1944.
[4] R.A. Notes No. 25, para. 1439.
[5] 21 Army Gp. No. 17626/4/RA of 28th September 1944.
[6] Notes on Ops. 21 Army Gp., p. 59.
[7] R.A. Notes No. 25, para. 1426.
[8] War Diary, R.A. 21 Army Gp., September 1944.
[9] R.A. Notes No. 33, para. 1810.
[10] R.A. Notes No. 25, para. 1463.
[11] R.A. Notes No. 19, para. 1125.
[12] War Diary, R.A. 21 Army Gp., January 1945.
[13] Gale Report on Airborne Forces in India and Far East.
[14] Note by Col. W. McC. T. Faithfull, D.S.O., late C.R.A. 6 A/B Div.

(15) R.A. Notes No. 25, para. 1464.
(16) R.A. Notes No. 27, para. 1574.
(17) R.A. 53 Div. No. RA245/12 of 12th November 1944.
(18) War Diary, R.A. 12 Corps, January 1945.
(19) B.A.O.R., Battlefield Tour, Operation " Veritable ".
(20) War Diary, 5 A.G.R.A., February 1945.
(21) R.A. Gds. Armd. Div., Operation Instruction " Veritable " of 5th February 1945.
(22) 2 Operational Research Section Rpt. No. 28.
(23) R.A. 30 Corps, Operation Instruction No. 32 of 3rd February 1945.
(24) S.H.A.E.F. Air Defence Review, April 1945.
(25) 2 O.R.S. Report No. 29.
(26) " Normandy to the Baltic ", by Field Marshal Montgomery, p. 196.
(27) War Diary, R.A. 21 Army Gp., February 1945.
(28) " Effect of Arty. Fire in Operation Veritable ", Report by O.C. 1. Gordons, 26th February 1945.
(29) R.A. Notes No. 30, para. 1698 (b).
(30) 2 O.R.S. Report No. 26.
(31) B.A.O.R., Battlefield Tour, Operation Plunder.
(32) War Diary, R.A. 7 Armd. Div., March 1945.
(33) R.A. 12 Corps, Technique Instruction, " The Crossing of a Wide River Obstacle ".
(34) Notes on Arty. Sp. for 18 U.S. A/B Corps, Operation Varsity, by C.C.R.A. 12 Corps, 23rd April 1945.
(35) R.A. 6 A/B Div., O.O.7 of 12th March 1945.
(36) Operational Research in N.W. Europe, Joint Rpt. No. 4, p. 104.
(37) " The Final Offensive in Italy ", by General McCreery, R.U.S.I. Journal, February 1947.
(38) War Diary, R.A. 5 Corps, April 1945.
(39) Operations of 2 N.Z. Div., 9th-16th April, 1945.
(40) Report on A.A. Demarcation of Line for Hy. Brs., by 12 A.A. Bde., 9th April 1945.
(41) " The Desert Air Force ", by Roderic Owen, p. 202.
(42) Operations in N.W. Europe, 6th June 1944 to 5th May 1945, Despatch by Field Marshal Montgomery, p. 4449.
(43) 2 O.R.S. Rpt. No. 11.
(44) R.A. Notes No. 28, App. " A ", Sec. G.
(45) *Ibid*, App. " A ", Sec. C. (ii).
(46) *Ibid*, para. 1589.
(47) War Diary, R.A. 21 Army Gp., May 1945.
(48) Proceedings of Committee set up to Investigate the Accuracy of Predicted Fire, September 1945, p. 21.
(49) R.A. Notes No. 28, para. 1588.
(50) " The Desert Air Force ", by Roderic Owen, p. 238.
(51) Operational Research in N.W. Europe, Sec. 19.
(52) 2 O.R.S. Rpt. No. 7.
(53) R.A.T.M. No. 14 of June 1945.
(54) R.A. Notes No. 28, pp. 1, 18.
(55) W.O. File 20/AA/639.
(56) R.A.T.M. (AA) No. 15 of September 1945.
(57) R.A. Notes No. 29, paras. 1642, 1665 and 1666.
(58) S.H.A.E.F. Air Defence Review, April 1945.

PART VI

THE WAR IN THE FAR EAST

CHAPTER XV

THE JAPANESE OFFENSIVE

Plates Relevant to this Chapter

Nos.
39. The "Baby" 25-pr.
40. The 25-pr. on Jury axle.
41. Japanese bunkers.
42. View of Ngakyedauk Pass from Hill 1070.
43. Kohima. Objectives of Key 2 and 4. 4th May 1944.
43A. Carriage, 3.7 in. how., Mk. 2P., Towed by Jeep.
44. Kohima. Panorama showing objectives for Operation Key. 4th May, 1944.
45. Mist in the mountains.

The Jungle as an Enemy

From December, 1941, when the Japanese first arrived in Malaya, to September, 1942, when they met their first serious military reverse at the hands of the Australian forces at Milne Bay in New Guinea, British troops had been fighting in the shadows. There was, first, the shadow of Dunkirk, which had made itself felt even at this distance in time and space; and secondly, the shadow of the jungle, which was then practically an unknown quantity and, as such, was felt to be almost as hostile as the enemy himself.

There was no ostensible reason why this should be so. In the course of its history, the British Army had met the forest and the jungle as early and as often as it had met the desert, and rarely, if ever, had it failed to accommodate itself to conditions as it found them. It had never, it is true, mastered either with the scientific thoroughness of the German, yet it had recently shown an aptitude for desert fighting which, if not entirely natural, was quickly acquired and which had proved a great asset in its first decisive encounters with the Italian Army. Yet now, in its initial encounters with the Japanese, it was to find itself at a considerable disadvantage in the jungle. In Malaya, "the Japanese ability to cross rivers, swamps, jungle, etc., came as a surprise."[1] In Burma, wrote General Alexander, "the technique of jungle fighting, as understood by the Japanese, was virtually non-existent in my force."[2]

From the gunnery point of view, the jungle was certainly most uninviting. The desert had at least held out promises, even if they were not always fulfilled; but the jungle offered nothing: no view, no gun positions, no facilities for movement. Later on, closer acquaintanceship was to prove it less forbidding than it at first appeared, but in the meantime the role of the guns was very limited. Even the Japanese, in their drive down the Malay Peninsula, relied for fire support chiefly on infantry guns and mortars, with "blitz" tactics by tanks along the roads. Our own field artillery, though at times quite effective, was seldom able to make full use of its fire power owing to the difficulties of observation, the lack of suitable gun positions, and the greater mobility of the enemy resulting from his greater familiarity with the jungle and his command of the sea and the air. Moreover, in a road-bound army, the normal allotment of field artillery could seldom be accepted in the forward areas, where tracks were scarce and apt to be congested.(¹)

With the loss of Malaya and of Burma, there had been a further heavy drain upon our scanty stocks of war material, and India found herself confronted with a situation distressingly similar to that which had faced the United Kingdom two years earlier, without the great industrial resources of the latter or the sure shields of Fighter Command and the Royal Navy behind which to exploit such resources. In March, 1942, when Rangoon fell, the number of A.A. guns available was less than 150 against an estimated requirement of some 1,500 necessary to defend Calcutta (her largest city), her most important war industries and other V.Ps., which were, or were soon likely to be, within effective range of the enemy bombers. For the air defence of Calcutta, one fighter squadron was available, with eight serviceable Mohawks. Airfields in eastern India were quite inadequate and the warning system was only in a rudimentary stage.(³) Finally, when the Burma Army withdrew to Imphal in May, 1942, it had with it only 10×25 prs., 11×3.7-in. hows. and 4×2-pr. anti-tank guns. All its tanks and A.A. guns had been lost owing to a sudden rise in the River Chindwin; and to reinforce it, India had no formation fully trained and equipped.(⁴)

But what her economic and military resources could not do for her, her size and her geography could. The military strength of the Japanese, already severely taxed, could for the moment be stretched no farther, and after two carrier borne air attacks on Colombo and Trincomalee, which were met and defeated by relatively strong fighter and A.A. defences with a recently installed radar early warning system, and minor raids on two small ports on the eastern seaboard, the offensive against India came to a halt.

Once again the British forces had been given a breathing space in which to ponder the lessons of past disasters and to prepare for the future. It was obvious that the first thing to be done was to get to know the jungle. Apart from that, the problems that presented themselves to the gunner were the same as they had been in Europe after Dunkirk: the dive bomber, the tank and the mortar; which, as the Japanese were never again in a position seriously to exploit the potentialities of the first two, practically resolved themselves into the single problem of the mortar. The Japanese, like the German, used his mortars with considerable skill, and they were of course particularly suitable for jungle warfare.

The British Attack in Arakan, December, 1942 to May, 1943

The matter was brought to a head by the operations in Arakan from December, 1942 to May, 1943. In an attempt—and, as it subsequently appeared, a successful attempt—to stave off a Japanese attack on India, it was decided to stage a limited offensive in Arakan. The original idea was to capture Akyab by a sea-borne operation, with the 14th Indian Division making a purely diversionary advance along the coast from Chittagong. Owing, however, to the prior claims of North Africa and Sicily, the landing craft and other facilities could not be made available, and the 14th Indian Division was left to do what it could single-handed.

Its artillery consisted of the usual two field and one mountain regiment, plus one L.A.A. regiment. It could also count on the support of a few tanks.

But unfortunately, owing to administrative difficulties, there was a delay of ten days during a rather critical stage of the advance, which enabled the Japanese to bring up reinforcements and strengthen their positions. When, therefore, the advance was resumed on 6th January, 1943, it came up against well prepared defences, which could not be overcome with the resources available. The first attack failed mainly because of the difficulty of locating the enemy machine-guns and mortars; and three more attacks, after some initial successes, failed to drive the enemy from the battlefield. Although our troops were able to penetrate some distance into his positions, they could not deal with his underground strong points, or " bunkers ", which remained in action behind them regardless of the defensive fire brought down upon their heads by their own guns, mortars and machine-guns.([5])

As a tactical ruse, this was not new. It had been successfully used by the Australians when they helped to break Rommel's first attack on Tobruk (see p. 79), and it was indeed the accepted method for dealing with an attack by armoured formations. But it was disconcerting to troops who lacked the means, or had not yet acquired the art, of destroying the bunkers and forcing their garrisons into the open; and our discomfiture was completed when the enemy, in his counter-attack, once more exploited his greater familiarity with the jungle and so got round our flanks. By the start of the monsoon, our forces in Arakan were back approximately in the positions from which the advance had begun five months earlier.

Reorganization of the Divisional Artillery

Clearly, it was necessary not only that we should get to know the jungle, as we had got to know the desert, but also that we should overhaul our whole system for giving fire support to the infantry. If ever it was true, as some gunners maintained, that all artillery support within the division was close support, then it was true in the jungle. In the " free for all " jungle mix-ups, close shoots predominated and F.O.Os. not in the front line were practically useless.

These conditions were not peculiar to Arakan. The whole Indo-Burmese frontier, on which our troops were to fight for the next two years for the defence of India, was mountainous, heavily forested and quite undeveloped. The height of the hills rose from about 2,000 feet in Arakan to over 10,000 feet at the north-eastern end of the frontier, and their sides were mostly covered with jungle so dense that it was not possible to move without cutting paths.

Nor was the jungle the only obstacle to movement. In Arakan, the " chaungs " (waterways), with which the coastal strip was intersected, were almost as great an obstacle as the hills and the jungle; and during the south-west monsoon in the summer, the rice-growing areas, which covered most of the plains, were turned into muddy swamps that were quite impassable to wheeled transport until proper roads had been constructed. In Assam and Burma also, the heavy rains between May and October made the native tracks almost impassable and turned the rivers and streams into formidable obstacles.([6])

In New Guinea, the Australians had to contend with a terrain that was even more primitive and forbidding to the stranger. They felt indeed that they were fighting " not only the Japanese, but also the country "([7]), and at first they had thought that in such country the use of artillery was out of the question. As their experience of the jungle increased, however, they changed their opinion, and with the arrival of the Lethbridge Mission from the United Kingdom in the latter half of 1943, much discussion ensued about what the organization and equipment of the divisional artillery should be.

In the Indian Army, which was designed primarily for the defence of the north-west frontier, the divisional artillery was composed of two ordinary field regiments and one mountain regiment, the latter equipped with 3.7-in. hows., which had a maximum range of about 6,000 yards and which were entirely pack transported. On the north-east frontier, it was evident, greater cross-country mobility would be required. The 25-pr., good gun as it was—and it was considered by many to be the most successful gun of the war—was for once unable to do everything that was required of it. It was simply impossible to get it forward, at any rate in the early stages of an operation; and, as a substitute, the 3.7-in. how. lacked the range to deal with the Japanese 75-mm. infantry gun, which could fire up to 7,500 yards. Moreover, even if its range could be increased—as it was, later, to 6,800 yards—there were still other difficulties to be overcome. Production capacity existed only in India and was limited to about 12 equipments a month. There was also a shortage of mules and of personnel of the correct " classes " in India. Finally, if guns and mules and personnel could be found, there remained the problem of feeding large quantities of animals in a country where fodder was scarce and transport already seriously overtaxed.

The introduction of a new establishment for a mountain regiment, allowing for a combination of pack and mechanical transport, helped to ease the problem but did not entirely solve it. Various other special equipments were considered, but all were turned down for one reason or another. The American 75-mm. pack howitzer, for example, had the range but not the weight of shell considered necessary. A new 25-pr. pack howitzer would have had the great advantage of using the same projectile as the existing field gun; and the 95-mm. infantry gun, if re-designed as a pack howitzer, would have given better shell power than any of the others.([8]) But these were both long term projects and were in consequence abandoned, attention being concentrated on increasing the range of the 3.7-in. how. to 6,800 yards.

It appeared that the only way out of the difficulty was to follow the example of the enemy and to make more use of the mortar. In North Africa and in Europe, it will be remembered, there had been some argument about who should bear the responsibility for counter-mortar measures and for the handling of the 4.2-in. mortars in our own Army. Since their effectiveness depended largely on the use of gunner fire control methods, 4.2-in. mortar teams had received their initial training under the supervision of Cs.R.A., and in the later stages of the war superfluous anti-tank gunners had sometimes been used in this role.

Here in the jungle, it was a question not merely of dealing with the enemy mortars, but also of using our own mortars in the normal field artillery role. Though slightly disturbing at first to the conventionally minded, who felt that they were losing caste by being armed with a weapon of such paltry range, the idea was logically flawless. Since the weapon of the artillery was the shell and not the gun, there could be no objection to the substitution of a mortar for a gun. What mattered was that the infantry should at all times be accompanied by supporting weapons manned by artillerymen and capable of giving adequate and guaranteed quick support. In the jungle, mobility was of far greater importance than range and weight of shell, and for mobility nothing could equal the 3-in. mortar.

Thus, in the general reorganization that took place in 1943, each divisional artillery (except those of the armoured and assault divisions) was given a proportion of 3-in. mortar and 3.7-in. how. batteries, some on a mule and others on a jeep-cum-porter basis (*see* Table K). In view of the relatively slight air and armoured threat in the jungle, the ordinary divisional A.A. and anti-tank regiments were condensed into one mixed regiment, as in the armoured divisional artillery of 1938 (*see* p. 18). The two A.A. batteries were armed initially with 12 Bofors each, which were to be replaced by 18 × 20-mms. as soon as these became available. The two anti-tank batteries were eventually to be equipped with 6-prs., but as these guns were still scarce, some units received 57-mms., of which a consignment had recently arrived from America, and others retained the 2-pr. The adoption of the Middle East portee mounting for the 2-pr. was considered, but was ruled out for general use because of the length of its wheel-base, which made it unsuitable for use in Assam and similar country.

In New Guinea, where, as has been mentioned above, the practicability of employing any kind of artillery was at first questioned, a reduction of the divisional artillery to two regiments—one of 25-prs. and one of light pack howitzers—was recommended ; the idea being that the third field regiment per division should be held in corps reserve, in addition to the normal corps artillery, and be used whenever opportunity offered.

The Jungle Field Regiment

The peculiar feature of the new Indian divisional artillery organization was the jungle field regiment, composed of two batteries each of 8 mechanized 3.7-in. hows. and one battery of 16 jeep-transported 3-in. mortars. The 3.7-in. batteries were to be employed in the same way as 25-pr. batteries, the main advantage of the new weapon being that it could be towed by a jeep or taken to pieces quite easily for loading into boats, aircraft or other improvised means of transport.

Mortar batteries were also to be used as far as possible as field batteries, with the troop—or occasionally the section—as the fire unit, and with a normal engagement range of 400 to 1,200 yards. Link shoots could be undertaken, so that the fire of all 16 mortars could be brought down on a single target as the result of ranging by one mortar ; and predicted shoots, including three or four lines of a barrage, could also be fired with satisfactory results—provided that targets were chosen in some depth or to a flank and not in close proximity to our own troops. The necessary degree of accuracy was obtained by departing from the normal infantry drill and relaying after every round. Although this slowed down the rate of fire slightly, it greatly reduced the zone, especially the breadth zone.[9]

The short range of the 3-in. mortar—at that time limited to 1,600 yards—undoubtedly interfered with flexibility of fire and made frequent changes of position necessary in an attack. It also greatly reduced its effectiveness in the counter-mortar role. But by strengthening the base plate it was possible to increase the range to 3,500 yards (see p. 170) without materially affecting the weight, and hence the portability, of the weapon.

The "Baby" 25-pr. and the Jury Axle

Meanwhile attempts were being made to improve the mobility of the ordinary field gun in the jungle. In the S.W. Pacific area, the Australians had produced a light—or "Baby"—25-pr. by shortening the piece. It had of course certain disadvantages: its range was less than that of the ordinary gun, and, because its balance had been upset, it was apt to be unstable when firing, and it was not an easy equipment to tow. But the facility with which it could be dismantled and reassembled, and transported on small craft, small vehicles or sledges, appeared to outweigh these disadvantages. It was therefore decided, in that theatre, to make it the standard equipment of one battery in every field regiment.

In the operations in New Guinea in September 1943, ending with the recapture of Lae, this decision was considered to have justified itself. For the first time, Australian artillerymen were parachuted into action, and, owing partly to the increased mobility of the light 25-pr., an adequate number of guns was kept in range of successive objectives during a quick advance, without disrupting sea and land communications by giving undue priority to the movement of artillery. Thus, sufficient support was always available to the infantry, and 22 guns, including 2 × 155-mm, were in action within easy range of the final objective on the day resistance ceased.[10]

In the India Command the problem had been tackled in a different, and apparently no less successful, manner. On the north-east frontier the chief obstacle to movement was the narrowness of the jungle paths, and it was found that by shortening the axle of the 25-pr., its mobility could be considerably increased. This entailed some minor adjustments to the trail fittings and other parts of the carriage, but it did not seriously affect the stability of the gun in action or reduce its range, as did the shortening of the piece in the Australian pattern of light 25-pr. It was therefore accepted in lieu of the latter, and its subsequent performance in action during 1944 and 1945 was satisfactory.

Inter-communication and Observation

After mobility, the two greatest problems were inter-communication and observation. In dense jungle it was extremely difficult to find ground O.Ps., which had often to be within 50 yards of the enemy positions. The limited field of view, and the difficulty of moving about, sometimes necessitated the use of as many as four O.Ps. to each troop[11]; and if the jungle was very thick, there might be no field of view at all and observations might have to be based on sound alone.[12] Hence communications were long and their maintenance was not easy, although a partial solution was found by laying trunk lines along the axis of advance of each battalion, to which connections could be made by light cable run from O.Ps. and troop positions.

The multiplicity of O.Ps. led inevitably to an increase in the establishment of signallers, and, as in Tunisia and Italy (see p. 167), field artillery O.Ps.

were converted, as required, from a wheeled to a pack basis. For this purpose, extra mules were allotted as a pool and held on the establishment of the mountain regiments.

The value of wireless as an alternative means of inter-communication was limited by the interference, or screening effect, that was characteristic of all mountainous—and to some extent also of jungle—country; and by the difficulty of combining power and mobility in the wireless instrument. The No. 11 set, which provided the minimum amount of power necessary for O.P. work, required eight men to transport it for any considerable distance; and for maintaining touch between F.O.Os. and infantry, there was at that time no absolutely reliable set of the "walkie-talkie" type—though, with really well-trained operators, a great deal could be got out of the 48 Set.([10])

The tank O.P., which had proved so useful in North Africa and in Europe, was not at this time available; and later, when it became available, it proved of little value for fighting at close quarters in the jungle. When closed down, the F.O.O. could not observe, and when opened up, he was immediately picked off by a sniper. For co-operating with tanks, therefore, the F.O.O. was regarded as better employed in a static O.P. on a hill-top, with a set on the tank frequency, over which the squadron or troop commander could call for fire.([13])

The easiest way out of all these difficulties was of course air observation, and during the early operations in New Guinea some valuable assistance was given by the Wirraways of a Royal Australian Air Force army co-operation squadron. But the indication and identification of targets here interposed further difficulties, which could not always be surmounted. There was a similarity and monotony about jungle landscapes that was very confusing to air pilots, and even if the correct area could be found, the target itself might still remain invisible or indistinguishable from its surroundings. Smoke, as an aid, would often fail through the blanketing effect of the foliage, or the irregular behaviour of the containers on a hillside (*see* p. 31), and the normal difficulties of ranging were thereby greatly increased.

Hence close liaison and constant practice between gunners and air observer was of more than usual importance, and the advantages to be derived from the use of an air O.P. needed no emphasizing. At first, like so many other things, the air O.P. had been a luxury denied to our forces in this theatre. Now that the critical stages of the war in Europe were over, and victory over Germany appeared to be assured, equipment began to trickle eastwards.

The question was, could the necessary landing grounds be found, or improvised, for the use of the air O.P. in jungle country? The general opinion was that it was worth trying, and by the end of February, 1944, the first air O.P. flight was in action with 15 Indian Corps in Arakan, and later a squadron less a flight joined 4 Corps in the Imphal area.

"Bunker Busting"

There remained the important problem of the "bunker", which had proved so troublesome a feature of the Japanese defensive systems both in Arakan and in the S.W. Pacific. Of all the tactical devices that earned the temporary notoriety of a nickname, the bunker was alone to win permanent recognition as an original feature of the Second World War, and was thus to take its place beside the pill-box, which was its European counterpart of the First World War.([14])

The difference between them lay mainly in their structure and siting. The bunker was built of timber and earth, instead of concrete, and was often dug well down into the side of a hill, where, concealed by the undergrowth, it offered cunningly sited fire positions for its own weapons and solid shelter for its garrison against the fire of other weapons whether directed by friend or foe.

Both were pin-point targets and had to be clearly seen, therefore, before they could be effectively engaged. In the jungle, more often than not, this meant the preliminary disclosure of the bunker by the removal of the undergrowth that concealed it. For this purpose, the 25-pr. and the 3.7-in. how., firing H.E., proved very suitable.

To destroy such a target by indirect methods was a lengthy and expensive proceeding if undertaken with a weapon like the 25-pr., which had not the shell power to achieve its object with a single direct hit. Thus we find among the lessons of the Arakan fighting in the spring of 1943, that if a frontal attack, however small, had to be made against a Japanese prepared position, it should form the subject of a divisional fire plan and receive the support of Vengeance dive bombers or of 6-in. hows., which were the only weapons then available that were capable of dealing with the enemy bunkers.([15])

With the arrival, later in the year, of some 5.5 in. guns, " bunker busting " by medium artillery became quite fashionable. The method usually adopted was as follows. The enemy position was first thoroughly reconnoitred, both from the air and from the ground. The softening of the area was then carried out by a series of slow destructive shoots on known enemy strong points. Each round would be observed and the whole area would be systematically covered. If necessary, the shoot would begin with the clearing of the scrub, and the bunkers thus uncovered would be destroyed by single guns or sections of 5.5-in., with an average expenditure of 15 rounds.([16])

At the same time extensive trials were held, which, although confirming existing theories about the indirect engagement of bunkers, showed that the 25-pr. and 3.7-in. how. could do the job by firing direct, with H.E. fuze 231, from a range of about 600 yards. If the H.E. did not appear to be having the desired effect, the bunker could be " softened " by the use of 25-pr. A.P. shot.([17])

This was a step towards the " pick and shovel " method that was later to be developed in Europe (*see* p. 254) for the attack of concrete, and during the next bout of fighting in Arakan, in January, 1944, the same procedure was followed by the 75-mm. guns of Lee tanks; for example, in the attack on the Razabil Fortress by the 161st and 123rd Indian Infantry Brigades. After a preliminary air bombardment by the strategic air force and by dive bombers, and an artillery bombardment by medium, field and mountain guns, the tanks moved forward to carry out—from ranges of 100 to 300 yards—a systematic destruction of the bunkers that had been pin-pointed. First, superquick H.E. was used to clear the undergrowth; then A.P. shot was used to loosen the earth about two to three feet below the timbered fire rest; and finally, delay action H.E. shell were fired through the now unprotected structure and burst inside the bunker.([18])

From here it was but a short step to the use of the 6-pr. anti-tank gun, which became fairly common during the later stages of the war in Burma. The chief problem was of course to get the gun within effective range—about 75 to 300 yards—of the target. In one A.A./anti-tank regiment this was done by digging a pit in the selected position under cover of darkness, and bringing in the gun either dismantled or manhandled on its wheels or on a toboggan. As soon as it was possible for the layer to see the slit of the bunker through his telescope, he opened fire with A.P. shot, and when the slit had been sufficiently enlarged, changed to H.E. and fired another 10 to 50 rounds through the hole. In some cases, when the slit was big, it was not necessary to fire A.P. shot at all.([19])

Fire Plans in the Jungle

The conditions of jungle warfare had not hitherto offered much opportunity for the use of artillery fire on a large scale. The Japanese, for their part, usually employed their guns singly. Misled perhaps by their easy successes in China and Malaya, they had clung to the simple tactics that had won them those victories: the extensive use of direct fire and the frequent relegation of artillery units to an " accompanying " role in direct support of the infantry. Rarely did more than two guns engage a target simultaneously, and then they fired only a few rounds at a time.

At first we tended to follow their example, but as our troops became more familiar with the jungle, and the systems of inter-communication and observation of fire were improved, the principles of massed artillery fire were found to be as applicable to jungle as to any other kind of warfare. In spite of the many difficulties with which it was faced, artillery survey soon began to function well, both in the S.W. Pacific and in S.E. Asia, and with its aid predicted shoots were often carried out. Mobile meteorological sections helped to overcome the inevitable meteor difficulties, and when maps were non-existent or unreliable, the air burst grid, as used in the desert (*see* p. 150), offered a quick means of putting the guns of a regiment, or of a divisional artillery, into harmony with each other. In the jungle, however, air bursts were not always easy to see, and the method was therefore seldom if ever used in action.

What distinguished the Far Eastern from the European theatres was the great distances, the lack of roads and railways in most areas, and the thick scrub which abounded almost everywhere and especially on the steep hill features. In such circumstances, it was maintenance that was the greatest problem, and the supply of ammunition became the limiting factor in the preparation of fire plans. During the early operations in New Guinea, where ammunition had on one occasion to be carried by porters across four miles of trackless jungle, it took 20 men a whole day to collect 20 rounds.([12]) Later, with the introduction of the jeep and the development of air supply, the situation improved, but at no time could the artillery indulge in the lavish expenditure of ammunition that was customary in N.W. Europe.

Partly for this reason, and partly because of the terrain, the barrage was seldom used. It was expensive in ammunition, and timing was difficult as the rate of advance was unpredictable. It was also apt to embarrass our own infantry—as it did in the Reichswald (*see* p. 267)—through premature bursts among the trees.

On the other hand, pre-arranged concentrations were often impracticable owing to the difficulty of locating the enemy strong points. Even when, by clearing the jungle with H.E. fire, the strong points were exposed to view, there was still the problem of how to cover the infantry across the last few yards of their ascent to the objective.

The Razabil fighting, just mentioned, took place over open paddy fields, which provided good fields of fire and an easy tank approach to the objective. Yet the first two attacks failed because the Japanese bunker system was more elaborate than had been thought and because there was too long a pause between the cessation of tank fire and the time the infantry reached their objective. On the second occasion, when the tanks stopped firing, the Japanese crept out of their trenches and dropped grenades on the Dogras beneath them; and when, at the request of the battalion commander, the tanks opened fire again with A.P. and H.E. delayed action, the Japanese still succeeded in beating off the attack by light automatic fire from a neighbouring locality.

It was the problem of Keren over again (see p. 56), and it was only finally solved by the closest co-operation between infantry, tanks, artillery and the air force. In this way, a technique was evolved that was expected to reduce the last 100 yards to 10 yards. The tanks lived with the infantry before the attack and got to know the country; the gunners carried out their deliberate destructive shoots against known strong points; and then, at zero hour, guns and mortars put down a heavy concentration, under cover of which the infantry moved to the start line and the tanks to their pre-arranged fire positions. When the artillery concentration lifted, a pause was usually necessary to allow the smoke and dust to drift away and enable the tank gunners to see their targets. The infantry crossed the start line as the first tank fired, and the tanks continued to fire H.E. until the infantry were about 25 yards from the objective. They then changed to A.P. shot, and finally to co-axial Browning, which was fired immediately over the heads of the infantry as they moved onto the top.

For the sake of surprise, a pause might be introduced during the progress of the assault, to tempt the enemy to leave their shelters and see what was happening, whereupon they would be caught by a burst of fire from the tanks, the artillery, and sometimes the cannon-firing Hurrifighters.[18]

The success of this method depended of course upon the ability of the tank to approach close to the objective and, by taking advantage of its high velocity, flat trajectory gun, to cover the infantry almost the whole of the way up to the objective. When tanks were not available, concentrations by corps and divisional artilleries were not always satisfactory. The jungle might be destroyed, or thinned, and a certain amount of damage would be done to the enemy defences, but the infantry still had to assault the top of the hill without artillery support and were either driven off or prevented from capturing their objective by fire from the position itself or from supporting localities. Success, therefore, was not reasonably certain and the expenditure of ammunition was high. It was found that the best results were obtained by a slower rate of fire over a longer period. For example, for the support of an infantry brigade, one 25-pr. regiment and one medium battery would concentrate on the objective—the latter in the initial stages only—while one close support regiment was employed on the neutralization of the objective or its supporting localities at the discretion of the C.R.A.'s representative with the infantry. The object was to destroy all known bunkers before the attack, and subsequently to keep them under intermittent fire ending with a short bombardment of maximum intensity as the attack went in (*cf.* p. 236). Fire was stopped either on a timed programme or when ordered as the infantry approached the objective.[16]

The Battle of the Administrative Box

In February 1944, when the Japanese began their counter-offensive in Arakan, the situation was not altogether unlike that at Gazala in May 1942. The 5th and 7th Indian Divisions were spread out—as was inevitable in this country—in brigade areas, and the Japanese plan was, by infiltrating through the jungle that separated them, to pass through and round the left flank of the 7th Indian Division, attack it in rear, isolate it from the 5th Indian Division, and then destroy each formation in detail.

But for once infiltration failed to produce for the enemy the results he had so confidently anticipated. With sufficient command of the air, and enough transport aircraft, to make supply from the air possible, the loss of a land L. of C. was no longer decisive. The three brigades of the 7th Indian Division dug in on their positions—which were referred to, reminiscently, as "boxes"—and a fourth defended area was hastily prepared to cover the administrative base at the eastern entrance to the Ngakyedauk Pass (*see* Map 21).

Side by side with command of the air went control of the ether. By making full use of wireless, the physical isolation of the four boxes was prevented from interfering with the centralized control of the artillery. Thus, flexibility of fire within the division was maintained, and the guns, closely sited in the brigade boxes, were able to fire on divisional targets throughout the whole period; sometimes to deal with attacks inside the administrative box and sometimes to assist outside. Indeed assistance was also obtained from the guns of the 5th Indian Division on the other side of the Mayu range, and corps (Victor) targets were engaged.

The result was a complete victory. Though closely invested by the Japanese, and subjected to frequent attacks supported by 150-mm. guns and fighter-bombers, not one of the boxes was lost. By 20th February, the Japanese troops in rear of the 7th Indian Division began to try and escape; and by 24th February, the enemy offensive in this area had been finally defeated.

The greatest cause of anxiety to the gunners during this period was the difficulty of identifying one's own troops, and the extremely close shooting often demanded. This was characteristic of all jungle fighting, especially against the Japanese, who had been trained to take advantage of the cover offered by the jungle and, by gaining and maintaining the closest contact with our troops, to escape the worst effects of our defensive fire. Under these conditions, the 3.7-in. how. proved a valuable adjunct to a defended locality, and the mortar " possibly the most useful weapon we had."[20] A number of the latter, found in the ordnance depot, were quickly distributed for use by the divisional anti-tank regiment.

The Japanese Offensive Against Imphal and Kohima

Thus the mistakes of 1942 had been avoided and the principle of concentration had been vindicated. But the Japanese had not yet "shot their bolt", and early in March, 1944, they began their last all-out offensive against India with twin thrusts up the Manipur River and Kabaw valleys. Again, by infiltration through the jungle, their troops got round the flanks of our foremost formations and isolated the small British garrison at Kohima from the main 4 Corps defended area at Imphal. But again the loss of a land L. of C. was counterbalanced by the use of air power, and the over-bold initial advance of the enemy proved his undoing. Reinforcements were rushed, by air and by rail, from Arakan, where the enemy threat was now completely liquidated, and the 2nd Division of 33 Indian Corps was brought by similar means from Bombay, where it had been training for combined operations.

In the four days that were available, this Division was re-equipped and reorganized in accordance with its new role. The "Priests" (see Table K) were replaced by 25-prs., and the 6-gun 3.7-in. how. batteries were organized into two troops each of 4×3.7-in. hows., thus bringing them into line with the 25-pr. batteries and simplifying their subsequent conversion to 25-pr. batteries for the advance from the Chindwin to Mandalay. At the same time the anti-tank batteries were armed with 3-in. mortars as their secondary weapon, in anticipation of close country and a scarcity of Japanese tanks.

Neither air nor rail transport facilities could compete with the artillery vehicles. The majority of the latter had to move by road, so that there were delays of up to 16 days in their arrival, and in the meantime some of their detachments again had an opportunity of proving their adaptability. In Arakan, anti-tank gunners had turned themselves at short notice into mortar detachments. Here a field regiment was hurriedly equipped with two 5.5-in. medium guns, extracted from the base ordnance depot at Dimapur, and for nearly two months these guns, manned by scratch detachments from the Divisional Artillery, represented the Corps medium artillery.

The base was saved and soon operations were on foot for the relief of Kohima. In spite of the difficult terrain, massed artillery fire was provided by the 2nd Divisional Artillery; occasionally from positions that were very unorthodox and were perhaps only rendered possible by the feebleness of the enemy's counter-battery organization. For example, for the attack on milestone 88, there were 2×5.5-in., 8×3.7-in. hows. and 8×25-prs. lined up in that order from front to rear, all jostling each other in a courtyard that was already fairly full with tanks and brigade M.T. On the opposite side of the road was a 3.7-in. how. battery in action in line ahead, and in the only other possible gun position—on the road some three miles further back —were another 25-pr. battery and a troop of mediums. Before nightfall the guns were registered and the next morning, after a heavy artillery concentration, the infantry advanced and found only one live and dazed Japanese on the position.

Throughout the operations at Kohima covering fire, as in Arakan, had to be brought down extremely close to our own troops. At one time our night perimeter enclosed a crowded hill top, not more than 300 yards by 250 yards in extent, with the Japanese only about 20 to 50 yards away to the north and south. All movement by day was made hazardous by the activities of Japanese snipers, and many smoke screens were put down to cover the necessary programme of reliefs. By night, harassing fire was directed against the most important of the enemy localities at intervals of about half-an-hour.(13)

It was in the assault that the closest support became necessary, and here the combined fire of tanks and artillery again proved most successful. Whenever possible, all available weapons—infantry mortars, M.M.Gs., tank 75-mms., 6-prs., and Bofors—were brought into the fire plans, and the mortars were brigaded so that control was easier and the results of their fire more effective, especially against reverse slope positions that could not be reached by the guns. It also helped to conserve artillery ammunition, which was very short. But the infantry " had constantly to be reminded to bring them into fire plans and to use them for D.F. and S.O.S. tasks "(13); a sign perhaps that here, as elsewhere, we still had something to learn from the enemy regarding the handling of this weapon (see p. 170).

The general procedure for the assault was similar to that employed by the 78th Division in its attack in the mountains of Tunisia (see p. 166). The operation would begin with a concentration by guns and mortars for up to 20 minutes, to clear the jungle and camouflage from the Japanese bunkers, and to allow time for the infantry to creep forward to their assaulting positions. Then there might be a pause to allow the infantry to make any necessary adjustments to their positions, after which the concentration would be repeated for 10 to 20 minutes, without the medium guns and with 25-prs. and 3.7-in. hows. firing capped fuzes so that the infantry might work forward as close as possible. This concentration would end with a one-round salvo from all guns, using some coloured smoke if available. The tanks, 6-prs. and Bofors would then open up, with the M.M.Gs. firing just ahead of the tanks: a kind of miniature "pepperpot" (see p. 264). The infantry would put up 77 grenade smoke every 30 to 50 yards and the "pepperpot" would lift accordingly. Meanwhile the divisional artillery would lift on to all possible covering positions, using a high proportion of smoke and "flick" concentrations if the positions were numerous. The medium guns, after the initial bombardment, would devote their attention to known or suspected enemy guns and mortars (see Map 22).

As in all timed programmes, success depended on the infantry maintaining the rate of movement expected of them. In the jungle this was more than usually difficult to guarantee, not so much because of enemy interference as of the thick undergrowth and the difficulty of estimating the distance to be traversed. For this reason, the infantry forming-up position was sometimes indicated by 77 grenade smoke, and was adjusted by the brigade commander if he did not think it was close enough to the enemy. When satisfied, he would inform all concerned of the time at which the artillery bombardment would start.(13)

As an example of how close this support might be, one might take the attack by a company of Gurkhas on a Japanese defended locality known as Gun Spur. At "H" – 1 minute, after the customary preliminary bombardment—which on this occasion included tanks—the mediums and 3.7-in. hows. switched and the company advanced to within 50 yards of the 25-pr. shell bursts. At "H" hour the tanks changed from H.E. to A.P. and continued firing about 10 yards in front of the leading infantry, whose flank men wore white towels on their backs to indicate their positions to the tank commander. As the attack went in there was a cloud burst, and the C.O., not being able to see the white towels, thought the company was late in starting and ordered the tanks to continue firing for another five minutes. In fact the company had started on time, and while waiting for the fire to lift, the leading troops crept closer, with the result that they went in less than 10 yards behind the covering fire and found many of the Japanese still crouching in their trenches. Out of a garrison of about 60, 20 were killed and buried, 20 more were probably killed, and 20 got away.[21]

Counter-battery Difficulties

Throughout these operations, we were handicapped by the shortage of medium artillery, and the short range of the few 5.5-in. guns that were available. The new 80-lb. shell for this equipment (*see* p. 179) had not yet reached India, and without it our guns lacked the range necessary to deal with the Japanese 105-mms. Hurribombers were, however, successfully used for counter-battery work with the aid of " block plot " air photographs (*see* p. 183) and, when available, a large scale map.[22]

The climate was another factor that often interfered with counter-battery and harassing fire arrangements; for example, during the advance to the Chindwin in July 1944, when 33 Indian Corps came up against a strongly entrenched Japanese position in the Shenam area, above Palel. For the attack on this position, a corps artillery group of two field and one medium regiment and one H.A.A. battery was formed, and, with the assistance of two squadrons of Hurribombers, was to have carried out a ten-day preliminary programme of harassing and counter-battery fire. On eight out of the ten days, however, there was almost continuous mist over the enemy positions, which were 5,000 feet above mean sea level. Day after day it was impossible to " soften up " or even register corps targets, and it was only with difficulty that targets for the attack could be registered; but two 5.5-in. were emplaced in the open and effectively softened one of the most important Japanese hill positions, while a troop of 25-prs., after a most difficult trek round the flank, was able to shoot up another of these positions from the rear.

When the attack by the 23rd Indian Division went in on 24th July, the corps artillery group remained in support of the whole divisional front under command of the C.C.R.A.; an arrangement due to the configuration of the ground, the difficulty of inter-communication, and the wide front on which the Division was to attack. The enemy artillery—4 × 150-mm. guns, 12 × 105-mm. and 24 field guns—had by this time mostly been pin-pointed, and the attack was a complete success. The Japanese withdrew, disorganized, down the road leaving much gun ammunition behind them.

Over the 17th Indian Divisional area, in the Bishenpur-Moirang plain, the recently arrived air O.P. proved very useful, and later, in November 1944, when an air O.P. flight had at last joined 33 Indian Corps, it also proved invaluable in the flat wooded country of the Kabaw Valley. In the mountainous jungle, however, up to 90 per cent. of the sorties were ineffectual.[23]

Flash spotting and sound ranging were seldom practicable in the jungle, chiefly because of the Japanese habit of using only one gun at a time, but also because of the difficulty of providing O.Ps., microphone bases and communications.([24]) Altogether it was a difficult problem, and the Japanese themselves made little attempt to exploit the range of their 105-mm. guns in a C.B. role. Both here and in New Guinea, their counter-battery methods consisted mainly of infantry attacks by organized parties about 20 to 30 strong, which infiltrated into our positions by day and attacked the gun positions after dark. The best weapons for countering such attacks were the grenade and the bayonet, and it was therefore evident that in the jungle as elsewhere—indeed in the jungle more than anywhere else—every officer and man in an artillery unit should be armed with a personal weapon, either carbine or rifle.([25])

It followed that battery and troop commanders should carefully organize their gun positions against this form of attack, and exercise the strictest fire control in the use of small arms. In the 7th Indian Division, for example, each gun pit, command post and small unit was made responsible for its own defence and was surrounded by trip wires, in addition to the normal wiring of a troop position. No sub-unit went to the assistance of another, and anything seen above ground by night was shot. This avoided casualties in a local "civil war".

It was found inadvisable for gunners to sleep in gun pits, as these were invariably the target for Japanese grenades. Hence sleeping trenches were dug radially outwards from the pit, as shown below, provided with overhead cover and finished off with a fighting pit at their outer extremities. Two sentries to each gun pit were on duty and each man of the detachment had a cord tied to his ankle so that he could be awakened to take post silently.

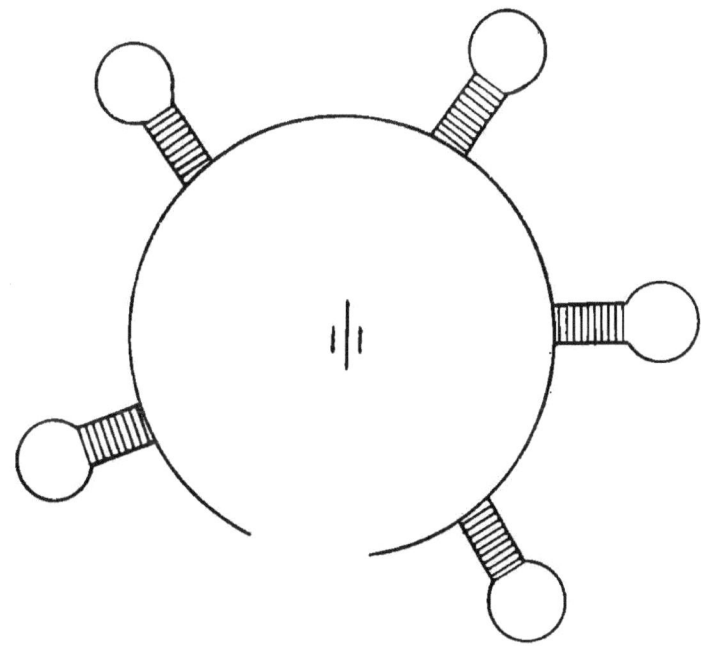

Upper Register Firing

Another constant source of trouble to the gunner was the enemy reverse slope position. Similar difficulties had been experienced in Italian East Africa, Tunisia and Italy, but with the growth of our superiority in the air and the development of direct air support, they had on the whole been successfully overcome. In S.E. Asia we had not yet built up the same overwhelming superiority in the air, and in any case direct air support was sometimes impracticable owing to the difficulty of identifying targets from the air. At Kohima, as has been seen, the problem was tackled by the use of brigaded infantry mortars. But the range of the 3-in. mortar was limited, and there was an insistent demand for high angle fire by guns, particularly the 3.7-in. how. and the 25-pr.([26])

It was for this purpose that incremental charges had been introduced for the 25-pr. in Italy (*see* p. 180), and the same arrangements were made by the Australians in New Guinea.([24]) But these incremental charges did not go far enough and still greater angles of descent were sought by means of upper register firing.

There were certain technical difficulties to be overcome, and in Europe the use of upper register firing was not generally considered to be worth the trouble that it entailed (*see* p. 241). In South-East Asia, however, no trouble could be too great that would help to solve the problem of the reverse slope position. Trials carried out at the School of Artillery (India) showed that the 3.7-in. how. was entirely suitable for this kind of firing, and in July, 1944, a trial was held by 33 Corps to investigate the possibilities of the 3.7-in. H.A.A. gun. The results in this case were disappointing. It was found that at high angles of elevation (in the neighbourhood of 75 degrees) and with full charge, the shell, on approaching the apex of its trajectory, developed instability which resulted in inaccurate shooting. At lower elevations in the upper register it appeared possible to obtain accurate results, but it was doubtful whether the angles of descent would then be great enough to achieve the objects of upper register firing.([27]) The project was therefore abandoned.

Indeed in general, the use of upper register firing was confined to the engagement, by observation, of pin-point targets on steep reverse slopes. Though used with airburst fuzes for counter-battery and harassing fire in Arakan in August, 1944, its accuracy was not considered reliable enough for other types of predicted shooting. The trouble was largely meteor correction, which was tremendous, unpredictable and continually changing. Accuracy was good for a short time after the m.p.i. had been adjusted, but it then rapidly deteriorated.

The "Golf Bag" Principle

The emergency issue of mortars to an anti-tank regiment in Arakan and of 5.5-in. guns to a field regiment during the Kohima fighting, and the valuable services rendered by them, offered practical confirmation of the adaptability of the modern gunner, on which the so-called "golf bag" principle had originally been based (*see* p. 253). More premeditated examples of this principle in action are to be found in the temporary re-equipment of assault field regiments with "Priests" for the Normandy landings (*see* p. 180) and of jungle field regiments in the Indian theatre with 3.7-in. hows. and 3-in.

mortars. In November, 1944, there was to be a further application of the principle when the divisional and corps artilleries were again reorganized. The operations during the first half of 1944 had shown the need, for fighting under Far Eastern conditions, of a standard infantry division that could be readily transported by rail, sea, M.T. or air; and it was decided that the artillery of this division should consist of two field regiments (instead of the existing one field and one jungle field), one mountain regiment of three (instead of the existing four) batteries each of 4×3.7-in. hows., and one anti-tank (instead of the existing A.A./anti-tank) regiment of three batteries each of 12×6-prs. and 12×3-in. mortars.([6]) One of the field regiments was to be equipped with shortened axles (*see* p. 288), and all 25-prs. were to be adapted to fire in the upper quadrant. For the anti-tank regiment, 36×3-in. mortars were to be available as an alternative to the 6-prs. when operating in country that was unsuitable to tanks. Finally, 2×7.2-in. hows. were to be held by each corps and manned as required by any artillery unit that happened to be available; probably by the H.A.A. regiment, whose personnel were being trained in their use.([28])

There had also been a demand in some quarters for the retention of the now obsolescent, but still popular, 2-pr. anti-tank gun as one of the " clubs " in the golf bag. In jungle fighting the need was felt for something that could be more easily manhandled than the 6-pr. or 57-mm., and that could be towed by something less conspicuous than the F.A. tractor. The demand was disallowed and the difficulty overcome by the production of a new Indian pattern F.A. tractor, which was less conspicuous than the old, and by the fitting of castor wheels to the 57-mms. so that they could be more easily manhandled.([29]) For anti-tank work in very hilly country, the 3.7-in. how., equipped with hollow charge ammunition, was expected to provide a satisfactory answer.([30]) Some 53,000 rounds of this ammunition were manufactured in late 1944 and 1945, and the penetration achieved under trial conditions was from 126-mm. at 0° to 70-mm. at 55° angle of impact.

Thus one additional burden of the ordnance services was avoided; and it was well that this was so, for it was becoming evident that the capacity of the " golf bag " was in danger of being over-taxed. " Too many clubs "—as it was wittily observed at the time—" might necessitate a larger golf bag, and an increase in the size of golf bags might in turn call for structural alterations in the club-house."

A.A. and C.D.

Apart from the general unpreparedness to meet an attack from the north-east, the greatest difficulty in planning the A.A. defence of India had been the distances that separated one vulnerable area from another. From the oilfields at Digboi, in North-East Assam, to the advanced base at Dimapur (Manipur Road) is about 150 miles; from Dimapur to Chittagong (the advanced base for Arakan) about 270 miles; from Chittagong to Calcutta about 220 miles; and from Calcutta to Jamshedpur (one of the main industrial centres) about 150 miles; and all these figures represent the distances as flown, not as driven over country roads, across difficult and often unbridged rivers, and sometimes along narrow mountain tracks, where " wash-outs " were not uncommon in the rainy season.

There was, therefore, little scope for flexibility in the A.A. defences as a whole. The move of A.A. guns from one of these areas to another was a matter of days—sometimes of weeks—rather than of hours, and even fighter aircraft allotted for the defence of Calcutta could not readily intervene at other places, owing partly to the lack of airfield facilities and partly to the gaps in the early warning system. Radar sets, even if available in sufficient quantities, could not easily be sited or maintained in the vast jungle no-man's land that separated the two armies, and mobile observation posts equipped with wireless sets (for inter-communication) could not be expected to cover more than a fraction of the requisite area.

During the monsoon of 1942, therefore, the greatest care had to be taken in deploying A.A. regiments as they became available, so that the many vulnerable areas and airfields would be protected by the end of it. In the event, when the Japanese began to raid in October, 1942, he was adequately and successfully engaged wherever he came and in fact all vital areas had some degree of A.A. protection. There was a certain waste of effort in deploying guns outside the probable range of enemy air activity, but this was unavoidable owing to strong demands by the U.S.A. and Indian civilian authorities.

In the three moderate raids made on U.S.A. airfields in N.E. Assam in October, 1942, the attackers lost about 20 per cent. of their aircraft, and this may well have acted as a deterrent and accounted for the small scale and limited scope of subsequent raids. It was fortunate that it was so, because the effect of even token raids on the coolie labour at Manipur Road base, the Brahmaputra crossing at Gauhati, and airfields under construction would probably have been very serious.

Partly because of all this dispersion, there was no attempt to reproduce the system of command that had grown up in A.D.G.B., with its heavy overheads in A.A. divisional and corps staffs. At one time in the Eastern Army there were five A.A. brigades whose local administration was carried out by field formations or L. of C. areas, while the operational and training command was exercised by a brigadier with five staff officers.

This was only a portion—if the most important portion—of the A.A. problem. About 400 and 900 miles S.S.W. of Calcutta lay Vizagapatam and Madras, which, as subsidiary ports for operations in the Bay of Bengal, had to have some defences. Still further away, on the Malabar Coast, was Cochin, and even Bombay at one time was not altogether exempt from the threat of carrier-borne air attack. Finally, there was Ceylon, which was vital to the Royal Navy and had therefore a high priority in the scale of A.A. defence.

Fortunately, once the equipment had arrived from the United Kingdom, an adequate supply of personnel could be obtained by using the largely untapped resources of southern India. Madrassi recruits, with the aid of selected N.C.O. instructors sent out from A.A. Command, and of a vast new A.A. training centre built up out of nothing at Mehgaon in the Central Provinces, were soon turned into good A.A. gunners, who acquitted themselves well on the few occasions on which they came into action.

That these occasions were not more numerous was again owing largely to geographical factors. The Japanese forces, already operating far from their home bases, were never able to put much weight into their air attacks, and Calcutta alone of the rear installations received more than a fleeting visit. Even the Calcutta attacks, judged by western standards, were not serious; and though some quite heavy high level attacks were made against some of our shore installations in the S.W. Pacific area, there was nothing unusual about them and they brought out no new lessons.

From the A.A. point of view, the major problem in the jungle was the "hedge-hopper", who could make his approach almost at tree-top level and shoot up an air strip or other ground installation and be away again within a matter of seconds. This was the sort of target that cried out for a 20-mm., but unfortunately, owing to the early lack of a self-destroying element in the Oerlikon and Polsten, it was a long time before any such gun was available. The requirement for self-destroying ammunition was not registered until 1943, and the first rounds of this nature were, therefore, only approved in November, 1944.

Radar was of little use for early warning at these very low levels, and natural O.Ps. were practically non-existent in the jungle and other densely wooded areas. When the tactical situation permitted, a solution was found by mounting the Bofors on a tubular steel tower, which could be built up in sections to a height of 60 feet or more.

The inactivity of the Japanese Air Force, however welcome to the rest of the Army, did nothing to relieve the strain on the A.A. gunner, whose endurance was severely taxed by the necessity of keeping continuously alert in such an oppressive climate. By maintaining a high standard of morale and discipline, the deleterious effects of monotony were successfully resisted, and A.A. personnel were later able to give a good account of themselves when transferred to other roles as units or as drafts to other arms.

After the loss of Singapore, the Royal Navy began to feel the need of bases in the Indian Ocean, and for this purpose it was decided to instal coast and air defences at Addu Atoll, Diego Garcia and the Cocos Islands. A complete M.N.B.D.O. (*see* p. 64) was not available, nor were there any mobile coast batteries ready to meet an emergency of this kind; but with the aid of certain Royal Marine parties, some old-fashioned coast artillery equipments were installed, and they were subsequently manned and maintained from India.

Conclusion

By the end of this period, the jungle, once regarded as an enemy, was at least neutral, if not indeed a friend. With the aid of the mortar, and the tank, the close support problem had been definitely solved; and this in spite of immense physical difficulties. During the defeat of the final Japanese offensive, "battles had been fought at 5,000 feet and over, often in impenetrable jungle; and troops loaded with full equipment, struggled up from nullahs 2,000 feet below in the face of heavy small arms, grenade and mortar fire. . . . Tanks often proved the decisive factor in the fighting up and down these mountain ranges, where they climbed almost precipitous slopes to blast the Japanese bunkers at a range of 10 yards."([6])

List of References

(¹) Operations of Malaya Command, 8th December 1941-15th February 1942, Despatch by Maj.-Gen. Perceval.
(²) Report by Gen. Alexander on Operations in Burma, 5th March-20th May 1942.
(³) "Operations in Eastern Theatre, Based on India", March 1942-31st December, 1942, Despatch by C.-in-C., India.
(⁴) BM/G(P)/1/13/1 of 31st May 1942.
(⁵) "Operations in India Command, 1st January to 20th June 1943", Despatch by C.-in-C., India.
(⁶) Despatch by Gen. Giffard, C.-in-C. 11 Army Gp., S.E.A.C., 16th November 1943-22nd June 1944.
(⁷) "The Australian Army at War", p. 27.
(⁸) Lethbridge Mission, LETMI/77 of 6th December 1943.
(⁹) M.G.R.A.(I), Training Instruction No. 2 of September 1943.
(¹⁰) R.A. Notes No. 12, App. C.2.
(¹¹) R.A. Notes No. 6, App. G.
(¹²) R.A. Notes No. 18, para. 1026 (c).
(¹³) Extracts from C.R.A. 2 Div. letter.
(¹⁴) R.A. Notes No. 27, para. 1538.
(¹⁵) 26 Ind. Div. Rpt. of 11th June 1943.
(¹⁶) D.R.A.(I) Liaison Letter No. 5, quoted in R.A. Notes No. 17.
(¹⁷) R.A. Notes No. 13, App. O.
(¹⁸) R.A. Notes No. 21, para. 1213.
(¹⁹) R.A. Notes No. 32, para. 1771.
(²⁰) D.R.A.(I) Liaison Letter No. 6, quoted in R.A. Notes No. 17.
(²¹) Report by O.C. 4/1 G.R. of 30th September 1944.
(²²) C.C.R.A. 4 Corps RA/59 of 23rd April 1944.
(²³) C.C.R.A. 4 Corps RA/37a/388 of 6th June 1944.
(²⁴) 220 Military Mission, Rpt. No. 32 of 31st December 1943.
(²⁵) G.H.Q.(I) u.o. 54234/RA1 of 7th February 1944.
(²⁶) Report by No. 1 Ind. Operational Research Section of 7th February 1944.
(²⁷) Report by C.C.R.A. 33 Corps.
(²⁸) R.A. 11 Army Gp. No. 11313/RA of 23rd November 1944.
(²⁹) G.H.Q.(I) u.o. 23676/RA1 of 7th February 1944.
(³⁰) R.A. 11 Army Gp. No. 10833/RA of 2nd November 1944.

TABLE K

RE-ORGANIZATION OF THE DIVISIONAL ARTILLERY—INDIA COMMAND, 1943

Type of Division	Numbers and Types of Units	Fd. Guns		3.7-in. Hows.	3-in. Mortars	L.A.A.		Anti-Tank		57 mm. SP	Remarks
		25 prs.	Priests			40-mm.	20-mm.	2-pr.	6-pr.		
Light ...	1 Lt. fd. regt.	24	—	—	—	—	—	—	—	—	Each lt. mtn. regt. had two btys. each of 4×3.7-in. hows., and one battery of 16 mortars.
	2 Lt. mtn. regts.	—	—	16	32	—	—	—	—	—	
	1 L.A.A./A. Tk. regt.	—	—	—	—	24	—	24	—	—	
A. and M.T. ...	1 Fd. regt.	24	—	—	—	—	—	—	—	—	*3.7-in. how. btys. in the jungle fd. regt. were T.D. and had 8 guns. *or 36×20-mm.
	1 Jungle fd. regt.	—	—	16*	16	—	—	—	—	—	
	1 Mtn. regt.	—	—	16	—	—	—	—	—	—	
	1 L.A.A./A. Tk. regt.	—	—	—	—	24*	—	—	24	—	
M.T. ...	1 Fd. regt.	24	—	—	—	—	—	—	—	—	*or 36×20-mm.
	2 Jungle fd. regts.	—	—	32	32	—	—	—	—	—	
	1 L.A.A./A. Tk. regt.	—	—	—	—	24*	—	—	24	—	
Armd. Div. ...	2 Fd. regts.	32	16	—	—	—	—	—	—	—	* 6 pr./57 mm. * incl. 18 S.P.
	1 A/Tk. regt.	—	—	—	—	—	—	—	36*	12	
	1 L.A.A. regt.	—	—	—	—	54*	—	—	—	—	
Assault Force:— 2 Div., 36 Ind. Div.	3 Asslt. fd. regts.	24	24	18*	—	—	—	—	—	—	*T.D.
	2 Asslt. fd. regts.	16	16	12	—	—	—	—	—	—	
	1 Lt. bty.	—	—	6*	—	—	—	—	—	—	
Force Tps.	1 A/Tk. regt.	—	—	—	—	—	—	—	48	—	*or 126 Bofors and 72×20 mm.
	3 L.A.A. regts.	—	—	—	—	162*	—	—	—	—	

CHAPTER XVI

THE DEFEAT OF JAPAN

PLATES RELEVANT TO THIS CHAPTER

Nos.
- 46. Ferrying guns and mules.
- 47. 25-prs. firing from beached "Z" craft.
- 48. 25-pr. being manhandled through mud on river bank near Rangoon.
- 49. The 4.7 recoilless gun.

Preparations for the Reconquest of Burma

Twice, in rapid succession, had air supply proved its ability to defeat a Japanese offensive against India. It remained to show that it could be as potent a factor in achieving victory for a British offensive into Burma. As the year 1944 drew to its close and the end of the war in Europe was seen to be approaching, more attention could be given to the needs of those who were fighting Japan in the Far East.

Already the degree of air support available was imposing when compared with what it had been in 1943, when six Blenheims and six Hurricanes were all that could be allotted to the 14th Indian Division for its offensive in Arakan. Nor was it in quantity only that improvements had been effected. The quality of the support given, and the degree of co-operation between the air and the ground forces, were fast approaching—if they had not already reached—the high standards achieved in Italy and N.W. Europe. The operations by the 5th Indian Division along the Tiddim road in August, 1944, " were distinguished by the highly successful co-operation of air, tanks, artillery and infantry, which inflicted severe casualties on the enemy and maintained the speed of the advance."[1]

In 1943, there had been no medium or heavy artillery, so that for the attack of bunkers, reliance had had to be placed on Vengeance dive bombers, without the aid of coloured smoke to indicate the targets on them. Now every corps had its quota of medium artillery, and a few 7.2-in. hows., manned as a rule by H.A.A. personnel and incorporated in medium regiments. Coloured smoke was also available for the indication of targets beyond the scope of the guns. Better still—since smoke could not always be relied on in the jungle or on a mountain side—the visual control post for the direction of close support aircraft working on the "cab-rank" system was now in operation, and was often placed directly under the control of the C.R.A. or his representative. In a country like this, where almost every opportunity was a fleeting one, and lightning decisions were generally required on whether the job could best be done by gun or aircraft, the resultant flexibility of fire control was invaluable.

Within the division, the artillery had been restored to its original strength by the adoption of the jury axle for one regiment of 25-prs. and the consequent elimination of the jungle field regiment (*see* p. 287). At the same time an adequate degree of close support had been ensured by the alternative 3-in. mortar establishment for the divisional anti-tank regiment, and by the brigading whenever necessary of the infantry mortars. The S.P. field guns of the assault divisions, which had originally been intended for use in combined operations (*see* Table K), and distributed on the scale of one battery per regiment, were now concentrated in an "army" reserve regiment and made available for the British counter-offensive overland into Burma. In the later stages of this operation, when the country became more suitable for tanks, they were to provide useful support for armoured units.

The V.T. Fuze Rejected

Among the most successful of the devices developed in the European theatre was the variable time (V.T.) fuze, in which a miniature radar set was used to produce, automatically, an air burst at a suitable height above the target. But for jungle warfare its value was open to question. In February 1945, when the matter was considered by the operational research group of the Fourteenth Army, the opportunities for the use of air bursts did not appear to be very numerous. During the greater part of 1944, worth-while artillery targets had consisted almost entirely of well dug-in positions with head cover; latterly, when the battle had begun to move more rapidly, positions in the plains were too widely dispersed to offer suitable targets for the artillery. For counter-battery work and for defensive fire, the V.T. fuze, it was admitted, had definite possibilities; but against the weak Japanese artillery, the need for counter-battery fire was almost negligible, and the possibility of having to fight on the defensive again was remote. It was the same with harassing fire. Although the V.T. fuze would undoubtedly be more effective than a direct action fuze for this type of fire, the general effectiveness of such fire in the jungle had proved so slight that the introduction of V.T. fuzes solely on this account could hardly be justified.

There was still the question of the slit trench position to be considered. For this kind of target, under normal conditions, the air burst was again indisputably superior to the ground burst. But conditions in the jungle were not normal. Most slit trenches so far encountered had been sited under trees or huts close to a crest, so that if V.T. fuzes had been used, the radar mechanism would have tended to function prematurely and the advantage of its accuracy would thus have been lost.([2]) Indeed so difficult was this problem of the slit trench, and so important was it to keep down the ammunition expenditure and thus ease the strain on the administrative services that, on the recommendation of the Director of Research at Delhi, trials had been carried out the year before with the 20-mm. Theoretical calculations showed that, weight for weight, the 20-mm. should be about 16 times as effective as the 25-pr., and that, by virtue of its high rate of fire, it could achieve its results in about one-third of the time.

Unfortunately, the trials, which were carried out early in July 1944, were a failure. The only guns available were Hispanos, and the only ammunition H.E.I. (incendiary) with an insensitive fuze. The guns constantly jammed, and the length zone proved too big for accurate firing. Owing to the imminent withdrawal of the Hispano, and its replacement by the Polsten, no further action was recommended, and the problem therefore remained unsolved.([3]).

There was, it seemed, no alternative to the 25-pr. Yet the V.T. fuze was still not considered worth introducing into the Fourteenth Army. Its fragility, some thought, and the complications it would cause in the ammunition supply, would outweigh any advantage it might possess in action. Hence it was decided to restrict its issue to A.A. units.([2])

Later, as the result of experience in the Irrawaddy valley, where actions were fought in the open over soft or flooded ground, the need for air bursts was more acutely felt. Under such conditions fuze 119 was ineffective, and fuze 231 on graze was seldom usable owing to the steep angles of descent.([4])

The Rocket in Jungle and Chaung Warfare

The 30-barrelled rocket projector, which had done such good work with the First Canadian Army in N.W. Europe, weighed 21 cwt. and was considered too cumbersome for use in S.E.A.C. To take its place, a 16-barrelled projector was designed, which weighed only 835 lb. and which could be towed by a jeep.([5])

A critical factor in assessing the possibilities of using rockets in the Far East was the stability of the propellant, which was apt to break down at high temperatures. By May 1945, the design had not yet been finally cleared, and it was therefore unlikely to be ready in time for use in this way.

The question was, could the "land mattress" (see p. 247), as it then stood, be profitably introduced into the jungle armoury, or "golf bag"? Because of its inaccuracy, it compared unfavourably with the medium gun, and the bulkiness of its ammunition was likely to present a serious maintenance problem. Thus rough calculations showed that, against a target area of 100 square yards, 2,000 rockets were the equivalent of 100 × 5.5-in. shells; from which it followed that the shipping or air space required was 150 times greater if rockets were used instead of medium artillery. On the other hand, the rocket projector itself was relatively light and portable, and to its proven value in a seaborne landing might be added its possibilities as a supporting weapon for airborne forces before medium artillery could be flown in and assembled.([6])

After much discussion it was agreed that the "land mattress" should be regarded as alternative equipment, not for a medium regiment, but—as in Europe—for a corps L.A.A. or anti-tank regiment; and that the scale of issue should be 12 equipments per corps, to be held forward in corps ordnance field parks.([7])

Meanwhile, in the U.S. Army, rocket launchers had been developed for use in amphibians: the 4.5-in., with a range of 1,100 yards, designed to provide supporting fire during the last phases of the "run-in" to an enemy-held beach; and the 7.2-in., with a range of 275 yards, which was originally designed as an anti-submarine weapon to be fired from surface craft, but which offered a suitable means of attacking Japanese bunkers or emplacements.([5]) These equipments promised to be of great value in coastal operations such as those undertaken by 15 Corps in Arakan during January and February, 1945. The coast along which this campaign was fought was intersected by numerous tidal "chaungs", which were navigable by light craft at certain states of the tide, and which, in the absence of roads, formed the framework of what came to be known as "chaung warfare". They were used not only as L. of C., but also as a means of penetration behind the enemy's front, which forced him to stand and fight in an endeavour to extricate himself.([8])

For this type of warfare, it appeared, the 7.2-in. rocket would be useful for breaking down the steep river and chaung banks and thus enabling the amphibians to climb out, and for supporting an assault on a strong point near a chaung. It could also be used at any time for the demolition of such obstacles as log barricades and stone or coral walls, and for the breaching of minefields. The amphibian-mounted 4.5-in. rocket would be needed in place of the L.C.T.(R) and L.C.S.(R) when a shallow water barrier or a fringe of reefs prevented these craft from getting within range of the landing beach, or in river estuaries and chaungs where the movements of craft were restricted and S.P. artillery could not get forward. It was therefore decided to ask for an amphibian support regiment with 20 L.V.Ts.; half equipped with 7.2-in., and half with 4.5-in., rockets.([9])

Mobility Compensates for Lack of Fire Support

While the 25th Indian Division cleared the Mayu Peninsula as a preliminary to a sea-borne assault on Akyab, the 81st and 82nd West African Divisions, moving further inland, struck through the jungle towards the Kaladan River, which flows down to Akyab from the north. These two divisions were weak in artillery, having each only one light regiment of three 3.7-in. how. and one mortar battery, and one anti-tank regiment of three batteries each of 12 × 6-prs. At first, when the jungle was very dense, this was no handicap. In fact, owing to the complete lack of roads, the 81st Division had to leave behind its jeep-drawn 3.7-in. hows., while its anti-tank/mortar regiment functioned as infantry because its mortars were porter-borne, and manpower difficulties were such that porters could not be provided. It was therefore reinforced by one mountain regiment with 16 mule-borne 3.7-in. hows.

In December, 1944, as this Division pushed on down the Kaladan River, it became increasingly apparent that "the period of our superiority in artillery fire power had come to an end and that we were both outnumbered and out-ranged in this respect."([8]). The fly-in of additional field and some medium artillery was considered but was abandoned, owing to the technical difficulties involved in the fly-in itself and in the subsequent process of maintenance and movement. Mountain artillery was available, but the feeding of the mules would increase the maintenance problem, and the additional 3.7-in. hows. would not extend the reach of the divisional artillery, which was what was really required. Hence it was finally decided to take a "wide hook" through the hills to the east.

This was the kind of operation that had won a quick victory at the Mareth Line (see p. 163), and that might have done the same at Keren had our troops possessed the right kind of mobility.([10]) It was exploiting to the full the power of movement, to compensate for the lack of supporting fire; and once again it proved a cheap and expeditious way of winning a battle, especially when reinforced by a generous degree of air support. From 29th to 31st December, the Japanese concentration in this area was attacked by 240 fighter-bomber and 213 light bomber sorties, which dropped a total of about 230 tons of bombs and 1,320 gallons of incendiary oil. This was a heavy strike for S.E. Asia, and the results were completely successful. The Japanese preparations for a counter-offensive were "nipped in the bud", and the 81st West African Division was enabled to attain its objective without serious loss.([8])

Coastal Operations by 15 Indian Corps in Arakan

In the Mayu Peninsula, the 25th Indian Division had been moving with one brigade on each side of the central spine; that on the coastal plain being supported by one field regiment, with a troop of medium guns under command, and by two destroyers with observation by an air O.P. The second brigade, operating down the Kalapanzin River, moved on a water-borne basis, with field artillery support limited to one troop owing to a lack of R.E. folding boat equipment. Two mountain and one mortar battery were allotted for close support, the former starting on a full mule basis. As the advance progressed, however, the mules became more of a liability than an asset. Feeding them was difficult, and the crossing of water obstacles became harder and harder as the chaungs widened and multiplied in number. Swimming was often impossible, and ferrying the mules over by raft and boat was a very slow business. They were therefore returned to base and the batteries continued their advance by water, coming into action on the banks when necessary. Later, they resumed their pack role and marched over to join the 82nd West African Division in the lower Kaladan valley.([11])

Akyab fell to an adventurous air O.P., whose pilot, looking in vain for suspected A.A. gun positions, circled lower and lower and finally landed, to receive an enthusiastic welcome from the local inhabitants. So 15 Corps pushed on and carried out its first assault landing at Myebon on 12th January, 1945. From an artillery point of view, this operation was peculiar in that the guns accompanying the first flight were confined to one medium gun and three Bofors, owing chiefly to the lack of suitable landing craft and the conflicting claims of the tanks. The latter were considered the more necessary, and results seemed to justify the decision.

Preceded by heavy air strikes and a preliminary naval bombardment by H.M.I.S. Narbada and Jumna, the 3rd Commando Brigade made an assault landing at Myebon at 0830 hours which achieved a complete tactical surprise. The bombardment caught the Japanese at breakfast and prevented most of them from manning their posts. Only light opposition was therefore encountered by the first wave, which was covered by a smoke screen laid by the Hurricanes.([8]) The tanks were brought into action on " D " + 1 and became a major feature of the ground operations. The medium gun and the three Bofors were ashore and in action by the afternoon of " D "+1.

The difficulties of landing artillery proved even greater than those of landing tanks, but much valuable support was given by a troop of 25-prs. mounted on a Z craft: a large lighter with a flat iron deck and end loading ramp. The gun platforms were bolted to the deck and ammunition was stacked along the sides. The wheelhouse made an excellent command post, and, with dinghy and outboard motor for inter-communication, the troop was entirely self-supporting. Shooting was not possible while the craft was under way, but as the attack progressed, the lighter was beached and the guns continued to fire from it in support of the infantry advancing up the Myebon peninsula.([11])

During the subsequent fighting at Kangaw, between 22nd January and 18th February, the enemy brought into action what was for him an unusual amount of artillery. By 2nd February, at least one battalion of field artillery appeared to be in action, in addition to some 105-mm. hows. and 25-prs.

Up to 600 rounds a day had been fired at our positions and at targets on an extremely vulnerable stretch of paddy between the landing beach and the small hill features on which our troops were established.([6])

This was in fact the heaviest shelling that had yet been encountered, and it was unfortunate that our counter-battery measures were hampered by survey difficulties. It was impossible to get forward more than small survey detachments, and a flash spotting post succumbed early in the operations to a direct hit from a 105-mm. shell. On the other hand, the 25th Indian Divisional Artillery had achieved its maximum concentration of the whole campaign, with all its guns in action less one battery and one troop, and with one troop of medium guns under command. At least two "Uncle" targets were engaged on the orders of the C.R.A., and, with the aid of the air O.P., valuable assistance was obtained from the guns of the supporting ships. Thus, although the enemy guns could not always be silenced, our own artillery was able to manifest its superiority by the support that it gave to the attack and by its retaliatory fire against the Japanese positions.

In the next, and final, landing at Ru-Ywa on 22nd February, the difficulties of providing covering fire in this sort of terrain were most clearly illustrated. The landing beach, instead of being on an open sea front, was tucked away in the folds of a tortuous estuary and had to be approached by a series of inland waterways entailing a journey of some 45 miles from Myebon. The landings had to be made in heavy mud and through a mangrove swamp on a beach so narrow that only two landing craft could be beached at a time.

The return of the Z craft had been demanded by Inland Water Transport, and artillery support for the initial landing and the subsequent build-up of the beachhead seemed almost impossible. However, a night reconnaissance by commando parties revealed an island some four miles from the proposed beachhead on which suitable gun positions might be found. Three days before the assault, two field batteries and one troop of medium guns were unobtrusively ferried to this island, and there, heavily screened by mangrove trees, they waited in readiness to support the attack on a completely unsuspecting enemy. A light air strip was also made and an adequate supply of ammunition for the guns was dumped.([8])

Air support throughout was controlled through R.A. channels. Each brigade and H.Q.R.A. had a tentacle, and for immediate support, brigades made their demands direct to Army Air Support Control through the C.R.A.'s representatives with them. Larger fire plans were co-ordinated by the C.R.A., and demands were placed over the H.Q.R.A. tentacle.

The use of wireless among the leading waves of the attack was now well established. Early difficulties (*see* p. 289)—sometimes the result of inexperience rather than of inadequate equipment—had been definitely overcome, and in one armoured regiment a "forward tank officer" went dismounted with a walkie-talkie set and directed the final covering fire, usually with reference to his own person.

Thus, despite the limitations imposed by the shortage of craft, artillery and air support combined had generally done all that had been asked of it, and had contributed in good measure to the ultimate victory. And the secret of its success seems to have lain chiefly in good wireless communications. There had been times during this war, in Europe and elsewhere, when the early promise of wireless had appeared chimerical; and there were still experienced gunner officers who distrusted "on call" concentrations as a method of covering fire because of the difficulty of ensuring that the calls would get through. But perhaps because the need was great, the response was great also. With no prolonged period of semi-static warfare in which to grow dependent upon cable, units maintained their wireless equipments and skills in a high state of efficiency, and although the guns were nearly always separated from their O.Ps. by wide stretches of water, on no occasion did communications fail. It had not been a divisional artillery operation; the nature of the country had prohibited that; but in the words of the C.R.A., the divisional artillery had "at least shown its flexibility and its capacity for improvisation", and it was for consideration whether this flexibility might not be further exploited. "We may well consider" he wrote "whether we are not often wrong in insisting on deploying so many guns; whether we could not with more careful siting and the use of alternative positions, achieve equally effective results with a less number of guns, thus helping our administrative problem."[11]

Modification of Naval Bombardment Procedure

Throughout these operations, co-operation with the Royal Navy had worked smoothly and well. The senior bombardment liaison officer—bombardment liaison officer—brigade bombardment liaison officer—forward observer bombardment organization, it appeared, could not be bettered.[11] But the scope of the operations had been small, and control at the higher levels had not been tested. For the large scale assault landings that were contemplated as the war was carried nearer to the Japanese homeland, a special bombardment control headquarters (B.C.H.Q.) was to be established, first in the assault force headquarters ship and later ashore at the headquarters of the highest military formation being supported. In charge of the B.C.H.Q. would be a commander naval bombardment whose function would be to direct the naval fire to meet the needs of the Army. This officer would have no staff of his own, but would operate through the bombardment staff at the headquarters from which he was operating. Afloat there would be the assault force gunnery officer, the S.B.L.O. (*see* p. 182), and two carrier-borne air liaison officers; the latter provided by the Army to deal with air spotting requirements. Ashore there would be a naval liaison officer bombardment, a staff officer bombardment—an army officer who, when the senior bombardment liaison officer was afloat, advised the C.R.A. ashore on the employment of divisional F.Os.B.—and two air liaison officers.[12]

For inter-communication purposes, bombardment control headquarters had seven wireless channels, provided when afloat by the sets and operators of the assault force headquarters ship, and when ashore by a mobile bombardment communications unit. They were:—

(1) Bombardment calling wave.

(2) Bombardment liaison wave.

(3) Force auxiliary wave.

(4) Air liaison officers spotting briefing wave.

Plate 42—View of Ngakyedauk Pass from Hill 1070.

Plate 43—Kohima. Objectives of Key 2 and 4, 4th May, 1944.

Plate 43A—Carriage, 3.7-in. How., Mk. 2P, Towed by Jeep.

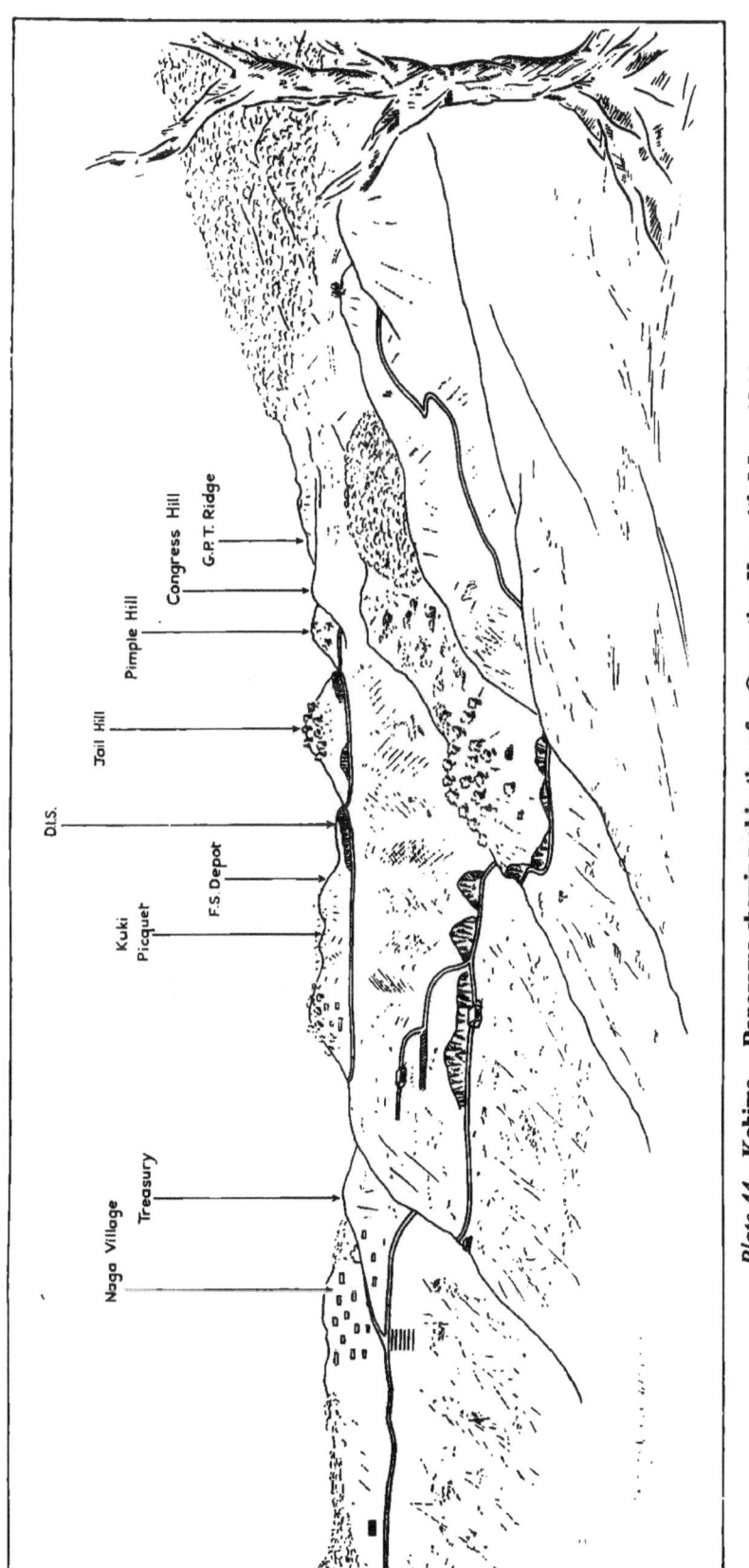

Plate 44—Kohima. Panorama showing objectives for Operation Key, 4th May, 1944.
(Taken from Punjab Hill)

Plate 45—Mist in the mountains.

Plate 46—**Ferrying guns and mules.**

Plate 47—25-prs. firing from beached " Z " craft.

Plate 48—25-pr. being manhandled through mud on river bank near Rangoon.

Plate 49—The 4·7-in. recoilless gun.

(5) Spotting wave.

(6) Channels to air commander.

(7) C.R.A.'s wave.

At the same time experience gained with the assault field regiments in the Normandy landings (*see* p. 207), and more recently—though on a much smaller scale—in Arakan, led to further experiments in the firing of guns from assault craft. The 3.7-in. how., the 75-mm. pack how. and the 25-pr., it was found, could be fired satisfactorily from a Dukw or a L.V.T.(4), and in June, 1945, it was agreed by the Service Ministries that an organization for the fire control of such 25-pr. flotillas was required. Each flotilla of nine craft (18 guns) was to have an establishment capable, once the craft had beached, of functioning as a battery. In addition there was to be a control staff for each assault force so that flotillas might be either fired as a regiment or grouped under the infantry divisional field regiments. The personnel for the organization were ultimately to be provided by the Royal Marines, though, as a short term policy, some of the control staff might be gunners.[13]

Yet even this degree of flexibility was not enough for some of the operations in the S.W. Pacific area. For example, for the landing on the Brunei peninsula in N.W. Borneo, the use of assault craft and folding boat equipment had to be abandoned owing to their indifferent performance in surf and the problem of trans-shipment. Rubber reconnaissance boats, reinforced with steel mesh lining, were too frail, and the method eventually adopted was to enclose the equipment in light timbered crates, wrapped in two layers of malthoid, with seams and folds tacked down and treated with bitumen. The 75-mm. how. was found to break up conveniently into six loads, of which the heaviest was the cradle and bottom sleigh, which when crated weighed 468 lb.[14]

The Overland Invasion of Burma

The lack of landing craft and other facilities for a major offensive against the Japanese in Burma had forced attention to be turned to the forbidding problem of an overland invasion. The natural difficulties were enormous, as they had always been, but with the development of air transport there was every prospect that they might be successfully overcome.

There were other factors, too, which helped to ease the situation; among them the introducton of the jury axle for the 25-pr. and the exploitation of the full offensive possibilities of the mortar in the hands of artillery personnel. During the advance of 4 Corps from Tamu to the Pakokku area, the Lushai Brigade, after moving through the Chin Hills without supporting arms, came up against determined opposition at Gangaw. A field battery equipped with jury axles was rushed up from Tamu and was able to give valuable support, much of it with observation by an air O.P. The mortar batteries had also completely justified themselves. The use of Everest pack equipment for manhandling the equipments proved very satisfactory, and in general it was clear that the problem of close support in jungle country had been finally mastered.[15]

During the subsequent operations in the Irrawaddy valley, the effect of mortar concentrations sometimes proved quite devastating; and at the crossing of this river, mortars were able to give much-needed close support in the bridgehead. For example, the 7th Indian Division crossing—at Nyaungu on 13th/14th February 1945—had to be made diagonally, over a distance of about a mile, to a far bank lined with 40-foot cliffs and intersected by deep chaungs every few hundred yards; and in the initial stages of the operation the guns were about 7,000 yards from the bridgehead. Support, therefore, was not easy, and the existence of mortars within the divisional artillery was undoubtedly a great advantage. Again, during the set-piece attacks by the 17th Indian Division at Meiktila, the combination of infantry and artillery mortars was used to good effect. All available weapons were brigaded under artillery control, by affiliating battalion mortars to the anti-tank/mortar batteries. Each pivot mortar was put on to the divisional grid by means of survey, and the parent anti-tank battery laid a line to each mortar platoon under its command. Infantry mortar platoon commanders were taught to use the artillery board and plotter, and to read a task table, and as a result many successful concentrations from up to 70 mortars were fired.([16])

Once in the open country, the full deployment of the divisional artillery became possible and our superiority in this arm was persistently exploited. For example, for the crossing of the Irrawaddy by 33 Indian Corps near Myinmu in February 1945, a corps artillery group of 80 guns was formed to support in turn the assaults of the 20th Indian and the 2nd Division. It was made up of 8 × 6-in. hows., 12 × 5.5-in. guns, 4 × 7.2-in. hows. (manned by H.A.A. personnel), 16 × 3.7-in. H.A.A. guns, 24 × 25-prs. and 16 × 105-mm. S.P. (Priests). As a preliminary to the crossing of the 20th Indian Division on the night of 12th/13th February, the R.A.F., at 1600 hours on 12th February, put down a carpet of bombs and inflammable oil on an area, some 2,000 yards square, in which most of the Japanese guns were in action. This was followed by heavy artillery concentrations on all known hostile gun positions, and as a result nearly every Japanese battery spent that night moving to alternative positions, and our infantry never had a round fired at them for the first 48 hours.

In 4 Corps, continuous support was assured to the infantry by linking regiments within the division and placing all O.Ps. on the frequency of the regiment in close support of the attacking brigade. The C.O. of this regiment, acting as the C.R.A.'s representative, was able to control the fire of all the available guns, and the maximum weight of covering fire could be given to a brigade or battalion attack without the delay incurred in the making of a set-piece fire plan.([16]) Battery commanders would accompany battalion headquarters with one set on the C.R.A.'s representative's net, and one set on their own battery net. Troop commanders would move with the leading companies, with 22 or 48 sets on their battery nets.([17])

We were fortunate in being able to bring the Japanese to battle mainly in dry, open country, to which his tactics and training were not suited, and in which our superiority in aircraft, tanks and guns could be simultaneously exploited. By this means, the Japanese resistance was broken in a series of decisive actions, in which aircraft prepared the way, the artillery continued the "softening" process and enabled the tanks to get close enough to destroy any enemy positions that remained "alive", and the infantry then went in and "mopped up". The Japanese had no satisfactory answer to our medium tanks, which were able to establish a tactical superiority on the battlefield unequalled in other theatres since the palmy days of the Matilda in 1940-1. "The impact of 100 bombers, 100 or so guns, 80 × 3-in. mortars and 100 tanks, followed up by well-trained, determined infantry, was too much for even the most fanatical and determined foe in his strong village positions."[16])

The end came with the Japanese attempt to break out from the Irrawaddy valley during the night 20th/21st July. In the centre sector, where the heaviest fighting took place, the 17th Indian Division was spread out over a front of 74 miles, with its artillery distributed in groups so that in vital areas it was possible to concentrate the fire of three or four field batteries and one medium battery. For this purpose, several sub-units were on two regimental nets and the H.Q.R.A. net, and an all-round field of fire at every gun position was practically essential. Never perhaps had the 3.7-in. H.A.A. gun shown up to such advantage in the ground rôle as now, when its central pivot mounting enabled it to join at short notice in a concentration at any point of the compass; unlike the 5.5-in. medium gun, which frequently delayed the firing of a concentration while a big switch was being applied.

In this country, where most of the enemy movement was over flooded ground, the lack of a V.T. fuze was found very inconvenient. Had it been available, the number of casualties inflicted on the enemy would probably have been much greater.

The main difficulty, however, was observation. The ground was flat and what view there was was generally obstructed by jungle, tall elephant grass or other obstacles. F.O.Os. accompanied the infantry to the limit of the resources available, and several successful shoots were directed by infantry officers (cf. p. 309); but even so, up-to-date information about the position of our own troops was often not available to the artillery, and as a result both air strikes and artillery concentrations had to be postponed while these positions were being verified.

Observation from the air was no less difficult. The Japanese were well trained in concealment in this type of country, and it was often impossible to see any movement from the air, even from a very low altitude. Moreover, the Taylorcraft air O.P. had failed to stand up to the weather conditions and had had to be withdrawn even before the monsoon had started in earnest. Nevertheless, some useful work was done by two L5 aircraft borrowed from the Corps Inter-communication Flight and used as air O.Ps. with untrained observers from field regiments carried as passengers. In one of the most successful engagements, two 7.2-in. hows. fired air bursts.

Inter-communication was almost as great a problem as observation. Owing to the great distances involved, the artillery had sometimes to share a main artery with other users and this often led to long delays in the passage of information and the application of fire plans. Here indeed was an opportunity for wireless to prove its worth, and, despite hourly variations in range during the monsoon, and the enforced use of continuous wave after 1700 hours, it generally did what was required of it.

Smoke was used effectively to indicate objectives to the infantry and targets to the supporting aircraft, but smoke screens were sometimes impracticable in the flooded country. Direct air support was, as usual in this theatre, controlled by H.Q.R.A., with which were located two visual control posts and a tentacle. The type of air support required was often unpredictable, and in consequence, aircraft would arrive without bombs when bombs were required. "Cab ranks" were not a success, because aircraft came from such distances that they could only stay on the rank for 10 to 20 minutes. Again, owing to the wide frontage on which the Division was operating, they could not carry 1-in. maps, and smaller maps gave rise to briefing difficulties, which were added to by the short range of the V.H.F. sets in use by the visual control posts. The indication of targets by artillery smoke was a help, but many targets were out of artillery range.

But the jungle had by now been mastered, and difficulties of this sort existed only to be circumvented or overcome. As in the desert five years before, what orthodoxy could not do was done by ingenuity and improvisation. Where only a railway existed, and no road, 25-prs. were mounted on small railway flats towed by a jeep train, and fired from the flats. A small railway trolley, propelled by a motor-cycle mounted on it, was used by F.O.Os. On other occasions F.O.Os. went out in armoured cars, jeeps, boats, and on foot with 22 sets carried by coolies, mules and even elephants.[18]

The Mortar as an Artillery Weapon

If it could not be said that the enemy mortar had been completely mastered, it had undoubtedly been proven that, by making proper use of their own mortars, British and Indian troops could hand back equal if not greater punishment than that which they had hitherto been forced to take. True, the short range of the 3-in. mortar exposed it to the risk of heavy casualties if used in concentrated lay-outs, but this risk could be greatly reduced by quick changes of position, as practised by the Germans; or, if alternative positions were scarce, as they often might be in the jungle, by using the mortars only for vital tasks and withdrawing them in the intervals to a suitable harbour area.[15]

It was also possible to extend the scope of the 3-in. mortar merely by strengthening the base plate, which would increase its range to 2,800 yards; and by the beginning of 1945, measures were being undertaken in the United Kingdom to strengthen the barrel and boost up the charge so that a range of 3,500 yards could be attained. Then there was the 4.2-in. mortar, which, after a rather shaky start, had done well in Tunisia and afterwards, and which, in April 1945, was accepted in A.L.F.S.E.A. as a replacement for the 3-in. mortar in all anti-tank regiments other than West African.[19]

As an example of what this weapon could do, one might cite the experience of an Australian anti-tank regiment in British Borneo. A certain village had been reported as strongly held by the Japanese. The field artillery could not get near enough to engage it, owing to the nature of the terrain; so two 4.2-in. mortars—with 60 rounds of H.E. and two native canoes—were moved up by jeep train, carried 3,000 yards over very rough country to a stream, and there loaded into the canoes and quietly pushed downstream for about four miles, with the unit "carriers" acting as infantry covering party. The hollowed out stump of a coconut palm was found to provide a good platform for the base plate of each mortar, and, having thus solved a difficult siting problem, the detachment was able to engage the enemy successfully.

Supply, however, was dependent on the United Kingdom, and it was not very satisfactory. In December, 1944, it had been agreed between Fourteenth Army and the R.A. Directorate at Delhi that 900 long range 3-in. equipments were required, but on 10th March, 1945, the B.R.A. Fourteenth Army complained that the supply of technical stores and ammunition—such as range scales, range tables, lensatic sights and long range bombs—had not kept pace with the supply of mortars. The net effect was that the regiment had adopted and was using an equipment that had "lost the reliability traditionally associated with gunner weapons."[20]

To regain that reliability, steps were now being taken to produce a rifled medium mortar, and on 19th September, 1945, it was recommended by the M.G.R.A. (India) that, pending the development of this new equipment, the 3-in. mortar should be retained in anti-tank regiments. In the meantime some infantry 4.2-in. mortars had arrived in the theatre, and during the advance on Rangoon they had added considerably to the effect of the divisional mortar concentrations under the C.R.A.'s control.

From the maintenance point of view, however, the situation was not altogether satisfactory. There were now three types of mortar in the field: the 3-in. unmodified, the 3.-in. long range, and the 4.2-in.; and the resultant complications in the ammunition supply were specially vexatious in formations operating on a system of air supply.[16]

Thus we ended the war, as we had begun it, on a note of improvisation and makeshift: a reminder, if such were needed, that in modern total war, shortcomings in the equipment situation cannot be made up so readily during the progress of a war as they could be in the past, when the industrial capacity of the nation was never fully taxed by military requirements.

The Rôle of Mountain Artillery

Throughout this campaign, mountain artillery had rendered good service. In the Naga Hills, six mountain ranges were crossed on hill paths, and on one occasion 1,005 steps had to be cut to get the mules down a particularly steep slope.[21] But the guns were always there when needed, and without them really close support could probably not have been guaranteed.

It was the same in the Kaladan valley, in November, 1944, when the two mountain batteries from the 25th Indian Division were put back on to a mule basis and joined the 82nd West African Division at Paletwa (*see* p. 308). While moving down the valleys, marches would sometimes have to be made for long stretches through water up to a maximum depth of over three feet, so that some of the small army transport mules were lifted off their feet and were only kept afloat by the buoyancy of their loads. At other times, while crossing over from one valley into the next, gradients were so steep—up to 1 in 1—that loads had to be removed from the mules and manhandled, or a track had to be cut almost under the noses of the advancing mules.[22]

Some fine feats of endurance were also performed during the final advance into Burma. For example, one Indian mountain battery left Imphal on

1st February, 1945, and marched 415 miles to Myitsin on the Shweli river, where, on 7th March, it joined its parent division. It had crossed two major rivers, the Chindwin and the Irrawaddy; the former on bamboo rafts, the latter by motor ferry. From Tamu to Katha on the Irrawaddy, a distance of about 150 miles, supply was entirely maintained by air.

To crown all these performances, trials carried out early in 1945 showed that mules could be successfully dropped by parachute.[23] Nevertheless there were difficulties attached to the feeding of so many animals, and there were occasions, both in the chaung country and in the hills, when even the mule was defeated and recourse had to be made to boats or to porters.

The Recoilless Gun

The problem was to find a weapon that could go where the "screw gun" could go, and give the same degree of support to the infantry, without being dependent on animal transport. The development of the recoilless gun appeared to offer a possible solution to some aspects of this problem, in particular in the design of very light manhandled weapons capable of firing a limited number of powerful shell against bunkers, etc., at close range. This development was initiated in the latter half of 1942, and weapons of the light close support type just failed to reach maturity in time to be tested in the war.

The basic principle of the recoilless weapon is that the momentum of the shell is exactly balanced by the momentum of a large volume of propellant gases discharged at high velocity to the rear. The absence of recoil thrust, eliminates the need of a recoil system and of providing a strong anchorage for supporting the lower carriage; thus a very light carriage is adequate for such a weapon.

The designer of these guns, in addition, utilized the principle of a large chamber, which fits in well with the recoilless principle, as this needs a very large cartridge. The large chamber principle leads to a more even, and lower peak, pressure in the gun, which can thus be designed with very thin walls. Through the combination of these two principles a very light equipment results, and, in fact, weapons were designed at between one-half and one-third of the weight of orthodox weapons of similar range and shell power.

The comparative advantages of manœuvring such weapons are clear, and if a prolongation of the war had allowed of the completion of some of these projects, they would no doubt have proved useful in some roles. For the more orthodox use as a substitute for existing field weapons of comparable range and effect, however, a very great disadvantage is the weight and size of the complete round of ammunition. This, in general, is twice that of the orthodox weapon in weight and considerably more in size. Hence the supply of ammunition at normal field usage rates would quickly outweigh, in the overall supply problem, the saving in the weight of the equipment. Back blast from the jets is another disadvantage, the full implications of which were not tested by the user.

In 1943 and 1944 the designs of a heavy anti-tank and demolition weapon (7.2-in.), a light field howitzer (95-mm.), and an anti-tank gun (3.7-in.) were put in hand. Late in 1944 all the above weapons were demonstrated at Ardeer, and by March, 1945, the 95-mm. field weapon was demonstrated at the School of Artillery at Larkhill. About this time, too, the development of a 4.7-in. weapon was started, in lieu of the 7.2-in. howitzer. This was to go on the same carriage as the 95-mm. howitzer and to be used for demolition purposes and for flat trajectory shooting against heavy armour, bunkers, etc. The war ended before any user trials of these weapons could be carried out.

Fire Plans

The war in the Far East had been on a very much smaller scale than in Europe, and in the jungle it was not often that more than 100 guns participated in a single fire plan. Yet even then the ground was sometimes so cut up that our infantry found it almost impossible to dig themselves in owing to the looseness of the earth.([24])

During the later stages of the operations, in the railway valley, occasional crashes might come down from 168 guns and 72 mortars as a maximum([25]), but while ammunition was being supplied by air the paramount need was its economy, so that heavy and prolonged bombardments were seldom possible. For the same reason barrages were as a general rule administratively impracticable, even if they were tactically sound, and there were some who would grant this only in exceptional circumstances. "Concentrations, well handled," wrote the C.C.R.A. 4 Corps on 31st July, 1945, "will nearly always be more effective than barrage fire. The latter is insufficiently flexible, does NOT neutralize the ground over which it passes, and all surprise is lost. The only occasions I can see where a barrage is justified is when one has been unable to locate the enemy's localities, either by photos, reconnaissance, etc., or by a careful scrutiny of the map, putting oneself in his place."([26])

This agreed with American opinion (*see* p. 280), and indeed did not conflict in principle with the doctrine laid down in the British Army in the pre-war period (*see* p. 2). The point at issue was, how often could accurate information of the enemy dispositions be expected in moving warfare? Would it be seldom, as implied in pre-war theory, or would the proper exploitation of modern facilities—such as the air O.P., air photography and radar—make it the rule rather than the exception?

There was another aspect of this problem that was perhaps still more important. The old controversy of "barrage *versus* concentration" was based simply on the accuracy with which covering could be put down on the enemy positions as they existed at the moment of going into battle. It was tacitly assumed that both methods of fire would be applied in accordance with a timed programme, based, inevitably, on a preconceived opinion of the physical and moral factors that were likely to affect the rate of progress of the attack.

But with the development of wireless and improved methods of cable communication, there had come the possibility of making the fire plan really flexible by substituting the "on call" for the timed concentration. During 4 Corps' advance to Rangoon, except for the initial concentrations that led up to the first objective, the fire plan normally consisted of concentrations on call, and despite the extra strain put on the gunner's reputation for consistency and accuracy, the results were generally satisfactory. With accurately calibrated guns and the excellent 1/25,000 maps that were available, predicted fire proved quite effective, and provided that the target could be located on the map, it was seldom necessary to do more than fire a "tester."([16])

The same principle could of course be applied to the barrage, or moving stonk, and during the operations in Bougainville, where the country was the usual thick jungle, it was found convenient to combine the directional value of the barrage with the flexibility of the "on call" system. Covering fire for the assault was generally in the form of a barrage, planned as a series of linear concentrations fired on call from the F.O.O., who moved with the forward troops.

Harassing fire, though not generally very effective in the jungle (see p. 305), was sometimes used with success; and it is interesting to note that, in one Australian artillery unit in the S.W. Pacific, a slow but prolonged rate of fire was found to give better results than a few bursts of greater intensity (cf. pp. 236, 292). For example, during the Aitape-Wewak campaign, this unit was allotted 300 rounds a day for H.F. tasks, which at first were engaged at the rate of 5 to 10 rounds of gunfire by a troop or battery—according to the size of the area—not more than once or twice a day. As no apparent results were obtained, a new system was tried by which selected targets were engaged by single guns for several hours at the rate of approximately four rounds an hour, fired at irregular intervals. Information received from prisoners at the end of the campaign showed that this fire had been very demoralizing.

Artillery smoke screens were not much used, owing partly to the technical difficulties presented by flood water, jungle and mountain; and A.A., or area, smoke screens of the kind that had proved so valuable at Cassino and at the battle of the Rhine, were beyond the available resources. Nevertheless it was decided in January, 1945, to train L.A.A. units in the operation of small local smoke screens with No. 24 generators, and to use No. 1 Indian Smoke Company, then under command of the 9th A.A. Brigade and earmarked for combined operations, for the provision of a smoke blanket over the enemy's position. If our infantry were trained to fight in their own smoke, it could often be of great advantage to them. For lack of such training, the smoke screen was often unjustly regarded as a double-edged weapon and therefore to be avoided.([26])

The small scale use of smoke shell, for the extrication of patrols or tanks from difficult situations, was sometimes practised. Directed, as opportunity offered, from a suitably situated ground O.P., such "covering fire" proved invaluable.

Proposals for New Field Artillery Equipments

Even more controversial perhaps than the relative merits of barrage and concentration, or of timed and "on call" fire plans, was the question, does the gunner aim to kill or merely to frighten? There were many who maintained, logically enough, that unless artillery fire maintained a reputation for deadliness, it would ultimately cease to frighten. But war experience proved, what the psychologist had long been saying, that under the stress of emotion the human animal is not so rational as had once been supposed.

A bang, especially if it occurred in the air above him, was apt to be unreasonably frightening. Moreover casualty lists showed that the number of people killed by an artillery bombardment was surprisingly small, and that the field gun achieved its purpose mainly by making the enemy keep his head down during critical periods.

Hence it was proposed, early in 1945, to introduce a new field artillery equipment with a lighter shell and a longer range. Although it was admitted that a number of heavy shell would neutralize a defensive position or break up an attack more effectively than an equal number of light shell, it was nevertheless considered that " there is a point at which the price paid for a heavier shell—in range, mobility, fatigue or ammunition supply—becomes uneconomical ", and that, " contrary to the accepted tenets of our enemies, our allies and some of ourselves ", the weight of the field artillery shell might safely be reduced to 20 lb.([27]) With modern improvements in shell design, it seemed likely that this reduction could be made without much, if any, loss of lethal effect; and even if this were not so, the importance of keeping the infantry close up to the covering fire provided a strong argument in favour of the lighter shell.

The main characteristics of the new weapon were to be: a minimum range of 16,000 yards; air portability, including the possibility of breakdown and reassembly by R.A. personnel in loads not exceeding 300 lb.; upper register firing, with an angle of descent of not less than 45 degrees and a 360 degree arc of fire in both upper and lower registers; and a shield extending to the ground level and giving immunity to small arms armour piercing fire at 500 yards. Its tractor was to be wheeled (6 × 6), to have a radius of action of 200 miles and as low a silhouette as possible, to be air portable without breakdown, and to be fitted with anti-mine armour for the protection of the crew.

At the same time, a new light artillery equipment was proposed in lieu of the 75-mm. and 3.7-in. pack howitzers. It was to be capable of being carried in 10 mule loads, and was to have a maximum range of 12,000 yards, an arc of fire—with split trail—of not less than 60 degrees, and an upper register performance as for the new field gun. It was to be equipped with a shield giving protection against ordinary small arms fire at 500 yards, and was to be air portable and capable of being dropped in parachute loads. Its tractor was to have a silhouette and radius of action as for the field gun tractor, and was to be capable of being dropped by parachute without breakdown.([28])

In A.L.F.S.E.A. the idea of the new field gun was not very favourably received; in particular, the theory that neutralization was the main role of the field gun. Experience in dealing with Japanese bunkers pointed rather to the opposite conclusion, and some even maintained that, if other nations were likely to adopt the Japanese tactics, the field gun would no longer be required in its present form. In its place we should require, for offensive action, weapons of destruction rather than neutralization; for example, heavy field (or medium) guns, firing shell of 100 lb. and upwards, to carry out the preliminary bombardment of the enemy positions, and mobile close support weapons, such as S.P. guns and tanks, to accompany the attack and deal the knockout blow to positions not already destroyed by the preliminary bombardment. In defence, the R.A. contribution should be direct fire weapons, using H.E. and A.P., and more automatics. This would stop the hostile infantry and tanks once they were committed to the assault, and, to disorganize his forces while forming up for the attack, we should have the heavy field guns and, above all, the air. "To sum up," wrote one of the chief proponents of this theory, "neutralization has 'had it'. It is an outworn tactic ; armour and digging in has defeated it."[29]

In apparent support of this argument was the fact that the Churchill tank could operate safely inside a field artillery barrage (see p. 210). Yet advantage had never been taken of this fact in battle, and it seems fair to conclude that the neutralizing effect of artillery fire against armoured troops was not yet negligible.

In short, opinion was divided, and in view of the potentialities of the recoilless gun, D.R.A., India, preferred that the matter should be left open for the time being. "I feel," he wrote, "that we should be very sure that the future of field and especially mountain artillery does not lie in this principle before we embark on a new programme on orthodox lines."[28] Meanwhile the problem remained, as it had always been, to get the infantry on to their objectives as soon as possible after the covering fire ceased.

Trouble with the Medium Gun

What he regarded as of immediate importance was an improvement in the supply of medium artillery. Here indeed was another example of the difficulty of making good initial deficiencies in the course of a modern, total war. It was not that the need for medium artillery had been overlooked ; but in the pre-war programme of modernization it had had to take precedence below both A.A. and field guns (see p. 12), and once the war had started there were so many other urgent claims on industrial capacity that the lee-way could never be made up.

Unfortunately, too, the 5.5-in. gun—the only medium gun in use in this theatre—had revealed such serious defects that it lost for a time the confidence of commanders and troops and its use had to be restricted. Prematures had in fact occurred in other theatres, but the incidence was much lower than in Burma. In the autumn of 1944 a " Premature Investigation Party " of experts was formed in the United Kingdom and sent to Normandy and Belgium to obtain first-hand information and make recommendations. However, no immediate solution was found, and as a temporary expedient in S.E.A.C., it was decided to revert to the old 6-in. howitzer. The difficulty here was the shortage of spares and the lack of maintenance facilities for an obsolete weapon of this sort. Hence, of the nine medium regiments then in S.E.A.C., only three could be thus re-equipped. The U.S. 155-mm. howitzer was not regarded as an acceptable alternative, owing to its short range, and it was therefore decided to retain the 5.5-in. gun in the other six regiments but to use only the light (80-lb.) shell, with which prematures, though not entirely unknown, were much less frequent.

Counter-battery and Counter-mortar become Counter-bombardment

That the effect of these weaknesses was not more severely felt was owing to the numerical and tactical inferiority of the Japanese artillery. Individually, the enemy guns were usually well sited, concealed and protected ; and in the attack battalion guns were boldly handled and frequently came into action at ranges of about 200 yards. Collectively, however, their handling was poor. The Japanese methods of fire remained to the end " illogical, unco-ordinated, and confined mostly to harassing tactics against our infantry."[30] At most a short concentration, following a long harassing programme at a slow rate, might be used as a prelude to an infantry attack.

Except on a few occasions, such as the siege of Meiktila, therefore, the calls made on our counter-battery organization were inconsiderable. Yet some useful experience was gained in the application of sound ranging and flash spotting procedures to jungle conditions. The chief difficulties were of course observation and inter-communication. Flash spotting O.Ps. were hard to find, and when found, could not always sort out the flashes they saw, owing to the avoidance by the Japanese of sustained fire. Sound ranging bases took some time to establish—24 hours in thick jungle, with survey assistance; four to six hours in open scrub, without survey assistance —and the protection of isolated microphone positions, as indeed of flash spotting O.Ps., was sometimes impossible to arrange owing to the shortage of infantry. The radio link in the sound ranging battery (*see* p. 37) was not used because of the interference with wireless signals that was so often experienced in the jungle. The equipment was old and difficult to maintain, and in view of the reduced scale of transport on which the troops were operating, it was left behind in store.[30]

Counter-mortar activities were equally slight. The Japanese mortars, like their guns, were few in numbers and were not used " *en masse* " even at Meiktila and in the bridgehead areas during the crossing of the Irrawaddy. Hence the lack of a special counter-mortar organization was not severely felt in Burma.[31] For assault landings, however, the need for such an organization was more urgent. Experience in Normandy had shown what a nuisance the hostile mortar could be in an operation of this nature, and it had been confirmed by later experiences in the Far East. Mortars were a menace not only to the assaulting troops themselves, but also to such naval craft as might be operating within their range. To counter this threat, trials were under way in July 1945 with the F.A. No. 3 Mk. 2 radar set mounted in the landing craft gun (medium).[32]

The development of radar in the ground role had been making steady progress, and in addition to the counter-mortar set there were now two other types under trial; one for the observation of fire and the tracking of moving vehicles, the other to act as a radar sentry for the initial detection of moving vehicles and for the indication of targets to the " tracker ". Another promising line of investigation was the development of a light radar equipment for self-location by airborne troops, reconnaissance units, long range penetration groups, patrols and front line units. If sufficient accuracy could be obtained, such a set offered the prospect of a quick artillery survey without the publicity involved in the use of an air burst grid (*see* p. 156); but by August 1945 experiment had not gone further than to show that existing R.A.F. equipment could provide locations: with static transmitters, to a distance of 120 miles with an accuracy of 100 to 300 yards; or with mobile transmitters, to a distance of 40 to 60 miles, with an error in position of anything up to a mile.[33]

In July 1945, a War Office Committee was formed to review the whole field of artillery survey and the existing methods of ground location of hostile movement, guns and mortars. This committee recommended the formation of a corps observation regiment to combine the functions of survey, observation, sound ranging and radar. In future, it suggested, counter-battery and counter-mortar should be considered as one subject and known as counter-bombardment. Policy within each corps should be co-ordinated by a corps counter-bombardment officer (G.S.O.1), with a counter-bombardment officer at each divisional headquarters and a divisional observation troop, to take the place of the existing counter-mortar organizations.[34]

The Air O.P. and the Visual Control Post.

In Arakan, at the crossing of the Irrawaddy, and during the final defeat of the Japanese attempt to break out from the Pegu Yomas, the air O.P. had shown how well it could adapt itself to Far Eastern conditions. It had even repeated, on a small scale, its co-operation with tanks, which had been so successful a feature of the pursuit in Italy and in N.W. Europe. The tank commander would keep a listening watch on the gunner frequency, and by this means would pick up all information sent down as quickly as the guns. There were indeed occasions on which tanks were deployed straight away as a result of this information.[35]

In the S.W. Pacific, the air O.P. was also frequently used by the U.S. forces, on at least one occasion taking off for its initial flight from the deck of a carrier. Missions—which included the observation and engagement of enemy guns—were generally flown at a height of 1,500 feet, and seldom above 2,500 feet, owing to the thick clouds which normally surrounded the islands in the Pacific above these levels.[36]

The production of an amphibian O.P. aircraft for use in the Far East had been under consideration at the War Office and the Air Ministry since the middle of 1944 (*see* p. 239). The idea was that it should be capable of operating from the sea or from inland waterways in the absence of suitable landing grounds. It soon became evident, however, that the provision of such an aircraft was a long term project, and the War Office agreed that its requirements would be met by a machine with an interchangeable chassis—that is, wheels or floats.[37]

Another suggested means of solving this problem was the portable airfield, which was based on the principle that an aircraft could land or take off from a 500-foot cable by means of a hook permanently attached to its superstructure. Since, however, the cable weighed well over 1,000 lb., and it seemed probable that wherever conditions permitted its erection, it would be equally possible to prepare a landing strip, the idea was not proceeded with.[38]

Opportunities for night work by air O.Ps., though not perhaps so numerous as in Europe, were worth cultivating because of the Japanese habit of making all major movements by night. Had such action been possible, harassing fire could have been much more economically and effectively applied and the casualties inflicted on the enemy might have been considerably increased.[4]

The combination of air O.P. and visual control post for the control of close support aircraft was particularly valuable in jungle country, where there were few landmarks to guide pilots and smoke could not always be relied on to give an accurate indication of the target. At the visual control post, a V.H.F. set would keep in touch with the supporting aircraft, while a 48 set maintained communication with the guns and the air O.P. First, the target would be indicated to the bombers by smoke shell, aimed to fall 300 yards plus and minus, followed 30 seconds later by a troop salvo of H.E. directly on the objective. Then, as the first bomb landed, the air O.P. would give an observation, which would be transmitted *via* the visual control post to the bombers and would usually reach them within 15 to 20 seconds.([39])

On one occasion, when the target was too close to our own troops for a coloured smoke indication by the artillery, and our infantry were too tightly pinned to the ground to make use of their own 2-in. mortars for this purpose, the difficulty was overcome by getting the Hurribombers to carry out a dummy dive first and by noting the accuracy of this dive as observed from the air O.P. When satisfied, the visual control post confirmed the bombing and the operation continued.([40])

Artificial Moonlight

In view of the Japanese activities by night, and their skill at concealing and protecting themselves against artillery bombardment by day, the introduction of some form of artificial moonlight was clearly desirable. There were no searchlights available for this purpose in S.E.A.C., but during the coastal operations in Arakan, F.O.B. parties in L.C.S., aided by star shell, had observed and engaged enemy movements ashore.([6]) In the S.W. Pacific, also, the Australians, early in 1945, carried out successful trials with the 25-pr. star shell as a means of beach defence illumination.([41])

In the U.S.A., experiments carried out with the 60-in. A.A.S.L. showed that targets could be illuminated, under favourable conditions, up to ranges as great as 10,000 to 12,000 yards, and that, under the direction of a forward observer, areas could be searched for suitable targets. The main problem seemed likely to be—as it had been in Europe—the protection of the searchlights against retaliatory fire by the enemy. For this reason, it was considered that lights and guns should be so co-ordinated that the former might be employed alternatively, each individual light remaining in action for a very short period. It might even be possible, if lights were mobile, to move them, while doused, to alternative positions.

At the same time it was found that, by the use of an infra-red filter, patrolling and similar activities could be assisted, in open country, up to ranges of two or three miles.([42])

Meteor

Inaccuracies in meteor had, as usual, presented a big problem, and the organization of a meteor service had been slow in developing. In February, 1944, the only meteorological detachment under command of 4 Corps was without equipment, its own having been lost on the L of C. Hence reliance had to be placed on the R.A.F. meteor station at Imphal for predicted shooting at Tamu, which was 60 miles away and 1,700 feet lower, and at Kennedy Peak, which was 100 miles away and 5,700 feet higher. In the circumstances, units sometimes preferred to produce their own meteor, assuming the ballistic temperature to be the same as the air temperature at ground level, and the pressure to be 30 inches less the height correction, and ignoring the wind, which was usually light.[43]

The fact was that, in the organization of the meteor service, it had never been possible to reconcile completely the requirements of the War Office and Air Ministry. The 1943 reorganization (*see* p. 197), which had provided meteorological sections with every divisional artillery and A.G.R.A., had proved a heavy strain on R.A.F. resources, and in March, 1945, the Air Ministry, taking note of the increasing tendency in N.W. Europe to centralize control of artillery operations at corps headquarters, proposed a corresponding centralization of meteorological resources. Divisional artillery and A.G.R.A. sections, and the meteorological officers with survey regiments, were to be withdrawn and their duties undertaken by a strengthened meteorological section at corps headquarters, plus a mobile observing unit per corps for deployment as necessary to meet special requirements. With this, however, the War Office were unable to agree, since it would not be suitable for all theatres.

As the war was ending, the War Office made another attempt to solve the problem by proposing that the provision of meteor should become an artillery responsibility, as it was in the Canadian, American and German armies ; but this time the Air Ministry could not agree. The meteor service, they contended, was inseparable from weather forecasting, which was indisputably a R.A.F. responsibility.[44]

Calibration

The provision of a reliable meteor telegram was only half the problem of making the guns shoot accurately. The other half was calibration. In September, 1945, after six years of war experience, some of which had been bitter, a training memorandum was issued on this subject.[45] Calibration, it said, should be a continuous process ; beginning with the formal calibration of a new gun under practice camp conditions, and continuing as comparative calibration—by means of datum point shoots, air burst ranging, and observed shooting against suitable targets—throughout the whole life of the gun. If during this process, any gun gave a markedly different performance from the remainder of its troop, its M.V. would be checked as soon as possible by one of the accepted methods. Thus excessive spread in a regimental or divisional concentration would be avoided, and the infantry would be enabled to keep closer to the covering fire in an attack.

A.A. Defence

Throughout this campaign, enemy air activity was slight and at no time were the A.A. defences seriously tested. What problems there were were connected with the jungle and with the system of air supply, which necessitated the provision, and the protection, of forward airfields. In 4 Corps, for example, there were never less than two airfields to be protected, and for this purpose one H.A.A. and one L.A.A. battery moved well forward in the leading formation column.[16] For the rest, fronts were wide and river crossings numerous, so that A.A. resources were as a rule dispersed in small quantities reminiscent of the early days in the Western Desert; and now, as then, owing to the lack of enemy air effort, this dispersion, if not entirely justified, was at least unpunished.

Early warning presented a more than usually difficult problem. Radar could not always be relied on in the jungle, and the use of visual O.Ps. put an additional strain on an already overburdened communications system. The enemy, naturally, continued to take advantage of these conditions and was skilful in his use of the low level attack to evade radar.([44]). Indeed, so difficult was the gunnery problem presented by the "hedge-hopper" that, at the request of the Army Commander, a small number of balloons were preserved from disbandment—owing to the need for economy in material and manpower, and to the difficulty of supplying the hydrogen— and were installed for the defence of the very important crossing of the Chindwin at Kalewa.

The system of I.A.Zs. and G.D.As., as developed in Europe, was not used in this theatre, because of the wide dispersion of vulnerable areas, the difficulty of controlling our own aircraft (in many cases there was no contact with R.A.F. controllers other than the commanders of adjacent airfields), and the extent of our air superiority. Instead a general rule was laid down that guns were not to open fire without permission of the R.A.F. controller unless a hostile act had been committed. But in view of the unreliability of the early warning system, this was not a satisfactory state of affairs, and had the Japanese air force been more active, it is probable that, at the more important V.Ps., a rigid application of I.A.Z. rules would have become necessary.([46]).

The problem would have been simplified if a really reliable means of radar identification (I.F.F.) could have been provided. By March, 1945, a new system, the I.F.F. Mk. 5 (United Nations Beacon), was being developed on a high priority in the U.S.A. Its main advantages over the I.F.F. Mk. 3 were a greatly improved security against compromise and counter-measures, improved discrimination in range and bearing, and increased "traffic handling" capacity. It was not, however, expected to be completely installed in the S.W. Pacific and S.E. Asia areas until the end of 1946.([47])

At the same time research and development of A.A. radar equipment were aimed at pick-up ranges of at least 80,000 yards and a capacity for accurate following down to half a degree in elevation.([48]) Meanwhile experience in action against the V.1 and the new jet propelled aircraft in N.W. Europe had shown the necessity of automatic following when dealing with high speed targets, and by July, 1945, new equipments, the A.A. No. 3 Mks. 4 & 7, embodying this principle, were in course of production for despatch to the Far East.([49])

List of References

[1] Despatch by Gen. Giffard, Commanding 11 Army Gp., 23rd June-10th November 1944.
[2] H.Q. Fourteenth Army, 542/1/—/ORG. of 1st and 25th February 1945.
[3] Report by No. 1 Ind. O.R.S. of 6th February 1944.
[4] Account of Operations by 4 Corps from 6th May to 15th August 1945.
[5] R.A. Notes No. 28, App. "F".
[6] Notes by Brig. "G" Research, November 1944.

(⁷) A.L.F.S.E.A. No. 10868/RA of 7th January and 28th February 1945.
(⁸) 15 Ind. Corps History, Arakan Campaign, 1944-45.
(⁹) S.A.C.S.E.A. No. SAC/5149 of 19th March 1945.
(¹⁰) "The Pattern of War", by Lt.-Gen. Sir Francis Tuker.
(¹¹) 25 Ind. Div. Arty., Lessons from Campaign, 12th December 1944 to 20th March 1945, by C.R.A.
(¹²) Combined Operations H.Q. Monthly Information Summary No. 26, Sec. A, 15th July 1945.
(¹³) R.A. Notes No. 29, para. 1686.
(¹⁴) R.A. Notes No. 34, para. 1843.
(¹⁵) D.R.A.(I) Liaison Letter No. 5, quoted in R.A. Notes No. 15 of April 1944.
(¹⁶) Account of Operations by 4 Corps from October 1944 to capture of Rangoon.
(¹⁷) R.A. 5 Ind. Div. Operation Instruction No. 22 of 10th June 1945.
(¹⁸) R.A. Notes No. 38, App. "B".
(¹⁹) A.L.F.S.E.A. No. 10844/RA of 23rd April 1945.
(²⁰) B.R.A. Fourteenth Army, No. 82624/100/RA of 10th March 1945.
(²¹) D.R.A.(I) L.L. No. 10, quoted in R.A. Notes No. 25 of February 1945.
(²²) D.R.A.(I) L.L. No. 11, quoted in R.A. Notes No. 26 of March 1945.
(²³) R.A. Notes No. 28, para. 1603.
(²⁴) R.A. Notes No. 28, App. "C".
(²⁵) A.L.F.S.E.A. No. 12053/GT of 1st June 1945.
(²⁶) R.A. 4 Corps Training Instruction No. 2 of 31st July 1945.
(²⁷) D.R.A./OML/16 of 19th February 1945.
(²⁸) D.O. No. 397/RA1 of 19th April 1945.
(²⁹) C.C.R.A. 15 Corps No. 3150/51/9/RA of 9th March 1945.
(³⁰) B.R.A. Fourteenth Army No. 82214/23/RA of 12th March 1945.
(³¹) Report on C.M. work in Burmese Theatre by GSO1 (L), March 1945.
(³²) R.A. Notes No. 30, para. 1733.
(³³) R.A. Notes No. 31, para. 1751.
(³⁴) R.A. Notes No. 35, para. 1873.
(³⁵) D.R.A.(I) L.L. No. 13, quoted in R.A. Notes No. 32 of September 1945.
(³⁶) R.A. Notes No. 27, para. 1542.
(³⁷) D. of Air, Monthly L.L. No. 13, 23rd August-22nd September 1944.
(³⁸) Brit. Army Staff, Washington, RA22/1 of 25th January 1945.
(³⁹) Extracts from News Letters, A.L.F.S.E.A. No. 11313/RA of 8th March 1945.
(⁴⁰) R.A. Notes No. 33, para. 1797.
(⁴¹) R.A. Notes No. 33, para. 1806.
(⁴²) R.A. Notes No. 34, App. "F".
(⁴³) Report by No. 1 Ind. ORS of 6th February 1944.
(⁴⁴) W.O. File 79/Mob/5966.
(⁴⁵) R.A.T.M. No. 15 of September 1945.
(⁴⁶) First Report by GSO1(L)AA, War Office, 15th March 1945.
(⁴⁷) R.A. Notes No. 26, para. 1525 and No. 28, App. "J".
(⁴⁸) R.A. Notes No. 28, para. 1629.
(⁴⁹) R.A. Notes, No. 30, para. 1729.

CHAPTER XVII
GENERAL CONCLUSIONS

The Second World War had been fought in the main with artillery equipments of familiar pattern. The anti-tank gun, first introduced in 1938, was the only new type of weapon to take the field until the end of 1944, when it was joined by the rocket; and even the latter was no stranger to the Royal Regiment, having flourished for a brief spell and then faded away just over a century ago.

New tactical uses of artillery there had of course been, to meet the expanding scope of air and armoured warfare; but, up to 1945 at any rate, they had not involved the provision of special weapons. Airborne and self-propelled artillery had so far been produced by relatively minor modifications to existing British and American equipments. In the field artillery, the 25-pr. had been a definite success, and the policy of combining the qualities of a gun and a howitzer in one weapon was generally felt to have been vindicated. But it was in the control and flexibility of artillery fire that the most striking developments had occurred, and here the Royal Regiment may fairly claim to have led the world. The application of modern radio technique to divisional and corps artillery concentrations had paved the way to a more effective, as well as a more economical, use of the gun. As the war went on, the control of artillery fire became more and more centralized, until ultimately it was highly effective at the corps level; and there were occasions—such as the crossing of the Rhine—when, with two corps operating side by side, control might have been successfully exercised by army. If the radio link between infantry and guns could be made as reliable as the artillery net, the substitution of "on call" for timed covering fire might make possible a similar economy in the employment of the shell.

To the A.A. gunner, radar had rendered services of a different, and still more decisive, nature. By its ability to find and to track the unseen target, it had helped to solve a hitherto insoluble problem; and later, in the target-operated (V.T.) fuze, it had provided him—in the nick of time—with the means of defeating the flying bomb (V.1) attacks on the United Kingdom and on Antwerp. Its application to field artillery problems, though less advanced, was full of promise, and before the war was over, some progress had been made in the location and engagement of hostile mortars and in controlling the height of air burst H.E.

In short, if the First World War had been distinguished by the development of the petrol engine and the conquest of the air, the Second World War was made equally remarkable by the development of the wireless valve and the conquest of the ether. It was this conquest that had so extended the scope of fire control systems and that now opened the way for further extensions in the range and mobility of artillery weapons. There were several promising novelties in the offing as the war ended, such as the recoilless gun and the rotated rocket, which might ultimately have a revolutionary effect upon the art of warfare.

There is another new factor in the world situation to-day, which is perhaps of even greater importance. In the past, the superior industrial capacity of Great Britain and her command of the sea have enabled her to make up for a bad start. In the future, that may not be so, and final success may depend more on immediate readiness for war and less on mobilization potential.

It is therefore worth recalling the occasions on which, in this Second World War or in our preparations for it, we were slow in adapting ourselves to new ideas or to changing circumstances. There was the failure to develop the S.P. gun in 1930; the delay in applying radar to the problem of A.A. fire control; the failure to develop a counter-mortar organization immediately after our experiences in France and Belgium; the delay in the development of time fuzes and the use of air burst H.E.; and the rejection of artificial moonlight when it was first offered in the autumn of 1942.

And the causes? In the opinion of the then D.G. of A., " the radical weakness of our weapon policy lay in the lack of knowledge, both theoretical and practical, of the principles of weapon technology and performance in the quarters responsible for its formulation and decision . . . In principle, most of the major weapons developed for the war owed their origin as policy projects to the Technical Staff. Few, if any, were originated by definite General Staff statements of military characteristics." Even the 25-pr. was from start to finish a creation of the Technical Staff, with outside support coming mainly from the School of Artillery.

It was not, however, only in our weapon policy that faults were to be found. There is evidence in these pages of a lack of co-operation between the various arms and services. There was the early neglect of artillery in the armoured battle; the original tendency for A.A. artillery to develop into a " private army "; the ever recurring difficulty of combining guns and infantry mortars in a single comprehensive fire plan; and the tardy realization of what could be done by really intimate co-operation between the artillery of the ground and of the air.

It is not difficult to find excuses for this early separation between the airman and the soldier, the mortar and the gun, the armour and the artillery, even the A.A. from the field gunner. Faced with a war on a scale, or of a kind, for which it was not prepared, each arm and each service was too preoccupied in making sure of its own position to give much attention to the needs of its fellows. But the results were deplorable, and by none were they more acutely felt than by the gunner, whose role is essentially an auxiliary one and who cannot by himself win battles. Among them, surely, was the apparent lack of faith in the gun during the gloomy days of 1941, when what little artillery we had was scattered about in " small packets " and was offered no chance of concentrating its fire power at the decisive time and place.

The breach within the regiment, between A.A. and field artillery, was completely mended before the war was over. By the end of 1944 the H.A.A. gun was being used extensively in the ground role and A.A. gunners were expected to man the 7.2-in. how. as an alternative weapon. The Bofors also had proved its value both for the direct engagement of attacking infantry and for the direction—by tracer—of our own troops in the assault; and in the later stages of the war in N.W. Europe, the L.A.A. guns played an important part in the " pepperpot " concentrations which achieved results as unexpected as they were remarkable. Thus the Royal Artillery, which had started the war in two separate branches, learned to fight its guns as one regiment.

Co-operation with the other arms was similarly improved by mutual trust begotten upon the battlefield and ripened by victory after victory. Yet these very successes were sometimes a source of error through the hypnotic effect of habit, which led to the perpetuation of tactics that were no longer suitable to the occasion. The misuse of the anti-tank portee and of the Jock column could both be attributed to over-confidence born of victories that could not be expected to repeat themselves under changed conditions; and when at last centralized control, good radio drill, and good liaison between the arms and services, had laid the foundations of victory at El Alamein, there was the same tendency for this new technique to develop into a fetish, so that the "colossal crack" became on occasion more of a hindrance than a help.

It was in fact never a technique that won a battle, but the selection and exploitation of a particular principle of war. At Sidi Barrani, in December, 1940, it was surprise that was the master principle, and as usual on such occasions, victory was complete and the price cheap, whether expressed in terms of lives lost or of ammunition expended. During the remainder of the first Cyrenaican, and much of the Eritrean and Abyssinian campaigns, it was mobility that won the day and proved that, if "sweat saves blood", petrol may save ammunition. At Keren and at El Alamein, where surprise and mobility could no longer be brought into play, concentration became the key to victory and the amount of ammunition dumped rose from 50 r.p.g. (at Sidi Barrani) to 500 r.p.g. at Keren and 1,000 r.p.g. at El Alamein. At Tobruk, Alam El Halfa and Medenine, defensive battles were won by "sitting still" and letting the enemy batter himself in vain against well sited anti-tank and A.A. gun positions; but final victory depended upon a return to the offensive. The A.A. and the anti-tank gun might hold the dive bomber and the tank, but our own aircraft and tanks had to drive them off the field of battle, helped in the later stages of the war by the air O.P. and the S.P. gun. In the American and the Russian armies, the principle was carried to its logical conclusion by the transformation of anti-tank into tank-destroying units.

In the conflict with the enemy mortar, a purely defensive attitude was rarely, if ever, successful owing to the difficulty of locating it. A counter-mortar organization was indeed necessary, and after much experimentation it finally became embodied with counter-battery in a single counter-bombardment organization; but the final answer to the enemy mortar—in Europe and, particularly, in the Far East—was a better mortar, and better mortar tactics, of our own.

So, in the preparation of artillery fire plans, there was no royal road to success. The increasing use of air transport made economy of ammunition of greater importance than ever, and for this reason, as well as because of its inflexibility, there are some, including the Americans, who believe that the old-fashioned creeping barrage is "dead." At its best in the First World War, when trench lines were continuous from the Channel to the Alps, it was in the Second World War often a "blow in the air." Yet it had its successes, especially when in support of armour; as witness El Hamma and Caen (Operations "Goodwood" and "Totalize"), the Garigliano, the Reichswald (Operation "Veritable") and the Senio (Operation "Buckland").

Opinion is equally divided on the question whether the primary role of the gun is to neutralize or to destroy. In Europe, at the end of the war, there was a feeling in favour of the former and a consequent proposal to reduce the weight of the field artillery shell in the interests of greater range and mobility. In S.E. Asia experience seemed to point to an exactly opposite conclusion. Against the Japanese bunker, neutralization was no good. It was destruction that was wanted.

Lastly, we find even the ancient controversy about the close support gun springing into life again with the development of jungle and airborne warfare. With good, or indifferent, roads and good radio drill, the field artillery of the division may be able to put their shell wherever the infantryman can go. But in trackless jungle, or in the early stages of an airborne assault, this becomes impossible.

It was hoped, in 1945, that the answer to this problem might be in the development of the recoilless gun. Here was a weapon, it seemed, that might combine the handiness of the infantry gun with the "punch" of the anti-tank gun or "concrete buster", and thus achieve at last the genuine dual purpose weapon and eliminate some at least of the disadvantages of the "golf bag principle". The war ended, however, before any user trials of these weapons could be carried out, and the matter remained therefore undecided.

These are the sort of problems that faced the gunner at the end of the Second World War, and they are not very different from those that faced his predecessors three centuries ago. "The Art is like to a circle without end", and in his journey round the perimeter of that circle, the gunner is continually striking a new balance between old principles. There is nothing abstruse about these principles; they are so simple that a child could understand them. There is, therefore, little logical foundation for the widely held belief that battles are lost through ignorance or neglect of them. They are of course often broken, because the principles of war are mutually contradictory and one cannot indulge one of them except at the expense of another. The difficulty lies in knowing where to put the emphasis at any particular moment, and in preventing a battle drill from degenerating, under the intoxicating effects of an early success, into an empty ritual.

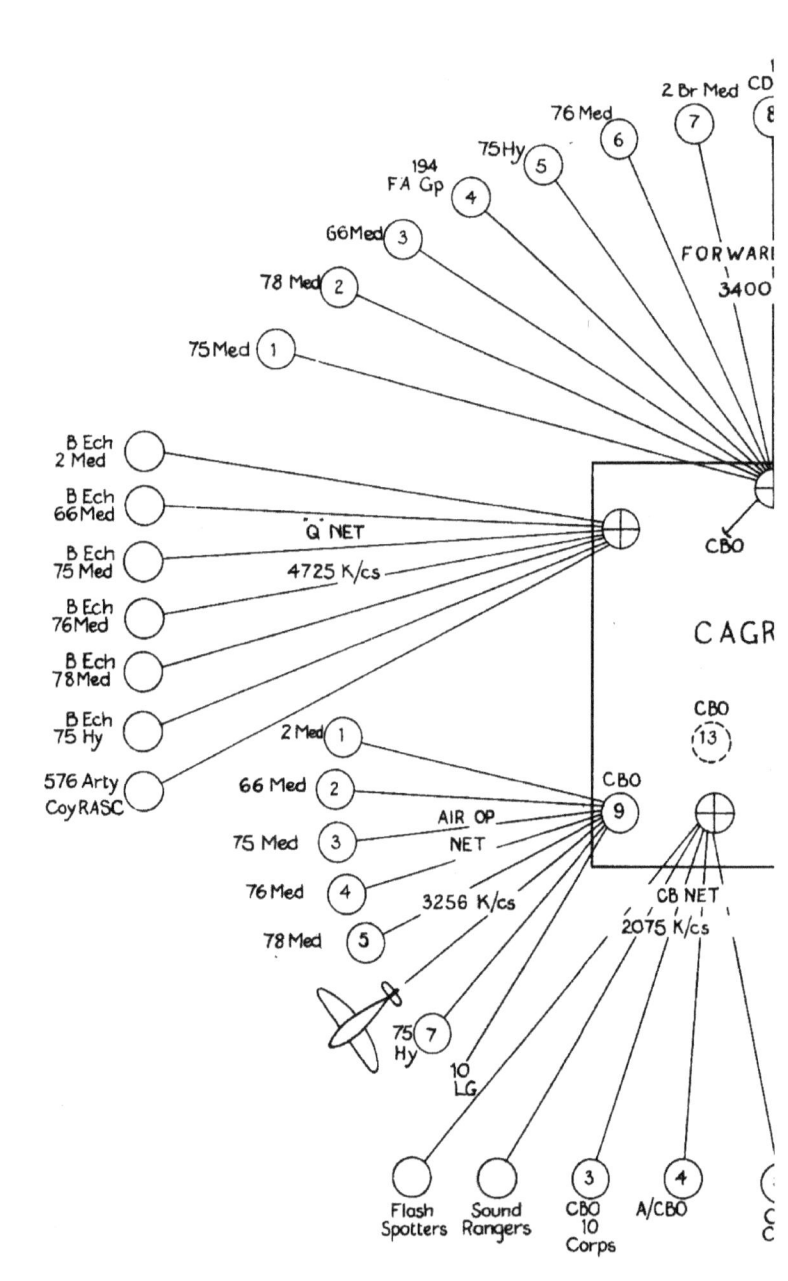

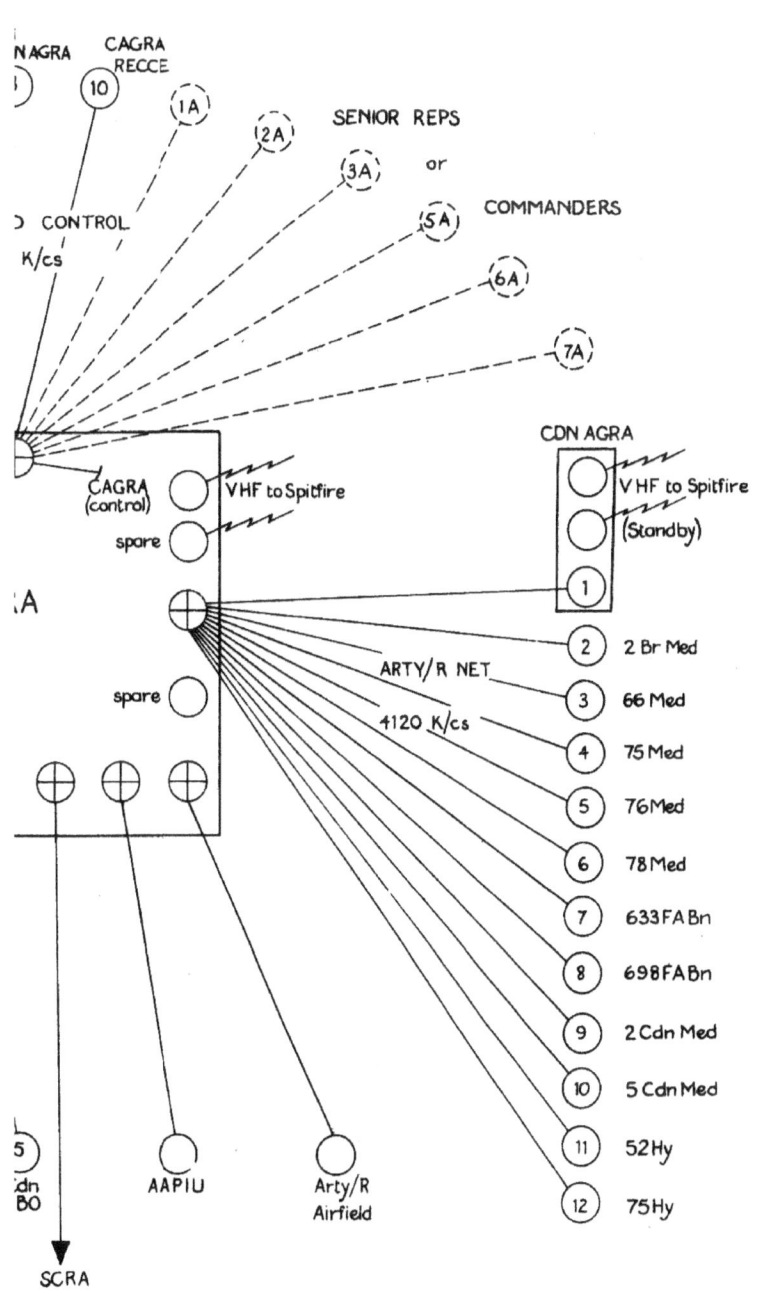

Diagram 5
Wireless Communications of 6 AGRA for Attack on Gustav Line 12 May '44

INDEX

NOTES.—Many of the subjects included in this index are dealt with very briefly in the text. The references that cover them are intended merely as a guide to the reader, who will, it is hoped, be able to trace without difficulty the technical or other work to which he should turn for fuller information.

Battle actions and engagements are *not* included in this Index, but are listed separately at the end of the volume.

	Page
AGREED POINT METHOD OF SHOOTING WITH AIR OBSERVATION	198, 266
AIR BOMBARDMENT—	
comparison of artillery and	103, 130, 228–9
distance at which attacking troops should follow	222, 228–9, 245, 271
moral and material effects of	38, 69, 71–2, 84, 116–7, 167, 183, 218, 244–5, 247, 271, 273, 313
scales of	163, 167, 183, 196, 217, 225, 227, 244, 269, 307, 312
AIRBORNE DIVISIONAL ARTILLERY—	
command of	205, 261
equipment of	205–6, 261, 271
forward observer unit for	207, 218, 246, 261, 271
organization of	205–7, 261
origins of	205
reinforcement of	206–7, 218–9, 261, 271
supply of ammunition for	219
AIR BURSTS—	
calculating error of moment	101, 230
calibration	101
counter-battery fire	148, 244, 298, 305
counter-mortar fire	209, 213, 231, 241–2
covering fire	226, 306, 313
defensive fire	222, 305
engagement of infantry in trenches	148, 170
harassing fire	298, 305
in jungle	291, 298, 305
indicating bomb line	238, 275, 276
indicating end of timed programme	166
moral effects of	170, 281
ranging	101, 170, 230
survey	150, 156, 291
AIRCRAFT FIGHTING ZONE—	
origins of	20
use of	33, 176, 221, 258
AIRCRAFT, PILOTLESS (*see* FLYING BOMB).	
AIR DEFENCE BRIGADE—	
organization of	18
renaming of	21
AIR DEFENCE COMMITTEE IN M.E.—	
abolition of	174
formation and functions of	61
AIR DEFENCE COMMANDER, functions of	174, 201
AIR DEFENCE DIVISION IN S.H.A.E.F., formation and functions of	249
AIRFIELDS—	
A.A. defence of (*see* A.A. DEFENCE).	
permanent allocation of A.A. formations to defence of	152, 174
silence as means of defence against night air attack of	130
sited in advance of main bodies in pursuit	149
AIR LIAISON OFFICERS	310

	Page
AIR OBSERVATION—	
essential in C.B. fire	278
in desert, difficulties of	45
in jungle, difficulties of	289, 313
in night operations, growing demand for	278
procedure for shooting with	6–7, 31, 57–8, 80, 99–100, 198, 266
AIR O.P.—	
air burst ranging assisted by	230
amphibious and air portable	239, 322
co-operation with tanks by	210, 322
co-operation with direct support aircraft by	277
co-ordination of arty/R and	214
counter-battery fire controlled by	188, 197, 216, 225, 238, 240, 309
counter-flak fire controlled by	172, 197, 224
counter-mortar fire controlled by	186, 224, 278
first use of	162
helicopter as	239
in assault landings	188, 219, 239, 322
in bocage country	224
in jungle	289, 296, 311, 313
in mountains	216
in pursuit	238–9, 277
in river crossings	191
in Western Desert, effect of lack of	156
large observed concentrations controlled by	172, 197
limitations of	158–9, 172, 197
naval covering fire controlled by	188, 308, 309
night operation of	172, 224, 238, 322
oblique photographs used by	172, 238
organization of	158, 239, 278
origins of	7, 31, 158
portable airfield for	322
protection against damage by own shells of	224
protection against enemy fighters of	159, 224, 278
radar control of	238
reconnaissance of gun areas by	197
registration shoots conducted by	172
scale of provision of	158, 278
smoke screens checked by	197, 237
tank hunting by	238
towed portee behind tanks in pursuit	278
AIR SUPPORT—	
as alternative to medium and heavy artillery	16, 31, 157, 179
as substitute for artillery covering fire	206, 226
carpet bombing as feature of	225, 312
controlled through R.A. channels	304, 309, 314
co-ordination of artillery and	170–1
dummy runs as feature of	275, 323
AIR SUPPORT—	
evolution of close (direct)	102–3, 129–30, 198, 207, 264, 292, 304, 312–3
in airborne operations	206, 245, 270
in assault landings	184, 187, 309
in attack of bunkers	290
in counter-battery role	142, 171, 198, 226, 243, 245, 296, 312
in counter-flak role	270
in jungle, difficulties of	298
Rover system of control of	163, 198, 214, 275, 276–7, 304, 309, 314, 322–3
shortcomings in 1940-1	54, 67, 68, 116–7
AIR TRANSPORT, turns the scale in S.E.A.C.	293, 294, 304
ALTERNATIVE LAY-OUTS, L.A.A.	72–3

	Page
ALTERNATIVE POSITIONS for field artillery	28, 56
AMALGAMATION OF FIELD AND ANTI-TANK REGIMENTS	119, 137

AMMUNITION—
- air supply of ... 317
- anti-tank ... 173, 211
- care and storage of ... 5–6, 197
- dumping of ... 29, 48, 50, 58, 142, 167, 193, 213, 226, 263, 268–9, 274, 277
- diversity of ... 7–8, 196, 262
- expenditure of 51, 57, 60, 142, 145, 167, 187, 192, 196, 228, 237, 244–5, 266, 271
- neglect of ... 102, 197
- returns, importance of ... 229
- shortage of ... 44, 46, 132, 212, 295
- sorting of ... 5–6, 197, 262
- supply the dominating factor in artillery dispositions ... 194
- supply the dominating factor in jungle fire plans ... 291, 317
- waste of ... 114–5, 229

AMPHIBEAN SUPPORT REGIMENT	207–8, 218, 276, 306, 311

A.A. ARTILLERY—
- in assault landings, proportion of ... 189, 219
- in ground role (*see* SECONDARY ROLES).
- misuse of ... 114
- origins of ... 7

A.A. ARTILLERY EQUIPMENTS—
- 20-mm ... 40, 115, 133–4, 184, 199, 212, 220, 258, 287, 301, 305
- 2-pr twin ... 19
- 40-mm ... 19, 40, 133, 199
- 3-in ... 18, 27
- 3·7-in (mobile) ... 18, 257, 313
- 3·7-in (static) ... 18, 258
- 4·5-in ... 18
- 5·25-in ... 211
- intermediate ... 133, 258
- rockets (*see* ROCKETS IN A.A. ROLE).
- S.P. (*see* SELF-PROPELLED ARTILLERY, A.A.).

A.A.-CUM-A.TK WEAPON FOR INFANTRY, proposal	40

A.A. BRIGADE—
- inadequacy of " base and forward " establishment ... 28
- introduction of ... 21
- reorganization of ... 35
- used as A.G.R.A. ... 252

A.A. DEFENCE—
- commander, role of ... 34, 132, 153, 175, 201, 220, 250
- difficulties in India ... 299–300
- early warning in (*see* EARLY WARNING).
- gun densities ... 20, 33, 131
- in assault landings ... 189–90, 219–21
- in forward areas ... 21–2, 58, 62–4, 82, 91–2, 114–5, 173–4, 249–50, 257, 324–5
- layouts, H.A.A. ... 20, 82, 131, 256, 258–60
- layouts, L.A.A. ... 20, 72–3, 82, 257, 258–60
- of airfields ... 34, 63, 114, 130, 151, 152, 174, 189, 221, 250, 324
- of ports 33, 34, 39, 61–2, 69, 71, 82, 92–3, 114, 131–2, 152, 173, 174, 175, 177, 189, 195, 201, 202, 220, 250, 259–60
- of small V.Ps. ... 20, 63, 220, 281
- policy, control of ... 22, 33, 34, 60, 62, 174, 201, 249, 300
- priorities of ... 63, 173–4, 249
- scales of 20, 33, 69, 70, 82, 130, 131, 152, 173, 175, 177, 201, 202, 219–20, 250, 260, 324–5
- use of decoy in ... 153

A.A. FIRE—	
deterrent *versus* lethal effect of	39, 132, 174
restriction of	21, 34–5, 93, 132, 201, 202, 221, 250, 325
A.A. AND FIELD ARTILLERY FIRE, comparison of	177
A.A. RESOURCES, dispersion of	58, 62, 91, 173, 324–5
A.A. OPERATIONS ROOM—	
functions of	34, 189, 220, 250, 251, 276, 278
mobile	257
A.A. UNITS BEAR MAIN BURDEN OF AIR DEFENCE	82, 131, 219, 259–60, 281
A.M.T.B. DEFENCE	94–6, 251
ANTI-TANK ARTILLERY—	
concrete busting by	187, 199, 254
bunker busting by	291
in the attack, follow-up of	128, 163, 191, 223
in the field artillery role (*see* SECONDARY ROLES).	
in support of a tank attack	128
offensive use of	32, 79, 90, 104, 106, 113, 151
origins of	16–7
portee (*see* PORTEE ANTI-TANK GUN).	
A.TK ARTILLERY EQUIPMENTS—	
37-mm	46, 67, 78–9
2-pr	16–7, 35–6, 53, 66, 67, 89, 102, 106, 113, 117, 119, 126, 287, 299
A.TK ARTILLERY EQUIPMENTS—	
57-mm	287, 299
6-pr	17, 36, 67, 89, 117, 119, 126, 128, 135, 151, 155, 162, 299
17-pr	126–7, 135, 150, 155, 162–3, 199, 203, 211, 223, 254
32-pr	211
3-in 20-cwt A.A. gun as make-shift	127
S.P. (*see* SELF-PROPELLED ARTILLERY, A.TK).	
A.TK. COMPANY OF INFANTRY BDE, introduction of	32
A.TK. DEFENCE—	
co-ordination of	17, 32, 112, 151
digging in of guns in	112, 113, 128
lay-outs	17, 32, 45–6, 78, 79, 104, 112–3, 124, 127, 128, 151
opening ranges	17, 32, 35, 45, 106, 112–3, 123, 128
scales of	32, 138, 151
25-pr as core of	78, 106–5, 107, 112, 124, 128
A.TK MINEFIELDS (*see* MINEFIELDS).	
A.TK OBSTACLES—	
destruction of (by artillery)	52
in desert, lack of	113
A.TK REGIMENT—	
corps	36, 181
divisional, organization and equipment of	17, 36, 137, 150, 181, 223, 287, 299
temporary break-up of	119
A.TK SCREENS, enemy use of	106, 109–10, 143, 147–8, 167
AREA SHOOTS—	
in desert, necessity of	116
special types of quick	208
ARMOUR, race between gun and	36, 126–7, 135, 211
ARMOURED CARRIERS FOR ASSAULTING INFANTRY, use of	227, 269
ARMOURED DIVISIONAL ARTILLERY—	
command of	47, 118, 239
need for med arty in	180, 210, 239
organization of	32–3, 46–7, 53, 118, 125, 137, 181
origins of	9, 18

Page

ARMOURED O.P.—
    communication with tanks and infantry by 140
    in mountain warfare, unsuitability of 57
    origins of 10
    scale of provision of 36, 54
    vehicles 54, 90
ARMOURED SUPPORT GROUP FOR ASSAULT LANDINGS 208, 218
ARMY GROUP, R.A.—
    decentralization to divisions of units of 185, 240
    in the pursuit, handling of 167–8, 216, 240
    maximum strength of 240
    origins of 158
    signals company required for 217
ARTIFICIAL MOONLIGHT—
    organization of special units for 280
    origins of 134, 171, 177, 209–10
    use of 221, 228, 243, 244, 254, 263, 268, 269, 274, 276, 280–1, 323
ARTIFICIAL PORT, A.A. defence of 219–20
ARTILLERY FIRE—
    as means of deception (*see* DECEPTION).
    denies ground to enemy 55, 73–4, 120, 126
    holds front in Tunisia 161, 168
ARTY/R AIRCRAFT—
    allocation of 159, 214, 265, 266, 278
    early difficulties over 7, 37, 67, 68, 80, 146, 156, 162, 195
ARTY/R PILOTS, need for training of 7, 58, 99, 278, 289
ASSAULT DIVISIONAL ARTILLERY 218, 303
ASSAULT LANDINGS—
    airborne troops in C.B. role in 184
    comparison of naval and military fire units in 182
    defence of beach-heads in 184–5, 189–90, 219–21
    naval covering fire for 182, 187, 207, 217–8

BABY 25-PR 288
BALLOON BARRAGES 20, 34, 189, 195, 201, 220, 258, 325
BALLOONS ON TRAINS, use of 131
BARRAGES, A.A.—
    anti-torpedo 189
    control of 82, 84, 154, 220, 257
    directional 189
    geographical 61–2, 92–3, 131
    origins of 21, 39,
    porcupine 83, 189
    predicted (radar controlled) 82, 84, 131, 154, 175, 257
    preponderance of 132
    radial 220
    sun 175–6, 189
    umbrella 71, 84, 189, 220, 281
BARRAGES, FIELD ARTILLERY—
    box 51, 163
    creeping—
        as bomb line 163–4, 170
        compared with concentrations 2, 143, 235–7, 266, 279–80, 317
        corps (block) 263–5, 279
        crooked 29, 164, 265
        density of 29, 143, 164, 167, 225, 226, 227–8, 265, 279
        depth (number of rows) of 194, 208, 265
        depth of penetration of 225, 227, 265, 276, 279
        directional 164, 208
        dummy 200, 275

BARRAGES, FIELD ARTILLERY—*cont.*
    creeping—*cont.*
        dwelling on opening line 144, 167, 200, 265
        enemy D.F. mistaken for own 200
        frontages of 2, 143, 164, 167, 215, 225, 226, 227, 265, 276
        in forest and jungle 267, 291
        in mountains 59
        lethal effect of 144
        lifts, size of 28–9, 170, 265
        longest duration of 266
        marker line, use of 144
        on call 318
        pauses in 200, 215, 225, 227, 265
        quick 99, 156, 277
        rate of advance with infantry
            3, 51, 144, 167, 170, 191, 194, 214, 215, 222, 227, 235, 265, 275–6
        rate of advance with tanks 28, 164, 225, 227–8, 236
        recall or stopping of 144–5
        standard 99
        time required to prepare 29, 156, 279
        two-way 200
    standing 3, 51, 275–6
BATTLE GROUPS 124–5, 137
BIRCH GUN 9
BISHOP, THE 89, 180
BLOCK PLOTS (*see* SKELETON BLOCK PLOTS).
BOCAGE COUNTRY, effects of 222, 231–2
BOMBARDMENTS—
    air (*see* AIR BOMBARDMENTS).
    artillery—
        duration *versus* weight of 236–7, 292–3, 318
        feint (*see* DECEPTION).
        moral and material effects of
            1–2, 50, 144, 193, 214, 218, 236–7, 245, 247, 248–9, 266, 267–8, 270, 271, 273, 313, 318–9
        number of shells *versus* weight of 268, 279
        naval 51, 103, 116, 182, 187, 218, 225, 244, 310
BOMBARDMENT—
    control headquarters 310
    forward observer 103, 116, 182, 184, 187–8, 310
    liaison officer 103, 116, 182, 187, 310
    liaison unit 184
    softening 244, 263–5, 269, 274, 290, 312–3
BOMB LINE—
    creeping barrage as 163–4, 170
    for guidance of supporting aircraft 184, 238, 275, 276
BOX, DEFENSIVE 104, 109, 120–4, 293
BRIGADE GROUPS IN M.E., formation of 118
B.A.A., appointment of 60, 114, 152
B.B.C. TIME SIGNALS, use of (*see* TIMED PROGRAMMES).
BUFFALO, 25-pr fired from 276
BUNKERS—
    co-operation of tanks and artillery in the attack of 290, 292, 295–6
    use of artillery for the destruction of 289–91, 319
    use of rockets for the destruction of 306

CABLE COMMUNICATIONS—
    in the artillery battle 58, 74, 151, 288, 313
    in A.A. lay-outs 201, 220

	Page
CALIBRATION—	
policy	5, 101, 142, 145, 197, 324
troop, formation of	197
CANNON-FIRING FIGHTER AIRCRAFT, development of	73, 115, 130, 131
CASUALTIES, comparison of causes of	142, 231, 242, 277
CAVALRY (HORSED) ATTACK GUNS	56
CENTRALIZED CONTROL OF ARTILLERY, growth of	279, 293, 326
CLOCK CODE SYSTEM OF AIR OBSERVATION	6, 99
CLOSE SUPPORT—	
aircraft (*see* AIR SUPPORT).	
guns	9, 11, 138–9, 328–9
in jungle, problems of	56, 292, 295–6, 304
in mountains, problems of	56
tanks in jungle	292, 295–6, 301
wireless problems	54, 178, 289
COAST ARTILLERY—	
developments after First World War	7, 22
in Indian Ocean	301
in Italy	251
in M.E.	64, 94, 134–5, 155
in North Africa	176
in N.W. Europe	250–1
mobile battery	134–5, 155
radar (*see* RADAR).	
COLOUR PLOTTING, for tracking of low-flying air attacks	153
COLOURED SMOKE (*see* SMOKE).	
COLUMNS, mobile	43, 47, 53, 54, 68, 88, 91, 103, 119–120
COMMAND OF FIELD ARTILLERY, system of	36, 47, 59, 118
COMMAND OF A.A. ARTILLERY, system of	34, 60, 62, 114, 118, 152, 201, 300
COMMAND OF COAST ARTILLERY, system of	176
C.C.M.A.	4, 145, 158
C.C.R.A.	4, 59, 62, 118, 141, 151, 158, 159, 167, 296
COMMUNICATIONS (*see* CABLE and WIRELESS).	
CONCENTRATION, revival of principle of	138, 141, 143–5, 156, 212, 291, 293, 312
CONCENTRATIONS—	
abuse of	229
against tanks, use of	80, 88, 126, 146–7, 162–3, 188
compared with barrages (*see* BARRAGES, FIELD ARTILLERY).	
corps and greater	142, 193, 200, 215, 222, 236, 266, 293, 317
depth of	208
divisional	5, 142, 161, 166, 188, 195, 277, 293, 294, 309, 312
grouping and naming of	235
observed	161, 167
on call	167, 200, 225, 226, 227, 235, 244, 269, 275, 317
rate of advance of timed	141
regimental	10, 36, 224
standard	143–4
CONCENTRATIONS—	
terror	200, 229
time required for preparation of	5, 150, 156
timed programme of	48, 81, 141, 166, 201, 295
CONCRETE BUSTING	187, 199, 254, 263, 264
CORPS ARTILLERY, frequent changes in composition of	239
COUNTER-BATTERY—	
aircraft (*see* AIR SUPPORT).	
allotment of guns for	4, 51, 80, 86, 141–2, 215, 225, 228, 244, 265, 270, 276
co-ordinate section	194
degree of concentration used for neutralization	100, 109, 141–2, 167, 186–7, 213, 223, 265, 266
during period of consolidation, difficulty of	279

COUNTER-BATTERY—*cont.*
- Festa ... 241
- importance of observation in ... 279
- in jungle ... 309, 320–1
- milk round system ... 213, 215, 270
- neutralization versus destruction ... 80, 100, 240
- officer ... 4, 86, 171, 183, 194, 214, 242, 243
- retaliatory shoots ... 162, 226, 241
- silent registration ... 142
- smoke screen as feint to discover enemy gun positions ... 144, 265

COUNTER-BOMBARDMENT ORGANIZATION ... 322, 328

COUNTER-FLAK—
- allotment of guns for ... 37, 58, 223
- as cover for arty/R aircraft ... 223, 241
- in support of airborne operations ... 253–4, 270–1
- standardization of procedure for ... 198–9, 225

COUNTER-MORTAR—
- allotment of guns for ... 86, 194, 209, 213, 215, 242, 265
- and counter-battery, attempt to combine ... 209
- co-ordination of guns and mortars in ... 209, 231, 242
- four pen recorder (*see* SOUND RANGING).
- in airborne division ... 261, 271
- in armd. division in rapid pursuit ... 242
- in jungle ... 321
- locations, accuracy of ... 241
- officer ... 209, 242, 271
- origins of ... 37–8, 209
- radar (*see* RADAR).
- retaliatory shoots ... 241, 246

COUNTER-PREPARATION ... 3, 100, 195–2

COUNTER-RADAR ... 202, 203, 221

COVERING FIRE—
- closeness with which own troops should follow ... 3, 29, 99, 144, 166, 186, 200, 229, 236, 249, 265, 267, 279, 295–6
- inf. objectives determined by facilities for ... 59
- types of ... 2

CREST CLEARANCE PROBLEMS, examples of ... 56, 58, 74

DATUM POINT, use of ... 57, 101, 230
DEACON, the ... 147, 180
DECENTRALIZATION OF ARTILLERY IN DIFFICULT COUNTRY ... 185, 240

DECEPTION—
- aggressive use of artillery fire as means of ... 212
- changes in nature of artillery as means of ... 55
- dummy barrage as means of ... 200, 275
- dummy bombardment as means of ... 203, 243, 269, 275
- dummy smoke screen as means of ... 144, 265
- pause in fire plan as means of ... 292
- tracer ammunition as means of ... 154

DECOYS IN A.A. DEFENCE, use of ... 153

DEFENCE IN FIRST WORLD WAR, predominance of ... 1

DEFENSIVE FIRE—
- air bursts used in ... 222
- brought down on own F.D.Ls. ... 79, 285
- divisional tasks in ... 145
- infantry mortars used for ... 295
- lack of flexibility in ... 37
- stonk as form of ... 208
- tasks, numbering and grouping of ... 208
- use of ... 3, 55, 59, 79, 151, 188, 195, 222, 246

	Page
DEPLOYMENT OF ARTILLERY, problems in	50-1, 168, 186, 193-4, 213, 263, 268-9, 274, 294
DESERT WARFARE, compared with naval warfare	134
peculiarities of	44-6, 116
DESPATCH RIDERS IN THE DESERT, failure of	46, 92
DISCARDING SABOT	211

DIVE BOMBING—
- at the zenith of its power ... 72
- defence by H.A.A. guns against ... 71, 83
- defence by L.A.A. guns against ... 38, 83
- mastered by fighters ... 129
- moral effect of ... 38, 66
- origins of ... 19
- parried by A.A. guns ... 82–5, 96

DIVISIONAL ARTILLERY—
- organization of ... 27, 118, 137, 285–7, 299, 304
- simplification of ... 11–12

DUAL PURPOSE WEAPONS ... 40, 253, 258
DUMMY FIRE PLANS (*see* DECEPTION).
DUMMY POSITIONS, A.A. ... 83, 115
DUMPING OF AMMUNITION (*see* AMMUNITION).

EARLY WARNING—
- A.A. guns used for broadcasting ... 130, 176
- in assault landings, standard grid for ... 184
- O.Ps. ... 130, 153, 257, 300, 301, 325
- radar used for (*see* RADAR).
- systems ... 34, 64, 69, 70, 73, 82, 130, 153, 257–8

ENEMY TACTICS (*see* TACTICS).

EQUIPMENTS—
- in First and Second World Wars, similarity of ... 1, 325
- shortage of ... 27, 32, 36, 43–4, 56, 62, 66–8, 74, 76, 85–7, 91, 102, 120–1, 125, 157, 160, 179, 284
- time factor in the production of artillery ... 22–3, 67
- types of (*see* A.A., FIELD, ETC. ARTILLERY).

FIELD ARTILLERY EQUIPMENTS—
- 18-pr ... 12, 27, 44, 54, 56, 78, 80, 102
- 4·5-in how ... 12, 27, 44, 54, 56, 78, 80
- 25-pr ... 12, 27, 35, 44, 47–8, 50, 53, 75–6, 79, 88, 104–5, 112, 119, 147, 163, 288, 290, 314
- proposed new ... 319–20
- S.P. (*see* SELF-PROPELLED ARTILLERY, FIELD).

FIELD REGIMENT, organization of ... 10–1, 36, 44, 87, 119, 137
FIGHTER AIRCRAFT AND A.A. DEFENCES, co-operation between
    93–4, 96, 202, 211, 219, 258–9
FIGHTER-BOMBERS IN C.B. ROLE (*see* AIR SUPPORT).
FIGHTER NIGHTS ... 93, 202

FIRE PLANS—
- inadequate preparation of ... 135, 147, 247
- inclusion of infantry weapons and tanks in ... 295
- in the jungle ... 291–3, 295, 317–8
- need for elasticity in ... 169, 200, 217, 310
- over-elaboration of ... 36, 267
- quick ... 99, 107, 222, 234–5
- time factor in (*see* TIME FACTOR).

FIRE UNIT—
- divisional artillery as ... 138, 141, 143–4
- field regt. as ... 10

FLAG SIGNALS FOR MANOEUVRE IN DESERT ... 45

FLARE SHELL (*see* SHELL).
FLASHLESS PROPELLANT 133, 148, 169, 173, 196, 199, 211, 249
FLASH SPOTTING—
    achievements of 37, 57, 142, 169
    against V2s 260
    in jungle 297, 321
    in mountains 169, 186
    not affected by artificial moonlight 243
    troop 91
FLEXIBILITY IN A.A. DEFENCES, need for 73–4
FLYING BOMB, THE 258–60
FORWARD AREA SIGHTS FOR L.A.A. GUNS 19, 84, 115, 132
F.O.Os., principles governing employment of
    10, 57, 160–1, 169, 217, 231, 235, 246, 288–9, 309, 312, 313, 318
FORWARD OBSERVER UNITS, R.A. (*see* AIRBORNE ARTILLERY).
FOUR PEN RECORDER (*see* SOUND RANGING).
FUZES—
    mechanical time 170, 211
    photo-electric 86
    powder filled 170, 230, 241
    reintroduction of time 101, 148
    variable time (*see* RADAR).
FUZE SETTER, MECHANICAL 211, 257

GERMAN TACTICS (*see* TACTICS).
GOLF BAG PRINCIPLE, THE 180, 253, 298–9
GROUPS, USE OF TEMPORARY ARTILLERY 109, 145, 166, 296, 312, 313
GUN DEFENDED AREA 21, 201, 221, 250, 325
GUN DENSITIES (*see* A.A. DEFENCE).
GUN OPERATIONS ROOM 34–5, 64, 70, 82, 153–4, 176, 212, 220
GUN OPERATIONS ROOM, mobile... 175

HARASSING FIRE 6, 212, 305, 318
H.A.A. REGIMENT, organization of 21
HEAVY ARTILLERY—
    concrete busting by 199, 263
    in the pursuit 216
    in jungle 304
    lack of 163, 213
HEAVY AND SUPER-HEAVY ARTILLERY EQUIPMENTS—
    6-in gun 15–6, 31, 157
    155-mm gun 157, 179, 219, 254
    7·2-in how 37, 157, 166, 179, 199, 214, 242. 265
    8-in how 16, 31, 157, 214
    8-in gun 157, 179, 213, 260–1
    9·2-in how 16, 31, 37, 157, 179
    9·2-in gun 16, 31, 261
    12-in how 15, 31, 179, 199
    240-mm how 179, 214, 260–1
    18-in how 16, 261
    in First World War 15
    role of 16
    theatre pools of 179
HEAVY REGIMENT, organization of 16
HEDGE-HOPPER, THE 18–9, 39–40, 130, 153, 184, 258, 301, 325
HELICOPTERS FOR AIR O.P. (*see* AIR O.P.).
HOSE-PIPE SYSTEM OF L.A.A. FIRE CONTROL 19

IDENTIFICATION OF AIRCRAFT (*see* RADAR).
INCREMENTAL CHARGES FOR 25-PR 180, 298

	Page
INDICATION OF DIRECTION BY BOFORS TRACER ...	... 154, 166, 228, 276
INDICATION OF OBJECTIVES—	
by flare shell	... 269
by smoke	... 314
INDICATION OF POSITION—	
to forward troops by shell bursts	145, 239
by forward troops by screens	... 59
by forward troops by smoke	184, 264, 295
by forward troops by towels	... 296
INDICATION OF TARGETS TO AIRCRAFT BY—	
dummy dive	... 323
map refs	... 296
flare shell	... 196, 238, 264, 275
S.L. beams	... 134
smoke	130, 166, 171, 207, 238, 264, 277, 289, 314, 323
INDICATOR BELT ...	... 94
INDIRECT FIRE—	
against tanks	17, 75, 80–2, 88, 104, 119, 123, 126, 146, 162, 188, 192
by anti-tank guns	... 251
by tanks	... 140
INFANTRY DIVISION, reorganization of ...	118, 137, 160
INFANTRY GUN	89, 139
INFANTRY TANK—	
by night, first use of	109
able to operate inside barrage	210, 320
dominates battlefield	47–8, 66, 88, 99
early emphasis on ...	32
INNER ARTILLERY ZONE ...	21, 201, 221, 249, 325
INTELLIGENCE, BUILD-UP OF ARTILLERY	194
INTER-COMMUNICATION PROBLEMS IN JUNGLE ...	288, 313
JAPANESE TACTICS (see TACTICS).	
JET AIRCRAFT, effect on H.A.A. lay-outs of	256
JOCK COLUMNS	87–8, 119–20, 156
JUNGLE WARFARE—	
close support in	286–7
difficulty of siting guns in	294
pack transport for O.Ps. in	289
peculiarities of	...283–4, 285–6, 288–9, 291–2, 294, 313–4
railway transport for field artillery in	314
JUNGLE FIELD REGIMENT	... 287–8, 304
JURY AXLE FOR 25-PR	288, 299, 311
KILLER BELT	94
LADDER RANGING	100
LANDING BARGE FLAK	220
LANDING CRAFT GUN	182,
LANDING CRAFT ROCKET...	182, 184,
LANDING GROUNDS, A.A. defence of (see AIRFIELDS).	
LIAISON OFFICERS, use of	46, 166, 169, 207, 271
LIFTING OUT PROCEDURE IN TIMED CONCENTRATIONS ...	201
LIGHT ARTILLERY—	
airborne division	... 205–6, 246
armoured division	18
infantry division	9
Crete...	70
Italy ...	206, 234
Sudan	55

	Page
LIGHT ARTILLERY—*cont.*	
Tunisia	160
proposed new equipment	319
L.A.A. ARTILLERY, introduction of	21
L.A.A. REGIMENT—	
corps	27, 33
divisional	40
organization of	63, 114
L.A.A. AND A.TK REGIMENT	18, 53, 62, 287, 299
L.A.A. AND S.L. BATTERY	176, 221
LIGHT WARNING SET (*see* RADAR).	
LINKING OF BATTERIES AND TROOPS	10–1
LISTENING POSTS FOR CONTROL OF A.A. BARRAGE	84
LITTLEJOHN CONVERSION OF 2-PR A.TK GUN	126
LOW-FLYING AIR ATTACKS BY DAY	18–9, 39–40, 68, 69, 73, 115, 131, 153
BY NIGHT	212
M.G.A.A., introduction of	34
MAN-POWER, effects of shortage of	87, 150, 180, 232
MAPS—	
accuracy of	183, 230
pre-war policy	5
vertical air photos and skeleton block plots as substitute for	183
MAP REFERENCES, indication of targets by	235, 246, 296, 318
MAP SPOTTINGS, as basis of divisional grids in pursuit	234
MECHANIZATION OF THE ARTILLERY	9–10
MEDIUM ARTILLERY—	
early shortage of	15, 141, 179
equipments—	
60-pr	15, 43, 48, 80, 86
6-in how	15, 43, 48, 57, 67, 74, 87, 102, 129, 290, 312, 320
155-mm how	87, 102, 125, 129, 320
4·5-in gun	15, 51, 67, 74, 125, 129, 219
5·5-in gun	15, 129, 163, 179, 199, 254, 290, 313, 320
in armd. division, need for	180, 210, 239
increase in amount of corps	180
mobility of	216
MEDIUM GUNS, trouble with	129, 320
METEOR—	
as an artillery responsibility	324
inaccuracies in	6, 45, 57, 80, 215–6, 230, 323–4
telegram—	
frequency of issue of	146
inadequacy of early system of production of	50, 80
introduction of	6
METEOROLOGICAL EXPERTS, shortage of	133
METEOROLOGICAL UNITS—	
formation of corps mobile	146
in jungle, mobile	291
organization of	197, 324
MINEFIELDS, use of artillery against	52, 102, 172, 199
MINE-LAYING AIRCRAFT, defence against	34, 62, 84, 221
MOBILE COLUMNS (*see* COLUMNS).	
MOBILE DIVISION, artillery in the	18, 46
MOBILITY-COMPENSATION FOR LACK OF FIRE SUPPORT	307
MOONLIGHT—	
artificial (*see* ARTIFICIAL MOONLIGHT).	
infantry attacks by	142, 149, 163, 171, 213
registration of guns by	149
tank attacks by	109, 164

Page

MORAL EFFECT OF ARTILLERY FIRE (*see* BOMBARDMENT).
MORTARS—
    as artillery weapons 214, 231, 286–8, 293, 311–2, 314–5
    compared with field artillery 140
    included in artillery fire plans, infantry 214, 275, 295, 304, 312
    introduction and use of 4·2-in 170, 186, 214, 231, 271, 275, 314–5
    introduction of rifled 315
    modification of 3-in 170, 314
    pack equipment for 311
MORTAR FIRE, moral effect of 169
MOUNTAIN ARTILLERY—
    equipments—
        3·7-in how 180, 234, 286, 290, 293, 298, 311
        75-mm 180, 286, 311
    in the Indian division 11, 160, 286
    in the Rhine crossing 269
    mules—
        difficulties of feeding 286, 307–8, 316
        dropped by parachute 316
    use of 59, 75, 160, 234, 247, 269, 307, 315–6
MOUNTAIN DIVISION, organization of 234
MOUNTAIN O.P. TROOP, proposal 234
MOUNTAIN REGIMENT, organization of 234, 286
MOUNTAIN VILLAGE, the problem of the 199
MOUNTAIN WARFARE—
    difficulty of finding gun positions in 56, 74, 185
    pack transport for O.Ps. in 161, 167
    the problem of covering fire in 56
MOVEMENT LIGHT (*see* ARTIFICIAL MOONLIGHT).
MULBERRY, the A.A. defence of a (*see* ARTIFICIAL PORT).

NAVAL BOMBARDMENT (*see* BOMBARDMENT).
NAVIGATOR IN DESERT WARFARE, appointment of 45
NEBELWERFERS 169, 213, 242
NEUTRALIZATION VERSUS DESTRUCTION, as object of artillery fire 2, 319–20
NIGHT ATTACKS—
    by moonlight (*see* MOONLIGHT).
    increasing frequency of 142, 148, 149
    in darkness 164, 166, 193
    tracer ammunition for maintaining direction in 154, 166, 228, 276
NIGHT BOMBER—
    defence against the 40, 84
    effect of blind flying by 212
NIGHT MARKER SHELL (*see* SHELL).

OBLIQUE AIR PHOTOS (*see* PHOTOGRAPHS).
OBSERVATION OF FIRE—
    by infantry and R.A.C. 231, 309, 313
    by moonlight 149
    in C.B. role, importance of 279
    in desert, difficulties of 45, 48
    in jungle, difficulties of 288–9, 313–4
OBSERVATION POLE OR LADDER, use of 45
OBSERVATION REGIMENT, corps 322
OBSERVED FIRE—
    as basis of fire plan 48
    concrete busting by heavy artillery dependent on 263
    increased importance of 100–1, 230
OBSERVED VERSUS PREDICTED FIRE 4, 6, 101, 197, 229–30
OPENING RANGES FOR A.TK GUNS (*see* A.TK DEFENCE).
OPEN SIGHT FOR 25-PR FOR A A.TK ROLE, modification of 113

	Page
PACK ARTILLERY IN ASSAULT LANDINGS	184, 311
PARATROOPS, defence against	69, 71

PASSIVE AIR DEFENCE—
    control of ... 61, 249, 251
    importance of ... 83
    object of ... 20, 61
    as sole means of defence ... 68, 70, 73, 173

PATTERN TARGETS	208
PEPPERPOTS	264, 268, 269, 279, 295, 327
PERSONAL WEAPONS IN ARTILLERY UNITS	69, 73, 128, 297
PERSONNEL PROBLEMS	44

PHOTOGRAPHS—
    gridded air ... 198
    oblique air ... 172, 238
    vertical air ... 54, 109, 141–2, 145–6, 169, 183, 194, 198, 223, 266, 296
    vertical air, misleading effect of ... 164

PHOTOGRAPH INTERPRETATION UNIT, air	219
PISTOL OR POCKET GUN PROCEDURE IN FIELD ARTILLERY	99, 149–50
PISTOL OR POCKET GUN PROCEDURE IN A.G.R.A.	240
PIVOT GROUP IN THE MOBILE DIVISION, role of	46
PLOTTER, A.A., SEMI-AUTOMATIC, introduction of	132, 154
POLSTEN, THE	184, 258
POOLS OF EQUIPMENT, theatre	179
POOLS OF STANDARD GUNS	197
PORTEE A.TK GUN	46, 75–6, 79, 89, 106, 113, 128, 135, 150, 287
PORTEE FIELD GUN	139

PORTS, A.A. defence of (*see* A.A. DEFENCE).

PREDICTED FIRE—
    control points for ... 194
    in absence of arty/R, importance of ... 44
    inaccuracies in ... 6, 80, 198, 203, 216, 247, 278
    in First World War ... 4
    predominates in later stages of war in Europe ... 229
    versus observed fire (*see* OBSERVED FIRE).

PREDICTORS—
    H.A.A. ... 7, 203, 212, 260
    L.A.A. ... 19, 84, 92, 115, 132

PRIEST, THE	140, 172, 180, 188, 190, 312

PROPAGANDA SHELL (*see* SHELL).

PROTECTION OF—
    air O.P. (*see* AIR O.P.).
    a.tk guns ... 112, 113, 128
    gun pits in jungle ... 297
    L.A.A. guns ... 72, 115–6

PROXIMITY SHOOTS	5, 246, 293, 294–5

RADAR—
    coast artillery ... 22, 202, 280
    control of air O.P. ... 238
    control of close support aircraft ... 264, 275
    counter-mortar ... 209, 230–1, 241–2, 265, 277, 321, 326
    early warning ... 20, 73, 130, 153, 184, 257–8
    field artillery ... 280, 321, 326
    G.L. III, first use of ... 196, 202
    H.A.A. ... 20, 69, 82, 84, 92, 175, 196, 202, 325
    identification of aircraft ... 73, 201, 250, 325
    L.A.A. ... 20, 73, 153, 212
    light warning set ... 73, 153, 184, 202
    limitations in mountains ... 69, 175
    mats for G.L. II ... 92

RADAR—*cont.*
 meteor (wind) measured by 230
 navigation by 247, 251, 274
 navigational fix of ships and floating artillery by 188, 207
 origins of 20, 33, 76, 96
 regiment, R.A., formation of 231
 searchlight 94, 154, 176, 202, 211
 survey by 321
 time fuzes 259, 262, 281, 305
RADIO LINK IN SOUND RANGING BATTERY, introduction of 37
RAILWAY MOUNTINGS—
 9·2-in guns on 16, 31, 261
 25-prs on 314
RANGE VERSUS SHELL POWER 15–6, 23, 157
RECOGNITION SIGNALS BY AIRCRAFT, use of 21
RECOILLESS GUNS 316–7, 320, 329
RECONNAISSANCE—
 aircraft regulations for engagement of 22
 groups in pursuit, artillery 150
REGIMENTAL FIRE, first use of 10
REGISTRATION—
 by moonlight 149
 silent 4–5, 50
REHEARSAL OF FIRE PLANS, use of 48
REMOTE CONTROL GEAR, H.A.A. 211, 256
REORGANIZATION OF ARTILLERY IN FIRST HALF OF WAR, frequent 155
REPRESENTATIVES, C.R.A'S AND C.C.R.A'S   161, 169, 217, 270, 271, 293, 304, 309, 312
RETALIATORY SHOOTS (*see* COUNTER-BATTERY and COUNTER-MORTAR).
REVERSE SLOPE POSITIONS, attack of 298
RIVER CROSSING, the problem of the 190–2, 193–5, 268–71, 312
ROCKETS—
 compared with medium artillery 306
 German long-range (V2) 260
 in A.A. role 85–6, 259
 in chaung warfare 306–7
 in field artillery role 247–8, 264, 269, 306–7
 in landing craft (*see* LANDING CRAFT, ROCKET).
 origins of 85
ROVER SYSTEM OF CONTROL OF AIR SUPPORT (*see* AIR SUPPORT).
ROVING POSITIONS, use of 28, 274

SCORPION, development of 172
SCREENS, use of infantry 59
SEARCHLIGHTS, A.A.—
 dazzle effects of 20, 34
 in ground role (*see* SECONDARY ROLES).
 in support of fighters 20, 33, 62, 94, 154, 176, 202, 211, 221, 258
 in support of H.A.A. guns 20, 34, 40, 82, 84, 154, 221, 258, 260
 in support of L.A.A. guns 20, 34, 62, 154, 176, 221, 258
 origins of 7, 18
SEARCHLIGHT—
 beams used to indicate targets to aircraft 134
 marker beacons for guidance of friendly aircraft 260
SEARCHLIGHT REGIMENT, organization of 40
SEAWARD DEFENCE COMMANDER 251
SECONDARY ROLE FOR A.A. UNITS—
 a.tk defence as 78, 104, 112, 114, 151
 coast defence as 155, 177, 250–1
 concrete busting as 254
 field artillery role as   63, 114, 124, 154, 170, 199–200, 244, 252, 264, 313, 327

SECONDARY ROLE FOR A.A. UNITS—*cont.*	*Page*
heavy artillery as	299, 304
infantry role as	189, 252
manning of rocket projectors as	248, 306
operation of smoke generators as	214–5
SECONDARY ROLE FOR A.A.S.LS., artificial moonlight as (*see* ARTIFICIAL MOONLIGHT).	
SECONDARY ROLE FOR A.TK UNITS—	
concrete busting as	187, 199
field artillery role as	52, 185, 192, 199, 251, 264, 269, 291
infantry role as	252, 307
manning of mortars as	214, 231, 293, 294, 299, 304
manning of rocket projectors as	306
SECONDARY ROLE FOR FIELD ARTILLERY—	
a.tk defence as	16–7, 32, 35, 79, 104–7, 110–3, 121–3, 128, 135, 161
coast defence as	134
manning of medium guns as	294
SECONDARY ROLE FOR MOUNTAIN GUN, a.tk defence as	299
SECOND-IN-COMMAND, introduction of	11
SECTOR AIR DEFENCE COMMANDER	189, 201
SELF-DESTROYING ELEMENT IN L.A.A. PROJECTILES	19, 133–4, 301
SELF-PROPELLED ARTILLERY—	
A.A.	181
A.tk	36, 90, 147, 181, 190, 218, 223
distinction between roles of tanks and	181
field	9, 89, 137, 140, 172, 180–1, 185
in assault landings	184, 188, 190, 207, 218
increase in proportion of	210
infantry gun	139
in jungle	304–5
medium	210
overhead cover demanded for	223
SEXTON, THE	180
SHELL—	
C.P. for concrete busting by 12-in how	199
for 5·5-in med. gun, 80-lb	179, 296, 320
night marker or flare	238, 264, 269, 275
propaganda	196, 245, 277,
shrapnel	11, 39
smoke	31, 148
star	171, 209, 323
SHELL LINE	217
SHELLING REPORTS	4, 57, 146, 186
SHELLS USED TO SAVE LIVES	177, 232
SHOT—	
A.P., for 25-pr	17, 147, 290
A.P.C.B.C.	173, 211
D.S.	211
SILENT ATTACKS	166, 190–1, 193, 194
SKELETON BLOCK PLOT	183, 296
SLIT TRENCH POSITION, the problem of the	305
SMOKE—	
coloured	130, 171, 207, 238, 264, 275, 277, 304
companies for defence of beachheads	185, 190
for indication of targets to aircraft	130, 166, 171, 207, 264, 277, 289, 314, 323
for indication of objectives to infantry	314
for indication of stages in progress of fire plan	265, 295
for maintaining direction	194–5, 314
generators in ground role	190, 196, 203, 214, 238, 266, 269, 318
grenades for indicating f.u.p. for infantry in jungle	295
materials in major operation, consumption of	214–5

SMOKE—*cont.*
   screens, artillery—
      as covering fire 3, 31, 48, 237, 295, 318
      as means of deception 144, 265
      limitations to use of 182–3, 237
      on call 244, 266
      quick 99
      to blind enemy O.Ps. 167, 214, 227, 266
      to neutralize enemy tank and a.tk weapons 112, 147, 155
      to screen flanks of attack 109, 227, 237, 266
   screens, A.A. 175, 185, 190, 195, 220
   screens laid by supporting aircraft 308
   shell (*see* SHELL).
SOUND RANGING—
   achievements 142, 149
   against V2s 260
   battery, radio link in 37
   four pen recorder 209, 231, 241, 261, 277
   in jungle 297, 321
   in mountains 57, 74, 186, 243
   troop 91
SPECIALISTS IN THE ARTILLERY, shortage of 44, 102
STANDARD GUNS, pools of 197
STAR SHELL (*see* SHELL).
STATIC H.A.A. MOUNTINGS, introduction of 18
STIFFKEY STICK 132
STONK—
   as D.F. 208
   as quick barrage, moving 208, 267, 318
   introduction of 144, 150
SUPER-HEAVY ARTILLERY EQUIPMENTS (*see* HEAVY AND SUPER-HEAVY ARTILLERY).
SUPER-HEAVY GROUP, formation of 260–1
SUPPORT GROUP 18, 32–3, 46–7, 53, 68, 103–4, 118
SUPPORT GROUP, R.M. armoured 208, 218
SURPRISE SAVES SHELLS 60, 230
SURVEY—
   company, R.A. 5
   for calculation of meteor, use of 50
   in desert 50–1, 150
   in mobile operations 5, 161, 234, 277
   in jungle 291, 309
   observation parties, introduction of 5
   party, regimental 11, 36
   regiment, reorganization of 91
   troop, role of 91
SURVEYOR, introduction of regimental 4–5

TACTICS—
   German—
      aircraft in C.B. role 81, 83, 250
      air support 35, 76, 152
      a.tk screen ... 89, 106, 109, 123, 138, 143, 147, 155, 164, 167, 226, 228
      armoured 35, 78–81, 89, 106, 109–10, 142, 155
      artillery 52, 186, 190, 223, 230, 234, 268
      defensive 187, 214–5, 217–8, 243–5, 268, 273
      dive bomber 38, 66, 71–2, 81, 83, 161
      machine-gun 159, 170, 190, 199, 227
      minefield 106, 138, 149, 155, 160
      mortar 37–8, 86, 159, 169, 186, 199, 212, 234, 242
   Italian 47, 56

	Page
TACTICS—*cont.*	
Japanese—	
artillery	291, 308–9, 321
bunker defences	285, 292
counter-battery	297
infantry gun and mortar	283, 321
use of jungle	283–5, 293–4
reverse slope positions	298
TALLY-HO PROCEDURE FOR CONTROL OF NIGHT FIGHTERS	93
TANKS—	
co-operation of guns with	17–18, 109, 116, 172–3
infantry (*see* INFANTRY TANK).	
TANK-BUSTING AIRCRAFT	129
TANK DESTROYER—	
a.tk gun as	90
gun as primary	110–2
TANK HUNTING BY AIR O.P. (*see* AIR O.P.).	
TANK O.P. IN THE JUNGLE, limitations of	289
TIGER TANK	162–3, 203
TIME FACTOR IN—	
air support	207, 275, 276
control of artillery/R sorties	216
counter-battery	162, 241
counter-flak	224, 270
counter-mortar	242
establishment of sound ranging base	149
preparation of artillery fire plans	
29, 99, 100, 107, 145, 147–8, 149–50, 156, 194, 268, 279	
production of air photographs	145–6
TIME FUZES (*see* FUZES).	
TIME ON TARGET (T.O.T.) PROCEDURE	129, 215, 236
TIMED PROGRAMME—	
duration of	225, 245, 266
infantry held up by	235–6
infantry unable to keep up with	81, 105, 166, 195, 214, 222, 227, 267, 276, 295
on call targets as alternative to	235
use of B.B.C. time signals for control of	129
TOWERS FOR L.A.A. GUNS, TUBULAR STEEL	301
TRACER AMMUNITION FOR L.A.A. GUNS, introduction of longer burning	133
TRACTORS, ARTILLERY	10, 55–6, 139, 216, 240, 299, 319
TRANSPORT—	
shortage of	27–8, 43
defects of artillery	178
TRENCH WARFARE IN FIRST WORLD WAR, influence of	1–2
UNSEEN FIRE CONTROL SYSTEM FOR L.A.A. GUNS	212, 259
UPPER REGISTER FIRING	192, 241, 298, 299
VALENTINE TANK CHASSIS, 17-pr a.tk gun on	181
VARIABLE TIME FUZES (*see* FUZES).	
VISUAL CONTROL POST	276–7, 304, 314, 322–3
WAR ESTABLISHMENTS, inadequacy of early	28
WINDOW (*see* COUNTER-RADAR).	
WIRE CUTTING BY ARTILLERY	1, 16, 33, 52, 102, 200
WIRELESS—	
centralized control of artillery made possible by	140–1, 293
close support aircraft controlled for first time from ground by	163
continuity of fire support in fast-moving battle ensured by	235
co-ordination of artillery fire plans by	168

WIRELESS—*cont.*
    discipline, importance of good 169
    equipments, need for power and portability in 178, 289
    establishments, inadequacy of early 11, 54
    flexibility of fire control increased by use of 10, 169, 310, 317
    limitations of 46, 58, 74, 200, 289
    nets
        101, 140–1, 169, 210, 218–9, 235, 238, 239, 246, 269, 277, 280, 310–1, 312, 313
    sets 92, 101, 140, 160–1, 238, 280, 289, 312, 314
Z CRAFT IN ASSAULT LANDINGS, 25-prs in 308–9

List of Battles, Actions and Engagements Mentioned in Text

Name of Action	Date	Page
The Dyle	May 1940	37
Dunkirk (A.A. defence)	Jun. 1940	39
Sidi Barrani	Dec. 1940	47–50
Bardia (first attack on)	Jan. 1941	50–51
Tobruk ,, ,,	,,	51
Beda Fomm	Feb. 1941	53
Gallabat	Nov. 1940	55
Keren	Feb.–Mar. 1941	56–60
Corinth Bridge (A.A. defence of)	Apr. 1941	69
Crete	May 1941	70–72
Proasteion Ridge	Apr. 1941	75
Tobruk (defence of)	Apr.–Nov. 1941	78–87
Capuzzo	Jun. 1941	88–89
Valletta (coast artillery action)	Jul. 1941	94–96
Sidi Rezegh	Nov. 1941	103–104
Taib-el-esem	Nov. 1941	104
Sidi Omar	,,	104–105
Bir el Hurush	,,	105
El Duda	,,	106
Gazala	Dec. 1941	107
Bardia (second attack on)	Dec. 1941–Jan. 1942	109
Gazala	May–Jun. 1942	121–124
Knightsbridge Box	Jun. 1942	123–124
Deir el Shein	Jul. 1942	125–126
Malta (A.A. defence of)	Mar.–May 1942	131–132
Alam el Halfa	Aug.–Sep. 1942	138
El Alamein	Oct.–Nov. 1942	142–143
Agheila	Dec. 1942	149
Homs	Jan. 1943	149
Medenine	Mar. 1943	150–152
Sidi Nsir (Tunisia)	Feb. 1943	162
Beja	,,	162–163
Mareth Line	Mar. 1943	163–164
Wadi Akrit	Apr. 1943	164–166
Heidous	,,	166–167
Tunis	May 1943	167–168
Pantelleria	Jun. 1943	183
Straits of Messina	Sep. 1943	186
Salerno	,,	187–190
The Volturno	Oct. 1943	190
The Trigno	,,	191
The Sangro	Nov. 1943	191–192
The Moro	Dec. 1943	192
Ortona	,,	192

Name of Action	Date	Page
Orsogna	Dec. 1943	192–193
Monte Camino	,,	193
The Garigliano	Jan. 1944	193–195
Anzio	,,	195–196
Bari (A.A. defence of) ...	Dec. 1943	202
Cassino	May 1944	213–215
Forme d'Aquino (Hitler Line)	,,	215–216
Normandy landings	Jun. 1944	217–222
Caen (Operation Epsom)	,,	222
Caen (Operation Goodwood)	Jul. 1944	225–226
Caumont (Operation Bluecoat)	,,	226–227
Caen (Operation Totalize)	Aug. 1944	227–228
Falaise	Aug. 1944	237
Arezzo	Jul. 1944	237
Fortunata Ridge (Rimini)	Sep. 1944	237
Gothic Line	Sep.–Oct. 1944	242–243
Le Havre	Sep. 1944	243–244
Boulogne	,,	244–245
Arnhem	,,	245–246
Walcheren	Oct.–Nov. 1944	246–247
Geilenkirchen	Nov. 1944	248–249
Reichswald (Operation Veritable)	Feb. 1945	263–268
The Rhine (crossing of)	Mar. 1945	268–273
The Senio ,, ,, ...	Apr. 1945	273–276
Arakan	Jan. 1943	284–285
Razabil (Arakan)	Jan. 1944	290, 292
Ngakyedauk Pass	Feb. 1944	293
Kohima	Mar.–Apr. 1944	294–296
The Kaladan (Arakan)	Dec. 1944	307
Myebon ,, ...	Jan. 1945	308
Kangaw ,, ...	Jan.–Feb. 1945	308–309
Ru-ywa ,, ...	Feb. 1945	309
Nyaungu (Irrawaddy crossing)	,,	312
Myinmu ,, ,, ...	,,	312
Meiktila	Mar. 1945	312
The Irrawaddy valley (final attempt at break-out by Japanese)	Jul. 1945	313

BAOR
BATTLEFIELD TOUR GUIDES

You don't get much better than this for first-hand information from the officers who commanded the formations and units carrying out these operations, these collected before time had blurred their memories of events

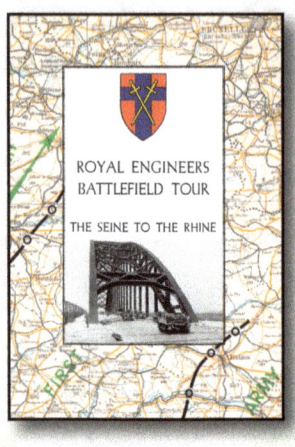

BAOR ROYAL ENGINEERS BATTLEFIELD TOUR
THE SEINE TO THE RHINE

Vol. 1 – An account of the operations included in the tour
Vol. 2 – A guide to the conduct of the tour

SB: 9781783316717
HB: 9781783317714

BAOR ROYAL ENGINEERS BATTLEFIELD TOUR
NORMANDY TO THE SEINE

SB: 9781783317516
HB: 9781783317813

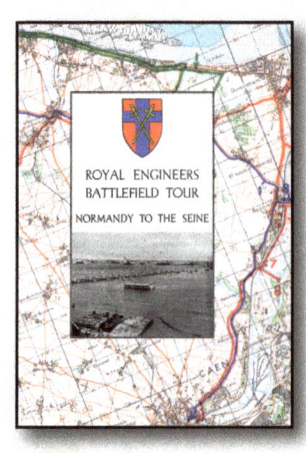

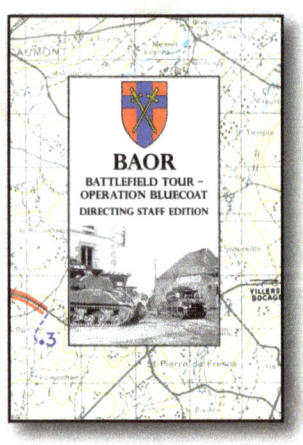

BAOR BATTLEFIELD TOUR
OPERATION BLUECOAT
– Directing Staff Edition

SB: 9781783318124
HB: 9781783318438

BAOR BATTLEFIELD TOUR
OPERATION VERITABLE
– Directing Staff Edition

SB: 9781783318131
HB: 9781783318421

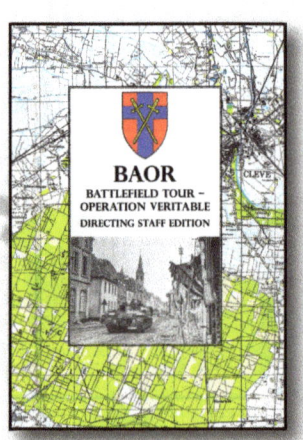

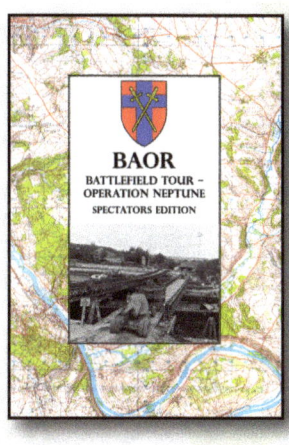

BAOR BATTLEFIELD TOUR
OPERATION NEPTUNE
– Spectators Edition
43(W) Division Assault Crossing of the River Seine
25-28 August 1944

SB: 9781474535298
HB: 9781474535311

BAOR BATTLEFIELD TOUR
OPERATION PLUNDER
– Directing Staff Edition

SB: 9781474535328
HB: 9781474535335

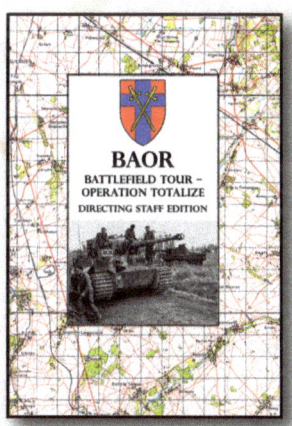

BAOR BATTLEFIELD TOUR
OPERATION TOTALIZE
– Directing Staff Edition

2 Canadian Corps Operations Astride the Road Caen-Falaise 7-8 August 1944

SB: 9781474535342
HB: 9781474535359

BAOR BATTLEFIELD TOUR
OPERATION VARSITY
– Directing Staff Edition

Operations of XVIII Unites States Corps (Airborne) in Support of the Crossing of the Rhine 24 & 25 March 1945

SB: 9781474535366
HB: 9781474535373

www.ingramcontent.com/pod-product-compliance
Lightning Source LLC
Chambersburg PA
CBHW040740300426
44111CB00027B/2993